Ambrose Milton Shotwell

Annals of our Colonial Ancestors and their Descendants

Or our Quaker Forefathers and their Posterity

Ambrose Milton Shotwell

Annals of our Colonial Ancestors and their Descendants
Or our Quaker Forefathers and their Posterity

ISBN/EAN: 9783337154455

Printed in Europe, USA, Canada, Australia, Japan

Cover: Foto ©Andreas Hilbeck / pixelio.de

More available books at **www.hansebooks.com**

THE BOWNE HOMESTEAD AT FLUSHING, LONG ISLAND,

Built in 1662, and yet standing (1895) in perfect preservation.

From a lithograph made before 1842.

Reproduced from the Report of Proceedings at the Bi-Centennial Celebration of New York Yearly Meeting of Friends held at Flushing, 1895 (p. 59).

By permission of Friends' Book & Tract Committee, New York.

" The banishment of Bowne by Gov. Peter Stuyvesant, 1662 was the harbinger of a better day for New Netherland."—Brodhead.

ANNALS

OF

OUR COLONIAL ANCESTORS

AND THEIR DESCENDANTS;

OR,

OUR QUAKER FOREFATHERS

AND THEIR POSTERITY.

WHO, WHERE, WHEN, AND WHAT HAVE THEY BEEN? AND WHAT HAVE THEY DONE
OR UNDERGONE THAT MIGHT BE OF INTEREST TO THEIR
RELATIVES IN TIME TO COME?

EMBRACING

A GENEALOGICAL AND BIOGRAPHICAL REGISTER OF NINE GENERATIONS
—ABOUT TWO HUNDRED PARTICULAR FAMILIES—OF THE
SHOTWELL FAMILY IN AMERICA, ARRANGED
ALPHABETICALLY BY HOUSEHOLDS;

TOGETHER WITH

THE PEDIGREE AND NEAR KINDRED OF THE AUTHOR'S PARENTS, NATHAN AND PHEBE B.
(GARDNER) SHOTWELL, OF JACKSON COUNTY, MICHIGAN, IN VARIOUS PATERNAL
AND MATERNAL LINES OF DESCENT, INCLUDING NOT LESS THAN FORTY
DISTINCT PATRONYMICS, CHIEFLY SEVENTEENTH-CENTURY FAMILIES
OF NEW JERSEY, LONG ISLAND, AND RHODE ISLAND, MANY OF
WHOM WERE MEMBERS OF THE RELIGIOUS SOCIETY OF
FRIENDS, COMMONLY CALLED QUAKERS.

COMPILED BY

AMBROSE M. SHOTWELL,

Of Concord, Jackson Co., Mich.

1895-7.

Printed for the Author by
ROBERT SMITH & CO., PRINTERS AND BINDERS,
LANSING, MICH.

NOTE.—Any reader who may be able and willing to supply omissions or correct errors observed in these pages, will confer a favor by sending promptly to the compiler, A. M. Shotwell, at Concord, Mich., any such items of information for use in a supplemental sheet, pamphlet, or volume (or possibly a revised edition of this work), which, if demanded, will be issued in the near future.

NOTE.—Any reader who may be able and willing to supply omissions or correct errors observed in these pages, will confer a favor by sending promptly to the compiler, A. M. Shotwell, at Concord, Mich., any such items of information for use in a supplemental sheet, pamphlet, or volume (or possibly a revised edition of this work), which, if demanded, will be issued in the near future.

TO THE COMPILER'S FAITHFUL BROTHER,

Manly M. Shotwell,

THROUGH WHOSE KIND AND CAREFUL CO-OPERATION

HE HAS BEEN ENABLED

TO BRING INTO THE PRESENT PERMANENTLY ACCESSIBLE FORM

THE DATA HERE PRESENTED,

AND TO WHOSE PATIENT AND CORDIAL ASSISTANCE

IN OTHER UNDERTAKINGS

HE HAS BEEN LIKEWISE DEEPLY INDEBTED,

This Volume

IS AFFECTIONATELY INSCRIBED.

CONTENTS CHART.

ABBREVIATIONS USED IN THIS WORK.

Abr.	stands for	Abraham.
b.	" "	born.
bapt.	" "	baptized.
Benj.	" "	Benjamin.
cert.	" "	certificate.
ch.	" "	children.
Chas.	" "	Charles.
C. W.	" "	Canada West.
d.	" "	died.
dau.	" "	daughter.
desc.	" "	descendant or descended.
d. s. p.	" "	died *sine prole*.
dw.	" "	dwelt.
E.	" "	east.
Geo.	" "	George.
H. & R. M. M.	" "	Hardwick and Randolph Monthly Meeting (of Friends).
Hic.	" "	Hicksite.
Jas.	" "	James.
Jno.	" "	John.
Jos.	" "	Joseph.
Jr.	" "	Junior.
L. I.	" "	Long Island.
l. l.	" "	left at liberty (by the Monthly Meeting to consummate intended marriage according to the discipline of Friends); i. e., past meeting.
m.	" "	married.
M. M.	stands for	Monthly Meeting (of Friends).
mo.	" "	month.
N.	" "	north.
Orth.	" "	orthodox.
p.	" "	page, *pp.* pages.
P. O.	" "	Post Office.
q. v.	" "	which see.
res.	" "	residence.
R. & P.	" "	Rahway & Plainfield.
S.	" "	south.
s.	" "	son.
s. p.	" "	*sine prole*; without issue.
Thos.	" "	Thomas.
Tp.	" "	Township.
U. C.	" "	Upper Canada.
unm.	" "	unmarried.
W.	" "	west.
wd. or wid.	" "	widow.
Wm.	" "	William.
W. R. & P.	" "	Woodbridge, Rahway and Plainfield.
&	" "	and.
+	" "	not earlier than.
-	" "	not later than.
±	" "	about.

"*Superior figures*" *exponents*, following proper names, indicate the generation reckoned from an ancestor, thus, John^4.

PREFATORY.

——— ———

"HE who cares nothing about his ancestors will rarely achieve anything worthy of being remembered by his descendants."
"In treasuring up the memorials of the fathers, we best manifest our regard for posterity."—*Rev. Abner Morse, A. M.* "When we see," says Gibbon, "a long list of ancestors so ancient that they have no beginning, so worthy that they ought to have no end, we feel an interest in all their fortunes, nor can we blame the generous enthusiasm or harmless vanity of those who are allied to the honors of the name."

Another writer says: "No virtuously disposed mind can look back upon a long line of truly venerable ancestors without feeling his motive to a virtuous life strengthened. He can scarcely help feeling that it is not for him to be the first to bring disgrace upon his lineage. It will, moreover, lead him to reflect that his posterity also will be looking back and comparing his life with that of his progenitors."

Familiar to the reader may be the thought, if not the language, of the question and answer: "*Does blood tell?*" Not in that narrow sense in which the blue blood of royalty has been quoted to sustain the divine right of kings, but in the broad philosophical sense which seeks for each result a cause. Can a stream rise higher than its fountain? And, if the source be muddy, will not the stream be, to a certain extent, impure also? We know that in the career of nations, races and civilizations, history constantly repeats itself. Does it not also repeat itself in families, in the reproduction of certain well-marked traits, characteristics and capacities, even to the remotest generations? Is there not, therefore, a philosophical reason for the existence in the human mind of a certain pride in and respect for honorable ancestry entirely apart from and independent of the merely adventitious circumstances of rank and fortune? We have been taught that pride of birth is a sign of weakness and folly, and I grant, with truth, if it be founded upon mere outward distinctions; but I believe there is in every soul an inborn feeling of respect for the memory of one's ancestors. This is by the Chinese exaggerated into worship, and in many European countries is little less. As Americans, we have gone to the opposite extreme, and attempted, in our boasted equality, to make every person look upon his own ancestors in exactly the same light as another's; which is no more natural or possible than for us to look upon other people's brothers and sisters as we do upon our own; nor does the fact that we do not and can not, detract aught from their worth. While, therefore, we concede to all an equal weight in the broad scale of humanity, we cannot be blind, either to those real differences that exist, or to those ideal ones which are no less natural; and we may, without shame, confess to that pride of birth which, being both natural and reasonable, is rather to be commended than rebuked, and which I, for one, will never disown."

"However indifferent some may affect to be regarding this question of ancestry, those who have a good pedigree will usually have a natural pride of it." And the recent rapid growth of patriotic hereditary societies like Sons and Daughters of the Revolution, the Society of Colonial Wars, Society of the War of 1812, Colonial Dames, Society of the Mayflower Descendants, the Holland Society, and other organizations in which eligibility to membership depends upon the deeds of ancestors, rather than upon any personal qualifications of the members, has resulted in a great revival of the study of genealogy in America, since to become a member of any of these, a record of the family history is required. "It is an injustice to characterize this movement as merely a society fad or passing fancy. It is much more; it stimulates a desire for genealogical and historical research, a pleasing and interesting study; it leads to a proper respect for one's ancestors, and creates a desire to emulate their work for the good of one's family and country; it revives an interest in American history and promotes patriotism, good citizenship and love of country. Therefore the movement is one to be commended; and thousands are now making a study of their family history. In fact, every person should compile and preserve such a family record, for it may be of great value to future generations, if not to himself."

The object of this compilation is to perpetuate the genealogical history of the Shotwells of America, and of a certain group of other early colonial families—largely members of the Society of Friends—of New Jersey, Long Island and Rhode Island in a form such as to render accessible to their numerous descendants and connections all the available information they may wish concerning them. It is designed to embrace, in addition to the register of the various Shotwell households in the United States and Canada, concise records of the compiler's direct ancestors bearing other names—Allen, Anthony, Berry, Bowne, Carr, Cock, Cowperthwaite, Fones, Gardner, Greene, Hallett, Hartshorne, Holden, Ilsley, King, Langford, Martin, Moore, Olney, Pound, Rice, Robins, Smith, Stafford, Sweet, Thorne, Watson, Webster, Westcott, Whipple, Winthrop, Woolsey, etc.—and their brothers and sisters, together with brief lineages of distinguished kinsmen and many living relatives (other than those bearing the Shotwell name) who have manifested a lively interest in the completion and publication of the annals.

Part I, after an outline index to the compiler's lines of descent from about forty distinct colonial families, presents: (I.) Outlines of the ancestry of his paternal grandfather, which as subsequently amended,* includes surnames Bowne, Browne, Cock, Feake, Fones, Hallett, Martin, Shotwell, Thorne, Winthrop, Woolsey and others. (II.) Ancestry of his paternal grandmother,† embracing surnames Bishop, Carr, Cowperthwaite, Hartshorne, Ilsley, King, Moore, Pound, Robins, Taylor, Webster, etc. (III.) Ancestry of his maternal grandfather,‡ including Gardner, Smith, Stafford, Sweet, Watson, Westcott and other Rhode Island family names. (IV.) Ancestry of his maternal grandmother, including names of Allen, Anthony, Berry, Dungan, Greene, Holden, Langford, Latham, Olney, Rice, Whipple, etc., with royal and noble forefathers and distinguished descendants of John Greene, surgeon, of Warwick, R. I.; to all of which is appended (pages 50–57) an alphabetical lineage table of the fathers and mothers of the 441 households originally sketched for insertion in Parts I and II of this volume to which groups of families numerous additions have been elsewhere inserted during the progress of the work through the press. Part I. was printed in 1895.

Part II presents, after a synopsis of six generations, (pages 81–3), the detailed records of the known Shotwell households in North America, arranged alphabetically, according to fathers' given names; the accounts of the several households being introduced by concise outlines of the parents' records as elsewhere more fully set forth in sketches of the grandparents' households.

Following these are the addresses of the Shotwells mentioned in American city directories for the year 1895, some of whom have failed to acquaint the compiler with their personal annals or their connection with the traced branches of the family.

The data given in the body of the book are supplemented by a register of the marriages of members of the Society of Friends in Essex (now Union) and Middlesex counties, N. J., prior to the close of the Revolutionary war, and several pages relating to the history and statistics of the Society of Friends, including notices of Plainfield, Rahway and Mendham meetings, and of the persecution of Quakers on Long Island. Abstracts of wills of Shotwells probated in New Jersey in the eighteenth century (pages 211–215) are followed in the appendix (1) by supplemental data concerning several branches of the Shotwell family, designated by the given names of their respective ancestors in the fifth generation, and (2) by concise tables of Bills, Fish, Beebe, Cope, Cock, Willson, Vail, Lundy, Hallett, Pound, Cowperthwaite, Webster, Kester, King, Robins, Moore, Gardner, Pattison, Hicks and Greene families, and numerous individual lineages of relatives in other names.

Indexes to principal families and topics, to Shotwell given names, to other surnames, and to lineages of early patrons, etc., are supplied. And, in the plan of the work, the alphabetical arrangement, with some notable exceptions, prevails, thus rendering, it is hoped, the somewhat varied contents conveniently accessible to the reader.

No attempt is made in the concluding indexes to discriminate between different persons bearing the same name, nor between references to personal sketches or records and allusions to persons merely mentioned in outline lineages of some of their descendants or otherwise. And where there are several references to a particular name, the one desired may often be most conveniently found by consulting also the patronymic of his or her mother, wife or husband in the index to surnames, or the given name (if of a Shotwell) of another member of the same family.

In the several individual notices it has been the endeavor as far as practicable to complete the personal record of each relative sketched—the birth, occupation, residence, removals, postoffice address or death and burial, church relations, official positions and other remarks—before registering his or her marriage or marriages, family connections and descendants.

Of so many of the departed is it recorded that in their death not only their respective families but the whole community in which they lived had met with a great loss, etc., that we have for the

* See pages 4–6, 85, 132–6, 203–14, 239–5, 264–5.
† See pages 6–24, 116–7, 266–76.
‡ See pages 24–37, 277–290.
、 See pages 37–49, 241–2.

most part restricted this register to definite events and experiences, with few attempts at even the briefest characterization; but, not having the vanity to suppose that any reader would prefer our own restatement of facts beyond our knowledge, we have freely borrowed the language of more authoritative obituary notices. And we can only regret that others have not more fully responded to our requests for precise information of this kind concerning themselves and other descendants of our ancestors of whom they had knowledge, and again respectfully and earnestly invite them to kindly contribute revised accounts for use in the preparation of future editions of, or supplements to, this work.

The numerical exponents, ¹, ², ³, etc., affixed to many names indicate that the individuals so marked were of the 1st, 2d, 3d, etc., generation—reckoned commonly from an emigrant ancestor, though not always in the direct male line, a Shotwell daughter's descendants, for example, being frequently traced through her to "Father Abraham" Shotwell, founder of the New Jersey line— and thus serve in a measure to distinguish each from others of the same name in earlier or later generations. There have been so many different members of the Shotwell family bearing the same names—Abraham, Benjamin, Daniel, John, Joseph, William, Elizabeth, Mary, Sarah, etc.—with numerous intermarriages among related branches, living in many cases within a few miles of the ancient homestead, and retaining, for the most part, their membership in the Society of Friends, that it is often very difficult to determine with certainty to which branch of the family they severally belong. Thus, in the synopsis of six generations (at pages 81–83) no less than seventeen different John Shotwells are mentioned, and the subsequent pages of the Shotwell genealogy register children of thirty different fathers so named.

One who has had little or no experience in genealogical work can hardly be expected to appreciate the great labor, the many perplexities or the pecuniary expense necessarily involved in the execution of a task of this kind. But to one able and willing, with patient, painstaking industry and carefulness thus to render his kindred a lasting service, such a labor of love can scarcely fail to bring its own reward.

The Friends' meeting records in Union county, New Jersey, long in the custody of the late Abel V. Shotwell of Rahway, covering 1,500 or 2,000 pages of closely written manuscript, and extending back to the year 1686, have been reviewed, and from them have been gleaned much information relating to the families sketched in this volume. To the works of Mr. J. O. Austin we have been indebted for much material relating to early Rhode Island families; and to Rev. J. W. Dally's history of Woodbridge for some New Jersey items. To many kind relatives who have passed away during the past twelve years—Abel V. Shotwell of Rahway, George R. Pound of Plainfield, N. J., Catherine S. (Pound) Hampton, of E. Hamburg, N. Y., Sunderland P. Gardner of Farmington, N. Y., Mary S. Reed (and family) of Perinton, N. Y., Emma (Webster) Stover (and family) of Norwich, Ont., Canada, Arrison Shotwell and Titus Shotwell of Ohio, Edward R. Shotwell of Missouri and others—have we been indebted for valuable assistance in the collection of materials for the work. Our grateful acknowledgments are likewise due to Hugh D. Vail of Santa Barbara, Cal., Mary C. Vail of Quakertown, N. J., O. B. Leonard, Catharine R. Webster, Margaret R. S. Laws and Wm. H. Moore of Plainfield, N. J., Albert Shotwell of Pike county, Mo., George H. Greene of Lansing, Mich., George T. Fish, of Rochester, N. Y., George W. Cocks of Glen Cove, L. I., John Cox, Jr., of New York, Benjamin D. Hicks of Old West- bury, L. I., and to very many other surviving relatives who have kindly supplied much useful information in their possession. In short, nearly all of the patrons listed at pages 283–5, and many others, to whom specific credit has not been invariably expressed in connection with their individual records in the body of the book. Without such cordial coöperation on the part of the numerous representatives of the several branches to be sketched, no work of this kind could reach a satisfactory measure of success.

In records of this kind we think that, as far as practicable, the original forms of dates should be preserved. Dates of events—births, deaths, removals, marriages, etc.—relating to persons who were at the time consistent members of the Society of Friends, should usually be expressed in the Friends' customary notation, designating the months by numbers, rather than by their popu- lar names. Other dates not obtained from Quaker records should be given in the more common notation, without needless translation. And in either case old-style dates, prior to March 25 in any year previous to 1752–3, should as far as possible retain the twofold units' figures to avoid ambiguity.* Errors—not always easy to rectify—have likewise arisen from unskillful attempts to translate the original designation of months (especially in old-style statistics) from the Roman or popular to the numerical or Quaker phraseology, or *vice versa*; as, calling "September" "ninth month" (it was *seventh* month), or calling "first month" "January" (it was *March*). In Great

* Thus, George Washington was born February 11, O. S., 1731-2, equivalent to February 22, N. S., 1732. To say he was born either "February 11, 1731," "February 11, 1732," or "February 22, 1732," leaves the intelligent reader in uncertainty as to the date meant, and without ready means of determining the point if the day of the week is not also accurately stated nor the style of the calendar indicated.

Britain and the protestant American colonies, the year began on March 25 until after the reformation of the calendar, which took effect in September, 1752.

In a few instances, the approximate date of birth has been computed from other data upon the supposition that the date of death and age of the decedent are accurately stated in the epitaph, obituary or other record. But epitaphs and family registers are not invariably accurate in their statements of ages or dates; nor are they always to be implicitly accepted as to the forms of the names which it is their purpose to preserve. For these and other reasons, the diligent genealogist or historian is frequently compelled to raise doubts concerning long-trusted dates and events. But in all observed cases of disagreement or evident inaccuracy, an honest effort has been made to arrive at the truth. And where the discrepancies have not been explained or the facts determined with a high degree of assurance, the alternative forms of names and dates are parenthetically retained.

Despite the utmost diligence on the part of the editor and proof readers, it can scarcely be hoped that a work of this kind will be found wholly free from typographical or other errors. But most of the blanks, omissions and discoverable inaccuracies (which none, more than the compiler, can regret) are due to the failure of many to respond to requests for exact information. In very many cases, proof slips have been sent to the relatives whose residences were known and who seemed most likely to be able and willing to rectify errors, with an earnest request for prompt revision and correction of the same. But in view of the fragmentary and unsatisfactory form in which the present account leaves certain branches, it is proposed, in the course of a few years, to issue either a revised edition of the entire work or a supplementary volume to embody all the appropriate addenda that may in the meantime be collected, including the female branches— descendants of daughters who, through marriage, have lost the family name. Each reader is therefore cordially invited to at once prepare and send to the compiler a careful statement of any noticed inaccuracies, and to supply any additional items of personal or family history, with references to other sources of like information.

In the consciousness of having been able, with the kind coöperation of interested friends, to place these memorials and statistics beyond the possible reach of any single fire or other untoward event, and having thus rendered them permanently accessible even to those who, through the negligence of their predecessors or through the now rapid dispersion of individual members and households from decade to decade, from state to state, and from denomination to denomination, would otherwise find themselves unable to trace the current of their descent, the compiler feels a sincere satisfaction. Many hindrances have been unavoidably encountered, and circumstances beyond present control have compelled the omission of much valuable material already collected. But in the conviction that a real and lasting service has been rendered, that the execution has not fallen below the promise made, and that all reasonable expectations will be met, and trusting to be of further service in the future, the compiler heartily salutes his kindred and takes leave.

A. M. SHOTWELL.

SCHOOL FOR THE BLIND,
    Lansing, Mich , 11–30, 1897.

OUR COLONIAL ANCESTORS

AND THEIR DESCENDANTS.

PART I.

ANCESTRY OF

AMBROSE MILTON[8] SHOTWELL

OF CONCORD, MICHIGAN,

Son of Nathan[7] and Phebe B. (Gardner) Shotwell, of Jackson Co., Mich., formerly of Genesee Co., N. Y., and descendant of Isaac M[6]., Richard[5], Benjamin[4], John[3], John[2], Abraham[1].

INDEX OF ANCESTRAL NAMES,

WITH THE AUTHOR'S LINE OF DESCENT FROM EACH.

The following concise synopsis of the compiler's known ancestors includes in the pedigree of his paternal grandfather, Isaac M[6.] Shotwell, the patronymics of Shotwell, Burton, Thorne, Hallett, Bowne, Cock, Martin, and Burling; in that of his paternal grandmother, Edna C. (Pound) Shotwell, those of Pound, Webster, Cowperthwaite, Taylor, Hartshorne, Carr, King, Moore, Ilsley, Robins, and Bishop; in that of his maternal grandfather, George Washington[3] Gardner, those of Gardner, Long, Wilkinson, Watson, Smith, Gereardy, Sweet, Westcott, and Stafford; and in that of his maternal grandmother, Diana (Berry) Gardner, those of Berry, Greene, Tattersall, Anthony, Allen, Langford, Rice, Holden, Dungan, Latham, Whipple, Olney, Small, and Thomas.

Allen, Increase[1] (wife's name not ascertained) had Mary[2], who married John[3] Greene [of James[2], John[1]] and had Joseph[4] Greene: [Langford[5], Bathsheba[6], Diana[7] Berry, Phebe B[8]. Gardner, Ambrose M[9]. Shotwell, the compiler *et al.*]

Anthony, John[1], m. Susanna .... and had Elizabeth[2], who m. James[2] Greene [of John[1]]

and had John[3]: [Joseph[4], Langford[5], Bathsheba[6], Diana[7] Berry, Phebe B[8]. Gardner, Ambrose M[9]. Shotwell.]

Berry, Jonathan[1], m. Bathsheba[6] Greene [of Langford[5], Joseph[4], John[3], James[2], John[1]] and had Diana[7], who m. George Washington[3] Gardner [of John[4], John[3], William[2], George[1]] and had Bathsheba Phebe[4], called Phebe B., who m. Nathan[7] Shotwell [of Isaac M[6]., Richard[5], Benjamin[4], John[3], John[2], Abraham[1]] and had Ambrose M[8]. Shotwell.

Bishop, Moses[1], had Christiana[2], who m. Joseph[4] Moore [of Samuel[3], John[2], Samuel[1]] and had Sarah[3]: [Sarah[4] King, Edna C[5]. Pound, Nathan[6] Shotwell, Ambrose M[7].]

Bowne, John[1], m. Mary Cock [of James] and had Amy[2], who m. Richard[4] Hallett, and had Ame[3]: [Richard[4] Shotwell, Isaac M[5]., Nathan[6], Ambrose M[7].]

Burling, Elizabeth[1], m. Isaac[1] Martin and had Mary[2], who m. Richard[5] Shotwell [of Benjamin[4], John[3], John[2], Abraham[1]] and had Isaac M[6].: [Nathan[7], Ambrose M[8].]

Burton, Elizabeth, m. John[2] Shotwell, Sr. [of

Abraham[1]] and had John[2], Jr., who m. Mary Thorne, Jr. [of Joseph], and had Benjamin[3]: [Richard[4], Isaac M.[5], Nathan[6], Ambrose M[7].]

Carr, Robert[1], had Margaret[2] who m. Richard Hartshorne and had Sarah[3], who m. Thomas Taylor, and had Anna[4]: [Catharine[5] Webster, Hugh[6] Pond, Edna C[7]., Nathan[8] Shotwell, Ambrose M[9].]

Cock, James[1], m. Sarah ______ and had Mary[2], who m. John Bowne and had Amy[3], who m. Richard[4] Hallett and had Ame[5]: [Richard[6] Shotwell, Isaac M[7]., Nathan[8], Ambrose M[9].]

Cowperthwaite, Hugh[1], m. Elizabeth ________ and had John[2], who m. ____________ and had Susannah[3], who m. William Webster [of William] and had John[4], who m. Anna Taylor [of Thomas] and had Catharine[5]: [Hugh[6] Pound, Edna C[7]., Nathan[8] Shotwell, Ambrose M[9].]

Dungan, William[1], m. Frances (Latham) West [of Lewis Latham] and had Frances[2], who m. Randall Holden, and had Elizabeth[3], who m. John Rice and had John[4]: [Barbara[5], Phebe[6] Langford, Langford[7] Greene, Bathsheba[8], Diana[9] Berry, Phebe B[10]. Gardner, Ambrose M[11]., Shotwell.]

Gardner, (sometimes anciently written *Gardiner*) George[1], m. Hored (Long) Hicks and had William[2] who m. ________ and had John[3], who m. ________ Wilkinson and had John[4], who m. Bathsheba[5] Watson [of Jeffrey[3], John[2], John[1]] and had George Washington[5] Gardner, who m.[?] Diana Berry [of Jonathan] and had Bathsheba Phebe[6], called Phebe B., who m. Nathan[8] Shotwell [of Isaac M[7]., Richard[6], Benjamin[4], John[3], John[2], Abraham[1]] and had Ambrose M[9]., *et al.* George[1] and wife Hored (Long) Gardner had also Dorcas[2] who m. John Watson and had John[3] who m. Hannah ________ and had Jeffrey[4]: [Bathsheba[5], George Washington[6] Gardner, Phebe B[7]., Ambrose M[8]. Shotwell.]

Gerardy, John[1], m. Renewed Sweet [of John] and had Phillis[2], who m. John Smith [of John] and had John[3]: [Bathsheba[4], Bathsheba[5] Watson, George Washington[6] Gardner, Phebe B[7]., Ambrose M[8]. Shotwell.]

Greene, John[1], of Warwick R. I. [of Richard[3], Richard[2], Robert[1]] m. Joanna Tattersall and had James[2] who m. Elizabeth Anthony [of John] and had John[3], who m. Mary Allen [of Increase] and had Joseph[4], who m. Phebe[3] Langford [of John[2], Thomas[1]] and had Langford[5], who m. Abigail Thomas [of George] and had Bathsheba[6], who m. Jonathan Berry and had Diana[7], who m. George Washington[5] Gardner [of John[4], John[3], William[2], George[1]] and had Phebe B[8]: [Ambrose M[9]. Shotwell.]

Hallett, Richard[1], m. Amy Bowne [of John] and had Ame[2], who m. Benjamin[4] Shotwell [of John[3], John[2], Abraham[1]] and had Richard[5], who m. Mary Martin [of Isaac] and had Isaac M[6].: [Nathan[7], Ambrose M[8].]

Hartshorne, Richard[1], m. Margaret Carr [of Robert] and had Sarah[2], who m. Thomas Taylor and had Anna[3], who m. John[3] Webster [of William[2], William[1]] and had Catharine[4]: [Hugh[5] Pound, Edna C[6]., Nathan[7] Shotwell, Ambrose M[8].]

Holden, Randall[1], m. Frances Dungan [of William] and had Elizabeth[2], who m. John Rice and had John[3], who m. Elnathan[3] Whipple [of John[2], John[1]] and had Barbara[4]: [Phebe[5] Langford, Langford[6] Greene, Bathsheba[7], Diana[8] Berry, Phebe B[9]. Gardner, Ambrose M[10]. Shotwell.]

Ilsley, William[1], m. Barbara ________ and had Mary[2] who m. Samuel Moore and had John[3] [Samuel[4], Joseph[5], Sarah[6], Sarah[7] King, Edna C[8]. Pound, Nathan[9] Shotwell, Ambrose M[10].]

King, Joseph[1] m. ________ and had Joseph[2] who m. Mary ________ and had Nathan[3], who m. Sarah[5] Moore [of Joseph[4], Samuel[3], John[2], Samuel[1]] and had Sarah[4], who m. Hugh[5] Pound [of Samuel[4], Elijah[3], John[2], John[1]] and had Edna C[6].: [Nathan[6] Shotwell, Ambrose M[7].]

Langford, Thomas[1], m[2]. Sarah ________ and had John[2], who m. Barbara[3] Rice [of John[2], John[1],] and had Phebe[3], who m. Joseph[4] Greene [of John[3], James[2], John[1]] and had Langford[4]: [Bathsheba[5] Greene, Diana[6] Berry, Phebe B[7]. Gardner, Ambrose M[8]. Shotwell.]

Latham, Lewis[1] m. Winifred ________ and had Frances[2], who m.[2] William Dungan and had Frances[3] who m. Randall Holden and had Elizabeth[4]: [John[5] Rice, Barbara[6], Phebe[7] Langford, Langford[8] Greene, Bathsheba[9], Diana[10] Berry, Phebe B[11]. Gardner, Ambrose M[12]. Shotwell.]

Long, Hored, (or Herodias), m[2]. George Gardner (or Gardiner), and had William[2]: [John[3], John[4], George Washington[5], Phebe B[6]., Ambrose M[7]. Shotwell.] She had also Dorcas[2] Gardner, who m. John Watson and had John[3]: [Jeffrey[4], Bathsheba[5], George Washington[6] Gardner, Phebe B[7]., Ambrose M[8]. Shotwell.]

Martin, Isaac[1], m. Elizabeth Burling and had Mary[2], who m. Richard[5] Shotwell [of Benjamin[4], John[3], John[2], Abraham[1]] and had Isaac Martin[6] Shotwell: [Nathan[7], Ambrose M[8].]

Moore, Samuel[1], m. Mary Ilsley [of William] and had John[2] who m. Hope Robins [of Daniel] and had Samuel[3] who m. Mary ________ and had Joseph[4], who m. Christiana Bishop [of Moses] and had Sarah[5], who m. Nathan[3] King [of Joseph[2], Joseph[1]] and had Sarah[6]: [Edna C[7]. Pound, Nathan[8] Shotwell, Ambrose M[9].]

Olney, Thomas[1], m. Mary Small and had Mary[2], who m. John Whipple [of John] and had Elanthan[3]: [Barbara[4] Rice, Phebe[5] Langford, Langford[6] Greene, Bathsheba[7], Diana[8] Berry, Phebe B[9]. Gardner, Ambrose M[10]. Shotwell.]

Pound, John[1] m. Esther ________ and had John[2], who m. ________ and had Elijah[3] who m. Elizabeth ________ and had Samuel[4], who m. Catharine[4] Webster [of John[3], William[2], William[1]] and had Hugh[5], who m. Sarah[4] King [of

Nathan[3], Joseph[2], Joseph[1]] and had Edna C[6]., who m. Isaac M[6]. Shotwell [of Richard[5], Benjamin[4], John[3], John[2], Abraham[1]] and had Nathan[7]: [Ambrose M[8].]

Rice, John[1], m. Elizabeth Holden [of Randall] and had John[2], who m. Elnathan[3] Whipple [of John[2], John[1]] and had Barbara[4] who m. John Langford [of Thomas] and had Phebe[5]: [Langford[6] Greene, Bathsheba[7], Diana[8] Berry, Phebe B[9]. Gardner, Ambrose M[10]. Shotwell.]

Robins, Daniel[1], m. Hope ———— and had Hope[2], who m. John Moore [of Samuel] and had Samuel[3]: [Joseph[4], Sarah[5], Sarah[6] King, Edna C[7]. Pound, Nathan[8] Shotwell, Ambrose M[9].]

Shotwell, Abraham[1] m. ———— and had John[2], who m. Elizabeth Burton, and had John[3], Jr., who m. Mary Thorne, Jr., [of Joseph[1]] and had Benjamin[4], who m. Ame Hallet [of Richard] and had Richard[5], who m. Mary Martin [of Isaac] and had Isaac M[6]. who m. Edna C[6]. Pound [of Hugh[5], Samuel[4], Elijah[3], John[2], John[1]] and had Nathan[7] who m. Bathsheba Phebe[6] Gardner, called Phebe B. [of George Washington[5], John[4], John[3], William[2], George[1]], and had Ambrose M[8]., the compiler *et. al.*

Small, Mary[1], m. Thomas Olney and had Mary[2], who m. John Whipple [of John] and had Elnathan[3]: [Barbara[4] Rice, Phebe[5] Langford, Langford[6] Greene, Bathsheba[7], Diana[8] Berry, Phebe B[9]. Gardner, Ambrose M[10]. Shotwell.]

Smith, John[1], m. Margaret ———— and had John[2], who m. Phillis Gereardy [of John] and had John[3], who m. Mercy[3] Westcott [of Amos[2], Stukely[1]] and had Bathsheba[4], who m. Jeffrey[3] Watson [of John[2], John[1]] and had Bathsheba[5]: [George Washington[6] Gardner, Phebe B[7]., Ambrose M[8]. Shotwell.]

Stafford, Thomas[1], m. Elizabeth ———— and had Deborah[2], who m. Amos Westcott [of Stukely] and had Mercy[3]: [Bathsheba[4] Smith, Bathsheba[5] Watson, George Washington[6] Gardner, Phebe B[7]. Ambrose M[8]. Shotwell.]

Sweet, John[1], m. Mary ———— and had Renewed[2], who m. John Gereardy and had Phillis[3]: [John[4] Smith, Bathsheba[5], Bathsheba[6] Watson, George Washington[7] Gardner, Phebe B[8]., Ambrose M[9]. Shotwell.]

Tattersall, Joanna[1], m. John Greene [of Richard[3], Richard[2], Robert[1]] and had James[2]: [John[3], Joseph[4], Langford[5], Bathsheba[6], Diana[7] Berry, Phebe B[8]. Gardner, Ambrose M[9]. Shotwell.]

Taylor, Thomas[1], m. Sarah Hartshorne [of Richard] and had Anna[2], who m. John[3] Webster [of William[2], William[1]] and had Catharine[3]: [Hugh[4] Pound, Edna C[5]., Nathan[6] Shotwell, Ambrose M[7].]

Thomas, George[1], m. ———— and had Abigal[2], who m. Langford[5] Greene [of Joseph[4], John[3], James[2], John[1]] and had Bathsheba[3]: [Diana[4] Berry, Phebe B[5]. Gardner, Ambrose M[6]. Shotwell.]

Thorne, Joseph[1], m. ———— and had Mary[2], Jr., who m. John[3] Shotwell, Jr., [of John[2], Abraham[1]] and had Benjamin[3]: [Richard[4], Isaac M[5]., Nathan[6], Ambrose M[7].]

Watson, John[1], m. Dorcas Gardner [of George] and had John[2], who m. Hannah ———— and had Jeffrey[3], who m. Bathsheba[4] Smith [of John[3], John[2], John[1]] and had Bathsheba[4], who m. John[4] Gardner [of John[3], William[2], George[1]] and had George Washington[5] Gardner: [Phebe B[6]., Ambrose M[7]. Shotwell.]

Webster, William[1], m. Mary ———— and had William[2], who m. Susannah[3] Cowperthwaite [of John[2], Hugh[1]] and had John[3], who m. Anna Taylor [of Thomas] and had Catharine[4], who m. Samuel[4] Pound [of Elijah[3], John[2], John[1]] and had Hugh[5]: [Edna C[6]., Nathan[7] Shotwell, Ambrose M[8].]

Westcott, Stukely[1], m. ———— and had Amos[2], who m. Deborah Stafford [of Thomas] and had Mercy[3], who m. John[3] Smith [of John[2], John[1]] and had Bathsheba[4]: [Bathsheba[5] Watson, George Washington[6] Gardner, Phebe B[7]., Ambrose M[8]. Shotwell.]

Whipple, John[1] m. Sarah ———— and had John[3], who m. Mary Olney [of Thomas] and had Elnathan[3], who m. John Rice [of John] and had Barbara[4]: [Phebe[5] Langford, Langford[6] Greene, Bathsheba[7], Diana[8] Berry, Phebe B[9]. Gardner, Ambrose M[10]. Shotwell.]

Wilkinson, ————, m. John[3] Gardner [of William[2], George[1]] and had John[4] Gardner: [George Washington[5], Phebe B[6]., Ambrose M[7]. Shotwell.]

THE AUTHOR'S FOREFATHERS.

I.

ANCESTRY OF HIS PATERNAL GRANDFATHER,

ISAAC M[c]. SHOTWELL, OF ELBA, N. Y.

[Of Richard,[5] Benjamin,[4] John,[3] John,[2] Abraham.[1]]

Abraham[1] Shotwell, dw. Elizabethtown.

John[2] Sr., dw. Staten Island, m. 1679, Elizabeth Burton.

Joseph Thorne, dw. Long Island, m.

James Cock, of Long Island, m. Sarah ----------

John Bowne, dw. Long Island, m. Mary Cock, b. ---------- 1655.

John[3], Jr., b. ------ 1686 ±, d. 15 of 6 mo. 1762. m. 8 of 9 mo. 1709. dwelt Shotwell's Landing, N. J.

Mary Thorne, Jr., b. ------ 1686 ±. d. 11 of 11 mo. 1708

Richard Hallett d. ---------- 1746. m. dwelt Newtown, L. I.

Amy Bowne.

Benjamin[4] Shotwell, m. ----- of 8 mo. 1746, b. 23 of 1 mo. 1726, d. 15 of 5 mo. 1793, dwelt Shotwell's Landing, Rahway, N. J.

Ame Hallett b. ---------- 1727. d. 15 of 9 mo. 1796.

Isaac Martin, m. ... Elizabeth Burling b. -----------, d. 12 of 7 mo. 1781, dwelt New York City, N. Y.

Richard[5] Shotwell, b. 25 of 7 mo. 1756, d. 17 of 6 mo. 1833, m. 10 of 4 mo. 1782, Mary Martin, b. 1 of 7 mo. 1756, d. 27 of 3 mo. 1844, dwelt Essex Co., N. J., Farmington and Elba, N. Y.

ANCESTORS AND CHILDREN OF ISAAC M[c]. SHOTWELL, 1786-1860, OF ELBA, N. Y., [of Richard[5], Benjamin[4], John[3], John[2], Abraham[1]], who married, 1813, Edna C[6], Pound, 1796-1872 [of Hugh[5], Samuel[4], Elijah[3], John[2], John[1]], and had:—

| 1 Sarah P., b. and d. 1814. | 2 Anna P., 1815-1851. | 3 Mary S., 1817-1869. | 4 Isaac M., b. 1819, | 5 Amy, 1821-1850. | 6 Hugh P., b. 1825. | 7 Nathan, b. 1826. | 8 Sarah E., 1830-1854. | 9 David B., b. 1833. | 10 Catherine E., 1836-1857. |

Note.—For more detailed accounts of members of the Shotwell family proper the reader is referred to Part II of this work.

Abraham[1] Shotwell, the earliest of the name of whom we have definite knowledge, was at Elizabeth Town, the capital of East Jersey, as early as 1665. He was probably one of the many Englishmen who fled from the mother country after the restoration of Charles II. He was certainly an active defender of the cause of the settlers in opposition to the collection of burdensome quit-rents exacted by the Governor, Capt. Philip Carterett, on behalf of the non-resident lords proprietors, in consequence of which he was forced into exile and his New Jersey real estate was confiscated, being sold at auction 25 Apr. 1675, and a few days later was in possession of the Governor. On 29 Sept. 1677, he received patent of a grant of 38½ acres of land in the southeast side of Manhattan

Island, including a water mill on Sawmill Creek, which property, on 6 Nov. 1679, he conveyed "with consent of his son John," to John Robinson. He probably died soon afterward. The name of his wife and the names of his children other than John have not been certainly ascertained, although he is believed to have been the father also of Daniel of Staten Island, the progenitor of the Richmond county branch of the family.

John[2] Shotwell, Sr., dwelt on Staten Island but removed to Woodbridge, N. J., in the second decade of the eighteenth century and there died 22 of 7 mo. [Sept.] 1719. To him his father's confiscated land in Essex Co., N. J., was restored by order of the new governor and counsel, 12 May 1683. The date and manner of the final disposal of this property has not been ascertained, but it must have gone out of the possession of the family at a very early date. John Shotwell was a leading member of Woodbridge Monthly Meeting of Friends as early as March, 1707-8, and soon afterward had religious meetings appointed periodically at his house on Staten Island. He married in New York, in Oct. 1679, Elizabeth Burton. Of her parents and their family nothing further has been learned. John and Elizabeth (Burton) Shotwell had six sons and two daughters, as shown in the accompanying exhibit of the author's line of descent.

ONE LINE OF DESCENT FROM ABRAHAM SHOTWELL

of Elizabethtown, N. J., 1665, exiled 1675; disposed of New York property, "with consent of his son John," 1679, had:

1. JOHN[2], SR.,   2. (?) Daniel of Staten Island.

of Staten Island and Woodbridge; b. 1650±, d. 22 of 7 mo. 1719, m. Oct. 1679, Elizabeth Burton and had:

1. JOHN[3], JR.,   2. Elizabeth. 3. Sarah. 4. Abraham.

of Shotwell's Landing (now Rahway); b. 1686±, d. 15 of 6 mo. 1762, m. 3 of 9 mo. 1709, Mary Thorne, Jr., daughter of Joseph, and had:

Children: 1. Joseph. 2. John. 3. Elizabeth. 4. Mary. 5. Abraham. 6. Jacob. 7. Samuel.

8. BENJAMIN[4],

of Shotwell's Landing, now Rahway, N. J.; b. 23 of 1 mo. 1726, d. 15 of 5 mo. 1793, m. in 8 mo. 1740, Ame Hallett; b. 1727 d. 15 of 9 mo. 1794, daughter of Richard and Amy (Bowne) Hallett of New Town, L. I., and had:

Children: 1. Sarah. 2. Anie. 3. Mary. 5. Benjamin. 6. Elizabeth. 7. Thomas. 8. William. 9. Lydia. 10. Sarah.

4. RICHARD[5],

of Farmington and Elba, N. Y.; b. 25 of 7 mo. 1756, d. 17 of 8 mo. 1833, m. 10 of 4 mo. 1782, Mary Martin; b. 1 of 7 mo. 1756, d. 27 of 3 mo. 1844, daughter of Isaac and Elizabeth (Burling) Martin of New York and had:

Children: 1. Elizabeth. 2. Amy. 4. Benjamin. 5. Mary. 6. Elizabeth. 7. Benjamin. 8. Ahbe. 9. Lydia. 10. Sarah.

3. ISAAC MARTIN[6],

of Elba, Genesee Co. N. Y.; b. 24 of 9 mo. 1786, d. 19 of 10 mo. 1860, m. 4 of 2 mo. 1813, Edna C. Pound, b. 2 of 1 mo. 1796, d. 14 of 1 mo. 1872, daughter of Hugh and Sarah (King) Pound of Farmington, N. Y. [of Samuel[4], Elijah[3], John[2], John[1]], and had:

Children: 1. Sarah P. 2. Anna P. 3. Mary S. 4. Isaac M. 5. Amy. 6. Hugh P. 8. Sarah E. 9. David B. 10. Catharine E.

7. NATHAN[7],

of Elba, N. Y., and Concord, Mich.; b. 14 of 5 mo. 1826, m. 2 of 5 mo. 1850, Bathsheba Phebe Gardner (called Phebe B.), b. 23 of 2 mo. 1831, daughter of George Washington and Diana (Berry) Gardner of Elba, N. Y. [of John[4], John[3], William[2], George[1]], and had:

Children: 1. Rozilla P. 2. Ambrose M. 5. Manly N.

3. CASSIUS F[8].,   **4. IDA A[8].,**

of Concord, Mich.; b. 29 of 7 mo. 1855, m. 19 Aug. 1885, Edith M. Briggs; b. 5 Feb. 1866, daughter of William C. and Elizabeth (Lewis) Briggs of Concord, Mich. [of Richmond[3], Pardon[2], John[1]], and had *Owen Briggs Shotwell,* b. 17 Sept. 1886.

b. 23 of 2 mo. 1857, m. 8 July 1886, Jehiel K. Davis, b. 26 of 6 mo. 1848, son of Jehiel[4] and Phebe T. (Dean) Davis of Troy, Oakland Co., Mich. [of Kittridge[3], Thomas[2]], and had Jehiel Shotwell Davis (called J. S.), b. Concord, Mich., 5 March, 1892.

JAMES COCK, [latterly more commonly written Cocks or Cox, sometimes Coxe], yeoman, great grandfather of the wife of Benjamin[4] Shotwell, was at Setauket, Suffolk Co., L. I., as early as 1659; Oysterbay, Queens Co., L. I., 1662; Killingworth (since Matinecock), L. I., 1669. The names of his children appear on the records of the Society of Friends of New York, and vicinity, as children of James and Sarah Cock. They had:—(1.) Mary, b. 1655, m. (as 3rd wife) John Bowne. (2.) Thomas, b. 1658, m. Esther Williams. (3.) Martha, 1661 1670. (4.) John, b. 1666, m[1]. __________ m[2]. Dorothy __________ (5.) Hannah, b. 1669, m.

James de la Plaine. (6.) Sarah, b. 1672, m. (as 2nd wife) Henry Franklin. (7.) James, b. 1674, m. Hannah Feke. (8.) Henry, 1678-1742, m¹. Mary Feke or Feeks; m². Martha Pearsall. (9.) Martha, (again) b. 1680. John Cox, Jr., of New York and George W. Cocks, of Glen Cove, L. I., have in preparation a genealogy of this family.

JOHN BOWNE, of Long Island and his 3rd wife Mary, nee Cock, b. 1655, had a daughter *Amy*, who m. *Richard Hallet*, who dwelt at Newtown, L. I., and d. before the marriage of his daughter Ame in 8 mo. (October) 1746. *Ame* (*or Amy*) *Hallett*, b. 1727, m. Benjamin⁴ Shotwell, of Shotwell's Landing, laterally called Bricktown (now Rahway), N. J., and there d. 15 of 9 mo. 1796. She was probably sister to Lydia [or Elizabeth], second wife of Abraham⁴ Shotwell, son of John⁴, Jr., and Mary (Thorne) Shotwell, and brother to Benjamin.

Benjamin's son Richard⁵ Shotwell, of Essex Co., N. J. and Genesee Co., N. Y., m. in New York City 10 of 4 mo. 1782. Mary Martin, daughter of Isaac and Elizabeth (Burling) Martin of New York. Among the witnesses to this marriage appear the names of Elizabeth, Burling, Isaac, Elizabeth, Abigail, and Gulielma Martin. Mary's father, *Isaac Martin*, "departed this life the 12th of seventh mo. 1781." His son Isaac, in his Journal p. 3 says of him:— "My dear father, Isaac Martin, was an upright, honest Friend; one that feared God, and loved the truth. Being much concerned on his children's account that they might have the Lord for their portion, he watched over us for our good, often caused us to read the holy scriptures, and other good books, and took us to religious meetings. He had a dispensation of the gospel ministry committed to him and hath left a good savour behind him. In his last illness, he expressed that death was no terror to him; and there is cause to believe that he is admitted among the faithful followers of the Lamb, in that 'city which hath foundations, whose builder and maker is God.'"

ISAAC AND ELIZABETH (BURLING) MARTIN, had:—(1.) James, b. 27 of 5 mo. 1753, d. "the beginning of the 7th mo. 1753." (2.) Burling, b. 6 of 1 mo. 1755. (3.) Mary, b. 1 of 7 mo. 1756, d. 27 of 3 mo. 1844. For fuller sketch, see account of Richard Shotwell in family of Benjamin⁴ in part II, of this work. (4.) Isaac, Jr., b. 16 of 1 mo. 1758, d. 9 of 8 mo. 1828, m. 12 of 4 mo. 1780, Elizabeth Delaplaine, daughter of Joseph. Isaac was a hatter, an apothecary, and a minister of the Society of Friends at Rahway, N. J., and traveled much in the work of the ministry. (5.) James (again), b. 26 of 1 mo. 1760, d. 23 of 5 mo. 1761. (6.) ____________, b. 4 of 9 mo. 1761, d. 7 of 5 mo. 1763, "suddenly." (7.) Elizabeth, b. 13 or 19 of 2 mo. 1764, d. 31 of 12 mo. 1812, m. 27 of 6 mo. 1793, Webster Thorn, son of Abraham⁴ and Susanna (Webster) Thorne [of Mary⁸ Shotwell, Daniel², Abraham¹]. (8.) Abigail, b. 21 of 8 mo. 1765, d. at Plainfield, 14 of 8 mo. 1817, m. ___________________ (9.) James (again), b. 10 of 2 mo. 1767. (10.) Jane, b. 7 of 3 mo. 1770.

II.

ANCESTORS AND NEAR RELATIVES OF THE

AUTHOR'S PATERNAL GRANDMOTHER,

EDNA C. POUND, DAUGHTER OF HUGH AND SARAH (KING) POUND,
OF FARMINGTON, NEW YORK.

[Of Samuel,⁴ Elijah,³ John,² John.¹]

In Hotten's Lists of Emigrants to America 1600-1700 no mention is made of the name Pound, but it is recorded that Thomas Pond, aged 21, was one of the passengers who embarked 20 Apr. 1635, in the Elizabeth and Ann,—Roger Cooper, Master, with certificates from the minister of the parish and justices of the peace of their conformation to the Church of England, to be transported to New England.

It is said that "three brothers" (1.)________, (2.) John, and (3.) Benjamin Pond or Pound came from Yorkshire, England, near the close of the seventeenth century, and settled near Plainfield, N. J.; that a legacy fell to the family, to be controlled by the eldest son, but as he was intemperate and too poor to establish his claim, and his brothers thinking it would only be wasted refused to assist him, it is said to be still in the possession of the British Government. One of these brothers is said to have been the great grandfather of Benjamin F⁵. Pound of Kansas and California [of Daniel¹, Elijah¹, John², John¹?] whose daughter, Julia F. (Pound) Wyland of Smith Center, Kans., reports this tradition.

JOHN¹ POUND, was an early settler in the township of Piscataway, Middlesex Co., N. J., and d. there 21 Feb. 1690-91. His wife's name was Esther _________. They had a daughter Mary, b. 25 Dec. 1682, and are believed to have been the parents also of *John[2]*, *Jr.*, and William who died 4 Dec. 1694; also of Vinefruct who m. in Piscataway, N. J., 15 Oct., 1691, Robert Rosly.

JOHN[2] POUND, of Piscataway, N. J., m. -------- (perhaps Esther) and had (1.) Thomas b. 18 July 1708. (2) *Elijah*, b. 8 July, 1712, d. 17 of 3 mo. 1780, m[1]. Bathsheba --------, m[2]. Elizabeth --------, who was b. ---- 1718, d. 9 of 10 mo. 1793. (3.) Joseph, b. 25 June, 1715.

The following extracts are from the minutes of the Monthly Meeting of Friends for Woodbridge, Rahway and Plainfield, N. J.: "19th of 5th mo. 1757 -------- This Meeting is Inform'd that Elija Pound desires to b Joyn'd in unity with friends. John Webster and David Laing are appointed to Inquire into his life & Conversation & make Report thereof to next Monthly Meeting." On the 16 of 6 mo. these friends "Report they Rec'd a good account of him. This Meeting accepts him a member." He was a member of the committee appointed by the Friends at Rahway in 1778, for the relief of sufferers under the laws against non-combatiants but being compelled to affirm his allegiance to the Continental Congress to avoid being thrown into prison, was therefore allowed to resign from the committee.

Samuel[4] m. 1772 Catherine[4] Webster (Samuel[4] 1745-1826; Catherine[4] Webster 1756-1836)

- Elijah[3], b. 1712, m. Elizabeth, 1718--1793
  - John[2], m.
    - John[1] Pound, m. Esther.
- John[3] m. Anna[2] Taylor
  - William[2] Webster, m. Susannah Cowperthwaite.
    - William[1], m. Mary
    - John[2]
      - Hugh[1], m. Elizabeth.
  - Thomas[1] Taylor, m. Sarah[2] Hartshorne,
    - Richard[1] Hartshorne, m. Margaret[2] Carr.
      - Robert[1],

Nathan[3] King, m. 19 of 3 mo. 1771, Sarah[3] Moore (Nathan[3] b. 3 of 5 mo. 1750, d. ------- 1825; Sarah[3] Moore b. 15 of 5 mo. 1752, d. 18 of 12 mo. 1825)

- Joseph[2] King, m. Mary
  - Joseph[1] King, 1683-1761, m. ------------
- Samuel[3] 1709-1751 m. Mary d. 1811.
- Joseph[4] b. 9 Jan. 1731, d. 6 of 10 m. 1793, m. Christiana Bishop
  - John[2] b. 1674, m[1]., 1699;
    - Samuel[1] Moore, d. 1688, m[2]. Mary[2] Ilsley
      - William[1] m. Barbara.
  - Hope[2] Robins, b. 1681;
    - Daniel[1] Robins, m. Hope.
  - Moses[1] Bishop

Hugh[5] Pound, b. 3 of 6 mo. 1773, d. 17 of 10 mo. 1852, m. 24 of 4 mo. 1794, Sarah[4] King, b. 28 of 3 mo. 1776, d. 4 of 7 mo. 1863, dwelt Farmington, N. Y.

ANCESTORS OF EDNA C[6]. POUND, b. 2 of 1 mo. 1796, d. 14 of 1 mo. 1872 [of Hugh[5], Samuel[4], Elijah[3], John[2], John[1]], who m. 4 of 2 mo. 1813, Isaac M[6]. Shotwell, b. 24 of 9 mo. 1786, d. 19 of 10 mo. 1860, dwelt Elba, N. Y. [of Richard[3], Benjamin[4] John[3], John[2], Abraham[1]].

ELIJAH[3] POUND, of Piscataway, N. J., by 1st wife Bathsheba, had three sons:

1. *David*[1], b. 10 November 1736, d. in Middlesex Co., N. J., 19 of 6 mo. 1819, aged 83 years, buried at Plainfield.

2. *Zachariah*, b. 9 of 9 mo. (September), 1738, dwelt Essex Co. N. J., near Plainfield and there d. 19 of 5 mo. 1822, m. early in 1761, Elizabeth Smith, b. 27 of 9 mo. 1744, d. 23 of 10 mo. 1831, and had, (1.) Bathsheba, b. 14 of 5 mo. 1763, d. 1 of 12 mo. 1848, m. 24 of 1 mo. 1781, Benjamin[5] Shotwell 1759-1848 [of Benjamin[4], John[3], John[2], Abraham[1]]. (2.) Zachariah, Jr., dwelt Plainfield, N. J., m. ----------------- (3.) Samuel, b. 18 or 11 of 12 mo. 1767, d. 1 of 2 mo. 1854, m[1]. 20 of 4 mo. 1790, Susannah Webster, b 15 of 10 mo. 1768, d. 29 of 8 mo. 1809 or 1802 [of Hugh and Sarah (Marsh) Webster]; m[2]. Catharine Cole, who d. 8 of 9 mo. 1859. (4.) Sarah, m. Samuel Webster, son of Hugh and Sarah (Marsh) Webster.

3. *Benjamin*[4] b. 6 of 8 mo. (August) 1740, m. 23 of 2 mo. 1763, Elizabeth Laing [of David and Mary (Thorn) Laing], and had (1.) Susannah, b. 2 of 7 mo. 1764. (2.) John, b. 3 of 5 mo. 1766, d. Eden, N. Y., unm. (3.) Jacob, dwelt Eden, N. Y., and in the West, m. -------- ----- (4.) David, Jr., b. 23 of 5 mo. 1768, d. 18 of 11 mo. 1848, m[1]. 27 of 10 mo. 1790, Mary Shotwell, daughter of Abraham[4] and Mary (Jackson) Shotwell, [of Joseph[3], Daniel[2], Abraham[1]]; m[2]. 27 of 9 mo. 1828, Penelope (Sisson) Coggshall [of Joseph and Ruth Sisson]. (5.) Elijah, b. 18 of 11 mo. 1770, d. 11 of 3 mo. 1850, m. Sarah Brotherton, daughter of Henry[4] and Mercy (Schooley) Brotherton, [of Ann[3] Shotwell, Daniel[2], Abraham[1]]. (6.) Mary, b. 9 of 6 mo. 1777, d. 10 of 8 mo. 1846, m. 10 of 10 mo. 1798, William Hampton, son of William and Sarah[5] (Shotwell) Hampton [of Benjamin[4], John[3], John[2], Abraham[1]]. (7.) Joseph, b. 8 Feb. 1783, d. 28 Aug. 1834, m[1]. Sarah --------- m[2]. ---------- 1814±, Mary Corbin, b. 24 Oct. 1799, d. 31 July, 1861.

ELIJAH[3] POUND, by 2d wife Elizabeth, had:—

4. *Samuel*[4], b. 15 of 6 mo. 1745, d. 21 of 11 mo. 1826, m. 26 of 8 mo. 1772, Catharine Webster, b. 23 of 6 mo. 1756, d. 18 of 1 mo. 1836, dau. of John[3] and Anna (Taylor) Webster [of Wm[2]., Wm[1]], (children recorded later).

5. *Bathsheba*[4], b. 13 of 1 mo. 1747, m. 22 of 3 mo. 1769, Jacob[5] Shotwell, b. 29 of 8 mo. 1746, son of John[4] and Grace (Webster) Shotwell [of John[3], John[2], Abraham[1]], (for children see family of Jacob[5] Shotwell in part II).

6. *Daniel*[4], b. 1 of 1 mo. 1751, removed from New Jersey, about 1790 to the Black Creek settlement of Friends, locating in the present township of Bertie, Upper Canada about 9 miles from Buffalo, and there died; m. Prudence Jones, and had: (1.) Sarah, d. in Bayham township, C. W., aged 78, m. Jeremiah Moore. (2.) William, d. aged 40, m[1]. Elizabeth Tuttle; m[2]. Susannah Crawford, [of James and Amy (Peacock) Crawford]. (3.) Elijah, d. aged 40, m. Idalia Ward. (4.) Elizabeth, b. in Bertie, Upper Canada, 19 of 11 mo. 1791, d. 29 of 11 mo. 1878, m. 26 May, 1811, Jacob Zavitz, b. 13 of 6 mo. 1790, d. 11 of 12 mo. 1876, son of Jacob and Catharine (Learn) Zavitz. (5.) David, d. 1886± in 90th year, m[1]. Elizabeth (--------) Laing, widow; m[2]. Mary Herod. (6.) John, (Twin of David), d. Malahide, Ont., aged 82, m. Athelia Ward. (7.) Rachel, d. Burford, Brant Co., Ont., aged 86, m. Abel Schooley [of Azaliah]. (8.) Daniel, d. in Humberston, C. W., aged 40, m. Sarah Schuhfelt or Suffeldt. (9.) Mercy, d. near Ottawa, Ill., aged 80±, m. (as 2nd wife), Samuel[6] Shotwell, b. 1802, son of Benjamin[5] and Bathsheba (Pound) Shotwell [of Benjamin[4], John[3], John[2], Abraham[1]]. (10.) Benjamin Franklin, b. 8 of 10 mo. 1805, dwelt (1890), Ionia Kansas, m. 26 of 5 mo. 1827, Rebecca L[1]. Shotwell, who d. at Odell, Ill., daughter of Thomas[6] and Tamer (Lundy) Shotwell [of Benjamin[5], Benjamin[4], John[3], John[2], Abraham[1].]

7. *Sarah*[4], b. 20 of 8 mo. 1752, d. 18 of 12 mo. 1770, m. 27 of 3 mo. 1769, Samuel Smith, b. 1748 [of Shubel or Shobel], and had William, b.--------- 1770.

8. *Elizabeth*[4], b. 16 of 11 mo. 1754, m. 25 of 3 mo. 1772, William[5] Shotwell, son of John[4] and Grace (Webster) Shotwell [of John[3], John[2], Abraham[1]]. (For children, see family of William[5] Shotwell in Part II.)

9. *Elijah*[4], b. 19 of 11 mo. 1756, was a conspicuous minister among Friends, m. ------- 1784, Isabella Sharp, and had: (1.) Thomas, b. 13 of 11 mo. 1784. (2.) Jacob, b. 6 of 1 mo. 1787, m. 31 of 1 mo. 1811, Rhoda Jones, b. 25 of 5 mo. 1791 [of John and Miriam (--------) Jones] (3.) Margaret, b. 30 of 4 mo. 1788, d 14 of 8 mo. 1880, m. 29 of 11 mo. 1810, Samuel Hance b. 12 of 3 mo 1781, d. 5 of 10 mo. 1872 [of Benjamin[3], Samuel[1]]. (4.) David, b. 9 of 5 mo. 1790, m. 2 of 5 mo. 1811, Ann Hance, daughter of Benjamin and Sarah Hance. (5.) Daniel, b. 18 of 4 mo. 1792, was an esteemed minister of the Society of Friends, removed from Junius, N. Y., about 1831, to the Holland Purchase, becoming a member of Collins Monthly Meeting of Hicksite Friends; m. Sarah Webster [of William S.]. (6.) Elizabeth, b. 21 of 10 mo. 1793, m. 2 of 3 mo. 1814, Benjamin Hance, Jr., b. 31 of 1 mo. 1792 [of Benjamin[2], Samuel[1]]. (7.) Jonathan, b. 14 of 9 mo. 1795, m. 3 of 9 mo. 1817, Deborah Webster, daughter of William and Susannah Webster. (8.) Asa, b. 2 of 3 mo. 1797, d. in Ohio, 1858±, m. 4 of 3 mo 1819, Mary Hance [of Benjamin and Sarah Hance]. (9.) Bathsheba, b. 2 of 7 mo. 1798, m. 22 of 9 mo. 1819, William Rathbun [of Acors and Sarah Rathbun]. (10) Joel, b. 12 of 11 mo. 1799, dwelt (1874) Chippewa Falls, Wis., m. Ann

ISAAC MARTIN[5] SHOTWELL, 1786-1860,
Of Elba, Genesee Co., N. Y.,
SON OF RICHARD[5] AND MARY (MARTIN) SHOTWELL,
of Farmington and Elba, N. Y., and Descendant of Benjamin[4] and
Ame (Hallett) Shotwell, John[3] and Mary (Thorne) Shotwell,
John[2] and Elizabeth (Burton) Shotwell, Abraham[1]
Shotwell, of Elizabethtown, N. J., 1665.

EDNA C. (POUND) SHOTWELL, 1796-1872,
WIFE OF ISAAC M[6]. SHOTWELL,
of Elba, N. Y., Daughter of Hugh and Sarah (King) Pound, of Pis-
cataway, N. J., and Farmington, N. Y., and Granddaughter
(1) of Samuel and Catharine (Webster) Pound, of
Piscataway, Middlesex Co, N. J., and (2) of
Nathan and Sarah (Moore) King, of
Amwell and Rahway, N. J.

Coleman. (11.) Elijah, Jr., b. 10 of 5 mo. 1802, he was living in 1870 with his sons Albert E. and Thaddeus C. and his grandchildren, at Chippewa, Falls, Wis. From an interesting sketch of Thad. C. Pound in the Western Monthly (Chicago) for April, 1870, we gather that Elijah' m'. Judith Coleman who d. 1839±, [of Thaddeus Coleman]; m². 1843 ± .... who d. 1847±.

10. *Thomas'*, b 14 of 12 mo. 1758.

11. *Easter'* [Esther], b. 17 of 3 mo. 1761, m. (as 2nd wife) Henry Brotherton, Jr., b. 26 of 8 mo. 1757, son of James' and Alice (Schooley) Brotherton [of Ann' Shotwell, Daniel², Abraham'], and had: (1.) Rachel, m. Thomas Evers. (2.) Elijah, m. Rebecca Brotherton, [of William and Sarah (Dell) Brotherton. (3.) Margaret, died unmarried.

SAMUEL' POUND, 1745–1826, of Piscataway, Middlesex Co., N. J. [of Elijah', John², John'], m., 1772, Catharine Webster, 1756–1836 [of John', William², William'], and had :

1. *Hugh'*, b. 3 of 6 mo., 1773, in Piscataway township, Middlesex Co, N. J., whence he removed with his family, in a covered wagon, in 1803, to Farmington, Ontario Co., N. Y., and located upon a farm, where he resided until his death, 17 of 10 mo., 1852. After the separation in 1828 he remained a member of the Society of Friends, called Hicksite, until his death, also his children except Edna and William. He m. in the Old Friends meeting-house at Rahway, N. J., 24 of 4 mo. 1794, Sarah King, b. 28 of 3 mo. 1776, d. 4 of 7 mo. 1863, daughter of Nathan³ and Sarah (Moore) King, of the borough of Elizabeth, Essex (now Union) Co., N. J. [of Joseph², Joseph']. They were very active in the work of their religious society and their old family Bible has the following inscription : " Genesee Yearly Meeting of Friends was established and opened at Farmington [N. Y.] the second day after the second first day in sixth month, eighteen hundred and thirty-four." Sarah was clerk of Farmington Monthly Meeting as early as 2d mo. 1811. (Children and grandchildren recorded later.)

2. *Anna'*, b. 26 of 7 mo. 1775, dwelt Plainfield, N. J., and there died at the house of her nephew, George R. Pound, 4 of 3 mo. 1851, having been an esteemed minister in the Society of Friends for more than 40 years ; m. 22 of 6 mo. 1796, Jediah Shotwell, 1775–1847, son of Isaiah³ and Constant (Lippincott) Shotwell—q. v. in Part II—[of John', John³, John', Abraham']. They had no children of their own but were foster parents to 20 young orphan relatives, all of whom remained to the age of 21 or until marriage, excepting one, who, at the age of 18, went elsewhere to learn her trade.

3. *John'*, b. 10 of 1 mo. 1779, in Piscataway, near Plainfield, N. J., became member of Saratoga Monthly Meeting of Friends by certificate

from Rahway and Plainfield M. M., dated 25 of 11 mo. 1802 ; dwelt for a time in Canandaigua, N. Y.; was a butcher in Farmington, N. Y., but meeting with financial reverses he removed, about 1824, to Lockport, N. Y., and there d. 28 of 11 mo. 1832 ; m. 8 of 10 mo. 1803, Alice Smith (called Elsie), b. Adams, Berkshire Co., Mass., 22 of 3 mo. 1779, d. Lockport, N. Y., 30 of 3 mo. 1832, daughter of Joseph and Rhoda (Thornton) Smith of Farmington, N. Y. [of Samuel and Mary]. Having removed to Lockport his wife Alice and their 5 minor children, Amy, Joseph Smith, Samuel, Alexander, and John Waterman, became members of Hartland M. M., by certificate from Farmington M. M., dated 26 of 2 mo. 1824, and John himself received a similar certificate, dated 21 of 9 mo. 1826, which states that his outward affairs were unsettled.

4. *Elizabeth*,³ called Betsey, b. 16 of 1 mo. 1782, dwelt Poughkeepsie, N. Y., and Philadelphia, Pa., d. 13 of 8 mo. 1815, m. (as 1st wife) George Robinson, a tanner and courier, of New York and Philadelphia, a native of England, who d. 24 of 4 mo. 1831 ; they had : (1.) Abigail, who died in Philadelphia unmarried. (2.) Catharine, who m. (as 2nd wife) Samuel Keys, a minister among Friends. (3.) Mary, m. Dr. William Gibbons, a physician and druggist of Philadelphia, Pa., formerly teacher at Poughkeepsie, N. Y.; removed to California. (4.) Anna, b. 1808±, d. unmarried. (5.) Elizabeth, d. at Poughkeepsie, N. Y., unmarried. (6.) Susan, dw. (1888) Poughkeepsie, N. Y., m. Levi Arnold.

5. *William'*, b. 21 of 3 mo. 1784, in Piscataway, N. J.; dwelt there and at Amboy, removed to town of Boston, Erie Co., N. Y., returned to N. J. about 1814, but after 2d marriage went back to Erie Co., N. Y., and there d. 2 of 1 mo. 1857 ; m'. Mary Vail, b. 17 of 1 mo. 1787, d. 20 of 12 mo. 1811, daughter of David³ and Phebe (Jackson) Vail of Greenbrook, N. J. [of Margaret' Laing, Elizabeth³ Shotwell, John², Abraham']; m². 1812±, Abigail Shotwell, who d. 17 of 4 mo. 1831, daughter of Samuel³ Shotwell of Rahway, N. J. [of Abraham', John³, John², Abraham']; m³. Elizabeth Blair. By the 1st wife William had: (1.) Jackson, died in infancy. (2.) Jackson, b. 1 of 12 mo. 1808, farmer and baker, d. in Plainfield, N. J., m. Mary Ann Steward. (3.) Catharine Shotwell, b. 19 of 11 mo. 1810, dw. E. Hamburg, Erie Co., N. Y., and there d. 5 of 5 mo., 1889, m. 30 of 11 mo. 1831, Asa Hampton, b. 20 of 4 mo. 1806, d. 23 of 7 mo., 1886, son of William and Mary³ (Pound) Hampton [of Benj'., Elijah³, John², John']. By the 2d wife, William³ Pound had: (4.) William Tuttle S., b. 12 of 8 mo., 1813, dw. Chicago, Ill., m. Eleanor ________ (5.) Samuel S., b. 30 of 2 mo. 1815, d in New York, m. Mary Hatfield [of Henry]. (6.) George Fox, b. 5 of 6 mo. 1817,

dwelt Iowa, m. Mary Johnson ; m². _________
(7.) Elizabeth M., b. 4 of 5 mo. 1823, d. in Spring Brook, N. Y., m. Henry Pate. (8.) Ann S., b. 4 of 6 mo. 1825, d. Boston, N. Y., m. John Owens. (9.) Hugh, b. 11 of 5 mo. 1827, served in war of the rebellion, m. Almina _________.

6. *Samuel L'.*, b. 27 of 3 mo. 1786, in Piscataway, N. J., 1½ miles from New Market, was a farmer there on the homestead of his father, whence in 1836 he removed with his family to Plainfield, and engaged in the business of a butcher, with meat market on E. Front St., opposite Peace St., d. 23 of 2 mo. 1840, m. 24 of 6 mo. 1807, Anne Laing (called Nancy), b. 8 of 2 mo. 1789, d. 11 of 6 mo. 1857, daughter of John² and Susannah (Webster) Laing [of David¹, Elizabeth³ Shotwell, John², Abraham¹], and had: (1.) Hugh L., b. 2 or 7 of 6 mo. 1810, d. 18 of 10 mo. 1819. (2.) Mahlon, b. 15 of 4 mo. 1812, d. 13 of 9 mo. 1877, m. 30 of 12 mo. 1840, Hannah Barclay. (3.) William L., b. 29 of 1 mo. 1815, d. Newark, N. J., m. _________ Jones. (4.) George Robinson, b. 17 of 9 mo. 1817, dwells, 29 East 3rd. St., Plainfield, N. J., dealer in hides, tallow, etc., since 1860, formerly a butcher; an exemplary Friend and a worthy representative of the old time people whose sterling character is well worthy of emulation; m¹. 25 of 11 mo. 1840, Rachel Webster Vail, b. 24 of 3 mo. 1821, d. 5 of 9 mo. 1860, daughter of John A. and Deborah (Harned) Vail [of Abraham¹, Margaret¹ Laing, Elizabeth³ Shotwell, John², Abraham¹]; m². 19 of 9 mo. 1871, Josephine T. LaFetra, b. 22 of 2 mo. 1836, daughter of Edward B. and Mary D. (Brinley) LaFetra of Monmouth Co., N. J. [of Joseph]. (5.) Elizabeth R., b. 21 of 9 mo. 1822, d. 23 of 6 or 5 mo. 1862, m. Thomas Barclay.

HUGH² POUND, 1773-1852, of Piscataway, N. J., and Farmington, N. Y., [of Samuel¹, Elijah³, John², John¹], m. 1794, Sarah King, 1776-1863 [of Nathan³, Joseph², Joseph¹], and had:

1. *Edna C'.* b. 2 of 1 mo. 1796, d. 14 of 1 mo. 1872, m. 4 of 2 mo. 1813, Isaac Martin⁵ Shotwell, 1786-1860, son of Richard³ and Mary (Martin) Shotwell of Farmington, and Elba N. Y., [of Benjamin⁴, John³, John², Abraham¹]. (For fuller sketch and names of children see Part II.)

2. *Nathan King',* b. 18 of 1 mo. 1798, d. 3 of 1 mo. 1882, m. 7 of 11 mo. 1824, Hannah G. Lane, b. 25 of 6 mo. 1799, and had: (1.) Addison L., b. 13 of 6 mo. 1826, m. 11 of 12 mo. 1845, Chloe Gurnee, b. 13 of 1 mo. 1828. (2.) Edward H., b. 9 of 2 mo. 1828, dwelt Ontario, N. Y., m. Lucy Pease. (3.) Jacob M., b. 25 of 6 mo. 1830, d. _________, m. _________ (4.) Stephen B., b. 14 of 1 mo. 1833, dwells Lincoln, Neb., m. Laura Biddlecome. (5.) William N. C., b. 27 of 6 mo. 1839, d. 25 of 1 mo. 1841.

3. *Asher',* b. 19 of 1 mo. 1800, dwelt for a time in Pennsylvania, and afterward for many years in S. Perinton, Monroe Co., N. Y., and

after death of his wife, went to live with his son Ira B. at Richmond, Macomb Co., Mich., and there d. 11 of 2 mo. 1881; m. 28 of 1 mo. 1819, Mary Birdsall, b. 8 of 2 mo. 1803, d. 9th September 1878, daughter of Joseph and Hannah Birdsall (or Burtsall), and had: (1.) Ira B., b. 9 of 11 mo. 1819, m. 16 Aug. 1844, Marion C. Groff, b. 26 Aug. 1828 [of Peter]. (2.) Sarah Ann, b. 26 of 1 mo. 1823, d. 26 Aug. 1861, m. 1 May 1845, Seymour G. Allen, who d. 1887 ± [of Timothy]. (3.) Maria B., b. 6 of 12 mo. 1825, d. 26 or 24 of 7 mo. 1850, m. 1st Jan. 1844, Stephen B. Katkamier. (4.) Emiline Jane, b. 3 of 3 mo. 1828, d. 23 Dec. 1844, unmarried. (5.) Clarkson A., b. 19 of 11 mo. 1829, dw. Highland Lake, Weld Co., Colo., formerly (1854 1872) in Cedar Co., Iowa, m. 10 Nov. 1853, Mary A. Gage. (6.) Mary Jane, b. 4 of 11 mo. 1835, dw. Oshtemo, Kalamazoo Co., Mich., m. 11 Nov. 1853, Marshall Cass⁵ Lapham, son of William S'. and Betsy (Cass) Lapham [of Abraham¹, Joshua³, John², John¹]. (7.) Albert O., b. 9 of 8 mo. 1844, dwells Blair, Neb., m. 19 Nov. 1866, Alice Hibben.

4. *William⁵,* b. 12 of 12 mo. 1801, d. 27 of 8 mo. 1853, m¹. 21 of 12 mo. 1818, Betsey Warner, b. 22 of 2 mo. 1803, d. 18 of 10 mo. 1828 [of Jonathan and Mary]; m². 3 Feb. 1830, Mary J. Goodell, b. 28 or 23 Apr. 1801, d. 8th July, 1885. By 1st wife he had: (1.) Mary Jane, b. 28 of 6 mo. 1820, m¹. William Ellison, b. 18 of 7 mo. 1819, d. 1 of 11 mo. 1845 [of John]; m². Cyrus Cole. By 2nd wife, William⁵ had: (2.) Edwin Hathaway, b. 9 of 7 mo. 1831, was a Union soldier in the war of the rebellion; m¹. _________; m². Jenny _________ (3.) Sarah Abigail, b. 7 of 12 mo. 1832, dwells Gibbon St., Canandaigua, N. Y., m. Elisha Watson⁵ Gardner, b. 23 of 11 mo. 1826, son of Elisha W', and Sarah (Pattison) Gardner [of Wm'., John³, Wm²., George¹].

5. *Jediah Shotwell⁵ Pound,* b. 26 of 8 mo. 1804, d. 5 of 2 mo. 1882, in W. Walworth, N. Y., where he had lived for many years; m¹. 29 of 1 mo. 1829, Edith Laing, b. 11 of 2 mo. 1806, d. 12 of 5 mo. 1852, dau. of John and Achsah (Lundy) Laing [of John⁴, Samuel³, Wm²., John¹); m². 7 of 6 mo. 1853, Prudence P. Shotwell, b. 7 of 10 mo. 1826, d. 27 of 6 mo. 1876, daughter of Benjamin⁶ and Catharine (Pugsley) Shotwell [of Benjamin⁵, Benjamin⁴, John³, John², Abraham¹]. By 1st wife, he had: (1.) Anna S., b. 27 of 4 mo. 1832, m. 23 Apr. 1861, Dr. Jacob Rickabaugh. (2.) Harvey H., b. 28 of 7 mo. 1834, is a merchant with his brother William at Williamston, Wayne Co., N. Y., m. 15 of 11 mo. 1870, Martha Pearsall (called Matty). (3.) Jediah S., Jr., b. 20 of 4 mo. 1837, d. 5 of 6 mo. 1852. (4.) Hugh, b. 10 of 7 mo. 1839, dw. Madison, Wis., m. 19 of 7 mo. 1873, Ida Beach. (5.) William, b. 29 of 12 mo. 1843, m. 15 of 1 mo. 1873, Mary L. Boynton. By 2nd wife, Jediah S'. Pound had: (6.) Edith Laing,

b. 8 of 3 mo. 1854, dwells N. Perinton, N. Y., m. 30 Jan. 1889, Oliver B. Furman.

6. *Anna*[6], b. 17 of 2 mo. 1807, d. 15 of 2 mo. 1886, m. 2 of 12 mo. 1824, Nathan Comstock, b. 10 of 2 mo. 1802, d. 8 of 10 mo. 1845, son of Otis and Huldah Comstock, and had: (1.) Caroline A., b. 2 of 5 mo. 1826, President of Granger Place School, Canandaigua, N. Y., since 1876. (2.) Huldah Ann, b. 11 of 12 mo. 1829, dw. Fairport, N. Y., m. 12 Oct. 1854, Jeremiah S. Ramsdell, b. 1 of 8 mo. 1822, son of Gideon and Hannah (Smith) Ramsdell. (3.) William Otis, b. 8 of 1 mo. 1836, d. 12 of 5 mo. 1861, unm.

7. *Catharine Eliza*[6], b. 27 of 9 mo. 1809, d. 21 of 11 mo. 1884, m. 27 of 11 mo. 1827, Seth W. Bosworth, b. 13 of 11 mo. 1806, d. ______ ____________, [of John], and had: (1.) Elizabeth J., b. 31 of 8 mo. 1828, m[1]. 6 of 6 mo. 1849, Henry Gilbert Zavitz, b. 21 of 10 mo. 1824, d. 5 of 8 mo. 1875 [of Henry and Catharine Zavitz], m[2]. 7 of 2 mo. 1878, William Cornell, b. 24 of 12 mo. 1820 [of Jesse and Ann]. (2.) Mary G., b. 3 of 2 mo. 1830, dw. Rochester, N. Y., m. 1 of 1 mo. 1855, Richard Hallett Herendeen, b. 20 of 4 mo. 1822, d. 28 of 12 mo. 1876, son of James and Elizabeth[6] (Shotwell) Herendeen [of Richard[3], Benjamin[4], John[3], John[2], Abraham[1]]. (3.) William H., b. 9 of 8 mo. 1832, d. 14 of 1 mo. 1885, m. 27 Dec. 1860, Susan Jennings. (4.) Sarah K., b. 10 of 8 mo. 1834, m. 11 of 4 mo. 1855, Nathanial B. Sheldon, b. 26 of 2 mo. 1824, d. 31 of 7 mo. 1886. (5.) John H., b. 9 of 8 mo. 1838, dw. Rochester, N. Y., m. 22 of 5 mo. 1859, Mary B. Cline, b. 22 Sept., 1838.

(8.) *Sarah K*[6], b. 8 of 10 mo. 1813, d. 6 of 9 mo. 1832, m 25 of 11 mo. 1830, George Daily, b. 12 of 3 mo. 1805, d. ___________, and had, Sarah Elizabeth, b. 9 of 12 mo. 1831, d. 26 of 6 mo. 1832.

CHILDREN AND GRANDCHILDREN OF JOHN[3] AND ALICE (SMITH) POUND OF LOCKPORT, N. Y., [OF SAMUEL[4], ELIJAH[3], JOHN[2], JOHN[1].]

1. *Philander*, b. 8 of 8 mo. 1804, Ontario Co., N. Y., d. 16 of 8 mo. 1810.

2. *Amy*[5], b. 27 of 9 mo. 1806, d. Lockport, N. Y., aged more than 70 years, m. 23 of 9 mo. 1824, Lyman Austin Spalding, who d. at Lockport, N. Y., 7 Jan. 1885, and had: (1.) Alice Jane b. 1 of 5 mo. 1826, dw. 158 High St., Lockport, N. Y., m. 6 Aug. 1845, Charles Evans of Batavia, N. Y., who d. 8 Sept. 1865, aged 44 [of David]. (2.) Amy Ann, b. 10 of 9 mo. 1827, d. young. (3.) Catharine Elizabeth[5], called Kate E. b. 8 of 10 mo. 1829. (4.) Lyman Austin, Jr., b. 22 of 12 mo. 1832, dw. Market St., Lockport, N. Y., was appointed by President G. Cleveland, in 1887, U. S. Consul at Aix la Chapelle, transferred in 1888 to the consulate of Brunswick, Germany; m. 15 May, 1867, Caroline Amy Lapham, dau. of William and Rebecca T[6].

(Smith) Lapham [of Mary[5] Shotwell, Richard[3], Benj[4]., John[3], John[2], Abraham[1]].

3. *Joseph Smith*[5], b. 1 of 5 mo. 1808, d. 24 of 9 mo. 1859, was an Orthodox Friend; m. 12 of 10 mo. 1829, Lavinia Dillingham, who d. ______ 1887, aged 75+, and had: (1.) Sarah Jane, who d. in infancy. (2.) Lyman Joseph, resided on the old Pound homestead, 114 Chestnut St., Lockport, N. Y., and there d. 17 Oct. 1888, unm. By prudence and careful investment he amassed a small fortune, estimated between $30,000 and $35,000, the greater portion of which he bequeathed to the Lockport Home for the Friendless. He also bequeathed to his cousin and housekeeper, Elizabeth Almina Pound [dau. of Samuel], the sum of $5,000, together with household furniture, books, household goods, beds, bedding, and pictures, and left smaller legacies to "Miss Ella Vail Thorne of Plainfield, N. J.," "Miss Kate Spaulding of Lockport, N. Y.," L. Austin Spaulding, John W. Pound and Lucretia Sophia Griffis, Frederick Few, Robert Duff and Eliza J. Howe, all of Lockport, N. Y., and directed his remains to be placed by the side of his father and mother in the Friends' burial plot in Cold Springs cemetery in Lockport, and that a stone slab or monument be placed thereat of the same general character as the one lately erected by him at the graves of his parents.

4. *Samuel*, b. 25 of 7 mo. 1810, dw. with son, Waterman S., at Lockport, N. Y., m. 1 of 1 mo. 1832, Lucinda Andrews, who d. _________, 1845, and had: (1.) Waterman Smith, dw. 45 Niagara St., Lockport, N. Y., m. 1864 Addie McNeil, who d. ______, 1888. (2.) John W., d. aged 4 yrs. (3.) Elizabeth Almina, b. 1841, dw. 114 Chestnut St., Lockport, N. Y., unm., 1888.

5. *Alexander*, b. 22 of 11 mo. 1812, dw. 504 High St., Lockport, N. Y., a farmer, m. 22 of 11 mo. 1842, Almina Whipple, niece of wife of Samuel, and had: (1.) John E., b. ____ 1844; was youngest member of New York Assembly, session of 18..; Assistant U. S. Attorney 1874; U. S. Commissioner 1884, office 55 Main St., res. 345 High St.; m. Catharine Hurd. (2.) Edwin, d. young. (3.) Alexander. (4.) Cuthburt Winfield, b. 1864±; is a lawyer with his brother John E., in Lockport, N. Y.; State senator 1895; m. ______ June 1887, Emma White.

6. *John Waterman*, b. 14 of 7 mo. 1818, was a gardner; dw. 244 Pine St., Lockport, N. Y., m. 1855± Lucretia Watson and had: (1.) John, d. aged 6 yrs. (2.) William R. W., dw. 244 Pine St., Lockport, N. Y.

OUR WEBSTER ANCESTORS AND THEIR FAMILIES.

Nathan Webster, one of the freeholders in Woodbridge, Middlesex Co., N. J., who, about 1670, shared in the first division of public land of the township, receiving a lot of 93 acres as his portion, is not thought to have been the progenitor of the Quaker Websters of New Jersey.

WILLIAM[1] WEBSTER probably came from Scotland with the Scotch settlers of Amboy, about 1685; he was certainly a freeman of the town of Woodbridge and a consistent Friend as early as 1695. In the minutes of Woodbridge preparative meeting of the Society of Friends the earliest Webster name, that of William Webster, is first found as one of the witnesses to a certificate given 18 of 2 mo. 1706, to William Sutton and Jane his wife, who were intending to remove from Piscataway to Burlington. But from Dally's History of Woodbridge (p. 86) we learn that William Webster was a consistent Friend there more than ten years before.

On the 1 of Oct. 1695, the Woodbridge town meeting voted to pay to the town minister, Rev. Samuel Shepard, £50 per annum, or its equivalent in the current pay of the colony, which was pork, peas, wheat and other agricultural productions. This was to be raised by direct tax upon all the townsmen. To this action, on the ground of conscientious scruples, the Quakers objected. The old town book says: "William Webster, pretending that it was contrary to his conscience to pay anything toward the maintenance of a minister, Capt. John Bishop hath engaged in open town meeting to free the said Webster from the said charge and to pay the said Webster's part so long as the said Bishop shall live." Dally remarks that so far as we have any account this was the first decided stand against the tax for the support of the town minister, and was the beginning of the controversy which eventuated in the complete separation of civil from ecclesiastical affairs. Two years later the Rev. Samuel Shepard's salary was raised to £60 a year. The Quakers strongly opposed an indiscriminate assessment for this purpose as unjust. They were contributing for the support of their own society and considered it not equitable that they should be compelled to pay the tax for the support of a ministry which they did not and could not enjoy. In 1700 the salary was ordered to be raised by subscription, but in 1702 it was again paid out of the town rates in spite of the protests of the Quakers.

William[1] Webster of Woodbridge and wife Mary had:

1. *Mary*, b. 31 July 1690, undoubtedly in Woodbridge, N. J., as these dates of birth were taken from the Woodbridge town book.

2. *Hannah*, b. 18 Sept. 1691.

3. *William*, b. 19 Jan. 1692-3, at Woodbridge, N. J., m. ------------ of 3 mo. (May) 1717, Susannah Cowperthwait, daughter of John, and granddaughter of Hugh, who was born in England about 1648, and died at Flushing, L. I., 20 May 1720; his wife Elizabeth died at Flushing, L. I., 15 Dec. 1697. Hugh and Elizabeth Cowperthwait, settled at Flushing, 1674. The following is copied from the rec-

ords of the Society of Friends: — "Att our monthly meeting held att onr meeting house att Woodbridge ye 18th day of the 2 mo. 1717. Grace Kinsey and Mary Trenury presented William Webster & Susanna Cowperthwait to this meeting who declared their intention of taking each other in marriage, it being the first time. This meeting appoints John Laing & John Shotwell, Jun., to report in ye man's clearness in respect to marriage with any other and into his conversation." And on "ye 16th of the 3rd month, 1717, ------------ Elizabeth Shotwell and Ann Brotherton presented before this meeting [of Men Friends], William Webster & Susannah Copperthwait who declared their intentions of marriage, it being the second time and on enquiry made, nothing appearing to obstruct, this meeting leaves them to their liberty to consummate their intentions of marriage according to the good order of truth. And it was left to the care of John Kinsey to provide them a certificate." (Children recorded later.)

4. *Moses*, b. Oct. ye 5th, 1694.

5. *Sarah*, b. June ye 24, 1695 [Error in this or preceding date]; she was "left at liberty," by Woodbridge, M. M., 15 of 8 mo. 1719, to marry William Chambers.

6. *Rachel*, b. 1697. The father, William[1], for permitting a daughter to be "married by a priest" at his house before 15 of 12 mo. 1726-7, made satisfactory acknowledgment to Woodbridge Monthly Meeting of Friends, one month later.

7. *Aaron*, b. 1700.

8. *Benjamin*, b. 4 of 2 mo. 1709. One Benjamin Webster became member of Kingwood Monthly Meeting by certificate from Woodbridge, M. M., dated 17 of 8 mo. 1751, but he with his wife and children brought back a similar certificate dated 21 of 10 mo. 1756.

9. *Joseph*, b. 1710, m. 1733, Elizabeth Shotwell, daughter of John[3] and Mary (Thorne) Shotwell of Shotwell's Landing [of John[2], Abraham[1]]. They were left at liberty to marry by Woodbridge, M. M., 15 of 9 mo. 1733; and the orderly consummation of this marriage was reported to the meeting of 10 mo. 20th, 1733.

WILLIAM[2] WEBSTER, JR., b. 1692-3, of Plainfield, N. J. [of William[1]], m. 1717, Susannah[3] Cowperthwait [of John[2], Hugh[1]], and had:

1. *John[3]*, b. 22 of 2 mo. (Apr.) 1718, d. 29 of 9 mo. 1800; built the first Grist Mill in Plainfield and put his son Taylor, into it. "Att our Monthly Meeting held att Woodbridge the 20th 7th mo. 1763, ------------ A proposal from Plainfield preparative meeting for holding a meeting circular at the house of John Webster & Zachariah Pound, at 4 o'clock afternoon on first days from this time to ye 1st of ye 10th mo. next was made and agreed to." He m. 24 of 11 mo. (Jan.), 1743-4, Anna Taylor, b. 1726, d. 20 of 5 mo. 1762, daughter of Thomas and Sarah (Hartshorn) Taylor. The minutes

of Woodbridge M. M. show that John Webster and Anna Taylor, also Samuel Smith and Masse Taylor were married with the unity of Friends, between 11th mo. 19th and 12th mo. 16th 1743-4. Jonathan Harned and Edward Fitz Randolph, Jr., being the committee appointed to attend both marriages and see that good order was observed at the same. (Children recorded later.)

2. *Mary*, b. 26 of 5 mo. 1721, d. 23 of 11 mo. 1736.

3. *William*, b. 27 of 7 mo. 1723, d. .... 1750, s. p., m. 1749, Mary Thorn, daughter of Jacob and Susannah³ (Shotwell) Thorn [of Daniel², Abraham¹].

4. *Grace²*, b. 4 of 9 mo. 1725, m. between 17 of 9 mo. and 15 of 10 mo., 1743 (as 2d wife), John⁴ Shotwell of Plainfield [of John³, John², Abraham¹]. (For children, see family of John¹ Shotwell in part II.)

5. *Rachael²*, b. 22 of 8 mo. 1727, d. .... of 12 mo. 1779, m. 1744 Abner Hampton, d. .. of 2 mo. 1780. Dally in his History of Woodbridge, p. 215-16, says: "Several soldiers under Col. Samuel Hunt seized the horses and wagon of Abner Hampton on the 24 of May 1760, as he was driving leisurely along the road, nine miles from home. They wanted the team for the transportation of their baggage, a distance of twelve miles. They endeavored to pursuade Abner to drive for them or procure a teamster, promising a generous remuneration. He declared that conscientious scruples forbade either his performing the task or receiving any reward therefor. The wagon was laden and the soldiers disappeared with it, the worthy Quaker pursuing his lonely way homeward on foot with no very bright hope of seeing his horses again. But, on the 27th, who should drive up to Abner's door but Azaliah Dunham with the team all safe and sound! Such instances of devotion to their time-honored anti-war principles served to strengthen the Friends in Woodbridge and its vicinity." Abner and Rachel had: (1.) .... a son who d. 26 of 7 mo. 1749. (2.) William, who d. at Rahway 24 of 2 mo. 1781, m. 28 of 9 mo. 1768, Sarah³ Shotwell, daughter of Benjamin⁴ and Ame (Hallett) Shotwell, [of John³, John², Abraham¹]. (3.) Mary, d. 1755. (4.) Isaac, d. 2 of 3 mo. 1763. (5.) Abner. On the 17 of the 11 mo. 1773, Abner Hampton's son .... was apprenticed to Isaac Thorn. On 21 of 2 mo. 1782, Abner Hampton was disowned by the Monthly Meeting for assisting military enterprises. (6.) Joseph; m. 4 mo. 1782, William Webster agreed to keep Abner Hampton's son Joseph one year, and from the M. M. minutes of 12th mo. 17, 1783, we learn that Joseph Hampton had been bound as an apprentice to William Webster. He m. 23 of 10 mo. 1805, Elizabeth Cook of Bridgetown (Rahway), who d. there 30 of 7 mo. 1825, aged 44. In 11 mo. 1772, the parents, with their 5 children then at home, became members of Rahway and Plainfield Monthly Meeting by certificate from Kingwood M. M., and it is remarked that two daughters were old enough to support themselves.

6. *Hugh²*, Sr., b. 20 of 3 mo. 1730, d. Plainfield, N. J., 17 of 7 mo. 1815; he suffered for his peace principles during the French and Indian war. J. W. Dally (History of Woodbridge, p. 215), says: "In 1758, Hugh Webster was drafted and taken three miles from his dwelling. Capt. Benjamin Stiles, before whom he was taken, demanded that he should go into the service himself or furnish a substitute. Hugh positively refused to do either; so he was led away eight miles further to a spot where the guard expected to find the company assembled. The soldiers, however, had marched away. He was left to take care of himself and returned to his residence, stopping at Capt. Stiles house to inform him that his men had set him free." He m. in 1753, Sarah¹ Marsh, b. 21 of 1 mo. [March] 1737, d. 24 of 2 mo. [Feb.] 1791, daughter of Samuel³ and Mary Marsh of Rahway [of Joseph² b. 1 Apr. 1663, Samuel¹, b. 1623±, who settled at Elizabethtown, N. J., 1666]. Hugh Webster with Sarah Marsh, and Sarah Webster with William Marsh, passed meeting in Woodbridge at the same time, 15 of 11 m. 1753, and their marriages were consummated between that date and that of the next Monthly Meeting, 20 of 12 mo. 1753. Hugh and wife Sarah had: (1.) William, b..... of 3 mo. 1755, d. 11 of 6 mo. 1793, m. .... of 5 mo. 1775, Sarah Smith who d. 26 of 4 mo. 1813. (2.) John, called John III., b. 1756±, d. 19 of 11 mo. 1817, m¹. "by a priest" before 20 of 12 mo. 1775, Mary Morris; m² 2 of 2 mo. 1809, Isabel Smith, b. 19 of 6 mo. 1783 [of Charles and Lydia]. (3.) Mary, b. 10 of 10 mo. 1758, d. 1832±, m. 1782 (between 21 of 11 mo. and 18 of 12 mo.) Edward⁴ Fitz Randolph b. 23 of 4 mo. 1749, d. 4 of 1 mo. 1831, son of Edward³ and Phebe (Jackson) Fitz Randolph [of Edward², Edward¹]. (4.) Martha, b. 30 of 7 mo. 1760, d. 20 of 1 mo. 1790, m. 1781, (as 1st wife) Thomas³ Laing, b. 5 of 10 mo. 1759, d. 11 of 2 mo. 1827, son of Isaac² and Annabella (Edgar) Laing [of Elizabeth³ Shotwell, John², Abraham¹]. (5.) Samuel, b. 1 of 8 mo. 1762, d. .... of 7 mo. 1843, m¹. 1789, Sarah³ Pound, daughter of Zachariah⁴ and Elizabeth (Smith) Pound [of Elijah³, John², John¹]; m², Martha Thorn [of Hugh]. (6.) Hugh, b. .... 1764, d. 24 of 11 mo. 1811; m. 1786, Mercy Pound. (7.) Isaac, b. 19 of 6 m. 1766, d. 27 of 11 mo. 1823, m. 24 of 10 mo. 1787, Mary³ Laing, b. 11 of 8 mo. 1768, daughter of John² and Susannah (Webster) Laing [of David⁴, Elizabeth³ Shotwell, John², Abraham¹]. (8.) Susannah, or Susan, b. 15 of 10 mo. 1768, d. 20 of 11 mo. 1802, m. 20 of 4 mo. 1790, Samuel Pound, b. .. of 12 mo. 1767, d. 1 of 2 mo. 1854, son of Zachariah⁴ and Elizabeth (Smith) Pound [of

Elijah[3], John[2], John[1]]. (9.) Marsh, b. 27 of 8 mo. 1771, d. 28 of 10 mo. 1819, m. 1794, Rebecca[6] Vail, b. 7 of 5 mo. 1778, daughter of David[5] and Phebe (Jackson) Vail [of Margaret[4] Laing, Elizabeth[3] Shotwell, John[2], Abraham[1]]. (10.) Sarah, b. 27 of 11 mo. 1773, d. 1 of 7 mo. 1789. (11.) Anna, b. 13 of 3 mo. 1777, d. 12 of 7 mo. 1845, m. 23 of 7 mo. 1794, Joseph Laing, b. 21 of 2 mo. 1773, son of John and Susannah (Webster) Laing [of David[4], Elizabeth[3] Shotwell, John[2], Abraham[1]]. (12.) Joseph, b. 17 of 3 mo. 1779, d. 20 of 12 mo. 1854, m. 23 of 9 mo. 1802, Amy King, b. 15 of 7 mo. 1784, d. 26 of 4 mo. 1876, daughter of Nathan[3] and Sarah (Moore) King [of Joseph[2], Joseph[1]]. (Child later).

7. *Susannah[3]*, b. 15 of 6 mo. 1732, m. 22 of 6 mo. 1750, Abraham Thorne, b. 14 of 1 mo. 1728-9, son of Abraham and Mary[3] (Shotwell) Thorne [of Daniel[2], Abraham[1]], and had: (1.) William, b. 5 May 1751. (2.) Hugh, b. 16 June 1753, m. 1780±, ... (3.) Elizabeth, b. 12 June 1755. (4.) Abraham, b. 1 of 4 mo. 1757, d. 6 of 2 mo. or 3 mo. 1822, in Galien, N. Y., m. between 18 of 7 mo. and 15 of 8 mo. 1781, Elizabeth Smith, b. 7 of 6 mo. 1757, d. 25 of 5 mo. 1833. (5.) John, b. 10 March 1759, went to Nova Scotia at close of Revolutionary War. (6.) Mary, b. 20 Apr. 1762. (7.) Isaac, b. 24 Nov. 1763. (8.) Rachel, b. 21 Sept. 1765. (9.) Webster, b. 6 Aug. 1767, d. young. (10.) Susannah (twin), b. 6 Aug. 1767. (11.) Jacob, b. 15 Nov. 1768. (12.) Webster (again), b. 8 of 10 mo. 1770, removed from Lockport, N. Y., to Raisin Tp., Lenawee Co., Mich., and there d. at the house of Nathan and Sarah[6] (Shotwell) Chase; m.[1] 27 of 6 mo. 1793, Elizabeth Martin, daughter of Isaac and Elizabeth (Burling) Martin of New York; m[2]. Ruth Mosher [of Joshua]. (13.) Sarah, b. 13 June 1773.

8. *Martha*, b. 15 of 4 mo. 1734, m. 22 of 6 mo. 1750, Joseph Marsh, b. 7 of 8 mo. 1730 [of Samuel and Mary].

9. *Mary[3]*, b. 9 of 4 mo. 1736, m. 22 of 9 mo. 1756, John Smith[4] Shotwell, son of John[1] and Elizabeth (Smith) Shotwell [of John[3], John[2], Abraham[1]]. (For children see family of John Smith[4] Shotwell, in Part II.)

10. *Sarah[3]*, b. 22 of 5 mo. 1738, m. .. of 11 mo. 1753, William Marsh, b. 1734, son of Samuel and Mary Marsh of Ash Swamp, N. J., and had: (1.) William, Jr., b. 12 of 8 mo. 1754, m. 1775 .... (2.) Isaac, b. 16 of 4 mo. 1756. (3.) Mary, b. 23 of 2 mo. 1758. (4.) Samuel, b. 6 of 4 mo. 1760. (5.) Ziporah, b. 11 of 2 mo. 1762. (6.) Hugh, b. 16 of 10 mo. 1763. (7.) Sarah, b. 15 of 12 mo. 1764, m. 26 of 8 mo. 1784, Joseph Laing, son of David[4] and Mary (Thorn) Laing [of Elizabeth[3] Shotwell, John[2], Abraham[1]]. (8.) John, b. 9 of 3 mo. 1767, m. 26 of 8 mo. 1790, Phebe Allen. (9.) James, b. 10 of 9 mo. 1768, m. 21 of 5 mo. 1792, Margaret Elston, b. 6 of 12 mo. 1774, d. 21 of 3 mo. 1820, daughter of Samuel and Margaret. Her's is the first Elston [or Alston] name in the record of births of members of Rahway and Plainfield M. M. (10.) Mulford, b. 20 of 6 mo. 1771. (11.) Charles, b. 24 of 5 mo. 1773. (12.) Gideon, b. 28 of 3 mo. 1775. (13.) Elizabeth, b. 24 of 8 mo. 1776. (14.) Rachel, b. 15 of 11 mo. 1778.

11. *Elizabeth[3]*, b. 8 of 2 mo. 1741, probably the Elizabeth Webster who m. between 17 of 5 mo. and 21 of 6 mo. 1759 (as 1st wife), John Laing, supposed son of Samuel[3] and Elizabeth (Smith) Laing [of Wm[2]., John[1]]. John Laing m. again before 16 Jan. 1765, to his former wife's 1st cousin, contrary to Friends' discipline, for which he was dealt with by the Monthly Meeting of Rahway and Plainfield, which meeting, on 20 of 12 mo. 1769, granted a certificate of membership to John Laing and wife and children, directed to Hardwick M. M. A similar certificate to the same or another John Laing and family was granted 18 of 4 mo. 1770. According to a record by John Laing of Cass City, Tuscola Co., Mich., "as he knew it to be from memory, with the part sent him as found in Edwin Schmock's library," we gather that *John[1] Laing*, a native of Scotland and a Quaker, emigrated to New Jersey, married Hannah Webster of Plainfield and had 6 children, Elizabeth, William, Samuel, John, Joseph and Elijah. But the tradition that this John Laing came from Scotland is distrusted.

John[3] Webster, 1718-1800, of Plainfield, N. J. [of William[2], William[1]], m. 1743-4, Anna Taylor 1726-1762 [of Thomas], and had:
1. *William*, b. 15 of 9 mo. 1744, d. 2 of 3 mo. 1763.
2. *Sarah[4]*, b. 30 of 11 mo. 1746-7, m. 24 of 12 mo. 1766 (as 1st wife), Isaac Thorn, b. 22 of 5 mo. 1741, son of Abraham and Ann[4] (Laing) Thorn [of Elizabeth[3] Shotwell, John[2], Abraham[1]], and had: (1.) Anna, m. .... Saunders. (2.) Catharine, called Katy, m. .... Ballard. (3.) Margaret.
3. *Taylor[4]*, b. 18 of 11 mo. 1748-9, m. .... of 2 mo. 1769, Hannah Jackson. They with their minor children William, Phebe, Rebecca, Susannah and John became members of the Monthly Meeting at Westland, Pennsylvania, by certificate from Rahway and Plainfield M. M., dated 18 of 11 mo. 1790.
4. *John, Jr.*, b. 22 of 9 mo. 1750, m. 28 of 2 mo. 1776, Christiana Vail, b. 10 of 12 mo. 1753, d. 1776, s. p. daughter of John jr., and Mary[4] (Laing) Vail [of Elizabeth[3] Shotwell, John[2], Abraham[1]].
5. *Susannah*, b. 22 of 4 mo. 1753, m. David Lenox.
6. *Catharine[4]*, b. 23 of 6 mo. 1756, d. 18 of 1 mo. 1836, m. 26 of 8 mo. 1772, Samuel Pound, b. 15 of 6 mo. 1745, d. 21 of 11 mo. 1826, son of Elijah[3] and Elizabeth (.........) Pound [of John[2], John[1]]. (Children elsewhere recorded.)

7. *Hugh*[1], *Jr.*, b. 27 of 7 mo. 1758, d. 19 of 3 mo. 1834, at Norwich, C. W., m. 29 May 1781, Sarah Moore, b. 31 of 8 mo. 1764, d. 14 of 8 mo. 1842, daughter of Samuel[1] and Rachel (Stone) Moore [of Samuel[3], John[2], Samuel[1],] and had: (1.) Anna, b. 5 of 6 mo. 1783, d. 18 of 3 mo. 1875, m. 24 of 6 mo. 1801, Nathan Vail, b. 3 of 5 mo. 1777, d. 4 of 5 mo. 1857, son of John[3] and Catharine (Fitz Randolph) Vail [of Margaret[4] Laing, Elizabeth[3] Shotwell, John[2], Abraham[1].] (2.) Rachel, b. 13 of 12 mo. 1784, d. 19 of 9 mo. 1805, m. 23 of 6 mo 1803, John A. Vail, b. ____ of 2 mo. 1777, d. 28 of 6 mo. 1832, son of Abraham[4] and Margaret (Fitz Randolph) Vail [of Margaret[4] Laing, Elizabeth[3] Shotwell, John[2], Abraham[1]]. (3.) Catharine, b. 17 of 4 mo. 1786, d. 10 of 11 mo. 1832, m. James Beach. (4.) Edward b. 14 of 12 mo. 1787, d. 14 of 7 mo. 1817. (5.) Crowel, b. 4 of 9 mo. 1789, d. 2 of 11 mo. 1867, m. Margaret Vail, b. 18 of 1 mo. 1791, d. 15 of 5 mo. 1861, daughter of David[3] and Phebe (Jackson) Vail [of Margaret[4] Laing, Elizabeth[3] Shotwell, John[2], Abraham[1]). (6.) Phebe, b. 16 of 4 mo. 1791, m. Thomas Sackrider. (7.) Samuel, b. 7 of 2 mo. 1793, d. 7 of 3 mo. 1795. (8.) Sarah M., b. 31 of 7 mo. 1794, d. 1823, m. (as 1st wife) Jonathan[4] Harned, Jr., b. 10 of 10 mo. 1791, son of Jonathan and Sarah[5] (Laing) Harned [of Jacob[4] Laing, Elizabeth[3] Shotwell, John[2], Abraham[1]]. (9.) Susan L., b. 27 of 3 mo. 1796, d. 2 of 4 mo. 1866, m. Stephen[7] Vail, b. 16 of 3 mo. 1794, d 18 of 1 mo. 1871, son of Samuel[6] and Prudence (Vail) Vail [of Stephen[5], Jr., Ester[4] Smith, Sarah[3] Shotwell, John[2], Abraham[1]]. (10.) John, b. 6 of 3 mo. 1798, d. 7 of 9 mo. 1813. (11.) Hugh, D., b. 25 of 1 mo. 1800, d. 2 of 2 mo. 1880, m. 17 of 1 mo. 1829, Lydia C. Cornell, b. 22 of 6 mo. 1805, d. 1892± [of Joshua and Rebecca]. (12.) William T., b. 18 of 10 mo. 1801, d. 31 of 3 mo. 1867, m. 10 Sept. 1827, Mary Stover b. 15 Feb. 1807, d. 1876, daughter of Michael and Polly (____) Stover [of Adam]. (13.) Emma, b. 14 of 8 mo. 1803, dwelt Norwich, Ont., and there d. ____ 1892±, m. 17 of 1 mo. 1827, John Stover, b. 3 of 2 mo., 1800, d. 15 of 10 mo. 1858 [of Adam[3], Jr., of Norwich, Adam[2], native of Dutchess Co., N. Y., Jacob[1] Staufer, a native of Germany]. To her and to the widow of her brother Hugh D., we are indebted for valuable data. (14.) Lindley Moore, b. 11 of 9 mo. 1805, d. 29 of 11 mo. 1878, m. 1852 Sarah (Goodfellow) Welch [widow of James Welch].

8. *Anna*[4], b. 16 of 9 mo. 1760, d. 20 of 2 mo. 1822, suddenly in Plainfield meeting-house, after having preached for about one hour; m. Jacob Fitz Randolph, who d. aged 86± [of Isaac], and had: (1.) Sarah, b. 1782, d. 14 of 9 mo. 1815, m. 24 of 5 mo. 1798, Nathan[5] Shotwell, b. 1768, son of Jacob[4] and Katharine (Tilton) Shotwell [of John[3], John[2], Abraham[1]]. (2.) Susan, m. Joseph D. Everingham. (3.) Elizabeth, m. 22 of 3 mo. 1804, Joseph Dobson Shotwell, son of Henry[4] and Sarah (Dobson) Shotwell [of Joseph[4], John[3], John[2], Abraham[1]]. (4.) John, d. at Richmond, Staten Island, was a physician, m. ______. (5.) Hugh, m. Sarah Armstrong. (6.) Jacob, m. ________. (7.) Samuel, b. 1798±, m. Sarah Runyon. (8.) Isaac, m. ______.

CARR AND HARTSHORNE LINE.

ROBERT[1] CARR, 1614–1681, of Newport, R. I., tailor, embarked in ship Elizabeth and Ann at London in 1635, aged 21, bringing with him his younger brother Caleb; was admitted an inhabitant at Portsmouth 21 Feb. 1639, and a freeman at Newport 16 Mar. 1641. On 26 Oct. 1670, he and five others were appointed to make a rate for Conanicut Island, and on 30 Jan. 1671, he was allowed £9 for several public services theretofore done by him and his sloop and hands. On 11 June 1677, the Assembly met at his house at 8 o'clock in the morning. His will of 20 Apr. 1681, proved 4 Oct. 1681, names as executors his wife ______ and sons Caleb and Robert, declares his intention of starting on a voyage to New York and New Jersey, and mentions children Caleb, Elizabeth, Mary, Robert, Esek and Margaret, to the last of whom he bequeaths all his sheep at Jamestown and proceeds of the sale of horseflesh, except a colt given to his son Caleb.

1. *Caleb*[2] *Carr* [of Robert], to whom the father had given all his lands at Jamestown, died in 1690 leaving a will, proved Mar. 3, 1690; he m. Phillip Greene, b. 7 Oct. 1658, d. 1690+, daughter of John[2] and Ann (Almy) Greene [of John[1] of Warwick], and had: (1.) Robert, b. 2 July 1678. (2.) Caleb, b. 21 Mar. 1679. (3.) William, b. 16 Oct. 1681. (4.) Robert again. (5.) Job. (6.) Mary. (7.) Phillip, b. 8 Dec. 1688.

2. *Elizabeth*[2], d. 1683+, m. James Brown, d. 1683, son of Chad and Elizabeth, and had: (1.) John, b. 1671. (2.) James. (3.) Esek, b. 8 Mar. 1679.

3. *Mary*[2], m[1]. John Hicks, m[2]. Ralph Earle, 1660 1757, son of William and Mary (Walker) Earle, and had: (1.) Robert. (2.) Abigail. The will of Mary's father gave to John Hicks and his children by Mary[2] £20.

4. *Robert*, of Newport, R. I., merchant, d. 1704, his will of 8 July, 1703, being proved 5 Feb. 1704. He m. Elizabeth Lawton, who d. 1724, daughter of George and Elizabeth (Hazard) Lawton.

5. *Esek*[2], d. 1741, of Little Compton, R. I., m. Susanna ____________ and had: (1.) Mary, b. 14 July 1685, m. John Brownell. (2) Sarah, b. 19 Mar. 1689, m. ___________ Thurston. (3.) Elizabeth, b. 29 July, 1691, m. Samuel Wilbur. (4.) Esek, b. 23 Aug. 1693, d. before date of father's will of 16 May 1739; m. ____________ (5.) Anna, b. 28 Feb. 1696, m. Jonathan Wood. (6.) Martha, b. 29 May 1698. (7.)

Susanna, b. 20 Sept. 1700, m. Thomas Wilbur. (8.) Margaret, b. 16 Jan. 1703, m. ________ Dosson. (9.) Robert, b. 24 Feb. 1706, executor of his father's will. (10.) Thankful, b. 27 Apr. 1709, m. William Lake. For further particulars concerning the foregoing children of Robert' Carr, the reader is referred to J. O. Austin's Genealogical Dictionary of Rhode Island.

6. *Margaret*, m. 27 of 9 mo. [Nov.] 1670, Richard Hartshorne, an eminent Friend or Quaker of Middletown, Monmouth Co., N. J., b. at Halhearne, Leicestershire, Eng., 24 Oct. 1641, came to New Jersey, certainly as early as 1669, settled in the township of Middletown, Monmouth Co., N. J., at the Navisink Hills, Sandy Hook now Portland, and there d. ______ of 3 mo. [May] 1722, son of William, of Halhern, Eng. He was High Sheriff of Monmouth Co. and Speaker of the Colonial Assembly. George Fox when in this country in 1672 visited him and mentions him in his Journal.

From Barber and Howe's Historical Collections of New Jersey, (1845 p. 354) we take the following: " Richard Hartshorne, an English Friend or Quaker, emigrated to this [Monmouth] county in May 1666, and settled about that time on the Navisink river. This was among the first, if not the first permanent settlement made in Middletown. His place, called Portland Point, now [1845] remains in the possession of his descendants. 'About this time, this part of the county was a great resort for industrious and reputable farmers. Many of the English inhabitants were from the west end of Long Island, and by degrees extended their settlements to Freehold and vicinity. Some Dutch and Scotch, also, early settled in the township. In 1682 Middletown was supposed to consist of 100 familes; several thousand acres were allotted for the town, and many thousands for the out plantations. John Bowne, Richard Hartshorne, and Nicholas Davis, had each well improved settlements here; and a court was held twice or thrice a year for Middletown, Piscataway, and their jurisdictions.'"

The same authors state that " This township was incorporated in 1798," and that its greatest length was fifteen miles, breadth 10 miles, and that it was bounded, N. by Raritan and Sandy Hook bays, E. by the Atlantic Ocean and Shrewsbury, S. by Shrewsbury and W. by Freehold and South Amboy, Middlesex Co. " Its surface is the most uneven of any in the county, and the highlands of Navisink are in the eastern part." The village of Middletown is in a fertile country, near the heart of the township, 16 m. N. E. of Freehold, and 45 m. from Trenton." The village of Middletown Point, is upon a narrow point of land formed by two branches of the Matteawan creek, 3 m. from Raritan bay, and 12 from Freehold. It was early settled by Scotch, and called New Aberdeen."

Keyport is situated on Raritan bay, about 2 miles from Middletown Point, and 22 from New York. There is from the village a splendid view of the bay, Staten Island, the Narrows, Sandy Hook, and the ocean. It was laid out about the year 1830 by a company who sold building lots. The noted highlands of Navisink extend along Sandy Hook bay for nearly five miles. The range is about 300 feet in height and comes boldly down to near the waters edge. On Beacon hill, near the southern terminus were erected the " Highland Lighthouses " during the administration of Jno. Q. Adams.

RICHARD' HARTSHORNE, 1641-1722, of Middletown, Monmouth Co., N. J. [of William of Halhern in Leicestershire, Eng.], m. 1670, Margaret² Carr [of Robert' of Newport, R. I.] and had:

1. *Hugh*, b. 15 of 3 mo. [May] 1673, d. young.

2. *Mary*, b. 14 of 6 mo. 1676, m. ____ Clayton.

3. *William*, b. 22 of 11 mo. [Jan.] 1678-9, m'. Catharine Bowne; m². Helena Willets; m³. Elizabeth Lawrence.

4. *Catharine*, b. 2 of 3 mo. [May] 1682; d. 13 of 8 mo. 1759, m. Edward Fitz Randolph, who d. 23 of 2 mo. 1760, son of Nathaniel² and Mary (Holley) Fitz Randolph of Woodbridge, N. J. [of Edward'].

5. *Hugh*, again, b. 2 of 4 mo. [June] 1685, m. ________ Tilton.

6. *Sarah*, b. 3 of 5 mo. [July] 1687, m. Thomas Taylor or Tailor, and had certainly a daughter *Anna*, who m. with the approval of Woodbridge (N. J.), M. M. of Friends 24 of 11 mo. [Jan.] O. S., 1743-4, John Webster of Woodbridge, N. J., b. 1718, son of William, Jr., and Susanna (Cowperthwait) Webster [of William].

7. *Mercy*, b. 12 of 3 mo. [May] 1693, m. William Lawrence].

THE KING LINE.

JOSEPH' KING, SR., b. 1683, d. 10 of 12 mo. 1761, in the 78 year of his age, was a member of Kingwood Monthly Meeting in Hunterdon Co., N. J., m. ________ and had *Joseph*, Jr., who m. Mary ________ and had 6 daughters and 2 sons, namely: (1.) Mary, m. 8 of 4 mo. 1756, David Marsh. (2.) Mercy, m. 12 of 2 mo. 1761, John Stevenson. (3.) Nathan, b. 3 of 5 mo. [July] 1750, was a teacher in Plainfield afterward a miller there and elsewhere; removed after m. from Amwell to Plainfield and thence to Milton within the present limits of the city of Rahway, and there d. 15 of 9 mo. 1825, m. at a meeting of Friends appointed for that purpose and held in a new barn erected by the bride's father in Amwell, Hunterdon, Co., N. J., 19 of 3 mo. 1771, Sarah' Moore, b. 15 of 5 mo. 1752, d. 18 of 12 mo. 1825, daughter of Joseph'

WILLIAM HARVEY[1] MOORE,

ELECTRICIAN,

930 West Front St., Plainfield. N. J.

Son of Harvey S.[6] and Susan (Van Winkle) Moore, of New Jersey, and grandson of
Samuel[5] and Elizabeth L. (Shotwell) Moore,—the former a Descendant of Samuel[4]
and Rachel Stone) Moore, Samuel[3] and Mary (———) Moore, John[2] and Hope
(Robins) Moore, Samuel[1] and Mary (Ilsley) Moore, all of Woodbridge Town-
ship, Middlesex Co., N. J., and the latter a daughter of William[5] and
Elizabeth (Moores) Shotwell, of Bricktown (Rahway), N. J., (of Benj.[4]
and Ame (Hallett) Shotwell, John[3] and Mary Thorne) Shotwell,
John[2] and Elizabeth (Burton) Shotwell, Abraham[1]
Shotwell, all of Essex (now Union Co., N. J.)

and Christiana (Bishop) Moore of Amwell, N. J. [of Samuel[3], John[2], Samuel[1]]; they were buried in the Friends ground in Lower Rahway, whence many graves have been removed to Hazlewood cemetery near the site of the Marmaduke Hunt homestead, a short distance outside the city. They and their children, Ann, John, Joseph, Amy, Asher and Christian became members of the Friends Meeting at Buckingham, Pa., by certificate from Rahway and Plainfield M. M., dated 21 of 5 mo. 1795. (4.) Jane. (5.) Anna. (6.) Hannah. (7.) George, b. 21 of 10 mo. [Dec.] 1743. (8.) Alice Mans.

NATHAN[3] KING, 1750–1825 of Amwell, and Milton (now Rahway), N. J., m. 1771, Sarah[3] Moore, 1752–1825 and had:

1. *Mary*[4], b. 11 of 1 mo. 1772, d. before 1839, m. 25 of 7 mo. 1793, John Fitz Randolph, who d. 1839± [of James[4], Edward[3], Edward[2], Edward[1]], and had: (1.) Amelia, d. unm. (2.) Joseph, d. unm. (3.) Sidney, m. Orlando Wilcox. (4.) James, d. 1838±, m. Elizabeth Pound, daughter of Samuel[4] and Susannah (Webster) Pound [of Zachariah[4], Elijah[3], John[2], John[1]]. (5.) Hannah, m. James D. Merritt or Merret, of Purchase, N. Y. (6.) Harriet, m. Erastus Denison. (7.) Edmund, d. unm. (8.) Sarah, m. Daniel Westcott or Wescot.

2. *Ann*[4], b. 21 of 10 mo. 1773, d. 21 of 12 mo. 1820, m. George D. Clark, b. 5 of 5 mo. 1774, d. 26 of 11 mo. 1812, and had: (1.) Edwin, b. 30 Jan. 1799. (2.) Eliza, b. 19 May 1801, d. unm. (3.) William, b. 17 Dec. 1804. (4.) Joseph W., b. 7. Dec. 1806. (5.) Almira, b. 30 Sept. 1809, d. 8 July 1853, m. 22 Apr. 1829, Robert J. Street, b. 23 July 1805, dw. (1889), Adrian, Mich., only son of Alfred and Ann (Johnson) Street, of New York.

3. *Sarah*[4], b. 28 of 3 mo. 1776, d. 4 of 7 mo. 1863, m. 24 of 4 mo. 1794, Hugh Pound, b. 3 of 6 mo. 1773, d. 17 of 10 mo. 1852, son of Samuel[4] and Catharine (Webster) Pound of Piscataway, N. J. [of Elijah[3], John[2], John[1]]. For records of her father's family and her own (elsewhere presented), we are largely indebted to her old family bible, published in Edinburgh in the year 1807, and now in the possession of her granddaughter Huldah A. (Comstock) Ramsdell at Fairport, N. Y.; it is printed on linen paper and in the old style of type having the form of the s resembling the f. This family, with many of the *ante-bellum* Friends, would use nothing made of cotton produced by slave labor. They often paid exorbitant prices to obtain *free cotton*, as they also did for *free sugar*. They were practical philanthropists and had the courage to live up to their convictions.

4. *Elizabeth*, b. 18 of 3 mo. 1778.

5. *John*[4], b 21 of 10 mo. 1779, m[1]. Joann Blanchard; m[2]. Ann ________ and had: (1.) Sarah Ann, dw. Newark, N. J., m. William Phillips. (2.) Asher, m. Ann or Joanna ______

6. *Joseph*[4], b. 3 of 2 mo. 1782, in Amwell, N. J., owned a farm in Woodbridge township about 1½ miles from Milton and lying between the farm of his father-in-law, Thomas Laing, and that of James Hunt at the head of "Duky's Lane" so called. This upon the death of his brother, Asher, in 1820, he exchanged with his father's co-partner, Henry Shotwell, for the latter's half interest in the Milton mill, which with his father he continued to carry on during the father's life time, and which he managed until about the year 1831, when he exchanged the mill with Thomas Salter of Elizabethtown, for land in Morrow Co., Ohio. Joseph with his family removed to Granville, Ohio, about 6 miles from Newark. He was, for many years, a hat and shoe dealer in company with his son Nathan in Newark, O., and occupied much of his time as a scrivener, and there d. 31 of 3 mo. 1859. He and his family became members of the Friends Meeting at Alum Creek, O., by certificate from Rahway and Plainfield M. M., (Hicksite) dated 20 of 6 mo. 1838, including wife Catharine and 3 minor children, Hugh, Anna, and Joseph; also his older son William L.

Joseph[4] m. 24 of 1 mo. 1805, Catherine[5] Laing, b. 6 of 10 mo. 1787, d. 25 of 4 mo. 1841, daughter of Thomas[3] and Martha (Webster) Laing, [of Isaac[4], Eilzabeth[3] Shotwell, John[2], Abraham[1]], and had: (1.) Julia C., b. 20 of 6 mo. 1806, d. 5 of 2 mo. 1878, m. 16 of 9 mo. 1830, Samuel Fisher Voorhies, b. 2 of 3 mo. 1805, d. 14 of 4 mo. 1880, son of Cornelius and Elizabeth Voorhies, of Rahway, N. J. (2.) Thomas L., b. 6 of 4 mo. 1808. (Sketch and family later.) (3.) Nathan, b. 23 of 12 mo. 1810, d. ________ 1882, m[1]. Adeline Granger, who d. 17 of 9 mo. 1860; m[2]. ________ (4.) Martha L., b. 21 of 3 mo. 1813, m. 3 of 8 mo. 1837, James Knight. (5.) Sarah K., b. 7 of 11 mo. 1814, d. 25 of 5 mo. 1869, m. 21 of 3 mo. 1833, J. Madison Houghton, who d. 9 of 7 mo. 1870. (6.) William L., b. 14 of 10 mo. 1816, d. 14 of 10 mo. 1885, m. 14 of 10. mo. 1841, Caroline Purdy. (7.) Hugh L., b. 26 of 2 mo. 1819, d. 6 of 1 mo. 1873, m[1]. 19 of 5 mo. 1848, Catharine Brock, who d. 15 of 12 mo. 1860; m[2]. 5 of 11 mo. 1862, Amelia Voorhies. (8.) Anna, b. 2 of 8 mo. 1821, d. 7 of 6 mo. 1844, m. 13 of 12 mo. 1842, Abner W. Dennis. (9.) Joseph, b. 2 of 5 mo. 1825, d. 17 of 12 mo. 1867, m. 1 of 9 mo. 1846, Eliza J. Hickrott. (10.) Asher, b. 31 of 8 mo. 1831, d. ________ of 6 mo. 1833.

7. *Amy*[4], b. 15 of 7 mo. 1784, d. 26 of 4 mo. 1876, m. 23 of 9 mo. 1802, Joseph[4] Webster, b. 17 of 3 mo. 1779, d. 20 of 12 mo. 1854, son of Hugh[3] and Sarah (Marsh) Webster [of William[2], William[1]], and had: Nathan, b. 20 of 9 mo. 1803, d. 17 of 11 mo. 1827, m. 21 of 1 mo. 1824, Catharine Vail, b. 1 of 9 mo. 1806, d. 29 of 3 mo. 1825, daughter of Nathan and Anna (Webster) Vail [of John[5], Margaret[4] Laing, Elizabeth[3]

3

Shotwell, John², Abraham¹]. To their daughter Catharine R. of Plainfield, N. J., b. 6 of 3 mo. 1825, we are indebted for valuable data.

8. *Asher*, b. 15 of 6 mo. 1787, d. 6 of 12 mo. 1820, unm.

9. *Christianna*, b. 30 of 4 mo. 1789, m. as 2nd wife) Jonathan Harned, b. 10 of 10 mo. 1791, d. at Adrian, Mich., son of Jonathan and Sarah (Laing) Harned [of Jacob¹ Laing, Elizabeth³ Shotwell, John², Abraham¹].

10. *Nathan*, Jr., b. 6 of 6 mo. 1797, d. young.

THOS. L. KING, b 6 of 4 mo. 1808, in Woodbridge tp., Middlesex Co., near Rahway, N. J.; became member of Friends Meeting at Cherry st., Phila., by certificate from R. & P. M. M., dated 18 of 6 mo. 1828; was a hatter at Newark, Ohio; afterward dw. at Locus Farm in Springdale tp., Hamilton Co., O., whence in 1870, he removed with his family to 223, 8th ave., Topeka, Kensas, and there d. 10 of 10 mo. 1894; buried at Spring Grove, Cincinnati, O. He revisited New England and his native state in summer of 1887.

He married¹ in Cincinnati, O., 14 of 8 mo. 1838, Ann Maria Harkness, b. 22 of 2 mo. 1820, d. Cincinnati, O., 21 of 8 mo. 1860. He married² in Cincinnati, O., 3 June 1863, Alice Gray, b. 18 of 8 mo. 1847, at Lawrenceburgh, Dearborne Co., Ind., dw. 223 8th ave., Topeka, Kansas, daughter of John and Rebecca (Livingston) Gray of Lawrenceburgh, Ind., the former a native of Scotland, and the latter, a daughter of John and Rebecca (Allen) Livingston, the former of these a grandson of Philip Livingston, one of the signers of the Declaration of Independence, and the latter niece of Ethan and Ira Allen of Vermont, of revolutionary fame. The Livingstons were of Scotch ancestry.

Thos. L³. King, 1808-1894 [of Joseph⁴, Nathan³, Joseph², Joseph¹], m¹. 1838, Ann Maria Harkness, 1820-1860, and had: (1.) Mary Catharine, called Kate, b. 21 of 6 mo. 1839, in Cincinnati, O., dw. Sandiego, Cal.; m. in Cincinnati, O., 7 of 12 mo. 1859, Daniel Woodmansee. (2.) Louisa Harkness, b. 21 of 3 mo. 1841, in Cincinnati, O.; dw. Locus Farm, Springdale tp., Hamilton Co., O.; m. in Cincinnati, O., 6 of 5 mo. 1863, Chester M. Poor. (3.) Alice Maria, b. 12 of 6 mo. 1843; dw. Kansas City, Mo., m. J. K. Lemon. (4.) Anthony Harkness, b. 9 of 12 mo. 1845, in Cincinnati, O.; dw. Kansas City, Mo.; is a farmer, and in politics a R. (5.) Joseph Edward, b. 24 of 3 mo. 1848, Cincinnati, O.; d. at Wilmington, N. C., 6 Mar. 1865. (6.) Chas. Gano, b. 24 of 9 mo. 1852, at Locus Farm, Springdale, O.; d. in New York City, 12 Mar. 1893, leaving a wife and one daughter. (7.) William Oren, b. 5 of 3 mo. 1855, Locus Farm, O., dw. Indianapolis, Ind.; m. ---------. (8.) Thos. L., b. 17 of 9 mo. 1857, Locus Farm, O., and there d. 17 of 8 mo. 1859. (9.) Anna Maria, b. 13 of 8 mo. 1860, Locus Farm, O., dw. Indianapolis, Ind., m. Chas. Lemon.

Thos. L³. King, 1808-1894, of Topeka, Kan., formerly of Hamilton Co., O., m². 1863, Alice Gray, b. 1847, and had: (10.) Thos. L., b. 22 Apr. 1864, at Locus Farm, O., and there d. 14 June, 1864. (11.) Frank Sewall Livingston King, b. 29 June, 1866, Locus Farm, O.; dw. City of Mexico; occupation, assayer; in politics a Republican, in religion an Episcopalian; unm. 1895. (12.) Thos. Laing King, Jr., b. 8 May 1872, at Topeka, Kan.; attended the military academy at Chester, Pa., for 3 years, studied civil engineering; is Rock Island ticket agent at Atchinson, Kans.; is a Republican and Episcopalian, unm. 1895.

THE MOORE LINE.

SAMUEL¹ MOORE called Moores in Savage's Genealogical Dictionary, removed from Newbury, Mass., to Middlesex Co., N. J., about 1666, certainly soon after the session of the Province of New Jersey by the Duke of York to John Lord Berkly and Sir George Carteret in the year 1664. Locating at Woodbridge he filed surveys for a number of tracts of land in Woodbridge and Piscataway townships; and on the 27 Dec. 1667, a patent was issued to him for 70 acres of land, at a yearly rental of half-penny sterling per acre. This 70 acre lot is situated in the lower end of what is now called Lower Rahway; and part of the old tract remained in the family until the latter part of the 19th century. His house lot at Woodbridge contained sixteen acres of land.

Samuel¹ Moore and Robert Dennis were chosen delegates to represent the town of Woodbridge in the 2nd General Assembly of the Province of East Jersey which convened at Elizabethtown 3rd Nov. 1668, Phillip Carteret being Governor. At that session, the Legislature passed an act imposing a tax of £12 sterling on the 6 towns then composing the province, namely Elizabeth, Newark, Woodbridge, Middletown, Shrewsbnry, and Bergen, 40 shillings on each town, for defraying the public charges.

"By a law passed in May of the same year, the taxes were to be paid in winter wheat at five shillings per bushel; summer wheat at four shillings & six pence; Indian corn at three shillings; rye & barley at four shillings; beef at two pence & half penny per pound; & pork at three pence and half penny; to be paid into the hands & custody of Jacob Mollins of Elizabethtown."

Samuel Moore was appointed Treasurer of the Province of E. Jersey, 4 Dec. 1675 and reappointed in 1678, his compensation being nine pence per pound; in 1682 he was ordained by an act of the Legislature one of the Commissioners for laying out highways, bridges, landings and ferries in the county of Middlesex.

At the first division of the public land of Woodbridge among the freeholders, about 1670 he received a double portion, 356 acres, his brother Matthew receiving but 177 acres. His fellow townsmen elected him to various positions of trust, as follows: Assistant justice of the township court, 1669-71, 1675 and 1681; President of the court 1672-74; Marshal 1676; Clerk of the court 1676-87, Overseer of the highway 1669-70; Rate-maker [Assessor] most of the time from 1672 to 1687; Rate-gatherer 1675-79, and 1683, Overseer of the poor 1682; Deputy in the General Assembly 1669, 1670, 1683, and 1688; Lieutenant of the military 1675. During the year 1683 he held the offices of high sheriff of Middlesex Co., Deputy to the Assembly; Messenger of the House of Deputies, Town clerk of Woodbridge and Tax collector for the township. And in June of that year, according to the Woodbridge town meeting records, he was " by a unanimous Vote Made Choice of to keep ordinary [an inn] for this towne, and whilst Rum is to Be had from the Merchant at three Shillings or two Shillings and six pence for Gallon, he is to afford it for Money at three pence for gill, Six pence the half pint, and Eighteen pence the Quart; if he gives more then to Raise the price." Dally states that this first tavern set up in Woodbridge, probably occupied the site upon which Dr. Samuel E. Freeman's drug store now stands, [1873], this being the spot assigned for his residence in the record and by tradition. The same historian justly remarks that, he appears to have been a capable, faithful, and honest servant of the township and Province, and as such will ever be held in honor.

Samuel[1] Moore, second Town Clerk of Woodbridge N. J., 1669-88, died there 27 May 1688, he m[1]. in New England, 3 May 1653, Hannah Plummer, who d. 8 Dec. 1654; m[2]. in Newbury, Mass., 12 Dec. 1656, Mary Ilsley, b. 1638±, d. about June 1678 (after birth of twins), daughter of William and Barbara Ilsley of Newbury; m[3]. 23 Dec. 1678, Ann Jaques or Jaquish.

His father-in-law, *William Ilsley*, b. 1608, came from South Ampton, Eng., in the Confidence in Apr. 1638, aged 20 years, occupation shoemaker, with wife Barbara aged 20. He served Philip Davis, 12 years; d. at Newbury, Mass., 22 or 23 July 1681 (Coffin says aged 73.) His will of 26 Feb. 1679 mentions his wife Barbara, 3 sons and 2 daughters. William and Barbara had: (1.) Mary, 1638±-1678, m. 12 Dec. 1656 (as 2nd wife), Samuel[1] Moore or Moores, of Newbury, sketched above, with whom she removed to Woodbridge, N. J., about 1666. (Children later). (2.) John, b. 14 Sept. 1641. (3.) Elisha, d. 16 Jan. 1691, m. 14 March 1668, Hannah Poor [of John]. (4.) William, b. 23 Feb. 1648, was great grandfather of Capt. Isaac Ilsley, a man of distinction in Maine in the 18th century. (5.) Joseph, b. 30 Oct. 1649, d. 15 Oct. 1704, m. 1 Mar. 1682, Sarah Little. (6.) Isaac, b. 23 June 1652, a soldier in Appleton's company, wounded in the great Narragansett fight, 19 Dec. 1675; m. Abigail Plummer [of Joseph]. (7.) Sarah, b. 8 Aug. 1655, m. 21 July 1673, Samuel Hale.

Samuel[1] Moore, of Woodbridge, N. J., d. 1688, by 2d wife Mary, *nee* Ilsley, 1638±-1678 [of William], after removal to New Jersey, had: (1.) Elizabeth, b. 20 July 1668. (2.) Samuel, b. 31 March 1670; either he or a younger Samuel was one of the three freeholders of Woodbridge, who at the town meeting of 19 June 1749 were added to a standing committee, appointed 20 Apr. 1744 to hear complaints and correct mistakes growing out of the division of the public lands of the township. He m[1], 29 Oct. 1693, Sarah Higgins; m[2]. 2 June 1718, Mary Harrison. (3.) Thomas, b. 26 July 1672, m. 25 Dec. 1690, Mary White. (4.) *John*, b. in Woodbridge, N. J., May ye 20th 1674, m[1] by John Bishop, justice in Woodbridge, 18 March 1699, Hope Robinds, b. Woodbridge, N. J., 10 Dec. 1681, daughter of Daniel and Hope (........ ....) Robinds of Woodbridge, N. J.; m[2]. by John Bishop, justice, in Woodbridge, Nov. ye 21st, 1717, Mary Oliver. (Children later.) Dally states that about 1714-16, "John Kinsey and John Moore were chosen pursuant to an act of the General Assembly to consult and coöperate with the justices in respect to the building of a 'gaol' and a court-house." It is said that the father's land in lower Rahway descended to his son Matthew [John] and from Matthew [John] to Samuel 2d, and from him to Edward of Rahway, brother to our Joseph. The mansion house and a part of the land was owned and occupied in 1863 by Hannah, widow of Edward's son Isaac Moore. (5.) Enoch, b. 3 June 1678. (6.) Frances (twin), b. 3 June 1678. By 3d wife Ann *nee* Jaquish, Samuel[1] had (7.) Sarah, b. 16 Sept. 1681, d. .. Jan. 1687-8, a little more than 4 months prior to her father's death. There may have been older children born in New England prior to 1667.

John[2] Moore, of Woodbridge township, Middlesex Co., N. J., b. 1674 [of Samuel[1]] m[1]. 1699, Hope Robinds [of Daniel], and had: (1.) John, b. 3 Dec. 1700, in ye town of Freehold, N. J. (2.) Joseph, b. 5 Oct. 1703. (3.) Benjamin, b. 10 Oct. 1705 in Elizabethtown, N. J. His name in the minutes of Woodbridge Monthly Meeting of Friends, is first met with in connection with his declaration of intention of marriage with Elizabeth Shotwell, 15 of 12 mo. O. S. 1727-8, m. between 21 of 1 mo. and 18 of 2 mo. 1728, Elizabeth Shotwell, who d. 31 of 9 mo. (Nov.) 1750, daughter of Daniel[2] and Elizabeth (.....) Shotwell of Staten Island [of Abraham[1]]. (4.) Enoch, b. 7 of 10 mo. (Dec.) 1707, d. 18 of 10 mo. 1755, m. .. of 6 mo. 1735, Grace Brotherton, b. 2 of 6 mo. 1719, daughter of Henry and

Ann³ (Shotwell) Brotherton [of Daniel², Abraham¹]. (5.) *Samuel*, b. April ye 4, 1709, probably in Woodbridge township, was a carpenter, afterward a merchant in lower Rahway; d. about 1751. His will of 3 May 1750, gives his age as 40, and his occupation as Merchant, appoints as executors his wife Mary and his brother Euoch, and names his five sons, Joseph, Edward, Isaac, John and Samuel. He m. 1729± Mary ...., who d. 17 of 5 mo. 1811, aged 97 years, 9 months and 14 days; i. e., b. about 3 Aug. 1713, buried in the Friends new burying ground at Rahway. (Children later.) (6.) Daniel, b. 24 Aug. 1711. (7.) Rachel.

John² Moore, b. 1674, m². 1717 Mary Oliver, and had: (8.) Mary, b. 17 Jan. 1718–19. (9.) William, b. 30 Aug. 1720. (10.) Hannah, b. 31 Mar. 1722. (11.) John, b. 13 May 1725. (12.) Deborah, b. 28 Mar. 1727. (13.) Sarah, b. 6 Dec. 1728.

After the death of Samuel² Moore, about 1751 [of John², Samuel¹], his widow, Mary who is believed to have come from Holland, m² .... Elston or Alston, and after his death, she m³ .... Hays, who absconded with part of her property. She was laterally known as Granny Hays. On 3 Aug. 1804, a chart was made out by her grandson Edward Moore II, by which it appears she had then living 4 children, 34 grand children, 98 great grandchildren and 17 great great grandchildren. In the latter part of her life time she was blind, and was much pleased when any of her descendants came to see her. She is said to have given birth to 13 children, 5 of whom had offspring. In the summer of 1888 the compiler of this volume met several persons who remembered having seen this, his great grandmother's great grandmother, and examined a chart of the given names of her posterity born before her death, which was drawn by her great grandson Clayton Moore, at Bridgetown, 26 July 1818, for his friend and cousin, Hugh D. Webster, from one drawn by Isaac Moore, 13 May 1811, at which time she was living, and all but 4 of the descendants therein mentioned. The list was said to include 6 children, 34 grandchildren, 116 great grandchildren and 47 great great grandchildren, making with herself a total of 204; but for some of them blank lines in place of names were given in the chart; all her descendants' surnames and the dates of their birth were omitted, also, all mention of her son John Moore. Beside her Moore children, the chart indicates that she had a son Thomas Elston, whose children are given as "Wallis, Mary, Benjamin, Lewis, Susan and Latisha" [Letitia], for none of whom are descendants named. The chart indicates that Thomas Elston's brother Isaac (probably the 3d son, Isaac Moore, is meant) had a son Isaac whose daughter Anna had a daughter Anna. There was in 1888, standing below Jane H. Van Winkle's residence in Rah-

way, an ancient dwelling which A. V. Shotwell remembered having heard called many years ago "the Captain Tom Elstone House," but as the names of Thomas and Isaac Elston, or Dr. De Camp, do not occur in the Rahway Meeting records, it is concluded that they were not members of the Society of Friends. On the 18 of 5 mo. 1774, Samuel Elstone and Margaret Elstone were by their request admitted as members of Rahway and Plainfield Monthly Meeting of Friends.

SAMUEL³ MOORE, 1709–1751±, of Woodbridge, now Rahway, N. J., m. Mary .... 1713±– 1811, and had:

1. *Mary*, called Polly, m. Morris DeCamp, who was sergeant in Col. Sheldon's Light Dragoons, a famous soldiery in the Revolutionary War; this regiment was part of the time in Connecticut, then in New Jersey and part of the time in Delaware. He was wounded on Staten Island on the 23 of Aug. 1777. They had: (1.) Susan, m. Samuel Marsh. (2.) Catharine, m. .... Marsh. (3.) Gideon, m..............

2. *Joseph*,¹ b. 9 Jan. 1731–2, in Woodbridge township now Rahway, N. J., was a miller; became a member of Woodbridge, Rahway and Plainfield, M. M. by request, 21 of 9 mo. 1763, and in 1766, he with his wife and children received a certificate of membership directed to Kingwood M. M.; he settled at Amwell, Hunterdon Co., N. J., and there d. 6 of 10 mo. 1793, of yellow fever contracted while attending Philadelphia Yearly Meeting, at the close of a very wearisome journey to Detroit, undertaken in the vain expectation of being present at a proposed general Indian treaty which failed of consummation, mainly on account of the unyielding demand of the Indians in Ohio, that the whites should not be allowed to continue their settlements north of the Ohio river. His very interesting journal of that expedition, together with Jacob Lindley's somewhat fuller account of the same, and a short memorial of Joseph Moore, was issued in pamphlet form in 1892, by the compiler of this work, and is yet to be had at 25 cents a copy. Joseph was buried on his plantation in Amwell; the neighbors were so fearful of the disease that not one of them dared venture near the house. An undertaker in the neighborhood made a coffin and left it in sight of the house to be taken away by some of the family. Joseph's two daughters with the aid of a colored man prepared and buried the remains, one neighbor at the last coming forward to render some assistance. John Moore, Joseph Moore and Samuel Moore, shoemaker, were names of inhabitants of Woodbridge township in 1757, as we learn from a list of the subscribers toward the building of a certain stone bridge there in that year. Joseph m. 21 of 2 mo. [Feb.] 1751, Christiana Bishop, who d. in 1791,

daughter of Moses. Moses Bishop's 4 daughters married 4 Josephs—Joseph Moore, Joseph Gilman, Joseph Williams and Joseph Martin. (Children later.)

3. *Edward*, b. 6 Nov. 1733, dwelt on the westerly side of Main St., near Commerce, in Lower Rahway, N. J., and there d. 8 of 3 mo. 1822; he became a member of Rahway and Plainfield M. M. by request, 15 of 8 mo. 1764. He was a carpenter by trade and sometimes acted as undertaker. A bill for services of this kind has been seen in which a coffin was charged 20 shillings (about $2.50), and this was for one of the wealthiest and most prominent men of the neighborhood. "Uncle Eddy Moore," as he was familiarly called, had peculiarities of which the old people sometimes speak; one was that he would not reply or respond when addressed as "*Mister* Moore." A committee for the relief of sufferers in the Revolutionary War was formed in 1778, consisting of Abraham Shotwell, William Smith, Hugh Webster, John Vail, William Thorne and Elijah Pound. Subsequently Thorne resigned and Edward Moore was chosen in his place. Thorne said in the November meeting at Rahway that he was compelled to affirm his allegiance to the Continental Congress several months before—having no choice except to do that or be thrown into prison. Elijah Pound did the same thing and was therefore allowed to resign his position on the committee. Dally in his history of Woodbridge, p. 220, says that "on a warrant issued by Henry Freeman, justice, Edward Moore was visited three times during 1780, by Daniel Compton, the constable, for the collection of a tax of £29, and a fine of £500," and was thus on account of his anti-war principles deprived of 2 tables, 2 calves, an iron pot, a hand-saw, an auger, a square and compass, broadax, drawing-knife, hammer, grindstone, spade, a hand-saw file, and a cow. He m¹. ....; m².......... Shotwell [of Abraham.] By 1st wife he had: (1.) Thomas, removed about 1790 from Rahway to the neighborhood of Lundy's Lane, in Bertie, C. W., and there d.; m. 1775± .... (2.) Deborah, m. 26 of 7 mo. 1787, (as 2d wife), Titus³ Shotwell I, 1758-1835, son of Daniel¹ and Deborah (Shotwell) Shotwell [of Joseph³, Daniel², Abraham¹]. (3.) Isaac, b. 1772±, was a surveyor and examiner, dwelt at the homestead in Lower Rahway, and there d, 25 of 9 mo. 1850, m¹. 1831±, Elizabeth ...., who d. 21 of 10 mo. 1831, aged 55; m². Hannah Price, d. .... of 3 mo. 1870, daughter of Ichabod and Susan⁶ (Moore) Price [of John⁵, Joseph⁴, Samuel³, John², Samuel¹]. (4.) Edward.

4. *Sarah*, b. 31 July 1735.

5. *Isaac*, b. 10 July 1737.

6. *John*, b. 11 May 1739.

7. *Samuel*, b. 4 Apr. 1742, at Rahway, N. J.; member of the M. M. for Rahway and Plainfield, by request, 16 of 11 mo. 1774; dwelt, before the Revolution, at Uniontown, 2 miles from Rahway, whence, having the reputation of being a Tory, he went, during the war, to New York, and at its close, like many others, he took refuge in Nova Scotia, his property near Rahway being confiscated; his family accompanied him excepting his son Elias and daughter Sarah. On 15 of 7 mo. 1802, he received a certificate of membership from R. & P. M. M., directed to Nantucket M. M., the few Friends in Nova Scotia being under the care of that meeting. He returned to New Jersey about 1808-10, and after the death of his wife he removed to the township of Norwich, district of London (now South Riden), county of Oxford, Upper Canada, buying 2,000 acres of land in Norwich, and there d. ....

He m. 8 of 11 mo. 1763, Rachel Stone, b. 21 Sept. 1743, d. 7 Dec. 1813, at Elizabethtown, N. J., and had : (1.) Sarah, b. 31 of 8 mo. 1764, in Uniontown (now Menlow Park), Middlesex Co., N. J., d. in N. Norwich, C. W., 14 of 8 mo. 1842, m. in New York city, 31 of 5 mo. 1781, Hugh⁴ Webster, Jr., b. 27 of 7 mo. 1758, d. 19 of 3 mo. 1834, son of John³ and Anna (Taylor) Webster [of William², William¹]. (2.) Joseph, dwelt near Chilicothe, O., m. .... (3.) Crowell, m. Experience Clarkson. (4.) Phebe, dwelt (1840) 9 miles from Digby, N. S., and on opposite side of Anapolis river, m. Moses Shaw. (5.) Enoch, m. Elizabeth .... (6.) Rachel, dwelt (1840) Digby, N. S., m. Joseph Young. (7.) Elias, member of Canadian Parliament, 1837±, m....... (8.) John, m¹. Anna Gillam ; m². Deborah Stogden. (9.) Samuel, Jr., m¹. 1808±, Charity Gifford, who d. 1812± ; m². 28 of 9 mo. 1815, Elizabeth L. Shotwell, 1795-1827, daughter of William⁵ and Elizabeth (Moore) Shotwell [of Benjamin⁴, John³, John², Abraham¹]; m². 1829±, Margaret Moores, b. 16 of 8 mo. 1788 [of Robert]. (10.) Lindley Murray, b. 31 of 5 mo. 1788, was a teacher, d. at Rochester, N. Y., m. at Mamarineck, N. Y., 1814±, Abigail L. Mott, who d. 6 of 9 mo. 1846, dau. of Adam and Anne (......) Mott.

ACCOUNT OF JOSEPH MOORE.

"About the year 1791 a misunderstanding existed between the United States and several of the Indian tribes. On this occasion the meeting for Sufferings, held in Philadelphia, addressed a memorial to Congress, the object of which was to show the expediency of pursuing pacific measures toward settling the disputes with the Indians. Their representation was well received, but the measures they recommended were not then adopted, and the calamities of war still continuing to prevail on the western frontiers of the States, the Yearly Meeting, held in 1792, appointed a large committee to unite with the meeting for Sufferings in deliberating on this momentous subject and if practicable to recommend such measures as would be most likely to promote peace and frindship with the Indians.

"Early in the year 1793 deputies from several Indian nations visited Philadelphia with a view of forwarding an accommodation of differences with the United States, and, Government having agreed that a treaty should be held in the Indian country, near Detroit, during the summer following—those Indian deputies repeatedly urged that some Friends should attend the negotiations, stating that the nations they represented had a special confidence in Friends as a people who, from their first settlement in America, had manifested a steady adherence to the maintenance of peace and friendship with the natives. In accordance with the desire which Friends had long felt to promote peace, the proposal was acceded to, and six Friends were deputed to accompany the commissioners appointed by Government, on this occasion, after having obtained the President's approbation."—Friends Miscellany, 2nd edition, Vol. II., pp. 49-50.

The journal of Joseph Moore, to which reference has been made, begins thus: "On the 17th of 4th mo. 1793, I set out for Philadelphia and attended the meeting for sufferings, where were divers Friends, who had given up to attend the Indian treaty proposed to be held at Sandusky, on the waters of Lake Erie—having previously obtained certificates from our several monthly meetings for that purpose. The commissioners appointed by Government are General [Benjamin] Lincoln, Colonel [Timothy] Pickering, and Beverly Randolph. Lincoln goes by water to Albany, &c.; William Savery, Jacob Lindley, [of Chester Co., Pa.], and William Hartshorn go with him, and John Parish, John Elliott and myself, with Timothy Pickering and Beverly Randolph, go through the country by land."

On the night of 26 of 5 mo. 1793, Joseph Moore, with the other Friends, on their way to Detroit, lodged at the house of Jeremiah Moore, near Niagara river.

Joseph Moore in his journal in Friends Miscellany, Vol. VI. pp. 334-5, gives the following list of families of Friends in Canada whom he had visited in the summer of 1793, namely: Asa Schooley, Joseph Havens, Obadiah Dennis, Abraham Webster, John Cutler, John Hill, Benjamin Hill, Jeremiah Moore (Abraham Laing and Benjamin Canby, single men), John Taylor, Joshua Gillam, Joseph Marsh, Adam Burwell, Daniel Pound, Wm. Lundy, Thos. Rice, James Crawford, Enoch Scrigley, Samuel Taylor, Ezekiel Dennis and several others.

As they approached Philadelphia on their homeward journey, they continued to hear alarming reports of the yellow fever pestilence in that city, yet they persisted in their purpose to attend the yearly meeting there. When near Germantown, they met Sarah Lundy also on her way to attend the yearly meeting and to make a proposed visit to the southern states.

On the 21st of 9th mo. 1793, Joseph Moore attended the select yearly meeting at 4th St., in Philadelphia, and on the 24th 2 sittings of the yearly meeting, and others on the succeeding days. But his fatigue and exposure had left him ill prepared to resist the attack of the fever then raging to a distressing extent in the city. The journal ends on the 26th of 9th mo. 1793, at the res. of John Johnson, closing thus:

"The meeting [yearly, in Philadelphia] assembled again at nine o'clock, and the business concluded before twelve, in solemn quiet, and, I believe, to the satisfaction of all present. After which I dined with my friend David Bacon, and returned to Germantown with my kind friend, John Johnson, who had also attended all the sittings of this Yearly Meeting. The sickness in town continues as heretofore. Divers friends in the city are paying constant attention to the sick—providing necessaries, nurses, coffins, and carriers of the dead. At which I feel glad, and hope they will be rewarded for their labours in so great and charitable a work."—Friends Miscellany, Vol. VI, p. 343.

The following essay appears to have been the commencement of a Testimony from Friends of Kingwood monthly meeting, concerning Joseph Moore.

"Our beloved friend, Joseph Moore, was born at Woodbridge in New Jersey, in the year 1732, of parents not professing with us; but as he advanced to manhood, a merciful extension of Divine regard so opened his understanding in the path of true religion, that he joined in communion with Friends.—Soon after his marriage he came to settle within the limits of our meeting. He had not long resided with us before he received a gift in the ministry; in the exercise of which he appeared very much to our edification and comfort. He was well qualified for the discipline of the church, and diligently labored therein for the promotion of peace and good order; nor were his pacific endeavours altogether confined to the religious society of which he was a member, but he was also usefully employed in promoting peace and harmony in his neighbourhood, where very few Friends resided.

"He was of an affable disposition, greatly delighting in the company and conversation of his friends. His upright life and social, engaging manners, together with his exemplary conduct, procured him an extensive acquaintance with people of all denominations, by whom also he was generally beloved. His gospel labours in the work of the ministry were chiefly confined to this and the neighbouring meetings, until the year 1786, when he performed a religious visit, in company with his near and dear friend, Abraham Gibbons, to Friends, and those professing with us in Nova Scotia. In this journey they travelled in much harmony, and their gospel labours were to the satisfaction of the visited. In the following year accompanied by William Wilson, of Philadelphia, he proceeded a second time to Nova Scotia with a donation from Friends, to be distributed amongst the poor in that country. This important trust and service he was enabled diligently to perform, to the satisfaction of Friends.

"This our dear friend was a true sympathizer with the sick and afflicted, either in body or mind, among the different religious denominations; and frequent were the calls which he made to this class, when he not only administered assistance and relief to the maladies of the body, but also was an instrument of spiritual consolation to the tired and desponding mind."

"In addition to the foregoing testimony it may be stated, that Joseph Moore was educated by his father for a mariner and he made one voyage to sea in the capacity of supercargo, at the age of sixteen. As he approached to manhood, it is probable those religious impressions, to which allusion is made, influenced him to decline a further prosecution of that design.

On the 21st of the 2d month, 1751, when a little over nineteen years of age, he was married, and not long after, settled on a farm about three miles from Flemington, and nine from Kingwood meeting. As his children grew up around him, the difficulties of getting them to meeting at such a distance, must have increased. It is probable this circumstance, in connection with his desire for the welfare and improvement of his neighbours, induced him, in 1772, to make application to the monthly meeting, requesting a meeting to be held at his house. The sympathetic and brotherly feeling of Friends at that day, induced them to grant his request, and a meeting was accordingly held there.

"Sometime previous to this, Joseph had acceptably appeared in the ministry, but he was not recommended as a minister until the year 1774. Not long after this period, Kingwood monthly meeting had the following named ministers belonging to it, who frequently travelled abroad in Truth's service: Joseph Moore, Sarah Lundy, Gabriel Willson and Henry Widdifield. It is said when Joseph Moore and Abraham Gibbons visited Nova Scotia, they travelled on foot; but no reasons are assigned for this mode of proceeding. In the year 1791, he met with a close trial in the decease of his wife.

"The preceding account of his journey to attend the Indian treaty, is the only Journal of his life that we [Editor of Friends Miscellany] have seen. On his return from that arduous and deeply exercising travel, he attended the Yearly Meeting held in Philadelphia, during the prevalence of the yellow fever.

He then proceeded on his way toward home, as far as Solebury, in Bucks county. Here he rested a day or two at his son in-law, Tomas Carey's and attended Buckingham meeting.—He was somewhat indisposed at the time, but proceeded to his own habitation, and thence to the week-day meeting at Kingwood. His indisposition continued; and though importuned to stay with his friends at Kingwood, he felt most easy to return home. The disorder, which was believed to be the yellow fever increased upon him, and in a few days terminated his course of probation. He was buried near his own dwelling house."

The following is a copy of a memorandum in the family register, said to have been written by Henry Clifton: "Our dear father Joseph Moore, departed this life, after a short illness, on the 7th of 10th month, 1793, and second of the week, in the sixty-second year of his age; expressing a few days before his departure, that if it was the Lord's will to remove him at this time he felt an entire resignation thereto."

Joseph[4] Moore, 1731-2-1793, of Amwell, Hunterdon Co., N. J., formerly of Woodbridge, N. J. [of Samuel[3], John[2], Samuel[1]], m. 1751, Christiana Bishop, who d. 1791 [of Moses] and had:

1. *Sarah*, b. 15 of 5 mo. 1752, d. at Rahway, N. J., 18 of 12 mo. 1825, m. in Amwell, N. J., 19 of 3 mo. 1771, Nathan King, 1750–1825, son of Joseph[3] and Mary (......) King of Amwell, N. J. [of Joseph[1]]. (Children and grandchildren recorded elsewhere.) According to an account published in 1863 by her nephew, John Moore of Marksboro, N. J., she was known to have had 9 children, 34 grandchildren, 54 great-grandchildren and 12 great-great-grandchildren; total, 109. Her brother Samuel, 3 children and 4 grandchildren; her sister Rachel, 5 children; Benjamin, 4 children and 3 grandchildren; Hannah, 12 children, 33 grandchildren and 50 great grandchildren, total 95; John, 7 children,—of whom Susan (Moore) Price had 12 children, 25 grandchildren and 2 great-grandchildren; Joseph, 5 children, 20 grandchildren and 4 great-grandchildren; Cowperthwaite C., 1 child; John, 8 children and 24 grandchildren; and Christiana (Moore) Cadwallader, 6 children and 10 grandchildren;—total for John, 7 children, 32 grandchildren, 79 great-grandchildren and 6 great great-grandchildren.

2. *Huldah*, d. in Bucks Co., Pa., unm.

3. *Samuel*, m. ...... Praul and had: (1.) Deborah, m. ....., and had Henry, Jesse, John and Deborah, b. before 1811. (2.) Jemima, m. .... and had Ambrose and Deborah, b. before 1811. (3.) Mary.

4. *Ann*, never married.

5. *John*, was a miller, dwelt at Quibbletown, now Newmarket, Middlesex Co., N. J., and at Brousetown, in the vicinity of Plainfield, becom-

ing member of the Friends meeting there by certificate from Hardwick M. M., dated 9 of 8 mo. 1787, also his wife Hannah and 3 children, Susannah, Joseph and Copwerthwaite. Soon after the death of his wife, in the last decade of the 18th century, he, in company with Asher Adkinson of Flemington, went to Pittsburg, Pa., purchased a flat-boat load of produce, descended the Ohio and Mississippi rivers to New Orleans, then a Spanish province, sold the cargo, and Adkinson returned home. John went on to Apalachian, or Apalachicola, at that time in the Spanish colony of Louisiana now in Florida. In 1816, after an absence of over 20 years, he returned to New Jersey. During the whole of that time his friends had no certain intelligence of his whereabouts. At the time of leaving home he had left in the hands of a brother-in-law two bonds for collection, for which he had taken a receipt; this he brought back with him. He d. in Bucks Co., Pa., about 1818, m. between 20 of 3 mo. and 16 of 4 mo. 1783, Hannah Copeland, who d. near Plainfield [of Cowperthwaite, a tailor, of Scotch descent], and had : (1.) Susan, b. 10 Feb. 1784, at Rahway, N. J.; d. 4 May 1871; m. in New York city, 12 May 1804, Ichabod Price, b. in Elizabethtown, N. J., 4 Oct. 1781, d. 22 Feb. 1862, grandson of Benjamin Price of Elizabethtown. (2.) John, b. 1789±, two years before his mother's death, dw. at Marksboro, N. J., and there d. .. Nov. 1877 ; compiled and published in 1863 chart and account of the Moore family, from which many names were first obtained; but his statements are not always accurate. Of Jo-

seph[1] Moore's descendants he had obtained the names of 8 children, 40 grandchildren, 104 great-grandchildren, 181 great-great-granchildren and 22 great-great-great-grandchildren,—total 358, and estimated the number of names not obtained at 150. He m[1]. 1814, Sara Hull, who d. in Marksboro, N. J.; m[2]. Amy Hance [of Sylvanus[2], John[1] and Ann (Lundy) Hance]. Amy d. at Plainfield, N. J. 1890±. (3.) Joseph was a tanner and shoemaker, dw. from age of 14 at Millbrook in Randolph township, Morris Co., N. J., about 1 mile from Dover, and there d. ; m[1]. Catherine Hand; m[2]. Gulielma Williams, niece of former wife. (4.) Cowperthwaite C., m. 1810±, ------ Horton. (5.) Ambrose. (6.) Jesse, d. in infancy. (7.) Christiana[6], m. Yardly Cadwallader.

6. *Rachel*[5], m. Thomas Head of Bucks Co., Pa., and had: (1.) Miranda. (2.) Joseph. (3.) David. (4.) Lewis. (5.) Hulda.

7. *Benjamin*[5], m. ------- and had : (1.) Nathan, m. ----- (2.) Susan. (3.) Joseph. (4.) Ann.

8. *Hannah*[5], m. Thomas Cary of Buckingham, Bucks Co., Pa., and had: (1.) Joseph, m. Eliza Wilson. (2.) Julia, d. among the Shakers at Lebanon, O., m. Charles Hampton. (3.) John, m. Isabella Nelson. (4.) Christiana, m. Moses Phillips. (5.) Mary, m. Robert T. Smith. (6.) Hannah, m. Samuel Fowler of Alliance, O. (7.) Anna, m. John Williamson. (8.) Moore, m. Ellen ---------. (9.) Elizabeth, d. unm. (10.) Sarah, m. Emmet Robeson. (11.) Rebecca, m. Stephen Price. (12.) Thomas, m. ---------.

9. *Miranda*, m. Edward Blackfan of Bucks Co., Pa., but died s. p.

III.

ANCESTORS AND NEAR RELATIVES OF THE

AUTHOR'S MATERNAL GRANDFATHER,

GEORGE WASHINGTON[5] GARDNER, OF ELBA, N. Y.,

SON OF JOHN[4] AND BATHSHEBA (WATSON) GARDNER, OF WASHINGTON CO., R. I., AND LIVINGSTON CO., N. Y.

[Of John[3], William[2], George[1].]

Eighth month 1st, 1638. In a catalogue of the persons who by the general consent of the Company were admitted to be "inhabitants of the island now called Aquidneck, having submitted themselves to the government that is or shall be established according to the word of God therein," is found the name of George Gardner.

Tenth month 17th, 1639. George Gardner, Robert Stanton and others are "admitted and embraced as freemen into this body politick" at Newport. At the General Court of Elec-

tions, held on the 12th day of the first month, 1640, there were present, George Gardner, Robert Stanton and others. On first month (March), 10th, 1640, George Gardner had 58 acres recorded. The Court Roll of Freemen of the town of Newport, dated March 16th, 1641, contains among others the names of George Gardner and Robert Stanton. At the General Court of Elections, held the 16th and 17th of March, 1642, at Newport, George Gardner and William Freeborn were chosen constables; George Gard-

GEORGE MILTON GARDNER, SR., BORN 1835,

Of Jackson, Mich.,

SON OF GEORGE WASHINGTON GARDNER AND SECOND WIFE DIANA,
NEE BERRY,

Late of Elba, Genesee Co., N. Y., and Grandson (1) of John and Bathsheba
(Watson) Gardner, of Washington Co., R. I., and Livingston Co.,
N. Y., and (2) of Jonathan and Bathsheba (Greene)
Berry, of Rensselaer Co., N. Y., and
Lenawee Co., Mich.

MRS. PHEBE B. (GARDNER) SHOTWELL, BORN 1831,

WIFE OF NATHAN[1] SHOTWELL,

Of Concord, Mich., formerly of Elba, N. Y., sister to G. M. Gardner, of
Jackson, Mich., and daughter of G. Washington and Diana
(Berry Gardner, late of Elba, Genesee Co., N. Y.

ner being elected senior sergeant, and Robert Stanton junior sergeant. At the election at Newport, 13th of first mo. 1644, George Gardner was chosen ensign in the R. I. troops, and Robert Stanton was chosen sergeant. On 29 June 1660, George Gardner appears as witness to a deed from T. Socho or Sosoa an Indian captain of Narragansett, to Robert Stanton, *et al.* (i. e., the trustees of the company of 76 men of Warwick and Providence), of a large tract of land at Pettaquamscutt called Misquamicoke or Misquomicoke *alias* Misquamicutt or Haversham, being to the westward of Pawcatuck river, and comprising the present town of Westerly. On 28 Oct. 1662, George Gardner was chosen a commissioner for the town of Newport. On 2 June 1668, he was made one of the overseers of his father-in-law, Robert Ballou's will. Oct. 22, 1673, he was chosen juryman.

From the Rhode Island Colonial Records relating to the original grant of lands to the early settlers of Newport, R. I. (printed in Newport Historical Magazine, Vol. II, pp. 66-7), we copy the following:

Land of George Gardner.   (Vol. I, p. 24.)

WHEREAS, According to certain orders, etc., be it known, therefore, that George Gardiner, having exhibited his bill, under the treasurer's

---

ANCESTORS AND CHILDREN OF GEORGE WASHINGTON[5] GARDNER, 1785-1849, ELBA, N. Y.

[Of John[4], John[3], William[2], George[1]], m[1]. 1814, Phebe N. Garbutt, 1784-1828 [of Zachariah]; m[2]. 1830, Diana Berry, b. 1810 [of Jonathan].

John[4] Gardner, b. 17 June 1745, d. ———— Sept. 1815, m. 30 Apr. 1767, Bathsheba[4] Watson, b. 1744±, d. 23 Aug. 1812. dw. Washington Co., R. I., and Livingston Co., N. Y.

- John[3], d. 1800, m. Mary (?) Wilkinson. (weaver.)
  - William[2], m. Alice (?). d. 1711.
    - George[1] Gardner, d. 1677±, dw. Newport, R. I., m.[1] 1640±. Hored (Long) Hicks, b. 1624±.
  - John[1] m[1]. Dorcas[2] Gardner. d. 1726.
    - George[1] Gardner, d. 1677±, dw. Newport, R. I., m.[1] 1640±. Hored (Long) Hicks, b. 1624±.
- Jeffrey[3] Watson, b. 3 Aug., 1712, m. 30 Nov. 1732, Bathsheba[4] Smith, b. 7 Apr. 1710. dw. S. Kingstown, R. I.
  - John[2] m. Hannah, dw. S. Kingstown, R. I.
    - John[2] m. Phillis[2] Gereardy. d. 1730. (Phillis[2] Gereardy, d. 1729±.)
      - John[1] Smith, d. 1677, dw. Prudence Island, R. I., m. Margaret.
      - John[1] Gereardy m. Renewed[2] Sweet. { John[1] Sweet m. Mary.
  - John[3] m., 1708, Mercy[3] Westcott.
    - Amos[2], m[2]. 1670, Deborah[2] Stafford, 1631-1685, dw. Warwick, R.I. 1651-1706.
      - Stukeley[1] Westcott, 1592-1677, dw. Warwick, R. I.
      - Thomas[1] Stafford, 1605-1677, dw. Warwick, R. I., m. Elizabeth.

Children by first wife.

1. Jeremiah Hazard, b. 4 Sept. 1819.
2. Elizabeth, 1822-1892.
3. George W., jr., 1824-1825.

Children by second wife.

4. Bathsheba Phebe, b. 29 of 2 mo. 1831.
5. Malinna A., 1833-1883.
George Milton, b. 23 of 6 mo. 1835.
Mary Jane, 1837-1844.

hand, into the sessions held on the 10th of March, 1640, wherein appears full satisfaction to be given for the number of 58 acres of land, lying within the precincts of such bounds, as by the committee, by order appointed, did bound it with all, viz.: To begin upon Mr. Jeoffreys' westerly line and so to extend by the marsh side (only leaving two rods breadth thereby, for fronting of the said marsh), to a marked tree by Robert Stanton and so from thence, upon a straight line to a marked stump upon the rocks this side Mr. Coddington's marsh, with a home lot and three cows' hay, one in the harbour marsh, next Goodman Bull's and two at the east end of Southmead, with three acres more of cow common, lying upon the swamp, upon the hill, all which parcels of land amounts to his proportion. This, therefore, doth evidence and testify that all those parcels of land before specified, amounting to the aforesaid number of fifty-eight acres, more or less, is fully impropriated to the said George Gardiner and his heirs forever."

Following this, in similar form and same date is the land of Robert Stanton, bounded thus: "To begin upon George Gardiner's line, and so to run by the harbour marsh, to a marked stake, and so upon a straight line to a marked tree upon the rocks, with a home lot and two cows' hay; west upon George Gardiner in Southmead and one cow's hay in harbour marsh; north upon Mr. Jeoffreys and 3 acres and 3 quarters of cow common lying west upon George Gardiner's by the water and swamp, all which parcels of land amounts to his proportion."

From the following extract from the Rhode Island Colonial Record, Vol. I, p. 51, we gather a revised description of George Gardiner's land and an explanation of the addition made to his original grant: "One parcel containing thirty-nine acres, more or less, lying southerly upon the harbour marshes, bounded on the east by Mr. Jeffreys' farm, and on the west by Robert Stanton's land, and butting upon the common with the south end, and north upon the harbour marsh (a driftway passing there through toward the end of the island) and for as much as the parcel was adjudged and laid forth primarily for forty acres, and upon due measure, falling short, satisfaction was allowed forth for want, as well as for the rocks, and in consideration of a drifting way there through, the number of eighteen acres, lying at Newport cliffs, bounded on the highway southwest and northwest, southeast upon the common, and northeast upon Robert Stanton's land; with a parcel of meadow lying at the east end of Southmead, next Mr. Brassees' farm; with another parcel of marsh adjoining to Henry Bull's marsh and Marmaduke Ward's; with a home lot of four acres, and another parcel of night common, lying next to Robert Stanton's night common upon the Hill, on the west side of the swamp, in all which parcels is contained the said allowance of fifty

acres, more or less, with eighteen acres more granted to him by the town, 13 acres of which lies at Newport cliffs, north upon the sea or harbour, south upon the highway, east upon Edward Robinson's land, and west upon Edward Andrews' land; with another parcel of five acres, more or less, adjoining to the aforesaid night common, bounded by Southmead driftway and the swamp."

George¹ Gardner married (1.) 1642±, Hored or Herodias (Long) Hicks, b. about 1624. On the 11 of 3d month (May) 1658, she came with her babe at her breast, from Newport to Weymouth, to deliver her religious testimony, for which she was carried to Boston before Governor John Endicott, who sentenced her to be whipped with ten lashes, as well as her companion, Mary Stanton, who came with her to help bear her child. After the whipping with a three-fold knotted whip of cords, she was continued for fourteen days longer in prison. The narrator (Bishop's New England Judged), says: "The woman came a very sore journey and (according to man), hardly accomplishable, through a wilderness of about sixty miles, between Rhode Island and Boston." "After the savage, inhuman and bloody execution upon her, of your cruelty, aforesaid, kneeled down and prayed the Lord to forgive you."

In an account of the barbarities toward Friends in New England, William Sewel, in his "History of the Rise, Increase and Progress of the Christian People called Quakers," written originally in low Dutch, and translated by himself into English about the year 1720 (Vol. I, p. 251, Friends Book Store edition), after mention of the whipping of Sarah Gibbons and Dorothy Waugh in Boston, under Gov. John Endicott, and the fact that in the house of correction they were kept from victuals three days before and three days after being whipped, though they had offered to pay for food, thus relates the foregoing circumstances:

"Not long after, Hored Gardner, an inhabitant of Newport in Rhode Island, came with her sucking babe and a girl to carry it, to Weymouth, whence, for being a Quaker, she was hurried to Boston, where both she and the girl were whipped with a three-fold knotted whip. After whipping, the woman kneeled down and prayed the Lord to forgive those persecutors:—which so reached a woman that stood by that she said, 'surely she could not have done this if it had not been by the spirit of the Lord.'"

On 3 May 1665, George Gardner was before the Assembly or court upon petition of Hored Long, alias Gardner, his reputed wife. She declared that when her father died (in England), she was sent to London and was married unknown to her friends, to John Hicks privately in the under church of Paul's, called St. Faith's Church, she being between 13 and 14 years old. She then came to New England with her husband and lived at Weymouth two and a half years, thence coming to Rhode Island about the year 1640, and there lived ever since till she came to Pettacomscott. Soon after coming to Rhode Island, there happened a difference between her and her husband, John Hicks, and he went away to the Dutch, carrying with him most of her estate, which had been sent her by her mother, her father and brother having lost their lives and estate in his majesty's service. After her desertion by John Hicks, Hored knew not what to do, she being not brought up to labor and being young and having no friends, in which strait she was drawn to George Gardner to consent to him so far as she did for her maintenance, and by whom she had many children.

In answer to the court, George Gardner plainly says that he cannot say that ever he went on purpose before any magistrate to declare themselves or to take each other as man and wife, or to their approbation as to the premises. But testimony as to her marriage to George Gardner was given by Robert Stanton, who declared that one night at his house both of them did say before him and his wife, that they did take one and the other, as man and wife. Hored Gardner having lived with her last [second] husband eighteen or twenty years, now desired of Assembly "that the estate and labor he had of mine, he may allow it me, and house upon my land I may enjoy without molestation, and that he may allow me my child to bring up, with maintenance for her, and that he be restrained from troubling me more." She afterward married 3d John Porter.

George Gardner (or Gardiner) married 2d, Lydia Ballou, who d. _________ not later than 1722, dau. of Robert and Susanna Ballou. After his death, she married 2d, 14 June 1678, Wm. Hawkins, of Providence R. I., who d. 6 July 1723, son of Wm. and Margaret Hawkins, of Providence.

J. O. Austin, in his "Genealogical Dictionary of Rhode Island," says, "1688, Nov. 30. His [George Gardiner's] daughter Mary gave a receipt for £13, to her father-in-law (i. e. stepfather), William Hawkins, of Providence, being balance of legacy of £20, bequeathed by last will of her father, George Gardiner, of Newport, deceased. It is assumed that he had a daughter Dorcas, who became the first wife of John Watson. Possibly his son Samuel was by his first wife, rather than his second. Possibly also, Jeremiah was a grandson rather than son."

The same authority states that the following record made in an old family bible, 1790, July 11, by William C. Gardiner is evidently erroneous in many important particulars, but not more so than traditionary statements of families are often found to be: "Joseph Gardiner the youngest son of Sir Thomas Gardiner, Knight, came over among the first settlers, and died in Kings county, Rhode Island state, aged 78 years. Born A. D. 1601, died A. D. 1679. Left six sons, viz.: Benoni, died 1731, aged 104, Henry, died 1737, aged 101, Wm., died at sea by pirates, George, lived to see 94 years, Nicholas and Joseph lived also to a great age," etc.

The Newport Historical Magazine (Vol. II, p. 6,) prints from the Rhode Island Colonial Land Evidence, the following abstract of deed: "John Porter, of Petticomscott, R. I., for £400 sterling conveys to Richard Smith, of Newport, merchant, a parcel of land in Portsmouth, R. I., containing 210 acres, bounded N. by land of Wm. Baulston; W. by the sea; S. by land of Thomas Hazard; E. by the common, Sept. 6, 1671. Witnessed by Francis Brinley, John Almy, Richard Bailey. Release of dower and jointure by Horad, wife of John Porter, Sept. 30, 1671. Witnessed by Samuel Wilson, Geo. Hicks, Geo. Gardner. Recorded by John Sanford, recorder, Oct. 7, 1671, Vol. I, p. 3."

GEORGE[1] GARDNER, of Newport, R. I., d. 1677±, m. at the house of Robert Stanton, 1642±, Hored [Horod or Herodias] (Long) Hicks, b. 1624±, and if the supposition be correct that the Gardiners from King's Province were identical with the family of George Gardner of Newport, the following were their children:

1. *Benoni*[2], d. 1731±, dwelt in Kings Town, (now N. Kingstown), R. I. In testimony given in 1727, he calls himself aged ninety years and upwards, but it may well be thought that he did not come so near as his brother Henry in counting the lapse of time. We are forced to question the accuracy of the tradition which appears to be based largely upon an entry made in an old family bible by William C. Gardiner on 11 July 1790, to the effect that Benoni was b. in 1630, and d. at the age of 104 years, that his father was Joseph Gardiner, b. in 1601, who came from Yorkshire to America, settled about 1628 or 1630 in what is now S. Kingstown, Washington Co., R. I., and there d. in 1679, and that he Joseph was the youngest son of Sir Thomas Gardiner, Kight. Benoni m. Mary _________, b. 1645, d. at her son-in-law Job Sherman's at Portsmouth, 16 Nov. 1729, and had: (1.) William, jr., (so called probably to distinguish him from his uncle William), b. 1671, d. 17 Dec., 1732, m. Abigail Remington, b. 1681, d. 6 Mar. 1763, dau. of John and Abigail (Richmond) Remington. (2.) Nathaniel. (3.) Stephen. (4.) Isaac, b. 7 Jan. 1687, m. _____ (5.) Bridget.

2. *Henry*[2], 1645-1744, dwelt Kings Town, R. I. J. Warren Gardiner of North Kingstown, R. I., in an article entitled, "The Pioneers of Narragansett" in the Narragansett Historical Register, Vol. II, p. 114, states that soon after the Indian war, during which every house in Narragansett was destroyed and the inhabitants entirely driven out, they returned and com-

menced again their settlements, and in a petition of the inhabitants of Narragansett dated July 29th, 1679, we find among the signatures, the following: Ben'jn, Henry, George, William, Nicholas Gardiner, James, John, Daniel Greene, Daniel Sweet. Some of these seem to have been of Pettaquamscutt. The inhabitants of Pettaquamscutt as given in May 1671, by the Court of Commissioners included Ben., Henry and Nicholas Gardiner.

Henry², m¹. Joan ...., who was living in 1715. He m². Abigail (Richmond) Remington, 1656-1744, widow of John Remington, who d. 1688, and daughter of Edward and Abigail (Davis) Richmond, and had by 2d wife: (1.) Henry, b. 25 Feb. 1691, in Kingstown, R. I., m. .... (2.) Ephraim, b. .. Jan. 1693, m. 28 April 1713, Penelope Eldred, dau. of Samuel and Martha (Knowles) Eldred, of Kings Town, R. I., [of Samuel]. (3.) William, b. 27 Oct. 1697, d. before 20 July 1744, m. in Kings Town, R. I., 12 June 1718, Margaret Eldred, dau. of Capt. John² and Margaret (Holden) Eldred, of N. Kingstown, R. I., [of Samuel¹].

3. George³, dwelt Kings Town, R. I., d. 1724, m. Tabitha Tefft, b. 1653, living in 1722, dau. of John and Mary Tefft, and had: (1.) Joseph. (2.) Nicholas. (3.) Samuel. (4.) Robert. (5.) John. (6.) George. (7.) Hannah, was living 1756, m¹. 1 Jan. 1701, Josiah Westcott of Providence, b. 1675±, d. 11 Nov. 1721, son of Jeremiah and Eleanor (England) Westcott, of Warwick; m² (as 2d wife) Thomas Burlingame, b. 6 Feb. 1667, d. 9 July 1758, second son of Roger and Mary Burlingame. (8.) Tabitha. (9.) Joanna. (10.) Henry (possibly son of Benoni), d. 1704.

4. William², dwelt in Kingstown, R. I., d. 1711, m. Elizabeth ...., who d. 1737. (Further sketch and children later.) The late Sunderland P. Gardner of Farmington, N. Y., 1802-1893 [of Elisha W⁵., William⁴, John³, William², George¹], was authority for the statement that this William² (son of George and Hored, of Newport), d. in Mar. 1748, that he was a farmer, tanner and currier, and dwelt 3 miles east of Kingston, R. I., that he m. Alice ...., and had sons John, William and Allen, and perhaps Thomas, and that John's wife .... née Wilkinson was sister to the wife of Jeremiah Browning; but his supposition that William's mother Hored was sister to Mary Dyer, who was hanged in Boston, 1 June 1660, for persistently bearing testimony against their cruel and unjust laws against the Quakers, and to Anne Hutchinson of Colonial celebrity, has been proved incorrect.

5. Nicholas³, 1654-1712±, dwelt Kings Town, R. I.; said to have had descendants living in Scipio, Cayuga Co., N. Y.; m. Hannah ....., and had: (1.) Nicholas, jr., dwelt Kings Town, R. I., m. 13 Oct. 1709, Mary Eldred. (2.) Ezekiel, b. after 1693. (3.) George.

6. Dorcas³, m. (as 1st wife) John Watson, a tailor of North Kingstown, R. I., who d. 1728. His will proved in 1728, names as executor his son Samuel, and gives to daughter Frances Brown £20; to daughter Herodias Sheldon, £15.; to sons-in-law John Sheldon and Daniel Brown equally a share in cedar swamp in South Kingstown; to son John Watson, — s.; to son William Watson, 2 s.; to granddaughter, Ann Wells, a kettle, brass warming pan, etc.; and to son Samuel, rest of estate. On 7 Nov. 1673, John and Dorcas were witnesses to deed from George and Tabitha Gardiner to Nicholas Gardiner. On 14 May, 1683, he took John Straight for an apprentice to serve sixteen years from the first of March last past to learn his master's trade of tailoring. On 6 Sept. 1687, he was taxed 8s., 8½d.; was constable in 1687; on grand jury, 1688, Conservator of the Peace and Deputy, 1690. (Descendants later.)

7. Rebecca³, m. (as 2d wife) John¹ Watson, who d. 1728. On 4 Aug. 1702, John and wife Rebecca, deeded to his son John, all his farm, 90 acres, orchard, housing, etc. On 17 Nov. 1705, John and Rebecca signed a deed with her brothers Benoni, Henry, George, William and Nicholas Gardiner. On 28 Jan. 1707, John and Rebecca sold John Thomas 30 acres for £30.

George¹ Gardner, m². Lydia Ballou, who d. 1722—, dau. of Robert and Susanna Ballou, and had:

8. Samuel², b. 1662±, (perhaps son of 1st wife), dwelt Newport, R. I., and Swanzey, Mass., d. 8 Dec. 1696, m. 1683±, Elizabeth (Carr) Brown, widow of James Brown and dau. of Robert Carr, and had: (1.) Elizabeth, b. 1684. (2.) Samuel, b. .. Oct. 1685. (3.) Martha, b. 16 Nov. 1686. (4.) Patience, b. 31 Oct. 1687.

9. Joseph², b. 1669, d. 22 Aug. 1726, was a cooper in Newport, R. I., m. 30 Nov. 1693, Catharine Holmes, dau. of John and Frances (Holden) Holmes, and had: (1.) John, b. 17 Sept. 1697, d. 1764±, became deputy governor of Rhode Island, m. Frances Sanford. (2.) Robert, b. 16 Aug. 1699. (3.) Frances, b. 7 Sept. 1701. (4.) Joseph, b. 17 Apr. 1703. (5.) George, b. 4 Feb. or Apr. 1705, m. Mary Thurston. (6.) Catharine, b. 1 Feb. 1707. (7.) Lydia, b. 2 Mar. 1709. (8.) William, b. 1712, m. Mary Carr. (9.) Mary, b. 1718.

10. Lydia², d. 1723, m. 4 Apr. 1689, Joseph Smith, who d. 13 Jan. 1750, son of John and Sarah (Whipple) Smith, of Providence, R. I. [of John and Alice of Providence], and had: (1.) Israel, b. 13 Jan. 1690. (2.) Lydia, b. 25 May 1692. (3.) Sarah, b. 24 May 1694, d. about 1762 m. 8 Aug. 1724, Thomas¹ Olney, b. 18 Jan. 1695-6, d. 7 Dec. 1758, son of Thomas² and Lydia (Barnes) Olney [of Thomas², Thomas¹]. (4.) Joseph,

b. 18 Dec. 1695. (5.) Robert, b. 3 Mar. 1698. (6.) Alice, b. 25 Jan. 1700. (7.) William, b. 15 Mar. 1703. (8.) David, b. 10 Dec. 1705. (9.) Jeremiah.

11. *Mary.*

12. *Peregrine.* The late Hon. William R. Staples says, in his "Annals of Providence," page 493: "The *first* schoolmaster in Providence of whom any memorial remains, was William Turpin. *When* he came is not known, but he was here the 11th day of June, 1684. On that day he executed an indenture with William Hawkins, and Lydia, his wife, in which he covenanted to furnish Peregrine Gardner with board and schooling for one year for six pounds; forty shillings of which in beef and pork,—pork at two pence, and beef at three pence half penny per pound; twenty shillings in corn at two shillings per bushel, and the balance in silver money. He was to be instructed in reading and writing. This instrument is in the handwriting of Mr. Schoolmaster Turpin, and exhibits plenary proof of his ability to teach writing. It also proves conclusively that schoolmasters in those days were not very exorbitant in their demands."

13. *Robert*, b. ... May 1671, dwelt Newport, R. I., d. ... May 1731; was naval officer and collector of the port of Newport for many years.

14. *Jeremiah²*, dwelt Newport, R. I., m. Sarah ________, and had 1 dau. ____________, b. 23 Sept. 1712.

On 17 Nov. 1705, Benoni, Henry, George, William, and Nicholas Gardiner and John Watson, all of Kings Town, and their wives, Mary, Tabitha, Joan, Elizabeth, and Hannah Gardiner and Rebecca Watson, sold John Potter 410 acres, bounded partly by Point Judith Pond, for £150, said sum to be paid to Thomas Hicks, of Flushing, Long Island, who was a son of John Hicks, the first husband of Herodias. Neither Tabitha, Joan nor Hannah signed the deed, though the other witnesses did.

On 21st Jan. 1671, *William² Gardiner*, calling himself "son of George Gardiner, of Newport," bought 200 or 20 acres of John Porter of Pettaquamscutt and Horod, his wife. July 29, 1679, he signed the petition to the King. On 6 Sept. 1687 was taxed 9s., 1½d. In 1688, he was chosen constable and the same year on grand jury. May 23, 1701, he deeded son and daughter, Joseph and Ann Hull, 204 acres for love, etc. Jan. 18, 1706, he deeded 20 acres for love, etc., to son John Gould and Elizabeth his wife.

His will, dated 18 Jan. 1711, proved 12 Mar. 1711, names as executor his son William, and gives to wife Elizabeth, half of stock of creatures and half of household goods at her disposal, except £40 to be paid daughter Rebecca at eighteen; to wife, for life, his house, half the orchard, and negro man James; to daughter Rebecca, negro girl Zipporah and £40; to daughter Susannah, 50 acres and £20; to daughter Dorcas, negro boy Philip and £35; to daughter Tabitha, £60; to daughter Rachel, land and £60, to be paid by his son-in-law, John Gould, to whom he gave certain land; to daughter Elizabeth, wife of John Gould, £20; to Honour Huling, daughter of Alexander Huling, £5; to son William, all lands remaining, housing and rest of personal estate.

The inventory of his personal estate, amounting to £368, 9s., 10d., included beds, churn, wearing apparel, hat, gloves, pewter, 4 oxen, 12 cows, 7 three years, 3 two years, 5 horse-kind, 142 sheep, 50 lambs, £5, negro boy (4 years), girl (2 years), and a negro 17 years, cart, etc.

In the year 1697, the Friends Yearly Meeting for New England appointed the following named persons a committee to collect funds for the completion of the Friends Meeting House in Boston, viz.: In Newport, John Easton and Wm. Allen; in Portsmouth, Jacob Mott and Matthew Borden; in Jamestown, Ebenezer Slocum; in Kings Town, Joseph Hull and Wm. Gardner; in Warwick, Benjamin Barton; in Providence, Daniel Abbott; in Swansea, Wm. Chase; in Sandwich, Wm. Alden and Daniel Butler; and in Dartmouth, John Tucker and Jacob Mott, jr., as is learned from a historical account of the Friends Meeting House, Boston, published in Boston, in 1874.

WILLIAM⁴ GARDNER, d. 1711, farmer, tanner and currier, of Kingstown, R. I. [of George¹], m. Elizabeth __________, who d. 1737, and had:

1. *William⁴*, Jr., dwelt S. Kingstown, R. I., m. by Ephraim Gardiner, Justice, in S. Kingstown, R. I., 19 May 1744, Freelove Joslin, and had: (1.) Clarke, b. 3 Aug. 1737; he with his brother Thomas owned fisheries on Boston Neck, R. I.; was lost at sea when his dau. Freelove was about 12 years old; m. by William Waite, Justice, in S. Kingstown, 1 Nov. 1759, Amie Lillibridge. (2.) Thomas, b. 7 Mar. 1738-9, kept a tavern on Boston Neck, S. Kingstown, R. I., was a captain in the American Army during the Revolutionary war, stationed to defend the bridge near his abode and keep the British from coming up the sound; d. Rensselaerville, N. Y., probably the Thomas who m. by Jeremiah Crandall, Justice, in S. Kingstown, R. I., 4 Feb. 1765, Abigail Parker. (3.) Stephen, b. 7 June 1740. (4.) Mary, b. 13 Feb. 1744-5. (5.) Desire, b. 26 Nov. 1749. (6.) Gideon, b. 15 Nov. 1751.

2. *Ann⁴*, b. before 1690, d. 12 Sept. 1710, m. 1700±, (as 1st wife) Joseph Hull of Kings Town, R. I., 1670-1748 [of Joseph³, Tristram², Joseph¹], and had: (1.) Ann, b. 26 Oct. 1702, living at date of husbands will of 29 Nov. 1758;

m. 27 Apr. 1721, Robert Knowles of S. Kingstown, R. I., who d. 1759, leaving a valuable estate, son of William and Alice (Fish) Knowles [of Henry]. (2.) William, b. 9 June 1705. (3.) Alice, b. 28 May 1708.

3. *Elizabeth,* m. John Gould.

4. *Rebecca,* b. after 1693.

5. *Susannah.*

6. *Dorcas.*

7. *Tabitha.*

8. *Rachel.*

9. *John²* (not mentioned in father's will; mother's name said to have been Alice ------), d. -- Aug. 1800, aged over 80; was a weaver; m. -------- Wilkinson, sister to the wife of Jeremiah Browning. There is a tradition that John's wife once pushed a colored boy off the wharf into the Narragansett Bay, and that the man (John Gardner) whom she afterward married helped rescue him. (Descendants later.)

10. *Allen,* brother to John². (Perhaps sons by a former wife Alice, but not mentioned in will.)

In old times the taverns were sometimes called Ordinaries. On Sept. 26, 1709, a Town Meeting was called to elect Representatives to the General Assembly and was held at the house of William Gardiner, Ordinary keeper in South Kingstown.

JOHN² GARDINER, of Kings (now Washington) Co., R. I., weaver [of William², George¹], m. -------- Wilkinson and had:

1. *William²,* b. 1 Aug. 1743, in S. Kingstown, R. I., d. in the town of Otsego, N. Y., m. Sarah Watson, b. 11 Jan. 1743-4, d. Rensselaerville, N. Y., dau. of Jeffrey³ and Bathsheba (Smith) Watson [of John², John¹], and had: (1.) Wilkinson, m¹. Hannah Allen, who d. Rensselaerville, N. Y.; m². -------- Brewster, who d. s. p.; m³. ----------------- (2.) William, dwelt Rensselaerville,) now Westerlo), Albany Co., N. Y., and there d.; m. Jane St. John [of Matthew]. (3.) Elisha Watson, b. 8 of 5 mo. 1779, in S. Kingstown, R. I., became member of Farmington Monthly Meeting of Friends by certificate from Rensselaerville, M. M., dated 26 of 1 mo. 1815, d. Farmington, N. Y., 15 of 12 mo. 1869, m. in Rensselaerville, N. Y., 19 of 4 mo. 1801, Sarah Pattison, b. 8 of 7 mo. 1785, d. 20 of 12 mo. 1851, dau. of Sunderland² and Sarah (Utter) Pattison [of Thos¹.]. To their son, the late Sunderland P. Gardner, of Farmington, N. Y., we are indebted for valuable information concerning this branch. (4.) Mary, m. William Stanton, a silversmith, who d. in Rochester, N. Y. (5.) Bathsheba, m. ------ Briggs, of Block Island. (6.) Mercy, m. John Knowles. (7.) Amy, d. 8 of 6 mo. 1841, aged 54 years, 3 mos., 20 days, m. John Sheffield.

2. *Mary²* (twin of Wm.), b. 1 Aug. 1743, in S. Kingstown, R. I., d. Blenheim, N. Y., m. in Rhode Island, ------------ and had among others a son, Wilkinson, and another

son -------- who was a christian minister, also daughters in Blenheim.

3. *John²,* b. 17 June 1745 in S. Kingstown, R. I., lived on Rhode Island, at or near Newport, and owned slaves there, also ships and was engaged in trading to the West Indies, but meeting with heavy losses soon after the Revolutionary War, he removed with the most of his family and about 20 of his slaves to a place on Schoharrie creek in Albany Co., N. Y. He afterwards removed with his family to Hector, Ontario (now Schuyler) Co., N. Y., between Seneca and Cayuga lakes and finally to Big Tree (now Geneseo), locating on a farm on the west side of Genesee river near the site of the present village of Avon, N. Y., and there resided until the death of his wife, and, beside his own place, managed a tract of Wadsworth's land at Canawaugus or Cannewaygus on the Genesee river. Several of his slaves remained with him voluntarily after their emancipation by act of the New York Legislature. He d. in Farmington, N. Y., ... Sept. 1815, and was buried 1st in Welcome Herendeens' orchard, whence, about 1832, his youngest son, J. Hazzard Gardner of Genesee Co., moved his grave to the Gardner family burying ground, Elba, N. Y. The spot is marked by 2 large granite slabs. Four adjoining farms in the northern part of Genesee Co., N. Y., were contracted for and afterward became the homesteads of his 4 sons, John, J. Watson, G. Washington, and J. Hazzard Gardner. The 1st and 4th of these lie upon the west or Oakfield side of the town line established when that town was set off from Elba in 1842, and the other 2 farms adjoined these upon the east. He m. (by William Potter, justice), in S. Kingstown, R. I., 30 Apr. 1767, Bathsheba Watson, b. 16 Sept. 1748, d. Batavia (now Elba), N. Y., 23 Aug. 1812, dau. of Jeffrey³ and Bathsheba (Smith) Watson of S. Kingstown, R. I. [of John², John¹]. (Descendants later.)

4. *Allen* (or *Alan*), b. 3 June 1748, in S. Kingstown, R. I.

5. *Abigail,* d. Washington Co., R. I., m. Nicholas Northrup of Washington Co., R. I.

JOHN⁴ GARDNER, 1745-1815, of Washington Co., R. I., and Livingston Co., N. Y. [of John³, William², George¹], m. 1767 Bathsheba Watson, 1748-1812 [of Jeffrey³, John², John¹], and had:

1. *John²,* was a great reader; his nephew J. H. Gardner of Centreville, Mich., says: "Uncle John Gardner had a wonderful memory, and when I was a boy I was fond of going to hear him tell of their pioneer days. He could read a book and then relate all the incidents it treated and almost whole chapters verbatim." He and his brothers J. Watson, G. Washington, and J. Hazard with their families (except that of G. Washington, who was then unmarried)

settled in the town of Batavia in the northern part of Genesee Co., N. Y., in the year 1811, contracting with the Holland company for 4 adjoining farms, those of John and J. Hazard being in the part of the town which on 11 Apr. 1842 was set off from the town of Elba, and erected into the town of Oakfield. John's deed was dated Oct. 1, 1819. He m. Elizabeth Adams (called Betsey), who d. 24 Aug. 1832, aged 60, and was buried near the residence. They had: (1.) John, d. 24 July 1816 in 22d year of his age, unm. (2.) Joseph, d. 1854 in Ottawa, Ill., m[1]. 1824± Lucy Turner, who d. 27 Sept. 1828, aged 25 years; m[2]. Anna[5] (Laing) Lundy, b. 26 of 7 mo. 1804, d. E. Oakfield, N. Y., widow of Daniel Lundy and dau. of John[5] and Achsah (Lundy) Laing [of John[4], Samuel[3], William[2], John[1]]. (3.) Lydia, b. 1801±, d. Kingston, DeKalb Co., Ill., s. p., m. 1820±, Harry Holmes [of Peter]. (4.) William Robinson, (called Robi'son) b. 6 Feb. 1799 in Rensselaerville, Albany Co., N. Y., d. E. Oakfield, N. Y., 6 June 1882, m. 11 Sept. 1823, Harriet B. Nott, b. 16 Sept. 1802, Salisbury, Conn., died 12 April, 1895 [of Giles]. (5.) Eliza, dw. DeKalb Co., Ill., P. O. Kirkville, m. Ira Dibble. (6.) Abraham Vincent, d. 1853± in DeKalb Co., Ill., of cholera, m. Catharine Busch. (7.) Mary, m. ___________ (8.) Allen, d, 1855± in DeKalb Co., Ill., unm. (9.) Emeline, m. John Griffin, a native of Ireland, who was drowned in Kishawawkie river in Ill. before 1849.

2. *Jeffrey Watson[2] Gardner*. b. 2 Feb. 1775 on Boston Neck, in S. Kingstown, R. I., located in Schuyler Co., N. Y., 15 May 1804, and in Batavia (now Elba), Genesee Co., N. Y., 10 Jan. 1811, obtained deed to his farm there from the Holland Co. 26 July 1819; united with the Society of Friends in Elba, and there d. 25 Aug. 1853; m. 1800±, Freelove[5] Gardner, b. 2 Jan. 1775, d. 28 Aug. 1855, dau. of Clark[4] and Amie (Lillibridge) Gardner, of Kings (now Washington) Co., R. I. [of William[3], William[2], George[1]] and had: (1.) Bathsheba, b. 15 July 1801, d. 22 Jan. 1836 in Elba, N. Y., m. 19 Dec. 1820 Joel Gardner, b. 12 Feb. 1798 in Rensselaerville, N. Y., d. in Alexander, N. Y., 5 May 1878, son of Abiel and Polly (Jewell) Gardner [of Thos[4]., Wm[3]., Wm[2]., George[1]]. (2.) John Champlain, b. 15 May 1804 in Hector, Seneca (now Schuyler) Co., N. Y., d. Oakfield, N. Y., 29 May 1882 s. p.; he was justice of the peace in Oakfield for many years; member of New York assembly in 1849; m[1]. 26 July 1832 Atha Field, b. 12 May 1806; d. 6 Aug. 1861; m[2]. 5 Mar. 1865 (former wife's sister) Harriet D. (Field) Hoose, b. 3 Oct. 1821. d. 7 Aug 1870; m[3]. 18 Oct. 1872 Jane Britton, b. 4 Jan. 1811. (3.) Amy, b. 25 Dec. 1805, d. 18 Apr. 1873, unm. (4.) Jeffrey Watson, Jr., b. 5 Feb. 1808 in Schuyler Co., N. Y., dwelt Elba, N. Y., and there d. 1 May 1882; m. 11 July 1875

Martha Minerva (Turner) Atwater, b. 10 July 1845, dau. of Chancy P. Turner of Livonia, N. Y. [of Deacon William], and widow of Eli N. Atwater of Middlebury, N. Y. (5.) Mary, b. 11 Jan. 1811 in Batavia (now Elba), N. Y., m. 5 May 1836 William C[1]. Bradley, b. 22 Mar. 1814, d. ____ 1894, son of Reuben[2] and Thankful (Foster) Bradley [of Adad[1]]. (6.) Mercy, b. 16 June 1812, d. 11 May 1876, s. p.; m. 1860± (as 2d wife) Daniel Stringham, son of Isaac and Nancy. (7.) Betsy, b. 3 Feb. 1814, d. ____ 1865, m. Milen Perry. (8.) William C., b. 10 Oct. 1816, d. 10 July 1853. (9.) Freelove, b. 28 Mar. 1818, d. 12 Aug. 1850, unm. (10.) Hannah, b. 4 Mar. 1821, d. 26 Jan. 1845, unm; was blind.

3. *George Washington[2] Gardner*, b. 13 Mar. 1785 in Washington Co., R. I., was in Batavia (now Elba), N. Y., as early as the spring of 1810, acquired title to his homestead there by deed from the Holland Company 24 June 1824, for the sum of $980.70; the tract comprised lots 2 and 4 in section 7, township 13, range 2, containing 239½ acres. His first dwelling, of logs, stood near the old well north of the few old apple trees adjoining the orchard planted about 1860 by Nathan Shotwell on land conveyed in 1868 by P. McPhillips to Stephen Vail the present owner of the homestead. In 1827 he erected the roomy and substantial double-silled frame dwelling house which is yet standing little altered in external appearance, except that a wing has been added at the northwest corner, but the portion of the great chimney below the attic floor, with its 7 fire-places—3 on each floor, and one in the basement beside the bake oven—has been removed by the present owner. His heirs in alienating the western portion of the estate in 1882 have reserved the family burying ground, a few rods southwest of the old mansion for the descendants of John and Bathsheba (Watson) Gardner and their husbands and wives. In September and October 1835 he visited Ohio, Michigan, Indiana and Illinois, making the journey on horseback, his son J. H. keeping an interesting "journal of business" on the farm during his absence. On his way back he bought 2 tracts of land in southern Michigan, one in St. Joseph Co., which became the home of his son J. H.; the other in Cass Co., where his dau. Elizabeth and family resided for many years. He was very fond of arbor culture, and planted several rows of shade and ornamental trees across portions of his place, some of which together with fragments of his ample orchards and the residence remain to this day. He and his 1st wife united with the Society of Friends in Elba, about 1821, and he continued a liberal-minded member with the branch called Orthodox until his death which occurred 17 of 7 mo. 1849. He was a man of large-hearted hospitality and general benevolence.

He m'. ____ 1814, Phebe Nairn Garbutt, b 1 Oct. 1784, d. 9 of 9 mo. 1828, dau. of Zachariah and Phebe (Nairn) Garbutt, of Wheatland, N. Y. Her father was an extensive shoemaker in the city of Newcastle on Tine, Northumberland Co., Eng., whence, between 1784 and 1790 he removed to New York, dwelt for a time in the neighborhood of Sing Sing, and near the close of the 18th century settled in the town of Wheatland, N. Y. G. W. Gardner m². at his residence in Elba, N. Y., 11 March 1830 Diana Berry, b. 31 July 1810, dwells with eldest daughter at Concord, Mich., dau. of Jonathan and Bathsheba (Green) Berry. (Children later.)

Gen. McClure commanding the American forces at Ft. George on the west bank of Niagara river about 1 mile from Lake Ontario abandoned that post 12 Dec. 1813, on the approach of the British; having on 10 Dec. reduced the Canadian village of Newark (now Niagara), at the mouth of the river, to ashes. On December 19 a force of British and Indians surprised and gained possession of Ft. Niagara on the American side opposite Newark, and in revenge for the burning of the latter, the villages of Youngstown (1 mile south of Ft. Niagara), Lewiston (6 miles farther south), Manchester (now Niagara Falls), and the Indian Tuscarora village (3 or four miles east from Lewiston) were reduced to ashes, and on the 30th Black Rock and Buffalo were burned. These events caused many of the settlers on the Holland Purchase, among them J. Watson Gardner, to move their families to the Genesee river for safety, but the brothers, G. Washington, and J. Hazard having on their places considerable live stock, remained in Genesee Co., to care for the same, relying upon the friendly Tonawanda Indians to apprise them of the approach of the British and their savage allies.

4. Jeremiah Hazard³ Gardner, b. 11 May 1790, his son G. W. is authority for the statement that he moved into Genesee Co., in the winter of 1811–12, secured from the Holland Company a tract of land which he sold in the autumn of 1812, going back to Ontario Co., but returned in 1820 and bought the same land and thereon continued to reside until his death, which occurred while on a visit in Raisin township, Lenawee Co., Mich., on 2 or 4 of 12 mo. 1838; m. in Palmyra. N. Y., 28 Nov. 1811, Harriet Pattison, b. 12 Dec. 1792, d. 22 Feb. 1878, dau. of Sunderland and Sarah (Utter) Pattison [of Thomas] and had: (1.) George Washington, b. 27 Mar. 1813, d. E. Oakfield, N. Y., 5 Jan. 1879, m. 11 Feb. 1839, Miriam Forbush Grimes, b. 19 Jan. 1818, d. 19 July 1843. dau. of George and Polly (Forbush) Grimes of Walworth, Wayne Co., N. Y. (2.) Sarah Ann, b. 23 Apr. 1815, d. 8 Aug. 1834, m. 11 July 1833 (as 1st wife), Edmond Foster Bradley, b. 18 Jan. 1810, d. 20 Nov. 1884, son of Reuben and Thankful (Foster) Bradley. (3.) William Clark, b. 4 July 1817, supposed to have died in California about 1857, m'. (14 Dec. 1837, Prudence Shotwell Vail, b. 1 of 1 mo. 1818, d. 12 of 2 mo. 1842, dau. of Moses' and Mercy (Pound) Vail, of E. Oakfield, N. Y. [of Samuel⁶, Stephen⁵, Esther⁴ Smith, Sarah³ Shotwell, John², Abraham¹]; m². Ruhamah Spoor; m³. Hannah Shapley. (4.) Jeremiah H., Jr., b. 24 Oct. 1819, d. 15 Dec. 1842, m. 20 June 1839, Dinah Busch. (5.) Sunderland Pattison, b. 24 Nov. 1821, d. 6 May 1884, m'. 28 Dec. 1842, Sarah Ann Churchill, who d. 1860; m². Sarah Hammond. (6.) John Wilkinson, called California John, b. 27 Mar. 1824, m'. Irene Coon; m². Ellen (Harper) Fuller. (7.) Harriet Pattison, b. 29 Apr. 1826, d. at the residence of her son Jerry Hazard Vail, Rochester, N. Y., 3 Aug. 1889; m'. 28 Dec. 1842, Samuel M'. Vail, b. 14 of 7 mo. 1819, son of Moses' and Mercy (Pound) Vail [of Samuel⁶, Stephen⁵, Esther⁴ Smith, Sarah³ Shotwell, John², Abraham¹]; m². A. Edwin Jaquith of Oakfield, N. Y. (8.) Dorcas Pattison, b. 13 May 1828, d. 25 Feb. 1837. (9.) Elias Hicks, b. 7 Apr. 1830, dwells Pittsburgh, Mich., m. Mary Johnson.

*5. Bathsheba², b. 20 of 9 mo. 1769, d. in Farmington, N. Y.; m. Champlain⁶ Gardner, b. 18 of 8 mo. 1768, in S. Kingstown, Kings (now Washington) Co., R. I., d. 25 of 6 mo. 1846, in Farmington, N. Y., son of Clarke⁴ and Amie (Lillibridge) Gardner [of Wm'. Wm². Geo'.], and had: (1.) William, b. 14 of 9 mo. 1800, d. 3 of 11 mo. 1821, unm.

*6. Mercy³, b. 1 of 1 mo. 1773, d. in Walworth, N. Y., 31 of 3 mo. 1858, m. in S. Kingstown, R. I., Welcome Herendeen, b. 18 of 4 mo. 1769, son of Nathan and Huldah. After Welcome's death Mercy lived with her son Nathan in Farmington till his death, and afterward with her daughter Elizabeth Smith in Walworth. Mercy and Welcome had: (1.) Wilkinson, who m. Caroline Arnold (2) Elizabeth, who m. Daniel Smith, son of George. (3.) Nathan G., b. 21 of 2 mo. 1813, m. Jane Sage [of Giles].

*7. Desire³, m. Levi Hoag b. 13 of 12 mo. 1779, in Dutchess Co., N. Y., settled in Elba, N. Y., acquiring title to land there 3 July 1823; d. 1874± in Chautauqua Co., N. Y., and had: (1.) Abigail, m'. 1830±, James Robson who d. 1831±, son of Michael; m². 1833±, Asa Aldrich, son of Wanton and Amy⁶ (Shotwell) Aldrich of Elba [of Richard⁵, Benj'., John³, John², Abr'.]. (2.) Sarah, 1799–1869, an acknowledged minister among Friends; m. Benjamin⁶ Shotwell, 1793–1869, son of Richard⁵ and Mary (Martin) Shotwell of Elba, N. Y. [of Benj'., Jno'., Jno²., Abr'.]. (3.) Mercy, m'. ________ Mason; m². ____________. (4.) Benjamin, d. 1831±, m.

GARDNER L. HUNN, of Parma Township, Jackson Co., Mich.,

AND WIFE

MABEL A. (HUNN) GARDNER, of Albion, Mich.,

the latter wife of W. Scott Gardner, son of John and Maranda (Smith) Gardner, of Litchfield, Mich., the surviving children of Oliver B. and Malinna A. (Gardner) Hunn,
deceased, late of Sandstone township (near Parma village), Mich., and
grandchildren of George Washington[5] and Diana (Berry)
Gardner, late of Genesee Co., New York.

1830± Anna P[7]. Shotwell, 1815-1881, dau. of Isaac M[6]. and Edna C. (Pound) Shotwell, of Elba, N. Y. [of Richard[5], Benj[4]., John[3], John[2], Abr[1].]. (5.) Bathsheba, m. (as 1st wife) Nehemiah Hull. (6.) Levi, Jr., b. 11 of 2 mo. 1819, m. Jedida ________. (7.) Mary Ann, b. 18 of 6 mo. 1819, (error in this or preceding date), m. Russel Wing. (8.) John G., m. 27 of 6 mo. 1821, Eunice Douglass, b. 9 of 3 mo. 1801, dau. of Asa and Abigail (Hardy) Douglass [of Wm.].

8. *Dorcas*[3], b. 22 of 8 mo. 1782 in S. Kingstown, R. I., m. Sunderland[3] Pattison, Jr., b. 19 of 2 mo. 1779, son of Sunderland[2] and Sarah (Utter) Pattison, of Dutchess Co., N. Y. [of Thomas[1] and Elizabeth (Sunderland) Pattison]. He was a miller in Farmington, N. Y. He and wife Dorcas and 2 minor sons George and William having removed and settled in the township of Marengo, Calhoun Co., Mich., became members of Plymouth M. M. of Hicksite Friends by certificate from Farmington M. M. dated 23 of 11 mo. 1837. The children were: (1.) Elizabeth, b. 20 of 4 mo. 1801 in Rensselaerville, N. Y., d. in Farmington, N. Y., m. George Wilber, who d. in Farmington, N. Y. (2.) Mercy, b. 12 of 8 mo. 1803 in Hector, Seneca Co., N. Y., d Marengo, Mich., 12 Dec. 1885, s. p., m[1]. Alvah Wanzer; m[2]. Benson Ford; m[3]. Julius Foster. (3.) Sunderland Gardner Pattison, called Gardner, born 13 of 9 mo. 1811 in Palmyra, N. Y.; dw. Marengo, Calhoun Co., Mich., and there d. 19 Aug. 1882±; m[1]. in Pittsford, Monroe Co., N. Y., 10 Sept. 1831, Anna Maria Smith, b. 25 of 5 mo. 1813, in Farmington, N. Y., d. Marengo, Mich., 2 Oct. 1877, dau. of Peter and Ruth (Brown) Smith of Farmington, N. Y., and granddaughter of Dr. david and Sarah (Ballou) Brown of R. I. He m[2], ____________ (4.) Welcome H., b. 23 of 11 mo. 1814. (5.) George Washington, b. 5 of 5 mo. 1817 in Farmington, N. Y., was founder and proprietor of various periodicals, and laterally dealer in old books at No. 35 Michigan Ave., Detroit, residing at "Orchard Hill" near Birmingham, Mich., m[1.] Mary Ann Wright, who d. ________, dau. of Benj. and Sarah (_______) Wright of Marengo, Mich.; m[2]. Julia A. (Wright) Sturgis, sister to former wife. (6.) Amy, b. 25 of 9 mo. 1820. (7.) William Gardner, b. 15 of 8 mo. 1822, dwells Kalamazoo, Mich.; m. Nancy Benson, dau. of Abijah and Bernecia (Lapham) Benson, of Marengo, Mich., natives of Vermont. (8.) Dorcas, G., b. 7 of 3 mo. 1825 in Farmington, N. Y. At the separation in 1828 the following were among the members of Farmington M. M. who remained with the party called Hicksite Friends: Sunderland, Dorcas, Sunderland G., Welcome, George, and William Pattison, Mercy Wanzer, and Elizabeth Wilber.

9. *Abigail*[3], removed with her husband to Ohio as early as 1818, settling at Goshen, and

becoming a member of Salem (Ohio) M. M by certificate from Farmington, M. M. dated 25 of 5 mo. 1820; m. (as 1st wife) Scott (or Hugh Scott E.) Fuller and had: (1) Ervin, dw. Rolla, Phelps Co., Mo., m. Nancy __________ (2.) Abigail, d. Walworth, N. Y., m. Abel Smith, son of Wilmarth.

GEORGE WASHINGTON[5] GARDNER, 1785-1849, of Elba, N. Y. [of John[4], John[3], William[2], George[1]], m[1]. 1814±, Phebe N. Garbutt, 1784-1828 [of Zachariah], and had:

1. *Jeremiah Hazard*[6], b. 4 Sept. 1818 in Batavia (now Elba), Genesee Co., N. Y., was educated at Wyoming, N. Y. The pursuit of agriculture and land surveying have been his chief occupations, and united with industry and thrift have largely added to his moderate inheritance. He came first to Michigan in 1838 and commenced work upon his "Forest Home Farm" in Lockport township near Centerville, Mich., purchased by his father in 1835, to which he removed 1 July 1840. In 1841 he assisted in surveying a tract at and about the site of the present city of Petoskey, going thither by water from Michigan City. He was county Surveyor of St. Joseph Co., for 16 years and has held the positions of county commissioner, township supervisor, highway commissioner, director of First National Bank of Three Rivers, and for several years purchasing agent for the St. Joseph county grange, of the order of the Patrons of Husbandry; in politics he is a Republican and has long been one of the foremost men in the community where he resides. His efforts and plans were efficiently seconded and promoted by his worthy and capable wife. He m. in St. Joseph Co., Mich., 8 Oct. 1844, Anna Thomson, b. 22 Jan. 1825, in Rochester, N. Y., came to Dearborn, Wayne Co., Mich., in 1835, and to Constantine, St. Joseph Co., Mich., in 1837. On 3 Dec. 1888 she went to Whittier, near Los Angeles, Cal., for the advantage of her health, and there d. 30 Dec. 1888, at the residence of George W. Hazzard. Her body was brought back to the family residence, about two miles north of Centreville, where she had dwelt since 1844, and was laid to rest in Prairie River Cemetery, Centreville, on Thursday, 10 Jan. 1889, the funeral being conducted by Rev. A. Paige Peeke. Her fidelity in all relations of life and her excellences of character are well known. She was daughter of John and Ann (Wheeler) Thompson of Rochester, N. Y. J. H. and Anna (Thompson) Gardner had: (1.) Isabel, b. Elba, N. Y. 1846±, married 15 April 1895 Volney J. Patchin of Centreville, Mich.; (2.) Phebe Ann, b. St. Joseph Co., Mich. 1851±; (3.) Arthur W., b. 1854±, all of whom, except Isabel, dwell with their father near Centreville, Mich., unm. The mother's sister Harriet (Thompson) Albright's youngest 2 children, Elwin T. and Nellie, were after their mother's death given a

home in this family and reared with all the care and solicitude that parental love could supply until prepared to enter life's battles for themselves. In 1836, J. H. Gardner, with his father and stepmother visited Michigan. At Buffalo they fell in company with William Macy of New York City, and journeyed together by steamboat to Monroe, and thence by a hired wagon to Tecumseh, where they parted. Macy went on farther west, and bought two sections of land near Three Rivers and other lauds in other counties. About thirty years afterward his sons deeded the lands near Three Rivers to J. H. Gardner, who has since sold them out to Germans, and they are now nice farms.

2. *Elizabeth*[6], b. 29 of 4 mo. 1822 in Elba, N. Y., she and her family removed to Michigan in 1844, and were among the pioneer settlers of Mason township, Cass Co., Mich., where they located upon a tract of land previously purchased by her father chiefly with means from her mother's estate; here they remained until 13 July 1881, when having sold this farm, they removed to the vicinity of Knoxville, Tenn., and thence in Nov. 1890, to California, locating on a farm one mile north of the village of Santa Maria, 12 miles from the coast, where she d. 11 Jan. 1892. She m. 28 Dec. 1843 Benjamin Worth, b. 1824 at Niagara, N. Y., and had: (1.) George W., b. 16 Sept. 1846, served in the War of the Rebellion to its close, d. -- Mar. 1873, m. 23 Dec. 1866, Sophronia M. Curtis, b. 1849, dau. of Jothan Curtis of Adamsville, Mich. (2.) John L., b. 17 Sept. 1849, m. 15 Sept. 1869, Laura J. Kingsley. (3.) Frances A., b. 24 July 1852, d. 5 Aug. 1873, unm. (4.) Jerome B., b. 12 Sept. 1854, dw. Santa Maria, Cal. unm. (5.) Oscar C., b. 1 Mar. 1857, d. Ogden, Utah 1893±, m. 13 Oct. 1884, Lizzie M. Kelley, b. 7 Dec. 1856 [of Henderson N.]. (6.) Alice A., b. 16 Feb. 1859, d. 29 June 1875. (7.) Ella E., b. 21 Sept. 1861, m. 24 June 1883 Louis Blanc. (8.) Ida E., b. 24 Jan. 1864, d. 1 May 1870. (9.) Mina E., b. 2 Feb. 1867, d. Santa Maria, Cal. -------- 1892, m. Hugh Smith.

3. *George W., Jr.*, b. 23 of 10 mo. 1824, d. 1 of 4 mo 1825.

George Washington[5] *Gardner*, 1785-1849, m[2]. 1830 Diana Berry, b. 1810 dau. of Jonathan and Bathsheba (Greene) Berry, and had:

4. *Bathsheba Phebe*[6] (called Phebe B.), b. 23 of 2 mo. 1831, dwells Concord, Mich., m. 2 of 5 mo. 1850, Nathan[7] Shotwell, b. 1826, son of Isaac M[6]. and Edna C. (Pound) Shotwell [of Richard[5], Benjamin[4], John[3], John[2], Abraham[1]]. For fuller sketch and children, see part II.

5. *Malinna Ann*[6], b. 4 of 6 mo. (June) 1833 in Elba, N. Y., removed in 1853 to Parma township, Jackson Co., Mich., and thence about 1867 to the western half of section 19 in Sandstone township, about 2 miles north of the village of Parma, and there d. 7 Mar. 1883, and was interred in the Gardner family burying ground in the western part of the town of Elba, Genesee Co., N. Y.; m. in Elba, N. Y., -------- 1852 Oliver Bliss Hunn, b. 25 June 1826, in Springfield, Mass., d. 18 May 1884 in Sandstone township, buried in Parma cemetery, son of Ephraim Hunn of Genesee Co., N. Y. They had: (1.) Mabel Alice (called Bell), b. 19 June 1854, dwells Albion, Mich., m. 18 Feb. 1874, Winfield Scott[7] Gardner, b. 16 Jan. 1847, in Elba, N. Y., son of John[6] and Maranda (Smith) Gardner of Litchfield, Mich. [of Abiel[5], Thomas[4], William[3], William[2], George[1]], and had: (a.) Lena Ann, b. 19 Sept. 1879, d. 7 Mar. 1880. (b.) Ray, b. 21 Aug. 1881. (c.) Iva Ann, b. 6 Aug. 1884. (2.) Gardner Albert, b. 18 Jan. 1857, d. 18 July 1858. (3.) Gardner Lincoln, b. 7 July 1861, dw. Parma, Mich., m. 23 Nov. 1881, Mary Hawes, b. 8 Oct. 1862, dau. of Joseph and Mary Ann (Woodliff) Hawes of Concord township, Jackson Co., Mich., natives of England, and had: (a) Leroy Oliver, b. 20 June 1883. (b) George Joseph, b. 27 Sept. 1888. (c) Howard H., b. 29 Oct. 1891. (4.) Edward Rice, b. 4 Aug. 1865, d. 25 Aug. 1891, m. 11 Feb. 1885, Caroline Estella Welch, b. -- May 1867, dau. of George and Prudence (Jones) Welch of Spring Arbor township, Jackson Co., Mich., and had: (a) Malinna Ann, b. 8 Oct. 1885, d. 11 Oct. 1886. (b) Edna, b. 5 Aug. 1888. (c.) Edward R., b. 25 Mar. 1891.

6. *George Milton*[6], b. 23 of 6 mo. 1835 in Elba, N. Y., entered the drug store of Berry & Hart in Adrian, Mich., 1 June 1851, remaining there 3½ years and mastering the business of a practical druggist, graduated in June 1855 from Bryant, Spencer, Lusk & Stratton Commercial College, Cleveland, O.; visited in Michigan until January 1856 when he returned to his native place; took an active part in the first National Republican campaign, casting his first vote for Freemont and Dayton, and has since continued his allegiance to the principles of that G. O. P. Bought the central portion of the old homestead 30 Aug. 1856, and there followed the occupation of farming until the autumn of 1861, when he sold his farm in Elba, and visited Michigan in the winter of 1861-2; but returning to E. Oakfield N. Y., ran the sawmill of his father-in-law for one year. Removing with his family to Adrian, Mich., in the spring of 1863, he engaged in the flour, feed, and commission business with his mother's cousin Frank Green who died in July following. Closing the business there in September 1863, he bought the drug store of C. C. Blakeslee in Jonesville, Mich., which business he followed until early in 1870 when he sold his stock to Dr. G. Chaddock and spent that summer on the farm of George Gardner, in Scipio township. Returning to Jonesville in the autumn, he commenced the news and subscription business in the postoffice there and

about two years later again embarked in the drug trade. He was president of the village of Jonesville 1866-7, marshal and recorder 1872; made a member of LaFayette Lodge No. 16, F. & A. M. of Jonesville, Mich., 1863; Master Mason 1864; Royal Arch Mason of Jonesville Chapter No. 8, 1865; Royal and Select Master, Jonesville Council No. 5, 1866; resumed the pursuit of agriculture on a 40 acre farm adjoining that of his father-in-law in the township of Scipio, Mich., in 1874. Became a member of Litchfield Grange No. 107 of the order of Patrons of Husbandry in Jan. 1876, and during most of the succeeding 14 years was purchasing agent for this association, was elected Master of the Grange in 1888. In May 1880 he removed to a farm which he purchased in section 12 of Litchfield township, making a specialty of stock rearing. Disposing of this place in 1890, he removed to the village of Litchfield, and thence in the summer of 1891, to Parma, and finally, 1892, to Jackson, Mich., was elected justice of the peace in Litchfield in spring of 1891, and in Jackson in 1894-'95; is engineer and starchmaker for Potter M'fg Co.; dw. 206 W. Biddle St., Jackson.

He m. at the residence of Harry Field, J. P. in E. Oakfield, N. Y., 28 Feb. 1857, Jane Elizabeth[7] Gardner, b. 19 Feb. 1840, in Elba, N. Y., dau. of George[6] and Mary V. (Pugsley) Gardner, of Hillsdale Co., Mich., formerly of Genesee Co., N. Y. [of Abiel[5], Thos[4]., Wm[3]., Wm[2]., Geo[1].], and had: (1.) George Milton, Jr., b. 13 Jan. 1859 in Elba, N. Y., dwells No. 306 Webb St., Jackson, Mich., has also been actively identified with Republican party; elected alderman in second ward in 1895; occupation steel worker, foreman hoe and rake shop Withington, Cooley M'fg Co., m. in Litchfield, Mich., 7 Dec. 1880, Mary Luvilla Freeman, b. 1 June 1860, dau. of Reuben William and Mary Louisa (Mead) Freeman, of Litchfield, Mich., and had: (a) Don Bion, b. 20 Sept. 1889. (b.) Gladys Mary, b. 24 June 1895. (2.) Minnie May, b. 9 May 1866, in Jonesville, Mich., dwells with parents Jackson, Mich., unm. 1895.

7. *Mary Jane*, b. 13 of 5 mo. 1837 in Elba, N. Y., d. 11 June 1844.

THE WATSON LINE, ETC.

JOHN[1] WATSON, tailor, of N. Kingstown, R. I., d. 1728 (for fuller sketch see 6th and 7th children of George[1] Gardner of Newport, *ante*), m. Dorcas[2] Gardner, dau. of George[1] and Hored (Long) Gardner, and had: (1.) John, m. Hannah .... (Children later.) (2.) Samuel, d. 1762+, m.[1] Abigail Northup, dau. of Stephen and Mary (Thomas) Northup; m.[2] Hannah Hazard, b. .. Apr. 1714, d. 17 Dec. 1801, dau. of Jeremiah and Sarah (Smith) Hazard. (3.)

William, d. 1740+, m. Mercy Helmer, dau. of Rouse and Mary (......) Helmer. (4.) Frances, d. 1726+, m. Daniel Brown who d. 1726. (5.) Ann, m. 1705± (as 1st wife), Peter Wells, 1681-1732 [of Peter]. (6.) Herodias, m. 11 Apr. 1706, John Sheldon [of John].

JOHN[2] WATSON, of S. Kingstown, R. I., son of John[1] and Dorcas (Gardner) Watson, became freeman in Kings Town, R. I., in 1712, was deputy 1718 and 1721-26; on 29 Mar. 1731 he was appointed guardian to his neice Desire Brown, dau. of Daniel deceased; he m. Hannah .... and had: (1.) Hannah, b. 1 Mar. 1703-4. (2.) Ann, b. 27 Mar. 1709. (3.) John, b. 13 Mar. 1709-10. (4.) Jeffrey, b. 3 Aug. 1712 at Kingstown, R. I., was assistant in 1746, 7, 9, 52, and 53-5; m. by Christopher Allen, justice, in S. Kingstown, R. I., 30 Nov. 1732, Bathsheba Smith, b. 7 Apr. 1710, dau. of John[2] and Mercy (Westcott) Smith [of John[2], John[1], of Prudence Island]. Children later. (5.) Elisha, b. 14 Sept. 1714. (6.) Dorcas, b. 25 Oct. 1716, m. by Ephraim Gardiner, justice, in S. Kingstown, R. I., 29 Aug. 1734, Ezekiel Gardiner, son of Nicholas[3] and Mary (Eldred) Gardiner, of N. Kingstown [of Nicholas[2], George[1]]. (7.) Amie, b. 18 Oct. 1719.

JEFFREY[3] WATSON, b. 3 Aug. 1712, of S. Kingstown, R. I. [of John[2], John[1]], m. 1732, Bathsheba Smith, b. 1710 [of Jno[3]., Jno[2]., Jno.[1]], and had: (1.) Hannah, b. 2 June 1733, m. 13 Sept. 1750, Joshua Allen [of Caleb]. (2.) Jeffrey, Jr., b. 16 Oct. 1734, m. 24 Mar. 1757, Hannah Gardiner, of N. Kingstown. (3.) Elisha, b. 10 July 1736. (4.) Mercy, b. 10 July 1740. (5.) Dorcas, b. 5 June 1741. (6.) Sarah, b. 11 Jan. 1743-4, m. William[4] Gardner, son of John[3] and .... (Wilkinson) Gardner [of Wm[2]., Geo[1].] (7.) William, b. 25 Apr. 1745. (8.) *Bathsheba*, b. 16 Sept. 1748, in S. Kingstown, R. I., d. .... 1812 in Batavia (now Elba), N. Y., m. 30 Apr. 1767, John[4] Gardner, 1745-1815, son of John[3] (weaver) and .... (Wilkinson) Gardner [of Wm[2]., George[1]]. (For her children, see family of John[4] Gardner *ante*).

JOHN[1] SMITH, of Conanicut 1664, and Prudence Island 1673, d. not later than 1677. His widow Margaret m[2]. John Snook. John[1] Smith of Portsmouth (Prudence Island), R. I., and wife Margaret had: (1.) John, d. 1730, m. Phillis Gereardy who d. 1729+, dau. of John and Renewed (Sweet) Gereardy. For fuller sketch and abstract of will the reader is referred to J. O. Austins Geneological Dictionary of Rhode Island families. (2.) Jeremiah, d. 1720, m. 2 Jan. 1672, Mary Gereardy who d. 1722+ [of John and Renewed]. (3.) Mercy, m. Benjamin Clarke. (4.) Hannah, d. 1712, m. Joseph Case, 1654-1741 [of William and Mary]. (5.) Daniel, d. 1707.

JOHN[2] SMITH, d. 1730 of Portsmouth (Prudence Island), and S. Kingstown, R. I., ferryman at Boston Neck in Kings Town [of John[1]], m. Phillis Gereardy, who d. 1729+ [of John and Renewed (Sweet) Gereardy] and had: (1.) John[2], m. 8 Jan. 1707-8, Mercy Westcott, daughter of Amos[2] and Deborah (Stafford) Westcott [of Stukeley[1]]. (Children later.) (2.) Daniel. (3.) _________ a son. (4.) Hopestill, m. ______ Northup.

JOHN[3] SMITH, of Kings Town, R. I. [of John[2], John[1]], m. 1708, Mercy Westcott [of Amos[2], Stukeley[1]], and had: (1.) Margaret, b. 3. Oct. 1708. (2.) Bathsheba, b. 7 Apr. 1710, m. 30 Nov. 1732, Jeffrey[3] Watson, b. 3 Aug. 1712, living in 1762 [of John[2], John[1]]. (3.) John, b. 26 July 1712. (4.) Mary, b. 17 July, 1715. (5.) Mercy, b. 5 Aug. 1717. (6.) William, b. 9 Oct. 1719. (7.) Phillis, b. 29 Sept. 1723.

JOHN[1] SWEET, was in Salem, Mass., as early as 3 July 1632, when his land is described as "bounding Mr. Skelton's land on the north and near to Captain Endicott's." The name of "Sweet's Cove" was given to an inlet near his residence. In 1637 he had a grant of land in Providence, R. I., and after his death in 1637 his widow Mary received a grant of land in Providence; returning to Salem, she had a grant of land the same year in that place also.

She m[2]. 1638±, Ezekiel Holliman. The Rev. Hugh Peters of Salem, in a letter to the church at Dorchester dated 1 July 1639, alludes to her as one of those who had "the great censure passed upon them in this our church," and that "they wholly refused to hear the church, denying it and all the churches in the Bay to be true churches," etc. Her will of 31 July 1681, proved the same year, gives to her son-in-law John Gereardy and daughter Renewed, his wife, both formerly of Warwick, now of Providence, all interest in her house, lot, meadow and upland in Warwick.

John[1] Sweet and wife Mary had: (1.) John, dw. Warwick, R. I., d. 1677, m. Elizabeth, 1629-1684+ (2.) James, 1622-1695+, m. Mary Greene, b. 1633+, dau. of John and Joan (Tattersal) Greene. (3.) Meribah, name changed by her step-father to Renewed, and she married under this latter name to John Gereardy, a native of Holland, both were living at date of her mother's will in 1681. They had: (a) Mary. (b) John (c) Phillis, d. 1729+, m. John[2] Smith, who d. 1730 [of John[1] and Margaret of Portsmouth, Prudence Island, R. I.].

STUKELEY[1] WESTCOTT, b. 1592, d. 12 Jan. 1676-7, aged about 85, as he states in will of same date, which was finally approved by the Town Council 20 years later. For an abstract of the same and fuller particulars than can be presented here, the reader is referred to Austin's R. I. Genealogical Dictionary, which presents the records of 5 children, 38 grandchildren and 62 great-grandchildren. In 1636 he was received as an inhabitant and freeman at Salem, Mass. On 25 Dec. 1637 a house lot of 1 acre was allotted to him there, his family consisting of 8 persons. In 1638 he removed to Providence, R. I., and was 1 of the 12 persons who on 8 Oct. 1638 had a deed from Roger Williams of land which the latter had bought of Canonicus and Miantonomi, and had a lot granted him soon after. He and his wife were among those alluded to in the letter of Rev. Hugh Peters already mentioned. He was one of the twelve original members of the First Baptist Church in America, organized at Providence in 1639. On 27 July 1640 he, with 38 others of Providence, signed an agreement for their civil government. Became an inhabitant of Warwick in 1648, and thenceforth was one of the chief men of that place. In 1654 the Town Council met at his house; on 25 May 1655 he was appointed to keep a house of entertainment, a sign was to be set out at the most perspicuous place; and again in 1664 he was authorized to keep an ordinary for entertainment of strangers during the time the King's Commissioners held court in Warwick.

The children of Stukeley Westcott were: (1.) Damaris, d. 1678+, m. 17 Dec. 1640 Benedict Arnold, b. 21 Dec. 1615, d. 19 June 1678, son of William and Christian (Peak) Arnold. (2.) Robert, d. 1676, m. Catharine _____ (3.) Amos, 1631-1685 of Warwick, R. I., m[1]. 13 July 1667, Sarah Stafford, d. 1669 [of Thomas and Elizabeth]; m[2]. 9 June 1670, Deborah Stafford, 1651-1706 [of Thomas and Elizabeth]. (Children later.) (4.) Mercy, d. 25 Mar. 1700, m. Samuel Stafford, b. 1636±, d. 20 Mar. 1718 [of Thomas and Elizabeth]. (5.) Jeremiah, d. 1686, m. 27 July 1665, Eleanor England, who d. 1686 [of William and Elizabeth].

AMOS[2] WESTCOTT, 1631-1685, was Town Sergeant in Warwick, R. I.; also held the office of Water Bailey, was often Juryman, and Deputy, and in 1662 he had a lot in the division of Potawomut lands and also in the division of Toseunk lands. He m[1]. 13 July 1667 Sarah Stafford who d. 1669 [of Thos.], and had: (1.) Amos, 1668-1692 of Warwick, R. I., and Oyster Bay, N. Y. Amos[3], Sr., m[2]. 9 June 1670, Deborah Stafford, 1651-1706 [of Thos.], and had: (2) Solomon, d. 1711, unm. (3.) Sarah, b. 1673, m. Abraham Lockwood, 1670+-1747. (4.) Penelope, m. James Baker [of Thos. and Sarah]. (5.) Mercy[3], m. 8 Jan. 1708, John Smith, son of John and Phillis (Gereardy) Smith. (6.) Luranah. The father, Amos[2], was named as sole executor in his father's will of 12 Jan. 1676-7, which granted to him all the movable estate as cattle, goods, and chattles, and land at Potawamut Neck, meadow at Toseunk, and three-fourths of land at Coweset with privileges, etc.

THOMAS[1] STAFFORD of Newport, R. I., received in 1638 a grant of 17 acres of land in Newport, being then in the employ of Nicholas Easton.

"The first Stafford who came to this country was Thomas[1], born about 1605. He emigrated from Warwickshire, England, to Plymouth, New

England, in or about the year 1626 [or 1623] and was among the inhabitants admitted 'at the Toune of Nieu-Port since the 20th of the 3rd mo. 1638.' A few years later he removed to Providence, R. I., and from thence to Warwick, R. I., in 1652, where he died in 1677. Thomas Stafford is recorded, 1655, in 'the Roule of ye Freemen of ye Colonie' as 'Freeman of the Towne of Warwicke.' In 1662 he was granted fifty acres of land in Connecticut by the General Court, and may possibly have stayed there a few years. He was a millwright, and at Plymouth he built the first mill in this country for grinding corn by water. He constructed another at Providence near what is called Millbridge, and still another on his own place in Warwick, the site of which is still recognizable."

"In the will of Thomas' Stafford, made Nov. 4th 1677, just before his death, mention is made of his wife Elizabeth, and we know nothing farther of her." This will, proved 24 Apr. 1678 names also children, Thomas, Deborah Westcott, Samuel, Joseph, Hannah Bromley. There was also a dau. Sarah, who d. 1669, 1st wife of Amos' Westcott, 1631-1685 [of Stukeley], who afterward m. 9 June 1670 her sister Deborah, 1651-1706, and had: Mercy Westcott, who m. John' Smith and had Bathsheba, b. 1710, who m. Jeffrey' Watson and had Bathsheba, 1744±-1812, who m. John' Gardner and had Gorge Washington' 1785-1849, who m.' Diana Berry, b. 1810, and had Bathsheba Phebe, called Phebe B., b. 1831, who m. Nathan' Shotwell, b. 1826, and had among others Ambrose M. Shotwell, b. 1853, the compiler of the present work.

IV.

ANCESTORS AND NEAR RELATIVES OF THE

AUTHOR'S MATERNAL GRANDMOTHER,

DIANA (BERRY) GARDNER,

DAUGHTER OF JONATHAN AND BATHSHEBA⁶ (GREENE) BERRY, OF RENSSELAER AND ORLEANS CO'S, N. Y., AND LENAWEE CO., MICH.

[Of Langford⁵ Greene, Joseph⁴, John³, James², John¹, of Warwick, R. I.]

AND SECOND WIFE OF GEORGE WASHINGTON' GARDNER, OF ELBA, N. Y.

[Of John⁴, John³, William², George¹.]

JONATHAN BERRY was b. in Rensselaer Co., N. Y., 28 June 1790, dwelt in the town of Berlin, whence he removed by way of the Erie Canal in the spring of 1827 to Orleans Co., N. Y., settling in the town of Barre, one-half mile east of the schoolhouse that stood on the highway known as the Oak Orchard Road; thence in July 1835 to Mt. Vernon, Knox Co., O.; thence, in Apr. 1836 in a wagon to Adrian, Mich., and finally about 1840 to a farm in the township of Rome, Lenawee Co., Mich., and there d. 20 Oct. 1851. While residing at Adrian, Mich., he was a judge of the Circuit Court, and after removing to Rome was elected a member of the 9th Michigan Legislature, which commenced its session in Detroit 1 Jan. 1844. He and his wife are buried in Oakwood Cemetery, Adrian, Mich. His father .... Berry, d. in Berlin, N. Y., near the beginning of the century, and his mother Judith before 1825. He had a brother Elisha, who was rendered imbecile by the kick of a horse, and who d. before 1820, unm.; also an uncle Clark Berry who went west early in the century. Jonathan m. by Rev. .... Hull (Baptist) in Stephentown, N. Y., 3 Dec. 1809, Bathsheba⁶ Greene, b. 21

Aug. 1790 in Stephentown, N. Y., d' at the residence of her daughter, A. Emily Park, State St., Adrian, Mich., 26 Sept. 1879 in the 90th year of her age, was a consistent member of the Presbyterian Church; daughter of Langford⁵ and Abigail (Thomas) Greene of Stephentown, N. Y. [of Joseph⁴, John³, James², John¹]. They had:

1. *Diana⁷*, b. 31 July 1810 in Berlin, Rensselaer Co., N. Y. She was the oldest of 5 children. Her birthplace was about 25 miles east of the Hudson River. She removed with her parents in 1827 by the (then recently opened) Erie Canal to Orleans Co., N. Y. From early life she seemed to view her surroundings through distorted mental lenses, which fact made her life far from a happy one. Between 1838 and 1850, she spent several years with her parents in Lenawee Co., Mich., whither they had previously moved. After the death of her husband and the marriage of her eldest daughter, she lived partly upon the estate of the former and partly in the family of the latter. Since the summer of 1877, she has made her home in the family of her daughter Phebe B. Shotwell, at Concord, Mich. In May, 1882, her dower interest in her deceased husband's

estate was sold to the late Henry Bartels of E. Oakfield and the proceeds placed at interest, thus yielding her a larger income than the rental previously obtained. She still enjoys a good degree of physical health. She m. 11 Mar. 1830 (as 2d wife) George Washington[5] Gardner 1785-1849 [of John[4], John[3], William[2], George[1]], she was at one time teacher of a district school in Lenawee Co. On her 85th birthday anniversary, her son and other callers found her in usual health and accustomed to take long walks with her youngest great-grandson. The following is from the "Jackson Citizen" of Aug. 1892:

FOUR GENERATIONS IN REUNION.

On Sunday, July 31st, the home of Mr. Nathan Shotwell, one mile north of the village of Concord, was the scene of a very pleasant gathering, the occasion being that of the eighty-second birthday anniversary of Mrs. Shotwell's mother, Mrs. Diana Gardner, who for the past fifteen years has resided in the family of her daughter.

In her honor and much to her gratification all but one of her twenty-one living descendents participated in the family reunion, namely: Two children, Mrs. Phebe B. Shotwell of Concord, and Mr. George Milton Gardner of Parma; eight of her nine grandchildren, Miss Lilla P. Shotwell, Ambrose M., Cassius E., and Manly N. Shotwell and Mrs. Ida A. S. Davis, all of Concord, Mrs. Mabel A. Gardner of Litchfield, Mr. Gardner L. Hunn of Parma and Mr. G. M. Gardner jr., of North street and West avenue, Jackson; and her ten great-grandchildren, Owen B. Shotwell, J. S. Davis, Ray Gardner, Iva Gardner, Leroy O., George J. and Howard Hunn, Edna and Edward R. Hunn, and Don B. Gardner, together with the husbands and wives of the several descendants with the single exception of Mr. W. Scott Gardner of Litchfield, who was detained at home. His presence and that of his wife's cousin, Miss Minnie M. Gardner, of Parma, were alone wanting to make the reunion of four generations and their respective families complete. Mrs. Gardner's only other descendants who survived early childhood were Mrs. Malinna A. Hunn, who died at her home near Parma in 1883—wife of the late O. B. Hunn—and her youngest son, Edward R. Hunn, whose untimely death, from the effects of an accidental fall from being struck by a frightened horse in Jackson, occurred at Parma, in August last.

Each of the living descendants was presented with a solid silver spoon, appropriately engraved, and many pleasant reminiscences of departed days were rehearsed. The exercises were mostly of an informal character, music and an ice cream festival being prominent features. For one of her years the aged widow is in the enjoyment of a good degree of bodily vigor and feels a lively interest in the latest twigs of the family tree. Her sister, Mrs. John B. Schureman, of Adrian, aged 76, visited her and other relatives in Jackson county during the first week in July.   A. M. S.

ANCESTORS OF DIANA[3] BERRY, b. 31 July 1810 [of Jonathan[1]], m. 1830 George Washington[5] Gardner, 1785-1849, [of John[4], John[3], William[2], George[1]].

Jonathan[2] Berry, b. 28 June 1790, d. 20 Oct. 1851, m. 9 Dec. 1809, Bathsheba[6] Greene, b. 21 Aug. 1790, d. 29 Sept. 1879, dwelt Berlin, Rensselaer Co., and Barre, Orleans Co., N. Y., and Rome, Lenawee Co., Mich.

..........[1] Berry m. Judith ....

Langford[5] Greene, b. 18 Dec. 1766, m. .... Abigail Thomas, dwelt Stephentown, Rensselaer Co., N. Y.

George[1] Thomas m. ....

Joseph[4] Greene, b. 19 Feb. 1727-8, d. 1822, m. 24 Oct. 1751, Phoebe[3] Langford, b. 26 Apr. 1734, dwelt Stephentown, (now Berlin) N. Y.

John[3], m. 1709 Mary[2] Allen, 1685-1757, b. 1689

James[2] 1626-1698 m[2], 1665, Elizabeth[2] Anthony d. 1698†

John[1] 1597-1658 m[1], 1619 Joan Tattersall, John[1] Anthony m. Susanna

Richard[3], Richard[2], Robert[1]

Increase[1] Allen

John[2] Langford, 1705-1785 m. 1727 Barbara[3] Rice, 1706-1799, dw. E. Greenwich, R. I.

Thomas[1] Langford, d. 1709. m[2], Sarah ....

John[2] Rice 1675-1765 m. 1695 Elnathan[3] Whipple, dw. Warwick, R. I. 1674-5—1758†

John[1] 1616-1731 m. 1674 Elizabeth[3] Holden, dw. Warwick, R. I. b. 1652

Randall[1] Holden m. Frances[2] Dungan

William[1] Dungan m. Frances[2] Latham

Lewis[1] m. Winifred.

John[2] Whipple m. Mary[1] Olney

John[1] Whipple m Sarah .... Thomas[1] Olney m Mary Small.

2. *Langford Greene [3]Berry*, b. 19 June 1812, in Berlin, N. Y., removed to Lenawee Co., Mich., about 1835, to Arkansas about 1867, to Colorado 1871 and to California about 1873, settling at Oakland, where he d. 3 Apr. 1878, was Auditor General 1861–63, afterward U. S. Collector at the port of Detroit and for many years a very prominent man of the State; in religion a Presbyterian and at one time an Elder in that church. He m[1]. (by Rev. Gilbert Crawford) in Albion, N. Y., ____ Sept. 1841, Mary Ann Hart, b. 2 June 1817, d. 8 May 1849, dau. of Joseph and Lucy (Kirtland) Hart, of Orleans Co., N. Y. She was a devoted, earnest christian from 11 years of age, and a member of the Presbyterian Church. Her last words were:

"Jesus can make a dying bed
Feel soft as downy pillows are."

He m[2]. in Adrian, Mich., Margaret Ramsdell, who d. at Adrian, dau. of Thomas D. Ramsdell, a tanner. He m[3]. in Connecticut, Betsey Coyt, who d. 3 July 1868 in Adrian, Mich. He m[4]. in Cincinnati, O., Rosa Ludlow, who, after his death, removed from California to Illinois.

By the 1st wife he had: (1.) Benjamin Hart, b. 20 Aug. 1842. (2.) Emily Alice, b. 19 Mar. 1844, was a graduate of the Misses Rogers Female College at Lansing. Her literary acquirements were of a high order; she was a member of the First Presbyterian Church of Lansing; d. of pneumonia at the Massasoit Hotel, Springfield, Mass., Saturday, 27 Sept. 1879, while on a trip for her health with her husband, to New York and Boston; funeral from their residence at Lansing, Sept. 30; buried in Mt. Hope Cemetery. She m. 25 Dec. 1867 Schuyler Fisk Seager, b. 6 July 1842, d. 6 Nov. 1883 [of Rev. Schuyler]. (3.) Mary Hart, b. 6 Feb. 1849, d. Lansing, Mich., 26 Jan. 1863.

By his 2d wife, he had: (4.) Gertrude Margaret, dw. New York, N. Y., m. (as 2d wife) Schuyler F. Seager, 1842–1883, a very successful lawyer of Lansing, where he acquired a considerable property.

By the 3d wife, L. G. Berry had: (5.) Langford Greene, Jr., b. 1862, d. 20 Nov. 1882, at El Paso, Texas, was bookkeeper for R. R. Co.

3. *Ambrose Spencer Berry*, b. 12 Aug. 1814, in Berlin, N. Y., removed with his parents in 1836 to Lenawee Co., Mich., was for many years engaged in the dry goods business at Adrian, Mich.; d. at Corning, Ark., 3 Sept. 1878, of yellow fever, s. p.; m. at Albion, N. Y., 19 Aug. 1839, Lucy Kirtland Hart, b. 22 Jan. 1814, at Albion, N. Y., dw. with brother Samuel E. Hart, 13 State St., Adrian, Mich., daughter of Joseph and Lucy (Kirtland) Hart.

4. *Judith Juletta*, b. 18 Feb. 1816, dwelt with her younger sister, Mrs. A. Emily Park, 25 State St., Adrian, Mich., and there died 24 April 1895, s. p.; m. in Rome township, Lenawee Co., Mich., 14 July 1842, (as 2d wife) John Bogart Schureman, b. near New York city, d. Rome, Mich., __________ 1879.

5. *Abigail Emily*, b. 28 Oct. 1818, dw. Adrian, Mich., m. 1 Jan. 1850, Jonathan Stanton[3] Park, b. 12 June 1803, at Preston, Conn., d. 3 Aug. 1869. Was Postmaster at Salem, Conn., whence he removed in 1837 to Adrian, Mich., where he was a grocer until 1860—descendant of Shubael[7] Park, 1774–1846, Jonathan[6], 1752–76, Paul[5], 1720–1802, a Congregational Minister of Preston, Conn., Hezekiah[4], 1690±–1753, Robert[3], b. 1650±, Thomas[2], 1625±–1709, one of the first settlers at Preston, Conn., Robert[1] who came from England in 1630 and settled in Roxbury, Mass., whence about 1637 he removed to Wethersfield, Conn. They had: (1.) Anna Witter, b. 14 Feb. 1851. (2.) Ambrose Berry, b. 12 Nov. 1852, dw. 33 Church St., Adrian, Mich., is dry goods merchant, at No. 17 S. Main St., m. at Adrian, Mich., 19 Nov. 1879, Emma Maria Young, b. 26 Apr. 1857, dau. of Charles Young of Adrian. (3.) Emily Berry, b. 20 Aug. 1855, d. 8 Nov. 1856. (4.) Ida, b. 6 June 1858. (5.) Charles Sumner, b. 16 Feb. 1861, dw. 29 Dennis St. Adrian, Mich., m. 25 Sept. 1889, Nellie M. Johnson.

ORIGIN OF THE GREENE FAMILY.

ROYAL AND NOBLE ANCESTRY OF
JOHN¹ GREENE (SURGEON), OF WARWICK, R. I.,

GREAT-GREAT-GRANDFATHER OF GEN. NATHANIEL⁵ GREENE, OF REVOLUTIONARY FAME,

[Of Nathaniel⁴, Jabez³, James², John¹],

AND OF LANGFORD⁵ GREENE, OF RENSSELAER CO., N. Y.,

[Of Joseph⁴, John³, James², John¹].

For the following outline of the royal descent of the founder of our branch of the Greene family in America, and for other valuable information concerning our Rhode Island forefathers presented in these pages, we are indebted to Mr. George H. Greene, of Lansing, Mich. [of Augustus Werden⁸, Seneca⁷, Stephen⁶, Job⁵, Fones⁴, James³, James², John¹], who, during the past 20 years, has been collecting genealogical data relating to the Greene family. A genealogy of the same family is also in preparation by Gen. George Sears⁷ Greene, of Morristown, N. J. [of Caleb⁶, Caleb⁵, Samuel⁴, Samuel³, John², John¹].

1. *Egbert I*, first King of Eng. 802 to 837, m. Lady Redburga, first Queen of England, had:

2. *Ethelwolf*, King of Eng. 837 to 858, m. Osburga, dau. of Earl Oslac, had:

3. *Alfred the Great*, King of Eng. 871 to 901, m. Ethelbith dau of Earl Ethelran, had:

4. *Edward, the Elder*, King of Eng. m. Edgiva dau. of Earl Sigelline.

5. Princess Edgiva of Eng. m. (2d) Henry, Count de Vermandois and Toryes, France, had:

6. Hubert, Count de Vermandois, m. Lady Adelheld de Valois, had:

7. Adela, Countess de Vermandois, m. Hugh Magnus Count Vermandois, son of *Henry I, King of France*, had:

8. Lady Isabel de Vermandois, who m. (1st) Robert Baron de Bellomont, Earl of Mellent, created Earl of Leicester, had:

9. Robert, second Earl of Leicester, Lord Justice of Eng., who m. Aurelia de Waer, dau. of Ralph, Earl of Norfolk, had:

10. Robert, third Earl of Leicester, Steward of Eng., d. 1196, m. Petronella dau. of Hugh de Grentesmesmil, had:

11. Lady Margaret de Bellomont, who m. Saier de Quincey, created 1207, Earl of Winchester, d. 1219, who was one of the twenty-five Magna Charta barons, had:

12. Roger, second Earl of Winchester, Constable of Scotland, d. 1264, m. (1st) Helen, dau. of Alan, Lord Galloway, had:

13. Lady Elene de Quincey, who m. Sir Alan, Lord Zouche of Ashby, Constable of the Tower of London; Governor of the Castle at Northampton, d. 1269, had:

14. Eudo Le Zouche, second son, who m. Lady Millicent Cantalupe, widow of John de Montalt, had:

15. Lady Lucy Le Zouche, who m. as 1st wife Thomas de Greene b. 1292 (son of Sir Thomas de Greene, Lord of Broughton or Boughton), Northamptonshire, had:

16. Sir Henry de Greene, Lord of Green's Norton, Northampton, Lord Chief Justice of England, 1353, who m. Catharin dau. of Sir John Drayton, had:

17. Sir Henry de Greene, Lord of Green's Norton, Knt., who m. Lady Matilda, dau. of Thomas de Maudit. Sir Henry's descendant, Sir Thomas Greene, Lord of Green's Norton, was the father of Maud, who m. Sir Thomas Parr and was the mother of Queen Katharine Parr. Another dau. of Sir Thomas Greene, Anne, was second wife of Nicholas, Lord Vaux, whose first wife, Elizabeth, was the widow of Sir William Parr and grandmother of Queen Katharine Parr. Sir Henry's third son

18. Thomas Greene was [father of 19 .... and] grandfather of

20. Robert Greene of Gillingham, Dorsetshire, who was assessed to Henry VIII's Subsidy in 1545, and whose second son

21. Richard Greene of Bowridge Hill, Gillingham, was father of

22. Richard Greene of Bowridge Hill, whose fourth son

23. John Greene of Salisbury, Wilts, b. 1597, m. 4 Nov. 1619, Joanna Tattershall, who d. 1643. With his wife and children he arrived in Boston 3 June 1635, and settled in Providence, R. I., and later in Warwick, R. I., and is the founder of the Warwick Greenes.

NATHAN[1] SHOTWELL'S HOUSEHOLD.
Concord, Mich., July, 1894.

1 Nathan[1] Shotwell, of Elba, N. Y., and Concord, Mich., born 1826.
2 Wife, Phebe B. (Gardner) Shotwell, born 1831.
3 Mother-In-Law, Diana (Berry) Gardner, born 1810.
4 Daughter, Rozilla P. Shotwell (called " Lilla "), born 1851.
5 Son, Ambrose M. Shotwell, the Family Annalist, born 1853.
6 Daughter, Ida A. S[2]. Davis (wife of J. K. Davis), born 1857.
7 Son, Manly N. Shotwell, of Concord, Mich., born 1858.
8 Grandson, Owen B. Shotwell, born 1886, son of Cassius E.
9 Grandson, Jehiel Shotwell Davis born 1892, son of J. K. and Ida A. S. Davis.

RESIDENCE OF NATHAN[1] SHOTWELL,
of Concord Tp., Jackson Co., Mich.

Situated on the south side of the highway, 75 rods west of the center of Section 22, Township 3 South,
of Range 3 West, one-fourth mile east of the Concord and Albion road, one-half mile
east of the east branch of Kalamazoo river, and about one mile north of the
village of Concord.

1. *Hugh Capet*, King of France. Founder of the Capetian or third dynasty of French Kings. He is said to have been the ancestor of thirty-two French Kings, born about 940, began to reign 987, and died in 996. He was succeeded by his son

2. *Robert the Pious*, King of France, who had:

3. *Henry I*, King of France, who by wife Anne of Russia, had:

4. Prince Hugh Magnus, Count de Vermandois, who m. Lady Adela, Countess de Vermandois.

---

1. *Romanus II*, Emperor of Constantinople, A. D. 959, had: Lady Anne, who m. Woldomir, Grand Duke of Russia, and had:

2. Jaroslaus, Grand Duke of Russia, who had:

3. Lady Anne, who m. *Henry I, King of France*, and had:

4. Prince Hugh Magnus, Count de Vermandois, who m. Lady Adela, Countess de Vermandois, dau. of Count Hubert.

Foregoing arranged from Charles H. Browning's "Americans of Royal Descent," Feb. 25, 1899, by Geo. H. Greene of Lansing, Mich.

In America Heraldica, published by Brentano Bros, New York, -------- p. 58, plate 8, are given the Greene Arms, which are Azure, Three Stags, Trippant, Gold, Crest, a Stag's Head, Erased Gold; given also in a pamphlet entitled "Arms & Pedigree of Gardiner Greene of Boston, taken from the researches of Mr. H. G. Somerby & Original Documents in the Possession of the Family," from which also the following particulars respecting the origin of the family have been in part compiled.

The family of Greene, orginally written "de la Greene," derive their name from their ancient possessions in Northamptonshire, Eng., where they were seated as early as the time of Edward I. In 1320, Thomas de Greene succeeded to the estates and was Lord of the Manor of Boughton and Norton (afterwards Greene's Norton) where the family continued to flourish for several generations, sending off shoots into various counties. One of the branches as verified by the similarity of Arms recorded in the Herald's College, was seated in Dorsetshire in the early part of the reign of Henry VIII, when Robert' Greene of Gillingham, from whom an unbroken line of descent is traced, was assessed to the King's subsidy, as appears by the rolls of the Exchequer bearing date 1545.

As the Heralds' College recorded the Arms of Robert Greene of Gillingham 1545 as being the same as the Arms of the Greenes of Greene's Norton, there can be little doubt that they belonged to the same family. It is believed that the Greenes of Gillingham, Eng., Boston, Mass., and Warwick, R. I., descended from Thomas' Greene, third son of Sir Henry' Greene by his wife Matilda, dau. of Thomas Maudit. The pedigree of Sir Henry Greene is as follows:

Sir Thomas' Greene, Lord of the Manor of Boughton, Northampton, married Alice, dau. of Sir Thomas Boltsham, and had a son Thomas', who was born in 1292 and was twice married. By the first wife, Lucy, dau. and heiress of Eudo, Lord Zouch, he Thomas² Greene had a son Henry,' afterwards Sir Henry³ Greene, Lord Chief Justice of England, who married in 1353 Catherine, dau. of Sir John Dayton. They had 4 sons and 2 daughters, viz.: Sir Thomas; Sir Henry' who married Matilda Maudit; Richard; Nicholas; Amabelia and Margaret. The tomb of Lord Chief Justice Greene remains to this day perfect and ornamented with many Shields showing the different houses with which he was connected; conspicuous among them is the Coat of Arms of the Family.

Robert' Greene of Gillingham, Eng., was father of 3 sons and 2 daughters, namely: Peter, Richard, John, Alice, and Anne. Peter² Greene having died *sine prole*, his brother Richard became heir to the estate of Bowridge Hill in Gillingham, Eng., and died leaving 2 children, Richard' and Anne. Richard², by his wife Mary, had 5 sons and 4 daughters, namely: Peter, Richard, Robert, John, Thomas, Rebecca, Mary, Rachel, and Anne.

JOHN' GREENE, of Warwick, R. I., 4th son of Richard' and Mary (----) Greene of Bowridge Hill, Eng. [of Richard,² Robert'], was b. 9 Feb. 1596-7, probably at Bowridge Hill, Parish of Gillingham, Dorsetshire, Eng., where his father and grandfather resided; was a surgeon in Salisbury, Wilts Co., Eng.; sailed from Southampton, Eng., 6 Apr. 1635 in Ship James of London, 300 tons, William Cooper, Master; arrived at Boston 3 June 1635; went to Salem, where for a short time he was probably associated with Roger Williams, and in 1637 to Providence. On 1 Aug. 1637 he (called of New Providence) having spoken against the magistrates contemptuously, stands bound in 100 marks to appear at the next Quarter Court, by order of the Massachusetts authorities; and on 29 Sept. 1637 he was fined £20, and to be committed until fine is paid, and was enjoined not to come into the jurisdiction of Massachusetts upon pain of fine or imprisonment at the pleasure of the court, for speaking contemptuously of magistrates. On 12 Mar. 1637-8, a letter from him being received by the court at Massachusetts, wherein the court is charged with usurping the power of Christ over the churches and men's consciences, etc., he was ordered not to come into that jurisdiction under pain of imprisonment and further censure.

On 8 Oct. 1638, he was one of the 12 persons to whom Roger Williams deeded land bought of Canonicus and Miantonomi, and was one of the 12 original members of the First Baptist Church in America, organized in 1639. In November 1642 he bought land called Occupassuatuxet, of Miantonomi. This land was the first purchased of the Indians in Warwick, and remained in occupation of his heirs until 1782, when it was sold to John Brown of Providence, and is now occupied by his heirs, and is called "Spring Green farm." On 12 Jan. 1643, John Greene of Warwick and 10 others bought of Miantonomi, for 144 fathoms of wampum, tract of land called Shawomet (Warwick), a tract extending along the Bay from Gaspee point to Warwick Neck and 20 miles inland embracing the greater part of the present townships of Warwick and Coventry. In 1644 he and Samuel Gorton and Randall Holden, went to England to obtain redress for their wrongs, being obliged to take ship at New York, on account of the unfriendliness of Massachusetts authorities. He and Holden returned, successful in their mission, landing in Boston 13 Sept. 1646. He was Commissioner (equivalent to Representative) 1654-1657; was very active in all the affairs of the colony, and his name rarely failed to appear in the acts of or relating to Warwick during his life. He d. in 1658. The Genealogical Dictionary of Rhode Island presents an abstract of his will of 28 Dec. 1658, proved 7 Jan. 1658-9, and similar synopses of the wills of other ancestors of Langford[5] Greene of Stephentown, N. Y.

John[1] Greene 1596-7-1658, m. (1) in St. Thomas Church, Salisbury, Eng., 4 Nov. 1619, Joana Tattersall, who d. at Conanicut, Warwick, R. I.; she was the mother of his children. He m. (2) Alice Daniels, a widow of Providence, R. I., who d. in 1643. He m. (3) Philip .... of London, Eng., an unusual feminine name, probaby designed for Philippa, who survived him nearly 30 years, b. 1601, d. 10 Mar. 1687-8.

Our immigrant ancestor, John Greene, surgeon, of Warwick, R. I., is to be sharply distinguished from two other early settlers in Rhode Island, bearing the same name, to wit: John of Newport and John of Kings Town, the latter the progenitor of the so called Quidneset Greenes.

The children of John[1] Greene of Warwick were: (1.) John, baptized 15 Aug. 1620, in St. Thomas Church, Salisbury, Eng.; was Deputy Governor of Rhode Island; d. 27 Nov. 1708; m. Ame or Ann Almy, b. 1627, d. 17 May 1709. (2.) Peter, bapt. 10 Mar. 1621-2, d. 1659 s. p., m. Mary Gorton [of Samuel]. (3.) Richard, bapt. 25 Mar. 1623, d. young, in England. (4.) James[2], bapt. 21 June 1626 in Salisbury, Eng., d. 27 Apr. 1698; m. (1) Deliverence Potter 1637-1664±, dau. of Robert and Isabel (.......) Potter of Warwick, R. I. Her mother, Isabel, was among those who fled to the woods at the approach of the Massachusetts troops in 1643 under Capt. Cook, and as

Gorton says, "suffering such hardships as occasioned the death of divers of them, as the wife of John Greene, as also the wife of Robert Potter, Sept. 28, 1643." James m. (2) at Portsmouth 3 Aug. 1665, Elizabeth Anthony. dau. of John and Susanna (......) Anthony of Portsmouth. (5.) Thomas, bapt. 4 June 1628, d. 5 June 1717; m. 30 June 1659, Elizabeth Barton who d. 20 Aug. 1693 [of Rufus and Margaret]. Their son Nathaniel had a son Thomas who m. Elizabeth dau. of John Gardiner, whose father David was a son of Lion Gardiner of Gardiner's Island, called Lord Gardiner of the Isle of Wight. Benjamin Greene, a younger son of Nathaniel, m. Mary Chandler and had among other children Gardiner Greene, the prominent merchant of Boston, who left an estate worth $3,000,000. Thomas[2] Greene, his son Richard[3], grandson Richard[4] and great-grandson Thomas[5] lived in the Stone Castle in Warwick, R. I., the only house there not destroyed in King Philip's War. (6.) Joanna or Joan, bapt. 3 Oct. 1630, m. ...... Hade. (7.) Mary, bapt. 19 May 1633, m. James Sweet 1622-1695+ [of John and Mary]. They were progenitors of the bone-setting Sweets.

JAMES[2] GREENE 1626-1698 [of John[1]] lived at Nausunket at what is called the old James Greene homestead at the Buttonwoods on the north side of Coweset Bay, in Warwick, R. I., a portion of which is still (1889) owned and occupied by Henry Whitman Greene, one of his descendants. He subsequently took up his residence at Potowomut, East Greenwich, R. I., on the opposite side of Coweset Bay, upon lands that have continued in possession of his descendants. His will of 22 Mar. 1697-8, proved 2 May 1698, names as executor his son Jabez—grandfather of Gen. Nathanael Greene—and among numerous other bequests gives to his son John[3] 118 acres, other land, a bed, wearing clothes and £20 on coming of age. He m. (1) Deliverence Potter, 1637-1664± [of Robert], and had: (1.) James, b. 1 June 1659; m. Mary Fones [of Capt. John]. (2.) Mary, b. 28 Sept. 1660; m. James Reynolds [of James]. (3.) Elisha, b. 17 Mar. 1662-3; probably d. young. (4.) Sarah, b. 27 Mar. 1664; m. Henry Reynolds [of James].

James[2] Greene, 1626-1698, m. (2) 1665 Elizabeth Anthony, who survived her husband [of John and Susanna], and had: (5.) Peter, b. 25 Aug. 1666, m. Elizabeth Slocum [of Ebenezer]. (6.) Elizabeth, b. 17 Oct. 1668, m. (1) Francis Reynolds [of James]; m. (2) ..... Hull or Hill. (7.) John, b. 1 Feb. 1670, d. young. (8.) Jabez, b. 17 May 1673; m. (1) Mary Barton [of Benj.]; m. (2) Grace Whitman [of Valuntine]. (9.) David, b. 24 June 1677, m. (1) Mary Slocum [of Ebenezer]; m. (2) Sarah Barbar [of Moses]. (10.) Susannah, b. 24 May 1688 or '80, d. 1748, m. 1 Jan. 1712-13 (as 2d wife) Joseph Hull, 1670-1748 [of Joseph[3], Tristram[2], Joseph[1]]. (11.) Thomas, b. 11 Nov. 1682, probably d. young. (12.) John[3], b. 30 Sept. 1685, at Potowomut (Warwick), R. I., on the farm on which his grand-nephew, Gen. Nathanael Greene (son of Nathanael, the Quaker Preacher), was born; d. 8 Dec. 1757; was probably a member of the Society of Friends; m. 16 Feb. 1609, Mary Allen, b. 29 May 1689, daughter of Increase Allen of Dartmouth.

JOHN[3] AND MARY (ALLEN) GREENE of Warwick, R. I. [of James[2], John[1]], had: (1.) David, b. 4 Jan. 1710-11, m. Alice Hall [of Robert]. (2.) James, b. 14 Mar. 1712-13, m. Mary Nichol [of James]. (3.) Rachel, b. 16 Mar. 1714-15, d. s. p.; m. Henry Mathewson [of Francis]. (4.) Increase, b. 12 Apr. 1717; m. Phebe Mathewson [of Francis]. (5.) Elizabeth, b. 26 May 1719, m. Job Mathewson [of Francis]. (6.) Benjamin, b. ... Sept. 1721, m. .... (7.) Dinah, b. 21 Jan. 1723-4, m. Samuel Hall [of William]. (8.) Mary, b. 1 Jan. 1724-5, d. 13 Oct. 1727. (9.) *Joseph*,[4] b. 19 Feb. 1727-8, in Warwick, R. I , d. 1822, aged 94. Settled in Stephentown (now Berlin), Rensselaer Co., N. Y., in 1769, was the third eastern settler in the town; was a Quaker and a trusted friend of Gen. Stephen VanRensselaer, with whom he always stayed when he went to Albany. He m. 24 Oct. 1751, Phoebe Langford, b. 26 Apr. 1734, dau. of John[3] and Barbara (Rice) Langford of E. Greenwich, R. I. [of Thomas[1]]. (10.) Peter, b. 8 Jan. 1730-31.

JOSEPH[4] GREENE 1727-8-1822 of Rensselaer Co., N. Y. [of John[3], James[2], John[1]], m. 1751, Phoebe Langford, b. 1734 [of John[3], Thomas[1]] and had: (1.) Benjamin, b. 16 Feb. 1752, d. s. p.; m. Polly Brown. (2.) Jonathan, b. 24 Feb. 1754, m. Patience Terry. (3.) James, b. 14 Feb. 1757, dwelt Berlin, N. Y., where all his children were born, and where he d. 1857. He celebrated the 100th anniversary of his birth on 14 Feb. 1857. When visited by his grand-nephew, David Maxson Greene, in 1855, he could then dress himself and read without glasses. He was known as Deacon James Greene. He m. Joanna Terry. (4.) David, b. 12 May 1762, m. Russell or Sarah Thomas. (5.) Sarah, b. 21 June 1764, m. Rowland Thomas, a soldier in the Revolution, who d. at the age of 26, son of Peleg. (6.) *Langford*,[5] b. 18 Dec. 1766, dwelt Stephentown, N. Y., about 25 miles east of the Hudson River, and there d.; m. Abigail Thomas, dau. of George Thomas. (7.) John, b. 10 Nov. 1768, m. Ellen Randall. (8.) Phebe, b. 21 Nov, 1770, d. 7 April, 1831, m. Maj. Daniel Hull, b. 22 Apr. 1767, d. 2 Apr. 1842. (9.) Joseph, b. 25 May 1773, m. Molly Rice. (10.) Thomas, b. 19 May 1775, dwelt Berlin, N. Y., and there d. 1810, m. Hannah Rix, who d. 1810, sister to Thomas Rix of Berlin, N. Y. (11.) Barbara, b. 4 Feb. 1778; brought up in family of Maj. Daniel Hull, m. Joshua Godfrey.

LANGFORD[5] GREENE, b. 1766, of Stephentown, N. Y. [of Joseph[4], John[3], James[2], John[1]], m. 1789±, Abigail Thomas [of George], and had: 1. *Bathsheba*,[6] b. 21 Aug. 1790, d. Adrian, Mich., 26 Sept. 1879; m. 3 Dec. 1809, Jonathan Berry, b. 28 June 1790, was at one time a Colonel

in the New York Militia; member of Michigan Legislature 1844; d. Rome, Mich., 20 Oct. 1851. (Children and grandchildren already recorded, see pp. 37-39.)

2. *George*,[6] d. 1840±, m. Sally Reeves, and had: (1.) Harvy R., b. Stephentown, N. Y., dwelt 1880 Highland Park, Ill., was afterward an egg packer in Chicago; m. ...... Streeter [of Barzalleel]. (2.) Albina or Malvina. (3.) Lauche. (4.) Henry G., b. 1823±, d. 10 Sept. 1845, s. p.; m. 10 Feb. 1845, Mary Ann Wyatt, d. Feb. 1845, aged 20.

3. *Phebe*,[6] dwelt at the Langford Greene homestead in Stephentown, N. Y., d. 17 June 1866, m. William Jones, son of Major Jones, Sr., of the Revolution, and Catharine (Dennison) Jones, and had: (1.) Oscar, b. Stephentown, N. Y., lived near Niles, Mich., in 1855; m. .... (2.) Laura, m. .... (3.) Katharine or Catharine, m. Albert Dennison. (4.) Abigail, m. .... Hadsel [of Niles]; lived near Lebanon Springs, N. Y. (5.) William. (6.) Griswold, d. young. (7.) Hulburt.

4. *Joseph*,[6] m. Urania Hull, dau. of Peter Hull, and had: (1.) Caroline, m. .... Hicks. (2.) Jane, d. young. (3.) Abigail. (4.) Delos, m. Caroline Jones, dau. of Elias and Lydia (Sweet) Jones of Stephentown, N. Y. (5.) Daniel J., m. Palmyra Matteson.

5. *Benjamin*,[6] b. 27 Nov. 1798, d. 25 Apr. 1842, was a farmer and cheese buyer in Berlin, N. Y., m. 7 Oct. 1821, Rhoda Niles, b. 17 Aug. 1802, d. 5 Oct. 1849, dau. of Eliphalet and Rebecca (Greene) Niles of Berlin, N. Y.; she m. (2) Barzaleel Streeter. Benjamin[6] and Rhoda had: (1.) Louisa Antoinette, b. 8 Mar. 1823, dw. Akron., Peoria Co., Ill., and afterward (1880) Lawn Ridge, Marshall Co., Ill., m. in Berlin, N. Y., 8 Oct. 1846, Lavinus Stillman, b. 9 Dec. 1727, son of Perry and Asenith (Maxon) Stillman. (2.) Benjamin Franklin (called Frank), b. 22 Dec. 1825, in Berlin, N. Y.; was a flour and feed dealer under the firm name of Warner & Green at Adrian, Mich., and there d. 30 July 1863, m. 1 Jan. 1849, Mary Jane Hubbs, b. 29 Jan. 1828, dau. of Jonathan and Catharine (Brewster) Hubbs; dw. (1880) Jouesville, N. Y. (3.) Calvin Pardee, b. .. Feb. 1829, dw. Akron, La Prairie and Lawn Ridge, Ill., and (1880) Walkerville, Page Co., Iowa; removed from Berlin, N. Y., about 1850; was postmaster at Lawn Ridge, Ill.; m. 31 Jan. 1850, Emeline Jeannette Dodge, dau. of John and Melinda (Bates) Dodge. (4.) Rebecca, b. 8 Apr. 1831, d. 29 May 1842 at Berlin, N. Y. (5.) Abigail, b. 21 Feb. 1834, d. 17 Nov. 1854, m. Southampton, Ill., .. Apr. 1852, Hiram Rosencrans; went to California.

6. *Samuel*,[6] b. ... Aug. 1800, was a wealthy farmer in Rensselaer Co., N. Y., dw. 1853, Genoa, Cayuga Co., N. Y.; raised many apples and was called "Apple Greene;" m. (1) Lucy Rose; m. (2) By first wife, he had: (1.) Phebe, m. her cousin Wyatt Rose, dw. Dunlap, Peoria Co., Ill. (2.)

Jefferson, m. ______ (3.) George. (4.) Harry, dw. Morris, Ill. (5.) Maria, d. Geneseo, N. Y. (6.) Samuel. (7.) Abby.

7. *Hannah*[6], b. Stephentown, N. Y., 1802, m. Samuel Hull and had: (1.) Schuyler, was a farmer near Peoria, Ill., m. ______________ (2.) George Harry. Also two daughters:

SOME OF THE MORE DISTINGUISHED DESCENDANTS OF JOHN[1] GREENE, SURGEON, OF WARWICK, R. I.

The Gov. Greene line, as it is called, has the greater number, who arose to distinction, than any other single line, and runs as follows:

DEPUTY GOV. JOHN[2] GREENE, baptized Aug. 15, 1620, the oldest of the children of John[1], was Deputy Governor of the Colony from 1690 to 1700, d. Nov. 27, 1708, aged 88; m. Ann Almy, dau. of William of Portsmouth. Their youngest child was:

DEPUTY SAMUEL[3], b. Jan. 30, 1669–70. He was a deputy from Warwick in 1704, 7, 8, 14, 15, and 19; d. Sept. 18, 1720, aged 50; m. Mary Gorton, dau. of Capt. Benj. and grd. dau of Samuel. Their oldest child was:

GOV. WILLIAM[4], b. March 16, 1695–6. He was Deputy Governor in 1740, 42 and 43, and Governor in 1743, 44, 46, 48 to 55 and 57; d. Feb. 22, 1758; m. Catharine[4] Greene [of Benj[3]., Thomas[2], John[1]]. Their 3d child was:

GOV. WILLIAM[5], b. Aug. 16, 1731. He was made Chief Justice of the Superior Court in Feb. 1778, and in May 1778 was elected Governor and filled that office until May 1786, a period covering nearly the whole of the Revolutionary war. He d. Nov. 29, 1809; m. Catharine Ray, dau. of Simon and Deborah[4] (Greene) Ray [of Maj. Job[3], Dept. Gov. John[2], John[1]]. Their oldest was:

U. S. SENATOR RAY[6], b. Feb. 2, 1765. He was Attorney General of R. I. from 1794 to 1797, and U. S. Senator from 1797 to 1801; m. Mary M. Flagg, dau. of George Flagg of Charleston, S. C. Their 2d child was:

LIEUT. GOV. WILLIAM[7], b. Jan. 1, 1797. Lieut. Gov. 1866 and 1867.

Another of the children of the 2d Gov. WILLIAM[4] GREENE was:

PHEBE[5], who m. Col. Samuel[6] Ward, s. of Gov. Samuel and Anna[5] (Ray) Ward, and gr. s. of Simon and Deborah[4] (Greene) Ray (of Maj. Job[3] Greene, Dept. Gov. John[2], John[1]]. They had:

SAMUEL[7] WARD, the father of

MRS. JULIA WARD HOWE, the authoress and celebrated woman suffragist, widow of Dr. Samuel G. Howe, the philanthropist.

Another of the children (2d) of the first Gov. WILLIAM[4] GREENE was:

CAPT. SAMUEL[5], b. Apr. 28, 1727; m. Patience Cook, dau. of Ebenezer Cook of East Greenwich. Their first child was:

PATIENCE[6], b. May 13, 1754; m. Welcome Arnold, s. of Jonathan. Their 4th child was:

SAMUEL GREENE[7] ARNOLD, b. Jan. 20, 1778; m. Frances Rogers, dau. of John. Their oldest child was:

SAMUEL GREENE[8] ARNOLD, the historian, b. Apr. 12, 1821; d. Feb. 13, 1880. He was three times elected Lieut. Gov. of R. I.; U. S. Senator from Dec. 1862 to March 1863; author of the History of Rhode Island, in 2 vols.

The 4th child of JOHN[1] and JOANNA (TATTERSALL) GREENE was:

JAMES[2], bapt. June 21, 1626; m. (2) Elizabeth Anthony, dau. of John of Portsmouth. His 8th child was:

JABEZ[3], b. May 17, 1673; m. Mary Barton, dau. of Benj. and Susannah (Gorton) Barton and grd. dau. of Samuel Gorton. Their 5th child was:

NATHANAEL[4], b. Nov. 4, 1707, the Quaker preacher; m. (2) "eighteenth day of the second month 1739" Mary Nott, dau. of Jacob and Rest (Perry) Nott (the Perry family to which Commodore Oliver H. Perry of Lake Erie renown belonged). His fifth child was:

GENERAL NATHANAEL[5] GREENE of Revolutionary fame, b. "twenty-seventh day of fifth month 1742, about one or two o'clock in the afternoon of the third day of the week;" m. Catharine[6] Littlefield, dau. of John and Phebe[5] (Ray) Littlefield, and gr. dau. of Simon and Deborah[4] (Greene) Ray [of Maj. Job[3], Dept. Gov. John[2], John[1]]. Their 4th child was:

NATHANAEL RAY[6], b. Jan. 29, 1780; m. Annie Maria Clarke, dau. of Ethan and Anna[6] (Ward) Clarke, and gr. dau. of Gov. Samuel and Anna[5] (Ray) Ward [of Simon and Deborah[4] (Greene) Ray, Maj. Job[3] Greene, Dept. Gov. John[2], John[1]]. Their 2d child was:

GEORGE WASHINGTON[7] GREENE, of East Greenwich, R. I., the historian, b. Apr. 8, 1811; d. Feb. 2, 1883.

Another son of NATHANAEL[4], the Quaker preacher, was:

CHRISTOPHER[5], b. "third day of 5th month 1748, about one or two o'clock in the morning, on the first day of the week;" m. (2d) Deborah Ward, sister to former wife Catharine, and dau. of Gov. Samuel and Anna (Ray) Ward, etc. (See Nathaniel Ray Greene *ante*.) His 7th child was:

RICHARD WARD[6] GREENE, b. Jan. 21, 1792; d. 1875; an eminent lawyer of Providence, R. I., and Chief Justice of the Supreme Court of Rhode Island.

Another, the 9th and youngest child of Nathanael[5] the Quaker preacher (of Jabez[3], James[2], John[1]], was:

PERRY[6], b. "fifth day of 9th month 1749, about five o'clock in the morning on the first day of the week. His 2d child was:

Gen. Albert Collins[6] Greene, b. Apr. 15, 1792, of East Greenwich. A Major General of Militia; Attorney General of Rhode Island from 1825 to 1843, and U. S. Senator from 1845 to 1851; d. Providence, R. I., Jan. 8, 1863.

John[1] and Joanna (Tattershall) Greene had (5):

Thomas[2], bapt. June 4, 1628; d. June 5, 1717; m. Elizabeth Barton, dau. of Rufus of Warwick, R. I. His 7th and youngest child was:

Nathanael[3], b. Apr. 10, 1679; went to Boston; m. Ann Gould, dau. of Thomas and Frances (Robinson) Gould of Boston. Their 5th and youngest child was:

Benjamin[4], b. Jan. 11, 1712-13, in Boston; m. Mary Chandler. Their 6th child was:

Gardiner[5], b. Sept. 23, 1753, a wealthy merchant of Boston. He d. 1832 leaving an estate of over $3,000,000. His 3d wife was Elizabeth Clarke Copley, dau. of John Singleton Copley, the artist, and sister of John Singleton Copley, Jr., who was Baron Lyndhurst of London, and sometime Lord Chancellor of England.

Another son of Nathanael[3], above, was:

Rufus[4], b. May 30, 1707, d. Dec. 31, 1777; m. Katharine Standridge. Their 9th child was:

Sarah[5], b. Dec. 1, 1743, d. about 1774; m. Thomas Hickling, who was for many years U. S. Consul at the Azores at the Island of St. Michael. They had:

Catharine Greene[6] Hickling, b. Aug. 1, 1767; m. Judge William Prescott, son of Col. William of Bunker Hill fame. Their son was:

William Hickling[7] Prescott, the historian.

Dept. Gov. John[2] Greene [of John[1] and Joanna (Tattershall) Greene], m. Ann Almy. Their 5th child was:

Maj. Job[3], b. Aug. 24, 1656; d. July 6, 1745; m. Phebe Sayles, dau. of John and Mary (Williams) Sayles and gr. dau. of Roger Williams. Their 10th child was:

Judge Philip[4], b. Mar. 15, 1704-5; d. Apr. 10, 1791; m. Elizabeth Wickes, dau. of John and Sarah (Gorton) Wickes. Their 4th child was:

Col. Christopher[5] Greene, b. May 12, 1737, served as captain in the Canadian Expedition in 1775; repelled the Hessians at Red Bank, N. J., in 1777; was ruthlessly murdered on his picket line where he was passing the night with few attendants, by a detachment of Tories at Pine Bridge on the Croton River, Westchester Co., N. Y., May 13, 1781.

Capt. Peter[2] Greene, 5th child of Dept. Gov. John[2] and Ann (Almy) Greene [of John and Joanna], b. Feb. 7, 1654-5; d. Aug. 12, 1723; m.

Elizabeth Arnold, dau. of Stephen[2] [of William[1]]. Their 5th child was:

William[4] Greene, b. July 29, 1690; d. Mar. 17, 1766; m. Sarah Medbury. Their oldest was:

James[5] Greene, b. Sept. 8, 1713; d. May 30, 1792; m. Desire Slocum, dau. of Giles. Their 8th child was:

Capt. James[6] Greene, b. 1754; d. Oct. 14, 1825; m. Rebecca Pitman, dau. of Sanders and Mary (Kinnicut) Pitman of Providence. Their 2d child was:

Mary Kinnicut[7] Greene, b. Oct. 31, 1785; m. William Anthony, son of Daniel and Mary (Bowen) Anthony. Their 4th child was:

Henry Bowen[8] Anthony, b. Apr. 1, 1815; was elected Governor of R. I. in 1849 and again in 1850, and was U. S. Senator from 1859 to the time of his death, Sept. 2, 1884, a period of 25 years. At the time of his death he was the senior Senator and was called the father of the Senate.

Samuel[3] Greene, son of Dept. Gov. John[2] and Ann (Almy) Greene [of John[1]], b. Jan. 30, 1669-70; m. Mary Gorton. Their 3d child was:

Samuel[4], b. Oct. 22, 1700; d. Sept. 15, 1780; m. Sarah Coggshall, dau. of Joshua and Deborah (Nichols) Coggshall. Their 4th child was:

Capt. Caleb[5], b. Apr. 23, 1737; d. Apr. 23, 1813; m. Mary Tibbitts, dau. of George. Their 7th child was:

Caleb[6], b. June 17, 1772; d. Dec. 4, 1853; m. Sarah Robinson[6] Greene (see below). Their 2d child was:

Maj. Gen. George Sears[7] Greene, b. May 6, 1801; still living at the age of 94; a graduate of the Military Academy at West Point. He commanded the 3d Brigade, 2d Div. 12th Corps, called Greene's New York Brigade, in the battle of Gettysburg, which it is claimed saved the right and thereby won the day. His maternal line runs as follows:

John[1] and Joanna had (5th child):

Thomas[2], bapt. June 4, 1628; d. June 5, 1717; m. Elizabeth Barton, dau. of Rufus. Their 4th child was:

Richard[3], b. Mar. 5, 1666-7; d. Sept. 25, 1724; m. Mary Carder, d. of John and Mary[2] (Holden) Carder, and gr. dau. of Randall[1] Holden. Their 2d child was:

Richard[4], b. Apr. 17, 1702; d. Dec. 28, 1778; m. Elizabeth Godfrey, dau. of John. Their 2d child was:

Thomas[5], b. Oct. 11, 1729; d. Dec. 14, 1813; m. (2) Sarah Wickes, dau. of Robert and Margaret (Barton) Wickes. His 6th child was:

Sarah Robinson[6] Greene, b. Dec. 12, 1774; m. Caleb[6] Greene. (See above.) Their 2d child was:

Maj. Gen. George Sears[7] Greene, b. May 6, 1801. His son,

Samuel Dana[8] Greene, b. Feb. 11, 1840; a graduate of the U. S. Naval Academy of Annapolis. Was executive officer on the Monitor from the first until she foundered off Hatteras. In her encounter with the Merrimac when commander Worden was disabled, he took command.

Another of his sons,

COL. FRANCIS VINTON[4] GREENE, b. June 27, 1850; graduated from West Point 1870. During the Turco-Russian war he was Military attaché to the U. S. Legation in St. Petersburg, to observe the operations of the two armies. He is the author of "Army Life in Russia." "The Russian Army and its Campaigns in Turkey, 1877-8," "The Mississippi," the eighth of the series of "Campaigns of the Civil War," and "General Greene," of the "Great Commanders series."

ANTHONY AND ALLEN LINE.

JOHN[1] ANTHONY, b. 1607, came from Hampstead, Eng., in the ship Hercules to New England, arriving 16 Apr. 1634, and settled at Portsmouth, R. I., was an inn-keeper as well as having other occupations; was called planter in 1642; in Oct. of that year he sold to Richard Tew of Newport three parcels, 50 acres of land in Newport east from the Newport mill, within the tract called the great enclosure, 40 acres of which had been given him by town grant, and 10 acres as a servant; also two parcels of marsh. He was Corporal in 1644, Commissioner in 1661 and Deputy in 1666 and 1672. He d. 28 July 1675; m. Susanna ...., who d. prior to making of his will of 23 July 1675, proved 21 Aug. 1675. They had: (1.) John, b. 1642; d. 20 Oct. 1715; m. (2) Nov. 23, 1669, Frances Wodell, b. 6 July 1652 [of Wm. and Mary]; m. (2) 3 Jan. 1694, Susanna Albro [of John and Dorothy]. (2.) Susanna; 1716+; m. 7 Sept. 1665, John Tripp, b. 1640±; d. 20 Nov. 1719 [of John and Mary (Paine) Tripp]. (3.) *Elizabeth*[2], d. 1698+; m. 3 Aug. 1665, James[2] Greene, b. 1626; d. 27 Apr. 1698 [of John and Joanna (Tattersall) Greene of Warwick, R. I.]. (4.) Joseph, d. 1728; m 5 Apr. 1676, Mary Wait [of Thomas]. (5.) Abraham, d. 10 Oct. 1727; m. 26 Dec. 1671, Alice Wodell, b. 10 Feb. 1650, d. 1734 [of Wm. and Mary].

INCREASE[1] ALLEN, of Dartmouth, Mass., and wife .... had a dau. *Mary*, b. 29 May 1689; m. 16 Feb. 1709, John[3] Greene of Warwick, R. I., son of James[2] and Elizabeth (Anthony) Greene of Warwick, R. I. [of John[1]].

OUR LANGFORD LINEAGE AND CONNECTIONS.

Col. Thomas Lincoln Casey of Washington, D. C., in 1884 contributed an article in the Narragansett Historical Register, Vol. II, pp. 302–305, from which we abstract the statements in the following paragraph:

On the 20th of June, 1670, the General Assembly of the Colony of Rhode Island, in session at Newport, ordered the Sergeant to procure a boat and men to carry a delegation of Deputies over to Narragansett. The boat obtained belonged to Mr. Robert Carr and the men employed were *Thomas Langford*, and Jacob Pender. Thomas Langford was probably the first of this family in Rhode Island, and the name does not seem to have been widely distributed in New England. A Richard Lanckford appeared in the list of Colony Rates of Plymouth, January 2, 1632-3 taxed 9s, but his name is not on the list of Jan. 2, 1633–4, neither does it appear in 1643 on the lists of those between the ages of 16 and 60. Savage states that in 1645 one John Langford was a freeman in Salem, and may have moved to this town from Sudbury. He was living in Salem in 1689, and Thomas[1] of Newport may have been a descendant of this John of Salem.

THOMAS[1] LANGFORD, of Newport, R. I. (possibly son of John of Salem), is believed to have had two sons, Thomas and John. It is quite certain that in the latter part of the seventeenth century there were two men in Newport, R. I., bearing the name of Langford, viz.:

1. *Thomas*[2], a house carpenter, b. about 1670; d. intestate in June 1709. The inventory of his personal estate amounted to £182 7s. 11d. He was mentioned as one of the legatees in the will of John Greene of Newport, R. I., of 4 Sept. 1694; about 1697 he removed from Newport to E. Greenwich, R. I., where as early as 1698 he owned a farm. On 13 Feb. 1708 he and his wife Sarah sold Zachariah Jenkins of Sandwich, Mass., for £330, a farm of 90 acres in E. Greenwich, bounded partly by land belonging to heirs of John Smith, surveyor, of Newport, deceased. Thomas Langford m. (1) Comfort ......, who d. 1699±; m. (2) in 1701, Sarah ......, who was living in E. Greenwich in Jan. 1755, but died shortly after that date. On 13 Sept. 1711, she m. (2) Immanuel Rouse of E. Greenwich, who d. before 1755.

2. *John*[2], a merchant at Newport, made freeman of the Colony, 30 Apr. 1717. From the records of Trinity College of Newport, it would appear that his wife's name was Alida or Alleda, and that they had 5 children, Richard, Catharine, George, Alida, and John. They are believed to have had Northrup, b. soon after their removal from Newport, and who m. Mary ....

THOMAS[2] LANGFORD, 1670±-1709 of Newport (afterward of E. Greenwich), R. I., by 1st wife Comfort had: (1.) Thomas, b. 22 Mar. 1695, dw. E. Greenwich, R. I., and Dutchess Co., N. Y.; m. .. Dec. 1723, Hannah. By the 2d wife Sarah, Thomas[2] Langford had: (2.) Ruth, b. 19 Feb. 1702 in E. Greenwich; m. 20 Oct. 1720, Thomas Nichols, b. 13 Dec. 1691, son of John and Hannah (Forman) Nichols of E. Greenwich. (3.) Comfort, b. 1 Jan. 1703–4, d. 2 Apr. 1784, m. 22 Nov. 1728, Thomas Casey, b. 18 Nov. 1706, d. 20 Apr. 1797, son of Adam and Mary (Greenman) Casey of Warwick, R. I. (4.) *John*, b. 10 Oct. 1705, dwelt E. Greenwich, R. I.; d. 3d of 3 mo. 1785, was member of E. Greenwich Town Council many years; Justice of the peace as early as 1750; m. 19 May 1727 Barbara Rice, b. 24 Apr.

1706, d. 9 of 3 mo. 1799, dau. of John and Elnathan (Whipple) Rice of Warwick, R. I. [of John¹]. (5.) Jonathan, b. 20 Feb. 1707–8, d. 1738 between date of will 5 Nov. 1738 and the proving of the same, 1 Jan. 1738–9; m. 15 Nov. 1727, Ann Clappe.

JOHN³ LANGFORD, 1705–1785 of E. Greenwich, R. I. [of Thomas², Thomas¹]; m. 1727 Barbara³ Rice 1706–1799 [of John² and Elnathan (Whipple) Rice, John¹] and had: (1.) Thomas, b. 9 Sept. 1729, m. 29 Nov. 1753, Elizabeth Cornell, who d. 5 May 1759 [of Richard]. (2.) Sarah, b. 6 Oct. 1731. (3.) *Phebe*, b. 26 Apr. 1734; m. 24 Oct. 1751, Joseph⁴ Greene, b. 19 Feb. 1727–8, d. 1822, son of John³ and Mary (Allen) Greene of Warwick, R. I. [of James², John¹]. (4.) Eleanor, b. 12 May 1737, m. 13 Feb. 1763, Abraham⁵ Greene [of Rufus⁴, Jabez³, James², John¹]. (5.) John, Jr., 1740–1812, m. (1) 26 Nov. 1761, Desire Tucker, b. 15 Oct. 1742, d. 14 of 7 mo. 1790 [of Capt. Benjamin, of Newport]; m. (2) 16 Jan. 1793, Ruth Greene; b. 19 May 1748 [of James and Hannah of Warwick]. (6.) Barbara, b. 1745, m. 14 Oct. 1768, Stukely Wicks [of Benj.].

JOHN¹ RICE, b. 1646, d. 6 Jan. 1730–31; came from England with Edmund Calvery, who was in Warwick, R. I., as early as 1661; he was on Grand Jury there in 1687, and was Deputy in 1710; he m. 16 July 1674 Elizabeth Holden, b. .. Aug. 1652, dau. of Randall and Frances (Dungan) Holden, and had: (1.) *John*, b. 1675; d. 9 Jan. 1755, m. 25 July 1695, Elnathan Whipple, b. 2 Jan. 1674–5, d. 1753+, dau. of John and Mary (Olney) Whipple, of Providence, R. I. He was Deputy much of the time from 1705 to 1727, and Captain in 1721. The inventory of his personal estate amounted to £3,361 16s 2d—a large sum for those times. (2.) Randall, d. 1742±, m. Elizabeth ________, who d. 1745+.

JOHN² RICE, 1675–1755, of Warwick, R. I. [of John¹]; m. 1695 Elnathan Whipple 1675–1753 [of John¹], and had: (1.) John, b. 6 Apr. 1696. (2.) Elizabeth, b. 8 May 1698, m .... Spencer. (3.) Thomas, b. 26 Apr. 1700, m. Mary Holden, dau. of Randall² and Bethia (Waterman) Holden [of Randall¹]. (4.) Mary, b. 22 Sept. 1702. (5.) Nathan, b. 20 Jan. 1703–4 (6.) *Barbara*, b 24 Apr. 1706, m. 11 May 1727, John Langford [of Thomas², Thomas¹]. (7.) William, b. 25 Mar. 1708. (8.) Mary, b. 24 Jan. 1709 -10. (9.) Lydia, b. 30 Dec. 1711, m. ...... Sweet. (10.) Randall. b. 22 May 1714. (11.) Elnathan, b. 4 Aug. 1716, m. ...... Hill.

RANDALL¹ HOLDEN, b. 1612, d. 23 Aug. 1692; came from Salisbury, Eng., and on 4 Mar. 1636–7. he and Roger Williams were witnesses to the deed of Aquidneck &c, from Canonicus and Miantonomi to William Coddington, &c, for 40 fathoms of white beads and 10 coats and 20 hoes to be given by Miantonomi to the inhabitants (aborigines), who were to remove before winter. On 7 March 1637–8, he was one of the nineteen signers of the following compact at Portsmouth: "We whose names are underwritten do here solemnly in the presence of Jehovah, incorporate ourselves into a Bodie Politick, and as he shall help, will submit our persons, lives, and estates unto our Lord Jesus Christ, the King of Kings and Lord of Lords, and to all those perfect and most absolute laws of His, given us in His holy word of truth, to be guided and judged thereby." He was one of the 11 purchasers of Shawomet (Warwick) on 12 Jan. 1642–3 and was thenceforth one of the most prominent men of that town; was frequently Assistant 1647–76; and Commissioner 1652–63, Deputy 1666–86, and Justice of the Court of Common Pleas 1687–8; in 1651 he and three others agreed with the town to build a mill at their own cost, and to grind the town's corn for two quarts in a bushel, the town granting them a lot for their encouragement, and in 1683 he was appointed on a committee to draft a letter to the King.

He m. 1648 Frances Dungan, 1630±–1697, dau. of William and Frances (Latham) Dungan, and had: (1.) Frances, b. 29 Sept. 1649, d. 1679, m 1 Dec. 1671, John Holmes, b. 1649, d. 2 Oct. 1712 [of Obadiah and Catharine]. (2.) *Elizabeth*, b. .. Aug. 1652, m. 16 July 1674, John Rice, b. 1646, d. 6 Jan. 1730 -31. (3.) Mary, b. .. Aug. 1654, m. 1 Dec. 1671, John Carder, who d. 26 Oct. 1700 [of Richard and Mary]. (4.) John, b. .. Jan. 1655–6. (5.) Sarah, b. .. Feb. 1657–8, d. 1731, m. Joseph Stafford, b. 21 Mar. 1648, d. 1697+ [of Thomas and Elizabeth]. (6.) Randall, b. .. Apr. 1660, d. 13 Sept. 1726, m. 27 Jan. 1687, Bethiah Waterman, b. 1664±, d. 23 July 1742 [of Nathaniel and Susanna (Carder) Waterman]. (7.) Margaret, b. .. Jan. 1662–3, d. 1740, m. John Eldred or Eldridge, who d. 1724 [of Samuel and Elizabeth]. (8.) Charles, b. 22 Mar. 1666, d. 21 July 1717, m. Catharine Greene, b. 15 Aug. 1665 [of John² and Ann (Almy) Greene, John¹]. (9.) Barbara, b. 2 July 1668. d. 1707, m. 4 June 1691, Samuel Wickham, b. 16 June 1664, d. 1712±. (10.) Susannah, b. 8 Dec. 1670, d. 11 Apr. 1734, m. 21 Jan. 1689, Benjamin Greene, b. 10 Jan. 1665–6, d. 22 Feb. 1757 [of Thomas² and Elizabeth (Barton) Greene, John¹]. (11.) Anthony, b. 16 Oct. 1673.

LEWIS LATHAM, of Elstow in County Bedford, England, Gentleman, Falconer to King Charles I, and of whom an original, life-sized, canvass portrait in the possession of Maj. Fred'c A. Holden of "Roselawn," Hyattsville, Md., has been photographed, copies being furnished at $1 each, was descended from a junior branch of the Lathams of county Lancaster, England, and bore the same coat of arms as that family. For many generations the Lathams exerted a powerful influence in the county of Lancaster. The senior branch of the family had ended with Isabel, dau. and heiress of Sir Thos. Latham of Latham, who d. in 1385, and wife of Sir John Stanley, Knight, from whom were descended the Stanleys, Earls of Derby. The Latham estate thus passed into another name and was long held by the Stanley family.

He, Lewis Latham, was b. .... 1555, dwelt at Elstow, in Co. Bedford, Eng., and d. 15 May 1655. He was twice married.

By his 2d wife, Winifred, who was living in 1662, he had a dau. Frances[2] Latham, b. ...... 1611, d. early in Sept. 1677. In the Newport (R. I.) cemetery, her burial place, a tombstone erected to her memory has the following inscription: "Here lyeth ye Body of Mrs. France Vaughn, alius Clarke, ye mother of ye only children of Capt'n Jeremiah Clarke. She died ye 1 week in Sept., 1677, in ye 67th year of her age." She m. 1st Lord .... Weston; she m. 2d Wm. Dungan, who d. in Eng. in 1636, and by whom she had four children; she m. 3d Jeremiah Clarke, who d. ... Jan. 1651-2, with whom, soon after marriage, she and her four children came to New England, and by whom she had 7 more. She m. 4th Wm. Vaughan, who d. in 1677. Through her 11 children and 82 grandchildren, the blood if not the name of Lewis Latham has been largely perpetuated in Rhode Island and other parts of the United States.

WILLIAM DUNGAN, of St. Martins, London, Eng., d. 1636, m. *Frances*, 1611-1677, widow of Lord Weston, and dau. of Hon. Lewis[1] Latham, of Elstow, Eng., 1555-1655, and had: (1.) Barbara, b. 1628±, m. 1644 James Baker, 1623-1702. (2.) William. (3.) *Frances*, 1630±-1697, m. 1648 Randall Holden, 1612-1692. (4.) Thomas, d. 1688; settled in Pennsylvania, and is said to have been the first Baptist minister in those parts; m. Elizabeth Weaver.

Capt. Jeremiah and *Frances*[2] (Latham) Clarke [of Lewis[1] Latham], had: (5.) Walter, b. 1640, d. 23 May 1714, m. (1) 1660±, Content Greenman, b. 1636, d. 27 Mar. 1666; m. (2) .. Feb. 1666-7, Hannah Scott; b. 1642, d. 24 July 1681; m. (3) 6 Mar. 1682-3, Freeborn Hart (widow), b. 1655, d. 10 Jan. 1709-10; m. (4) 31 Aug. 1711, Sarah Gould (widow), b. .. Oct. 1664, living 1714. (6.) Mary, b. 1641, d. 7 Apr. 1711, m. (1) 1658, John Cranston, b. 1626, d. 12 March 1679-80; m. (2) John Stanton, b. .. Aug. 1645, d. 3 Oct. 1713. (7.) Jeremiah, b. 1643, d. 16 Jan. 1729, m. Ann Audley, who d. 15 Dec. 1732. (8.) Latham, b. 1645, d. 1 Aug. 1719, m. (1) Hannah Wilbur; m. (2) 20 Sept. 1698, Anne Newbury (widow), b. 1652, d. 19 Feb. 1731-2. (9.) Weston, b. 5 Apr. 1648, living in 1728; m. (1) 25 Dec. 1668, Mary Easton, b. 25 Sept. 1648, d. 16 Nov. 1690; m. (2) 21 Nov. 1691, Rebecca Easton (widow), b. .. Apr. 1662, d. 16 Sept. 1737. (10.) James, b. 1649, d. 1 Dec. 1736, m. Hope Power, b. 1650, d. 27 Feb. 1717-18. (11.) Sarah, b. 1651, living in 1706, m. (1) John Pinner, who d. 1674; m. (2) Caleb Carr, b. 1624, d. 17 Dec. 1695.

JOHN[1] WHIPPLE, b. 1617±, d. 16 May 1685, was at Dorchester, Mass., 1632-58 and afterward at Providence, R. I., 1659-85; was Deputy much of the time from 1666 to 1677, and was licensed to keep an ordinary in 1674. He was one of those "who staid and went not away'" in King Phillip's War, and so had a share in the disposition of Indian captives, whose services were sold for a term of years. He m. 1639±, Sarah ...., 1624±-1666, and had: (1.) *John*, b. 1640, dwelt Providence, R. I., where he repeatedly held the positions of Town Treasurer, Town Clerk, Deputy, Town Council, and Assistant, and there d. 15 Dec. 1700; m. (1) 4 Dec. 1663, Mary Olney, who d. 1676±, dau. of Thomas and Mary (Small) Olney; m. (2) 15 Apr. 1678, Rebecca Scott, who d. 1701+, widow of John Scott. (2.) Sarah, 1642-1687+, m. John Smith, who d. 1682 [of John and Alice]. (3.) Samuel, b. 1644, d. 12 Mar. 1711; m. Mary Harris, b. 1639, d. 14 Dec. 1722 [of Thomas and Elizabeth]. (4.) Eleazer, b. 1646, d. 25 Aug. 1719; m. 26 Jan. 1668-9, Alice Angell, b. 1649, d. 13 Aug. 1743 [of Thomas and Alice]. (5.) Mary, 1648-1698+; m. 9 Mar. 1666, Epenetus Olney, b. 1634, d. 3 June 1698 [of Thomas and Mary (Small) Olney]. (6.) William, b. 1652, d. 9 Mar. 1712, m. Mary ..... (7.) Benjamin, b. 1654, d. 11 Mar. 1704, m. 1 Apr. 1686, Ruth Mathewson [of James and Hannah (Field) Mathewson]. (8.) David, b. 1656, d. .. Dec. 1710, m. (1) 15 May 1675, Sarah Hearnden, who d. 2 Apr. 1677 [of Benj. and Elizabeth (White) Hearnden]; m. (2) 11 Nov. 1677, Hannah Tower, who d. .. Nov. 1722 [of John and Margaret]. (9.) Abigail, d. 19 Aug. 1725. m. (1) Stephen Dexter, b. 1 Nov. 1647, d. 1679 [of Gregory and Abigail (Fullerton) Dexter]; m. (2) .. Jan. 1681-2, William Hopkins, b. 1647, d. 8 July 1723 [of Thomas]. (10.) Joseph, b. 1662, d. 28 Apr. 1746, m. 20 May 1684, Alice Smith, b. 1664, d. 20 July 1739 [of Edward and Anphillis (Angell) Smith]. (11.) Jonathan, b. 1664, d. 8 Sept. 1721, m. (1) Margaret Angell [of Thomas and Alice]; m. (2) Anne ....., who d. 5 Mar. 1725.

JOHN[2] WHIPPLE, baptized at Dorchester, Mass., 9 Mar. 1639-40, dw. Providence, R. I., and there d. 15 Dec. 1700 [of John and Sarah]; m. (1) 1663, Mary Olney [of Thomas], and had: (1.) Mary, b. 4 Mar. 1665. (2.) John, b. 2 Oct. 1666, m. ...... (3.) Elnathan, b. 2 Jan. 1674-5, m. John Rice. John[2] Whipple, 1640-1700, m. (2) 1678, Rebecca Scott, widow of John, and had: (4.) Deliverence, b. 4 Feb. 1678-9; m. William Arnold. (6.) Dorothy.

THOMAS[1] OLNEY, 1600-1682, shoemaker, from St. Albans, Hertford Co., Eng., embarked in ship Planter of London for New England 2 Apr. 1635, aged 35, with wife Mary aged 30, and sons Thomas and Epenetus. He was elected Freeman at Salem, Mass., 17 May 1637, and received a grant of land there the same year, but went to Providence in 1638, where he was Treasurer for the town and again in 1669; was one of the twelve original members of the First Baptist Church (1639), and one of the 39 signers of the agreement for a form

CASSIUS E. SHOTWELL AND FAMILY.

Concord, Mich

1. Cassius Emmett[7] Shotwell, born 1855, son of Nathan and Phebe B.
    (Gardner) Shotwell, of Concord, Mich., and descendant of Isaac M.[6],
    Richard[5], Benjamin[4], John[3], John[2], Abraham[1].

2. Edith M., born 1866, wife of Cassius E. Shotwell, and daughter of
    Wm. C. and Elizabeth (Lewis) Briggs, of Jackson Co., Mich.

3. Owen Briggs Shotwell, born 1886, son of Cassius E. and Edith M.
    Briggs[1] Shotwell.

JEHIEL K. DAVIS AND FAMILY.

Concord, Mich.

1. Jehiel K. Davis, born 1848, son of Jehiel and Phebe T. Dean) Davis,
    of Oakland Co , Mich.

2. Ida A. S., born 1857, wife of J. K. Davis, and daughter of Nathan
    and Phebe B. Gardner) Shotwell, of Concord, Mich.

3. Grace B. Davis, born 1875, of Saline, Mich., daughter of Jehiel K. and
    Alma C. (Donaldson) Davis.

4. Jehiel Shotwell Davis (called J. S.), born 1892, son of Jehiel K. and
    Ida A. S. (Shotwell) Davis.

(FROM PHOTOGRAPH 1894.)

of government of the Colony, 27 July 1640, and subsequently held the positions of Assistant, Commissioner, Deputy, and Town Council. The Genealogical Dictionary of Rhode Island, has records of his 7 children, 21 grandchildren, and 60 great-grandchildren. He m. Mary Small, b. 1605, who d. before the date of his will of 21 Mar. 1678-9, proved 17 Oct. 1682, and had: (1.) Thomas, b. 1632, d. 11 June 1722, m. 3 July 1660, Elizabeth Marsh, who d. before 1722. (2.) Epenetus, b. 1634, d. 3 June 1698; m. 9 Mar. 1665-6, Mary Whipple, 1648-1698+ [of John and Sarah]. (3.) Nedabiah, baptized 27 Aug. 1637, d. young. (4.) Stephen, d. 1658±. (5.) James, d. .. Oct. 1676, unm. (6.) *Mary*, d. 1676±, m. 4 Dec. 1663, John Whipple, b. 1640, d. 15 Dec. 1700 [of John and Sarah]. (7.) Lydia, b. 1645, d. 9 Sept. 1724,

7

m. 17 Dec. 1669, Joseph Williams, b. 12 Dec. 1643, d. 17 Aug. 1724 [of Roger and Mary].

Thomas[1] and Mary (Small) Olney's daughter Mary[2] m. John[2] Whipple [of John[1]] and had: Elnathan Whipple, who m. John[2] Rice [of John[1]] and had Barbara Rice, who m. John[3] Langford [of Thomas[2], Thomas[1]], and had Phoebe Langford, who m. Joseph[4] Greene [of John[3], James[2], John[1], of royal descent], and had Langford[5] Greene, who m. Abigail Thomas [of George], and had Bathsheba Greene, who m. Jonathan Berry, and had Diana Berry, who m. George Washington[5] Gardner [of John[4], John[3], William[2], George[1]], and had Phebe B. Gardner, who m. Nathan[7] Shotwell [of Isaac M[6], Richard[5], Benjamin[4], John[3], John[2], Abraham[1]], and had Ambrose Milton Shotwell, the compiler of this volume, *et al.*

OUR PARENTS AND THEIR PARENTAGE.

A CONDENSED LINEAGE TABLE

OF THE

HEADS OF FAMILIES

WHOSE KNOWN CHILDREN ARE RECORDED IN

THE ANNALS OF OUR COLONIAL ANCESTORS AND THEIR DESCENDANTS.

(FIRST SERIES, 1895. PARTS I. AND II.)

NOTE—The following catalogue of fathers and mothers, whose children, so far as their genealogical records have been obtained, are duly registered in the body of the present volume, will, it is hoped, be found a convenient appendix, especially serviceable in tracing the various branches of one's ancestry elsewhere more fully presented in this book.

The "superior figures" or exponents affixed to the several names denote the generation, reckoned usually from the earliest American forefather of the same patronymic; and the numbers within brackets indicate the corresponding lines of this exhibit where the parents' names may be found. This list does not include the new names given in the appendix which presents the lineages of those relatives who have subscribed for copies of the volume prior to its publication.

In this alphabetical summary, the author's direct ancestors are indicated by the asterisk (*). Any reader able and willing to point out possible errors or supply additions, is cordially requested to report promptly to the compiler, A. M. Shotwell, at Concord, Mich., any observed inaccuracies or the omission of any known marriage dates, or of the names of parents of persons named Shotwell, or of parents who were sons or daughters of his forefathers * so marked, together with any data in such sender's possession relating to such omitted households or individuals—to the end that a revised and corrected table of the editor's kindred and their pedigrees may be completed at an early date.

The numbers prefixed to certain fathers' names in Part II of this work correspond, not to those of the same name in this table, but to those in a later Synopsis of six generations of the Shotwell family.

AMBROSE M. SHOTWELL'S ANCESTORS.
Mentioned in accompanying table.
No. 339.

Paternal . No. 254.

Grandfather.. Desc. of Nos 344, 190, 283, 282, 174, 8(a), 8(c), 20, 37, 40, 82(a), 83(a), 126, 410, 411.

Grandmother. Desc. of Nos. 149, 157, 147(b), 152, 151, 16, 22, 23, 86, 101, 103, 105, 106, 109, 130(a), 132, 133(a), 134, 168, 403, 430, 434, 435.

Maternal . No. 46(b).

Grandfather.. Desc. of Nos. 55, 54, 60, 44(a), 65, 394, 395, 396, 401, 402, 425, 426, 427, 436, 437(a).

Grandmother. Desc. of Nos. 5, 75, 73, 72, 70(b), 71, 77, 76, 78, 69, 68, 81, 80, 88, 35, 36, 2, 34, 3, 4, 32, 95, 116, 117, 118(a), 119, 137, 165, 166, 404, 438, 439(a).

---

1.   Aldrich, Wanton⁶ [of Asa] married 1805 Amy⁶ Shotwell [of 344].

2.*   Alfred⁵, The Great, King of England [of 30], m. Ethelbith—ancestors of the mother of the compiler's maternal grandmother. (See Nos. 5, 71, 81 and 88, and p. 40.

3.*   Allen, Increase¹, of Dartmouth, m. ——

4.*   Anthony, John¹, m. Susanna ——

5.*   Berry, Jonathan¹, m. 1809 Bathsheba⁶ Greene [of 75].

6. (a)   "   Langford G². [of 5] m. (1) 1841 Mary A. Hart.

   (b)   "   Langford G²., m. (2) Margaret Ramsdell.

   (c)   "   Langford G²., m. (3) Betsey Coyt.

7.   Bosworth, Seth W., m. 1827 Catharine E.⁶ Pound [of 149].

8. (a)* Bowne, John², (of Flushing, L. I. [of Thos¹.] m. (1) 1654 + Elizabeth² Feeke [of 37].

   (b)   "   John², (of Flushing, L. I.) [of Thos¹.] m. (2) 1679 + Hannah Bickerhoff.

   (c)*   "   John², (of Flushing, L. I.), [of Thos¹.) m. (3), 1692 + Mary² Cock [of 20].

9. (a)   Briggs, Richmond³, [of Pardon², John¹] m. (1) 1839 Caroline Chapman.

   (b)   "   Richmond⁴, m. (2) 1843 Mary Swift.

10.   "   William C⁴. [of 9 (a)] m. 1860 Elizabeth Lewis.

11.   Brotherton, Henry¹, m. 1713 Ann³ Shotwell [of 208].

12. Brotherton, Henry[3], Jr., [of James[2], of 11], m. (2) Esther[4] Pound [of 147 (b)].
13. Brown, James, m. Elizabeth[2] Carr [of 16].
14. Carr, Caleb[2], [of 16] m. Phillip[3] Greene [of John[2] and Ann (Almy) Green, John[1]].
15.   "   Esek[2] [of 16] m. Susanna ———
16.* "   Robert[1], of Newport, R. I., m. ———
17. Cary, Thomas, m. 1787 Hannah[5] Moore [of 132].
18. Clark, George D., m. Ann[5] King [of 100].
19. Clarke, Jeremiah[1], m. Frances[2] (Latham) Dungan [of 119].
20.* Cock, James[1], m. Sarah ———
21. Comstock, Nathan, m. 1824 Anna[6] Pound [of 149].
22.* Cowperthwaite, Hugh[1], of Flushing, L. I., m. Elizabeth ———
23.*   "   John[3], [of 22] m. 1690–1, Sarah Adams.
24. Curtis, Wilbur F., m. 1871 Rosetta A[4]. Dillingham [of 30].
25. Daily, George, m. 1830 Sarah K[4]. Pound [of 149].
26.(a) Davis, Jehiel[3], m. (1) 1810 Lydia T. Bentley.
   (b) "   Jehiel[3], m. (2) 1843 Phebe T. Dean.
27.(a) "   Jehiel K[4]. [of 26 (b)] m. (1) 1874 Alma C. Donaldson.
   (b) "   Jehiel K[4]., m. (2) 1886 Ida A[6]. Shotwell [of 339].
28. Dillingham, Isaac[4] [of 30] m. 1865 Martha A. Hosmer.
29.   "   Oscar[4] [of 30] m. 1872 Sarah H. Thistlethwaite.
30.   "   Stephen[4], m. 1833 Anna P[7]. (Shotwell) Hoag [254].
31.   "   Stephen N[4]. [of 30] m. 1863 Emeline E. Porter.
32.* Dungan, William[1], m. Frances[2] (Latham) West [of 119].
33. Ebert, Jacob, m. 1826 Nancy[6] (Shotwell) Vandolah [of 250].
34.* Edward[4], The Elder, King of England [of 2] m. Edgiva.
35.* Egbert[1], First King of England, m. Lady Redburga.
36* Ethelwolf[2], King of England [of 35].
37* Feake, Lieut. Robert[1], m. Elizabeth[2] (Fones) Winthrop.
38. Fitz Randolph, Jacob, m. Anna[4] Webster [of 430].
39.   "   "   John, m. 1793 Mary[4] King [of 100].
40.* Fones, Thos[1]., m. Anna Winthrop [sister to Gov. John, of Mass.]
41. Fuller, Scott, m. Abigail[5] Gardner [of 55].
42. Gardiner, Benoni[2] [of 44 (a)] m. Mary ———
43. Gardner, Champlain[5], [of Clark[4], Wm[3]., Wm[2]., George[1]], m. Bathsheba[5] Gardner [of 55].
44.(a)* Gardner George[1], [of Newport, R. I.] m. 1642 ± Horod (Long) Hicks.
   (b) "   George[1], m. [2] 1665 ± Lydia Ballou.
45.   "   George[2] [of 44 (a)] m. Tabitha Tefft.
46.(a) "   George Washington[5] [of 55] m. (1) 1814 Phebe N. Garbutt.
   (b)* "   George Washington[5] m. (2) 1830 Diana[2] Berry [of 5].
47.   "   George Milton[6] [of 46 (b)] m. 1857 Jane F[7]. Gardner [of Geo[6]., Abiel[5] Thos[4]., Wm[3]., Wm[2]., Geo[1].].
48.   "   George Milton[7] Jr., [of 47] m. 1880 Mary L. Freeman.
49.   "   Henry[2] [of 44 (a)] m. (2) Abigail (Richmond) Remington.
50.   "   Jeffrey Watson[5] [of 55] m. 1800 ± Freelove[5] Gardner [of Clark[4], Wm[3]., Wm[2]., Geo[1].].
51.   "   Jeremiah[2] of Newport, R. I., [of 44 (b)] m. ———

52. Gardner, Jeremiah Hazard[5] [of 55] m. 1811 Harriet Pattison [of Sunderland[2] Sr.]
53.   "   Jeremiah Hazard[6] [of 46 (a)] m. 1844 Anna Thompson.
54.* "   John[3] [of 60] m. ——— Wilkinson.
55.* "   John[4] [of 54] m. 1767 Bathsheba[4] Watson [of 425].
56.   "   John[5] [of 55] m. Elizabeth Adams.
57. Gardiner, Joseph[3] [of 44 (b)] m. 1693 Catharine Holmes.
58. Gardner, Nicholas[2] [of 44 (a)] m. Hannah ———
59.   "   Samuel[3] [of 44 (a)] m. 1683 Elizabeth[2]. (Carr) Brown [of 16].
60.* "   William[2] [of 44 (a)] m. Alice, Elsie, or Elizabeth ———
61.   "   William[3] [of 60] m. 1744 Freelove Joslin.
62.   "   William[4] [of 54] m. Sarah[4] Watson of [425].
63.   "   Winfield Scott[7], [of John[6], Abiel[5], Thos[4]., Wm[3]., Wm[2]., Geo[1].] m. 1874 Mabel A. Hunn, [of 100].
64. Genung, Lewis, m. 1850 Mary Jane[4] Dillingham [of 30].
65.* Gereardy, John[1], m. Renewed[2] Sweet [of 402].
66. Greene, Benjamin[6] [of 75] m. 1821 Rhoda Niles.
67.   "   George[6] [of 75] m. Sally Reeves.
68.* "   Henry[3], de, [of 81] m. 1353 Catherine.
69.* "   Sir Henry[4], de, [of 68] m. Matilda Maudit.
70.(a) "   James[2] [of 71] m. (1) Deliverence Potter.
   (b)* "   "   m. (2) 1665 Elizabeth[3] Anthony [of 4].
71.* "   John[1] (of Warwick) [of 77] m. 1619 Joana Tattershall.
72.* "   John[3] [of 70 (b)] m. 1709 Mary[3] Allen [of 3].
73.* "   Joseph[4] [of 72] m. 1751 Phoebe[4] Langford [of 110].
74.   "   Joseph[6] [of 75] m. Urania Hull.
75.* "   Langford[5] [of 73] m. 1789 ± Abigail[3] Thomas [of 404].
76.* "   Richard[2], of Bowridge Hill, England [of 78] m. ———
77.* Greene Richard[3] [of 76] m. Mary ———
78.* "   Robert[1], of Gillingham, England [grandson of 60] m. ———
79   "   Samuel[6] [of 75] m. (1) Lucy Rose.
80.* "   Sir Thomas[1], de la, m. Alice.
81.* "   Thomas[2] de, (born 1292) [of 80] m. (1) Lucy[15], Le Zouche (desc. of Eudo[14], Elene[13] de Quincy, Roger[12], (d. 1264), Margaret[11] de Bellomont, Robert[10] —3d Earl of Leicester (d. 1190), Robert[9], Isabel[8] de Vermandois, Adela[7] —consort Prince Hugh[6], Magnus of France, count Hubert[5], Princess Edgiva[5] of England, of 34, and desc. of 4 English and 3 French kings, 2 Russian grand dukes and 1 Emperor of Constantinople].
82.(a)* Hallet, Richard[3] [of 83 (a)], m. (1) 1717, Amy[3] Bowne [of 8 (c)].
   (b) "   Richard[3] [of 83 (a)], m. (2) Anne Miller.
83.(a)* "   Wm[2]. [of Wm[1]. of Hellgate], m. Sarah Woolsey [of Geo[1]. of Jamaica].
   (b) "   Wm., m. Elizabeth (Fones) Winthrop [of 40].
84. Hampton, Abner, m. 1744 Rachel[3] Webster [of 435].
85.   "   William[2] [of 84], m. 1768 Sarah[4] Shotwell [of 100].
86.* Hartshorne, Richard[1], of Middletown, N. J., from Hathern, Eng., m. 1670 Margaret[4] Carr [of 16].
87. Head, Thomas, m., Rachel[5] Moore [of 132].

88.* Henry[3], I, King of France [of Kings Robert[2], Hugh[1] Capet, and father-in-law of Countess Adela[7] de Vermandois (see 81)], m. Anne of Russia [of GrandDukes Jaroslaue[2], Woldomir[1], and the latter's consort Anne, dau. of Romanus II, Emperor of Constantinople].
89.   Herendeen, James[3] [of Joshua[2]], m. 1812, Elizabeth[6] Shotwell [of 344].
90.   "   Welcome, m. Mercy[6] Gardner [of 55].
91.   Hicks, John, m. Mary[2] Carr [of 10].
92.   Hoag, Benjamin[2] [of 94] m. 1830 Anna P[7]. Shotwell [of 254].
93.   "   Jacob, Jr., m. Sarah[6] Shotwell [of 344].
94.   "   Levi, m. Desire[5] Gardner [of 55].
95.* Holden, Randall[1] m. 1648 Frances[2] Dungan [of 32].
96.   Hull, Joseph[4] m. 1700± Ann[3] Gardner [of 60].
97.   "   Samuel, m. Hannah[6] Greene [of 75].
98.   Hunn, Edward R.[3] [of 100] m. 1885 Caroline E. Welch.
99.   "   Gardner L[3]. [of 100] m. 1881 Mary[2] Hawes.
100. "   Oliver B., m. 1852 Malinna A[6]. Gardner [of 46 (b)].
101.* Ilsley, William[1], m. Barbara ———
102. Kellogg, Charles H., m. 1872 Clara A[3]. Shotwell [of 256 (b)].
103.* King, Harmanus[1], m. ———
104. "   John[5], born 1779 [of 100] m. ———
105.* "   Joseph[2], Sr. (of 103) m. 1711± Mercy ———
106.* "   Joseph[3], Jr. [of 105] m. Mary ———
107. "   Joseph[3] [of 100], m. 1805, Catharine[5] Laing [of Thos[4], Isaac[3], John[2], John[1]].
108. "   Joseph[4] [of 111], m. (2) Anne(Large)Lundy.
109.* "   Nathan[4] [of 100] m. 1771 Sarah[6] Moore [of 132].
110. (a) "   Thomas L[4]. [of 107], m. [1] 1838 Ann Maria Harkness].
    (b) "   Thomas L[4]., m. [2] 1863 Alice Gray.
111. "   Wm[3] [of 105], m. Abigail Doughty.
112. Laing, John[2] (of John[1]) m. 1705 Elizabeth[3] Shotwell [of 282].
113. "   John[4] [of Samuel[3], Wm[2]., John[1]], m. Hannah Webster.
114. "   Smith[6] [of Joseph[5], of 113], m. 1815 Abbe[6] Shotwell [of 344].
115. Langford, John[2] [of 117] m. Alida ———
116.* "   John[3] [of 118 (a)] m., 1727 Barbara[3] Rice [of 166.]
117.* "   Thomas[1], of Newport, R. I., m. ———
118. (a)* " Thomas[2] of Newport, R. l., [of 117] m. (1) Comfort ———,
    (b) "   Thomas[2], m. (2) Sarah ———
119.* Latham, Lewis[1], of Elstow, Eng., m. Winifred ———
120. Loomis, Charles R., m. 1892 Kate M.[3] Shotwell [of 222 (a)].
121. Lundy, Jacob, Jr., m. 1783 Sarah[6] (Shotwell) Hampton [of 190].
122. "   Joseph, m. 1787 Elizabeth[6] Shotwell [of 190].
123. Maltby, Wm H., m. Sarah Florilla[6] Shotwell [of 222 (a)].
124. Marsh, Samuel, m. 1744 Mary[4] Shotwell [of 283].
125. "   William, m. 1753 Sarah[3] Webster [of 435].
126.* Martin, Isaac[1], m. Elizabeth Burling.
127. Moore, Benjamin[3] [of 130 (a)] m. 1728 Elizabeth[4] Shotwell [of 208].
128. "   Benjamin[5] [of 132] m. 1790 (—)
129. "   Edward[4] [of 134] m. ———
130. (a)* " John[3] [of 133 (a)] m. (1) 1699 Hope Robins [of 168].
    (b) "   John[3], m. (2) 1717 Mary Oliver.
131. "   John[2] [of 132] m. 1783 Hannah Copland.
132.* "   Joseph[4] [of 134] m. 1751 Christiana Bishop [of Moses].
133. (a)* " Samuel[1], m. (2) 1676 Mary[2] Ilsley [of 101].
    (b) "   Samuel[1], m. (3) 1678 Ann Jaques.
134.* "   Samuel[2] [of 130 (a)] m. 1730± Mary ———

135. Moore, Samuel[4] [of 134] m. 1763 Rachel Stone.
136. "   Samuel[5] [of 132] m. 1781 Amelia Prall [of Benj.].
137.* Olney, Thomas[1], m. Mary Small.
138. Osborne, Jonathan II., m. Martha[5] Shotwell [of 285 (b)].
139. Park, Jonathan S., m. 1850 Abigail Emily[2] Berry [of 5].
140. Pattison, Sunderland[3], Jr., m. Dorcas[5] Gardner [of 55].
141. Piatt, Capt. Wm., m. Sarah[5] Shotwell [of 285 (b)].
142. Piper, John D., m. 1884 Gertrude E[3]. Shotwell [of 251].
143. Pound, Alexander[6] [of 153] m. 1842 Almina Whipple.
144. Pound Asher[6] [of 149] m. 1819 Mary Birdsall.
145. "   Benjamin[4] [of 147 (a)] m. 1763 Elizabeth[4] Laing [of David[3], John[2], John[1]].
146. "   Daniel[4] [of 147 (b)] m. Prudence Jones.
147. (a) "   Elijah[3] [of 152] m. (1) Bathsheba ———
    (b)* "   Elijah[3], m. (2) Elizabeth ———.
148. "   Elijah[4] [of 147 (b)] m. 1784 Isabella Sharp.
149.* "   Hugh[5] [of 157] m. 1794 Sarah[5] King [of 109].
150. (a) "   Jediah Shotwell[6] [of 149] m. (1) 1829 Edith[6] Laing [of John[5], John[4], Samuel[3], William[2], John[1]].
    (b) "   Jediah, m. (2) 1853 Prudence P[7]. Shotwell [of 195.]
151.* "   John[1] m. Esther ———
152.* "   John[2] of Piscataway, N. J., [of 151] m.———
153. "   John[5] [of 157] m. 1803 Alice Smith.
154. "   John W[6]. [of 153] m. 1855± Catharine Lucretia Wilson.
155. "   Joseph Smith[6] [of 153] m. 1829 Lavinia Dillingham.
156. "   Nathan K[6]. [of 149] m. 1824 Hannah G. Lane.
157.* "   Samuel[4] [of 147 (b)] m. 1772 Catharine[4] Webster [of 430].
158. "   Samuel L[5]. [of 157] m. 1807 Anne[5] Laing. [of John[4], David[3], John[2], John[1]].
159. "   Samuel[5] [of 153] m. 1832 Lucinda Andrews.
160. (a) "   William[4] [of 157] m. (1) Mary Vail.
    (b) "   William[5], m. (2) 1812 Abigail[6] Shotwell [of 347].
161. (a) "   William[6] [of 149] m. (1) 1818 Betsey Warner.
    (b) "   William[6] m. (2) 1830 Mary J. Goodell.
162. "   Zachariah[4] [of 147 (a)] m. 1761 Elizabeth Smith.
163. Reed, John[2] m. 1839, Mary S[7]. Shotwell [of 254].
164. "   John Seley[3] [of 163] m. 1864 Mary Eliza[8] Shotwell [of 233].
165.* Rice, John[1], m. 1674 Elizabeth[2] Holden [of 95].
166.* "   John[2] [of 165] m. 1695 Elnathan[3] Whipple [of 430 (a)].
167. Robe, William Frank, m. (1) 1863 Mary Ellen[6] Shotwell [of 256 (a)].
168.* Robins, Daniel[1], of Woodbridge, N. J., m. Hope ———
169. Robinson, George, m. Elizabeth[5] Pound [of 157].
170. Sayre (or Sears), Ephraim, m. 1816 Charlotte[6] Shotwell [of 250].
171. Seaton, Maj. George C., m. 1820 Ester[6] (Shotwell) Smith [of 250].
172. (a) Shotwell, Aaron[5] [of 183] m. (1) ——— Martin.
    (b) "   Aaron[5], m. (2) ——— Freeman.
173. "   Abel[6] [of 260] m. 1810 Elizabeth[4] Vail [of 413].
174.* "   Abraham[1], of Elizabethtown and New York m. ———
175. "   Abraham[3] [of 282] m. 1712 Elizabeth[3] Cowperthwait [of 23].
176. (a) "   Abraham[4] [of 283] m. (1) 1742 Mary Potts.
    (b) "   Abraham[4] m. (2) 1767 Lydia Hallett [of 82 (b)].

177. Shotwell, Abraham[6] [of 310] m. 1751 Mary Jackson.
178. " Abraham[7] [of 200] m. Almyra Clark.
179. " Abraham[6] [of 172 (a)] m. —— Moore.
180. " Abraham F[6]. [of 200] m. ———
181. " Abraham V[6]. [of 348] m. ———
182. " Adoniram Judson[7] [of 189] m. 1872 Martha H. Graham.
183. " Albert[5] [of 292 (b)] m. (1) 1836 Catharine Geery.
184. " Alexander[6] [of 335] m. 1824 Eliza Smith.
185. " Alexander Hamilton, M. D. [of 337 (a)], m. 1861 Jennie Eliza McEntire.
186. " Alfred L[7]. [of 375] m. Gabriella Breckenridge.
187. " Alvin Theodore[8] [of 228 (b)] m. 1881 Mary Josephine Moore.
188. " Anson[7] [of 308] m. 1863 Lucinda Jane Cummins.
189. " Arrison[6] [of 230] m. 1835 Mary Dickerson.
190.* " Benjamin[4] [of 283] m. 1746 Ame[4] Hallett [of 82 (a)].
191. " Benjamin[4] [of 284] m. 1754 Elizabeth Manning.
192. " Benjamin[5] [of 190] m. 1781 Bathsheba[5] Pound [of 102.]
193. " Benjamin[6] [of 344] m. 1815 Sarah Hoag [of 94.]
194. " Benjamin[6] [of 373] m. Mary[4] Hunt [of James.]
195. " Benjamin[6] [of 192] m. 1825 Catharine Pugsley.
196. (a) " Benjamin H[7]. [of 364 (a)] m. (1) Susan L[7]. Thorn [of Samuel[5], Abr[5]., Abr[4]., Abr[3]., Jos[2]., Wm[1].].
(b) " Benjamin H[7]. m. (2) Paulina R. Davis.
197. " Benjamin W[8]. [of 231] m. 1849 Mary Hoyle.
198. " Benjamin H[8]. [of 391] m. 1876 Melissa Lowes.
199. " Benjamin F[8]. [220] m. 1887 Alice Bennett.
200. " Caleb[5] [of 346] m. Phebe (Hinckston) Gliddon.
201. " Caleb G[7]. [of 318] m. 1837 Sarah J. Carey.
202. " Carlos B[8]. [of 200] m. 1871 Eliza L. Williams.
203. " Cassius E[8]. [of 339] m. 1885 Edith M[5]. Briggs [of 10].
204. (a) " Charles Akin (b. 1846) [adopted s. of Mary[6], dau. of 372] m. (1) Alice DeMouliere.
(b) " Charles Akin m. (2) 1876, Agnes Brook.
205. " Charles[6] [of 275] m. ———
206. " Clarkson[7] [of 211] m. Mary Ross.
207. " Clarkson[6] [of 208] m. Keziah Freeman.
208. " Daniel[2] of Staten Island [of 174] m. Elizabeth ———
209. " Daniel[4] [of 310] m. 1753 Deborah[4] Shotwell [of 175.]
210. " Daniel[5] [of 209] m. Keziah Terrill.
211. " Daniel C[6]. (Hatter) [of 329] m. Martha[6] Pound [of Samuel[5], of 102].
212. (a) " Daniel[6] "on the hill" [of 264] m. (1) Mary[6] Shotwell [of 287 (b)].
(b) " Daniel[6] m. (2) Phebe Cole.
213. " Daniel[6], Jr. [of 210] m 1827 Margaret Ann Elizabeth Force.
214. " Daniel L[7]. [of 300(b)] m. Mary Iden.
215. " Daniel P[6]. [of 301] m. 1886 Sarah V. (Bond) Shotwell (see 333).
216. " David[5] [of 346] m. 1779, Elizabeth Fitz Randolph [of Hartshorne].
217. " David[6] [of 373] m. —— Prall.

218. (a) Shotwell, David[6] [of 200] m. (1) Polly Lewis.
(b) " David[6] [of 200] m. (2) Bulah Wood.
219. " David[7] [of 218 (b)] m. Delia Shute.
220. " David S[7]. [of 193] m. 1838 Eliza[3] Dillingham.
221. (a) " David[7] [of 342(b)] m (1) Permelia Clark.
(b) " David[7] [of 342 (b)] m. (2) Ann Berry.
222. (a) " David B[7]. [of 254] m. (1) 1860 Adaliza J. Wilder.
(b) " David B[7]. [of 254] m. (2) 1880 Margery A. (McPherson) Mason.
223. " David S[7]., Jr., [of 220] m. 1871 Adelia Bliss.
224. " Dea Abel[7] [of 318] m. 1847 Christi Ann Gordon.
225. " Eden[5] [of 262 (a)] m. Mary Haydock.
226. " Eden[6] [of 335] m. 1837 Ann M. Haas.
227. " Edmund[6] [of 200] m. Sarah R. Shepard.
228. (a) " Edmund V[7]. [of 211] m. (1) Freelove Laing.
(b) " Edmund V[7]. [of 211] m. (2) 1844 Jane H. Williams.
229. " Edmund[7] [of 363] m. 1834 Adna A. La Rue.
230. " Edward[6] [of 366 (b)] m. Miriam[6] Moore [of Edward[5], of 129].
231. " Edward R[7]. [of 341] m. 1835 Margaret H[7]. Shotwell [of 227].
232. (a) " Edward H[7]. [of 195] m. (1) 1865 Rosetta E. Corwin.
(b) " Edward H[7]. [of 195] m. (2) 1868 Eliza Jones.
233. " Edwin B[7]. [of 390 (b)] m. 1846 Sarah A. Harkness.
234. " Eli[7] [of 211] m. Emeliza Boyce.
235. " Elijah[6] [of 264] m. Jemima[2] Piatt [of 141].
236. " Elijah[6] [of 371] m. Martha Burtsall.
237. " Elijah B[8]. [of 383] m. ———
238. " Elmer E[8]. [of 233] m. 1884 Carrie B. Olds.
239. " Elvington M[8]. [of 188], m. 1891± Mary Lobdell.
240. " Ezra M[7]. [of 255] m. 1868 Theora Door.
241. " Freeman[7] [of 345] m. Nancy Nott.
242. (a) " George H[6]. [of 172 (a)] m. Mary E. A. Tudor.
242. (b) " Geo[7]. [of 242 (a)] m. ———
243. " George[7] [of 207] m. ———
244. " Greenleaf[8] [of 380] m. ———
245. " Harvey, of Pennsylvania, m. ———
246. " Harvey[6] [of 373] m. 1823 Louisa[6] Shotwell [of 335].
247. " Henry[5] [of 311 (a)] m. 1781 Sarah Dobson.
248. " Henry R[7]. [of 315] m. 1830 Margaret G[6]. Laing [of Wm[5]., Thos[4]., Isaac[3], John[2], John[1]].
249. " Hudson B[8]. [of 231] m. Emma J. Noe.
250. " Hugh[5] [of 285 (b)] m. 1783 Rosetta Arrison.
251. " Hugh P[7]. [of 254] m. 1850 Hannah Haines.
252. " Isaac[6] [of 263] m. 1770 Hannah[5] Shotwell [of 262 (a)].
253. " Isaac[5] [of 176 (b)] m. 1791 Catherine Moore.
254.* " Isaac M[6]. [of 344] m. 1813 Edna C[6]. Pound [of 149].
255. " Isaac[6] [of 366 (b)] m. Hope Stanton.
256. (a) " Isaac M[7]. [of 254] m. (1) 1843 Elvira L. Schofield.
(b) " Isaac M[7]. [of 254] m. (2) 1854 Delia A. Mattice.
257. " Isaac M[7]. [of 193] m. Mary P. Estes.
258. (a) " Isaac[7] [of 305] m. (1) Harriet Hobbs.
(b) " Isaac[7] [of 305] m. (2) Sadie Fowler.
259. " Isaac[7] [of 295 (b)] m. Mary Nickison.

260. Shotwell, Isaiah⁵ [of 285 (b)] m. 1772 Constant Lippencott.
261. " Jabez⁶ [of 289] m. 1815± Eliza Warder.
262. (a) " Jacob⁴ [of 283] m. (1) 1746 Eleanor Haydock.
   (b) " Jacob⁴ [of 283] m. (2) 1766 Katharine Tilton.
263. " Jacob⁴ [of 310] m. ——
264. " Jacob⁵ [of 285 (b)] m. 1769 Bathsheba⁴ Pound [of 147 (b)].
265. " Jacob⁷ [of 342 (b)], m. Dorcas Drake.
266. " Jacob 2⁵. [of 391] m. 1870 Arabella J. Cox.
267. " Jacob A⁷. [of 226] m. 1872 Susan E. Canfield.
268. " James⁵ [of 285 (b)] m. Elsie (Smalley) Runyan.
269. " James, m. 1772 Ann Moore.
270. " James⁷ [of 374] m. 1831 Phebe Ayers.
271. " James⁷ [of 356] m. Matilda Seley.
272. " James F. R⁷. [of 345] m. (1) Julia Caroline Welch.
273. " Capt. James A⁷. [of 213] m. 1876 Hattie A. (Cambell) Shotwell. (See 361.)
274. " James⁷ [of 181] m. ——
275. " James Luther⁵ [of 183] m. 1865 Sallie Magee.
276. " Jasper⁵ [of 286] m. ——
277. " Jasper⁷ [of 292 (b)] m. 1843 Ann McMillen.
278. " Jediah⁷ [of 363] m. 1845 Martha A. Provost.
279. " Jeptha⁷ [of 320] m. 1849 Nancy Cooper.
280. " Jermiah⁵ [of 176 (a)] m. 1781 Mary
281. " Joel⁷ [of 205 (a)] m. Sarah J. Blansfield.
282.* " John² [of 174] m. 1679 Elizabeth Burton.
283.* " John³ Jr. [of 282], m. 1709 Mary³ Thorne, Jr. [of 410]
284. " John³ [of 208] m. Lydia ——
285. (a) " John⁴ [of 283] m. (1) 1735 Elizabeth³ Smith [of Shobel², Samuel¹].
   (b) " John⁴ [of 283] m. (2) 1743 Grace³ Webster [of 435].
286. " John⁴ [of 175] m. 1752 + Anna ——
287. (a) " John Smith⁵ [of 285 (a)] m. (1) 1756 Mary³ Webster [of 435].
   (b) " John Smith⁶ [of 285 (a)] m. (2) 1782 Phebe⁴ Shotwell [of 175].
288. " John⁵ [of 311 (a)] m. 1760 Margaret Haydock.
289. " John⁵ (b. 1753) [of 286] m. Abigail Shipman.
290. " John⁶ [of 313] m. Phoebe Byron.
291. " John⁵ [of 101] m. Esther⁵ Fitz Randolph [of Joseph⁴].
292. (a) " John⁶ [of 280] m. (1) 1803 Rachel Dye.
   (b) " John⁶ [of 280] m. (2) 1809 Sally Burroughs.
293. " John⁷ [of 200] m. Susan St. C. Stratton.
294. " John⁶ [of 250] m. 1804 Sarah Shanklin.
295. (a) " John⁶ [of 371] m. (1) Grace Marsh.
   (b) " John⁶ [of 371] m. (2) 1833 Matilda Heaton.
296. " John⁵ [of 176 (b)] m. —— Freeman.
297. " John⁶ [of 210] m. —— Moore.
298. " John⁷ [of 292 (b)] m. 1840 Elizabeth Biggs.
299. " Rev. John M⁷. [of 318] m. (1) 1842 Salome L. Stone.
300. " John W⁷. [of 261] m. ——
301. " John Jr⁷. [of 295 (a)] m. Catherine Blansfield.

302. Shotwell, John⁷ [of 207] m. Sarah Johnson.
303. " John⁷ [of 342 (b)] m. ——
304. " John I⁷. [of 356] m. ——
305. " John B⁸. [of 291] m. 1871, ——
306. " John F⁸. [of 258 (a)] m. 1879 Ella R. Starbuck.
307. " John P⁸. [of 301] m. ——
308. " Jonathan⁶ [of 268] m. 1818 Phebe Willson.
309. " Jonathan L⁷. [of 304 (b)] m. 1857 Elizabeth Fitz Patrick.
310. " Joseph³ [of 208] m. 1716 Mary Manning.
311. (a) " Joseph⁴ [of 283] m (1) 1742 Sarah³ Cock [of Henry², Jas¹.].
   (b) " Joseph⁴ [of 283] m. (2) Phebe Allen.
312. " Joseph⁴ III [of 310] m. 1743 Elizabeth Jackson.
313. " Joseph⁵ [of 312 (?)] m. 1783 Sarah Wilson.
314. " Joseph⁶ [of 288] m. 1820 Margaret Elston.
315. " Joseph D⁶. [of 247] m. 1804 Elizabeth Fitz Randolph [of 38].
316. " Joseph L⁶. [of 260] m. 1809 Christiana⁴ Vail [of 413].
317. " Joseph [of 269] m. 1800 Sarah⁶ Thorn [of Abr⁵. of 406].
318. " Joseph⁶ [of 200] m. 1811 Sarah Randall.
319. " Joseph Smith⁶ [of 287 (b)] m. Deborah Fox.
320. " Joseph⁶ [of 250] m. 1821 Mary Arrison.
321. " Joseph⁶ [of 210] m. —— Ball.
322. " Joseph M⁷. [of 205 (a)] m. 1860 Martha Ferguson.
323. " Joseph D⁸. [of 248] m. Amelia Everett.
324. " Joseph M⁷. [of 378] m. 1860 Minnie Perrier.
325. (a) " Joshua⁷ [of 363] m. (1) 1834 Sarah A. Stillwell.
   (b) " Joshua⁷ [of 363] m. (2) 1842 Rebecca A. Stillwell.
326. " Josiah⁷ [of 318] m. 1850 Julia Cornell.
327. (a) " Levi L⁷. [of 390 (a)] m. (1) Nancy P. Pratt.
   (b) " Levi L⁷. [of 390 (a)] m. (2) Aseneth Williams.
328. " Levi S⁷. [of 193] m. 1840 Sarah Estes.
329. " Manning⁵ [of 191] m. 1783 + Mary Clarkson [of Robert].
330. " Manning⁷ [of 345] m. 1838 Lucy Ann Cannon.
331. " McCleery J. [of 337 (c)] m. 1881 Sarah M. Hardwick.
332. " Melancthon S. [of 337 (b)] m. 1867 Caroline R⁷. Porter.
333. " Merrett Elmer⁸ [of 301] m. 1877 Sarah V. Bond.
334. (a) " Montgomery⁸. [of 208] m (1) 1861 Elizabeth Robertson.
   (b) " Montgomery⁸ of [of 208] m. (3) 1882 + Cora Ellis
335. " Nathan⁵ [of 262 (b)] m. 1798 Sarah Fitz Randolph [of 38].
336. (a) " Nathan⁶ [of 289] m. (1) ——
   (b) " Nathan⁶ [of 289] m. (2) ——
337. (a) " Rev. Nathan, D. D., 1806-1800 [of 343]. m. (1) 1833 Lydia Baldwin.
   (b) " Rev. Nathan m. (2) 1841, Martha Ann⁴ Abbott.
   (c) " Rev. Nathan m. (3) 1852, Mary L. McCleery.
338. " Nathan⁷ [of 292 (b)] m. 1834 Catharine Geery.
339.* " Nathan⁷ [of 254] m. 1850 Bathsheba Phebe⁶ Gardner [of 46 (b)].
340. " Nathan T⁷. [of 226] m. 1867 Lizzie Smith.

341. Shotwell, Peter[6] [of 260] m. 1803 Phebe[4] Vail [of 413].
342.(a) " Ralph[6] [of 264] m. (1) Elizabeth Marsh.
(b) " Ralph[6] [of 264] m. (2) Hosea Tingley.
343. " Randolph (b. 1774), of Newark, N. J., m. 1800 Mary H. Gage.
344.* " Richard[5] [of 190] m. 1782 Mary[2] Martin [of 126.]
345. " Robert[6] [of 323] m. 1812 Martha[5] Fitz Randolph [of James[6]].
346. " Samuel[4] [of 283] m. 1749 Ame ——
347. " Samuel[5] [of 176 (a)] m. ——
348. " Samuel[5] [of 177] m. 1788 Hannah Lundy.
349. " Samuel E[6]. [of 260] m. 1817 Sarah C. Rich.
350.(a) " Samuel[6] [of 192] m. (1) 1821 Phebe[6] Laing [of Jos[5]., John[4], Samuel[3], Wm.[2], John[1]].
(b) " Samuel[6] m. (2) Mercy[5] Pound [of 146].
351. " Samuel[6] [of 200] m. ———
352. " Rev. Samuel R[7]. [of 318] m. 1842 Patience M. Bloss.
253. " Samuel H[7]. [of 194] m. 1874 Jane Elizabeth Everet.
354. " Samuel P[7]. [of 195] m. 1851 Maria Watson.
355. " Samuel B[8]. [of 352] m. 1872 Sarah A. Lansing.
356. " Smith[6] [of 371] m. Mary Crawford.
357. " Stuart B[7]. [of 376] m. 1851 Nancy Gaston.
358. " Stuart B[8]. Jr. [of 357] m. 1892 Caroline R. McIlvaine.
359. " Theodore[7] [of 211] m. Amelia Smith.
860. " Theodore[7] [of 376] m. Sarah B. Lucas.
361. " Theodore F[7]. [of 213] m. 1867 Hattie A. Cambell.
362. " Theodore F[8]. [of 299] m. 1876 Amanda McKinstrey.
363. " Thomas L[6]. [of 260] m. 1806 Elizabeth Satterthwait.
364.(a) " Thomas[6] [of 192] m. (1) 1808 Tamer Lundy [of Jonathan].
(b) " Thomas[6] [of 192] m. (2) 1819 Hannah[4] Lundy [of Daniel[2], Sam'l[1]].
365. " Thomas[6] [of 366(b)] m. Ellen Brown.
366.(a) " Titus[5], Sr., [of 209] m. (1) 1781 Sarah Marsh.
(b) " Titus[5], Sr., [of 209] m. (2) 1787 Deborah[5]. Moore [of 129].
(c) " Titus[5], Sr., [of 209] m. (3) 1807 Deborah Howell.
367. " Titus[6] [of 366 (b)] m. 1814 Susan Garrett.
368. " Titus[7] III. [of 255] m. 1852 Mary Doan.
369. " Walter L[8]. [of 270] m. 1861 Harriet Decker.
370. " Walter G[8]. [of 357] m. 1884 Belle McIlvaine.
371. " William[5] [of 285 (b)] m. 1772 Elizabeth[8] Pound [of 147(b)].
372. " William[5], nicknamed "Governor," [of 311 (b)] m. 1787 Sarah Hopkins.
373. " William[5] [of 190] m. 1792 Elizabeth Moore.
374. " William[6] [of 268] m. Mary Ayers.
375. " William[6] [of 289] m. Fannie Triplett.
376. " William[6] [of 250] m. 1819 Rhoda Beebe.
377. " William[6] [of 373] m. ———
378. " William[6] [of 172 (a)] m. Anna Marsh.
379. " Willian J[7]. [of 194] m. 1862 Mary N. Melick.
380. " William P[7]. [of 235] m. Harriett Pearce.
381. " William[7] [of 295 (a)] m. 1846 Susannah Keeter.
382. " William B[7]. [of 345] m. 1847 Phebe Compton.

383. Shotwell, William[5] [of 356] m. Martha Elizabeth Taylor.
384. " William Harvey[7] [of 217] m. 1851 Sarah Louisa[7] Shotwell [of 246].
385. " William S[7]. [of 227] m.———
386. " William[6] [of 208] m. 1809 Jemima Liter.
387. " Dr. William Edward[8] [of 299] m. 1885 Harriet C. Pierson.
388. " William[9] [of 275] m. ———
389. " Wilson (of 313) m. ———
390.(a) " Zachariah[4] [of 192] m. (1) Elizabeth[7] Lundy [of Levi[2], Samuel[1]].
(b) " Zachariah[5] [of 192] m. (2) Edna[2] Lundy [of Daniel[2], Samuel[1]].
(c) " Zachariah[6] [of 192] m. (3) 1828 Elizabeth H. Lundy [of Samuel].
391. " Zachariah P[7]. [of 364 (a)] m. 1835 Margaret Zavitz [of Jacob].
392. Smith, Benjamin[2] [of Samuel[1]] m. 1712 Sarah[3] Shotwell [of 282].
393. " David, m. Mary[6] Shotwell [of 344].
394.* " John[1], of Prudence Island, m. Margaret ———.
395.* " John[2] [of 394] m. Phillis[2] Gereardy [of 65].
396.* " John[3] [of 395] m. 1708 Mercy[3] Westcott [of 437 (b)].
397. " Joseph[3] [of John[2], John[1], of Providence] m. 1680 Lydia[2] Gardiner [of 44 (b)].
398. " Timothy, Jr., m. 1803 Esther[6] Shotwell [of 250].
399. " William Fred, m. (1) 1882 Edna A.[7] Shotwell [of 222 (a)].
400. Spalding, Lyman A., m. 1824 Amy[6] Pound [of 153].
401.* Stafford, Thomas[1] m. Elizabeth ———
402.* Sweet, John[1], m. Mary ———
403.* Taylor, Thomas[1], m. Sarah[2] Hartshorne [of 86].
404.* Thomas George[1], m. ———
405.(a) Thorne, Abraham[3] [of 410 m. (1) 1717 Mary[3] Shotwell [of 208].
(b) " Abraham[3] [of 410] m. (2) 1739 Ann[2] Laing of 112].
406. Thorn, Abraham[4] [of 405 (a)] m. 1750 Susannah[3] Webster [of 435].
407. " Isaac[4], [of 405 (b)] m. 1766 Sarah[4] Webster [of 430].
408. Thorne Jacob[2], [of 410] m. 1723 Susannah[4] Shotwell [of 208].
409. " John[2] (b. 1643) [of 411] m. Mary ———
410.* " Joseph[2] [of 411] m. 1680 Mary[3] Bowne [of 8 (a)].
411.* " Wm[1]., of Flushing L. I. m. Sarah ———
412. Townsend, John m. 1768 Susannah[5] Shotwell [of 285 (b)].
413. Vail, Abraham[3] [of 419 (a)] m. 1766 (?) Margaret Fitz Randolph.
414. " Abraham[3] [of 422] m. 1708 Margaret Fitz Randolph.
415. " Benjamin[3] [of 419(a)], m. Margaret Clarkson.
416. " Daniel[4] [of 419 (a)] m. 1774 Mary ———,
417. " David[4] [of 419 (a)] m. 1766 Phebe Jackson.
418. " Isaac[4] [of 419 (a) m. 1762 ———
419.(a) " John[2], Jr. [of 421 (a)] m. (1) 1731 Margaret[3] Laing [of 112].
(b) " John[2], Jr. [of 421 (a)] m. (2) 1751 Mary[3] Laing [of 112].
420. " John[3] [of 419 (a)] m. 1760 Catherine Fitz-Randolph [of Ed., Jr.].
421.(a) " Samuel[1], 1678-1733, m. (1) Abigail ———.
(b) " Samuel[1], 1678-1733, m. (2) Sarah ———.
422. " Stephen[2] [of 421 (a)] m. 1733-4 Esther[3] Smith [of 392].
423.(a) " Stephen[3] [of 422] m. (2) 1763 Sarah Smith [of Shobel].
(b) " Stephen[3] [of 422], m (3) 1771 ———
424. Vandolah, Peter, m. 1815 Nancy[6] Shotwell [of 250].

425.* Watson, Jeffrey² [of 427] m. 1732 Bathsheba⁴ Smith [of 306].
426.*   " John¹, m. (1) Dorcas² Gardner [of 44(a)].
427.*   " John² [of 426] m. Hannah ——
428. Webster, Hugh³ Sr. [of 435] m. 1753 Sarah Marsh.
429.   " Hugh⁴ Jr. [of 430] m. 1781 Sarah⁵ Moore [of 135].
430.*   " John³ [of 435] m. 1744 Anna² Taylor [of 403].
431.   " Joseph² [of 434] m. 1733 Elizabeth⁴ Shotwell [of 283].
432.   " Joseph⁴ [of 428] m. 1802 Amy⁵ King [of 109].
433.   " Taylor⁴ [of 430] m. 1769 Hannah Jackson.

434.* Webster, William¹, of Woodbridge m. Mary ——
435.*   " William² [of 434] m. 1717 Susannah³ Cowperthwait [of 23].
436.* Westcott, Stukeley¹, of Providence, R. I., m. ——
437.(a)*   " Amos² [of 436] m. (1) 1667 Sarah² Stafford [of 401].
(b)   " Amos², m. (2) 1670 Deborah² Stafford [of 401].
438.* Whipple, John¹, m. 1639 ± Sarah ——
439.(a)*   " John² [of 438] m. (1) 1663 Mary² Olney [of 137].
(b)   " John³, m. (2) 1678 Rebecca Scott.
440. Wintermute, Charles, m. 1809 Susanna⁶ Shotwell [of 250].
441. Worth, Benjamin, m. 1843 Elizabeth⁶ Gardner [of 46 (a)].

INDEX TO MOTHERS' MAIDEN NAMES
MENTIONED IN THE FOREGOING TABLE.

HON. JOHN E. POUND,

Lockport, Niagara Co., N. Y.,

SON OF ALEXANDER AND ALMINA (WHIPPLE) POUND,

Of Lockport, N. Y., grandson of John[5] and Alice Smith[4] Pound, of Lockport, N. Y.,
great-grandson of Samuel[4] and Catharine (Webster) Pound, of Piscataway, N. J.,
of Elijah[3], John[2], John[1], all of Middlesex Co., N. J.

ERRATA AND ADDENDA.

NOTE.—It is suggested that each owner of a copy of this work should enter in the following blanks accurate Genealogical and Biographical Records of himself and his own direct ancestors, in both paternal and maternal lineages, with the family and descendants of each (unless elsewhere presented herein), and should register any errors or omissions discovered in the body of this book, and report all such additions and corrections to the author, A. M. SHOTWELL, of Concord, Mich., for use in a proposed supplement or revised edition.

I.
ONE LINEAGE IN BRIEF.

1. A descendant's name in full, and date of birth:

--; --

MARRIED—(Date)...................................... to..

2. Name of father (of person first named) and date of birth:

--; --

MARRIED—(Date)..................................... to..

3. Grandfather's name, and date of birth:

--; --

MARRIED—(Date)..................................... to..

4. Great-grandfather's name, and date of birth:

--; --

MARRIED—(Date)..................................... to..

5. His father's name, and date of birth:

--; --

MARRIED—(Date)..................................... to..

6. His father's name, and date of birth:

--; --

MARRIED—(Date)..................................... to..

7. His father's name, and date of birth:

--; --

MARRIED—(Date)..................................... to..

Family of (*father's name*)...

Who was born in...

County of........................., *State of*........................., *on the*.........*day of*........................., *A. D.*........., *and d*

of........................., *on the*.................*day of*........................., *A. D.*........................., *in*...

aged........................*years*, ...*months, and*.................*days.   He was interred in*..

His occupation was that of a..*and he resided in*...

His father's name and residence were..

His mother's name before marriage was..

He was married the.................*time, the*.................*day of*........................., *A. D.*........., *to*...

....*described on the opposite page, by whom he had*.................*children, whose nam*

and history are recorded on the following blanks.

Given Name.	Date of Birth.	Place of Birth.	Place of Death.	Date of Dea

other's name before marriage ..

s born in.................................. ...

unty of......................, State of................. ...., on the...........day of.... ...., A. D.. ...; and died

.... the............day of......................., A. D.............in..

ed.............years,.............months,.............and days. She was interred in.......................................

er father's name was..Her mother's name was..

he was married the.............time, in..........................., on the...........day of...................A. D...........

y.....................................to.......................................described on the opposite page.

he resided before marriage, in.. By him she had.................children,

ho are recorded below.

Age at Death			Place of Interment.	If Married, to Whom.	Date of Marriage.			Occupation, Remarks and References.
rs.	Months.	Days.			Year.	Month.	Day.	

1. *Husband's full name, residence and, if living, his present postoffice address*..................................

....

2. *Date of birth and birthplace*...

3. *Place, date, and cause of death, and burial place if elsewhere*...

....

4. *Graduation, removals, occupations, political preference, offices held, church relations, characteris*

her remarks ....

....

....

5. *His father's full name and residence, and mother's full maiden name*..

....

6. *Full names and residences of both paternal and maternal grandparents, with earlier lineage of eit*

lown ....

....

....

7. *Manner, place and date of his (first, second or only) marriage*...

....

8. *Wife's full name, with name of former husband, if a widow*...

....

9. *Wife's birth-date and place of birth*..

10. *Place, date and cause of her death, etc*...

....

11. *Her parent's names and residence*...

....

12. *Her paternal and maternal grandparents, with the earlier lineage of either, if known*.....................

....

....

13. *Remarks concerning this family, the names of the children in order of birth (each to be afterwards ske*

above); later marriage of husband or wife, etc...

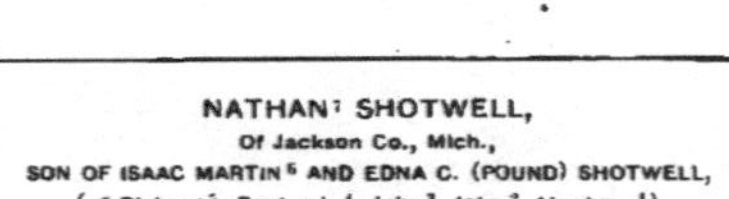

NATHAN[7] SHOTWELL,

Of Jackson Co., Mich.,

SON OF ISAAC MARTIN[6] AND EDNA C. (POUND) SHOTWELL,

(of Richard[5] Benjamin[4], John[3] John[2], Abraham[1]).

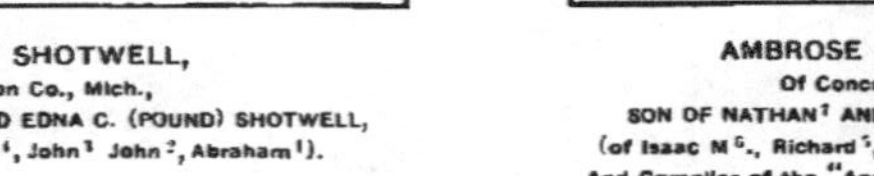

AMBROSE MILTON[8] SHOTWELL.

Of Concord, Jackson Co., Mich.

SON OF NATHAN[7] AND PHEBE B. (GARDNER) SHOTWELL,

(of Isaac M[6]., Richard[5], Benjamin[4], John[3], John[2], Abraham[1]),

And Compiler of the "Annals of our Colonial Ancestors and their Descendants."

OUR COLONIAL ANCESTORS

AND THEIR DESCENDANTS.

PART II.

THE SHOTWELL FAMILY

IN AMERICA.

NOTE.—After a preliminary synopsis of six generations of the family, the detailed accounts of the several households are presented, and, for convenience of reference, are arranged alphabetically by fathers' given names. And the reader who may wish to peruse the history in a more nearly chronological sequence should begin with the sketch of Abraham[1] Shotwell and family, seek next the children of John[2] and Daniel[2], then take up the members of the fourth, fifth, and sixth generations in the order indicated in the following synopsis, and finally read the sketches of the representatives of the seventh, eighth and ninth generations in alphabetical succession. The generation to which each parent belongs (if known) being denoted by an index figure following his or her name, and the lineage as far as traced being also usually given [within brackets].

An alphabetic list of the heads of families, with reference numbers denoting their relationship to one another, will, it is hoped, be found a convenient appendix, especially serviceable in tracing out the various branches of one's ancestry elsewhere presented in these pages.

In dates drawn from Quaker sources, the months of the year are commonly designated numerically; and in those prior to 1752 the months are usually reckoned from March, rather than from January, as the old-style year began on March 25th, instead of January 1st. The original forms of ancient dates have been retained as far as practicable.

I.

SYNOPSIS OF SIX GENERATIONS

OF THE MALE BRANCHES

OF THE SHOTWELL FAMILY.

I. FIRST THREE GENERATIONS.

1. Abraham[1] Shotwell, founder of the family in America, was in Elizabeth Town, N. J., as early as 1665, and in New York as late as 1679. He had certainly a son (2.) John[2], who dwelt chiefly on Staten Island, whence a few years before his death he removed to Woodbridge, Middlesex Co., N. J., and there died in 1719,—ancestor of the Shotwells of Rahway and Plainfield, N. J. (3.) Daniel[2], probably son (possibly nephew or younger brother) of the first Abraham, dwelt on Staten Island, and was the progenitor of the Richmond County (N. Y.) branch of the family.

2. John[2] Sr., married 1679 Elizabeth Burton, and had: (4.) John[3], Jr., (5.) Elizabeth, (6.) Sarah, (7.) Abraham[3].

3. Daniel[2], of Staten Island, m. Elizabeth —— and is believed to have had: (8.) Ann, (9.) Joseph[3], (10.) Mary, (11.) John[3], (12.) Susannah, (13.) Margaret, (14.) Elizabeth, (15.) Daniel, (16.) Martha.

NOTE.—For sons whose names are followed by index figures, children are registered in the proper places in this record.

FOURTH GENERATION.

II. Grandchildren of (2.) John[2], Sr.

4. John[3], Jr., of Shotwell's Landing, m. 1709 Mary Thorne, Jr., and had: (17.) Joseph[4], (18.) John[4], (19.) Elizabeth, (20.) Mary, (21.) Abraham[4], (22.) Jacob[4], (23.) Samuel[4], (24.) Benjamin[4].

7. Abraham[3] Shotwell [of John[2], Abraham[1]], m. Elizabeth Cowperthwaite, and had: (25.) Elizabeth, (26.) Sarah, (27.) Hannah, (28.) John[4], (29.) Abraham, (30.) Deborah.

For children of John[2] Shotwell's daughters, see synopsis following the account of his family in the proper alphabetic place.

III. Grandchildren of (3.) Daniel[2], of Staten Island.

NOTE.—For children of his daughters, see synopsis following the account of his family in the proper place hereafter.

9. Joseph[3], m. Mary Manning, and had: (33.) Joseph[4], III, (34.) Nicholas, (35.) Elizabeth, (36.) Mary, (37.) Daniel[4], (38.) Abraham[4], (39.) Isaac, (40.) Jacob[4], (41.) Elizabeth.
11. John[3], m. Lydia ———, and had: (43.) John, (44.) Benjamin[4], (45.) Joseph.

FIFTH GENERATION.

(a.) Line of (2.) John[2]., Sr.

IV. Grandchildren of (4.) John[3], Jr., of Shotwell's Landing.

17. Joseph[4], m. Sarah Cock, and had: (46.) John[5], (47.) Mary, (48.) Joseph[5], (49.) Sarah, (50.) Henry[5], (51.) James, (52.) Thomas, (53.) William[5], called "The Governor."
18. John[4], of Plainfield, m. (1) Elizabeth[3] Smith, and had: (54.) Elizabeth, (55.) John Smith[5].
18. John[4], m. (2) Grace[3] Webster, and had: (56.) Susannah, (57.) Jacob[5], (58.) William[5], (59.) Isaiah[5], (60.) James[5], (61) Sarah, (62.) Mary, (63.) Elizabeth, (64.) Martha, (65.) Hugh[5].
21. Abraham[4], m. (1) Mary Potts, and had: (66.) Phebe, (67.) Elizabeth, (68.) Naomi, (69.) Mary, (70.) Hester, (71.) Jeremiah[5], (72.) Samuel.
21. Abraham[4], m. (2) Lydia Hallett, and had: (73.) Isaac[5], (74.) Abraham, (75.) Ann, (76.) Aaron[5], (77.) John[5].
22. Jacob[4], m. (1) Eleanor Haydock, and had: (78.) Hannah, (79.) Eden[5].
22. Jacob[4], m. (2) Catharine Tilton, and had: (80.) Nathan[5].
23. Samuel[4], m. Ame ———, and had: (81.) Caleb[5], (82.) Thomas, (83.) Sarah, (84.) Mary, (85.) David[5], (86.) Elizabeth.
24. Benjamin[4], of Shotwell's Landing, m. 1746 Ame Hallett, and had: (87.) Sarah, (88.) Amy, (89.) Mary, (90.) Richard[5], (91.) Benjamin[5], (92.) Elizabeth—wife of Joseph Lundy and mother of Benjamin Lundy, the philanthropist, (93.) Thomas, (94.) William[5], (95.) Lydia.

V. Grandchildren of (7.) Abraham[3] Shotwell.

28. John[4], m. Anna ———, and had: (96.) John[5], (97.) Jasper.

(b.) Line of (3.) Daniel[2], of Staten Island.

VI. Grandchildren of (9.) Joseph[3] and Mary (Manning) Shotwell.

33. Joseph[4] III, of Woodbridge, m. Elizabeth Jackson, and had: (98.) Margaret, (99.) Phebe, (100.) Joseph[5].
37. Daniel[4], m. Deborah[4] Shotwell [of (30.) Abraham[3], John[2], Abraham[1]], and had: (102.) Hannah, (103.) Titus[5], Sr., (104.) Elizabeth, (105.) John, (106.) Mary, (107.) Daniel[5], (108.) Sarah.
38. Abraham[4], m. Mary Jackson, and had: (109.) Samuel[5], (110) Mary.
40. Jacob[4], m. ——— ———, and had: (111.) Isaac[5].

VII. Grandchildren of (11.) John[3].

44. Benjamin[4], m. Elizabeth Manning, and had: [113(a)] Daniel, (b) Charity, (c) Manning[5], (d) Mary, (e) Elizabeth, (f) John, (g) Joseph, (h) Lydia, (i) Benjamin, (j) David.

SIXTH GENERATION.

(a.) Line of (2.) John[2], Sr.

VIII. Grandchildren of (17.) Joseph[4].

46. John[5], m. Margaret Haydock, and had: (114.) Jane, (115.) Sarah, (116.) Margaret, (117.) Phebe, (118.) Joseph[6], (119.) Mary, (120.) Elizabeth, (121.) Hannah, (122.) Rebecca, (123.) Eleanor.
50. Henry[5], m. Sarah Dobson, and had: (124.) Joseph D[6]., (125.) Sarah, (126.) Margaret, (127.) Ann, (128.) Hannah M., (129.) Thomas, (130.) Elizabeth, (131.) Mary, (132.) Mary (again), (133.) Deborah.
53. William[5] (called "The Governor"), m. Sarah ———, and had: (134.) Sarah, (135.) Hannah, (136.) William, (137.) Mary, (138.) Elizabeth, (139.) Phebe.

IX. Grandchildren of (18.) John[4], of Plainfield.

55. John Smith[5] Shotwell, m. (1) Mary[3] Webster, and had: (140.) Samuel, (141.) William.
55. John S[5]., m. (2) (49.) Phebe[5] Shotwell [of Joseph[4], Joseph[3], Daniel[2], Abraham[1]], and had: (142.) Joseph Smith[6] Shotwell, (143.) Nathan, (144.) Mary.
57. Jacob[5], m. Bathsheba[4] Pound, and had: (145.) Mary, (146.) Sarah, (147.) Ralph[6], (148.) Daniel[6] ("on the hill"), (149.) John, (150.) Elijah[6].

58. William[5] (latterly of Upper Canada), m. Elizabeth[4] Pound, and had: (151.) Rachel, (152.) Catharine, (153.) Anna, (154.) Phebe, (155.) Elizabeth, (156.) Elijah[6], (157.) John[6], (158.) Smith[6], (159.) Sarah, (160.) Miriam or Mariam, (161.) William.

59. Isaiah[5], m. Constant Lippencott, and had: (162.) Mary, (163.) Jediah, (164.) Peter[6], (165.) Abel[6], (166.) Thomas L[6]., (167.) William, (168.) Grace, (169.) Joseph L[6]., (170.) Edmund[6], (171.) Samuel E[6]., (172.) Hugh.

60. James[5], m. Elsie (Smalley) Runyan, and had: (173.) William[6], (174.) Nancy, (175.) Clarissa, (176.) Clarkson[6], (177.) Charles, (178.) Jonathan[6].

65. Hugh[5], m. Rosetta Arrison, and had: (179.) John[6], (180.) Esther, (181.) Susanna, (182.) Charlotte, (183.) Nancy, (184.) William[6], (185.) Joseph[6], (186.) Arrison[6].

X. Grandchildren of (21.) Abraham[4].

71. Jeremiah[5], m. Mary ——, and had: (187.) George.

72. Samuel[5], m. —— ——, and had: (188.) Abigail.

73. Isaac[5], m. Catharine Moore, and had: (189.) Enoch, (190.) Lydia, (191.) Katy.

76. Aaron[5], m. (1) —— Martin, and had: (192.) Aaron, Jr., (193.) William[6], (194.) Abraham[6], (195.) George H[6].

76. Aaron[5], m. (2) —— Freeman, and had: (196.) Isaac Prall.

77. John[5], m. —— Freeman, and had: (197.) Abraham F.[6], (198.) —— (wife of B. M. Price), (199.) Lydia.

XI. Grandchildren of (22.) Jacob[4].

79. Eden[5], m. Mary Haydock, and had: (200.) Haydock, (201.) Robert.

80. Nathan[5], m. Sarah Fitz Randolph, and had: (202.) Catharine Ann, (203.) Louisa (wife of 242), (204.) Alexander[6], (205.) Jacob, (206.) Susan R., (207.) Ellen T., (208.) Eden[6], (209.) Sarah Elizabeth.

XII. Grandchildren of (23.) Samuel[4].

81. Caleb[5], m. Phebe (Hinckston) Gliddon, and had: (210.) David[6], (211.) Samuel[6], (212.) Amy, (213.) Robert, (214.) Joseph[6], (215.) Polly, (216.) Sarah, (217.) Phebe.

85. David[5], m. Elizabeth Fitz Randolph, and had: (218.) Charlotte, (219.) Samuel Hartshorn, (220.) Catharine.

XIII. Grandchildren of (24.) Benjamin[4], of Shotwell's Landing.

90. Richard[5], m. 1782 Mary Martin, and had: (221.) Elizabeth, (222.) Amy, (223.) Isaac Martin[6] Shotwell, (224.) Benjamin, (225.) Mary, (226.) Elizabeth (again), (227.) Benjamin[6] (again), (228.) Abbe, (229.) Lydia, (230.) Sarah.

91. Benjamin[5], m. Bathsheba[5] Pound, and had: (231.) Elizabeth, (232.) Thomas[6], (233.) Zachariah[6], (234.) Amy, (235.) Mercy, (236.) Benjamin[6], Jr., (237.) Samuel[6], (238.) Lydia, 94. William[5], m. Elizabeth Moore, and had: (239.) Benjamin[6], (240.) Elizabeth L., (241.) William[6], Jr., (242.) Harvey[6] (see 203), (243.) David[6].

XIV. Grandchildren of (28.) John[4].

96. John[5], m. Abigail Shipman, and had: 243 (a) Mary, (b) Charlotte, (c) Lydia, (d) John[6], (e) William[6], (f) Nathan[6], (g) Anna, (h) Phebe, (i) Jabez[6], (j) Abigail, (k) Priscilla.

(b) Line of (23.) Daniel[2] of Staten Island.

XV. Grandchildren of (33.) Joseph[4].

100. Joseph[5], of Perrytown, m. Sarah Wilson, and had: (244.) John[6], (245.) Thomas, (246.) Wilson[6], (247.) Joseph, (248.) Elizabeth, (249.) Rebecca, (250.) Mary, (251.) Isaac[6], (252.) (a) Catharine, (b) Margaret, (c), Sarah, (d) Alice.

XVI. Grandchildren of (37.) Daniel[4] and (30.) Deborah[4].

103. Titus[5], m. (1) Sarah Marsh, and had: (253.) Hope, (254.) Daniel.

103. Titus[5], m. (2) Deborah[5] Moore, and had: (255.) Edward[6], (256.) Titus[6], (257.) Miriam, (258.) Joseph, (259.) Thomas[6], (260.) Isaac[6], 103. Titus[5], m. (3) Deborah Howell, and had: (261.) Rebecca, (262.) Mahlon, (263.) Nathan, (264.) Sarah.

107. Daniel[5], m. Keziah Terrill, and had: (265.) John[6], (266.) Joseph[6], (267.) Daniel[6], Jr., (268.) Sarah, (269.) Susan, (270.) William.

XVII. Grandchildren of (38.) Abraham[4].

109. Samuel[5], m. Hannah Lundy, and had: (271.) Abraham V[6]., (272.) Joseph, (273.) James, (274.) Mary, (275.) Sarah.

XVIII. Grandchildren of (40.) Jacob[4].

111. Isaac[5], m. (73.) Hannah[5] Shotwell, and had: (276.) Eden, (277.) Joseph, (278.) Elizabeth, (279.) Catharine.

XIX. Grandchildren of (44.) Benjamin[4].

113(c). Manning[5], m. Mary Clarkson, and had: (280.) Robert[6], (281.) Daniel C[6]. (Hatter), (282.) Elizabeth, (283.) Lavinia, (284.) Rachel, (285.) Clarkson.

Note.—For the members of the seventh generation, see the families of three whose names are indexed in the foregoing outline of the sixth generation; namely, of Nos. 118, 124, 142, 147, 148, 150, 156, 157, 158, 163, 164, 165, 166, 169, 170, 171, 173, 176, 178, 179, 184, 185, 186, 187, 193, 194, 195, 197, 204, 208, 210, 211, 214, 223, 227, 232, 233, 236, 237, 240, 241, 242, 243, 244, 246, 251, 255, 256, 259, 260, 265, 266, 267, 271, 280, 282, 283, 287, and 289. These, with the other households of the male branches of the Shotwell family, will be found in alphabetic succession in the following pages.

II.

ANNALS OF SHOTWELL HOUSEHOLDS

ALPHABETICALLY ARRANGED BY FATHERS' GIVEN NAMES.

NOTE.—The numbers prefixed to certain heads of Families, correspond to those in the foregoing synopsis. The detailed records of the descendants of Shotwell daughters are, for the most part, reserved for a separate volume or series, as a little reflection will show that they must be far more numerous than the members of the male branches of the family. In the third or fourth generation, of almost any family, fully one-half of the members will be found to have lost the ancestral patronymic; and to this proportion each succeeding generation will add about fifty per cent of the remaining representatives. Hence those now bearing the Shotwell name are less than one-sixteenth of the living decendants of Abraham[1] Shotwell of Elizabethtown.

In the following pages, with few exceptions, the accounts of the children of the several particular families are introduced by concise synopses of the parents' records, more fully presented in sketching the members of the grandparents' households in their proper order elsewhere in this volume.

---

76. AARON[5] SHOTWELL, 1774±—1852, of Rahway, Essex Co., N. J., son of Abraham[4] and Lydia (Hallet) Shotwell of Essex Co., N. J., and descendant of John[3], John[2], Abraham[1], m. (1) ... *Martin*, and had:

1. *Aaron, Jr.*, m. ... Freeman, sister to his father's second wife and to the wife of his uncle John Shotwell. They left no heirs.

2. *William*[6]; dwelt Rahway, N. J., m. Ann Marsh.

3. *Abraham*[6], dwelt in Essex Co., N. J., near Rahway, m. ..... Moore, dau. of Thomas Moore of Woodbridge, N. J.

4. *George II*[6], left the farm of his father, near Rahway, when a boy, went to Cincinnati, O., where, during the latter part of his life, he was in the commission and real estate business; lived on George St., between Smith and John Sts., Cincinnati, O., and there d. 14 Jan. 1869; was fatally injured by the kick of one of his carriage horses 3 Jan. 1869; m. Mary E. A. Tudor, who spends a part of each year with children at Englewood, Chicago, Ill., and part with dau. Cordelia, Mrs. J. C. Campbell of 234 Lawrence St., Cincinnati, O.

76. AARON[5] SHOTWELL, 1774 ± — 1852, [of Abraham[4], John[3], Jno[2]., Abr[1].], m. (2) .... *Freeman*, and had:

5. *Isaac Prall*, dw. with his nephew, Robert Alex. Shotwell, near Rahway, unm.

6. *Sarah*, m. .... Rindle.

165. ABEL[6] SHOTWELL, 1779—1840, of Rahway, N. J., s. of Isaiah[5] and Constant (Lippincott) Shotwell of Plainfield, N. J. [of John[4],

John[3], John[2], Abr[1].], m. 1810, *Elizabeth*[4] *Vail*, 1782–1866, dau. of Abraham[3] and Margaret (Fitz Randolph) Vail [of John[2], Samuel[1]], and had:

1. *Margaret Randolph*, b. 15 of 10 m., 1812, Bridgetown, Rahway, Middlesex Co., N. J., dw. N. Plainfield, Somerset Co., N. J.; a wd., s. p., an Elder in Rahway and Plainfield M. M. of (Hicksite) Friends; clerk of R. and P. M. M. 15 of 5 mo., 1856, and for several years thereafter; m. at Greenbrook, Warren Tp., Somerset Co., N. J., 24 of 4 mo., 1873, Thomas Laws, b. in Delaware 26 of 8 mo., 1798, d. N. Plainfield, N. J., 12 of 6 mo., 1882, s. of Ludawick and Anna Laws.

2. *Abel Vail*, b. 18 of 10 mo., 1814, at Milton, Woodbride Tp. (now Rahway), N. J., dwelt Rahway, N. J., N. side of Elm Ave., W. of Bryant St., and there died 17 Dec., 1893, in his 80th year, s. p. He received a common school education. In 1834 he started life as a merchant, amassed a fortune and retired from active business in 1863. He afterward, however, engaged in banking and insurance business. In 1868 he assumed charge of the Rahway Fire Insurance Company, acting as its secretary for more than 20 years. His office was at the northeast corner of Milton Ave. and Main St. He was a director of the Rahway bank 1857–81, and when the National Bank of Rahway was established in 1865 he was elected Secretary to the Board of Directors, which position he held until poor health compelled him to resign. He was the first official of Rahway when the town was first incorporated, in 1858. He was a member of the Hicksite branch of the Society of Friends and was for many years clerk of Rahway and Plainfield Monthly Meeting. He was an authority on matters pertaining to the

early history of New Jersey, possessed many valuable papers in relation thereto, and to him and to the records of the Society of Friends in his keeping, extending back to the year 1686, we are indebted for very much of the information presented in these pages. In the autumn of 1885 he was stricken down by something between vertigo and paralysis, perhaps partaking of both, which disabled him at times from using or moving his left hand and foot: but, submitting to heroic treatment, blood letting and the galvanic battery, he apparently recovered his normal health, but in 1891 was again stricken with paralysis. Thos. L. King of Topeka, Kan., left Rahway in 1827; yet on revisiting the place sixty years later (June, 1887), he was recognized by Abel V. as soon as he entered the latter's office and spoke. A. V. Shotwell m. in Hamilton, O., 2 Nov., 1859, his second cousin, Rosetta S. Ebert, b. 18 Feb., 1830, in Cadiz, O., dau. of Jacob and Nancy[6] (Shotwell) Ebert of Harrison Co., O., (of Hugh[5], John[4], John[3], John[2], Abr[1].).

3. *Elizabeth Smith Shotwell*, b. 19 of 3 mo., 1818, Rahway, N. J., and there d. 27 of 8 mo., 1846, unm.

4. *Charles Cox*, b. 25 of 3 mo., 1824; d. Rahway, N. J., 7 of 8 mo., 1861, unm., buried in Hazelwood Cemetery near Rahway.

1. ABRAHAM[1] SHOTWELL, the first of the name of whom we have any definite account, was one of the earliest settlers, 1665, of Elizabeth Town, Essex Co., N. J., which was the seat of government for the province of East Jersey, originally called Nova Cesaria. Dr. Hatfield, in his History of Elizabeth, N. J. (p. 56), states that Abraham Shotwell was fourth in the list of the sixty-five persons in that town who on 19 Feb., 1665, took the oath of allegiance to King Charles II of Eng. and to the Lords Proprietors of the province. He was the owner of about five acres of valuable land in the heart of the town.

It is said that the name was originally Shadwell, and there is a vague tradition that, once upon a time, one of our English ancestors bearing this older form of the name was, with the King and his guard, engaged in an archery contest and Shadwell hitting the mark with greater precision than the rest, the King exclaimed, "Well done! Shot well!" and that thenceforth his associates, noting the resemblance of the latter part of the Royal expression to his name, used the modified appellation, Shot-well. In the early Friends' records of Flushing, L. I., the name is commonly written Chatwell.

Abraham Shotwell was probably one of the many Englishmen who fled from Great Britain after the death of Cromwell and the restoration of Charles II to the throne. In the contentions between the people of the town of Elizabeth and the proprietors, he was bold and outspoken in his opposition to the tyranical and oppressive exactions enforced by the Governor, Captain Philip Carterett, which course rendered him obnoxious to that officer. There is a tradition in the family that meeting the Governor on the bridge over the creek that passes through the town, they had a personal altercation and rencounter which resulted in Shotwell's pitching the Governor into the water. He became the victim of the Governor's wrath; certain it is that his house and grounds were confiscated and he himself forced into exile. His valuable property was sold at auction 25 April, 1675, and a few days afterward came into the possession of Gov. Carterett for the small sum of £14. He retired to the adjacent colony of New York and did not again reside permanently in New Jersey. He obtained a grant of land in New York, located, it is believed, not far from the present site of the Brooklyn bridge.

The following Patent (dated 29 Sept., 1677, recorded in Secretary of State's office at Albany, 4 Patents, p. 12,) was surveyed originally for George Elphinstone, who transferred his right to receive the patent to Abraham Shotwell:

"SIR EDMUND ANDROS, Governor, &c.,

"*To Abraham Shotwell:*

"WHEREAS, There is a certain piece of Land upon this Island, Manhattans, in ye South-east side thereof, ye which by virtue of my warrant hath been layed out for Abraham Shotwell, beginning at a certain mark't tree and running in breadth North-east from ye land of John Basset to ye land of Jacob Young, fifty-one rodd including ye run of water formerly called ye Saw Mill Creek, where now a Water Mill is set, together with ye pond, running into ye woods One hundred and twenty rodd being bounded to ye South-east [S. W.?] by ye land of John Bassett and to ye North-east by ye land of Jacob Young, and contains in all thirty eight acres and a quarter as by ye return of ye Surveyor may and doth appear. Conveys said premises to the patentee reserving a quitt rent of half a bushel of good winter wheat."

Riker, in his History of Harlem, p. 383, says, "Elphinstone had erected a leather mill and other buildings upon his tract, with the assistance of a copartner, Abraham Shotwell, late of New Jersey, to whom (probably in view of what follows) the patent was made out. On Oct. 30, 1677, Elphinstine sold all his interest in the farm houses and mill to Shotwell, who in payment gave his obligation in the form of a note for £52 10s."

Abraham Shotwell, "with consent of his son John," conveyed the farm and improvements to John Robinson by deed dated 6 Nov., 1679, and recorded in Secretary of State's office at Albany, 5 deeds, p. 208. He probably died in New York about the year 1680. The name of his wife has not been ascertained.

1. ABRAHAM[1] SHOTWELL, of Elizabethtown, N. J., 1665-75, and New York, 1677-9, married and had:

1. *John Shotwell*, b. probably in Eng., about 1650, dw. on Staten Island, but removed to Woodbridge, N. J., a few years before his

decease which occurred there 22 of 7 mo., 1719, and he was buried in the Friends' ground at Woodbridge. To him, his father's confisticated real estate in Elizabethtown, N. J., was, after Gov. P. Carterett's removal and death, restored, 12 May, 1683, as will appear from the following extracts from the " Record of the Governor and Council in East Jersie, *Anno Dom.* 1682–1703," in Smith's Documentary History of New Jersey, originally published before the revolutionary war, and reprinted in fac simile in 1877, by order of the Legislature.

At a meeting of Council held the 10th day of May, *Anno Dom.*, 1683,—" The peti'on of John Shotwell being here read and upon reading thereof it being alldged that the Lands for which he Desires a Survey and patent is now or late in the possession of Elizabeth Carterett wid., the Relict and Executrix of the late Governor, Capt. Philip Carterett, Deceased, Its agreed that the ffurther consideration thereof be Defered till the next Seventh Day Morning being the 12th instant at 8 of the clock in the fforenoon and that notice then be given to the Widow Carterett that she may then appear and if she has aught to allege ag'st substance of the pet'on, she may then be heard."

Eliz. Town May 12th, 1683.—" The matter of John Shotwell's peti'on came here into Debate and the Widow Carterett being also here p'sent and in writing gave in two papers as her Answer to the substance of the said pet'on, and it being asked the said Widow Carterett if she Desired any tyme to offer or object any thing ag'st the substance of the peti'on She said She had no ffurther answer than what she gave in writing. And it appearing that Abraham Shotwell was the possessor, occupant, clearer and improver of the Land mentioned in the petition. And that John Shotwell is the said Abraham Shotwell's Sonne and heire, Its therefore agreed and ordered that the Deputy Governor issue out a Warr't (to the) Surveyor generall and his Deputy to Survey the same Lands and make returns Thereof in order that the said Shotwell may have a pattent thereof according to the concessions."

In what manner John Shotwell disposed of his property after it was restored to him, has not been ascertained; but the next authentic record of him is found in the minutes of Woodbridge Monthly Meeting of Friends, as he was the first of the name who were members of the Religious Society of Friends called Quakers. In the records of that Monthly Meeting, the name of Shotwell first occurrs among the witnesses to a certificate dated 18th of 1st mo. (March), 1707–8, given to Benjamin Griffith of Amboy to clear his reputation for honesty on the island of Barbadoes from an accusation by Thomas Edwards, a hat maker formerly of Amboy, for which allegation the said Edwards was disowned by the Society 18 of 1 mo., 1707–8. The certifi-

cate is recorded after the minutes of 3 mo. 20th, 1708; and the following are the names of the witnesses thereto: John Kinsy, David Commer, Daniel Shotwell, John Shotwell, Nathaniel ffitz Randolph, Edward ffitz Randolph, Samuel ffitz Randolph, John Laing, William Robinson, John Vail.

The following are also from the book of minutes:

" Att a Monthly Meeting held at Nathaniel fitz Randolph's ye 16th of 12th month (Feb.) 1709–10 .... Our friend John Shotwell hath requested this Meeting to have a Meeting Settled at his house once every quarter, to which this Meeting Consented & it is to begin ye first day in ye next first Month and so continue quarterly."

" Att our Monthly Meeting held att Nath'l fitz Randolphs In Woodbridge ye 21st of 3rd mo., 1713 .... The Meeting y't was appointed att John Shotwell's att Statton Island is found Inconvenient to be on ye day it was appointed because it happened to Come ye same day w'th ye quarterly meeting att New York. therefore this meeting orders itt to be altered to ye Second first day in ye 4th 7th 10th & 1st mo. till further orders."

" Att our Monthly Meeting held att Nathaniel fitz Randolph the 19th of ye 8th mo., 1710 .... John Shotwell, William Sutton and John Laing iss apointed or any two of them to take Care in ye affairs of truth and to deal with disorderly persons in order to reclaim them if possible and bring them that will not hear them before ye meeting that they may be dealt further with and so give an account of their proceedings to this meeting if required."

His will presents several items of interest. It is as follows:

" In the Name of God Amen the seventeenth day of the fifth Month commonly called July in the year of our Lord God One thousand Seven Hundred and Nineteen and in the fifth year of His Magestie King Georg's Reigne over Great Brittain &c. John Shotwell of the Town of Woodbridge In ye County of Middlesex and Providence of New Jersey yeomen. Being not very well In Bodly health But of Sound and Perfect Mind & Memory (thanks be to God therefore) Do Make this My Last Will and Testament In manner and form following that is to say first of all I bequeath My Soul & Spirit into the hands of God My Heavenly Father by whom of his Mercy and only Grace I trust to be Saved & received into Eternal Rest, through the death of My Saviour and Redeemer Jesus Christ & only hope of My Salvation. My Body to be buried in the Earth with such charges as to my Executors named shall seem meet, hoping in ye joyfull Resurection of ye just that God will Raise it up A Glorious Body. And as touching ye distribition of My Worldly Estate I dispose of the same as followeth.

"My Will is and I do hereby Nominate ordain & Appoint My trusty & well beloved John Kinsey and My Son Inlaw John Laing to be My Executors or in case of death the Survivor of them to execute this My Will according to my true intent and meening in ye same Giving them full Power & Authority to sell and dispose of All and Singular My Real & Personal Estate to the Buyer or Buyers thereof, and to make them sufficient Title or Titles by Deed or Deeds of Conveyance to them their Heirs and assigns for each and My Will is that All such Deed or Deeds signed & sealed by my said Executors or ye Survivor of them shall be Deemed Esteemed and Judged to be As firm in ye law to All Intents & purposes as If I My self did sign & Seal & deliver the same in my Lifetime & to stand firm & Remain Against My Heirs or any other claiming by force or under them.

"I Will that all Such Debts as I owe shall be truly paid and also All my funeral charges and charges about proving my Will and also the charges About selling my Estate & turning them Into Money for to be disposed of according to this my Last Will & Testament and all other charges that My Executors shall be at about ye Presents shall be allowed them.

"Item. I Give My Son John Shotwell twenty pounds to be paid him or discounted out of the money that is in his hands of mine within three months after my decease.

"Item (I give to my Son Abraham Shotwell tweaty pounds) Error.

"Item. I give to my two daughters Elizabeth Laing & Sarah Smith Each of them a feather Bed.

"Item. I Give My Son Abraham Shotwell twenty pounds to be paid him or discounted out of the money that is in his hands of mine within three months after my decease.

"My Will is that my Executors before named presently After my Decease shall put to sale & sell as soon as they can conveniently My House & Lands whereon I live and Also All My Household Goods which I have not disposed off Allready both within doors and without of what quality or quantities So Ever and Likewise All My Husbandry Utensils & Joiners tools and All My Cattle & horses & My Negro Tom, Together with All other things not mentioned here that any manner of ways belong to My Real or Personal Estate be they of what Quality or Quantities so Ever not already disposed of. Further My Will is that the Money that shall arise from ye sale of ye above mentioned Personal and Real Estate. Together with all the Money due Me from My Children or any Body Else After My Just Debts & Legacies be paid Shall be put out to Interest In Safe hands by My Said Executors or the Survivor of them which Said Interest shall be for the Support & Maintenance of my well beloved Wife Sa—— . . . . .

(about 6 words cut off) . . . —— will is that after her decease, the above sd —— . . . . (10 or 12 words missing) . . . . —— children, and in case that any my sa —— . . . . —— to be my last will and testament as k—— . . . . —— commonly called July in ye year above c—— . . . . ——livered in the presence of us, Isabella F. . . . .

———

One of the witnesses was probably Isabella Fitz Randolph, the widow of Joseph, whose will was recently found by Benjamin Vail. The foregoing Will was proved at Amboy, 5 Oct., 1719, before John Barclay, and power to administer under it was granted by Barclay, Dep. Set'r on 7 Oct., 1719 to John Kinsey, one of the executors, who was a prominent Friend, residing in Woodbridge. John Barclay of Amboy, N. J., dwelt for many years in a house which in 1873 was yet standing in Amboy. He was a brother of Robert Barclay of Morayshire, Scotland; author of the *Apology for the People called in scorn Quakers*, who is styled by the poet Whittier " the Laird of Ury."

> " Nay I do not need thy sword,
> Comrade mine," said Ury's lord;
> " Put it up, I pray thee:
> Passive to his holy will,
> Trust I in my Master still,
> Even though he slay me."
>
> *　　*　　*　　*　　*
>
> " Woe's the day!" he sadly said,
> With a slowly shaking head,
> And a look of pity;
> " Ury's honest lord reviled,
> Mock of knave and sport of child,
> In his own good city!"

John Barclay, Gov. Laurie, John Reid, Miles Forester, and other prominent officials in the colonial government were Friends in Amboy and organized a meeting there, in or about 1686 but were subsequently lead off by the apostate George Keith.

The following is from the Records of the Society of Friends:—" Att our Monthly Meeting held att our Meeting house in Woodbridge the 21st day of the 11th mo., 1719.................. John Shotwell, Decease left five pounds for the Service of this Meeting."

He m. in New York, in October, 1679, Elizabeth Burton.

2. *Daniel*, of Staten Island. Dr. Hatfield in his history of Elizabethtown, says that Daniel Shotwell was probably son of Abraham and brother of John Shotwell Sr. He was living as late as 1721.

The following is from the Friend's Book of Minutes:—"Att our Monthly Meeting held att our Meeting house att Woodbridge, the 18th day of the 6th Mo., 1720,.................. Elizabeth Laing, the wife of John Laing, on Consideration not being willing to take [son of],

William Willis his apprentice, and Dan'l Shotwell offering to do it this Meeting consents thereto and desires the friends heretofore appointed to continue their care to bind him there accordingly;" and in the summer of 1721 Daniel for the sum of £16 agreed with the M. M. to take and bring up William Willis' son Nathaniel. Daniel m. Elizabeth________ who was certainly living at time of the marriage of Henry Brotherton and Ann Shotwell 25 of 6 mo., 1713.

7. ABRAHAM[3] SHOTWELL of Piscataway, N. J., formerly of Staten Island, s. of John[2] Sr. and Elizabeth (Burton) Shotwell of Woodbridge, N. J. [of Abraham[1]], m. 1712 *Elizabeth Cowperthwaite* of Flushing, L. I., dau. of John[2] and Sarah (Adams) Cowperthwaite of West Jersey, of [Hugh[1]], and had:

1. *Elizabeth*, b. 10 of 1 mo., 1716 in Tp. of Elizabeth, N. J.
2. *Sarah*, b. 5 of 4 mo., 1720 in Elizabeth, N. J.
3. *Hannah*, b. 23 of 12 mo., 1722-3.
4. *John[4]* b. 25 of 1 mo. (March), 1727 in Piscataway Tp., Middlesex Co., N. J., probably the John who m. Anna________ On record in the Surrogate General's office at Trenton, is the will of one John Shotwell of Middlesex Co., 1758, who mentions wife Anna and sons John and Jasper.
5. *Abraham*, b. 13 of 7 mo., 1732, in Piscataway, N. J., there were thus three Abraham Shotwells of near the same age, the others being (1) his cousin Abr., s. of John at the Landing, (2) Abr., s. of Joseph and Mary (Manning) Shotwell. He was possibly the Abraham who m. with the unity of Woodbridge M. M. ________ 1749-50, between 18 of 11 mo. and 15 of 12 mo., Mary Hampton.
6. *Deborah*, b. 12 of 3 mo., 1735; probably the Deborah of Piscataway who m. with approval of Woodbridge M. M. 24 of 1 mo., 1753, Daniel Shotwell, doubtless the Daniel b. 8 of 2 mo., 1725, s. of Joseph and Mary (Manning) Shotwell.

21. ABRAHAM[4] SHOTWELL, 1719-1801, of Essex (now Union) Co., N. J., s. of John[3] Jr. and Mary (Thorne) Shotwell of Shotwells Landing, [of John[2], Abraham[1]] m. (1) 1742, *Mary Potts* d. 1762, dau. of Thomas and Phebe Potts of Honey Neck, Conn., and had:

1. *Phebe[5]*, b. 5 of 2 mo., 1744, in Elizabethtown N. J.; m. 22 of 9 mo., 1763, Thomas Hallett of Queens Co., L. I.
2. *Elizabeth*, b. 5 of 7 mo., 1746, in Elizabethtown, N. J.
3. *Naomi[5]*, b. 2 of 4 mo., 1749, in Elizabethtown, N. J., m. (1) at Rahway, N. J., 21 of 11 mo., 1765, Israel Hallett of Long Island, member of Flushing M. M. She m. (2) Thurber Dunbar.

4. *Mary[5]*, b. 28 of 9 mo., 1751, in Elizabethtown, N. J., m. at Rahway N. J. 29 of 10 mo., 1778, Mordecai Marsh of Rahway, who d. there 24 of 7 mo. 1815, aged 80, buried in Rahway Friends ground; was a miller; his house was next to that of Samuel Marsh in Lower Rahway, but they were not Brothers.
5. *Hester[5]*, b. 13 of 7 mo., 1754, in Elizabethtown, N. J., m.________Townsend.
6. *Jeremiah[5]*, b. 23 of 3 mo., 1757, d. at Rahway, N. J.________1830, m. without the unity of Friends________1781, Mary________, b.______1762±, d. 17 of 5 mo., 1817, aged 55 yrs.; buried 18 of 5 mo., 1817, according to Rahway Friends Record.
7. *Samuel[5]*, b. 24 of 12 mo., 1759, lost membership in Rahway Preparative Meeting 15 of 5 mo., 1783; was murdered near Rahway, in latter part of 18th century, m. ________.

21. ABRAHAM[4] SHOTWELL, 1719-1801 [of John[3], John[2], Abr.[1]], m. (2) 1767, *Lydia Hallett*, 1738±—1815, [of Richard of Newtown, L. I.] and had:

8. *Isaac[5]*, b. 22 of 1 mo., 1769, was of borough of Elizabeth when he m. 24 of 11 mo., 1791, Catharine Moore of same place, dau. of Dr. ________ Moore.
9. *Abraham*, b. 31 of 10 mo., 1770.
10. *Ann*, b. 22 of 10 mo., 1772.
11. *Aaron[5]*, b. ________1774± d. in Tp. of Rahway (now Linden), Essex (now Union) Co., N. J., 29 of 12 mo., 1852, aged 78; was apprenticed to a Friend on Long Island, taking a cert. of membership to the meeting at Flushina, L. I., from R. and P. M. M. dated 16 of 6 mo., 1790; m. (1) ________ Martin; m. (2) ______ Freeman, m. (3) Sarah (Way) Brown, wd. of Amos, and dau. of John Jr. and Mary (Marsh) Way of Newtown, L. I.
12. *John[5]*, b. ________ d. near close of 18th century, m. ________ Freeman, sister to 2d wife of his brother Aaron, and to the wife of the latter's son Aaron, Jr.

38. ABRAHAM[4] SHOTWELL, b. 1726, of Woodbridge, N. J., s. of Joseph[3] and Mary (Manning) Shotwell [of Daniel[2], Abr.[1]], m. 1750-51, *Mary Jackson* and probably had:

1. *Samuel[5]*, was of Piscataway, N. J., when he m. at Plainfield, N. J., 21 of 5 mo., 1788, Hannah Lundy of Piscataway. They and their s. Abraham, took cert. of membership from R. and P. M. M. to the meeting at Kingwood (now Quakertown), N. J., dated 17 of 6 mo., 1789.
2. *Mary*, "daughter of Abraham and Mary" b. 20 of 11 mo., 1768, Piscataway, N. J., dw. Sussex Co., N. J., became member of Farmington (N. Y.) M. M., d. Collins, Erie Co., N. Y., 3 of 4 mo., 1820; m. Plainfield, N. J., 27 of 10 mo., 1790, David Pound, 1768-1848, s. of Benjamin[4] and Elizabeth (Laing) Pound of Piscataway, N. J. [of Elijah[3], John[2], John[1]]

FRIENDS' MEETING HOUSE AT RAHWAY, N. J.,

Erected in 1803-4, sold and removed in 1893, the Society (Hicksite) in
Rahway having become so small as to occasion the laying
down of the meeting there.

FROM AN OLD PHOTOGRAPH, THROUGH THE KINDNESS OF WILLIAM M. MOORE, OF PLAINFIELD.

194. ABRAHAM⁶ SHOTWELL, of Essex Co., N. J., s. of Aaron⁵ and .... (Martin) Shotwell of Rahway, N. J., [of Abraham⁴, John³, John², Abr.¹], m. .... *Moore* dau. of Thomas and had:

1. *Robert Alexander*, dw. near Rahway, N. J.
2. *George H.*, banker in New Orleans, La.

197. ABRAHAM F⁶. SHOTWELL, d. 1885, banker of Rahway, s. of John⁵ and .... (Freeman) Shotwell, [of Abr⁴., John³, John², Abr¹.], m. .... and had a large family whose records we have been unable to obtain. A son res. on the homestead of his grandfather John⁵ near Rahway.

271. ABRAHAM V⁶. SHOTWELL, of Samuel⁵ and Hannah (Lundy) Shotwell of Kingwood now Quakertown, N. J., [of Abraham⁴, Joseph³, Daniel², Abraham¹], m. .... and had:

1. *James⁷*.

ABRAHAM⁷ SHOTWELL, 1819± – 1891, s. of John⁶ and Phoebe (Byron) Shotwell of New York, [of Joseph⁵, Joseph⁴, Joseph³, Daniel², Abraham¹], m. *Almyra Clark*, and had:

1. *Alonzo B.*, continued the business of his father, i. e., the manufacture of cigars and tobacco, m. and has 2 daughters.
2. *Belle.*
3. *Ida*, m. Chas. Pettengill.
4. *Frank*, is in the railroad business.

ADONIRAM JUDSON⁷ SHOTWELL, b. 1848, of Boulder Co., Colo., s. of Arrison⁶ and Mary (Dickerson) Shotwell of Glenville, O., [of Hugh⁵, John⁴, John³, John², Abr¹.], m. 1872, *Martha H. Graham* of Washington, Ind., and had:

1. *Susan*, b. 2 Aug., 1874, Washington, Ind., dwells, 1893, Boulder, Colo.

ALBERT⁷ SHOTWELL, b. 1811, of Bowling Green, Pike Co., Mo., s. of John⁶ and Sally (Burroughs) Shotwell, of Mason Co., Ky., [of John⁵, John⁴, Abraham³?, John⁴, Abraham¹], m. (1) 1836, *Catharine Geery*, 1815–1892, dau. of James and Sally (Rice) Geery, and had:

1. *Louisa*, b. 30 Nov., 1836, dw. Bowling Green, Mo., m. 13 Sept., 1855, Wm. A. Hutcherson.
2. *Wm. Henry*, b. 8 Aug., 1840, d. 20 Sept., 1840.
3. *James Luther*, b. 11 Jan., 1848, dw. Farber, Audrain Co., Mo., m. 5 June, 1865, Sallie Magee.
4. ----------------.

204. ALEXANDER⁶ SHOTWELL, 1802–1884, of Salem, Ala., s. of Nathan⁵ and Sarah (Fitz Randolph) Shotwell, of Rahway and Blazing

Star, N. J., [of Jacob⁴, John³, John², Abr.¹], m. 1824, *Eliza Smith*, 1803–1879, and had:

1. *Elizabeth Greenleaf*, b. 9 of 2 mo., 1826, Rahway, N. J., dw. Lee Co., Ala., P. O., Salem, to her we are indebted for valuable information, m. near Salem, Ala. 21 of 11 mo., 1877, Lozla Edwards, father of judge Polk Edwards and other children, who d. Opelika, near Salem, Ala., aged about 82 yrs., after a lingering illness, of cancer in the throat, having gone for 43 days without any nourishment whatever, and leaving to his children and grandchildren the priceless heritage of an unblemished character to revere and emulate. " Strong in spirit, clear in judgement, he exhibited to the last moments a watchful and affectionate regard for all around him, losing sight of his own ills in provision for the interest of others. Honorable, upright, generous and amiable, he was extremely popular and without an enemy in the world."
2. *Julia S⁷.*, b. 7 of 9 mo., 1833, Macon, Ga., d. Atlanta, Ga., 28 Dec., 1890, aged 57 yrs., having gone there for medical treatment; was a most devoted Christian lady, and had been for a long time a faithful and earnest member of Trinity Church, Salem, Ala., the funeral took place from the res. of her son-in-law, Mr. D. W. Dixon, Salem, Ala., Dr. W. C. Hunter officiating. She m. W. Greene Andrews of Lee Co., Ala., who d. before 1890.
3. *Jennie⁷*, b. 25 of 5 mo., 1836, Macon, Ga., d. near Crawford, Ala., ... of 4 mo., 1886, aged 49 yrs., m. 23 of 2 mo., 1870, Alexander Lamb, b. 8 of 5 mo., 1820, dw. near Salem, Ala.

DR. ALEXANDER HAMILTON⁷ SHOTWELL, 1839–1862, of Rutherfordton, N. C., s. of Rev. Nathan and Lydia (Baldwin) Shotwell, [of Randolph], m. 1861 *Jennie Eliza Mc. Entire*, dau. of Dr. John of Rutherfordton, N. C., and had:

1. *John Hamilton*, b. Rutherfordton, N. C., 20 Apr., 1862, a few weeks prior to the death of his father at Richmond, Va., dw. with his mother at Smithwood, Knox Co., Tenn.

COL. ALFRED LAWRENCE⁷ SHOTWELL, b. 1809± of Jefferson Co. (now part of Louisville), Ky., s. of Wm⁶. and Fannie (Triplett) Shotwell of Mason Co., Ky., [of John⁵, John⁴, Abraham³?, John², Abraham¹], m. *Gabriella Breckenridge*, and had:

1. *Stephen B.*, b. 30 April, 1830, m........., dw. Louisville, Ky.
2. *William P.*, b. 15 April, 1835, d. 1 March, 1869.
3. .... (a daughter) b. 15 March, 1838; was living in Chicago in 1869, m. Robert M. Cannon, and had two sons.
4. *Alfred Ann* (called Annie), b. 14 Nov., 1843, m. (1) at her father's residence, Louisville, Ky., ..., 1862, Gabriel F. Tate, who d. at Henderson, Ky., ..., 1887. Being intemperate

he soon wasted the property given him by his father-in-law. He promised to do better, and was helped again and again; but failing to provide for his family, they at length separated. A few years afterward she married (2) .... Churchill. The following article, clipped (1887) from *The Rogersville Herald*, gives several interesting particulars relating to this branch of the family:

GABE TATE'S ROMANCE.

MARRIED, DIVORCED, GIVEN UP FOR DEAD, AND AGAIN MARRIED TO THE SAME WOMAN.

[From the St. Louis Globe-Democrat.]

The death of Gabe Tate at Henderson, Ky., brings to mind the romantic career of his life. Tate was born and raised in this country. His father was one of the prosperous planters of ante-bellum days. The large tract of land he owned was in Walnut Bottom, in the most productive part of this section. He had a large number of slaves and, better still, a large bank account. Gabe had grown in an atmosphere of luxury until luxuries were common. He had been accustomed to having his own way and to have every want supplied. When his father died the estate was divided between him and his sister, Mrs. Dr. J. A. Harding, who had gone to the home of her husband in Jefferson county, now a part of Louisville, Ky. There he met Miss Annie Shotwell, the daughter of Col. A. L. Shotwell, a man who was rich in a dozen different ways. His steam interest was only second to his landed estate, and his commission merchants business but barely outstripping his mining rights. The vast coal fields of Union county, now owned by Brown & Jones, the Pittsburgh coal kings, were his individually. At that time, in 1862, there were only two coal mines operated on the Ohio River below Pittsburgh, Pa., the one at Cannelton, Ind., and the Shotwell mines in Union county. So exhaustless is the supply of coal and so superior the quality that a railroad has just been completed to the mines from this city. Fabulous fortunes have been made from the fleets of coal sent South from these mines. It is seen by this what Oriental grandeur was in the reach of Gabe Tate and Miss Shotwell, with their fortunes, when united in marriage at the residence of Col. Shotwell, in Louisville. After marriage Mr. and Mrs. Tate went to the Shotwell mines, where the products of a thousand miners supplied their wants. For some years they lived at the mines, and all went well. Two or more children blessed their union. Mr. Tate left his home, and to this day the public do not know the cause. Surmises were plentiful, but no knowledge of the cause was ever had. It was known that his estate was gone, but that was of small importance for his wife was rich.

Some time after Mr. Tate left home Mrs. Tate procured a divorce, and shortly afterwards married Sam Churchill, a prosperous planter, who had lived near the mines, and with whom she was acquainted during her married life at the mines. In the meantime Andrew Tate, an old bachelor uncle, had died and left his vast estate to Gabe and his sister. Hugh Tate, another bachelor uncle, soon died, and added his fortune to that of his brother Andrew for the benefit of his nephew and niece. Not long after that Miss Nancy Tate died, and left her increased fortune from her own right and undivided interests in the estates of her two brothers, Andrew and Hugh, to Gabe Tate and his sister. These changes covered a period of nearly ten years. Notwithstanding the fact that considerable advertising had been done, nothing could be heard of Gabe Tate, and he was suspected to be dead. At last he was heard from at Cairo, Ill., and found. Arriving home, he found himself a rich man again. He wrote to his wife to send the children to him at Evansville, Ind., as he wanted to see them. She met him there with the children. Shortly afterwards a divorce was procured from Sam Churchill, the second husband, and speedily following that divorce was the marriage of Gabe Tate to the same woman who had procured a divorce from him years before.

5. *Frances T.*, b. 18 Feb., 1849, d. 24 Dec., 1868, unm. On the day preceding her death, she had been out to invite some lady friends to a social party to be given next day at her father's house, and having walked much in the city that evening, on going to bed she inhaled chloroform to quiet her nerves, and was found dead in bed the next morning.

6. *John T.*, b. 22 Sept., 1853, dw. Louisville, Ky., m. -------------

ALVIN THEODORE[6] SHOTWELL, b. 1846, of Fargo, Cass Co., N. D., s. of Edmund V[7]. and Jane H. (Williams) Shotwell of Plainfield, N. J., [of Daniel C[6]., Manning[5], Benj[4]. John[3], Daniel[2], Abraham[1]], m. 1881, *Mary Josephine Moore*, b. 1856, and had:

1. *Winthrop Babbidge*, b. 1 Dec., 1882, Plainfield, N. J.

2. *Florence Courtney*, b. 27 Aug., 1885, Fargo, Dak.

ANSON[7] SHOTWELL, b. 1839, of Linden, Genesee Co., Mich., s. of Jonathan[6] and Phebe (Willson) Shotwell of Long Bridge, N. J., [of James[5], John[4], John[3], John[2], Abraham[1]], m. 1863, *Lucinda Jane Cummins*, b. 1841, daughter of William (b. 1 June, 1800) and Marie (Middlesworth, b. 18 Jan., 1807) Cummins and granddaughter of Mathias and Hannah (Shakelton) Cummins of Vienna, N. J., and of John and Sarah (Reid) Middlesworth of Johnsonsburgh, and had:

1. *Elvington M.*, b. 19 May, 1864, m. ------ Nov., 1892, Mary Lobdell, called Mollie.

2. *Phebe Marie*, b. 10 Feb., 1867, a trained nurse, dwells Linden, Mich. To her we are indebted for valuable data relating to this branch.

3. *James A.*, b. 12 March, 1870; dw. Linden, Mich.

4. *Clarence Cecil*, b. 13 Feb., 1879, d. 6 May, 1879.

5. *Ray L. Anson*, b. 13 Jan., 1881.

186. ARRISON[6] SHOTWELL, 1812–1893, of Glenville, O., s. of Hugh[5] and Rosetta (Arrison) Shotwell of Harrison Co., O., [of John[4], John[3], John[2], Abraham[1]], m. 1835, *Mary[4] Dickerson*, 1817–1894, dau. of Baruch[3], [of Thomas[2], Joshua[1]], and had:

1. *Elizabeth*, b. 17 Sept., 1836, Washington Tp., Harrison Co., O.; dw. with parents Glenville, Cuyahoga, Co., O., unm. (1893).

2. *Rosetta*, b. 10 Dec., 1838, Washington Tp., O., where all the children were b., and where she d. 21 Dec., 1838.

3. *Victoria*, b. 10 Dec., 1839, dw., 1893, with parents, Glenville, O., s. p.; m. Glenville, O., 13 Feb., 1883, George Gooding.

4. *Adoniram Judson*, b. 21 Apr., 1842, dw. 1893, Boulder, Colo., a mining engineer; enlisted 17 Feb., 1864, in Company K., 11th Ohio Volunteers Cavalry and served on the Indian frontier at Forts Laromy and Hallock, honorably discharged 14 July, 1866; m. Washington, Davis Co., Ind., 27 May, 1872, Martha H. Graham.

5. *John Thomas*, b. Freeport, O., 1 Aug., 1845, dw. Deadwood, S. D., s. p.; manufacturer of lumber for more than 25 yrs., a Republican, Baptist, temperance, progressive. He m. St. Louis, Mo., 20 Apr., 1875, Evolyn McBrine, b. Chester, Ill., 18 Nov., 1856, dau. of Wm. McBrine of St. Louis, Mo., native of the North of Ireland.

6. *Austin*, b. 28 Aug., 1848, engaged in mining with brother, A. Judson, at Boulder, Colo., unm. (1893) formerly teacher of penmanship and drawing.

7. *Fremont*, b. 5 Aug., 1856, dw. Glenville, O., unm. (1893).

33. BENJAMIN⁴ SHOTWELL, 1726-1793, of Shotwell's Landing, Bricktown (now Rahway), Essex (now Union) Co., N. J.; s. of John³, Jr., and Mary (Thorne) Shotwell, at the Landing, [of John², Abraham¹], m. 1746, *Ame Hallett*, 1727-1796, dau. of Richard and Amy (Bowne) Hallett of Newtown, L. I., and had:

1. *Sarah⁵*, b. 3 of 3 mo., 1748, was a prominent minister of the Society of Friends; m. (1) at Rahway, N. J., 28 of 9 mo., 1768, Wm. Hampton of the borough of Elizabeth, N. J., dw. Woodbridge, N. J., d. Rahway, 24 of 2 mo., 1781; probably s. of Abner and Rachel (Webster) Hampton of Essex Co., N. J. The following from the minutes of the Society may be of interest: "At Our Monthly Meeting held at Woodbridge the 17th 8th mo., 1768, ... William Hampton & Sarah Shotwell appeared at this Meeting and declared their Intentions of Taking Each Other in Marriage, it being the first time, & he produced a Certificate from the Monthly Meeting of Chesterfield Signifiing that he was Removed from thence to live within the Verge of this Meeting and that his life & Conversation was tolerable orderly & a frequenter of Meetings and clear of Marriage Engagements and in Unity with friends there, which was satisfactory." At the next meeting, 9-21, 68, they were "left at Liberty to Consumate their Intended Marriage according to the good order used amongst Friends." And on 19 of 10 mo., 1768, "The Friends appointed to attend the Marriage of William Hampton and Sarah Shotwell report it was Orderly accomplished." In 6 mo., 1770, Wm. Hampton and his wife took a cert. of membership to Hardwick. M. M., but were received back by cert. to R. and P. M. M. 21 of 10 mo., 1772. On the 18 of 5 mo. 1774, we find, "This Meeting is inform'd that our Friend Sarah Hampton desired to attend the Quarterly Meeting at Crosswicks, which this Meeting approves of, She hav-

ing a Short testimony which is Satisfactory. The Clerk is desired to give her a Copy of this Minute." On 15 of 3 mo., 1781, "Our Friend Sarah Hampton inform'd this Meeting that for some time past She has been under a religious Concern to Visit Friends at Barnigat, Eggharbor, the Great Meadows, some part of New York, [and] New England." A cert. for this purpose was given her at the next M. M. On 16 of 10 mo., 1782, "Our esteemed Friend Sarah Hampton having returned from a religious Visit to Friends to the Eastward returned her Certificate as also a number of Certificates, viz.: One from the Yearly Meeting held at Westbury for Newyork Government & One from the Yearly Meeting held at Newport for New England, al·o divers from several Quarterly & Monthly Meetings all expressive of their Satisfaction with her Visit." Her travels in the ministry were continued on various occasions after her second marriage.

At the M. M. held at Rahway 18 of 9 mo., 1783, Jacob Lundy, Jr., of Hardwick, b. 30 of 5 mo., (July), 1751, d. 22 of 3 mo., 1806, s. of Jacob and Mary Lundy, produced a cert. from Kingwood M. M. dated 11 of 9 mo., 1783, recommending him as a Friend in Unity in order for Marriage with Sarah Hampton," and the written approbation of his parents. They, at this meeting, appeared the second time and were left at liberty to consummate their marriage agreeable to the orders established amongst Friends. This marriage was "orderly accomplished" on 25 of 9 mo., 1783. Sarah Lundy and two childen, Ame and Benjamin Hampton became members of Hardwick M. M. by cert. from R. and P. M. M., given 17 of 12 mo., 1783, but returned to membership in R. and P. M. M. 20 of 5 mo., 1784, by cert. from Hardwick, dated 8 of 4 mo., 1784, for herself, her husband Jacob Lundy, Jr., and her children, Amy and Benjamin Hampton. Jacob Lundy of Rahway Preparative Meeting and his wife Sarah, "a minister well approved," and three children, Benjamin and Amy Hampton and Mary Lundy, having removed within Kingwood M. M. took cert. thither from R. and P. M. M., dated 19 of 5 mo., 1785; also "his son-in-law [stepson], Wm. Hampton," son of Wm. Hampton deceased, having been apprenticed to Robert White, a Friend belonging to the M. M. at Chesterfield.

Isaac Martin, in his journal (1791 p. 18) says: "Our beloved friend, Sarah Lundy, having a concern to pay a religious visit to some parts of New England and Nova Scotia, my dear wife offered to accompany her; which I encouraged on account of the near unity I felt with the concern. William Shotwell of Plainfield being willing to go with them, I went on to New York with my dear wife, and they all embarked on board a vessel for Newport, Rhode Island." And on p. 40, we find the following entry: "Toward the latter end of the 8th month [1793], in company with my kinswoman, Sarah Lundy, who was going on a religious visit southward as far as Carolina and Georgia, I attended Buck's Quarterly Meeting held at the Falls. Had also the company of a large committee of Friends appointed by the Yearly Meeting, to visit the Quarterly and monthly meetings in order to afford such help as in wisdom might be furnished to stir up the members to a more lively concern in attending to meetings, particularly those near the middle of the week."

Sarah B. Brotherton, wd. of Sarah (Showell) Lundy's grandson, Dr. J. Lundy Brotherton of Philadelphia, has in her possession the small English trunk that Sarah carried on the horn of her saddle while making her religious visits on horse back.

2. *Ame* or *Amy*, b. 22 of 2 mo., 1750, was of the borough of Elizabeth when m. (1) at Rahway * Friends Meeting house 28 of 8 mo., 1788, Charles Brooks of Woodbridge; was of Rahway when she m. (2) at Rahway, 20 of 2 mo., 1794, Samuel Hicks of Westbury, Queens Co., L. I., to which place she took cert. of membership from R. & P. M. M., dated 18 of 6 mo., 1794.

3. *Mary*, called "Aunt Molly" b. 15 of 4 mo., 1752, lived for a time at Westbury, L. I., taking cert. to the meeting there dated 19 of 3 mo., 1795, and again 17 of 6 mo., 1801; dw. for many years with her brother Wm. at the Landing, and there d. 13 of 2 mo., 1823, unm., aged 71 yrs., buried Rahway; was remarkably plain in speech and apparel, and occasionally made high exhortations in meetings for worship.

It was sometimes facetiously said, "Aunt Molly Shotwell was so plain that she would not eat striped beans."

4. *Richard*[5], b. 25 of 7 mo., 1756, at Shotwells Landing, Bricktown (now Rahway), Essex (now Union) Co., N. J. Farmington M. M. records give date of birth as 24 of 7 mo., 1755. It is apparent from the record that Richard Shotwell had taken an active part in the war of the revolution on the side of the British government. In the minutes of the M. M. held at Plainfield 21 of 2 mo., 1782, occurs the following passage:—"The Monthly Meeting of New York have sent to this meeting a Copy of a Paper given into that Meeting by Richard Shotwell condemning his Conduct in taking up Arms and assisting other Armed Men in taking away People from the Jersey's and making them Prisoners: which was Satisfactory to that Meeting. Thomas Latham is appointed to read the same at the close of a first day Meeting at Rahway . . . . . . Benjamin Shotwell informed this Meeting that his Son Richard Shotwell of New York, requests our Certificate to that Meeting in order that he may proceed in Marriage with Mary Martin, a Friend belonging to that Meeting." The cert. was granted at the next meeting 21 of 3 mo., 1782. The cert. of

* Not at Plainfield as stated in O. B. Leonards Centennial Address, 1888.

this marriage states that "Richard Shotwell son of Benjamin Shotwell of Rahway in East New Jersey and Mary Martin Daughter of Isaac Martin of the City and Province of New York, deceased, and Elizabeth Martin . . . . . appeared in a Publick Meeting of said People [called Quakers] in the City of New York," and were there married "according to the good order used amongst them" on the 10 of 4 mo., 1782. The following is a list of the witnesses whose names are appended to this marriage cert.:

Elizabeth Martin,	Abigail Martin,
Burling Martin,	Henry Shotwell,
Isaac Martin,	Gulielma Martin,
Ame Shotwell,	Eden Shotwell,
Elizabeth Martin,	Saml. Bowne,
Elizabeth Shotwell,	Abigail Bowne,
Ann Burling,	Abr. Franklin,
John Burling,	Henry Haydock Jur.,
Thomas Burling,	James Parsons Junr.,
Richard Lawrence,	John B. Parsons,
Ann Webster,	James Parsons,
Benjn. Haviland,	James Burling,
Samuel Burling,	Sally Bowne,
John W. Haydock,	Esther Shotwell,
Thos. Dobson,	William Bowne,
Samuel Moore,	Mary Haydock,
Lindley Murray,	Edmund Prior,
Letitia Underhill,	Jos. D. Laplaine Junr.,
Rebecca Haydock,	Phebe Prior,
Penelope Hull,	Hannah Haydock,
Hannah Haydock Jur.,	Joseph De Laplaine,
Lydia Hunt Jun.,	Sarah Prior,
Mattw. Bowne,	Ebenezr. Haviland,
Henrietta Burling,	Jane Haviland,
Catharine Burling,	Phebe Haviland,
Priscilla Brown,	Ann Haviland,
Mary Cowper,	Thos. Robinson,
Ambrose Copland,	Wm. Nelson,
John Murray Jun.,	Phebe De Laplaine.
William Cowper Junr.,	

In 1784, Richard asked the advice of R. & P. M. M. in the settlement of trouble about money matters with Joseph Shotwell, of Perry Town (now called Uniontown), N. J.

"At a Monthly Meeting held at Rahway 20th of 5th mo., 1784, ... Certificates were produced to this meeting and read, one from Kingwood Monthly Meeting held at Hardwick the 8th of 4th mo. last recommending Jacob Lundy Jun., and Sarah his wife with her two children, Amy and Benjamin Hampton, to the care of this Meeting which was accepted. Also one from the Monthly Meeting of New York, dated 4th of the 12th mo., 1782, recommending Mary Shotwell, wife of Richard, which was also accepted." Richard with his family removed from Essex Co., N. J., in 1804, to Farmington, Ontario Co., N. Y., and thence about 14 yrs. later to the northern part of the town of Batavia (now Elba), Genesee Co., N. Y., locating on a farm at what is known as Lancton's Corners; his res. was on the E. side of the Oak Orchard road opposite the Shelly house built by his grandson Hugh P. Shotwell, about the year 1861; he d. there 17 of 8 mo.,

1833, of a cancer, "aged 78 yrs., 20 days." Richard, his son Isaac M., and son-in-law Wanton Aldrich were the three Trustees to whom on 30 July, 1819, four acres in the S. E. part of lot 2, Sec. 3, town 13, range 1, were conveyed by the Holland Co. for the use and benefit of Batavia (now Elba) Preparative Meeting of Friends. This deed is recorded in the Genesee Co. Clerks office, Liber 13, p. 9. At the separation in 1828, Richard and family and most of his grandchildren continued in membership with the Society of Friends called Orthodox.

His wife Mary, dau. of Isaac and Elizabeth (Burling) Martin of New York, was b. there 1 of 7 mo., 1756, lived for a time after her husband's death with their son Benjamin and afterward with their eldest dau. Amy Aldrich in Elba, N. Y., and there d. 27 of 3 mo., 1844, " aged 87 yrs., 9 mos., 22 days."

At one time during the revolutionary war, when it was thought that a bombardment of the city was imminent, part of the Martin family retired to the country and there lived with relatives for several months; but Mary, on learning that the prospect of military operations would not induce her father to forsake his home, or by any act of his give countenance to the warlike preparations, decided to remain with him at all hazards. During the bombardment they merely sought safety in the cellar. She had been carefully trained in the use of the needle; and, in the pursuit of her daily task, all unconscious of observation, was frequently noticed through their field glass by British officers who lodged not far away, and who, seeing her diligence and skill engaged her to make a considerable number* of fine linen shirts for Lord Cornwallis, then in command of the city, for which she was paid in silver at the rate of one Spanish dollar each. She afterward took this price to a goldsmith and had it made into, or exchanged it for, a set of solid silver spoons, one of which was afterward given to each of her married children. One of them is yet 1888, in the possession of each of the following grandchildren: D. Waterman Smith, Mary S. Reed, and Desire Estes. She retained her sight so perfectly that, at 80 yrs. of age, she was able to do fine sewing without the aid of glasses; but her hearing, like that of her husband and several of her children and grandchildren, was quite imperfect in the latter years of life.

5. *Benjamin*, b. 25 of 4 mo., 1759, d. at Marengo, in the town of Galen, Wayne Co., N. Y., 12 of 5 mo., 1848, in his 90th year; was a farmer, and a consistent Friend; his nephew Wm. Shotwell has been heard to say that this uncle, when at the house of his (Wm's) father, Penn-like ate his dinner without removing his hat; was very deaf for many years and his wife Bathsheba was blind; he m. in old Plainfield

meeting house 21 of 1 mo., 1781, Bathsheba⁵ Pound, b. 14 of 5 mo., 1763, d. Galen, N. Y., 1 of 12 mo., 1818, dau. of Zachariah⁴ and Elizabeth (Smith) Pound of the borough of Elizabeth, N. J., [of Elijah³, John², John¹]. Benjamin, Jr., and his wife Bathsheba, with their two minor children, Elizabeth and Thomas, having removed within Kingwood M. M., took cert. thither from R. and P. M. M. dated 15 of 8 mo., 1787, and subsequently removed from Warren Co., N. J., to Seneca (now Wayne) Co., N. Y., but not, their grandson Samuel L. Shotwell thinks, until after the marriage of all their children. Dally, in his History of Woodbridge, p. 288, says, "At the annual election in Woodbridge, Mar. 11, 1783, Benjamin Shotwell and Carlile Brown were chosen by the town meeting as ' the Survares of the Roads the year insuing.' "

6. *Elizabeth*, b. 17 of 4 mo., 1762, d________ 1794±, m. at Rahway, N. J., 26 of 4 mo., 1787, (as first w.) Joseph Lundy of Hardwick, Sussex (now Warren) Co., N. J., b. 29 of 3 mo., 1762, and d. 13 of 1 mo., 1846, and had one son Benjamin Lundy, the distinguished anti-slavery leader who first enlisted Wm. Lloyd Garrison in the same cause.

7. *Thomas*, b. 10 of 12 mo., 1764.

8. *William*, b. 27 of 4 mo., 1766, Rahway, N. J., inherited the homestead of his father and grandfather at the Landing in the borough of Elizabeth, and there engaged in farming and the manufacture of brick, shipping them to New York and elsewhere, and was also interested in vessels running to New York. About the beginning of the 19th century, twenty vessels, freighted with brick, sailed weekly from Shotwell's landing and the neighboring docks, to the New York markets. In 1879 not a brick was made within 7 miles of this place: Owing to the facilities furnished by the railroads, the commerce of Rahway river has been nearly ruined; occasionally a vessel from some other place brings a cargo of lumber, brick or other building material to the Landing, which is regarded as the head of sloop or steamboat navigation. In the early half of the 19th century many good sized vessels were built in the ship yards at the Landing; it was not uncommon to see two on the stocks in process of erection at the same time. The last vessel built there was for Wm. Shotwell, Jr., about 1850-55, when he was engaged in the lime and coal business.

When young, Wm. had the reputation of being the most rapid skater in that part of the country. Old people have been heard to say that, on one occasion, a man came from New York to try his speed with "Uncle Billy," and they skated from the Landing to Staten Island and back a distance of about 6 or 7 miles, when the New York man was so badly beaten that he went away quite crestfallen.

The spacious barn and outbuildings which were upon the farm at the Landing when Wm.

left it in 1836, have long since been burned by incendiaries. The commodious house which he built and occupied was standing in 1879, though fast falling to decay and in latter years was little occupied. An illicit distillery was at one time discovered to be in operation in the cellar. The dwelling was soon afterward destroyed by fire. There was, in 1879, yet remaining near the site of the residence a small apple orchard; our informant remembered having seen "Uncle Billy" engaged in grafting these trees about the year 1830.

He m. (1) Rahway, N. J., 25 of 10 mo., 1792, Elizabeth Moore of Woodbridge, who d. at the Landing 13 of 3 mo., 1826, aged 64 yrs.; m. (2) in Friends' meeting, Junius, Seneca Co., N. Y., 27 of 9 mo., 1827, Achsah (Lundy) Laing, wd. of John Laing and dau. of Samuel and Sarah (Willits) Lundy; she was b. 21 of 3 mo., 1777, d. 26 of 9 mo., 1854, aged 78±, having removed and settled with her husband at Rahway, became member of R. & P. M. M. by cert. from Junius M. M. dated 20 of 11 mo., 1827. About 10 yrs. later, William sold the old homestead at the Landing for what was deemed a very high price; it was believed at the time that he was influenced by his wife to make the sale, as she wished to return to her former home in N. Y. state, which they did, becoming members of the meeting at Junius, by cert. from R. and P. M. M., dated 18 of 1 mo., 1838, he purchasing a farm near Waterloo, N. Y.; but very soon afterward, the purchaser of the ancestral homestead failed to carry out his engagements, which resulted in William Shotwell's having to take back the place, property in Rahway having much depreciated in value. Returning to Rahway in 4 mo., 1855, after a short interim and meeting at the R. R. station a friend, A. V. Shotwell, who, at first sight, failed to recognize him as he appeared so broken down and feeble, he said that he had "come home to die." He went to the res. of his s. Wm. near the Landing and lived but a short time, departing this life on 26 of 4 mo., 1855; his remains were taken to the old meeting house in Lower Rahway, where in former years he had been a constant and exemplary attendant, and were buried in the Friends' ground near by on the 29 of 4 mo., 1855, leaving to his posterity a reputation of which they may well be proud,—that of a good and honest man. He was a man of great industry and of no less kindness. New Jersey became a free state about the year 1816, but Wm. Shotwell's negroes willingly remained with their old master after their emancipation.

9. *Lydia*, b. 27 of 7 mo., 1769, d. at the house of Azaliah Schooly near Waterloo, N. Y. ------ 1844±, s. p.; she was skilful with the needle, was at one time teacher in the Nine Partners Boarding School near Poughkeepsie, N. Y., becoming member of Nine Partners M. M. by cert. dated 19 of 7 mo., 1804; had previously taken a similar cert. to New York dated 21 of 11 mo., 1793; m. (1) at Nine Partners, N. Y., ------ 1808, Philip Dorland of Upper Canada, b. 9 of 9 mo., 1755, d. 18 of 12 mo., 1814, s. of Samuel[2] of Dutchess Co., N. Y., [of John[1] of L. I.], she becoming member of Adolphus M. M. by cert. from R. & P. M. M. dated 27 of 4 mo., 1808. After Phillips death she resided for several years with her brother William at the Landing; she m. (2) 29 of 1 mo., 1829, Isaac Griffin of Dutchess Co., N. Y., she becoming member of Nine Partners M. M. by cert. from R. and P. M. M. dated 17 of 6 mo., 1829.

Benjamin[4] Shotwell, 1726-1793, of Shotwell's Landing (now Rahway), N. J., married 1746, Ame Hallett, 1727-1796, daughter of Richard and Amy (Bowne) Hallett.

1. *Sarah*, b. 1749, m[1]. 1768, William Hampton, who d. 1781; m[2]. 1783, Jacob Landy, Jr., 1751-1806.
    1. Benjamin Hampton, b. 1775, m. 1807, Mary (Cox) Jackson, b. 1768.
    2. William, 1776-1859, m. 1798, Mary Pound, [of Benj[4]., Elijah[3], John[2], John[1]].
    3. Ame, or Amy.
    4. Mary Lundy, b. 1785, m[1]. John Stevenson; m[2]. David Willson, Jr.
    5. Elizabeth, 1787-1838, m. 1808, Abner Willson, [of Gabriel[2], Samuel[1]].
    6. Lydia, d. 1815 ±, m. Thomas Brotherton, b. 1786, [of William].
2. *Ame*, or Amy, b. 1750, m[1]. 1788, Charles Brooks; m[2]. 1794, Samuel Hicks.
3. *Mary*, 1752-1823.
4. *Richard[5]*, 1756-1833, m. 1782, Mary Martin, 1756-1814, [of Isaac and Elizabeth (Burling) Martin].
    1. Elizabeth, b. 1783.
    2. Amy, 1784-1858; m. 1805, Wanton Aldrich, 1780-1870.
    3. Isaac Martin[6], 1786-1860, m. 1813, Edna C. Pound, 1790-1872, [of Hugh].
    4. Benjamin, 1788-1793.
    5. Mary, 1790-1862, m[1]. David Smith, b. 1774; m[2]. James Peacock.
    6. Elizabeth, 1791-1874, m. James Herendeen, 1788-1873.
    7. Benjamin, 1793-1865, m. 1815, Sarah Hoag, 1799-1869.
    8. Abbe, 1795-1878, m. 1815, Smith Laing, 1793-1877, [of Joseph].
    9. Lydia, b. 1797.
    10. Sarah, 1799-1884, m[1]. Jacob Hoag, Jr.; m[2]. Nathan Chase.
5. *Benjamin*, 1759-1848, m. 1781, Bathsheba Pound, 1763-1848, [of Zachariah[4], Elijah[3], John[2], John[1]].
    1. Elizabeth, 1781-1857, m. Samuel Lundy, b. 1775, [of Samuel].
    2. Thomas, 1786-1857, m[1]. Tamer Lundy; m[2]. Hannah Lundy; m[3]. Anna Webster.
    3. Zachariah, 1788-1857, m[1]. Elizabeth Lundy; m[2]. Edna Lundy; m[3]. Elizabeth H. Lundy.
    4. Amy, 1790-1876, m. 1808, Asa Willson, 1786-1859 ±, [of Gabriel].
    5. Mercy, 1792-1836, m. 1814, Daniel Strang, 1780-1841.
    6. Benjamin, Jr., 1797-1878, m. 1825, Catharine Pugsley, 1806-1870 ±.
    7. Samuel, b. 1802, m[1]. Phebe Laing; m[2]. Mercy Pound.
    8. Lydia, 1805-1829, m. 1824, John Rogers, 1804-1837.
6. *Elizabeth*, 1762-1794 ±, m. 1787, Joseph Lundy, 1762-1846, had Benjamin, 1789-1830, the philanthropist, m. 1815, Esther Lewis, d. 1826 ±.
7. *Thomas*, b. 1764.
8. *William*, 1766-1855, m. (1) 1792, Elizabeth Moore, 1762 + — 1826; m. (2) Acsah (Lundy) Laing.
    1. Benjamin, 1793-1859, m. Mary Hunt, b. 1800 ±.
    2. Elizabeth L., 1795-1827, m. 1815, Samuel Moore, Jr., [of Samuel[4]].
    3. William, Jr., 1798-1870, m[1]. Catharine Pettit; m[2]. ----------; m[3]. ------------.
    4. Harvey, 1800-1848, m. 1823, Louisa Shotwell, 1800-1880, [of Nathan[4]].
    5. David, d. 1836, m. Margaret Prall.
9. Lydia, 1769-1844 ±, m[1]. Philip Dorland; m[2]. Isaac Griffin.

---

44. BENJAMIN[4] SHOTWELL, b. 1731, s. of John[3] and Lydia (......) Shotwell, [of Daniel[2]?, Abraham[1]], m. 1754, *Elizabeth Manning*, and had:

1. *Daniel*, b. 18 Jan., 1755.
2. *Charity*, b. 6 Sept., 1756.
3. *Manning[5]*, b. 14 Apr., 1758; m. Mary Clarkson, b. ..... 1762 ±, dau. of Robert and Rebecca[4] (Fitz Randolph) Clarkson, [of Edward[3] Fitz Randolph, Edward[2], Edward[1]].
4. *Mary*, b. 16 May, 1759.
5. *Elizabeth*, b. 20 Sept., 1761; m , 1784, Isaac Drake, b. 1760, s. of Nathaniel[2] (b. 1730) and Dorothy, *nee* Retan (m. 1750), [of Isaac[1] Drake].
6. *John*, b. 14 Oct., 1763, m. Esther[5] Fitz Randolph, dau. of Joseph[4] and Esther (Broderich) Fitz Randolph, [of Joseph[3] and Rebecca (Drake) Fitz Randolph, Joseph[2] and Hannah (Conger) Fitz Randolph, Edward[1] and Elizabeth (Blossom) Fitz Randolph].
7. *Joseph*, b. 18 Nov., 1765.
8. *Lydia*, b. 16 March, 1768, m. 1791, ... Tennent.
9. *Benjamin*, b. 5 Apr., 1770.
10. *David*, b. .. Dec., 1772.

91. BENJAMIN[5] SHOTWELL, 1759-1848, of Essex Co., N. J., and Wayne Co., N. Y., s. of Benjamin[4] and Amy (Hallet) Shotwell of Shotwell's Landing, N. J., [of John[3], John[2], Abraham[1]], m. 1781, *Bathsheba Pound*, 1763-1848, dau. of Zachariah[4] and Elizabeth (Smith) Pound of Essex Co., N. J., [of Elijah[3], John[2], John[1]], and had:

1. *Elizabeth*[6], b. 8 of 12 mo., 1781, in Independence Tp., Sussex (now Warren) Co., N. J., dw. Junius, N. Y., d. Waterloo village; Junius Friends Record says, she d. Galen, N. Y., 16 of 9 mo., 1857, aged 76; m. in N.J., Samuel Lundy, b. 18 of 5 mo., 1775, d. Waterloo, N. Y., of a cancer, s. of Samuel and Sarah (Willits) Lundy.

2. *Thomas*[6], b. 25 of 8 mo., 1786, Rahway, N. J., dw. Hardwick, N. J., whence about 1816 he removed to Galen, Seneca (now Wayne) Co., N. Y., and there d. 1 of 1 mo., 1857; was a farmer, and an exemplary Friend; m. (1) in N. J., 1 of 3 mo., 1808, or 9 of 3 mo., 1807, Tamer Lundy, b. 27 of 3 mo., 1786, d. Galen, N. Y., 3 of 7 mo., 1818, dau. of Jonathan and Rebecca (Heaton) Lundy; m. (2) in Galen Friends Meeting, 13 of 12 mo., 1819, Hannah Lundy of Galen, N. Y., b. 27 of 2 mo., 1789, d. Galen, N. Y., 6 or 26 of 3 mo., 1843, dau. of Daniel and Elizabeth (Laing) Lundy of Independence, N. J., [of Samuel], and cousin to the former wife; m. (3) at Mendon, N. Y., 27 of 11 mo., 1849, Anna Webster, b. 14 of 5 mo., 1788, d. Galen, N. Y., 22 of 2 mo., 1858, s. p., dau. of Wm. and Susannah Webster.

3. *Zachariah*[6], b. 8 of 8 mo., 1788, Hardwick, Sussex (now Warren) Co., N. J., was a farmer and an exemplary Friend, was in N. J., twice within the recollection of his son Samuel L., once with his family and once with a ministering Friend named Sarah Underwood, who afterward m. and settled in N. J. He d. Macedon Centre, N. Y., 18 of 9 mo., 1857, in 70th yr. of his age; m. (1) in Friends meeting house Hardwick, N. J., Elizabeth Lundy, b. 27 of 6 mo., 1792, in Sussex (now Warren) Co., N. J., d. Galen, Wayne Co., N. Y., 13 of 12 mo., 1816, dau. of Levi and Sarah (Tomer) Lundy of Hardwick, N. J., [of Samuel]; m. (2) in Hardwick Friends meeting house, Edna Lundy, dau. of Daniel and Elizabeth (Laing) Lundy, [of Samuel]. Zachariah and wife Edna L., and 3 minor ch., Levi L., Daniel L, and Edwin, having removed to the Holland Purchase received a cert. from Junius (N. Y.) M. M. directed to Hartland M. M. 28 of 4 mo., 1824. He dw. Elba, N. Y., when he m. (3) in Galen (N. Y) Friends meeting, 25 of 9 mo., 1828, Elizabeth H. Lundy, who d. 4. of 9 mo., 1857, aged 50 yrs. and 7 mo's., dau. of Samuel and Sarah (Lundy) Lundy of Independence, N. J., called Muncy Sammy. Elizabeth H. Shotwell, having removed and settled with her husband at Elba, N. Y., received cert. of membership from Junius M. M. of (Hic.) Friends directed to Rochester M. M. and dated 24 of 3 mo., 1829. On 16 Sept., 1833, Zachariah bought the N. part of Lot 9, Sec. 3 in Elba, by deed recorded in Genesee Co. clerk's office, liber 24, p. 436. Zachariah and wife Elizabeth H. and 4 minor ch., Daniel L., Edwin B., Samuel L., and Edna Ann, brought cert. to Farmington M. M. of (Hic.) Friends from Rochester M. M. dated 24 of 5 mo., 1839; the same except Daniel L. and Edwin B. took back a similar cert. 26 of 9 mo., 1844, but returned with a like cert. dated 24 of 7 mo., 1846.

4. *Amy*[6], b. 12 of 7 mo., 1790, Independence Tp, Sussex (now Warren) Co., N. J., d. Leslie Tp., Ingham Co., Mich., 14 of 11 mo., 1876; was of a quiet, peaceful nature and an exemplary member of the Society of Friends; m. Independence Tp., Sussex (now Warren) Co., N. J., 12 of 10 mo., 1808, Asa Willson, b. 31 of 10 mo., 1786, in N. J., removed from Warren Co., N. J., to Junius, Seneca Co., N. Y., and thence to Raisin, Lenawee Co., Mich., and there d. ...... 1859±, s. of Gabriel and Keziah Willson of Sussex Co., N. J.

5. *Mercy*[6] b. 3 of 8 mo., 1792, Independence, N. J., d. Macedon, N. Y., 15 of 5 mo., 1836; m. Junius Friends meeting, 28 of 12 mo., 1814, (as 2d wife) Daniel Strang of Galen, Seneca (now Wayne) Co., N. Y., b. Saratoga, N. Y., 9 of 5 mo., 1780, d. Hartland, Niagara Co., N. Y., 2 of 1 mo., 1841, s. of Gabriel and Catharine of Junius, N. Y. Daniel and two minor sons, Asa W. and Enoch D., took cert. of membership from Farmington M. M. of (Orth.) Friends to Hartland M. M. dated 25 of 4 mo., 1839.

6. *Benjamin*[6], *Jr.*, b. 23 or 27 of 7 mo., 1797, in Independence, N. J., removed with his family about 1830 from Galen to Elba, N. Y., becoming members of Rochester M. M. of (Hic.) Friends by cert. from Junius M. M. dated 21 of 6 mo., 1831, returned about 1839 to Wayne Co., N. Y., and thence with 5 ch. removed in 5 mo., 1852, to Bedford, Calhoun Co., Mich., bringing cert. of membership to Battle Creek M. M. of (Hic.) Friends from Junius M. M. dated 24 of 3 mo., 1852, mentioning himself, wife Catharine, and 3 minor ch., Mercy L., Mary D., and Edward, also certs. for daughters Elizabeth and Bathsheba. He removed thence in 1870 to Warrensburg, Mo., and finally in 1872 to Idana, Clay Co., Kans., where he took a homestead adjoining those of his s. Edward and dau. Mary, being then 75 yrs. of age, and there d. 30 of 3 mo., 1878; m. in Galen (N. Y.) Friends meeting 3 of 2 mo., 1825, Catharine Pugsley, b. 5 of 12 mo., 1806, d. Bedford, Mich., 2 of 2 mo., 1870, or 3 of 2 mo., 1869, dau. of Wm. and Prudence Pugsley of Galen, N. Y.; she was a worthy member of Battle Creek M. M.; her obituary in a local paper contained the remark that these aged Friends were not rich in the perishable things of this world but, if they were rich in faith realizing that they were equally children of our Father in Heaven, "heirs of God and joint heirs with Jesus Christ," then were the departed far better off than the most wealthy of those who make gold their god and ready pay their religion. Benjamin and Samuel Shotwell of the town of Palmyra, N. Y., are mentioned in a bond given by Scott Fuller of Elba, N. Y., to Joseph Hoag 26 Nov., 1822.

ZACHARIAH[c] SHOTWELL, 1788-1857,
At age of 62,
Of Genesee and Wayne Counties, N. Y., son of Benjamin[5] and Bathsheba [6]Pound
Shotwell, of Galen, Wayne Co., N. Y., and descendant of Benjamin[4],
John[3], John[2], Abraham[1].

ELIZABETH HANNAH (LUNDY) SHOTWELL, 1800-1857,
At age of 50,
THIRD WIFE OF ZACHARIAH[6] SHOTWELL,
And daughter of Samuel and Sarah [1]Lundy Lundy, of Independence, N. J.

7. *Samuel*[5], b. 23 of 8 mo., 1802, Independence, N. J., was farmer and lawyer, removed from Galen, Wayne Co., N. Y., to the little hamlet in Genesee Co., now known as East Oakfield, where he kept a saw mill and grist mill and owned the farm which was afterward the homestead of Moses Vail. According to records in the Genesee Co. clerks office (liber 28 p. 221 and liber 24 p. 284) he bought land in Elba (now Oakfield) on 1 May, 1831, and 18 July, 1832; but on 18 Sept., 1832, he and wife Mercy conveyed land there to Edmond F. Bradly. He afterward dwelt for many years at or near Ottawa, Ill., and there d.; lost one arm in a sorgum grinder in Ill.; dw. Galen, Seneca (now Wayne) Co., N. Y., when he m. (1) in Junius Friends meeting 31 of 1 mo., 1821, Phebe Laing, b. 7 of 8 mo., 1802, d. Elba, N. Y., soon after marriage, 1824±, dau. of Joseph[3] and Anna (Smith) Laing of Junius, N. Y., [of John[4], Samuel[3]?, Wm[2]., John[1]]; having removed to the Holland Purchase, they became members of Hartland M. M. by cert. from Junius M. M. dated 28 of 4 mo., 1824; m. (2) in Bertie, C. W., Mercy Pound, b. Ridgeway, Upper Canada, d. near Ottawa, Ill., aged 80±, dau. of Daniel[4] and Prudence (Jones) Pound of Canada West, [of Elijah[3], John[2], John[1]].

8. *Lydia*[6], b. 27 of 1 mo., 1805, Independence, N. J., d. Galen N. Y., 3 or 4 mo., 1829; m. in Galen Friends meeting, 2 of 12 mo., 1824, John Rogers of Galen, N. Y., b. Grandville, N. Y., 16 of 2 mo., 1801, d. 6 of 4 mo., 1837, s. of Matthew and Phebe Rogers of Galen; were Hicksite Friends and both d. of consumption.

227. BENJAMIN[6] SHOTWELL, 1793–1865, of Genesee and Monroe Co.'s, N. Y., s. of Richard[5] and Mary (Martin) Shotwell, of Elba, N. Y., [of Benj.[4], John[3], John[2], Abr.[1]], m. 1815 *Sarah Hoag*, 1799–1869, dau. of Levi and Desire (Gardner) Hoag, of Elba, N. Y:, and had:

1. *David Smith*[7] b. 6 of 2 mo., 1817, Batavia (now Elba), N. Y., removed thence to Cortland, Kent Co., Mich., 16 miles n. e. of Grand Rapids, and there d. 1 of 2 mo., 1872; m. in Elba Friends meeting house, 19 of 4 mo., 1838, Eliza S. Dillingham, b. 3 of 10 mo., 1820, dw. (1888) Cortland, Mich., dau. of Silvanus[2] and Judith (Marshall) Dillingham, [of John[1]]. On the evening of their marriage the log house in which they expected to live was destroyed by fire.

2. *Desire*[7], b. 22 of 8 mo., 1818, Batavia (now Elba), N. Y.; dw. Fairport, N. Y., a wd.; m. at same place and time as her brother David, 19 of 4 mo., 1838, Robert Estes of Wheatland, Monroe Co., N. Y., b. 13 of 5 mo., 1814, Augusta, Maine, came with his father's family in 1827, to Wheatland, N. Y., settling on a farm there, and thence in 1869 removed to Fairport, N. Y., and there d. at the house of his son Lindley, 10 of 11 mo., 1877; s. of Benjamin and Sarah (Curby

or Kirby) Estes of Wheatland, N. Y., funeral conducted from Wheatland Friends meeting house, buried in Friends ground; was a birthright member of the Society, whereof he continued a consistent member, and in every sense a Christian; held responsible positions in the Society and at time of his death he and his wife were Elders in their M. M.

3. *Bathsheba*[7], b. 14 of 7 mo., 1820, Batavia (now Elba), N. Y., d. 7 of 1 mo., 1875; m. in Collins, N. Y., Edward Sherman; went west.

4. *Mary Jane*[7], b. 15 of 9 mo., 1822, Elba, N. Y.; dw. Collins Centre, Erie Co., N. Y., m. in Collins, N. Y., Addison Smith; a carpenter who d. about 1878.

5. *Richard*, b. 22 of 11 mo., 1824, Elba, N. Y., d. Elba, N. Y., ————————, 1832.

6. *Levi S*[7]., b. 2 of 1 mo., 1827, Elba, N. Y.; dw. for a time Wheatland, N. Y., and afterward on the bank of Grand River, 3 miles n. of Portland, Mich.; P. O. Collins, Ionia Co., Mich., m. Wheatland, N. Y., ————————, 1840, Sarah Estes, b. Wheatland, N. Y., dau. of Allen Estes.

7. *Abigail*[7], b. 18 of 6 mo., 1829, Elba, N. Y., d. Wheatland, N. Y., ————————, 1853; m. Isaac[7] Cox, b. 1825±, s. of James[6] and Silva (Lewis) Cox, of Wheatland, N. Y., and ————————, Wis., [of Samuel[5], Joseph[4] Cock, Samuel[3], Henry[2], James[1]].

8. *Benjamin H.*, b. 28 of 3 mo., 1832, Elba, N. Y., went about 1850 from O., to Cal., and probably d. there; m. ————————, a Catholic who remained in O.

9. *Sarah A.*, b. 20 of 12 mo., 1833, Elba, N. Y.; d. ————————, 1853, unm.

10. *Isaac M*[7]., b. 22 of 10 mo., 1835, Elba, N. Y., dw. Corunna, Shiawassee Co., Mich., m. in Wheatland, N. Y., Mary P. Estes, dau. of Allen, and sister to wife of bro. Levi.

239. BENJAMIN[6] SHOTWELL, 1793–1859, of Blazing Star, Middlesex Co., N. J., s. of Wm[5]. and Elizabeth (Moore) Shotwell of Shotwells Landing, Rahway, N. J., [of Benjamin[4], John[3], John[2], Abraham[1]], m. *Mary Hunt*, dau. of James[3] and Sarah? Hunt, of Middlesex Co., N. J., [of Marmaduke[2], Solomon[1]], and had:

1. *Elizabeth V.*, dw. St. Clair, Mich., m. Elijah M. Bacon.

2. *Lydia D.*, dw. Milltown, N. J., m. Melvin Gordon.

3. *Harriet H.*, dw. St. Clair, Mich., m. Gen. Simeon B. Brown.

4. *Sarah S.*, d. ——————; m. John Hart.

5. *Wm. J*[7]., dw. Orange, N. J., formerly at Blazing Star; m. 1862, Mary N. Melick.

6. *Jeanette C.*, d. ——————

7. *Samuel H*[7]., b. 9 Jan., 1836, at Blazing Star, Middlesex Co., N. J.; received his education in district schools, finishing in a select school at Perth Amboy, N. J.; when 19 years of age, he went to New York City, where he

engaged with wholesale house of D. H. Decker, remaining there 14 years. Leaving N. Y., in 1873, he settled at Gloversville, N. Y., where he held the position of manager of the glove material house of Rose, McAlpin & Co., until Jan., 1885, when he purchased the business of his employers, which he has successfully conducted to the present time. He is in politics a Rep., was a trustee of the village in 1886; was elected a member of the board of education in 1890, and is a director in the Fonda, Johnstown and Gloversville R. R. He married by Friend's ceremony at Rahway, N. J., 8 of 12 mo., 1874, Jane Elizabeth Everit, b. 19 Mar., 1839, in New York City, daughter of Richard and Mary (Carle) Everit of New York.

8. *Esther E.*, d. .....

236. BENJAMIN[6] SHOTWELL, 1797–1878, of Bedford, Calhoun Co., Mich., s. of Benjamin[5] and Bathsheba (Pound) Shotwell, of Wayne Co., N. Y., [of Benj[4], John[3], John[2], Abraham[1]], m. 1825 *Catharine Pugsley*, 1806–1870±, dau. of Wm. and Prudence of Galen, N. Y., and had:

1. *William P.*, b. 1 of 11 mo., 1825, Galen, Wayne Co., N. Y., and there d. 25 of 12 mo., 1825, or 25 of 2 mo., 1826.

2. *Prudence P.*, b. 5 of 10 mo., 1826, Galen, N. Y., d. Walworth, Wayne Co., N. Y., 27 of 6 mo., 1876, of consumption; m. in Junius, Seneca Co., N. Y., 7 of 6 mo., 1853, (as 2d w.), Jediah S. Pound of Williamson, Wayne Co., N. Y., b. 26 of 8 mo., 1804, d. in W. Walworth, N. Y., 5 of 2 mo., 1882, s. of Hugh[5] and Sarah (King) Pound of Farmington, N. Y., [of Samuel[4], Elijah[3], John[2], John[1]].

3. *Samuel P.*, b. 14 of 5 mo., 1828, Galen, N. Y., removed from Wayne Co., N. Y., to Battle Creek, Mich., in 1851; kept a shoe store at Augusta, Mich., whence in the spring of 1871, he, with his wife and 4 daughters, removed to Five Creeks, Kans.; dw. Idana, Clay Co., Kans.; m. ...., 1851±, Maria Watson of Junius, N. Y., who d. 1 May, 1886, buried in Idana, Kans.

4. *Elizabeth*, b. 16 of 3 mo., 1830; m. George P. Russell, then a moulder in an iron foundry, Michigan City, Ind.

5. *Daniel*, b. 30 of 9 mo., 1831, Elba (now Oakfield), Genesee Co., N. Y., d. 8 of 5 mo., 1833.

6. *Bathsheba R.*, b. 20 of 9 mo., 1833, Elba (now Oakfield), N. Y., d. 6 Oct., 1886, buried in Monte Vista, Colo.; m. Marvin Mead of Bedford, Mich., whence, in 1884, they, with youngest two ch., removed to Henry (now Monte Vista), Rio Grande Co., Colo., where he dw., having m. (2) in O. in autumn of 1887 his cousin, Mary Gifford Robbins, a wd.

7. *Mercy Lydia*, called Lydia M., b. 4 of 6 mo., 1836, Elba, N. Y.; m. Wm. T. Simmons, of Bedford, Mich., b. 23 Nov., 1827, d. 27 Jan., 1886.

8. *Edward Hix*, b. 28 of 1 mo., 1838, Elba, N. Y., served in Union Army in war of the rebellion; removed in spring of 1884, with his 2d wife and four daughters from Warrensburgh, Johnson Co., Mo., to Henry (now Monte Vista), Rio Grande Co., Colo., P. O. Monte Vista; m. (1) 15 Oct., 1865, Rosetta E. Corwin, who d. Warrensburgh, Mo., 19 Sept., 1867, of typhoid fever, buried in Bedford (Mich.) cemetery; m. (2) .... Oct., 1868, Eliza Jones, of Warrensburgh, Mo.

9. *Mary D.*, b. 1. of 3 mo., 1840, Galen, N. Y., removed with her family in the fall of 1871 from Warrensburgh, Mo., to Clay Co., Kans., settling at Idana; m. 17 Oct., 1867, Hiram W. Bradley, b. Canada West, 17 of 11 mo., 1838, enlisted in Co. F. of 11 Mich. Cavalry, 22 Oct., 1863, for three yrs., and was discharged at the end of the war, 10 Aug., 1865, when the regiment was disbanded. They have known privation and hardship, like other pioneers of Kans., though they felt fortunate in being always warmed and fed from their own, while some of their neighbors had to look to others for sustenance, but more prosperous times have since supervened.

10. *Margaret Ann*, b. 2 of 7 mo., 1841, Galen, N. Y., d. 20 of 2 mo., 1845.

11. *George Emmor*, b. 1 of 3 mo., 1847, Galen, N. Y., and there d. 3 of 9 mo., 1851.

BENJAMIN HEATON[7] SHOTWELL, b. 1815, of Hadley, Lapeer Co., Mich., s. of Thomas[6] and Tamer (Lundy) Shotwell of Galen, N. Y., [of Benjamin[5], Benjamin[4], John[3], John[2], Abraham[1]], m. (1) *Susan L. Thorn*, b. 1813, dau. of Samuel[6] and Rachel (Laing) Thorn of Junius, N. Y., [of Abr[5], Abr[4], Abr[3], Jos[2], Wm[1].], and had:

1. *Rachel T.* b. ..... of 8 mo., 1842, in Galen, N. Y., dw. Hadley, Lapeer Co., Mich.; m. Junius, N. Y., Solomon Bishop.

BENJAMIN H[7]. SHOTWELL, b. 1815, of Hadley, Mich., [of Thos[6]., Benj[5]., Benj[4]., John[3], John[2] Abr[1].], m. (2) *Paulina (Richards) Davis*, and had:

2. *Katie B.*, b. Lapeer Co., Mich., dw. in Hadley, Mich., s. p.; m. in Mich., Cassius Hemingway.

3. *Ella*, b. Hadley, Mich.; there dw. with her father, unm. (1888.)

BENJAMIN WARDER[6] SHOTWELL, b. 1839, of Trenton, Mo., s. of Edward R[5]. and Margaret H. (Shotwell) Shotwell of Marengo, O., [of Peter[5] Isaiah[5], John[4], John[3], John[2], Abr[1].], m. 1869, *Mary Hoyle*, dau. of Edward and Sarah E. Hoyle of Brookfield, Linn Co., Mo., and had:

1. *Edward R., Jr.*, b. 11 Sept., 1885, Marengo, Morrow Co., O.

BENJAMIN HEATON[7] SHOTWELL, b. 1853 of Brainard, Butler Co., Neb., s. of Zachariah P[6]., and Margaret (Zavitz) Shotwell of Lobo, Ont., [of Thos⁶., Benj⁵., Benj⁴., John³, John², Abr¹.], m. 1876, *Melissa Lowes*, dau. of Caleb and Susannah Lowes of Blenheim, Ont., and had:

1. *Margaret Susannah*, b. 2 of 12 mo., 1876, in Lobo, Ont.
2. *Lawrence Elsworth*, b. 29 of 6 mo., 1878, in Lobo, Ont.
3. *Eli Lowes*, b. 5 of 2 mo., 1881, Plumcreek Tp., Butler Co., Neb.
4. *Lottie Pearl*, b. 30 of 4 mo., 1883, Plumcreek Tp., Neb.
5. *Charles Willis*, b. 1 of 5 mo., 1885, in Plumcreek Tp., Neb.
6. *Thomas Le Roy*, b. 5 of 2 mo., 1888, Plumcreek Tp., Neb.
7. *Ida Frances*, b. 5 of 1 mo., 1893.

BENJAMIN F⁸. SHOTWELL, b. 1862, of Cortland, Mich., s. of David S⁷. and Eliza (Dillingham) Shotwell of Cortland, Mich., [of Benjamin⁵, Richard⁵, Benjamin⁴, John³, John², Abraham¹], married 1887, *Alice Bennett*, daughter of Lyman and Celestia (Unger) Bennett of Cortland, Mich., [of Solomon], and had:

1. *Florence B.*, b. 14 July, 1888.
2. *Everett L.*, b. 1 June ,1891.
3. *Forrest L.*, b. 7 Aug., 1894.

81. CALEB⁵ SHOTWELL, b. 1749–50, of Saratoga Co., N. Y., s. of Samuel⁴ and Amy Shotwell of Rahway, Essex (now Union)Co., N. J., [of John³, John², Abr¹.], m. *Phebe (Hinckston) Gliddon*, and had:

1. *David⁶*, m. (1) Polly Lewis; m. (2) Bulah Wood of Port Byron, N. Y.
2. *Samuel⁶*, dw. near Hackettstown, N. J.; m.
-------- ----------
3. *Amy⁶*, m. John Randall.
4. *Robert*.
5. *Joseph⁶*, b. 27 Feb., 1789, Essex Co., or Greenwich, Cumberland Co., N.J.; d. near Barryville, Sullivan Co., N. Y., 6 Mar., 1869, aged 80 years and 7 days; was a very intelligent and pious man, truly able in the scriptures, and served as deacon in the Baptist church; "was one of the best men in York State," said his nephew David, who will never forget the welcome he received from his uncle Joseph as he stepped into his house, rising and exclaiming, "Come in! take a chair! This is Sarah's boy, David, is it?" He m., by Elijah Peck, in Half Moon, N. Y., 24 July, 1811, Sarah Randall of Burnt Hills, Saratoga Co., N. Y., b. 10 Dec., 1793, d. 3 Nov., 1877. Of their 10 ch. who grew to be men and women, 9 were hopefully pious.
6. *Polly*, d. Saratoga Co., N. Y., ____, 1838, s. p.; m. John R. Maxwell.
7. *Sarah⁶*, called Sally; m. 1824 ±, Richard Kells of Cayuga Co., N. Y., b. N. J., 1805 ±.
8. *Phebe⁶*, m. Thomas Kerns.

CALEB G¹. SHOTWELL, 1815–1873, of Barryville, Sullivan Co., N. Y., s. of Joseph⁶ and Sarah (Randall) Shotwell of Saratoga Co., N. Y., [of Caleb⁵, Samuel⁴, John³, John², Abraham¹], m. 1837, *Sally Jane Carey*, and had:

1. *Azubah Jane*.
2. *Fannie*, m. 1857, Charles Webb of New York City.

CARLOS BACON⁸ SHOTWELL, b. 1848, of Detroit, Mich., s. of John M⁷. and Saloma L. (Stone) Shotwell, [of Joseph⁶, Caleb⁵, Samuel⁴, John³, John², Abraham¹], m. 1871, *Eliza L. Williams*, b. 1851, daughter of Nicholas and Sarah (Nichols) Williams of Oswego, N. Y., and had:

1. *Clara Louise*, b. 17 March, 1873, in Detroit, Mich., is member of the M. E. Church of Detroit.
2. *Alice Williams*, b. 21 Jan., 1876, Detroit, Mich., d. 29 Feb., 1884, aged 8 yrs. and 8 days, passed away after an illness of only 48 hours, singing Gospel Songs learned in Sunday school and in the home circle, and her last moments were filled with Heavenly visions wonderful for a child to express.
3. *Sarah Eliza*, called Sadie, b. 22 Feb., 1878, in Detroit, Mich., is member of the M. E. Church there.
4. *Fred Meredith*, b. 16 Sept., 1880, Detroit, Mich.
5. *Edith Lillian*, b. 7 Sept., 1887, Detroit, Mich.

CASSIUS EMMETT⁸ SHOTWELL, b. 1855, of Concord, Jackson Co, Mich., s. of Nathan⁷ and Phebe B. (Gardner) Shotwell of Concord, Mich., [of Isaac M⁶., Richard⁵, Benjamin⁴, John³, John², Abraham¹], m. 1885, *Edith Myrtle Briggs*, b. 1866, dau. of Wm. C⁵., and Elizabeth (Lewis) Briggs of N. Concord, Mich., [of Richmond³, Pardon², John¹], and had:

1. *Owen Briggs*, b. 17 Sept., 1886, in the village of Concord, Jackson Co., Mich.

CHARLES AKIN SHOTWELL, born in New York, 22 June, 1846, now of 3501 Mather St., Philadelphia, Pa.; parentage unknown; was adopted in infancy by Mary⁵ Shotwell of Tremont, Westchester Co., N. Y., afterward (1855–70) of West Farms, N. Y., dau. of Wm⁵. and Sarah (Hopkins) Shotwell of New York, [of Joseph⁴, John³, John², Abraham¹], and 3d wife (m. 14 Feb., 1856) of Morris Shipley of Westchester Co., N. Y., formerly of Utoxeter, Staffordshire, Eng., who d. in 1859, and whose 1st wife was Mary's sister Sarah⁵ Shotwell—the mother of his 3 children, Joseph, Murray, and Annie. His (Shipley's) 2d wife was Ann Eddy of Rahway, N. J.

When about 14 years old, he (Charles A.) committed some boyish prank which so incensed his foster mother that she then for the first time told him that he was not her child and had no claim upon her. Further than this she would never go; the only thing she would say about his parentage was that some day the Lord would reveal it to him. In 1861 he ran away from home and joined the 62d New York Volunteers, being anxious to take part in the war for the Union, which had just broken out. His foster mother, however, discovered his whereabouts just before the regiment marched to the South, and as he was under 18 years of age, he was compelled to return with her; and to prevent a repetition of what she was pleased to term his "scandalous conduct," he was placed on board the ship Viking, of Boston, Capt. Townsend, and sent to California and China. In 1862 the vessel was wrecked in the Japan Sea; and the survivors ultimately found their way to Yokohama. There he joined the U. S. S. Jamestown and served in her till after the close of the war in 1865 returning home in October of that year.

In 1866 he again sailed for California in the ship David Crockett and after varied experiences in the gold mining districts of California, Nevada and Utah, he enlisted in Company K., 8th U. S. Cavalry and served through the Indian campaign in Arizona. In 1869 he sailed from San Francisco to Liverpool, England; in the British ship Queen of Beauty; thence to Quebec and Montreal spending the summer of that year on the great lakes, returning to England in the fall and sailing thence to various ports in South America. At the opening of the Suez Canal he started on a series of voyages to India, China and Africa. He joined Her Majesty's troop ship, Adventurer, and took part in the expediton to Abyssinia and the siege of Magdala. He was with Sir W. F. Roberts in the attack on Cabul in Afghanistan. In 1873 he was one of the survivors of the burning of the S. S. Riga in the straits of Sumatra, and was subsequently appointed by Capt. A. D. S. Denison [afterward Lord Londesborough] on the staff of Lt. Col. J. T. N. O'Brien of the military police in Port Louis, Isle of France (Mauritius). This last most lucrative position he was compelled to relinquish owing to a severe attack of the Dingue fever, a malignant form of fever and ague to which the dwellers in that far off isle are peculiarly subject. The Dingue fever was contracted through exposure on a coral reef whilst rescuing a native woman of Bengal from drowning in a sea swarming with sharks. For this he holds the Royal Humane Society's gold medal and a special medal presented by the Governor of Mauritius (vide) London Illustrated News, December, 1873. He got away just in time to save his life, and after a short sojourn in Australia, sailed thence to Oregon and California, where he remained till 1875, when he returned to England in the British ship Airlie.

During the whole of this last absence from home he had written frequently to his adopted mother, but for some reason, never explained, he received no replies. On his return to New York, in March, 1876, he found that Mary (Shotwell) Shipley had died in January of that year, also both her sisters and her step-daughter Annie Shipley. He did not make many inquiries, for he thought that most of the old lady's relatives regarded him as an interloper. He went for a short stay in Cuba, and on returning to New York joined the British ship George Thompson, carrying passengers to Melbourne, Victoria; he thenceforth resided in Australia for 17 years, returning in 1893 to his native land, chiefly to secure for his two sons a more liberal education than could be obtained for them at the Antipodes, and if possible to give them a better start in life than was vouchsafed to himself. His wife and family followed him, arriving in Philadelphia, in Nov., 1894. He is a prominent member of the G. A. R., Secretary of the Philadelphia Naval Veteran Association, and is one of the trustees of that portion of Independence Hall, Philadelphia, which has been allotted to the Naval Veterans of the Department of Pennsylvania, also a member by baptism and confirmation of the Church of England, Episcopal; he has also had the honor to fill the position of Grand Marshal of the Grand Lodge of Australasia, I. O. O. F.

He married (1) at Liverpool, Eng., *Alice De Mouliere*, who died at Warrington, Eng., in 1872 of phthisis, daughter of Claud Vevera and Marguerite De Mouliere, of the Isle of Jersey, British Channel, deceased.

CHARLES AKIN SHOTWELL, born 1846, now of Philadelphia, Pa., married (2) in Melbourne, Australia, in 1876, *Agnes Brook* born at Huddersfield, Eng., 30 Aug., 1846, eldest daughter of John and Ame (Gledhill) Brook of Melbourne, Victoria, and had six children, of whom the following are living with the parents in Philadelphia.

1. *Henry Shipley*, born 1882±.
2. *William Francis*, born 1885±.

CHARLES A.[9] SHOTWELL, b. 1867, of Audrain Co., Mo., s. of James L.[8] and Sallie C. (Magee) Shotwell, [of Albert[7], John[6], John[5], John[4], Abraham[3]?, John[2], Abraham[1]], m. *Mattie Smith*, and had:

1. *Blanche.*
2. *Orion.*
3. *Leona.*
4. ......, a daughter, b. ...., 1895.

CLARKSON[7] SHOTWELL, of Brooklyn, N. Y., s. of Daniel C[6]. and Martha (Pound) Shotwell of Greenbrook, N. J., [of Manning[5], Benj[4]., John[3], Daniel[2], Abraham[1]], m. *Mary Ross*, and had:

1. *Susan.*
2. *Waller.*
3. *Georgiana[7]*, d. ....; m. George Gwyn.

176. CLARKSON FREEMAN[6] SHOTWELL, b. 1789, of Pontiac, Oakland Co., Mich., s. of James[5] and Elsie (Smalley) Shotwell, of Long Bridge, N. J., [of Jno.[1], Jno.[2], Jno.[3], Abr.[1]], m. *Keziah Sutton*, dau. of Wm. and Annie (Harkins) Sutton, and step dau. of .... Freeman, and had:

1. *Anna*, who m. Philip Dyer, and had six children.

2. *Elsie*, who m. Joseph Linaberry, and had eleven children.

3. *Wm.*, dw. Oxbow, Oakland Co., Mich., and there d. 25 May, 1894; was member of the "Sons of the Revolution," of Detroit, Mich.; m. (1) Theresa Linaberry, who d. leaving three children; he m. (2) Elizabeth Fitzgerald, who d. leaving three children, who were reared in the family of William's sister, Mrs. Orrilla Worden.

4. *John*[1], d. 1887 ±; m. Sarah Johnson, who dw. (1893) Owosso, Mich., dau. of Ebenezer and Laura (....) Johnson.

5. *Mary* (twin of John), dw. in Whitelake Tp., Oakland Co., Mich., P.O., Oxbow; m. Wm. Gale, and had one son, Abram.

6. *Clarissa Ann*, who m. Wm. Bailey, and had ten sons.

7. *Caroline Matilda*, lives in Lum, Lapeer Co., Mich., a wid.; m. ...... Eastman and had eleven children.

8. *Jonathan*, dw. Nashville, Tenn.: m. Celinda Parkis; had four children who live Pontiac, Mich.

9. *Orrilla*, b. 1829, in New Jersey, came to Michigan in 1836, dw. in Whitelake Tp., Oakland Co., Mich., P. O., Oxbow, has lived on same farm since autumn of 1855; m. Archibald Warden. They have no children except by adoption.

10. *Prudence*, who d.; m. John P. Worden, who dw. five miles from Lowden, Cedar Co., Iowa; they had one son and one daughter.

11 *George Washington*, who m. (1) Angeline Toping, and had five children; after her death he m. (2) ...., and had one daughter.

3. DANIEL[1] SHOTWELL, of Staten Island supposed s. of Abraham[1] Shotwell of Elizabethtown and New York, m. *Elizabeth* ...., and probably had:

1. *Ann*[2], m. (1) with approval of Woodbridge M. M., 25 of 6 mo., 1713, Henry Brotherton of Woodbridge, N. J., who d. 1727 ±. Henry Brotherton, the first of the name in America, came from Manchester, Eng., about the year 1700, lived in Monmouth Co., N. J., then moved to Bridgetown (now Rahway) where his children were born; was a zealous Episcopalian of humble rank but possessed of a stout heart, active brain, and willing hands; and in order to raise the price of his passage to America, sold his services to a Friend, with whom he lived for several years. There is a tradition in the family that, feeling it to be his duty to convince his employer of certain errors in doctrine held by the Quakers, a friendly theological discussion was begun, which

resulted in Henry himself embracing Friends' views. He united with the Society. Most of his descendants have been active Friends and noted for their sympathy with the needy of all classes, regardless of sect, race or condition. The following is from Friends records: "Att our Monthly Meeting held att ye New Meet-Meeting house In Woodbridge ye 20th of ye 11th mo., 1714-15. It is Concluded by this Meeting that a Stable Shall be built of 25 foot in length & 16 foot in breadth w'th 6 foot between Sill & plate & to be Covered w'th Shingles over ye top, & on ye sides & ends w'th bords. John Luffberry and Henry Brotherton are desired to agree w'th Somebody to do it and make report to ye next Monthly Meeting." On 17 of 12 mo., 1714-15, Henry Brotherton was chosen Clerk of the M. M., which position he continued to hold for many years. Ann (Shotwell) Brotherton m. (2) with unity of Woodbridge M. M., ... 1728-9, between 16 of 11 mo. (Jan.) and 20 of 12 mo., Peter Wren, the M. M. insisting that before her 2d marriage something should be settled upon the Children of Henry Brotherton, deceased, out of his estate. Peter Wren was disowned by the Society 19 of 9 mo., 1730, for persisting in the intemperate use of intoxicating liquors.

2. *Joseph*[2], removed from Staten Island to Woodbridge, N. J., m. 20 of 7 mo., 1716, Mary Manning. The following is from the Friends' Book of Minutes: "Att our Monthly Meeting held att our Meeting House in Woodbridge ye 16th day of the 6th mo., 1716, ...Elizabeth Griffith & Eliza Laing presented Joseph Shotwell and Mary Manning before this Meeting who declared their intentions of taking each other in Marriage, it being the first time. Joseph Shotwell's father being here, Satisfied this Meeting of his & his wife's consent and Mary Manning produced a Certificate of her father & mother their consent to this intended marriage and Edward Fitz Randolph & John Shotwell were ordered to enquire into the clearness of Joseph Shotwell concerning precontracts of marriage with any other & make report thereof to the next Monthly Meeting."

One month later, 7-20, 1716, after a favorable report from the Committee, the record continues: "The S'd Joseph & Mary presented .... the Second time before this meeting and continuing their intentions of Marriage with each other were permitted by this meeting to consumate the same according to the good order of friends." In the Woodbridge M. M. minutes, this name is next met with under date of 5th mo. 16th, 1724, when Joseph Shotwell and Henry Brotherton were appointed as representatives to attend the next Quarterly meeting at Shrewsbury.

3. *Mary*[2], m......... 1717, Abraham Thorne of L. I. The following is from the minutes of

the Society of Friends: "Att our Monthly Meeting held att our Meeting house in Woodbridge the 19th day of ye Seventh month, 1717, Mary Shotwell & Eliza Shotwell presented before this Meeting Abraham Thorne and Mary Shotwell, who declared their intention of taking each other in Marriage, it being the Second time, and he producing a Certificate from the Monthly Meeting of Friends at Flushing of his clearness in conversation & in respect to Marriage, friends leaves them to their liberty to consumate their intention of Marriage according to the good order of truth." His parents were living at this time, as, at the previous meeting, 6-15, 1717, "A letter was also produced to this meeting from Abraham Thornes father and mother showing their consent to the marriage intended."

In the Woodbridge M. M. Minutes of 2d mo. 16th, 1724, it is stated that Abraham Thorne had taken Nathaniel, son of Wm. Willis, as an apprentice to learn his trade of a Weaver; and on 8th mo. 20th, 1736, the M. M. directed that this apprentice should serve the remaining part of his time with John Shotwell, he fulfilling his indentures.

4. *John³*, was the 3d of this name among the witnesses to the marriage of Henry Brotherton of Woodbridge and Ann Shotwell of Stateh Island, 25 of 6 mo., 1713. Probably the John whose will, 1745, mentions wife Lydia, and sons John, Benjamin and Joseph.

5. *Susannah³*, d. 26 of 7 mo., 1777; m. ______ 1723, Jacob Thorne, b. ________ 1700, d. 29 of 9 mo., 1759; s. of Joseph and Mary Thorne of Flushing, L. I. "Att our Monthly Meeting held att our Meeting house in Woodbridge the 18 day of 8th mo., 1722, ________, Jacob Thorne produced a Certificate from Flushing Monthly Meeting which was read and approved of by this Meeting." "Att our Mouthly Meeting held att our Meeting house in Woodbridge the 16th day of the 3d mo. 1723, ________ Mary Thorne & Susannah Webster presented Jacob Thorne & Susannah Shotwell before this meeting, who declared their intentions of taking each other in Marriage, it being the first time. This Meeting appointed John Shotwell & Abraham Thorne to enquire in Jacob Thorne his clearness in respect to any engagement of Marriage with any other & to make report thereof to the next Monthly Meeting." And at the next meeting, 4-20, 1723, " Mary Thorne & Ann Brotherton presented Jacob Thorne & Susannah Shotwell, who declared their intentions of taking each other in Marriage, it being the Second time: And the S'd Jacob presented a Second Certificate from the Monthly Meeting off Friends of Flushing, Long Island, (the first, being short, not mentioning his clearness in respect to Marriage) as the last did to the satisfaction of friends, and enquiry being made by the friends appointed, nothing appearing to the Contrary but that he was clear of all other Women, & their parents Consenting thereto, friends left them to their liberty [to] consummate their intentions according to the good order of truth. Daniel Shotwell & Henry Brotherton were appointed to attend the S'd Marriage to see that it be accomplished in the S'd good order." At the following meeting a member of this committee reported that the marriage had been duly consummated. On the 15 of 11 mo., 1735-6, Jacob Thorn was appointed an overseer by Woodbridge M. M. in the room of Benjamin Smith, deceased.

6. *Margaret*, (dau. of Daniel and Elizabeth), born 18 of 2 month (April), 1708, on Staten Island.

7. *Elizabeth³*, d. 31 of 9 mo. (Nov.), 1750; m. with unity of Woodbridge M. M. of Friends, ________, 1727-8, between 21 of 1 mo. and 18 of 2 mo. (Apr.), 1728, Benjamin³ Moore, b. Oct. ye 10th, 1705, in Elizabethtown, N. J., s. of John² and Hope (Robinds) Moore of Woodbridge, N. J., [of Samuel¹].

8. *Daniel*, received from Woodbridge M. M. a cert. of clearness with respect to marriage directed to Shrewsbury M. M. and dated 21 of 1 mo., 1733.

9. *Martha*, m. ________, 1732, between 20 of 2 mo. and 18 of 3 mo., Samuel Alling.

SYNOPSIS OF THE CHILDREN AND GRANDCHILDREN OF

DANIEL² SHOTWELL, OF STATEN ISLAND,

SUPPOSED SON OF ABRAHAM¹ SHOTWELL.

DANIEL² SHOTWELL, m. *Elizabeth* ________, and is supposed to have had nine children, namely:

1. *Ann³*, who m. (1) 1713, Henry¹ Brotherton, of Woodbridge, N. J., who d. about 1727±; she m. (2) 1728-9 Peter Wren. By the former husband she had: (1.) John Brotherton, b. 1714. (2.) Mary, b. 1715-16. (3.) Elizabeth, b. 1717. (4.) Grace, b. 1719; m. 1735 Enoch³ Moore, [of John², Samuel¹]. (5.) Ann, b. 1721. (6.) Henry, b. 1722. (7.) Henry (again), b. 1724, m. 1752 Masse (Mercy) Schooly, [of Wm. and Elizabeth]. (8.) James, b. 1726, m. 1754 Alice Schooly, sister to Mercy.

2. *Joseph³ Shotwell*, of Woodbridge, N. J., m. 1716 Mary Manning, and had: (1.) Joseph, III, b. 1717; m. 1743 Elizabeth Jackson. (2.) Nicholas, b. 1718. (3.) Elizabeth, b. 1720. (4.) Mary, b. 1722-3; m. 1745 Nathaniel Fitz Randolph, 1714-1780. (5.) Daniel⁴, b. 1725; m. 1753 Deborah⁴ Shotwell, b. 1735, [of Abraham³, John², Abraham¹]. (6.) Abraham, b. 1726; m. 1750-51 Mary Jackson. (7.) Isaac, 1727-1731. (8.) Jacob, b. 1729; m. (1) ---------; m. (2) ---------. (9.) Elizabeth, b. 1731-2; m. 1773 Samuel Smith, b. 1722-3, [of Shobal², Samuel¹].

3. *Mary³*, m. 1717 Abraham² Thorne, b. 1696±, s. of Jos². and Mary (Bowne) Thorne of Flushing., L. I., [of Wm¹.]; dw. Woodbridge, N. J., formerly of Flushing, L. I.; and had after removal to Woodbridge: (1.) Abraham, b. 1728-9; m. 1750, Susannah Webster. (2.) Hannah, b. 1731-2.

4. *John³*, d. about 1745; m. Lydia ---------, and had: (1.) John. (2.) Benjamin⁴, b. 1731; m. 1754 Elizabeth Manning. (3.) Joseph.

5. *Susannah³*, d. 1777; m. 1723 Jacob³ Thorne, 1700-1759, s. of Joseph² and Mary (Bowne) Thorne of Flushing, L. I., [of Wm¹.], and had: (1.) Mary, b. 1724; m. 1741 David Laing, 1714-1747-8, s. of John and Elizabeth³ (Shotwell) Laing, [of John² Shotwell, Abraham¹]. (2.) Sarah, b. 1726; m. 1749 Wm³. Webster, [of Wm²., Wm¹]. (3.) Susannah, m.? 1746-7 Wm. Morris. (4.) Martha, b. 1732. (5.) Jacob, b. 1734. (6.) Elizabeth, b. 1736. (7.) Joseph, b. 1737-8; m. ---------. (8.) Ann, b. 1740. (9) Martha (again), b. 1742. (10.) Margaret, 1741-1759. (11.) Jacob, b. 1746; m.? 1769 ---------.

6. *Margaret*, b. 18 of 2 m. (Apr.), 1708, on Staten Island.

7. *Elizabeth*, d. 1750; m. 1727-8 Benjamin³ Moore, b. 1705, [of John², Samuel¹], and had " a large family."

8. *Daniel*, m. at Shrewsbury, N. J., 1733, ---------

9. *Martha*, m. 1733 Samuel Alling.

37. DANIEL⁴ SHOTWELL, b. 1725, of Woodbridge, N. J., s. of Joseph³ and Mary (Manning) Shotwell, of Staten Island, [of Daniel², ? Abraham¹], m. 1753, *Deborah⁴ Shotwell*, b. 1735, dau. of Abraham³ and Elizabeth (Cowperthwaite) Shotwell, of Piscataway, N. J., [of John², Abraham¹], and had:

1. *Hannah*, b. 12 of 4 mo., 1756.

2. *Titus, I⁵*, b. 11 of 8 mo. or 17 of 11 mo., 1758, removed from Woodbridge, N. J., in 1792, to Woodland, Clearfield Co., Pa, taking cert. of membership for himself, his 2d wife, Deborah, and five minor children, Daniel, Hope, Edward, Titus, and Miriam, from R. and P. M. M., dated 20 of 9 mo., 1792, and directed to the meeting at Westland, near Redstone, Pa.; and about 1810 he removed from Chester Co., Pa., to Belmont Co., O., and there d. before 1835; m. (1) at Rahway, N. J., 26 of 4 mo., 1781, Sarah Marsh of Woodbridge Tp., N. J.; m. (2) at Rahway, N. J., 26 of 7 mo., 1787, Deborah Moore of Woodbridge Tp., dau. of Edward⁴ Moore of Lower Rahway, [of Samuel³, John², Samuel¹]; m. (3) 3 of 4 mo., 1807, Deborah Howell, d. at the home of her son Nathan Shotwell at Barnesville, O. One record or tradition gives the name of Titus' mother as Rebecca.

3. *Elizabeth*, b. 1 of 8 mo., 1760; m. Daniel Marsh.

4. *John*, b. 22 of 9 mo., 1762.

5. *Mary⁵*, b. 29 of 7 mo., 1764; d. 21 of 4 mo., 1841; dw. in Woodbridge Tp. when she m. at Rahway, 23 of 11 mo., 1786, Benjamin Thorn of Woodbridge, b. 23 of 2 mo., 1764, s. of Abraham and Ann (Laing) Thorn.

6. *Daniel⁵*, b. 8 of 6 mo., 1767; died 1838, buried in Friends' ground 1 of 3 mo., 1838; probably the Daniel of Woodbridge who m. with unity of Friends at Rahway 25 of 10 mo., 1787, Margaret Alstone or Elston of Woodbridge Tp., as among the witnesses to this marriage were Daniel Shotwell, Deborah Shotwell, Hannah Elston, Andrew Elston, Agnes Elston, Sarah Elston, Isaac Moore, and others. One Margaret Shotwell d. in Middlesex Co., N. J., 2 of 1 m., 1815, aged 63, buried at Rahway; a child Margaret (parentage not stated) d. Middlesex Co., N. J., 31 of 12 mo., 1814, aged 9 years, buried at Rahway. Daniel Shotwell m. (2 ?) Keziah Terrill, who d. Rahway, N. J., 26 of 12 mo., 1819, aged 44 years, and was buried at Rahway; became member of Friends' meeting at Rahway on application in 1805; was youngest of four children, William, John, Susan. and Keziah.

7. *Sarah*, b. 2 of 8 mo., 1772.

107. DANIEL⁵ SHOTWELL, b. 1767, of Woodbridge, N. J., s. of Daniel⁴ and Deborah (Shotwell) Shotwell of Woodbridge, [of Joseph³, Daniel², Abraham¹], m. 1787 ?, *Keziah Terrill*, who d. 1819, and had:

1. *Sarah*, d. 1832; m. Wm. Parker.

2. *Susan*, d. 1820.

3. *John*, b. 10 Oct., 1793; dw. Rahway, N. J.; d. 1837; was a shoemaker; m. Sarah Moore, b. 21 March, 1801, dau. of Joseph of Turkey Hill, N. J.

4. *Joseph⁶*, removed with his family to the west and there died 1862, m. Ann Ball, dau. of Deacon --------- Ball.

5. *Daniel⁶, Jr.*, b. 24 Oct., 1806, at Rahway, N. J.; lived there till after marriage, in 1827. During the following half century he moved 26 times and found life's pathway anything but smooth. In 1858 he went to Minnesota, in broken health, settled on the Otter Tail River (now called the Red), four miles below the present city of Fergus Falls. In 1860 he removed to the young village of Alexandria, Douglas Co, Minn., and soon afterward took a claim on lakes Geneva and Victoria, three miles east of Alexandria. Here his reverses included the grasshopper scourge, the

raid of the savage redskins, and the running of the railroad through the "Shotwell Place." During the alarm and peril of the Indian outbreak, he took refuge for 18 mos. in St. Cloud, but returned to his lakeside home, and there resided until three years before his death, when he with his wife returned to Alexandria, making his home with his son, Capt. James A. Shotwell, and there d. 5 Nov., 1882, aged about 76 years.

> "Life's race well run,
> Life's work well done,
> Life's crown well won."

Of Quaker parentage and training, he naturally sympathized very earnestly with the early anti-slavery movements. He was for many years an honored official member of the M. E. Church, but withdrew on account of the conservatism of that denomination respecting the question of emancipation; yet he continued a zealous Christian and a close Bible student all his life. He m. 10 Nov., 1827, Margaret Ann Elizabeth Force, b. 7 Oct., 1809, at New Dover, 5 miles from Rahway, N. J.,who died at Alexandria, Minn., 12 Jan., 1880, soon after their golden wedding, which was pleasantly commemorated at their residence, "Hope Cottage," near Alexandria. Of their eleven children (six surviving) and twenty-six grandchildren, but two children and eight grandchildren were present on that occasion, the others being scattered over various states, from New Jersey to Oregon. Margaret was sister to Jeremiah C. Force and daughter of Ezra and Nancy (Clarkson) Force of New Dover, N. J.

Both died of Appendicitis, and were buried in Kinkead cemetery, Alexandria, Minn.

281. DANIEL CLARKSON[6] SHOTWELL, 1791–1875, called "Hatter Daniel," of Greenbrook, N. J., s. of Manning[5] and Mary (Clarkson) Shotwell, [of Benjamin[4], John[3], Daniel[2], Abr[1].], m. *Martha Pound*, dau. of Samuel[5] and Susannah (Webster) Pound, [of Zachariah[4], Elijah[3], John[2], John[1]], and had:

1. *Edmund V[7].*, b. 25 Aug., 1816, Greenbrook, N. J., d. Plainfield, N. J., _________, 1888, "aged 71 yrs., 9 mos., 5 days," funeral from home of dau. Martha J. Cadmus, W. 4th St., Plainfield, N. J.; m. (1) Freelove Laing; m. (2) in Brooklyn, N. Y., 28 Apr., 1844, Jane H. Williams, b. 5 July, 1844, d. 22 June, 1868; m. (3) Elizabeth (Marsh) Olmstead, dw. Plainfield, N. J., s. p.

2. *Eli P.*, b. 5 Jan., 1818, Greenbrook, N. J.; d. Brooklyn, N. Y.; m. Emma Eliza Boice, dau. of David.

3. *Mary*, d. young.

4. *Clarkson[7]*, b. 12 June, 1821, dw. Brooklyn, N. Y.; m. Mary O. Ross.

5. *Elizabeth D[7].*, b. 28 March, 1823, dw. Plainfield, N. J., wd. (1888); m. Joseph Webster Vail, who d. _________, s. of Joel and Phebe (Webster) Vail of Ontario Co., N. Y.

6. *Susan W[7].*, b. 30 June, 1825; d. in Illinois, 1887 ±; m. in N. J., Joel D. Fitz Randolph, dw. Pontiac, Ill.

7. *Hugh Webster*, b. 22 June, 1828, in Greenbrook, N. J.; dw. Brooklyn, N. Y., s. p.; m. Rosamond Dettit.

8. *Rachel V.*, b. Greenbrook, N. J., and there d. unm.

9. *Mary Jane*, b. 6 Apr., 1831, in Greenbrook, N. J.; d. ________, N. J., s. p.; m. Abel Manning.

10. *Theodore V.*, d. young.

11. *Theodore[7]*, b. 3 Jan., 1833, dw. Brooklyn, N. Y.; m. Amelia J. Smith.

148. DANIEL[5] SHOTWELL, b. 1775, of Plainfield, N. J., called "Daniel on the Hill," s. of Jacob[4] and Bathsheba (Pound) Shotwell, [of John[4], John[3], John[2] Abraham[1]], m. (1) *Mary[5] Shotwell*, dau. of John Smith[3] and Phebe (Shotwell) Shotwell, [of John[4], John[3], John[2], Abraham[1]], and had:

1. *Mary[7]*, dw. Plainfield; d. 1877; m. 1826, James Breen.

2. *Elizabeth*, dw. at the Two Bridges, near Plainfield, N. J, d. 7 Oct., 1895, aged 85 years; m. 1828, Daniel Hatfield.

3. *Sarah*, dw. Plainfield; d. 1852; m. 1832, Cora Meeker.

4. *Rachel, W.*, dw. Plainfield, N. J.; d. 1872, m. 1837, Wm. Piatt Williamson.

5. *Emeline D[7].*, dw. Plainfield, N. J.; d. 1886; m. 1845, Mulford Cole.

6. *Jemima Piatt*, dwells (1896) New Brunswick, N. J., a wid.; m. (1) 1849, Silas Cole, half bro. to Mulford; m. (2) 1855, David Lenox.

7. *John S.*, merchant in Pearl St., N. Y., 1830 to 1837; d. 1878, in New York city, unm.

148. DANIEL[5] SHOTWELL, b. 1775, of Plainfield, [of Jacob[4], John[4], John[3], John[2], Abr[1].], m. (2) *Phebe Cole*, and had:

8. *William C.*, a clerk in New York; merchant on Pearl St., New York, 1830 to 1837, afterward a wanderer; left home in 1863, and was not afterwards heard from, was unm.

267. DANIEL[6] SHOTWELL, Jr., 1806–1882, of Alexandria, Minn., s. of Daniel[5] and Keziah (Terril) Shotwell, [of Daniel[4], Joseph[3], Daniel[2], Abraham[1]], m. 1827, *Margaret A. E. Force*, 1809 to 1880, dau. of Ezra and Nancy (Clarkson) Force of New Dover, N. J., and had:

1. *Annie Force*, dw. 23 Church St., Paterson, N. J.; m. Chas. Keeler. To her we are indebted for valuable data.

2. *Sarah*, dw. Alexandria, Minn.; m. Charles Canfield.

3. *James Albert[7]*, b. 20 May, 1837, at Newark, N. J., served as Captain in the Union army during the Civil War; after marriage he continued to reside at Alexandria, Minn., until 7 Sept., 1890, when he removed to Minneapolis, where he is a dry goods clerk; in politics a repub-

lican, and in religion a Baptist; m. by Rev. Geo. E. Stewart, at Alexandria, Minn., 1 Jan., 1876, Hattie Ann (Cambell) Shotwell, b. at Lebanon Springs, N. Y., 9 Mar., 1849, widow of his younger brother Theo. F., and daughter of Moses D. and Paulina (Whittemore) Cambell of Battle Creek, Mich., the former a native of Keene, Vt., [son of David and Sylvia (Taylor) Cambell], and the latter a native of New Hampshire.

4. *Walter S.*, d. Grand Rapids, Michigan, 1892±.

5. *Mary*, dw. Elizabeth, N. J.; m. ________ Edward James Denman.

6. *Theodore F.*, b. 26 July, 1841, at Newark, N. J. At six months of age a severe attack of whooping cough deprived him almost totally of the use of his sight. He entered the New York Institution for the Blind in 1852, graduating in 1860. The next year he went to Minnesota, and thenceforth devoted himself to his favorite calling, the profession of music. Several stirring battle hymns, of which he composed both words and music, bear witness to his earnest patriotism. In 1862 he commenced giving concerts, and during the remaining eight years of his life he gave 122 public entertainments and instruction in music to over 25,000 children, visiting in the pursuit of his art every western, nearly every eastern, and more than one southern state, usually attended by his brother Walter or some other young man. He kept a music store for a short time near his home, but his chief exertions were those of a composer and teacher of music. He died at the residence of his parents at Alexandria, Minn., 1 Oct., 1870, of a lingering disease of the liver, yet suddenly at the last. His were those solid virtues which grew by communion with the Source of Truth; and, could life's battle have been a less unequal one, they would have made him great in the eyes of men. A man of the strictest integrity of character, doing justice, loving mercy, and walking humbly with his God; and we trust that He in whose Light we shall see Light has released this prisoner of hope in the words of unutterable love, "Receive thy sight." In 1863 he was music teacher at St. Cloud (Minn.) Seminary, and gave two entertainments, both of which were participated in by his future wife, then a pupil in that excellent seminary, at the time of the Indian outbreak already referred to. He m. (by Rev. M. S. Harriman) at the residence of the bride's uncle, James Cambell, at Clearwater, Minn., 3 Dec., 1867, Hattie Ann Cambell, b. 9 Mar., 1849, Lebanon Springs, N. Y., dau. of Moses D. and Paulina (Whittemore) Cambell, [of David].

7. *Marcus A. K.*, b. 19 May, 1849, dw. San Francisco., Cal., unm. (1895).

DANIEL L[7]. SHOTWELL, 1819-1890, of Cass Co., Mich., s. of Zachariah[6] and Edna (Lundy) Shotwell, of Wayne Co., N. Y., [of Benj[5]., Benj[4]., Jno[3]., Jno[2]., Abr[1].], m. 1844, *Mary P. Iden*, b.

14

1820, dau. of Thos[2]. and Rachel A. (Parry) Iden, of Richland, Pa., [bf Geo[1].], and had:

1. *Helen Edna*, b. 10 July, 1846, in Johnstown, Barry Co., Mich., dw. ______, Kans.; m. at Dixon, Kans., 8 Aug., 1881, Enoch W. Waterhouse of Clear Lake, Polk Co., Wis.

2. *Mary Frances*, b. 10 Mar., 1848, in Johnstown, Mich., d. young.

3. *Charles Edwin*, b. 16 Aug., 1849, in Johnstown, Mich., dw. Pontiac, Mich., m. in Bloomdale, Van Buren Co., Mich., 3 Dec., 1874, Caroline Hike, dau. of Henry and Docy (Robinson) Hike.

DANIEL POUND[8] SHOTWELL, b. 1842, of Garrison, Butler Co., Neb., s. of Zachariah P[7]. and Margaret (Zavitz) Shotwell of Lobo, Ont., [of Thos[6]., Benj[5]., Benj[4]., John[3]., John[2]., Abr[1].], m. 1886, his brother Merritt E.'s wid., *Sarah V. (Bond) Shotwell*, b. 1859, dau. of John and Jane Bond, and had:

1. *Edgar Merritt*, b. 27 of 1 mo., 1887, in Butler Co., Neb., and there d. 15 of 2 mo., 1887.

2. *Cora Ethel*, b. 25 of 7 mo., 1888, Butler Co., Neb.

85. DAVID[5] SHOTWELL, of Essex Co., N. J., s. of Samuel[4] and Amy Shotwell, of Essex Co., N. J., [of John[3], John[2], Abr[1].], m. 1779, *Elizabeth[5] Fitz Randolph*, b. 1756, dau. of Hartshorne[4] and Ruth (Dennis) Fitz Randolph, [of Edward[3], Nathaniel[2], Edward[1]], of Morris Co., N. J., and had:

1. *Charlotte*, b. 20 of 3 mo., 1780; received cert. of membership from R. and P. M. M. 15 of 12 mo., 1802, directed to the meeting at Hardwick, she having settled there; was then unm.; m. Jacob Losee of Dover, N. J.

2. *Samuel Hartshorn*, b. 6 of 5 m., 1782, Rahway, N. J.

3. *Catharine*, she, and her sister Charlotte, became members of New York M. M. by cert. from R. and P. M. M. dated 17 of 5 mo., 1798; m. about 1807, Samuel B. Ives.

243. DAVID[6] SHOTWELL, d. 1836, s. of Wm[5]. and Elizabeth (Moore) Shotwell of Shotwell's Landing, [of Benj[4]., John[3], John[2], Abraham[1]], m. ____ Prall, dau. of Isaac of Woodbridge, N. J., and had:

1. ______________; m. ________ Schooley.

2. *William Harvey[7]*, b. Redbanks, Woodbridge Tp., N. J., dw. La Porte, Ind., a druggist; m. Waterloo, N. Y., 20 of 8 mo., 1851, his cousin Sarah Louisa Shotwell, b. 26 of 11 mo., 1827, in New York, dau. of Harvey[6] and Louisa (Shotwell) Shotwell of Shotwell's Landing, [of Wm[5]., Benj[4]., John[3], John[2], Abraham[1]].

210. DAVID[6] SHOTWELL, s. of Caleb[5] and Phebe (Hinckston) Shotwell, of Saratoga Co., N. Y., [of Samuel[4], John[3], John[2], Abr[1].], m. (1) *Polly Lewis*, and had:

1. *Phebe[7]*; m. David Crowell.

2.   *Ann'*, dw. Tryonville, Pa.; m. Aaron Lewis.

DAVID⁶ SHOTWELL, [of Caleb⁵, Samuel⁴, John³, John², Abr¹.], m. (2) *Bulah Wood*, of Port Byron, N. Y., and had:
3.   *Polly*, m. ---- Ackley; no issue.
4.   *Rebecca*, m. ---- Ikins.
5.   *David⁷*, dw. Nunda, N. Y.; m. Delia Shute of Livingston Co., N. Y.

DAVID⁷ SHOTWELL, of Nunda, Livingston Co., N. Y., s. of David⁶ and Bulah (Wood) Shotwell, [of Caleb⁵, Samuel⁴, John³, John², Abr¹.], m. *Delia Shute*, and had:
1.   *Gertrude*.

DAVID SMITH⁷ SHOTWELL, 1817–1872, of Cortland, Kent Co., Mich., s. of Benj⁶. and Sarah (Hoag) Shotwell, of Genesee Co., N. Y., [of Richard⁵, Benj⁴., John³, John², Abr¹.], m. 1838 *Eliza³ Dillingham*, b. 1820, dau. of Silvanus² and Judith (Marshal) Dillingham [of John¹], and had:
1.   *Sarah Jane*, called Jane, b. Elba, N. Y., 9 of 3 mo., 1839; removed with her parents to Kent Co., Mich., P. O. Rockford; m. (1) 2 Oct., 1858, I. M. Hunting, who served 1 year (1864–5), in the union army, was treasurer and supervisor of Cortland Tp., Kent Co., Mich., and there d. 27 Apr., 1879. She m. (2) Edwin Wilson.
2.   *Judith Ann*, called Anna, b. Elba, N. Y., 24 of 5 mo., 1840; removed to Cortland, Mich.; dw. Cedar Springs, Mich.; m. 25 of 12 mo., 1860, A. J. Provin, who enlisted 1862, and served 3 years in the union army, and was at one time Tp. supervisor.
3.   *Benjamin*, b. 20 of 6 mo., 1844; d. 11 of 7 mo., 1850.
4.   *David Smith⁸, Jr.*, called Smith; b. 7 of 12 mo., 1846, Collins, N. Y.; dw. Cortland, Kent Co., Mich., P. O. Rockford; is farmer and grafter; m. at Rockford, Mich., 22 Feb., 1871, Adelia Bliss, b. 7 Oct., 1846, in Livingston Co., N. Y., dau. of Wm. and Rachel (Deuel) Bliss, natives of Saratoga Co., N. Y., the former b. 5 Nov., 1813, d. -------- Oct., 1871, and the latter b. 19 July, 1813.
5.   *Sylvanus D'.*, b. 27 of 9 mo., 1849; owns the homestead where his father settled in Cortland Tp., Kent Co., Mich., P. O. Rockford; m. 21 Apr., 1872, Mary Whittall, of Cortland, Mich.
6.   *Benjamin Franklin⁸*, called Frank, b. Cortland, Kent Co., Mich., 29 Jan., 1862, dwells Cortland, Mich; P. O. Cortland Centre. Went from his native Tp. in the spring of 1885, to Buffalo, N. Y., and thence in summer of '86 to Detroit, Mich., to take charge of the retail department of W. S. Dillingham's cigar store; returned in the spring of 1888 to Cortland, Mich., and engaged in farming where he still resides; P. O. Cortland Centre, Mich. In

politics a Democrat, elected Treasurer of Cortland Tp. Apr., 1893. He m. 5 Oct., 1887, Alice Bennett of Cortland, Mich., elder of only 2 children of Lyman and Celestia (Unger) Bennett and granddaughter of Solomon and Sally (Merritt) Bennett of Warrensburg, N. Y., who removed in the summer of 1848 to Cortland, Kent Co., Mich., settling on the farm where the widow (b. in New York. N. Y., in 1810) and their two granddaughters, Alice and Emma, reside 1893. Solomon's son Lyman Bennett was b. Warrensburgh, N. Y. -------- 1839, d. 3 Nov., 1872, of Typhoid Fever; m. 25 Dec., 1867, Celestia Unger, who d. 28 Oct., 1872, leaving the two daughters, Alice less than 4 yrs. old and Emma aged 5 mo.

DAVID⁷ SHOTWELL, b. 1820, of California, s. of Ralph⁶ and Osy (Tingley) Shotwell, [of Jacob⁵, John⁴, John³, John², Abr¹.], m. (1) *Permelia Clark*, and had:
1.   --------, dw. Rahway, N. J.; m. Theodore Miller.
2.   --------, dw. Rahway, N. J.; m. Wm. Martin.

DAVID⁷ SHOTWELL, [of Ralph⁶, Jacob⁵, John⁴, John³, John², Abr¹.], m. (2) *Ann Berry*, dau. of John C. and Deborah (Cock) Berry.

DAVID BENJAMIN⁷ SHOTWELL, b. 1833, of Kalamazoo Co., Mich., s. of Isaac M⁶. and Edna C. (Pound) Shotwell, of Elba, N. Y., [of Richard⁵, Benj⁴., John³, John², Abr¹.], m. (1) 1860, *Adaliza J. Wilder*, 1839–1870, dau. of John and Rebecca Ann (Waller) Wilder of Elba, N. Y., and had:
1.   *Edna Ann*, b. 17 Aug., 1861, Elba, N. Y., d. in Barry Co., Mich., 19 Mar., 1883, was a member of the Presbyterian Church; m. by Rev. Milton Bradley of Richland Presbyterian church at res. of her father in Ross Tp., Kalamazoo Co., Mich., 31 May, 1882, William Fred Smith, b. 25 Feb., 1855, Barry Co., Mich., s. of Charles and Clarissa H. (DeWolf) Smith, the former a native of Onondaga Co., N. Y., and desc. of Stephen Gardner of Norwich, Conn., supposed son of Lord Gardner, and the latter, native of Genesee Co., N. Y., desc. from a distinguished French family. W. F. Smith served as postmaster at Hoskins, Dak., under President Arthur, was elected treasurer of McIntosh Co., Dak., by the republican party, 1886, was proprietor of a temperance hotel, the Lake View House, and a deacon of the Hoskins (now Ashley, N. D.) Congregational Church; dw. 1896, St. Paul, Minn., occ. Real Estate; he m. (2) 28 July, 1887, in Morenci, Lenawee Co., Mich., Agnes L. Green, and had three sons, Stanley Joy, Carl Oren, and Willard Fred, and one dau. Alice Luella.
2.   *Sarah Florella*, called Flora S., b. 24 July, 1863, in Elba, N. Y.; m. at res. of her late grand-

father, John Wilder, in Elba, N. Y., 6 Apr., 1887, Wm. Henry Maltby, b. 16 Dec., 1862, Elba, N. Y., s. of Wm. Henry and Emma Caroline (Irwin) Maltby of Elba, N. Y., [of Wm. H'., native of Vt.]; they dw. in town of Oakfield, N. Y., about 2½ miles w. of Elba village.

3. *Jay Wilder*, b. 19 Sept., 1865, removed from Jackson, Mich., in Feb., 1895, to Los Angeles, Cal., and thence in May following to San Bernardino, Cal., in the hope of recovering better health; m. ______ Mar., 1893, Mrs. Susan Elizabeth Langdon, a widow.

4. *Kate Maude*, b. 21 June, 1870, Ross, Mich., near Augusta; taught school in Elba, N. Y.; chosen first Sec. of Christian Endeavor Society, organized 25 Apr., 1890, connected with Elba Presbyterian Church; took active part in Sunday school and temperance work; dwells, Sherburne, N. Y.; m. by Presbyterian clergyman at Elba, N. Y., 5 July, 1892, Charles R. Loomis, b. E. Pembroke, N. Y., 2 May, 1858, Principal Sherburne High School, son of Samuel and Amanda M. (Babcock) Loomis, of East Pembroke, N. Y., and grandson of Russell and Rachel (Shepard) Loomis and of Reuben and Susan (Gould) Babcock.

(For David B's grandchildren, see synopsis of descendants of Isaac M⁶. Shotwell, of Elba, on a later page.)

DAVID B⁷. SHOTWELL, b. 1833, of Kalamazoo Co., Mich., [of Isaac M⁶., Richard⁵, Benjamin⁴, John³, John², Abraham¹], m. (2) 1880, *Margery Ann* (*McPherson*) *Mason*, b. 1845, wd. of Nelson Mason and dau. of James and Elizabeth McPherson of Le Roy, N. Y., and had:

5. *Clyde Raymond*, b. 25 July, 1881, in Ross, Mich.

6. *Clarence Hugh*, b. 13 Feb., 1883.

7. *Adaliza*, b. 13 Sept., 1884.

8. *Charles Edward*, b. 13 Oct., 1886, Ross Tp., Kalamazoo Co., Mich., d. in Charleston, same Co., Mich., 28 Feb., 1887.

DAVID SMITH⁸ SHOTWELL, JR., b. 1846, of Cortland, Kent Co., Mich., s. of David S⁷. and Eliza (Dillingham) Shotwell of Kent Co., Mich., [of Benj⁶., Richard⁵, Benj⁴., John³, John², Abr¹.], m. 1871, *Adelia Bliss*, b. 1846, dau. of Wm. and Rachel (Deuel) Bliss of Saratoga Co., N. Y., and had:

1. *William David*, b. 19 Dec., 1871, Cortland, Kent Co., Mich.

2. *Lillian Adelia*, b. 26 Dec., 1872, Cortland, Mich., dw. Cortland Centre, Mich., m. in Cortland, Mich., 18 March, 1895, Guy Shank, b. 19 Aug., 1873, Cortland, Mich.

3. *Jane Ann*, b. 18 May, 1875, Cortland, Mich.

4. *Clare Raymond*, b. 7 July, 1879, Cortland, Mich.

DEA ABEL⁷ SHOTWELL, 1825–1888, of Detroit, Mich., s. of Joseph⁶ and Sarah (Randall) Shot-well, of Saratoga Co., N. Y., [of Caleb⁵, Samuel⁴, John³, John², Abraham¹], m. 1847, *Christi Ann Gordon*, and had:

1. *Emma⁸*, dw. Detroit, Mich.; m. Charles Mosher of Detroit, Mich., who d.

79. EDEN⁴ SHOTWELL, b. 1755, of New York and Philadelphia, s. of Jacob⁴ and Eleanor (Haydock) Shotwell, of Rahway, N. J., [of John³, John², Abr¹.], m. *Mary Haydock*, and had:

1. *Haydock*, b. Philadelphia; a carpenter, a temperate, industrious, quiet man; disappeared very mysteriously in New York; the workmen in the shop could give no account of him.

2. *Robert*, d. in or near Brooklyn, N. Y.; m. ______

208. EDEN⁶ SHOTWELL, 1812–1896, of Bennet, Lancaster Co., Neb., s. of Nathan⁵ and Sarah (Fitz Randolph) Shotwell, of Middlesex Co., N. J., [of Jacob⁴, John³, John², Abr¹.], m. 1837, *Ann Mary Haas*, 1816–1892, dau. of Jacob and Susanna (Goode) Haas, and had:

1. *Sarah F. Randolph*, b. 1 of 4 mo., 1838, Hanover, Ind.; m. at age of 26 Charles W. Long, of Loda, Ill., formerly of Salem, Mass.

2. *Susan Haas⁷*, b. 14 of 5 mo., 1840, in La Porte Co., Ind.; m. 1859, James Welch, of Webster City, Iowa, son of Dr. Turner and Esther (Fallis) Welch of La Fayette, Indiana.

3. *Nathan Tilton⁷*, b. 12 of 9 mo., 1842, in La Porte Co., Ind.; lumberman at West Plains, Mo., m. in St. Louis, Mo., (____ 1869) Lizzie Smith, dau. of Wm. and Jennie Smith, of Scotch descent.

4. *Anna*, b. 18 of 7 mo., 1845, in La Porte Co., Ind.; d. in La Porte Co., Ind. 1848, aged 3 years.

5. *Catharine Ann*, b. 6 of 12 mo., 1847, La Porte Co., Ind.; m. (1) 1 of 3 mo., 1865, James B. Moore; m. (2) 31 of 12 mo., 1885, James W. Mussetter, now of University Place, Neb., b. in West Virginia.

6. *Jacob Alexander⁷*, b. 22 of 3 mo., 1850, in La Porte Co., Ind., dw. Wanatchee, Kittitass Co., Wash., a farmer; m. in __________, Kans., 6 of 8 mo., 1872, Susan E. Canfield, b. 19 of 12 mo., 1854, in Mason Co., Ill.

7. *Willis W. Hill*, b. 18 of 8 mo., 1852, in Valparaiso, Ind., d. Loda, Ill., 1859, aged 7 years.

8. *Joseph Pierce*, b. 26 of 9 mo., 1854, in Valparaiso, Ind., farmer in Wanatchee, Wash., unm.

9. *Luella*, b. 13 of 4 mo., 1858, Loda, Ill.; m. at age of 16, Benjamin E. Weaver, of Bennet, Neb.

10. *Harvey Eden*, b. 12 of 3 mo., 1860, in Loda, Ill., civil engineer in Wanatchee, Wash., unmarried; P. O. Mission.

170. EDMUND⁶ SHOTWELL, 1791–1866, of Rahway, N. J., s. of Isaiah⁵ and Constant (Lippincott) Shotwell, of Plainfield, [of John⁴, John³,

John², Abraham¹], m. *Sarah R. Shepard*, 1792–1860, dau. of Nathan and .... (Hart) Shepard of Philadelphia, and had:

1. *Catharine*, d. in childhood.
2. *Margaret Hart⁷*, b. 14 July, 1816, in Philadelphia, Pa.; d. Marengo, Morrow Co., O., 12 Nov., 1882; m. 9 of 5 mo., 1835, Edward R. Shotwell of Marengo, O., b. 11 Aug., 1811, Rahway, N. J., d. Trenton, Mo., 21 Nov., 1887, s. of Peter and Phebe (Vail) Shotwell of Rahway, N. J., [of Isaiah⁵, John⁴, John³, John², Abraham¹].
3. *Catharine Sheppard⁷*, called Kate, dw. with her dau. in Brooklyn, L. I., a wid. (1888); m. in Philadelphia Samuel Wonderly of Philadelphia.
4. *William Seymour⁷* (twin of Nathan S.), dw. Philadelphia, Pa.; m. (1) ...., m. (2) .....
5. *Nathan Sheppard* (twin of William), d.
6. *Henry L.*, d. in Cal. about 1850, unm.
7. *Lydia Hart⁷*, dw. Rahway, N. J.; m. George Williams.
8. *Sallie J.*, dw. in and claims the ownership of the residence known as " Shotwell's Folly;" unm. (1888).
9. *Nathan Sheppard*, II., d. Rahway, Middlesex (now Union) Co., N. J., 2 of 4 mo., 1853, aged 30 years, unm.

280. EDMUND V⁷. SHOTWELL, 1816–1888, of Plainfield, N. J., s. of Daniel C⁶. and Martha (Pound) Shotwell, of Greenbrook, N. J., [of Manning⁵, Benj⁴., John³, Daniel², Abraham¹], m. (1) *Freelove Laing*, and had:

1. *Delia*, d. young.
2. *Martha Jane⁷*, dw. W. 4th St. Plainfield, N. J.; m. Abram L. Cadmus.

EDMUND V.⁷ SHOTWELL, 1816–1888, of Plainfield, N. J., [of Daniel C⁶., Manning⁵, Benj⁴., John³, Daniel², Abraham¹], m. (2) 1844, *Jane H. Williams*, 1814–1868, and had:

3. *Alvin Theodore⁷*, b. 14 Dec., 1846; Treasurer (1887) Fargo, Cass Co., Dak.; m. Plainfield, N. J., 27 July, 1881, Mary Josephine Moore, b. 18 Apr., 1856.
4. *Emma Adelia*, dw. Boston, Mass.; m. George H. Appleton.
5. *Josephine R⁷.*, dw. Plainfield, N. J.; m. Rev. George C. Milen, now an actor.
6. *John Joseph*, dw. Fargo, N. Dak.; m......
7. *Jennie Estell*, dw. (1888) .... Dak.; m. H. D. Kohler, a native of Germany. She or an eighth child named Estell died.

EDMUND⁷ SHOTWELL, b. 1811, of Crosswicks, N. J., s. of Thos. L⁶. and Elizabeth (Satterthwaite) Shotwell, of Crosswicks, [of Isaiah⁵, John⁴, John³, John², Abraham¹], m. 1834, *Adra Ann LaRue*, d. 1887, and had:

1. *Letitia*, b. 20 of 10 mo., 1835, dw. with her widowed father at Crosswicks, N. J.; unm. (1893).

2. *Charles*, b. 2 of 6 m., 1837, d. 10 of 11 mo., 1856.
3. *Henry L.*, b. 4 of 5 mo., 1839, d. 4 of 8 mo., 1855.
4. *Alonzo*, b. 17 of 3 mo., 1844, dw. Philadelphia, Pa.; was delegate to the National Republican Convention in Chicago, 1888. One of the World's Fair Commissioners for the State of Pennsylvania, 1893; unmarried.
5. *Alexander J.*, b. 29 of 10 mo., 1847, d. 16 of 4 mo., 1855.

255. EDWARD⁶ SHOTWELL, 1788–1879, of Rahway, N. J., s. of Titus⁵ and Deborah (Moore) Shotwell, [of Daniel⁴, Joseph³?, Daniel², Abraham¹), m. *Miriam⁶ Moore*, dau. of Edward⁵ Moore [of Edward⁴, Samuel³, John², Samuel¹], and had:

1. *Clayton Moore*, b. N. J.
2. Several children dw. Rahway, N. J.

EDWARD R⁷. SHOTWELL, 1811–1887, of Morrow Co., O., s. of Peter⁶ and Phebe (Vail) Shotwell, of Rahway, N. J., [of Isaiah⁵, John⁴, John³, John², Abr¹.], m. 1835, *Margaret H⁷. Shotwell*, 1816–1882, dau. of Edmund⁶ and Sarah R. (Sheppard) Shotwell, of Rahway, N. J. [of Isaiah⁵, John⁴, John³, John², Abraham¹], and had 7 children, 4 of whom d. young, among them,

1. *Frances Emma*, b. 5 July, 1837, Philadelphia, Pa., and there d. 23 Oct., 1843, buried in Monument Cemetery. Those living to majority were:
2. *Benjamin Warder⁸*, b. 25 Jan., 1839, in Philadelphia, Pa., removed from Marengo, O., in Nov., 1886, to Trenton, Mo.; m. 12 Dec., 1869, Mary Hoyle, dau. of Edward and Sarah E. Hoyle of Brookfield, Linn Co., Mo.
3. *Hudson Burr⁸*, b. 3 July, 1842, dw. Marengo, O.; m. Emma J. Noe, dau. of George E. and Sarah Noe of Marengo, O.
4. *Laura E⁸.*, b. 18 July, 1847, in Bennington Tp., Delaware (now Morrow) Co., O.; d. Newark, N. J., 25 May, 1882, and buried in Hazelwood Cemetery, Rahway, N. J.; m. Galion, O., 4 May, 1868, William E. Tucker, of Philadelphia, b. there; he m. (2) Margaret Elizabeth Oliver, dau. of Washington B. and Mary M. (Allen) Oliver.

EDWARD H⁷. SHOTWELL, b. 1838, of Monte Vista, Colo., s. of Benjamin⁶ and Catharine (Pugsley) Shotwell, [of Benj⁵., Benj⁴., John³, John², Abr¹.], m. (1) 1865, *Rosetta E. Corwin*, d. 1867, and had:

1. *Mary Rose*, b. .... May, 1867, d. 1875±, aged nearly 8 yrs., buried in Warrensburg, Mo.

EDWARD H⁷. SHOTWELL, b. 1838, of Monte Vista, Colo., [of Benj⁶., Benj⁵., Benj⁴., John³, John², Abr¹.], m. (2) 1868, *Eliza Jones*, and had:

2. *Emma Hortense*, b. 4 July, 1869; m. 15 May, 1887, Sigel Heilman.
3. *Edith Lydia*, b. 30 Mar., 1871.
4. *Mary*.
5. *Albert Lee*, d. in infancy.
6. *Grace Edna*, b. 4 May, 1876.

EDWIN BENJAMIN[7] SHOTWELL, b. 1821, of Bunkerhill, Mich., s. of Zachariah[6] and Edna (Lundy) Shotwell, of Wayne Co., N. Y., [of Benj[5]., Benj[4]., John[3], John[2], Abr[1].], m. 1846, *Sarah Ann Harkness*, b. 1825, dau. of Daniel and Beulah (Estes) Harkness, and had:
1. *Mary Eliza[8]*, b. 30 Aug., 1848, Barre, Orleans Co., N. Y., dw. Perinton, Monroe Co., N. Y., P. O. Egypt; m. in Byron, N. Y., 29 July, 1864, John Seley Reed then of Elba, N. Y., b. there 25 Sept., 1842, s. of John and Mary S. (Shotwell) Reed. (For her children, see synopsis of descendants of Isaac M[6]. Shotwell of Elba, on a later page.)
2. *Elmer Edwin[8]*, b. 24 June, 1863, Elba, N. Y., dw. Bunkerhill Tp., Ingham Co., Mich., P. O. Fitchburg, a farmer; m. in Leslie, Mich., 22 Feb., 1884, Carrie B. Olds, of Leslie, Mich.

ELI[7] SHOTWELL, of Brooklyn, N. Y., s. of Daniel C[6]. and Martha (Pound) Shotwell, [of Manning[5], Benj[4]., John[3], Daniel[2], Abraham[1]], m. *Emeliza Boyce*, dau. of David Boyce, and had:
1. *Emeline*, dw. Los Angeles, Cal., s. p.; m. (1) --------------; m. (2) Frank Kernigan.
2. *Edgar*, dw. Fargo, N. D., m. ----------
3. *Charles*, dw. Indianapolis, Ind., unm.
4. *Mary*, dw. Westfield, N. J., m. Lewis C. Lightfoot, (1888).
5. *Fannie*, dw. Los Angeles, Cal.
6. *George*, dw. Fargo, N. D.
7. *David*, dw. Fargo, N. D.

150. ELIJAH[6] SHOTWELL, 1779–1861±, of Scotch Plains, Middlesex Co., N. J., s. of Jacob[5] and Bathsheba (Pound) Shotwell, [of John[4], John[3], John[2], Abraham[1]], m. *Jemima G. Piatt*, dau. of Capt. Wm. and Sarah (Shotwell) Piatt, and had:
1. *William Piatt[7]*, b. 12 of 3 mo., 1802, only child that lived to adult age, was a civil engineer, was assistant chief in the first survey of the New Jersey Central R. R.; d. at Scotch Plains, 30 Sept., 1841, leaving children there who were not Friends; m. 11 April, 1846, Harriet Parse of Scotch Plains, N. J.
2. *Greenleaf*, b. 5 of 8 mo., 1824, d. 1 of 2 mo., 1825.

156. ELIJAH[6] SHOTWELL, b. 1783, of Thorold and Yarmouth, C. W., s. of Wm[5]. and Elizabeth (Pound) Shotwell, of Upper Canada, [of John[4], John[3], John[2], Abraham[1]], m. *Martha Burtsall*, and had:

1. *Elizabeth B[7]*. (called Eliza) b. Pelham, C. W., 4 of 6 mo., 1807, d. Yarmouth, C. W., 8 of 3 mo., 1874, m. (1) in Pelham, C. W., John Taylor, d. Thorold, C. W.; m. (2) in Pelham, C. W., 13 of 3 mo., 1833, Amos Canby, b. ------, Md., 29 of 3 mo., 1802, d. Richmond, Mich., 29 Nov., 1879, son of Whitson and Mary Canby of Md. (children by both husbands).

ELIJAH BERNARD[8] SHOTWELL, b. 1857, of --------, Kans., s. of Wm[7]. and Martha E. (Taylor) Shotwell of Windham, Kans., [of Smith[6], Wm[5]., John[4], John[3], John[2], Abr[1].], m. -----------------, and had children.

ELMER EDWIN[8] SHOTWELL, b. 1863, of Ingham Co., Mich., s. of Edwin B[7]. and Sarah A. (Harkness) Shotwell, of Bunker Hill, Mich., [of Zachariah[6], Benj[5]., Benj[4]., John[3], John[2], Abr[1].], m. 1884, *Carrie B. Olds*, and had:
1. *Della Bell*, b. 11 Dec., 1884, Bunker Hill, Tp., Ingham Co., Mich.

ELVINGTON M[8]. SHOTWELL, b. 1864, s. of Anson[7] and Lucinda J. (Cummins) Shotwell, of Linden, Mich., [of Jonathan[6], James[5], John[4], John[3], John[2], Abr[1].], m. *Mary Lobdell*, and had:
1. *Charles L.*, b. 21 Apr., 1893.

EZRA MOORE[7] SHOTWELL, b. 1845, of Sioux Falls, S. Dak., s. of Isaac[6] and Hope (Stanton) Shotwell, of O., [of Titus[6], Sr., Daniel[4], Joseph[3], Daniel[2], Abraham[1]], m. 1868, *Theora Dorr*, and had:
1. *Hertha*, b. 15 Sept., 1869, New Sharon, Mahaska Co., Iowa.
2. *Edmund Dorr*, b. 31 Oct., 1873, Monroe, Jasper Co., Iowa.

FREEMAN[7] SHOTWELL, b. 1814, of Plainfield, N. J., s. of Robert[6] and Martha (F. R.) Shotwell, [of Manning[5], Benj.[4], John[3], Daniel[2], Abr.[1]], m. *Nancy Nott*, and had:
1. *Wm. H.*, dw. Plainfield, N. J., a grocer; m. Miriam Staats.
2. *Harriet*, m. ---------, J. S. Garretson.

195. GEORGE H[6]. SHOTWELL, d. 1869, of Cincinnati, O., s. of Aaron[5] and ------ (Martin) Shotwell of Rahway, N. J., [of Abraham[4], John[3], John[2], Abraham[1]], m. 1836, *Mary E. A. Tudor*, and had:
1. *Cordelia*, dw. 234 Lawrence St., Cincinnati, O., member of Methodist church; m. 1858, J. C. Campbell, M. D., of Leavenworth, Kans., afterwards of Cincinnati, O., who d. 1 Feb., 1894.
2. *Cassius*, dw. Englewood, Chicago, Ill., m. 1864, Virginia D. Bone, of Cincinnati, O.
3. *Mary*, dw. Englewood, Ill.; m. 1864, W. W. Backman.
4. *George*, (twin of Mary), dw. Bellevue, Campbell Co., Ky.; m. 1869, Annah K. Smith, of Cincinnati, O.

GEORGE[1] SHOTWELL, of Bellevue, Ky., s. of George H[6]. and Mary E. A. (Tudor) Shotwell, of Cincinnati, O., [of Aaron[5], Abraham[4], John[3], John[2], Abraham[1]], m. 1869, Annah K. Smith, of Cincinnati, O., and had:

1. *Irene.*
2. *Mary.*
3. *John Tudor*, dw. Bellevue, Ky.
4. *George.*
5. *Clifford Earle.*
6. *Edna*, d.

GEORGE WASHINGTON[1] SHOTWELL, b. 1833, ±, s. of Clarkson[6] and Keziah (Sutton) Shotwell, of Oakland Co., Mich., [of James[5], Jno[4]., Jno[3], Jno[2]., Abr[1].], m. (1) *Angeline Topping*, who d., and had 5 children.

GEORGE W[7]. SHOTWELL, b. 1833 ±, [of Clarkson F[6]. James[5], Jno[4]., Jno[3]., Jno[2]., Abr[1].], m. (2) ----------------, and had:

6. ----------------, a daughter.

GREENLEAF[7] SHOTWELL, s. of Wm. P[7]. and Harriet (Parse) Shotwell, of Scotch Plains, N. J., [of Elijah[6], Jacob[5], Jno[4]., Jno[3]., Jno[2]., Abr[1].], m. *Elizabeth Cleveland*, of Elizabethtown, N. J., and had:

1. *Wm. Piatt Greenleaf[8] Shotwell*, b. 16 Feb., 1848, at Scotch Plains, N. J., dw. 536 Swan St., Buffalo, N. Y. Early in February, 1896, he was knocked off the steps of a locomotive by a switch stand, at Black Rock, Buffalo, N. Y., while returning from the custom house, at the international bridge, to his office, having just stepped out of the gangway on the step without noticing the switch stand; was hit by it and thrown some distance upon the street crossing, severely injuring his knee joint and probably rendering him a cripple for life. In an experience of twenty-two years in railroad service, he had sustained no previous injury. He was yard master and assistant train master on the eastern division of the Penna. Co.'s lines for eighteen years and four months before going to Buffalo.

He m. 22 Nov., 1867, Margaret R. Stevenson, of Milton, Northumberland Co., Pa., who d. Conway, Beaver Co., Pa., 18 Feb., 1892, dau. of Wm.

HARVEY SHOTWELL, of -----------, Pa., m., and had:

1. *Harvey*, b. ----------, Pa., dw. Orchard St., New York, and there d. of ruptured blood vessel, 2 of 4 mo., 1831, aged 29 yrs.

242. HARVEY[7] SHOTWELL, 1800-1848, of Macon, Ga., s. of Wm[6]. and Elizabeth (Moore) Shotwell, of Shotwells Landing, N. J., [of Benj[4]., John[3], John[2], Abr[1].], m. 1823, *Louisa[6] Shotwell*, 1800-1889, dau. of Nathan[5] and Sarah (Fitz Randolph) Shotwell, of Middlesex Co., N. J., [of Jacob[4], John[3], John[2], Abraham[1]], and had:

1. *Anna F. R.*, b. 8 of 11 mo., 1824, New York City, dw. Orange, N. J.; m. Macon, Ga., 31 of 5 mo., 1845, Francis John Ogden, called Frank, of New York, 1821-1882.
2. *Sarah Louisa[7].* b. 26 of 11 mo., 1827, New York City; m. Waterloo, N. Y., 20 of 8 mo., 1851, her cousin Wm. Harvey Shotwell, s. of David[6] Shotwell, of Red Bank, N. J., [of Wm[5]., Benj[4]., John[3], John[2], Abr[1].].
3. *Lida C.*, b. 17 of 5 mo., 1837, Macon, Ga.; m. La Salle, Ill., 4 of 9 mo., 1856, Willis M. Hitt, real estate dealer of Chicago.

HARVEY H[7]. SHOTWELL, of Buffalo, N. Y., s. of John I[7]. and -------- Shotwell, of Colden, Erie Co., N. Y., [of Smith[6], Wm[5]., Jno[4], Jno[3]., Jno[2]., Abr[1].], m. ----------------, and had:

1. *Mary Adella*, b. ------------, 1879.
2. *Clara Daphne*, b. ------------, 1880.
3. *Elijah Ferdinand*, b. ---------, 1882.
4. *Harvey Lorne*, b. ------------, 1886.

50. HENRY[5] SHOTWELL, 1752-1821, of Rahway, N. J., s. of Joseph[4] and Sarah (Cock) Shotwell, of Rahway, N. J., [of John[3], John[2], Abr[1].], m. 1781, *Sarah Dobson*, and had:

1. *Joseph Dobson[6]*, b. 6 of 4 mo., 1782; d. 7 of 12 mo., 1856, was for many years Clerk of R. & P. M. M. and of Quarterly Meeting for Shrewsbury and Rahway, dw. Woodbridge Tp., when he m. at Rahway, 22 of 3 m., 1804, Elizabeth Fitz Randolph, of Woodbridge Tp., dau. of Jacob and Anna (Webster) Fitz Randolph, of Blazing Star, near Woodbridge, N. J.
2. *Sarah[6]*, b. 2 of 1 mo., 1784, d. 22 of 12 mo., 1860, was of Woodbridge Tp. when she m. at Rahway, 29 of 11 mo., 1810, (as 2d wife), Isaac Vail, of Woodbridge Tp., b. 1 of 8 mo., 1770, d. near La Porte, Ind., 1 of 10 mo., 1839, s. of John[3] and Catharine (Fitz Randolph) Vail, of Woodbridge, N. J., [of John[2], Samuel[1]].
3. *Margaret*, b. 30 of 8 mo., 1785; d. 21 of 7 mo., 1854. m. Aaron Bellanger of Bordentown, N. J.
4. *Ann[6]*, b. 11 of 2 mo., 1787, dw. Middlesex Co., N. J., d. 2 of 6 mo., 1834; m. Peter Cohu, a cloth manufacturer of Essex Co., N. J., who d. in Middlesex Co., N. J., 27 of 2 mo., 1823, aged 35, buried at Rahway.
5. *Hannah Murray*, b. 14 of 10 mo., 1788, d. Rahway, N. J., 8 of 8 mo., 1873, member of Oswego (N. Y.) M. M. by cert. from R. and P. M. M., dated 24 of 11 mo., 1825; had previously m. James C. Moore, of Rahway, N. J., who d. there 1 of 12 mo., 1868, aged 92 yrs., 6 mo., 29 days, s. of John and Eleanor Moore.
6. *Thomas D.*, b. 17 of 3 mo., 1790, d. 2 of 5 mo., 1812.
7. *Elizabeth*, b. 22 of 9 mo., 1791, d. Rahway, Middlesex Co., N. J., 26 of 7 mo., 1849, s. p.; m. (as 2d wife) John Harned, b. 16 of 3 mo., 1783, s. of Jonathan and Sarah (Lang) Harned, of Middlesex Co., N. J.

8. *Mary*, b. 6 of 5 mo., 1793, d. young.

9. *Mary*, b. 18 of 10 mo., 1795, d. Rahway, Middlesex Co., N. J., 16 of 7 mo., 1849, of Cholera, unm.

10. *Deborah*, b. 29 of 1 mo., 1797, d. 6 of 4 mo., 1801.

HENRY SHOTWELL, of Brooklyn, N. Y., m. ----, and had:

1. *William*, b. 1822, Brooklyn, N. Y., and there d. 21 of 3 m., 1831, of convulsions, aged 9 yrs., 1 mo., interred in N. Y. Friends ground.

HENRY RANDOLPH[7] SHOTWELL, 1806–1887, of Rahway, N. J., s. of Joseph D[6]. and Elizabeth R. (Fitz Randolph) Shotwell, of Rahway, N. J., [of Henry[5], Joseph[4], John[3], John[2], Abraham[1]], m. 1830, *Margaret G[6]. Laing*, dau. of Wm[5]. and Martha (Freeman) Laing,[of Thos[4]., Isaac[3], John[2], John[1]], and had:

1. *Joseph D[7].*, b. 25 of 8 mo., 1831, Rahway, N. J., dw. (1895) Hillside Ave., Orange, N. J., removing thither from Rahway in 1891, m. by Friends ceremony, in New York City, 9 of 10 mo., 1862, Amelia Everit, dau. of Richard and Mary Carle Everit, of New York.

2. *Katharine L.*, b. 26 of 11 mo., 1832, dw. Philadelphia, Pa.; m. (as 2d. wife), Edward J. Maginnis.

3. *Caroline A.*, b. 13 of 5 mo., 1839, dw. Philadelphia, Pa., member of Friends Meeting at Cherry St., Philadelphia, by cert. from R. and P. M. M., dated 18 of 4 mo., 1860; had previously m. Thomas S. Wood.

HENRY T[8]. SHOTWELL, b. 1862, of 72 Washington Ave., Brooklyn, N. Y., s. of Joseph F[7]. and Amy (Titus) Shotwell, [of Joseph S[5]., Jno. S[4]., Jno[3]., Jno[3]., Jno[2]., Abr[1].], m. 1886, *Alice Gardner*, and had:

1. *Willits Haviland*, b. 31 Jan., 1889.

HUDSON BURR[8] SHOTWELL, b. 1842, of Marengo, O., s. of Edward R[7]. and Margaret H. (Shotwell) Shotwell, of Morrow Co., O., [of Peter[5], Isaiah[3], John[4], John[3], John[2], Abraham[1]], m. *Emma J. Noe*, dau. of George E. and Sarah Noe, of Marengo, O., and had:

1. *Kleber Burr*, b. 22 of Mar., 1875, at Marengo, O.

2. *Frederick W.*, b. 24 July, 1877, in Marengo, O.

3. *Charles E.*, b. 23 Sept., 1878, Marengo, O.

4. *Francis A.*, b. 14 June, 1881, Marengo, O.

5. *Abel V.*, b. 7 Jan., 1883, Marengo, O.

6. *Sarah J.*, b. 25 Nov., 1884, Marengo, O.

65. HUGH[5] SHOTWELL, 1764–1854, of Freeport, Harrison Co, O., s. of John[4] and Grace (Webster) Shotwell, of Plainfield, N. J., [of John[3], John[2], Abraham[1]], m. 1783, *Rosetta Arrison*, who d. 1836, dau. of John, of Sussex Co., N. J., and had:

1. *John[6]*, b. 17 Apr., 1784, in N. J., dw. Fayette Co., Pa., near Brownsville, and there d. 15 Apr., 1869; m. (1) 14 June, 1804, Sarah Shanklin, of Fayette Co., Pa., b. in Ireland, 1 Dec., 1779, d. 9 Mar., 1851; m. (2) 2 Oct., 1854, Hannah Myers, b. 1812, Fayette Co., Pa.

2 *Esther[6]*, b. 30 Aug., 1785, in Sussex Co., N. J., after death of second husband she made her home in the family of her dau., Charlotte A. (Seaton) Riggs, in Pennsylvania, Ohio and Illinois, d. in Rockford, Ill., 10 June, 1870, aged 84 yrs., 9 mos., 11 days, buried, with three grandchildren, in Cedar Bluffs Cemetery, E. Rockford, Ill.; was for over 40 years a consistent member of the M. E. Church; m. (1) at Redstone, Pa., 13 Mar., 1803, Timothy Smith, Jr., of Brownsville, Fayette Co., Pa., who d. 1816 ±, s. of Timothy of Carmichael's, Greene Co., Pa.; m. (2) by Wm. Bailey, Esq., near Carmichael's, Pa., 25 or 30 Dec., 1820 (as 2d wife), Major George Clark Seaton, b. near Carmichel's, Pa., 2 June, 1783, d. in Beallsville, Washington Co., Pa., 13 Sept., 1849, s. of James and Mary (Clark) Seaton, who had removed from Apple Pie Ridge, Va., in 1775, to Greene Co., Pa., bringing with them eight slaves, and there purchasing 380 acres of land. George C. Seaton enlisted in the war of 1812, was Corporal, but on account of sickness was honorably discharged after serving but a few months; engaged in farming and buying and driving stock to eastern markets; removed from Carmichael's, Pa., in 1828 to Beallsville, Pa., where for a time he conducted a hotel; was P. M. 1832–1849; in the latter year he was incapacitated for business by a cancer on his right ear, from the effects of which he d. at his home in Beallsville as above stated, interred at his request in the family burying ground at Carmichael's; his religious preferences were those of an Episcopalian from childhood.

3. *Susanna[6]*, b. 6 Jan., 1789, Stillwater, N. J., d. at the res. of her son-in-law, Wm. W. Willett, near Allamuchy, N. J., 15 March, 1874, leaving 10 surviving children, 48 grandchildren, and 13 great-grandchildren, she was remarkable for her prudence and foresight in all the affairs of life, for the peace and harmony which her presence inspired and for the beautiful christian character she exhibited; had been for 47 years a worthy member of the Christian Church at Johnsburg; m. at Redstone, Pa., 20 Nov., 1809, Charles Wintermute, b. 16 Aug., 1784, d. Stillwater, N. J., 21 Feb., 1868, s. of George. Charles with two other young men went west on horseback in 1809 on a visit to Fayette Co., Pa., and there became acquainted with Susanna Shotwell; after their marriage her father gave her a pony and saddle and she rode 320 miles to his home at Stillwater, Sussex Co., N. J., where they settled on the Big Spring farm, subsequently owned by M. R. Dennis; seven years later they removed to the next farm below, and there dw. until his death 58 yrs. and 3 mos.

after marriage. They visited relatives in O.,
about the year 1828.

4. *Charlotte*[6], b. 17 Nov., 1790, Fayette Co.,
Pa., d. 25 Nov., 1827; m. in Cadiz, Harrison
Co., O., ---- Nov., 1816, Ephraim Sears or
Sayrs, of Tuscarawas Co., O.

5. *Nancy*[6], b. 15 Oct., 1796 or '95, in Redstone, Fayette Co., Pa., d. Hamilton, O., 1 Oct.,
1861; m (1) in Stillwater, O., 12 Oct., 1815,
Peter Van Dolah, a merchant of Cadiz, O.,
formerly from Brownsville, Pa., b. 26 Aug.,
1787; d. Cadiz, O., 4 Oct., 1823; m. (2) ----
Apr., 1826, Jacob Ebert a copper and tinsmith
at Cadiz, O., b. 9 Aug., 1800, at York, Pa., d.
Hamilton, O., 6 Apr., 1854, s. of John, of York,
Pa. Shortly after her 2d marriage they settled
at Hamilton, Butler Co., O., where he continued
the business of copper and tinsmith, and afterward with others conducted an iron foundry
and machine manufactury.

6. *William*[6], b. 29 Jan., 1798, Fayette Co.,
Pa.; was a farmer in Washington Tp., Harri-
son Co., O., until 1837, when he removed to
Cadiz, was a merchant there but did not succeed
well as such, and there d. 21 Jan., 1855; m. at
Cadiz, O., 24 Feb., 1819, Rhoda Beebe, b. 3
June, 1792, Wilbraham, Hampden Co., Mass.,
where she received a thorough education; d.
Cadiz, O., 22 Mar., 1876, aged nearly 84 yrs.
She went to Cadiz, O., first in 1817 to visit her
brother, Gen. Walter Beebe, and there made
the acquaintance of William Shotwell. She

was a daughter of Stuart Beebe, of Wilbraham,
(now Hampden), Mass., who was born in East
Haddam, Conn., 28 Feb., 1754, and granddaughter of Lieut. Samuel Beebe, who removed
from Middlesex Co., Conn., to Hampden, Mass.,
about the year 1772,—of English descent.

7. *Joseph*[6], b. 23 July, 1801, in Fayette Co.,
Pa., was somewhat of a military man and was
called Col. Shotwell, lived in Harrison Co.,
1813-1837, and there for a time kept the tavern
previously owned by his father about five miles
east of Cadiz, after which he engaged in farming, in the counties of Hamilton, Montgomery,
Butler, Allen, and Cuyahoga, O., and d. at
Glenville, O., 14 March, 1883; m. (1) in Delaware Co., O., 29 Nov., 1821, his 1st cousin,
Mary Arrison, who d. Lima, Allen Co., O., dau.
of Jeptha Arrison, of Delaware Co., O.; m. (2)
----, a wd., by whom he had no children.

8. *Arrison*[6], b. 19 Oct., 1812, Redstone Tp.,
Fayette Co., Pa., dw. Glenville, an eastern
suburb of Cleveland, O., and there d. 25 June,
1893; was for several years (about 1876-80)
treasurer of that village; visited New Jersey and
Philadelphia in 1876; to him we are indebted
for valuable data; m. by Wm. Wyckoff, Esq., in
Washington Tp., Harrison Co., O., 1 Oct., 1835,
Mary Dickerson, b. Cadiz Tp., Harrison Co.,
O., 30 Nov., 1815, d. 30 Nov., 1894, aged 79,
dau. of Baruch[3] Dickerson, who at time of
his death was sheriff of Harrison Co., [of
Thomas[2], Joshua[1]].

SYNOPSIS OF THE CHILDREN AND GRANDCHILDREN OF

HUGH[5] SHOTWELL, OF HARRISON CO., OHIO,

[OF JOHN[4], JOHN[3], JOHN[2], ABRAHAM[1].]

1. *John*[6], 1784-1869, m. 1804, Sarah Shanklin, 1779-1851, and had: (1.) Catharine, b. 1806,
m. 1825, Henry B. Goe, b. 1804 ±. (2.) Rosetta,
1808-1883, m. 1827, Robert Smith, 1799-1881.
(3.) Emily, d. 1809, m. 1838, Jacob Shearer, 1809-
1884, [of Frederick]. (4.) Susan C., 1811-1894,
m. 1832, Eli Cope, b. 1810. (5.) Caroline, b.
1813, m. 1835, Joel Strawn.

2. *Esther*[6], 1785-1870, m. (1) 1803, Timothy
Smith, Jr., d. 1816 ±, [of Timothy], and had: (1.)
John Shotwell, b. 1804, dw. Fairmont, W. Va.,
m. --------. (2.) Rosetta S., b. 22 Jan., 1806,
m. 1833 ±, James Johnson, who was merchant
and postmaster at Danville, Ky., and there d.
(3.) James, b. 1808, d. near Lexington, Ky. (4.)
Hugh Shotwell, b. 8 Aug., 1810; was farmer and
drover in Rush Tp., Tuscarawas Co., O., removed to Marion Co., Iowa, laying out on his farm
there in 1857 the village of Columbia; m. 29

Aug., 1833, Rebecca Johnson, b. 22 Jan., 1808,
d. 9 June, 1884, [of Joshua and Sarah]. (5.)
Timothy, Jr., b. 1812, was a soldier, drowned at
Dubuque, Iowa, m. ---------

Esther[6] (*Shotwell*) *Smith*, 1785-1870, m. (2)
1820 (as 2d wife) Maj. George Clark Seaton,
1783-1849, s. of James and Mary (Clark) Seaton,
and had: (6.) Jonathan Davis, b. 7 Nov., 1821,
was dry goods merchant, d. at Denver, Colo., 11
Feb., 1880, m. 10 Mar., 1845, Jane K. Lucas, b.
28 Apr., 1824, [of M. Ennis and Elizabeth Lucas].
(7.) Charlott Ann, b. 3 Nov., 1823, dwells at
Cambridge, Ill., m. 13 Dec., 1848, Edward R.
Riggs, b. 29 Sept., 1826, s. of John and Mary
(Phillips) Riggs.

3. *Susanna*[6], 1789-1874, m. 1809, Charles
Wintermute, 1784-1868, [of George], and had:
(1.) William Shotwell, b. 30 Sept., 1810, d. 10
Oct., 1879, m. 30 Oct., 1841, Eliza Fowler, d. 14

HUGH P.[7] SHOTWELL,
Of Elba, Genesee Co., N. Y.,
SON OF ISAAC M[6]. AND EDNA C. (POUND) SHOTWELL,
of Genesee Co., N. Y., and Descendant of Richard[5], Benjamin[4],
John[3], John[2], Abraham[1] Shotwell.

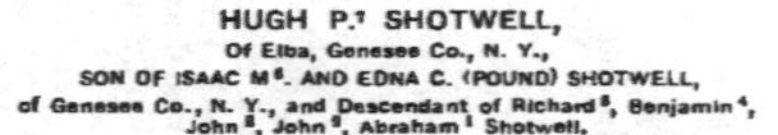

HANNAH (HAINES) SHOTWELL,
WIFE OF HUGH P. SHOTWELL,
of Elba, N. Y., and Daughter of Reuben and Anna (Hawley) Haines
of Shelby, N. Y.

Oct., 1872. (2.) Joseph Rhodes, b. 25 Oct., 1811, d. 19 Dec., 1864, m. 21 Mar., 1840, Judith Ann Shoemaker or Wolf. (3.) Rosetta A., b. 19 Sept., 1813, dw. (1888) Hackettstown, N. J., with her step dau., Mary Smith, to whom we are indebted for valuable data; m. 24 Mar., 1853, George S. Smith, b. 18 July, 1804, d. 30 Mar., 1874. (4.) Hugh Shotwell, b. 18 Apr., 1816, d. 2 Apr., 1869, m. 8 Nov., 1840, Mercy L. Luse. (5.) Esther S., b. 20 Apr., 1818, m. 3 Jan., 1843, Aaron B. Mitchell. (6.) John Shotwell, b. 2 June, 1819, d. 13 Mar., 1895, m. 9 May, 1847, Sarah B. Linaberry, b. 5 Nov., 1821. (7.) George Washington, b. 1 May, 1821, m. 18 Apr., 1850, Sarah M'. Middlesworth, b. 5 Dec., 1832, dau. of Abram and Mary C'. (Green) Middlesworth, [of Nancy' Shotwell, James', John', John', John', Abraham']. The name Wintermute is thought to have been formerly written Windemode, but is now spelled Wintermute, except by George, who writes it Wintemute. (8.) Caroline, b. 5 Feb., 1823, m. 26 Feb., 1845, John Mitchell, d. 9 Mar., 1879. (9.) Charlotta, b. 26 Nov., 1824, m. 15 Nov., 1847, Reuben Randolph, b. 10 May, 1821, d. 23 Jan., 1879. (10.) Abigail R., b. 6 June, 1826, m. 4 Mar., 1847, Cummins O. Harris. (11.) Howel Goodrich, b. 26 Feb., 1828, d. 20 Sept., 1831. (12.) Alice A., b. 25 Sep., 1829, dw. Allamuchy, N. J., has furnished valuable data for this work; m. 27 Dec., 1856, William W. Willett, b. 25 Feb., 1832, s. of Ananias C. and Mahala (Wintersteen) Willett. (13.) Oliver B., b. 15 Mar., 1832, m. 24 Mar., 1855, Alice Tunison.

4. *Charlotte*, 1790-1827, m. 1816, Ephraim Sears or Sayrs, and had: (1.) Hugh S. (2.) William S., m. ___________. (3.) Wesley. (4.) Nancy, b. 12 June, 1826, d. 19 Mar., 1886, at Howard, Knox Co., O., having never recovered from the shock occasioned by the heroic but melancholy death of her son, Sergt. David Columbus Ralston, who died of hunger in Camp Clay, near Cape Sabine, Ellsmore Land, 23 May, 1884, being a member of Lieut. Greely's party in the expedition in search of the North Pole. She m. at the res. of her uncle, Arrison Shotwell, in Harrison Co., O., 30 Dec., 1847, Lewis W. Ralston.

5. *Nancy*, 1796 or '95-1861, m. (1) 1815, Peter Van Dolah, 1787-1823, and had: (1.) William Hogg, b. 10 May, 1818, d. 7 July, 1861, m. (1) 1846±, Julia Walton; m. (2) ____. (2.) John Shotwell, b. 11 Mar., 1820, dw. 1885, Hutchinson, Reno Co., Kans., m. (1) 1845±, Amelia Parks, called Milla, [of John]; m. (2) Ester Haines. (3) Mary Matilda H., b. 20 Nov., 1822, d. 18 May, 1824.

Nancy (*Shotwell*) *Vandolah*, 1796-1861, m. (2) 1826, Jacob Ebert, 1800-1854, [of John], and had: (4.) Margaret Elizabeth, b. 28 Feb., 1828, at Cadiz, O., d. 11 Nov., 1882, unm. (5.) Rosetta Shotwell, b. 18 Feb., 1830, at Cadiz, O., m. at Hamilton, O., 2 Nov., 1859, her 2d cousin, Abel Vail Shotwell, b. 18 of 10 mo., 1814, d. at Rahway, N. J., 17 of 12 mo., 1893, son of Abel', and
15

Elizabeth (Vail) Shotwell, [of Isaiah', John', John', John', Abraham']. (6.) Sarah B., b. 26 Apr., 1832, at Cadiz, O., dw. with sister Rosetta S., at Rahway, N. J., m. at Hamilton, O., 22 July, 1851, John R. Lewis, b. 30 Sept., 1821, d. 10 Aug., 1861, s. p., son of Rev. David and Harriet (Bullock) Lewis. (7.) Jerome Buckingham, b. 4 Apr., 1835, at Cadiz, O., dw. (1888) Rahway, N. J., m. 6 Jan., 1870, Mary Doran, b. 1852, d. 1884, s. p. (8.) Joseph Henry, b. 3 June, 1837, d. 6 Sept., 1838.

6. *William*', 1798-1855, m. 1819, Rhoda Beebe, 1792-1876, [of Stuart', Samuel'], and had: (1.) Stuart Beebe, 1819-1890, m. 1851, Nancy Gaston, b. 1823, [of James', Hugh']. (2.) John, 1821-1822. (3.) Samuel, 1823-1824. (4.) William, Jr., 1825-1849, unm. (5.) Theodore b. 1828, dw. Minneapolis, Minn., m. Sarah J. Lucas, [of M. Ennis Lucas]. (6.) Walter B., 1831-1847. (7.) Rhoda Lauretta, b. 1834, m. 1855, Smiley Sharon, who d. 1870.

7. *Joseph*', 1801-1883, m. (1) 1821, his 1st cousin, Marry Arrison, [of Jeptha], and had: (1.) Jeptha, m. 1849, Nancy Cooper. (2.) George, m. _________. (3.) Louisa, m. _______ Gibson.

8. *Arrison*', 1812-1893, m. 1835, Mary Dickerson, 1815-1894, [of Baruch', Thomas', Joshua'], and had: (1.) Elizabeth, b. 1836. (2.) Rosetta, 1838-1838. (3.) Victoria, b. 1839, m. 1883, George Gooding. (4.) Adoniram Judson, b. 1842, m. 1872, Martha H. Graham. (5.) John Thomas b. 1845, m. 1875, Evolyn McBrine, b. 1856, [of William]. (6.) Austin, b. 1848. (7.) Fremont, b. 1856.

Hugh' and Rosetta (Arrison) Shotwell thus had eight children and 54 grandchildren.

HUGH P'. SHOTWELL, b. 1825, of Elba, N. Y., s. of Isaac M'. and Edna C. (Pound) Shotwell, of Elba, N. Y., [of Richard', Benj'., John', John', Abr'.], m. 1850, *Hannah Haines*, b. 1830, dau. of Reuben' and Anna (Hawley) Haines, of Ridgeway, N. Y., [of Jesse'], and had:

1. *Murray A.*, b. 3 of 9 mo., 1852, Elba, Genesee Co., N. Y., graduated from Cornell university, 1873, with degree of Ph. B., was for a time in the employ of his uncles, the Haines Bros., lumbermen in Buffalo, but afterward engaged in farming, purchasing the homestead of the late Peter Mattice, in Elba, N. Y., which he still owns, is an active member of the I. O. of Good Templars, and of the Society of Friends.

2. *Elvin H.*, b. 23 of 3 mo., 1855, Elba, N. Y., and there d. 19 of 9 mo., 1855.

3. *Anna H.*, b. 8 of 2 mo., 1857, Elba, N. Y., and there dw. with parents, unm.

4. *Edward R.*, b. 11 of 5 mo., 1859, Elba, N. Y., dw. Elba, N. Y., a farmer, owns the Schofield place, which he purchased from Stephen Shepperd; m. (1) at the res. of the bride's father, N. E. Cor. of State and North

Sts., Batavia, N. Y., 15 Apr., 1885, by Wm.
Dean of Bushville, N. Y., a minister of the
Society of Friends, to Lura Ann Edgerton,
who d. 1886, dau. of Alanson Edgerton of
Batavia; m. (2.) at the res. of the bride's par-
ents in W. Barre, N. Y., 3 March, 1890, Lillian
I. Avery, b. 18 Feb., 1867, dau. of Francis G. and
Sarah (Bliss) Avery.

5. *Gertrude E'.*, b. 29 of 9 mo., 1863, Elba,
N. Y., dw. Elba, N. Y.; m. at her father's res. in
Elba, N. Y., 7 of 2 mo., 1884, John Delos Piper,
b. 27 Aug., 1862, Mt. Morris, Livingston Co.,
N. Y., s. of Henry P. and Charlotte (Piper)
Piper, is an approved minister and pastor of
Elba Friends meeting.

6. *Nellie Haines*, b. 27 of 12 mo., 1871;
entered Oberlin college in the autum of 1892.

7. *Alice Evangeline*, b. 1 of 4 mo., 1873,
Elba, N. Y.; entered Oberlin college with her
sister Nellie in 1892.

111. Isaac⁵ Shotwell, of Rahway, and New
York, s. of Jacob¹, [of Joseph³ ?, Daniel²,
Abraham¹], m. 1770, *Hannah⁵ Shotwell*, b. 1749,
dau. of Jacob⁴, and Eleanor (Haydock) Shot-
well, of Lower Rahway, N. J , [of John³, John²,
Abraham¹], and had:

1. *Eden*, b. Rahway, N. J., was a minor in
1791, when he removed with his parents to N.
Y.; was a sea captain, lost at sea with ship and
all on board.

2. *Joseph*, went with his parents to New
York in 1791, taking cert. from R. and P.
M. M.

3. *Elizabeth*, b. before 1791.

4. *Catharine⁶*, b. before 1791, in Rahway,
N. J., d. in New York city; m. David R.
Jaques, who. d. at Blazing Star, N. J., of
yellow fever four days after leaving New
York.

73. Isaac⁵ Shotwell, b. 1769, of Essex
Co., N. J., s. of Abraham⁴, and Lydia (Hallot)
Shotwell, of Essex Co., N. J., [of John³, John²,
Abraham¹], m. 1791, *Catharine Moore*, dau.
of Dr. ____ Moore, and had:

1. *Enoch*, b. 4 of 11 mo., 1792.
2. *Lydia*, b. 12 of 5 mo., 1794.
3. *Katy*, b. 21 of 1 mo., 1799.

251. Issac⁶ Shotwell, 1802-1864, of Cincinnati, O., and Columbia, Cal., s. of Joseph⁵ and
Sarah (Wilson) Shotwell, of Perrytown, N. J.,
[of Joseph⁴, Joseph³, Daniel², Abraham¹], m.
________, 1828, *Elizabeth A. West*, 1809-1885,
dau. of Samuel and Anna (Goncher) West of
Philadelphia, and had:

1. *Sarah N. W.*, b. 1831, Philadelphia, Pa.,
dw. Vallejo, Solano Co., Cal.; possessed some
ability as a writer and artist; m. (1) in Cincinnati, O., about 1850, Olpha Bonney, who removed
with his family to California, and d. near Cincinnati, O. She m. (2) Capt. W. A. Hutchinson, of
San Francisco, a native of England, who dw.
Vallejo, Cal.

2. *Samuel W.*, b. 1833, Philadelphia, Pa., d.
in Cincinnati, O., aged 36, unm.

3. *Harriet W.*, b. 1835, Philadelphia, Pa.;
dwelt for 40 yrs. at Yellow Springs, O.; present
residence 247 Bell Ave., Cleveland, O.; m. (1) in
Cincinnati, O., 12 Nov., 1853, Dr. Joshua Biglow
Pennell, who d. in Yellow Springs, O., 2 Jan.,
1855; their only child d. in infancy. She m. (2)
at Yellow Springs, O., 1 Sept., 1862, Aaron Polhemus, who went out in the service of his country,
was wounded in battle at Cold Harbor, Va., in
June, 1864, and d. of his wound 2 Aug., 1864.

4. *William*, b. 1836, Philadelphia, Pa.; d. of
heart disease, in Nevada; never married.

5. *Joseph*, b. 1838, Phila, Pa.; d. of Cholera
in Cincinnati, in 1848.

6. *Mary Ellen*, b. 1840, Phila, Pa.; dw. Philadelphia, P.; m. W. Price Davis.

7. *Isaac*, b. 1842, Philadelphia, Pa., and there
d. of consumption, m. ______________.

8. *Elizabeth*, b. 1844, Philadelphia, Pa.; d. of
consumption in Cincinnati, O., 29 Aug., 1864;
m. 12 July, 1862, Charles E. Bennett.

9. *Anna*, b. 1847, Cincinnati, O.; d. aged 3
months.

10. *Anna* (again), b. 1851, Cinciunati, O.; d.
aged 3 weeks.

223. Isaac Martin⁶ Shotwell, 1786-1860,
of Elba, Genesee Co., N. Y., s. of Richard⁵
and Mary (Martin) Shotwell, of Genesee Co.,
N. Y., [of Benjamin⁴, John³, John², Abraham¹],
m. 1813, *Edna C⁶. Pound*, 1796-1872, dau. of
Hugh⁵ and Sarah (King) Pound, of Farmington, N. Y., [of Samuel⁴, Elijah³, John²,
John¹], and had:

1. *Sarah Pound*, b. 25 of 6 mo, 1814,
Farmington, Ontario Co., N. Y., and there
d. 15 of 9 mo., 1814, of whooping cough.

2. *Anna P'.*, b. 31 of 8 mo., 1815, Farmington, N. Y.; was a woman of sterling worth
in every relation in life; was one of the pioneer members of the Elba meeting of the
Society of Friends and remained · one of
exemplary fidelity and constancy to the last.
Only a few days before her death, she attended
religious meetings in Bushville, in her usual
health; but taking a severe cold, she rapidly
went down, and in spite of all that skill and
kindness could do, she departed this life in
great peace on the 26 of 10 mo., 1881, of
tyhoid pneumonia, aged 66 yrs., 1 mo., 26
days. She left six children, all of them active members in some branch of christian
fellowship. Her youngest living dau. Rosetta
Curtis, from Iowa, was visiting in Elba at the
time, and thus had the melancholy satisfaction
of sharing with the other children in kind
ministrations to the sick mother and in the
last sad rites of sepulture. She m. (I) in
Elba, N. Y., Friends log meeting house early
in 1830, Benjamin Hoag, who died. ____ 1831±,
about 18 mos., after marriage, s. of Levi and

Desire (Gardner) Hoag, of Elba, N. Y. At the time when Benjamin and Anna should have appeared the 2d time before the M. M., to receive the answer to their application for approval of proposed marriage, Benjamin was under arrest for refusing to train in the militia, but being thus prevented from attending the meeting through his faithfulness to the peace principles of Friends, his absence was readily excused and they were left at liberty to consummate their intended marriage. Anna P. (Shotwell) Hoag, m. (2) 21 of 11 mo., 1833, Stephen Dillingham, b. 28 of 2 mo., 1809, in the vicinity of Saratoga, N. Y., came to Caledonia, thence to Farmington, and in 1836, settled in Elba, and on a portion of the original farm which he then secured about one mile east of Elba village, since the property of John Crawford, he and his wife spent the remainder of their days; he d. 9 of 4 mo., 1881, of dropsy, aged 72 yrs., 1 mo., 11 days, s. of Silvanus and Judith (Marshel) Dillingham, of Saratoga Co., N. Y., and grandson of John Dilingham, whose wife's maiden name was Gifford. His parents being Quakers he continued in membership with the branch of that society called Orthodox Friends, and during the last few years of his life, he manifested a greatly increased activity in his religious life. Among his fellow citizens he was respected and honored as a man of inflexible integrity, kind and faithful in all his relations. Two brothers, three sisters, his wife and six children, survived him. His funeral service was conducted by Mary J. Weaver, of Bushville, assisted by Mrs. E. G. Underhill, and the Rev. E. A. Wheat, of Elba; both women were esteemed ministers of the Society of Friends. A very large gathering of neighbors attended his burial.

3. *Mary Smith*, b. 26 of 8 mo., 1817, in Farmington, N. Y.; taught school for several terms in early life; dw. latterly, Perinton, Monroe Co., N. Y., near Egypt, and there d. 11 of 12 mo., 1893, was a consistent member of Farmington M. M. of (Orth.) Friends; m. by a justice of the peace, in Stafford, Genesee Co., N. Y., 26 Sept., 1839, John Reed, b. 5 Dec., 1807, in Farmington, N. Y., was a carpenter, blacksmith and farmer; dw. in Genesee, Ontario, Wayne and Monroe Cos., N. Y.; d. in Perinton, N. Y., 31 of 3 mo., 1888, s. of Seley and Martha (Mills) Reed, of Farmington, N. Y. He united with the Friends after marriage, and was for many years an active member of Farmington M. M.; left the consoling evidence that it was well with him, saying that his prospect was peace and joy, and his heart was filled with praise. His funeral was conducted from his late res. in Perinton, N. Y., 3 of 4 m., 1888, and was largely attended. His parents d. in Wis. His maternal grandfather, John Mills, s. of John and Mary, was b. in N. Berwick, Scotland, 25

or 24 of 3 mo., 1755, and d. Farmington, N. Y., 21 of 3 mo., 1843, aged 87±. There is a tradition that John Mills in boyhood was taken to sea from the Scottish lowlands and kept on shipboard for 12 years and that an attempt was then made to press him into the British navy, but he ran away and settled in the town of Farmington, Ontario Co., N. Y., and there d.

4. *Isaac Martin, Jr.*, b. 3 of 12 mo., 1819, in Batavia (now Elba), Genesee Co., N. Y., was a farmer and removed, in Dec., 1854, from Elba to the town of Alabama, N. Y., thence, 1 Apr., 1859, to Careyville (now Oakfield), N. Y., thence 1 Apr., 1862, to Elba, thence in Jan., 1871, to Batavia, N. Y., purchasing a res. on State St., which he sold in 1888, and finally about 1891, to Buffalo, N. Y., dw. 150 Prospect Ave.; has held various local and county offices, was elected J. P. in Elba in 1863; is an insured member of the Masonic Fraternity and of the Royal Templars of Temperance. He m. (1) in Elba, N. Y., .. Oct., 1843, Elvira Levantia Scofield, b. 16 Sept., 1823, in Elba, N. Y., and there d. 11 Oct., 1852, dau. of Marlin and Eliza Scofield; m. (2) by the Rev. Dr. Gabriel S. Corwin, a Presbyterian minister, in Elba, N. Y., 14 Nov., 1854, Delia Alicia Mattice, b. 2 Dec., 1825, Elba, N. Y., dau. of Deacon Peter and Anna K. (Royce) Mattice, of Elba, N. Y., the former a native of Schoharie Co, N. Y., d. in Batavia, N. Y., .. Oct., 1883, s. of Nicholas Mattice of Shelby, N. Y., of Dutch ancestry, and the latter a native of Vermont.

5. *Amy*, b. 18 of 2 mo., 1821, Elba, N. Y., and there d. 21 of 11 mo., 1850, unm.

6. *Hugh Pound*, b. 23 of 2 m., 1825, Elba, N. Y., and there dw. a thorough and successful farmer and a faithful elder in the Society of Friends; taught school for ten years during the winter months, and served the town as superintendent of education for one year, owned the homestead of his father, whence about 1865, he removed to the farm known as the Dickey place, where he still resides; m. 23 of 10 m., 1850, Hannah Haines, b. in town of Ridgeway, Orleans Co., N. Y., 27 of 3 mo., 1830, dau. of Reuben² and Anna (Hawley) Haines of Shelby, N. Y., [of Jesse¹]. Her father was an esteemed minister of the Society of Friends.

7. *Nathan*, b. 14 of 5 mo., 1826, in Elba, N. Y. In addition to the meager educational advantages afforded in his own town, he spent several terms at Carey Collegiate Seminary in Oakfield and the Millville Academy in Orleans Co., earning, by his own exertions, as teacher, farm laborer, etc., the means needed to defray his expenses incurred in satisfying his thirst for knowledge. He engaged in orchard grafting from boyhood, nearly every spring, until 60 yrs. of age. By vocation a farmer, he has contributed to agricultural journals numerous articles upon horticultural and miscellaneous topics. He was the owner successively of three farms in

Elba, resided for a few months in East Oakfield in 1868, visited Michigan that summer and in Oct. of the same year removed to his present location on Sec. 22 in the Tp. of Concord, Jackson Co., Mich., about one and a half miles N. of the village of Concord, where he had purchased 106 acres of land; has since disposed of the rear portion of the place lying in Sec. 27, retaining 80 acres of improved land in Sec. 22, all of which is in an excellent state of cultivation. Always opposed to slavery and to the use of and traffic in intoxicants and narcotics, he adheres to the Republican party and has been an active and stedfast member of the I. O. of Good Templars and other temperance organizations, is a birthright member of the Society of Friends, but being liberal in his views, has freely contributed to the support of the local ministry of other denominations. He has been a Notary Public since 1881, was at one time Justice of the Peace in Concord, and has acceptably filled various other township offices. He m. in Friends meeting house, Elba, N. Y., 2 of 5. mo., 1850, Bathsheba Phebe Gardner, called Phebe B., b. 23 of 2 mo., 1831, dau. of George Washington^5 and Diana (Berry) Gardner, of Elba, N.Y., [of John^4, John^3, Wm^2, George^1]. She completed her school training at the Carey Collegiate Seminary, Oakfield, in 1850, a few weeks prior to her marriage. Her husband had at one time been her instructor in school district No. 9, Elba, N. Y., 1847-8. He had taught his first school the previous winter in the next district north; in the winter 1848-9 he taught in the Lanctons Corners district, and one year later in Wheatland. In the spring of 1854, Phebe B. visited her mother's relatives at Adrian and her sister at Parma, Mich., and again in the summer of 1868, accompanied on the latter trip by her husband and their second son, Cassius E., spent several weeks in southern Michigan, whither the family removed a few months later. With the exception of these slight interruptions and a few months of feeble health in recent years, her diligent attention to household cares has been as unremitting as it has been faithful and efficient. In the absence of her mother for several years before her marriage, the chief burden of domestic duties in her father's household had devolved upon her and had given her a most valuable practical preparation for the responsibilities, the industry and thrift of her subsequent life. Carding, spinning and weaving were among the avocations in which she had her full share of toil and discipline. A devoted and selfsacrificing wife and mother, a kind and obliging neighbor, ever ready in time of need to lend a helping hand, it has seemed to be her chief aim and care to relieve the suffering and promote the real welfare of all about her. Unpracticed in the pronunciation of denominational shibboleths she has yet been an earnest and humble follower of Him who of old went about doing good.

8.   *Sarah Edna*, b. 1 of 10 mo., 1830, in Elba, N. Y., taught school several terms in Elba, and there d. 26 of 2 mo., 1854, of consumption, aged 23 y., 4 m., 25 days., unm.

9.   *David Benjamin^7*, b. 8 of 5 mo., 1833, in Elba, N. Y., dw. Galesburg, Kalamazoo Co., Mich., a farmer; m. (1) in Elba, N. Y., 18 Jan., 1860, Adaliza Julia Wilder, b. 21 May, 1839, Elba, N. Y., d. Ross Tp., Kalamazoo Co., Mich., 16 Feb., 1870, aged 33 y., 4 m., 5 days, buried at Augusta, Mich., dau. of John and Rebecca Ann (Waller) Wilder, of Elba, N. Y. He m. (2) in Ross, Mich., 2 Nov., 1880, Margery Ann (McPherson) Mason, b. 5 July, 1845, in LeRoy, N. Y., wd. of Nelson Mason—by whom she had two daus., (1) Anna Elizabeth Mason, b. 6 Aug., 1872, and (2) Maud Mason, b. 4 Sept., 1874—and dau. of James and Elizabeth (McPherson) McPherson, of Genesee Co., N. Y.

10.   *Catharine Elizabeth*, b. 17 of 2 mo., 1836, in Elba, N. Y., was a teacher in Mt. Carroll Seminary, Ill., from Sept. 1855 to 1857, attained a high reputation as a scholar and a teacher; possessed the true teacher's spirit and taught from a love of her chosen calling. She d. at her home in Elba, N. Y., 9 Dec., 1857, of hemorrhage of the lungs, aged 21 y., 9 m., 22 days; unm.; united early in 1857, with the Mt. Carroll Baptist Church, and was an earnest devoted christian.

OF

ISAAC M[6]. SHOTWELL, OF ELBA, NEW YORK,

[of Richard,[5] Benj[4]., John[3], John[2], Abr[1].]

1. *Sarah P.*, b. 1814, d. 1814.

2. *Anna P[7].*, 1815–1881, m. (1). 1830, Benjamin Hoag, d. 1831, ±, [of Levi and Desire (Gardner) Hoag], and had: (1.) Sarah Edna, b. 3 of 4 mo., 1831, d. 6 of 4 mo., 1832.

Anna P[7]., m. (2) 1833, Stephen Dillingham, 1809–1881, [of Silvanus[2], John[1]], and had: (2.) Mary Jane, b. 23 of 3 mo., 1835, m. 24 Feb., 1859, Lewis Genung, b. 15 Mar., 1828, and had: (a) Lizzie A., b. 4 Sept., 1860, d. ..., m. 12 Sept., 1889, S. W. Randall. (b) Carl D., b. 1 Jan., 1866, m. ..., (c) Clara C., b. 1 Jan., 1866. (d) Mary Edith, b. 17 Feb., 1870, m. ...... (3.) William Dillingham, b. 14 of 9 mo., 1836, d. 24 of 9 mo., 1836. (4.) Maria L., b. 26 of 1 mo., 1838, m. 12 Mar., 1879, Lebbeus B. King, who d. 1895. (5.) Isaac, b. 24 of 10 mo., 1839, m. 1 Nov., 1865, Martha Achsah Hosmer, and had: George Simeon, b. 7. Aug., 1871, m. 1895, ____. (6.) Oscar, b. 21 of 6 mo., 1831, d. 8 of 2 mo., 1895, m. 21 of 3 mo., 1872, Sarah H. Thistlethwaite, and had: (a) James Irving, b. 3 of 2 mo., 1873. (b) Alfred Stephen, b. 25 of 2. mo., 1875. (c) Mary H., b. 28 of 1 mo., 1878. (d) Ethel Anna, b. 12 of 3 mo., 1885. (7.) Stephen N., b. 27 of 2 mo., 1843, m. 26 July, 1863, Emeline E. Porter, b. 18 Mar., 1844, and had: (a) William H., b. 22 July, 1865; d. 1 Jan., 1891. (b) Anna D., b. 24 Sept., 1866, m. 24 Sept., 1886, Henry A. Vail, [of Ephraim M.]. (c) Charles Stephen, b. 19 Oct., 1868. (d) Rosetta Maria, b. 2 Jan., 1874, m. 23 of 2 mo., 1890, John H. Field. (e) Emma J., b. 16 Dec., 1877. (f) Wilbur G., b. 31 Oct., 1881. (8.) Ann Loretta, b. 12 of 5 mo., 1845, d. 3 of 10 mo., 1848. (9.) Rosetta Anna, b. 24 of 5 m., 1850, m. 8 Nov., 1871, Wilbur Fisk Curtis, and had: (a) Louis Alfred, b. 5. Oct., 1872, d. 7 Nov., 1881. (b) Bertha Evelyn, b. 2 May, 1874. (c) Edna Ann, b. 16 Oct., 1884. (d) Ethel Mae, b. 29 Mar., 1887. (10.) Sarah Eliza, called Lizzie, b. 4 of 3 mo., 1855, d. 26 of 12 mo., 1859.

3. *Mary S[7].*, 1817–1893, m. 1839, John Reed, 1807–1888, [of Seley], and had: John Seley, b. 25 Sept., 1842, m. 29 July, 1864, Mary Eliza Shotwell, [of Edwin B[7]., Zachariah[6], Benj[5]., Benj[4]., John[3], John[2], Abraham[1]], and had: (a) Edwin John, b. 2 of 6 mo., 1865, d. 24 of 5 mo., 1866. (b) Charles Eugene, b. 19 of 9 mo., 1866, d. 2 of 7 mo., 1891. (c) William Elmer, b. 7 of 8 mo., 1869, m. 25 Feb., 1890, Etta Myrna Clark, and had: Myrna Beulah, b. 28 of 9 mo., 1890. (d) Albert Seley, b. 14 of 9 mo., 1871, d. 5 of 10 mo., 1872. (e) Sarah dna, b. 4E of 6 mo., 1873. (f) Martha Beulah, b. 13 of 8 mo., 1875. (g) Myrna Nellie, b. 12 of 8 mo., 1877. (h) David Smith, b. 25 of 6 mo., 1880. (i) Ruth A., b. 22 of 11mo., 1884.

4. *Isaac Martin[7], Jr.*, b. 1819, m. (1) 1843, Elvira L. Scofield, 1823–1852, and had: (1.) Mary Ellen, 1844–1871 (precise dates for Shotwell children and their consorts recorded elsewhere), m. 1863, William Frank Robe, b. 1841, and had: (a) Georgia Louise, b. 26 Mar., 1864, d. 2 Nov., 1865. (b) Herbert Jay, b. 10 Feb., 1867. (c) Nellie May, b. 23 May, 1871. (2.) Lester Lewellin, 1846–1848. (3.) Sarah Elizabeth, 1850–1887, m. (1) 1864, Henry Moreau; m. (2) 1877, Dr. Harry R. Nettleton.

Isaac Martin,[7] Jr., m. (2) 1854, Delia A. Mattice, b. 1825, and had: (4.) Clara Annie, b. 1856, m. 1872, Charles Henry Kellogg, b. 1852, and had: (a) Charles Henry, b. 10 July, 1873. (b) Kittie Clara, b. 16 Feb., 1876. (c) George Shotwell, b. 8 Dec., 1880. (5.) George M., b. 1860, m. 1881, Nellie Houghtaling.

5. *Amy*, 1821–1850.

6. *Hugh P[7].*, b. 1825, m. 1850, Hannah Haines, b. 1830, [of Reuben[2], Jessie[1]], and had: (1.) Murray A., b. 1852. (2.) Elvin H., b. 1855, d. 1855. (3.) Anna H., b. 1857. (4.) Edward R., b. 1859, m. (1) 1885, Lura Ann Edgerton, who d. 1886; m. (2) 1890. Lillian I. Avery. (5.) Gertrude E., b. 1863, m. 1884, John D. Piper, b. 1862, and had: (a) Murray Shotwell, b. 15 of 2 mo., 1890, d. 12 of 9 mo., 1890. (b) Nellie Evangeline, b. 24 of 7 mo., 1891. (6.) Nellie H., b. 1871. (7.) Alice Evangeline, b. 1873.

7. *Nathan[7]*, b. 1826, m. 1850, Phebe B. Gardner, b. 1831, [of George Washington[5], John[4], John[3], William[2], George[1]], and had: (1.) Rozilla Phebe, called Lilla P., b. 1851. (2.) Ambrose Milton, b. 1853. (3.) Cassius Emmett, b. 1855, m. 1885, Edith M. Briggs, b. 1866, and had: Owen Briggs Shotwell, b. 1886. (4.) Ida

Ann, b. 1857, m. 1886, Jehiel K. Davis, b. 1848, and had: Jehiel Shotwell Davis, b. 5 Mar., 1892. (5.) Manly Nathan, b. 1858.

8. *Sarah Edna*, 1830-1854.

9. *David B'.*, b. 1833, m. (1) 1860, Adaliza J. Wilder, 1839-1870, and had: (1.) Edna Ann, 1861-1883, m. 1882, William Fred Smith, b. 1855, and had: Edna Adele, b. 19 Mar., 1883. (2.) Sarah Florella, called Flora S., b. 1863, m. 1887, William Henry Maltby, b. 1862, and had: (a) Rebecca Delia, b. 28 July, 1889. (b) Frances Louise, b. 10 Sept., 1892. (c) Robert Irwin, b. 14 Feb. 1894. (3.) Jay Wilder, b. 1865, m. Mar., 1893, Susan Elizabeth Langdon. (4.) Kate Maude, b. 1870, m. 1892, Charles R Loomis, b. 1858, and had: Glen Shotwell Loomis, b. 10 Feb., 1895, at Sherburne, N. Y.

David B'., m. (2) 1880, Margery Ann (McPherson) Mason, b. 1845, and had: (5.) Clyde Raymond, b. 1881. (6.) Clarence Hugh, b. 1883. (7.) Adaliza, b. 1884. (8.) Charles Edward, 1886-1887.

10. *Catharine E.*, 1836-1857.

260. ISAAC[5] SHOTWELL, 1798-1845, of Ohio, s. of Titus[5], Sr., and Deborah (Moore) Shotwell, of Belmont Co., O., [of Daniel[4], Joseph[3] ?, Daniel[2], Abraham[1]], m. *Hope Stanton*, and had:

1. *Mary*, b. 18 of 12 mo., 1822; dw. (1895), Seneca, Kans.; m. ________ Vickers.

2. *Ruth*, b. 28 of 9 mo., 1824, dw. (1895), Seneca, Nemaha Co., Kans.; m. ______ Vickers.

3. *Titus*, called Titus III, b. 29 of 3 mo., 1826, dw. Latrobe, Athens Co., O.; has in his possession a pair of silver sleeve buttons with the initials T. S. inscribed on them, that were worn by his grandfather, the 1st Titus, when young, and which were to be passed down to the name of Titus Shotwell; many years after the death of Titus II, they passed to this nephew, but so far as yet known the name will run out with the present holder. Like his father before him, Titus III was very active in the working of the underground railroad in the *ante bellum* days, helping scores of oppressed and downtrodden Africans to start across the free states of the north to a land of liberty. He had a birthright membership in the Society of Friends, and after the division in 1828, both sides claimed him; when, however, he thought of marriage, both of the contracting parties, although members, did not wish to proceed according to the rules of the Society, and for this refusal they were disowned. He m. 20 of 10 mo., 1852, Mary Doan.

4. *Borden*, b. 6 of 12 mo., 1827, d. 10 of 7 mo., 1830.

5. *Jonathan*, b. 21 of 12 mo., 1829, d. 27 of 7 mo., 1844.

6. *Elias*, b. 22 of 3 mo., 1831, d. 27 of 12 mo., 1841.

7. *Charlotte*, b. 29 of 3 mo., 1833, d. 3 of 5 mo., 1847.

8. *Emily*, b. 20 of 3 mo., 1835, d. 9 of 3 mo., 1855.

9. *Thomas*, b. 6 of 3 mo., 1837, dwells Logan, Hocking Co., O.

10. *Susan L.*, b. 27 of 4 mo., 1839, dwells Little Hocking, Washington Co., O.; m. ______ Plumly.

11. *Eleanor*, b. 5 of 6 mo., 1841, dwells Twin Creek, Osborne Co., Kans.; m. ____ Ellis.

12. *Isaac*, b. 10 of 11 mo., 1843, dwells Rockland, Washington Co., O.

13. *Ezra Moore'*, b. 28 of 10 mo., 1845, 6 mos. and 11 days after the death of his father, dw. (1895), Sioux Falls, S. Dak., address 432 E. 12th St., of the firm of E. M. Shotwell & Co., successors to E. L. Smith & Co., proprietors of the coal and wood yard, Sioux Falls, S. Dak.; m. 5 Apr., 1868, Theora Dorr.

ISAAC[7] SHOTWELL, of 1508 N. 10th St., Philadelphia, Pa., s. of Wilson[6] and Sarah (Marsh) Shotwell, of Moorestown, N. J., [of Joseph[5], Joseph[4], Joseph[3], Daniel[2], Abraham[1]], m. *Catharine Dell*, dau. of Richard and Mary (Shotwell) Dell, and had:

1. *Thomas Dell'*, m. Adele Picot; has one daughter, Helen Picot Shotwell.

2. *Mary Dell.*

3. *Ida*, d ________ unm.

4. *Eliza Elliott.*

5. *Catharine.*

ISAAC MARTIN[7] SHOTWELL, b. 1819, of Elba and Buffalo, N. Y., s. of Isaac M[6]. and Edna C. (Pound) Shotwell, of Elba, N. Y., [of Richard[5], Benj[4]., John[3], John[2], Abr[1].], m. (1) 1843, *Elvira L. Schofield*, 1823-1852, dau. of Marlin and Eliza Schofield, of Elba, N. Y., and had:

1. *Mary Ellen[8]*, b 16 Sept., 1844, Elba, N. Y., and there d. 1 July, 1871; m. Elba, N. Y., 16 May, 1863, Wm. Frank Robe, b. 16 Apr., 1841, Elba, N. Y.; he subsequently married again.

2. *Lester Lewellin*, b. 16 Nov., 1846, Elba, N. Y., and there d. 30 Aug., 1848.

3. *Sarah Elizabeth*, b. 6 Feb., 1850, Elba, N. Y., d. Batavia, N. Y., 17 June, 1887, s. p.; m. (1) in Alexander, N. Y., ____ June, 1864, Henry Moreau; she obtained a divorce about 1873; m. (2) in Batavia, N. Y., 22 Feb., 1877, Dr. Harry Racine Nettleton, b. 1 Jan., 1848, dw. Rochester, N. Y., a practicing physician, s. of King David and Harriet Elizabeth Nettleton, of Nunda, N. Y.

ISAAC M[7]. SHOTWELL, b. 1819, of Elba and Buffalo, N. Y., [of Isaac M[6]., Richard[5], Benjamin[4], John[3], John[2], Abraham[1]], m. (2) 1854, *Delia A. Mattice*, b. 1825, dau. of Peter[2] and Anna K. (Royce) Mattice of Elba, N. Y., [of Nicholas[1]], and had:

4. *Clara Annie[8]*, b. 25 Apr., 1856, Elba, N. Y., dw. Buffalo, N. Y.; m. in Oakfield, N.

Y., 5 Oct., 1872, Charles Henry Kellogg, of Buffalo, N. Y., b. there 8 Nov., 1852, s. of Charles Kellogg.

5. *George M.*, b. 19 Sept., 1860, Oakfield, N. Y., was for several years a stenographer, employed in brass and clock works, New York city and Conn., notary public in both states; m. in Buffalo, N. Y., 30 June, 1881, Nellie Houghtaling, dau. of John and Margaret.

ISAAC M'. SHOTWELL, b. 1835, of Corunna, Mich., s. of Benj.' and Sarah (Hoag) Shotwell, of Elba, N. Y., [of Richard³, Benjamin⁴, John³, John², Abraham¹], m. *Mary P. Estes*, dau. of Allen Estes of Wheatland, and had:
1. *Sylvanus*, b. Wheatland, N. Y., d. young.
2. *Thurston*, b. Wheatland, N. Y., ------, 1850±.

ISAAC⁷ SHOTWELL, b. 1835±, of Smyrna, O., son of Thomas⁶ and Ellen (Brown) Shotwell, of Somerton, O., [of Titus⁵, Daniel⁴, Joseph³ ?, Daniel², Abraham¹], m. (1) *Harriet Hobbs*, and had:
1. *George Colson*, b. 20 Dec., 1856, Barnesville, Belmont Co., O., dw. Clark City, Mo.
2. *John F'''.*, b. 15 Dec., 1858, Barnesville, O., salesman, m. 23 Dec., 1879, Ella R. Starbuck, of Somerton, O., b. in Kans., 23 Mar., 1860, dau. of Wm. of Belmont Co., O.
3. *Emma Cornelie*, b. 1 Aug., 1863, in Barnesville, O., dw. there, unm. (1888.)

ISAAC⁷ SHOTWELL, b. 1835±, of Smyrna, O., [of Thos⁶., Titus⁵, Daniel⁴, Joseph³ ?, Daniel², Abraham¹], m. (2) *Sadie Fowler*, of Belmont Co., O., and had eight children.

ISAAC⁷ SHOTWELL, b. 1834, of Sparta, Ont., dw. Mt. Clemens, Mich., and Puyallup, Wash., s. of John⁶ and Matilda (Heaton) Shotwell, of Sparta, Ont., and Philadelphia, Pa., [of Wm⁵., John⁴, John³, John², Abraham¹], m. 1854, *Mary Martha Nickerson*, b. 1834, dau. of Nathaniel and Berthena, and had:
1. *Geo. B.*, b. 1856, Sparta, Ont., dw. Mt. Clemens, Mich.
2. *Alfred N.*, b. 28 Nov., 1857, Sparta, C. W. (Ont.), graduated from Detroit Medical College, 1884. Afterward practicing physician at Mt. Clemens, Mich., res. 98 Cass Bvd., office 36 Macomb St.
3. *Mortimer*, b. 1858.
4. *Charlotte Alma*, b. 1860, at Sparta.
5. *Agnes May*, b. 1868, at Lapeer, Mich. Either she or her sister m. Byron Thomas, and lives at 109 Taylor St., Seattle, Wash.
6. *Rolph S.*, b. Lapeer, Mich.

59. ISAIAH⁵ SHOTWELL, 1749-1832, of Plainfield, N. J., s. of John⁴ and Grace (Webster) Shotwell, of Plainfield, N. J., [of John³, John², Abraham¹], m. 1772, *Constant Lippincott*,

1753-1845, dau. of Remembrance⁴ of Shrewsbury, N. J., [of Wm³., Remembrance², Richard¹], and had:
1. *Mary⁶*, b. 23 of 9 mo., 1773, dw. near Rahway, but after death of her husband, lived with her deaf unm. dau. Rebecca in Plainfield, and there d. 7 of 10 mo., 1842, was an elder among Friends; m. at Plainfield, N. J., 23 of 1 mo., 1793, (as 2d wife), Thomas Laing, of Woodbridge Tp., N. J., b. 5 of 10 mo., 1759, in Woodbridge Tp., and there d. near Rahway, 11 of 2 mo., 1827, s. of Isaac and Annabella (Edgar) Laing of Turkey Hill, Middlesex, Co., N. J., [of John², John¹].
2. *Jediah*, b. 15 of 3 mo., 1775, in Plainfield, N. J., owned and resided in a house that was standing in 1876, and which had been occupied by his uncle Wm. Shotwell, previous to the latter's removal to Canada, in 1803, and there d. 12 of 8 mo., 1847, s. p.; m. in Plainfield, N. J., 22 of 6 mo., 1796, Anna Pound, b. 26 of 7 mo., 1775, d. 4 of 3 mo., 1851, dau. of Samuel⁴ and Catharine, (Webster) Pound, of Piscataway, N. J., [of Elijah³, John², John¹]; she had been an esteemed minister for more than 40 yrs., and as such, visited Canada about 1820.
3. *Peter⁶*, b. 2 of 6 mo., 1777, Plainfield, N. J., settled at Rahway, N. J., where as early as 1804, and for many yrs. thereafter, he kept a country store, and there d. 30 of 1 mo., 1845, buried in Friends' ground and afterward moved to Hazelwood cemetery; m. at Friends' meeting house, Plainfield, N. J., 31 of 8 mo., 1803, Phebe⁴ Vail, b. 16 of 5 mo., 1779, d. Upper Rahway, N. J., 19 of 9 mo., 1806, dau. of Abraham³, and Margaret (Fitz Randolph) Vail of Greenbrook, Warren Tp., Somerset Co., N. J., [of John², Samuel¹).
4. *Abel⁶*, b. 2 of 2 mo., 1779; learned the trade of a tanner with James Cox, a consistent Friend, whose son, Dr. Samuel H. Cox, was father of Bishop Arthur C. Coxe of the western diocese of N. Y. Abel took cert. of membership to New York M. M. from R. and P. M. M. dated 18 of 4 mo., 1798; followed the business of tanner and courier at Milton (now Rahway), N. J., and afterwards engaged in the business of grocer and baker in Upper Rahway, and there d. 20 of 2 mo., 1840; m. in Plainfield Friends' meeting house, 6 of 6 mo., 1810, Elizabeth⁴ Vail, b. 17 of 2 mo., 1782, d. Rahway, N. J., 15 of 8 mo., 1866, dau. of Abraham³ and Margaret (Fitz Randolph) Vail, of Greenbrook, Somerset Co., N. J., [of John², Samuel¹].
5. *Thomas Latham⁶*, b. 1 of 9 mo., 1781, was placed with Willet Hicks and given a cert. of membership from R. and P. M. M. 17 of 1 mo., 1799, directed to N. Y. M. M., d. near Crosswicks, Burlington Co., N. J., 21 of 8 mo., 1859; m. 8 of 5 mo., 1806, Elizabeth Satterthwait, b. 11 of 6 mo., 1786, dwelt Crosswicks, N. J., and

there d. 19 of 1 mo., 1843, one of the 14 children, (11 sons and 3 daughters), of Joshua Wright Satterthwait, of Crosswicks, N. J., b. 7 of 3 mo., 1755, d. 28 of 12 mo., 1816, and wife Ann, who d. 23 of 7 mo., 1834.

They became members of Chesterfield M. M. by cert. from R. and P. M. M., dated 16 of 7 mo., 1807.

6. *William*, b. 7 of 3 mo., 1783, Plainfield, N. J., and there d. at the res. of his brother Jediah, 17 of 12 mo., 1846, in 64th yr. of his age, unm; was not sane.

7. *Grace*, b. 21 of 4 mo., 1786, d. 4 of 6 mo., 1786.

8. *Joseph Lippincott*[6], b. 14 of 6 mo., 1787; dw. N. Plainfield, N. J., and there d. 12 of 10 mo., 1871; m. in Plainfield (N. J.) Friends meeting house 25 of 10 mo., 1809, Christiana Vail, b. 11 of 12 mo., 1788, d. N. Plainfield, N. J., 29 of 11 mo., 1871, dau. of Abraham[3] and Margaret (Fitz Randolph) Vail, [of John[2], Samuel[1]], and sister to the wives of Peter and Abel.

9. *Edmund*[6], b. 3 of 4 mo., 1791, learned the trade of bricklayer in Philadelphia, taking cert. of membership from R. and P. M. M. to the M. M. for the northern district of Philadelphia, dated 19 of 8 mo., 1812; dw. there for many yrs; d. in Rahway, N. J., 3 of 4 mo., 1866, aged exactly 75 yrs.; m. in Philadelphia, Pa., Sarah R. Shepard, b. 7 of 1 mo., 1792, in Philadelphia, Pa., d. Rahway, Middlesex Co., N. J., 21 of 7 mo., 1860, dau. of Nathan and .... (Hart) Sheppard, of Phila., granddaughter of Seymour Hart who came to America when a boy, and niece of Moses Sheppard who bequeathed an estate of one million dollars to found an insane asylum at Baltimore.

10. *Samuel Emlin*[6], b. 21 of 5 mo., 1793, Plainfield, N. J., was apprenticed to Henry Abbot, of Phila., becoming member of the M. M. for the northern district of Phila., by cert. from R. and P. M. M. dated 20 of 9 mo., 1810; dw. at Milton, (now Rahway), Middlesex (now Union) Co., N. J., and there d. 15 of 9 mo., 1823; m. at Friends' meeting house Middletown, Bucks Co., Pa., 13 of 2 mo., 1817, Sarah Carlile Rich, dau. of Joseph and Elizabeth Rich, of Attleboro (now Langhorn), Pa.

The following is a portion of an account of Samuel Emlin Shotwell, published in "Friends Miscellany," Vol. III, Second Edition 1845 pp. 130–4:

"From a child he was of a mild and pleasant disposition, and the sweetness of his spirit increased with his years. As he grew to the state of manhood, he became a true friend of the afflicted, was qualified to extend the hand of sympathy to those in distress—for trials of various kinds attended him, such as loss of property, and of professed friends, etc. He was just and upright in all his dealings among men; and when disappointments occurred, he bore them with much humility; trusting in that Almighty Arm which ever supports the faithful, and which he witnessed to be near him in his trials and difficulties.

"His mind had been exercised for some time, under a belief that some more active labors were required at his hands, respecting the discipline of the church; but considering his youth, he had not yielded to these impressions, till the last meeting for discipline which he attended. Feeling the renewing of this concern, he then thought he heard this language spoken in the secret of his soul, 'This is thy time and thy only time.' On which he gave up in obedience to apprehended duty, and spoke a few words to the business before the meeting. He afterwards remarked with thankfulness, that he never went from a meeting so well satisfied before, and whatever people might say, he enjoyed peace of mind as the result of obedience.

"After his marriage with Sarah Rich, of Buck's county, (Pa.), he was several times visited with sickness, which brought him very low,—several of his family were also afflicted with illness—all of which he bore with much composure and fortitude as dispensations from the Almighty. His constitution being but slender, his wife was anxious that he might get into some easy way of business for a livelihood. But he felt best satisfied to continue at his calling, under an apprehension that there would be a change in the family,—though he saw not in what way it might occur. In about a week after, being the 12th of the 9th month, 1823, he complained of feeling very much wearied, and retired to his bed . . . . . He several times expressed the love he felt for the whole human family. At one time, with much composure he said, 'There is nothing between me and the Almighty. If it is His will to take me, I am prepared.' He then with a pleasant countenance conversed with his wife on this very solemn event, greatly to the consolation of his tried mind."

11. *Hugh*, b. 10 of 8 mo., 1795, Plainfield, N. J., his last known place of residence about 1830, was in Darke Co., O., whence, it is said, he proposed to go with a drove of horses to Phila.; he m. in Morristown, N. J., Hannah Cole of Moorestown, Burlington Co., N. J., who d., s. p.

243. (i) JABEZ[6] SHOTWELL, 1791–1871, of Richmond, Ray Co., Mo., s. of John[5] and Abigail (Shipman) Shotwell of Mayslick, Mason Co., Ky., [of John[4], Abraham[3] (?), John[2], Abr.[1]], m. ...., and had:

1. *Ester Ann*, d. many years ago, leaving one son ...., who dw. (1891), in New Mexico, having married a Mexican lady and had two children and several grandchildren.

2. *Benjamin*, d. at age of 22, s. p.

3. *William*, b. 1824±, m. .... and has two daughters and one grandchild (b. before

Feb., 1891). One of the sons was a practicing physician at Richmond, Mo.; m. .... The other three children — Lucy, George and Mamie—dw. on a farm one mile from Richmond, Mo. Lucy taught in the college at Richmond. George was a farmer; m. Mercy Sanders. Their father Wm. Shotwell owns a farm one mile from Richmond, Mo.

4. *John W'.*, b. 1829±; is an attorney at law, notary public, and insurance agent at Richmond, Mo.; owns several farms, and the improvements on his home place cost about $8,000; in religion a Baptist; m. ....

5. *Jabez'*, b. 1831±, dw. near Odessa, in La Fayette Co., Mo., m. ....

6. *Charles*, dw. Gainesville, Texas; is a practicing physician; m. (1) ....; m. (2) ....

7. *Fannie*, dw. Lexington, Mo., m. .... Her son Charles, married and had one child. Her daughter Fannie was a widow in 1891.

JABEZ[7] SHOTWELL, b. 1831±, of La Fayette Co., Mo., P. O. Odessa, s. of Jabez[6] and .... (......) Shotwell, of Richmond, Mo., [of John[5], John[4], Abraham[3] (?), John[2], Abr.[1]], m. .... and had:

1. ...., a daughter, m. ....
2. ...., a daughter, m. J. E. Ball, a lawyer of Richmond, Mo., and had five children, one of whom m. a druggist of Odessa, La Fayette Co., Mo., and had one child.
3. *Alice.*
4. *Susie.*
5. *Milton.*
6. *Benjamin.*

22. JACOB[4] SHOTWELL, 1721-1793, of Rahway, Middlesex, (now Union), Co., N. J., s. of John[3] and Mary (Thorn) Shotwell, of Shotwell's Landing, N. J., [of John[2], Abraham[1]], m. (1) 1746, *Eleanor Haydock*, 1716±-1762, and had:

1. *Hannah*, b. 20 of 1 mo., 1749, Rahway, Middlesex (now Union) Co., N. J., d. in New York City; m. Rahway, N. J., 28 of 11 mo., 1770, Isaac Shotwell, a merchant of Rahway, N. J., s. of Jacob[4] [of Joseph[3], Daniel[2], Abraham[1]].

2. *Eden[5]*, b. 7 of 4 mo., 1755, in Lower Rahway, N. J.; having served an apprenticeship in New York and desiring to remain there, a cert. of membership was given him by R. and P. M. M. 16 of 9 mo., 1772, he returned with a similar cert. from New York M. M. dated 1 of 3 mo., 1775; James and Eden Shotwell became members of N. Y. M. M. by cert. from R. and P. M. M. dated 19 of 11 mo., 1777; James was disowned by Flushing M. M. 4 of 5 mo., 1780; Eden was afterward a merchant in Phila., Pa., and there d. before the memory of his nephew, Eden Shotwell; he m. Mary Haddock.

JACOB[4] SHOTWELL, 1721-1793, of Lower Rahway, N. J., [of John[3], John[2], Abraham[1]], m. (2) 16

1766, *Katharine Tilton*, of Shrewsbury, N. J., and had only:

3. *Nathan[5]*, b. ...., 1768, in Lower Rahway, N. J., was a merchant, dw. on the homestead at Rahway, afterward at Blazing Star, Middlesex Co., N. J., whence with his family in 1834, he removed to La Porte, Ind., and there d. aged 80 yrs., interred in Friends ground near that place; was a cripple for many yrs.; m. at Rahway, N. J., 24 of 5 mo., 1798, Sarah Fitz Randolph, b. 1782, d. Middlesex Co., N. J., 14 of 9 mo., 1815, dau. of Jacob and Anna (Webster) Fitz Randolph, of Blazing Star, N. J., [of Isaac[2], Jacob[1](?)].

40. JACOB[4] SHOTWELL, b. 1729, s. of Joseph[3] and Mary (Manning) Shotwell, [of Daniel[2], Abraham[1]], m. about 1750-54, ..., and had:

1. *Isaac[5]*, dw. Rahway, N. J., when he there m. with Unity of Friends and consent of parents, 28 of 11 mo., 1770, Hannah Shotwell, of Woodbridge Tp., b. 20 of 1 mo., 1749-50, dau. of Jacob[4] and Eleanor (Haydock) Shotwell, of Lower Rahway, N. J., [of John[3], John[2], Abraham[1]]. They and their minor children, Eden, Joseph, Elizabeth, and Catharine, having some time before 1791 removed to New York City, took cert. of membership to the M. M. there from R. and P. M. M., dated 21 of 7 mo., 1791.

57. JACOB[5] SHOTWELL, b. 1746, s. of John[4] and Grace (Webster) Shotwell, of Plainfield, N. J., [of John[3], John[2], Abraham[1]], m. 1769, *Bersheba Pound*, b. 1747, dau. of Elijah and Elizabeth Pound of Piscataway, N. J., [of John[2], John[1]], and had:

1. *Mary*, was a preacher and remained with the Orthodox Friends after the separation in 1828.

2. *Sarah*, b. 1 of 9 mo., 1772; d. at age of 29, unm.

3. *Ralph[6]*, b. 6 of 11 mo., 1773, Plainfield, N. J., and there d. 4 of 9 mo., 1826; m. (1) Elizabeth Marsh, called Betsey, a near relative, who d. 12 of 5 mo., 1812, buried at Plainfield, dau. of William of Ash Swamp; they were married out of meeting, for this, and being nearly related, they were under discipline by R. and P. M. M., but after many months deliberation both concluded to retain their right of membership in the Society. Ralph m. (2) in Plainfield, N. J., Osy Tingley, b. Plainfield, N. J., and there d. 17 of 5 mo., 18..., dau. of Jacob, of Washington Valley, N. J.

4. *Daniel[6]*, called "Daniel on the Hill," b. 28 of 7 m., 1775, d. 8 Aug., 1851, buried in Friends ground; m. (1) his cousin Mary[6] Shotwell, who d. when her only son was 3 years old, dau. of John Smith[5] and Phebe (Shotwell) Shotwell, [of John[4], John[3], John[2], Abraham[1]]; m. (2) Phebe Cole, dau. of William.

5. *John*, b. 24 of 10 mo., 1779, dw. Plainfield, N. J., and there d., s. p.; was an Orthodox Friend;

m. Mercy Smith, called "Massy," a minister among Orthodox Friends, dau. of Samuel, of Newark, and great-granddaughter of Shobel and Prudence (Fitz Randolph) Smith, of Woodbridge, N. J.

6. *Elijah*[6] (twin of John), b. 24 of 10 mo., 1779, d. Scotch Plains, near Plainfield, N. J., 9 of 5 mo., 1857, m. his cousin, Jemima G. Piatt, who d. near Pittsburgh, Pa., about 1868, dau. of Capt. Wm. and Sarah (Shotwell[5]) Piatt, [of John[4], John[3], John[2], Abraham[1]].

Jacob[7] Shotwell, b. 1804, of ____, Ill., s. of Ralph[6] and Elizabeth (Marsh) Shotwell, [of Jacob[5], John[4], John[3], John[2], Abraham[1]], m. *Dorcas Drake*, dau. of Noe Drake, of Washingtonville, N. J., and had a large family, among them:

1. *Jonathan*, (eldest son), was accidentally shot soon after removal with father's family to Illinois.

Jacob Alexander[7] Shotwell, b. 1850, of Wanatchee, Wash., s. of Eden[6] and Ann M. (Haas) Shotwell, of Bennett, Neb., [of Nathan[5], Jacob[4], John[3], John[2], Abr.[1]], m. 1872, *Susan E. Canfield*, b. 1854, and had:

1. *Henry Irving*, b. 21 of 11 mo., 1873, Topeka, Kans.
2. *Francis Eden*, b. 10 of 10 mo., 1875, Labette Co., Kan.
3. *Anna Lora*, b. 2 of 3 mo., 1884, Ellensburgh, Wash.
4. *Nora Edna*, b. 23 of 10 mo., 1885, Ellensburgh, Wash.
5. *Ralph Leroy*, b. 22 of 3 mo., 1887, Ellensburgh, Wash.
6. *Lyman Ray*, b. 5 of 3 mo., 1889, Wanatchee, Wash.

Jacob Zavitz[7] Shotwell, b. 1840, of Garrison, Butler Co., Neb., s. of Zachariah P.[7] and Margaret (Zavitz) Shotwell, of Lobo, Ont., [of Thos.[6], Benj.[5], Benj.[4], John[3], Jno[2]., Abr[1].], m. 1870, *Arabella J. Cox*, b. 1840±, dau. of Joseph, Jr., and Hannah (Briggs) Cox, of Scottsville, N. Y., and had:

1. *Catharine E.*, b. 13 of 3 mo., 1871, Butler Co., Neb.
2. *Joseph Cox*, b. 17 of 3 mo., 1873, Butler Co., Neb., and there d. in infancy.
3. *Wm. Merrit*, b. 8 of 10 mo., 1874, Pawnee Res., now Nance Co., Neb.
4. *Annette*, b. 16 of 8 mo., 1876, Pawnee Res., now Nance Co., Neb.
5. *Elizabeth May*, b. 11 of 8 mo., 1878, Platte Co., Neb.

60. James[5] Shotwell, b. 1752, of Long Bridge, Allamuchy, N. J., express rider under Washington during the Revolutionary War, s. of John[4] and Grace (Webster) Shotwell of Plainfield, N. J., [of John[3], John[2], Abraham[1]],

m. *Elsie (Smalley) Runyan*, b. 1758; dau. of Andrew Smalley of Harris' Lane, and had:

1. *William*, b. 18 of 4 mo. (Apr.), 1783, dw. Long Bridge, near Allamuchy, Independence Tp., Warren Co., N. J., and there d. when his children were young; m. at or near Hackettstown, N. J., Mary Ayers, dau. of Ezekiel Ayers.
2. *Nancy*, b. 13 of 7 mo. (July), 1785, m. (1) in Long Bridge, N. J., John Green, dwelt Green village and Drakesville, Morris Co., N. J., and there d. during the war of 1812, in which he served; m. (2) William Vliet of Vienna, N. J.; m. (3) Hardwick, N. J., John Schmuck, who dw. Warren Co., N. J., and there d.
3. *Clarissa*[6], b. 22 of 2 mo. (Feb.), 1787, dw. in Ohio; m. at Long Bridge, N. J., David Vliet.
4. *Clarkson*[6], b. 20 of 2 mo. (Feb.), 1789, removed with all his large family about 1830, from Warren Co., N. J., to Pontiac, Oakland Co., Mich., and there d.; m. in N. J., Keziah Sutton, step-daughter of ________ Freeman.
5. *Charles*, b. 20 of 12 mo. (Dec.), 1792, m. Ann Maines.
6. *Jonathan*[6], b. 25 of 9 mo. (Sept.), 1795, inherited the homestead of his father at Long Bridge, and there d. 14 Jan., 1850; in politics a democrat, was repeatedly a member of the New Jersey legislature from Warren Co., in the early half of the 19th century; was a birthright Friend but became a Methodist; m. at Allamuchy, N. J., 1 July, 1818, Phebe Willson, b. 18 July, 1796, d. at Longbridge, N. J., dau. of Mordecai and Anna (Larison) Willson. They were Friends.

James Shotwell, (parentage not ascertained), dw. Essex Co., when he m. in Friends meeting at Rahway, 27 of 5 mo., 1772, *Anna Moore*, of Essex Co., who afterward m. ________ Line, Lane or Laing, and d. in Eden, N. Y. Among the witnesses to this marriage in 1772, were Elizabeth Moore, Abraham Shotwell, Mary Shotwell, and Isaac Shotwell. James and Ann (Moore) Shotwell, had:

1. *Mary*[2], b. 18 of 2 mo., 1778, d. Eden, N. Y., 21 of 10 mo., 1862; m. in Rahway Friends' meeting 16 of 10 mo., 1800, Eber Willson, of Independence, N. J., b. 25 of 1 mo., 1779, s. of Gabriel[2] and Keziah (Decker) Willson, [of Samuel[1]). Among the witnesses to this marriage were Joseph, John, Margaret, Anne, Sarah and Phebe Shotwell, Gabriel, Kezia, Lydia, John, and James Willson, John, John, Jr., Bethiah, Elizabeth, Anna, Phebe, and Ann Moore.
2. *Elizabeth*; m. David Taylor.
3. *Joseph*[2], b. 25 of 4 mo., 1788, d. Eden, N. Y., 16 Mch., 1863; m. with approbation of R. and P. M. M. 26 of 7 mo., 1809, Sarah Thorn, b. 25 of 4 mo., 1790, d. Eden, N. Y., 23 Oct.,

1837, dau. of Abraham[3] and Elizabeth (Smith) Thorn, of Junius, N. Y., [of Abraham[2], Abraham[1]]; became members of Eden M. M. by cert. from R. and P. M. M., dated 23 of 8 mo., 1815, settled on the farm now occupied by their grandson, Joseph Kester, in Eden, Erie, Co., N. Y.

JAMES[7] SHOTWELL, 1810–1845, of Hackettstown, N. J., s. of Wm[6]. and Mary (Ayres) Shotwell, of Long Bridge, Warren Co., N. J., [of Jas[5]., John[4], John[3], John[2], Abr[1].], m. 1831, *Phebe Ayres*, b. 1812, and had:

1. *Archibald Ayres*, b. 10 Aug., 1832, dw. Hackettstown, N. J., a farmer, unm., 1888.
2. ____[8], a dau., dw. Hackettstown, N. J., and there d. ____, 1883 ±; m. Dr. Theodore Crane, of Hackettstown, N. J., dw. there on Washington St. (1888).
3. *Walter L'.*, b. 7 Sept., 1840, Hackettstown, N. J., dw. No. 77 Roseville Ave., Newark, N. J., salesman in a clothing house in New York City; m. at Stanhope, N. J., __ Nov., 1861 or '62, Harriet Decker.

JAMES[7] SHOTWELL, s. of Smith[6] and Mary (Crawford) Shotwell, of Thorold, Ont., [of Wm[5]., John[4], John[3], John[2], Abr[1].], m. *Matilda Seley*, and had:

1. *James*, dw. in town of Boston, Erie Co., N. Y.
2. *Cora E.*

JAMES FITZ RANDOLPH[7] SHOTWELL, b. 1822, s. of Robert[6] and Martha (Fitz Randolph) Shotwell, [of Manning[5], Benj[4]., John[3], Daniel[2], Abr[1].], m. (1) *Julia Caroline Welch*, and had:

1. *Martha Ann.*
2. *Mary Virginia.*
3. *Richard W.*

CAPT. JAMES A[7]. SHOTWELL, b. 1837, of Minneapolis, Minn., s. of Daniel[6] and Margaret (Force) Shotwell, of Alexandria, Minn., [of Daniel[5], Daniel[4], Joseph[3], Daniel[2], Abraham[1]], m. 1876, *Hattie A. (Cambell) Shotwell*, b. 1849, dau. of Moses D. and Paulina (Whittemore) Cambell, [of David], and had:

1. *Louis Barrett*, b. 10 Dec., 1876, at Alexandria, Minn; is salesman (youngest on the floor, aged 18), in the carpet department of Donaldson's Glass Block Store, Minneapolis, Minn., employed there since 1891.
2. *Daniel Bronson*, b. 28 Feb., 1880, at Alexandria, Minn.
3. *Marguerite Paulina*, b. 15 Oct., 1881.
4. *James Densmore*, b. 7 June, 1884.
5. *Roy Hayden*, b. 31 May, 1887.

JAMES[7] SHOTWELL, [of Abraham V[6], Samuel[5], Abraham[4], Joseph[3], Daniel[2], Abraham[1]], m. ____, and had:

1. *Dellie*, dw. (1895) Fredon, Sussex Co., N. J.
2. ________, a dau., dw. (1890) at Johnsonburg, Warren Co., N. J., m. John A. Stickles.

JAMES LUTHER[8] SHOTWELL, b. 1848, of Audrain Co., Mo., s. of Albert[7] and Catharine (Geery) Shotwell, of Bowling Green, Pike Co., Mo., [of John[6], Jno[5]., Jno[4]., Abraham[3] (?), Jno[2]., Abraham[1]], m. 1865, *Sarah Catharine Magee*, and had:

1. *Charles Albert[9]*, b. 5 June, 1867, Pike Co., Mo., is a farmer in Audrain Co., Mo., P. O., Farber; in politics a democrat; m. at Clarksville, Pike Co., Mo., __ March, 1885, Mattie Smith.
2. *Willie[9]*, b. 16 March, 1873; m. ________
3. *John R*, b. 30 July, 1875.
4. *Leona*, b. autumn of 1877; m. ____ Bishop, had a daughter b. 1895.
5. *James*, d. when 9 months old.

JASPER[3] SHOTWELL, of Ohio, s. of John[4] and Anna (__________) Shotwell, of Middlesex Co., N. J., [of Abr[3].(?), John[2], Abr[1].], is supposed to have had a son *David[4]*, who dw. in southern Ohio, perhaps identical with the David Shotwell of Boone Co., Ky., who left two married daughters living about two miles N. of Burlington, Ky.

JASPER[7] SHOTWELL, 1810–1849, of Mason Co., Ky., s. of John[6] and Sally (Burroughs) Shotwell, of Mason Co., Ky., [of John[5], John[4], Abr[3].(?) John[2], Abr[1].], m. 1843, *Ann McMillen*, 1825–1864 ±, dau. of Kinzie and Isabell (Givens) McMillen, and had:

1. *Malissa*, d. young.
2. *Eliza*, b. 6 May., 1847, dw. Kirkwood, St. Louis Co., Mo.; m. spring of 1869, William H. Biggs, who is Judge of the Court of Appeals of the State of Missouri.
3. *Sarah Isabel* (called Bell), b. about 1 Aug., 1849; dw. Kansas City, Missouri, m. __ Oct., 1870, James H. Caldwell.

JEDIAH[7] SHOTWELL, b. 1822, of Hightstown, Mercer Co., N. J., s. of Thos. L[6]., and Elizabeth (Satterthwait) Shotwell, of Crosswicks, N. J., [of Isaiah[5], John[4], John[3], John[2], Abraham[1]], m. 1845, *Martha Ann Provost*, and had:

1. *Ann Elizabeth*, b. 27 of 3 m., 1846.
2. *Thomas*, b. 29 of 6 mo., 1848.
3. *Erastus*, b. 30 of 9 mo., 1850; d. 12 of 2 m., 1851.
4. *Phebe T.*, b. 30 of 1 mo., 1853; d. 12 of 12 mo., 1856.
5. *Phebe Ella*, b. 17 of 6 mo., 1859.
6. *Jediah, Jr.*, b. 19 of 8 mo., 1862; d. 26 of 9 mo., 1863.

JEPTHA[7] SHOTWELL, b. 1824, of Allen Co., O., s. of Joseph[6] and Mary (Arrison) Shotwell, of Cleveland, O., [of Hugh[5], John[4], John[3], John[2], Abr[1].], m. 1849, *Nancy Cooper*, dau. of Thos. and Hannah, and had:

1. *Anna*, b. 1857, dw. with parents, Evandale, O., unm. (1888).
2. *Mary Louisa*, b. 1858, dw. Evandale, O.; m. 1877, George Bascom.
3. *Lenora*, b. 1860.
4. "*John Brough Shotwell*, was born on a farm near Delphos, Allen Co., Ohio, October 9, 1863, and was named in honor of the war governor, Brough of the State. Mr. Shotwell was educated in the public schools and at 18 began teaching in a country school in Hamilton county, Ohio. In 1885 he entered Hughes' High School (Cin.), where he graduated in 1888. He then resumed teaching in the country and followed the work for two years when he became a reporter on the Cincinnati Times-Star. In 1891 he was engaged on the Cincinnati Commercial Gazette, and for three years did local work and also traveled in all parts of the United States for his employers. In 1894, his health giving way, he visited California, and on returning took employment with the Times-Star, upon which journal he is now (1895) engaged. Mr. Shotwell enjoys the distinction of having dined with presidents and with eminent men of many professions. He has also written many newspaper and magazine sketches of more than local interest on matters of politics and on points visited by him in this country. During his newspaper career Mr. Shotwell studied law and was admitted to the bar. June 16, 1892, he was married to Miss Gena J. W. Phillips of Carthage, Ohio. Mr. Shotwell is a Republican and known in his party as a delegate to county and state conventions. He has held one office, that of member of the board of education at Evandale, O. Mr. Shotwell resides in Cincinnati, O., at this writing."
5. *Thomas*, b. 1867, dwells (1895) Cincinnati, O.

71. JEREMIAH[5] SHOTWELL, 1757-1830, of Rahway, N. J., s. of Abraham[4] and Mary (Potts) Shotwell, of Essex Co., N. J., [of John[3], John[2], Abraham[1]], m. 1781, *Mary* --------, 1762±-1817, and had:
1. *George*, dw. Milford, Pa., a physician.

JOEL[7] SHOTWELL, 1810-1880, of Garnett, Anderson Co., Kans., s. of John[6] and Grace (Marsh) Shotwell, of Kans., [of Wm[5]., John[4], John[3], John[2], Abr[1].], m. *Sarah Jane Blansfield*, and had:
1. *Matilda Elizabeth*, b. Lobo, C. W., dw. (1888) with her mother in Tenn. or Kans., unm., became member of Yarmouth M. M. of (Hic.) Friends by request 10 of 10 mo., 1860.
2. *John Blansfield*, b. Lobo, C. W. ------ 1844±, dw. Strathroy, Ont., a teacher; m. at Caradoc, Ont., 24 May, 1871.

2. JOHN[2] SHOTWELL, SR.,[*] d. 1719, of Woodbridge, N. J., formerly of Staten Island, s. of Abraham Shotwell, of Elizabeth Town, N.J., and New York, m. 14 Oct., 1679, *Elizabeth Burlon*, and had:
1. *John[3], Jr.*, b. about 1685-6, d. at his res. in Essex Co., N. J., 15 of 6 mo., 1762, in the 77th yr. of his age. In 1708, he brought from Friends' Meeting in Philadelphia, where he had been learning a trade, the following cert. to the Monthly Meeting at Woodbridge, N. J.:

"From our Monthly Meeting held at Philadelphia, this 20th Day of ye Eight Mo., 1708. To the Monthly Meeting of Friends at Woodbridge, Greeting: Whereas, John Shotwell, who came from your parts to Serve an apprenticeship in this City, which being fulfilled & he intending to return to ye place of his former abode, hath regularly applied to this meeting for a Certificate Concerning his Conversation (whilst among us) and Clearness with respect to Marriage. These are therefore according to ye wholesome and necessary Disipline of truth to Certify on his behalf that after due inquiry made we find his Conversation has bin orderly & his diligence in keeping to meetings Commendable as becomes our holy profession and as to Clearness relating to Marriage we have no Cause to think him under any Ingagements of that kinde. So recommending him to your Care with desires for his prosperity in ye blessed truth we Dearly Salute you & take leave. Your affectionate friends & Brethren.

Wm. Southby,	Tho. Griffith,
Richard Hill,	David Loyd,
Nicholas Wain,	Anthony Morris,
Hugh Dewboy,	Griffith Owen,
Nathan Stanbury,	Tho. Story,
Sam. Carpenter,	Ralph Jackson,
Wm. Hudson,	Christopher Blackburn.

"At a Monthly Meeting held att Nathaniel fitz Randolph [in Woodbridge], ye 20th Day of ye 8th Mo., 1709, ... John Shotwell, Jun., requested a Certificate of this Meeting of his Clearness in relation to Marriage & Conversation, he having bin hear but a little while Since he brought a good Certificate from Philadelphia which gave friends satisfaction that he is clear, ordered John Kinsy to gitt him one & Sign in ye behalf of ye Meeting."

"At Monthly Meeting in Flushing, 3d of ye 9 month, 1709, John Chatwell (Jr.) [of] Staten Island and Mary Thorn (Jr.) of Flushing [dau. of Joseph] appeared and delivered their consent and intention of marriage for the second time."

They were married at Flushing, L. I., 8 of 9 mo., 1709; she was b. about 1686, and d. 11 of 11 mo., 1768, aged 82 yrs. They settled about 1709, on the left or northwesterly bank of Rahway river, in Essex (now Union) Co., N. J. The place was long known as Shotwell's Landing, afterward Bricktown, within the corporate limits of the present city of Rahway, about one mile below the original town, formerly called Bridgetown or Lower Rahway. The property has passed out of the family. During the decade 1870-1880, streets were laid out through the farm, the sidewalks paved, the assessments for the so called improvements being more than the farm could be sold for, and it is ruined for agricultural purposes. Nothing now remains to mark the spot where John and his son Benjamin resided more than a century ago. A street called Lenington Ave., opened about 1866, passes over the ground where the dwelling stood and obliterated what, until that time, showed that a house and cellar had been there. Here John, Jr., had meetings of Friends appointed before their establishment in Rahway. On the last of 2d day in 5th mo., 1751, the Quarterly Meeting previously held only in Shrewsbury, assembled for the first time in Woodbridge; John Shotwell and Edward Fitz Randolph were the representatives from the Woodbridge M. M.

2. *Elizabeth*[3]; m. in Woodbridge, N. J., in 9 mo., (Nov.), 1705, John Laing, Jr., b. 1680 ±, who came from Scotland with his parents, John and Margaret Laing, as is believed, in the year 1685, when about 4 to 6 yrs. old. He resided at what was for a long time called Plainfield, in Piscataway Tp., Middlesex Co., N. J., and there d. in 1728, before 21 of 9 mo., leaving by his will half an acre of land on which to build a meeting house for Friends in that neighborhood, as it had been found inconvenient to attend the meetings in Woodbridge. Meetings had for several years previous to his decease been held on first and fourth days in his house; but the Monthly Meetings were held only at Woodbridge. On the ground given by him, a meeting house was built in the year 1736, which was occupied until the year 1788, when the present house was erected about two miles to the west, and was still called Plainfield Meeting, from which has grown up the present city of that name, one of the finest and most flourishing towns of the state.

3. *Sarah*[3], m. -- of 4 mo., 1712, Benjamin Smith, of Woodbridge Tp., N. J., b. there "Jan. ye 28th," 1687-8, d. 1735, s. of Samuel and Easter [Esther] Smith, of Woodbridge.

"At our Monthly Meeting held at Nath'l fitz Randolph's, in Woodbridge, ye 17th day of ye 2 mo., 1712, ... Benj'n Smith and Sarah Shotwell brought a paper to this meeting desiring our Consent to Marry among us. Fds. after a Serious Consideration of ye matter did Consent to permitt y'm to declare their Intentions of Marriage next Monthly Meeting, w'th this proviso, y't nothing appear to hinder by ye next Monthly Meeting."

"Att our Monthly Meeting held att Nathaniel fitz Randolph's, in Woodbridge, ye 15th of 3rd mo., 1712, ... Jane fitz Randolph and Eliz. Griffith presented to this [the Men's] Meeting Benj'n Smith & Sarah Shotwell who declared their Intentions of Marriage w'th Each other, it being the first time. This Meeting appoints Edmond Kinsey & Jno. Eastwood to Inquire Into ye clearness of ye young man in Relation to Marriage w'th any other & Conversation amongst [us] & to make report to ye next Monthly Meeting."

"Att a Monthly Meeting held att Nathanel fitz Randolph's, in Woodbridge, ye 19th of ye 4th mo., 1712, Jane fitz Randolph and Eliz. Griffith presented to this meeting Benj'n Smith & Sarah Shotwell who declared their Intentions of Marriage w'th Each other, it being ye Second time; and Inquiry being made concerning the young man's Clearness in relation to Marriage w'th any other and no objection made. They are Left att their Liberty to Consumate their Intended Marriage in ye fear of God."

Meetings were occasionally held at Benjamin Smith's house. "Att our Monthly Meeting held att ye new meeting house in Woodbridge ye 17th of ye 12th mo., 1714-15, ... Our friend Benjamin Smith hath propos'd to have a Meeting Settled att his house once a quarter, friends hath left it to ye Consideration of ye next Monthly Meeting." One mo. later, 1-17, 1714-15, "This Meeting in Answer to ye request of our fr'd Benj. Smith concludes to try one or two meetings att his house and if friends see y't it will answer ye end, to Settle farther."

"Att our Monthly Meeting held att our Meeting house in Woodbridge ye 17 day of ye 9 mo., 1720, ... Benjamin Smith reports that he hath brought twenty posts in order for fencing the burying ground." In the minutes of the M. M. 11-19, 1720-21, we find " William Willis requesting the Aid of this Meeting in the management of what Estate he hath for his best advantage. This Meeting appointed John Shotwell and Benjamin Smith for that Service and ordered them to make report of the proceedings which shall be made therein to the next Monthly Meeting." Benjamin was appointed an overseer in Woodbridge M. M., 21 of 9 mo., 1723, in the room of John Laing deceased. Smith died before 1736, Jacob Thorn being appointed overseer as his successor 15 of 11 mo., 1735-6.

There was another Benjamin Smith a weaver and a Friend. "Att our Monthly Meeting held att our Meeting house att Woodbridge ye 19th day of ye Second Month, 1716, . . . Samuel Fitz Randolph and James Clarkson were appointed to inquire into the life & Conversation of Benj'n Smith (Weaver), and of his clearness in respect of Marriage and make report thereof to the next Monthly Meeting." One month later 3-17, 1716, "On the enquiry made concerning Benjamin Smith (Weaver) things do not appear so clear as becomes the Simplicity of truth, So that Friends concludes to rest it awhile."

On 17 of 6 mo., 1721, in response to the "Proposals from the Yearly Meeting att London being made to the Monthly & Quarterly Meetings for the printing the book entitled The History of the Christian People called Quakers, in English, & written by our friend William Sewell in Holland. This Meeting agreed to the Sending for two of them." The following individual members of Woodbridge

M. M. on 18 of 2 mo., 1723, agreed to take one copy each of the same book: John Kinsey, John Laing, John Shotwell, Henry Brotherton, Dan'l Shotwell, and Benjamin Smith. In the small circulating library belonging to the Monthly Meeting, the most popular books, as Dally remarks, appear to have been Bishop's New England Judged, George Fox's Journal, Robert Barclay's Apology for the Quakers, Thomas Chalkley's Forced Maintenance, and "The History of the Christian People Called Quakers," by William Sewell of Holland, mentioned above, toward the publication of which in English, the Woodbridge Friends subscribed in 1721 and 1723.

4. *Abraham*, dw. Piscataway, Middlesex Co., N. J. During the building of the Woodbridge Friends' Meeting house we find in the Monthly Meeting minutes of 17 of 11 mo., 1711-12, "Abram Shotwell brought in his account of work done att the Meeting house w'ch at 4s per day amounts to £9 0s 0d, also John Vail brought his account att 4s per day amounting to £4 10s 0d. In all £13 10s 0d. In 9 mo., 1716, Abraham Shotwell was appointed to make a table with a draw and a lock to it for ye use of ye meeting. Under date of 16 of 6 mo., 1722, we find, "This meeting appoints Abraham Shotwell to remove the meeting house Stairs and to take down part of the gallery and make seats where it is needful." From the records of the M. M. at Flushing, L. I., it appears that Abraham Shotwell of Staten Island, son of John of Staten Island, m. at Flushing, L. I., fifth of ye tenth mo., 1712, Elizabeth Cowperthwaite of Flushing, dau. of John Cowperthwaite, of West Jersey. The minutes of Woodbridge M. M. of 16 of 8 mo., 1712, state that "Abram Shotwell hath proposed to this meeting to have a certificate of his Clearness relating to Marriage and Conversation whilst among us, to Flushing Monthly Meeting, in order to Marriage. Whereupon this Meeting orders Edward fitz Randolph and Dan'l Shotwell to Inquire Concerning him in Relation to those things and make report to ye next Monthly Meeting." At the next M. M. 9-20, 1712, Dan'l Shotwell and Edward Fitz Randolph makes report y't they have inquired Into Abram Shotwell's clearness in relation to Marriage and Conversation and find nothing but w't is well concerning him, ye s'd Abram who hath likewise produced a certificate from ye Philadelphia Monthly Meeting w'ch gives frn'ds here full satisfaction concerning him, whereupon ye meeting orders Jno. Shotwell to draw his brother a certificate against ye next first day, to be signed by as many of this meeting as may att that meeting in behalf of this."

At a M. M. in Woodbridge 15 of 9 mo., 1749, one Abraham Shotwell of Piscataway sent in a written confession of having been in the habit of taking strong drink to excess and of having been guilty of immoral conduct; but which of the numerous Abrahams was meant it is difficult to determine. In 12 mo., 1749, Abraham Shotwell and Mary Hampton were m. in Woodbridge. Abraham Shotwell and Mary Jackson were m. in the same place in 12 mo., 1751. In 1753 it is reported to the meeting that the wife of Abraham Shotwell of Piscataway has left; but the committee appointed in the case cannot ascertain the cause of her leaving him. Those bearing this name on record in 1753, comprised the following: (1) Abraham brother to John at the Landing; (2) his son Abraham b., 1732; (3) Abraham son of John at the Landing, b. 1719; (4) Abraham son of Joseph and Mary (Manning) Shotwell, b. 1726. But little is known concerning most of the descendants of Abraham' and Elizabeth (Cowperthwaite) Shotwell.

CHILDREN AND GRANDCHILDREN

OF

JOHN² SHOTWELL, SON OF ABRAHAM.

JOHN SHOTWELL, SR., 1650±-1710, of Woodbridge, N. J., formerly of Staten Island, married, 1679, Elizabeth Burton.

1. John³, Jr., 1686±-1762, of Shotwell's Landing, (now Rahway), N. J., married 1709, Mary Thorne, Jr., 1686-1768, daughter of Joseph.

1. Joseph, 1710-1787, m. (1) Sarah Cock; m. (2) Phebe Allen.
2. John, 1712-1779 ±, m. (1) Elizabeth Smith; m. (2) Grace Webster.
3. Elizabeth, 1715-1736, m. 1733 Joseph Webster, b. 1710.
4. Mary, 1717-1805, m. 1743-4, Samuel Marsh.
5. Abraham, 1719-1801, m. (1) Mary Potts; m. (2) Lydia Hallett.
6. Jacob, 1721-1793, m. (1) Eleanor Haydock; m. (2) Katharine Tilton.
7. Samuel, 1723-1777, m. 1748-9, Ame ....
8. Benjamin⁴, 1726-1793, m. 1746, Ame Hallett, 1727-1796.

2. Elizabeth, m. 1705. John Laing, Jr., 1680 ± -1728, of Piscataway, Middlesex Co., N. J., son of John and Margaret, from Scotland.

1. Sarah, b. 1706, m. 1734, John Heborn.
2. Elizabeth, b. 1707, m. 1731-5, George Parker.
3. John, b. 1709, m. 1741, Sarah Smith, b. 1721, [of Benj. and Sarah³].
4. Margaret, b. 1710, m. 1731, John Vail, Jr., 1709-1754, [of Samuel].
5. Ann, b 1712, m. 1739, Abraham Thorne.
6. David, 1714-1747-8, m. 1741, Mary Thorne, b. 1724, [of Jacob].
7. Martha, b. 1715, m. 1736, James Willson.
8. Mary, b. 1717, m. (1) John Vail, Jr.; m. (2) Samuel Hedger.
9. Abraham, b. 1718-19.
10. Isaac, 1720-1787, m. 1747±, Anabella Edgar, 1727-1803.
11. Jacob, b. 1722-3, m. (1) Sarah ....; m. (2) Ann Copling.
12. Christianne, b. 1724-5.

3. Sarah, m. 1712, Benjamin Smith, 1687-8-1735, of Woodbridge, N. J., son of Samuel and Easter of Woodbridge.

1. Esther, b. 1713, m. 1733-4, Stephen Vail, [of Samuel].
2. John, 1714-1714.
3. John, b. 1715.
4. Benjamin, 1717-1731.
5. Elizabeth, b. 1719, m. 1738, Samuel Laing.
6. Sarah, b. 1721, m. 1741, John Laing, [of John², Jr.].
7. Mary, b. 1723.
8. Abraham, b. 1724, m. 1754, Phebe Jackson.

4. Abraham, of Piscataway, N. J., formerly of Staten Island, m., 1712, Elizabeth Cowperthwaite, of Flushing, L. I., daughter of John, of West Jersey.

1. Elizabeth, b. 1716.
2. Sarah, b. 1720.
3. Hannah, b. 1722-3.
4. John, b. 1727, m. (?) Anna ....
5. Abraham, b. 1732, m. (?) 1749-50, Mary Hampton.
6. Deborah, b. 1735, m. 1753, Daniel Shotwell, b. 1725, [of Joseph].

---

4. JOHN³ SHOTWELL, 1686±-1762, of Shotwell's Landing (now Rahway), Essex (now Union) Co., N. J., s. of John², Sr., and Elizabeth (Burton) Shotwell, of Woodbridge, N. J., formerly of Staten Island, [of Abraham¹], m. 1709, *Mary³ Thorne*, Jr., 1686±-1768, dau. of Joseph² and Mary (Bowne) Thorne, of Flushing, L. I., [of Wm.'], and had:

1. *Joseph⁴*, b. 20 of 6 mo. (Aug.), 1710, dw. Main St., Rahway, N. J., on grounds now occupied by the National Bank building and there d. 8 of 4 mo., 1787; was clerk of the M. M. for several years, having been appointed to that position in the room of Jacob Thorn on 21 of 3 mo., 1741; on 17 of 11 mo., 1750-51, he was directed to "purchase a large book in folio for recording marriage certificates." From this and similar records of the Society of Friends, we have gathered much of the data presented in these pages.

At the Monthly Meeting held at Rahway, 19 of 5 mo., 1773, Joseph Shotwell, John Webster, and Benjamin Shotwell, were appointed pursuant to "a minute from the Meeting of Sufferings . . . . requesting acc'ts of the settlements of meetings in y's province &c. and that sa'd accounts be transmitted from y's to the Quarterly Meeting." From the report of this committee submitted to the M. M. 21 of 7 mo., 1773, we quote the following:

"At a Monthly Meeting at Woodbridge ye 16th 10th mo., 1742, a motion was made by divers Friends at Rahway to hold a meeting for three mos. at the House of Joseph Shotwell which was agreed to be held on the First Day of the Week and on the 17th 9th mo., 1743, it was agreed by the Mo. Meeting that a Meeting should be held twice a Week at S'd Jos. Shotwell's till the Middle of ye Second Mo. following on the first and fourth Days of ye Week. Which Meetings were Continued by appointments from year to year till a Meeting House was built on a Lot of Land given by S'd Jos. Shotwell for that Purpose in the year 1757. And then were removed to S'd Meeting house."

In 3d Mo., 1757, Joseph Shotwell gave to the M. M. one acre of land on Main St., Rahway, on which to build a Meeting House and for a Burying Ground. The house which was soon afterward built was occupied for that purpose until the year 1804, when the house now occupied was built on Irving St. The first house is standing in a good state of preservation and has been used for various purposes. No indications of a graveyard appear on the surface of the lot, in its rear, where John of the Landing and all his sons except John were burried.

At the M. M. held in Woodbridge on the 18 of 2 mo., 1751, it is stated that, "Some friends having been Con013 in Setting up grave Stones in our Burying ground, John Vail and Joseph Shotwell are desired to Treat with them and to desire them to have them Removed." Two months later a report was rendered that some had taken the stones down, but had laid them on the graves. Others had not done even that—the stones remaining in their original positions. On the 18 of 5 mo., however, it was reported that all the stones were taken down.

At the close of the Revolutionary war he was assessor and one of the treasurers of the school lands of Woodbridge. Among the papers of his great grandson, Henry R. Shotwell, was found the following:

"Memorial Concerning Joseph Shotwell.

"He was born in Statton Island in the Year 1710. Soon after his parents removed and settled near Rahway River. In the thirtieth year of his age, he Married and about that time built a house on one of the banks of Rahway River in which he passed the residue of his lifetime.

"About the twenty-fifth year of his age he was awakened to a close consideration of things pertaining to happiness, and however unpleasing it appeared to his natural inclination to walk in the path which leads thereto, through Divine assistance he very clearly evinced that it became his delight.

"He was favored with a good share of natural understanding, his judgment was strong, well qualified to give advice in difficult cases, settle disputes and as a ready willingness appeared to assist on these occasions his capacity and character induced to an extensive employ of his talents in benevolence. His favorable situation to entertain strangers and others gave opportunity to manifest his hospitality, and the sister virtue was also conspicuous in generously distributing to the poor and needy.

"The attendance of Religious Meetings appeared so interesting that the common concerns of life did not occasion his absence, neither did he think himself privileged to detain any of his family on trivial occasions but at the approach of the time appointed prepared his house for desertion. He had a clear discerning of the Manner our Discipline ought to be managed. And invested with a proper concern for the interest of Society, was enabled from time to time to impart advice, counsel, and admonition, suited to the various occasions.

"He much esteemed the practice of religious visits to families, was generally one of the number appointed to that service; one time he could not properly go to the Town proposed; at parting with his companions saluted them 'My heart goes with you.'

"He carefully attended to the welfare of his children, early instructed them in the propriety of a conduct according with the principles and manners of Friends, and this concern extended to his brethren pressing them to the like care in their families.

"He carried something about him so contrary to levity that libertines were awed, seldom offering their vain, frothy conversation in his company, but to the sincere, those who leaned to their real good, he was an example of encouragement.

"He was Clerk to our Monthly Meeting Thirty-one years and an Elder about the same length of time filled these stations with great propriety and meekly condescended to be employed in any of the smaller services.

"He cheerfully submitted to have meetings held in his house accommodated Friends five months in a year for the space of fourteen years and when it was concluded to build a house for the purpose gave the Meeting a Lot of Land to place it on.

[In] "His lively concern for the increase of piety and virtue the uniformity of his life he approached so near doing to those he had communication with as it was probable he might wish them to do to him, that he was beloved and his example admired.

"The 25th of 7th mo., 1787, he was taken unwell and chiefly confined to his bed, during his illness he said but little, appeared in a state of great composure, was favored to have his reason at times till almost the close. Our dear friend Joseph Delaplaine being informed it was apprehended he would shortly be removed from us, was constrained (by that love which long since dearly united them) to come and mingle the tear of sympathy, and bid him farewell, 4th of 8th mo., taking him by the hand asked if he knew him, he answered yes, then embracing each other took their last leave. Our esteemed friend William Jackson also taking him by the

ADAM [3] WINTHROP, 1498-1562,

of Groton, in Suffolk, England.

Grandfather of Gov. John [4] Winthrop of Boston, and ancestor of the compiler of the Shotwell Annals in the following line: Adam [4] Winthrop, 1548-1623, Anne [4] (Winthrop Fones, 1585-6--1618, Elizabeth [5] Fones Winthrop Feake, Hannah [6] 'Feake' Bowne, Mary [7] Bowne Thorne, Mary [8] (Thorne Shotwell, Benjamin [9] Shotwell, Richard [10] Isaac M. [11], Nathan [12], Ambrose M. [13] Shotwell of Concord, Mich.

hand affectionately repeated, 'This is our rejoicing the testimony of our conscience, that in simplicity and Godly Sincerity not with fleshly wisdom, but by the grace of God, we have had our conversation in the world; in a full belief this is thy happy experience I bid thee farewell.'

"Soon after, inclined much to sleep in the evening perceiving his breath was shorter, a number of friends and others collected and about half after eleven he quietly departed.

"His remains were carried into our Meeting House attended by a large number. Our beloved friend Joseph Delaplaine feeling his heart warmed with a measure of that love which burned in the hearts of the two brethren engaged him in testimony and the communications with them on their way to ________ was the subject. After meeting, was decently intered. Remember his grave deportment, temperance, humility and faithfuness. See him carefully passing on with an even thread in patience, the tenor of his life evinced he was bound for happiness, the course he steered pointed to the place prepared for the Righteous. "J. SHOTWELL."

The author, J. Shotwell, was probably either his son John or Joseph as the signature would answer for either of them. The latter part of the manuscript is much worn and difficult to make out. Joseph Delaplaine alluded to in the memorial was an ancient and prominent minister who resided in New York one hundred years since; he was the father-in-law of Isaac Martin of Rahway, N. J., brother to the wife of Richard Shotwell. The other friend, Wm. Jackson, spoken of in the Memorial was s. of James and Rebecca Jackson of Flushing, L. I., and brother to Phebe, wife of Edward Fitz Randolph of Woodbridge, and resided between Rahway and Plainfield.

Joseph Shotwell, like his father and uncle, went for a wife to Flushing, L. I.; he there m. (1) ________ of 1 mo., 1741-2, Sarah Cock, b. 14 of 12 mo., 1714-15, d. 11 of 8 mo., 1759, dau. of Henry[2] and Mary (Feeke) Cock, of Matinicock, L. I., [of James[1]]; she was educated among Friends on Long Island; entered the ministry early in life, became member of Woodbridge M. M. by cert. from Flushing, 16 of 7 mo., 1742; J. W. Dally in his history of Woodbridge (p. 214) states that she was a speaker and pattern of humility and faithfulness, a memorial of whom, written by John Webster and Abner Hampton, was adopted in the M. M. of 6 mo., 1760. Joseph m. (2) in Shrewsbury, N. J., in the summer of 1761, Phebe Allen, b. 1719±, d. Middlesex Co., N. J., 20 of 11 mo., 1815, aged 96 yrs., buried at Rahway.

2. *John*[1], b. 3 of 7 mo., 1712, at Shotwell's Landing, in the borough of Elizabeth, Essex, (now Union) Co., N. J. About the year 1735 he settled on the road to the Scotch plains near where the city of Plainfield now stands and at

17

the point where in 1876, the President of the N. J. Central R. R. resided, 9 miles from the Landing; it is said he was the only son who was willing to go out west to the "New Countries." He is distinguished as John of Plainfield; he there d. 1779± ; m. (1) in 11 mo. (Jan.), 1734-5, (between 11-16 and 12-20) Elizabeth Smith, b. 15 of 6 mo., 1718, dau. of Shobal[2] and Prudence (Fitz Randolph) Smith, of Woodbridge, N. J., [of Samuel[1]]; m. (2) at Woodbridge, N. J. ________, 1743, (l. l. 17 of 9 mo., 1743), Grace Webster, b. 4 of 9 mo., 1725, dau. of Wm[2]. and Susannah (Cowperthwaite) Webster, of Plainfield, [of Wm[1].].

3. *Elizabeth*[1], b. 9 of 2 or 2 of 9 mo., 1715, d. 17 of 4 mo., 1736; m. with unity of Friends in Woodbridge ________, 1733, (between 15 of 9 and 20 of 10 mo.), Joseph[2] Webster, b. 1710, s. of Wm[1]. and Mary Webster, of Woodbridge, N. J.

4. *Mary*[1], b. 9 of 2 mo., 1717, d. 20 of 10 mo., 1805; m. in Friends Meeting Rahway, 17 of 12 mo., 1743-4, Samuel Marsh, of Lower Rahway. On 21 of 12 mo., O. S., 1750-51, Richard Fitz Randolph, Samuel Marsh and Shobell Smith were appointed by the M. M. to promote subscriptions for the purpose of enlarging the Woodbridge Friends' Meeting house so as to accommodate the Quarterly Meeting which was to assemble there yearly on the last second-day of the 5th mo., (July), beginning in 5th mo., 1751. With the minute of this action, 12-21, 1750, closes the first Book of the Woodbridge Friends' Record. On the 18 of 10 mo., 1759, Samuel Marsh was appointed treasurer of Woodbridge M. M. in the room of Edward Fitz Randolph, who after long and acceptable service was, at his own request, discharged from that office and was directed in 11 mo., 1759, to pay over to his successor the funds of the meeting amounting to £13, 6s, 10d.

The house in which they resided in Lower Rahway, Middlesex, (now Union) Co., N. J., and where their son Samuel Marsh died in 1829, is yet standing at the corner of Main St. and Elm Ave., and in a good state of preservation; it is one story in height with a double pitched roof enclosed with shingles, and is probably older than the house of Jacob Shotwell. Their descendants are widely scattered.

5. *Abraham*[1], b. 8 of 3 mo., 1719, at Shotwell's Landing, N. J., settled on the left bank of Rahway River about a half mile below his father's place at the Landing, and at what was in 1879, the res. of his grandson Abraham F. Shotwell, and there d. 4 of 2 mo., 1801, in 82d yr. of his age, buried at Rahway; was appointed an overseer by Woodbridge M. M. 19 of 11 mo., 1755; m. (1) in Flushing, L. I., ________, 1742, (after 4 of 9 mo.), Mary Potts, who d. 31 of 3 mo., 1762, dau. of Thomas and Phebe Potts of Honey Neck, "Conattecut." He m. (2) in Flushing, L. I., in autumn of 1767, Lydia Hallett, b. 1738±, d. 19 of 9 mo., 1815, aged 77 yrs., buried at Rah-

way, dau. of Richard and Amy (Bowne) Hallet of Newtown, L. I. There was in 1755 another Abraham Shotwell, of Metuchen, who was under dealing for intemperance, and on 18 of 3 mo., 1756, the Abraham Shotwell and wife, of Piscataway, who in 1752-3, had an unhappy difference, were disowned by Woodbridge M. M. for continuing to live apart contrary to their engagements.

6. *Jacob*[4], b. 14 of 4 mo., 1721, was a merchant at Rahway; the dwelling in which he resided on Main St., in lower Rahway, nearly opposite Monroe St., is in good condition, enclosed with cedar shingles in place of siding and will last, if it meets with no accident, another century and a half. It was owned and occupied by the late Henry R. Shotwell, s. of Joseph Dobson[6] Shotwell, [of Henry[5], Joseph[4], John[3], John[2], Abraham[1]]. Jacob was killed 14 of 6 mo., 1793, by being thrown from his riding chair. Isaac Martin in his Journal (p. 38) under this date says: "Jacob Shotwell, an elder of our Meeting, being about a mile from home, was thrown out of his chair, and so much hurt by the fall that he died in about two hours after. Oh! the uncertainty of our time here! Yesterday he spent some time at my house; but now is summoned almost instantly from works to rewards. But I have faith to believe he is arrived where the wicked cease from troubling and the weary are at rest."

Dally in his history of Woodbridge, p 212, referring to the position taken by the society of Friends during the French and Indian war, has the following: "Several Mendham Quakers suffered some animadversion for redeeming their goods from the authorities which had been taken from them for refusing to 'train' with the militia. A committee of equity consisting of John Webster, Abner Hampton, William Morris, Jacob and Joseph Shotwell was instructed to go to Mendham and notify the culpable parties of dissatisfaction of the Woodbridge Quakers. In August the offending members, seven in number, acknowledged that they had done wrong and were penitent.

Jacob m. (1) on Long Island, 10 of 11 mo., 1746-7, Eleanor Haydock, b. 1716±, d. Philadelphia, Pa., 2 of 10 mo., 1762, in 46th year of her age; she was an elder among Friends. Memorials of Eleanor Shotwell and Elizabeth Haydock were drawn by John Webster and Abner Hamton and presented to the M. M. for W. R. and P. in 11 mo., 1763. He m. (2) at Shrewsbury, N. J., ..., 1766, Katharine Tilton, b. Shrewsbury, N. J.; a cert. of clearness to enable him so to proceed in marriage was granted by W. R. and P. M. M. 20 of 8 mo., 1766.

7. *Samuel*[4], b. 20 of 10 mo. (Dec.), 1723, at the Landing, Rahway, Essex (now Union) Co., N. J.; his farm now known as the Millington place adjoined that of his father on the west. On 18th of 6 mo., 1766, he was directed by the

M. M. to repair the Rahway burying ground fence, and on 20 of 2 mo., 1771, he was a member of a committee appointed by the M. M. to inquire into the dereliction of duty of the Woodbridge Friends, whose zeal for the work of the society had gradually declined for several years. Samuel Shotwell died 6 of 8 mo., 1777.

His great-grandson, Rev. John M. Shotwell, is authority for the tradition that he was a Tory and a man of wealth. Lord Howe made his home at his house and it is said that he loaned him £50,000, and that the British commander went away heavily in debt to him. The legislature of N. J., confiscated his real estate deeding it to his son Caleb then a soldier in the American army but he gave it back to his parents, who afterwards nearly disinherited him, giving nearly all of their lands to their younger son David.

A cert. of clearness on his application of marriage was granted by Woodbridge M. M. on 2 of 1 mo., 1748-9, directed to the M. M. at Mamaroneck, Westchester Co., N. Y. He there m. Ame .... who died 29 Oct., 1762. Samuel's executor was his brother Benjamin.

8. *Benjamin*[4], distinguished as Benjamin at the Landing, b. there 23 of 1 mo., 1726, and there d. of small-pox and was buried 15 of 5 mo., 1793. After the interment a meeting was held, doubtless in the meeting house, at the request of Samuel Smith and Rebecca Jones; both, as the account states, were "favored in testimony, and spoke of the uncertainty of time and the great necessity of making timely preparation for death." He received a cert. of clearness from marriage engagements, etc., from Woodbridge M. M., 18 of 7 mo., 1746, directed to the Flushing M. M., which, in 8th mo., appointed John Way and Richard Betts to see that the marriage was orderly accomplished; he m. .... of 8 mo., 1746, Ame Hallett, b. 1727, d. 15 of 9 mo., 1796, dau. of Richard and Amy (Bowne) Hallett, of New Town, L. I.

The following entry in the second book of records of the Woodbridge M. M., under date of 1st mo., 1757, indicates that Rahway members were growing restive: "Friends at Rahway have Repeatedly made application to the Monthly Meeting for leave to build a meeting house at that place, which friends at Woodbridge are oneasey with, and to put an end thereto it is Referred to the Consideration of the Quarterly meeting." The representatives to that body subsequently reported that it was the Solid Sence of that meeting that a meeting house ought to be built at Rahway." After citing the above, Dally, in his History of Woodbridge (p 213) says: " Without further opposition, the project was pushed forward. During February and March, much was done toward the new enterprise. Solomon Hunt, Samuel Marsh, Abraham Shotwell [of Rahway], and Benjamin Shotwell were appointed to purchase a suitable lot. Francis Bloodgood, Abner Hampton and Robert Willis were appointed to assist in selecting the ground and determining the size of the plot. It was decided that the new building should be thirty-four feet long and thirty feet wide." On 21 of 4 mo., 1757, meetings for worship were established on first days at Rahway, to begin at 4 o'clock P. M. On 20 of 2 mo., 1771, a committee composed of Samuel and Benjamin Shotwell, James Haydock and Solomon Hunt was sent from Rahway M. M. to inquire into the "slackness and Indifferency" of the Woodbridge Friends in the matter of regular attendance upon their Weekly Meetings for worship. They found that no meetings had been held during the winter, but a feeble effort was being put forth to recover the lost privileges.

On 19 of 4 mo., 1769, the M. M. had met in Woodbridge for the last time, and the Woodbridge Preparative Meeting had been removed to Rahway, and thenceforth the M. M. alternated between Rahway and Plainfield; it had since 5 mo., 1753, been held at Rahway, Plainfield and Woodbridge alternately. The Quarterly Meeting, which, up to this time, had assembled yearly in Woodbridge, was requested to be held thereafter at Rahway. At an expense of about £161 the meeting house there was enlarged for the reception of the delegates who met in it for the first time in 8 mo., 1769.

For several years the question of holding negroes in bondage had agitated the Society. On the 18 of 5 mo., 1768, the Monthly Meeting of Woodbridge, Rahway and Plainfield appointed a committee consisting of John Haydock, Benjamin Shotwell, Abraham Shotwell, Richard Dell, James Brotherton, Hugh Webster and Joseph Shotwell to treat with such Friends as then held Slaves; and on the 20 of 7 mo., 1768, they reported that with the exception of 2 members of the Mendham Preparative Meeting who had Slaves, only one other slave fit to be freed was owned within this M. M. On the 18 of 10 mo., 1759, Wm. Smith was taken under dealing by Woodbridge M. M. for having "purchased a Negro lately imported." On the 20 of 4 mo., 1774, having manumitted his negro man and negro woman, he made satisfaction to the M. M. for having bought them. On 15 of 5 mo., 1776, the fact was reported to the M. M. that Adam Miller had manumitted 2 Negro boys, Jack and Murr, and 1 Negro girl Quero, the boys to be free at 21 and the girl at 18 years of age.

Juduah Harned manumitted her negro man Jack in 9 mo., 1776. Jonathan Harned brought to the M. M. of 18 of 9 mo., 1776, the deed of manumission of his negro woman Mary. At the next M. M., 10-16, '76, it is recorded that Jonathan Harned, deceased, had, by his will, bequeathed the sum of £20 to the Society of Friends. On 16 of 4 mo., 1777, it is recorded that Solomon Hunt was the only member of R. and P. M. M. who owned a negro fit for freedom; and on the 17 of 9 mo., of the same year, '77, he was disowned by the Society for keeping his negroes in bondage. On 7 of 8 mo., 1777, Stephen Vail manumitted his negro. Josiah Wilson manumitted his negro woman, Inde, in 5 mo., 1778. On 19 of 11 mo., 1778, in compliance with a general order of the Yearly Meeting respecting the care and education of manumitted Slaves, Richard Dell, Wm. Smith, Isaac Hance, Benjamin Shotwell and John Vail were appointed to have the oversight of freed negroes within the limits of R. & P. M. M. Adam Miller in 8 m., 1780, manumitted his negro man Yammo.

SYNOPSIS OF THE CHILDREN AND GRANDCHILDREN OF

JOHN³ SHOTWELL, OF SHOTWELL'S LANDING.*

1. *Joseph⁴ Shotwell*, 1710–1787, of Rahway, N. J., married (1) 1741-2, Sarah Cock, 1715–1759, [of Henry², James¹], and had: (1) John, b. 1743-4, m. 1769, Margaret Haydock, 1752±–1815. (2.) Mary, b. 1746, m. 1766, John Haydock. (3.) Joseph, 1747–1817, m. 1774, Elizabeth Greenleaf. (4.) Sarah, b. 1750, m. 1771, Thomas Burling. (5.) Henry, 1752–1824, m. 1781, Sarah Dobson. (6.) James, b. 1754. (7.) Thomas, 1756–1760. (8.) William, b. 1759, m. Sarah ‑‑‑‑‑‑‑‑‑.

2. *John⁴*, 1712–1779±, of Plainfield, N. J., m. (1) 1734-5, Elizabeth Smith, b. 1718, and had: (1.) Elizabeth, b. 1736-7. (2.) John Smith, 1738-9–1801, m (1) 1756, Mary Webster, b. 1736, [of Wm.², Wm.¹], m. (2) 1782, Phebe Shotwell.

John⁴, of Plainfield, m. (2) 1743, Grace Webster, b. 1725, [of Wm.², Wm.¹], and had: (3.) Susannah, b. 1744, m. 1768, John Townsend, 1734±–1810. (4.) Jacob, b. 1746, m. 1769, Bathsheba⁴ Pound, b. 1747, [of Elijah³, John², John¹]. (5.) William, 1748–1841±, m. 1772, Elizabeth⁴ Pound, b. 1754, [of Elijah³, John², John¹]. (6.) Isaiah, 1749–1832, m. 1772, Constant Lippencott, 1753-1815. (7.) James, 1752–1795±, m. Elsie (Smalley) Runyan, a widow, b. 1758. (8.) Sarah, d. 1841±, m. (1) Ralph Smith; m. (2) Capt. William Piatt, killed by Indians in O., 1791; m. (3) ‑‑‑‑‑‑‑‑‑ Murray.

---

* According to surrogate records at Trenton, N. J., the will of John³ Shotwell, dated 10 of 3 mo., 1759, and probated 22 June, 1762, mentions wife Mercy and children John, Abram, Samuel, Benjamin, Jacob, Joseph, and Mary [wife of Samuel] Marsh.

(9.) Mary, m. John Stevens. (10.) Elizabeth, m. ________ Clayton. (11.) Martha, m. Jonathan Hand Osborne. (12.) Hugh, 1764-1854, m. 1783, Rosetta Arrison, 1764±-1836.

3. *Elizabeth*, 1715-1736, m. 1733, Joseph Webster, b. 1710, [of Wm'.], and probably had Susannah, who m, 1758, Samuel Kester.

4. *Mary*, 1717-1805, m. 1743-4, Samuel Marsh, of Rahway, N. J., and had: (1.) Elizabeth, b. 1744, m. 1761, Marmaduke Hunt. (2.) Jacob, 1746-1750. (3.) Mary, 1748-1816±, m. 1768, John Way. (4.) James, 1753-1764 (?). (5.) Anna, b. 1755. (6.) John, b. 1756, m. 1782, Sarah Fitz Randolph, 1763-1799 (?), [of Hartshorn]. (7.) Susannah, 1758-1829, m. Oliver Martin. (8.) Samuel, 1764-1829, m. Ann ________, d. 1823.

5. *Abraham*, 1719-1801, of Essex (now Union) Co., N. J., m. (1) 1742, Mary Potts, d. 1762, and had: (1.) Phebe, b. 1744, m. 1763, Thomas Hallett. (2.) Elizabeth, b. 1746. (3.) Naomi, b. 1749, m. (1) 1765, Israel Hallett; m (2) Thurber Dunbar. (4.) Mary, b. 1751, m. 1778, Mordecai Marsh, d. 1815. (5.) Hester, b. 1754, m. ________ Townsend. (6.) Jeremiah, 1757-1830, m. in New York, 21 June, 1781, Mary Barron, 1762±-1817. (7.) Samuel, b. 1759, m. ________

Abraham, of Essex Co., N. J., m. (2) 1767, Lydia Hallett, 1738±-1815, and had: (8.) Isaac, b. 1769, m. 1791, Catharine Moore. (9) Abraham, b. 1770. (10.) Ann, b. 1772. (11.) Aaron, 1774±-1852, m. (1) ________ Martin; m. (2) ________ Freeman; m. (3) Sarah (Way) Brown, widow of Amos. (12) John, m. ________ Freeman.

6. *Jacob*, 1721-1793, of Rahway, N. J., m. (1) 1746, Eleanor Haydock, 1716±-1762, and had: (1.) Hannah, b. 1749, m. 1770, Isaac Shotwell, [of Jacob', Joseph', Daniel', Abraham']. (2.) Eden, b. 1755, m. Mary Haydock.

Jacob, of Rahway, m. (2) 1766, Katharine Tilton, and had: (3.) Nathan, 1768-1848±, m. 1798, Sarah Fitz Randolph, 1782-1815, [of Jacob].

7. *Samuel*, 1723-1777, of Rahway, N. J., m. 1748-9, Ame ________, and had: (1.) Caleb, b. 1749-50, m. Phebe (Hinckston) Glidden, a widow, who d. 1819±. (2.) Thomas, 1752-1754. (3.) Sarah, b. 1754, d. unm. (4.) Mary, b. 1756. (5.) David, 1759-1797, m. 1779, Elizabeth Fitz Randolph. (6.) Elizabeth, 1761-1826, m. Thomas Bills, 1760-1845.

8. *Benjamin*, 1726-1793, of Shotwell's Landing (now Rahway), N. J., m. 1746, Ame Hallett, 1727-1796, [of Richard], and had: (1) Sarah, b. 1748, m (1) 1768, William Hampton, d. 1781; m. (2) 1783, Jacob Lundy, Jr., 1751-1806, [of Jacob]. (2.) Ame, or Amy, b. 1750, m. (1) 1788, Charles Brooks; m. (2) 1794, Samuel Hicks. (3.) Mary, 1752-1823. (4.) Richard', 1756-1833, m. 1782, Mary Martin, 1756-1844, [of Isaac]. (5.) Benjamin, 1759-1848, m. 1781, Bathsheba' Pound, 1763-1848, [of Zachariah', Elijah', John', John']. (6.) Elizabeth, 1762-1794±, m. 1787, Joseph Lundy, and had Benjamin, 1789-1839, the distinguished anti-slavery leader and philanthropist. (7.) Thomas, b. 1764. (8.) William, 1766-1855, m. (1) 1792, Elizabeth Moore, 1762±-1826; m. (2) 1827, Achsah (Lundy) Laing, 1777-1854, [of Samuel]. (9.) Lydia, 1769-1814±, m. (1) 1808, Philip Dorland, 1755-1814; m. (2) 1829, Isaac Griffin.

NOTE.—Since the matter of Part 1, pp. 1-3 and 5 was put in type, we have obtained the following additional data concerning the maternal ancestors and near relatives of the foregoing family of John³ and Mary (Thorne) Shotwell of Shotwell's Landing, and of their son Benjamin's wife, Ame, *nee* Hallett, chiefly as the result of the investigations of our kind kinsmen, Geo. T. Fish of Rochester, N. Y., Geo. W. Cocks of Glen Cove, L. I., and the several authors cited in these notes:

MARY³ THORNE'S FOREFATHERS AND NEAR KINDRED.

OUR THORNE, BOWNE, FEAKE, FONES AND WINTHROP LINES.

THORNE.

WILLIAM¹ THORNE, probably of Essex, Eng., was made Freeman at Lynn, Mass., on the 2d of May, 1638, and the same year he had 30 and 10 acres of land there. In 1645 he was in Flushing, L. I., the original patent of that town granted by Gov. Kieft on the 19 Oct., 1645, naming him among the eighteen patentees. In 1646 he was granted a plantation at Gravesend. In 1657 he was one of the proprietors of Jamaica, N. Y., and probably resided there for a time. Bergen's "Early Settlers of King's County," p. 301, says: "This is probably the William Thorne who with other Englishmen (as per p. 68, Vol. II, of Thompson's L. I.) arrived from Vlissingen in the Netherlands at N. A. and finally located at Flushing."

There seems to be reason to believe that this William¹ Thorne was the ancestor of all the early Thornes who have lived in the neighborhood of New York. The name is written either with or without the final e, the same branch of the family sometimes adopting one form at one time and later another. But Thorne seems to be the original orthography.

It is probable that William and Sarah Thorne, the immigrants, were buried in the grounds of Friends Meeting house at Flushing. Many of the Flushing Thornes are still Friends, as well as those who have settled elsewhere; but probably the larger number now go in other directions.[*]

They had at least four sons and one daughter as follows:

1. (?) *William*[2], of Flushing and Great Neck, L. I., name on record 1697-8 Will Thorne. The early records of Flushing show one document with names of William Thorne, Sen., and Wm. Thorne, Jr. They are thought by some to be father and son, and by others to be contemporaneous Williams with perhaps but little difference in their ages. Wm. Jr. m. Winifred --------, of Hempstead, who is understood to have d. 1713; but 1698 a William Thorne had wife Catharine, perhaps dau. of Henry Linnington. Wm. and Winifred probably had: (1) Richard, m. 1699 Phebe Denton. (2) Margaret, m. Thomas Rattoon. (3) Elizabeth m. 1696, Richbell Mott. (4) Sarah m. 1698, Roger Pedley.

2. *John*[2], b. 1643, dw. Flushing, L. I., d. 1709; m. 1664, Mary Parsell, of Flushing, dau. of Nicholas and Sarah -------- Parsell, and had: (1.) William[3], m. 2 Feb., 1708-9, Meribah Alling. (2.) John, m. Katharine --------. (3.) Joseph[3], m. 1695, Martha Johannah[3] Bowne, b. 1673, dau. of John[2] and Hannah (Feke) Bowne, of Flushing, L. I., [of Thos.[1]]. (4.) Mary, m. Wm. Fowler. (5.) Elizabeth[3], m. Frederick Schureman. (6.) Hannah[3], m. Richard Cornell. (7) Sarah, m. Joshua[3] Cornell, s. of John[2] and Mary (Russell) Cornell [of Thomas[1]]. The foregoing is made up to some extent of probabilities, being culled from various records, including John's will.

3. *Joseph*[2], of Flushing, L. I., d. 1727; m. 1680, Mary[3] Bowne, b. 6 Jan., 1660-61, dau. of John[2] and Hannah (Feke) Bowne of Flushing, L. I., [of Thomas[1]], and had 12 children: (1.) Hannah, b. 26 Oct., 1680, m. Thomas Field. (2.) Joseph, b. 22 Sept., 1682; m. Catharine Smith, widow. (3.) William, b. 7 Nov., 1684; m. 1729, Mary Fitz Randolph. (4.) Mary, b. 22 Aug., 1686; m. 1709, John[3] Shotwell, 1696-1762, s. of John[2] and Mary [Burton] Shotwell, [of Abraham[1]]. (5.) Susannah, b. 18 June, 1688; m. Eliakim Hedger. (6.) John, b. 5 Oct., 1690; m. Ann Hinchman. (7.) Thomas, b. 1 March, 1692-3; m. Letitia Hinchman. (8.) Benjamin, b. 6 Jan., 1694-5; m. Sarah Balding. (9.) Abraham, b. 1 Sept., 1696; m. 1717, Mary[3] Shotwell, supposed dau. of Daniel[2] and Elizabeth (----) Shotwell of Staten Island, [of Abraham[1]]. (For children see synopsis of

Daniel[2] Shotwell's grandchildren, p. 103, *Ante*.) (10.) Isaac, b. 4 Nov., 1698; m. Hannah Haight, and was great-grandfather of Jonathan[6] Thorne, (b. 1801) of New York, (mentioned with outlines of ancestry by ex-Gov. Alonzo B. Cornell in a pamphlet entitled "Some Beginnings of Westchester County (N. Y.)." (11.) Jacob[3], b. 20 May, 1700, d. 1759; m. 1723, Susannah[3] Shotwell, who d. 1777, supposed dau. of Daniel[2] and Elizabeth, of Staten Island, [of Abraham[1]]. (For their 11 children see synopsis of Daniel's grandchildren, p. 103, *Ante*.) (12.) Sarah, b. 20 Jan., 1702-3; m. 1726, James Jackson.

4. *Samuel*, b. 1657, d. 1732; m. Susannah

----

5. *Susannah*, m. 10 July, 1667, John Kissam or Lockissam (Lockerson, T. C. Cornell).

Hannah[3] *Thorne*, dau. of John[2] and Mary (Parsell) Thorne of Flushing, [of William[1]], m. Richard[3] Cornell, s. of John[2] and Mary (Russell) Cornwell, [of Thomas[1]], removed about 1725 to Scarsdale, they had: (*a*) Mary, b. 1703, d. 1762; m. Henry Sands. (*b*) Deborah, b. 1705, d. 1772; m. Matthew Franklin. (*c*) Richard, b. 1708, m. Mary Ferris. (*d*) Joseph, m. Phebe Ferris. (*e*) Hannah, m. Joshua Quimby. (*f*) Phebe, b. 1715; m. Ebenezer Haviland. (*g*) John, b. 1717, d. 1781, s. p. (*h*) Rebecca, b. 1718; m. Edward Burling. (*i*) Elizabeth, b. 1720, d. 1795; m. (1) Aaron Palmer; m. (2) Aaron Quimby. (*j*) Benjamin, b. 1723, d. 1771; m. 17 of 9 mo., 1742, Abigail Stephenson, dau. of Stephen and Jane (Clement) Stephenson, and had 10 children. One of them, Silas, the surveyor of Rochester, N. Y., b. 1789, d. 1864, was father of Thomas C., the author of "Adam and Ann Mott," which see.

BOWNE.

THOMAS[1] BOWNE, b. 1595, bapt. 25 July, 1595, Mattock, Derbyshire, Eng.; d. 18 Sept., 1677, Flushing, L. I., N. Y. Thompson's History of Long Island, says: "John Bowne and his father Thomas Bowne were among the earliest and most venerable inhabitants of Flushing." J. T. Bowne, in New England Register, XXV., 294, says: "Thomas Bowne with son John and daughter Dorothy (who afterward married Edward Farrington) came to Boston from England in the latter part of 1648 or early in January, 1649, and thence to Flushing in 1651." Thomas Bowne and wife -------- had:

1. *Truth*, remained in England; was living 1676.

2. *John*[2], b. 9 May, 1627, Mattock, Eng., bapt. in parish church there 29 May, 1627; arrived in Boston 1648-9±; returned to England Dec., 1650, and again arrived in America in 1651, arriving in Boston, Mass., 25 July; on 15 Aug. of that year he visited Flushing with Edward Farrington. His family soon afterward settled in Flushing. He built his house

there in 1601, and there d. 20 Dec., 1695, buried at Flushing on the 23d. He m. (1) 7 July, 1656, Hannah Feake, who d. in London 2 Feb., 1677-8, dau. of Robert and Elizabeth (Fones Winthrop) Feake. (See Fones and Winthrop.) Some records erroneously give the name as Hannah Field, (N. Y. Biog. Record, XI., 12). He m. (2) 1679, Hannah Bickerstaff, who d. 25 June, 1690. He m. (3) 1693, Mary Cock, b. 1655, dau. of James and Sarah (........) Cock, of Matinecock, L. I. (Children later.)

3. *Dorothy*, b. 1631 ± ; m. in America, Edward Farrington.

JOHN[2] BOWNE, of Flushing, L. I., by first wife Hannah, *nee* Feake, had :

1. *John*, b. 13 March, 1656-7, d. 1673.
2. *Elizabeth*, b. 8 Oct., 1658; d. 14 Oct., 1721; m. (1) 2 Nov., 1678, John Prier (or Prior) of Killingworth; m. (2) (as 2d wife) Samuel Titus, who d. 1 Jan., 1732-3, aged about 75, s. of Edward and Martha (Washburn) Titus.
3. *Mary*, b. 6 Jan., 1660-61, m. 1680 Joseph[2] Thorne, of Flushing, L. I., s. of William and Sarah of Flushing, L. I., *Ante*.
4. *Abigail*, b. 5 Feb., 1662-3, d. 16 June, 1688; m. 25 March, 1686, Richard Willits, b. 25 Dec. 1660, d. 14 May, 1703, s. of Richard and Mary Willets, and had Hannah, b. 24 Jan., 1687-8. The father m. (2) ....June, 1689, Abigail Powell, dau. of Thomas, and had 6 other children.
5. *Hannah*, b. 10 Apr., 1605; m. Benjamin Field, youngest son of Susanna Field.
6. *Samuel*, b. 21 Sept., 1667; d. 30 May, 1745; He was overseer of will of Nathaniel Pearsall 1703. (Am. Ancestry X, 74.) m. (1) 4 Aug., 1691, at Flushing, L. I., Mary Becket, who d. 21 Aug., 1707; m. (2) Hannah Smith; m. (3) Grace Cowperthwaite. He had a son Samuel.
7. *Dorothy*, b. 29 March, 1669, m. Henry Franklin.
8. *Martha Johannah*, b. 17 Aug., 1673, m. 1695, Joseph[2] Thorne, s. of John[2] and Mary (........) Thorne of Flushing, L. I., [of Wm[1].].

JOHN[2] BOWNE, by second wife Hannah, formerly Bickerstaff, had :

9. *Sarah*, b. 14 Dec., 1680, d. 1681.
10. *Sarah*, (again), b. 17 Feb., 1681-2, m. ....Foord.
11. *John*, b. 10 Sept., 1683, d. ....
12. *Thomas*, b. 26 Nov., 1684, d. 1684.
13. *John*, (again), b. 9 Sept., 1686, m. Elizabeth Lawrence.
14. *Abigail*, (again), b. 5 July, 1688.

JOHN[2] BOWNE, by third wife Mary, *nee* Cock, had :

15. *Amy*, b. 1 Apr., 1694, m. Richard Hallett, of New Town, L. I. Their dau. Ame Hallett, 1727-96, m. 1746, her mother's cousin Benjamin[4] Shotwell, 1726-93, [of John[3], John[2], Abraham[1]].
16. *Ruth*, b. 30 Jan., 1695-6, d. young.

FEAKE.

ROBERT FEAKE of Watertown, Mass., 1630, came probably in the fleet with Winthrop. He was one of the earliest and largest proprietors. Requested 19 Oct., in that year to be made Freeman, and was admitted 18 May, 1631; selectman 1637, '39, '40; representative 1634 (first court), 1635, 1636; appointed by the Court 4 Sept., 1632, a lieutenant under Capt. Daniel Patrick, and is said to have united with him in the purchase of Greenwich, Conn. [Winthrop, I, '69]. Trumbull's history of Connecticut (I, 118) names him among the purchasers of Greenwich, 1640; but his residence was at Watertown, where he was several years deprived of reason. He was one of the committee that reported Dorchester bounds 28 May, 1636. On May 25, 1636, he was appointed one of those deputed to keep the court for those towns which afterward became the county of Middlesex.

He signed the original covenant of Dedham, Mass., and was present at a number of meetings there. On 23 Nov., 1638, he proposed to lay down his whole estate at Dedham for twenty marks of English money, when his lands were sold. It was agreed to. On 7 Aug., 1639, he is called in Dedham records "of Watertown." See early records of Dedham, by D. G. Hill, town clerk, Vol. III, Index. "1636, Oct. 10, Agreed by the consent of the Freemen these 11 Freeman shall dispose of all civil affairs of the towne for one whole yeare." "Thomas Mayhew, Robert Feke, ... John Sherman. . . . . . ." 1639. Thomas Mayhew . . . Robert Feake, . . and ten others were appointed for one year to order all civil affairs of the town. He sold his homestead in Watertown, a house and ten acres, to Thomas Bright, who for £60 sold it 17 Dec., 1640, to Col. Ramborn.

Henry Feake (whether a relative is not ascertained) was admitted Freeman 14 May, 1634, and magistrate of Newtown, R. I., 1656, and '57 (Bond's Watertown).

Mount Feake, in Waltham, was named for Lieut. Feake, as was also Feake Isle, on the ocean side of the eastern shore of Virginia, but the name of the latter seems to have been corrupted to Fetches Island. In Frothingham's history of Charlestown, his name is printed Heake, as a witness to a grant of land from Indian Sachems. In a description of Waltham in 2 Hist. Coll., III, 261, it is said the name of the mountain is perpetuated (Winthrop, I, 69). Hazard, II, 214, has erroneously given his name as Fenner. Winthrop, I, 69, says he represented Watertown in the 1, 2, 3, 4, 5, 6, 7, and 9 Courts of Deputies. Trumbull, I, 116, says, "He united with Patrick 1640 in the purchase of Greenwich, Conn." For location of his Watertown lands, see Bond's Watertown Map. Daniel Patrick and Lieut. Robert Feake's wife were authorized by him to dispose of his property. Doc. Col. Hist., II, 144, says, "Daniel Patterick & Elizabeth Feac duly authorized by her husband Robert Feac, now sick, have resided two years about five or six leagues east of the Netherlands," etc. Dated 9 Apr., 1642.

ROBERT[1] FEAKE, b. ......; Freeman 18 May, 1631, at Watertown, Mass.; d. 1 Feb., 1660-61, Watertown records (1663, Savage and Bond); m. before the end of Jan., 1632, Elizabeth (Fones) Winthrop, wid. of Henry[5] Winthrop, [of John[4]], and dau. of Thomas and Anne (Winthrop) Fones.

He came to Mass. Bay in 1630 with the Winthrop fleet. He d. at the house of Samuel Thacher, who disposed of his estate to defray expenses. Inventory .... Feb., 1662-3, £9, 9s, 2d. (Bond).

She subsequently m. Wm. Hallett, and removed to Flushing and Newton, L. I., N. Y. Robert and Elizabeth (Fones Winthrop) Feake had:

1. *Elizabeth*, b. 1633±; m 1659, (as 3d wife), Capt. John Underhill, b. 1600±, d. 21 Sept., 1672, s. of John, an officer in the English army.

He was for a time a fellow soldier with Miles Standish in Holland. He sailed from Yarmouth 7 Apr., 1630, with John Winthrop and his fleet of 900 immigrants for Boston under an agreement to train the militia of the new settlement. Freeman of Boston 18 May, 1631, and was one of the first deputies to the general court. On 28 Sept., 1630, the court ordered £50 to be raised for Mr. Underhill and for Mr. Patrick, who was training another company. Capt. Underhill and Capt. Daniel Patrick were fellow soldiers in several Indian fights. Capt. John Underhill and his Netherland wife, Helena Kruger, were members of the old South Church.

On 7 Nov., 1637, he was banished from Massachusetts. In 1638 he returned to England and there printed a book called "News of America, by Capt. John Underhill, a commander in the warres there." On his return to America he went to Dover, N. H., where he was chosen governor. He afterward went to Boston and made confession of immorality and promised amendment. After much controversy he was again admitted to communion, and after six months of good behavior the court relieved him from sentence of banishment. Gov. Winthrop's journal says, "The governor and Capt. Underhill being on a journey" were bountifully entertained by Capt. Elliott. "In April, 1640, Capt. Daniel Patrick bought Indian lands near Norwalk, and soon after this date Capt. John Underhill was settled in Stafford, making occasional visits to New Amsterdam. In 1643 he was representative to the general court at New Haven. The inhabitants of New Netherlands were having serious difficulties with the Indians and in sore distress. They asked Capt.

Underhill to come to their aid with a company of English troops (N. E. Register, VIII, 269). On Sunday afternoon, June 2, 1644, a Dutch soldier called at Capt. Underhill's house while the people were at church, and finding Capt. Patrick there, charged him with having misled them, and shot him dead. As in other campaigns, Capt. Underhill was successful in subduing the Indians and returned to New Amsterdam in triumph. Later he took part with the English against the Dutch. After peace, he obtained from the Matinecock Indians a tract of land in Oyster Bay, where he settled for the remainder of his life. He named the place Kenelworth after the Kenelworth of the Earl of Leicester in Warwickshire, near where the Underhill family had lived for many generations. The name was corrupted to Killingworth. His second marriage brought him under Quaker influence, and he became a member of the society. He died at Killingworth 7 Sept., 1672, and was buried on his own place. Will dated 18 Sept., 1671, gives use of his whole estate to his " wife Elizabeth Under' hill during her widowhood; but if she marrythen my brother John Bowne and Henry Townsend and Matthew Pryor and my son John Underhill, I impower hereby that they see to ye estate that ye children be not wronged nor turned off without some proportionable allowance, as ye estate will afford, and that my son Nathaniel remain with his mother until 21 years," 'etc. [Queens Co. Records, Liber B, p. 91]. For his autobiography, see 3 Mass. Hist. Coll., VI. For his descendents by second wife, see Bolton's "Hist. of Westchester Co." See Thompson's L. I., also Cornell's "Adam and Ann Mott."

John and Elizabeth (Feake) Underhill of Killingworth, L. I., had: (1.) Deborah, b. 29 Nov., 1659, m. Henry Townsend. (2.) Nathaniel, b. 22 Feb., 1663-4, m. 1685, Mary Ferris. (3.) Hannah, b. 2 Dec., 1666, m. Thomas Alsop. (4.) Elizabeth, b. 2 July, 1669, m. Isaac Smith. (5.) David, b. -- Apr., 1672, m. Hannah ......

2. *Hannah*, b. 1637, m. 1656, John[2] Bowne, of Flushing, L. I., s. of Thomas[1] of Flushing. (See Bowne, *Ante*.)

3. *John[2]*, b. Greenwich, Conn., d. at Killingworth, L. I., -- May, 1727; he was a farmer and member of the society of Friends, and Friends' meetings were frequently held at his house; m. 1670, Elizabeth Prier, b. -- Aug., 1656, d. 25 Feb., 1702, dau. of Matthew and Mary (......) Prier, and had: (1.) Elizabeth, b. 9 June, 1674, m. Benjamin Field. (2.) Hannah, b. 6 Oct., 1675, m. James Cock. (3.) Mary, b. 30 Apr., 1678, m. Henry Cock. (4.) John, b. 10 July, 1679, d. 19 Dec., 1683. (5.) Robert, b. 22 June, 1683, d. 11 Apr., 1773, at Matinecock, L. I., he was a farmer, blacksmith, mill owner, and pastor of the Baptist church at Oyster Bay, L. I.; m. Clemence Ludlam (American Ancestry, X.,

77.) (6.) Sarah, b. 17 Feb., 1685-6, d. young.
(7.) Martha, b. 27 Oct., 1688, m. John Carpenter. (8.) Abigail, b. 7 Aug., 1691, m. Josiah Coggeshall. (9.) Deborah, b. 5 Jan., 1695, m. Thomas Whitson. (10.) Freelove, d. young. (Am. Ancestry, X., 77).

4. *Robert*, bapt. 17 July, 1642, in Dutch church. For grandchildren of Robert Feake, see N. Y. Biog. and Gen. Record, III., p. 184, taken from Friends' records.

5. *Sarah*, bapt. -- Apr., 1647.

FONES.

FOWNES, Devonshire, resident in that county for more than two centuries. (Previously of Saxby Saphy, county Worcester), also of Cornwall. "Bear," says Burke, "Azure two eagles displayed in chief and a mullet in a base argent."

1. *William* *Fownes*, of Saxby, Esquire, m. ---- Hyelton, dau. of Robert Hyelton, Knight, who must have lived about A. D. 1400. They had a son (2.) George.

2. *George* *Fownes*, [of Wm.'], m. ---- Milbranck, dau. of ---- Milbrauck of Malpas. They had a son (3.) William.

3. *William* *Fownes* or Fones, of Saxby, m. ---- Telham, dau. of ---- Telham. They had a son (4.) John.

4. *John* *Fones*, m. ---- Bradley, dau. of ---- Bradley. They had a son (5.) John.

5. *John* *Fones*, m. ---- Lewell, dau. of ---- Lewell of Lewell. They had six sons: Robert, (6.) *John*, Thomas, Humphrey, Nicholas, and William.

6. *John* *Fones* was of Dedford in the Parish of Bramsgrove, now Brownsgrove (?), Worcestershire. He had three sons: William of Bristol, who d. s. p. (7.) Thomas of Bristol. (8.) Richard of Bristol.

7. *Thomas* *Fones*, [of John, John, John, Wm., Geo., Wm.], son and heir, had son (9) Thomas.

8. *Richard* *Fones*, [of John, John, etc.], of Bristol, m. Joane Twidall, dau. of ---- Twidall of the Isle of Axholme in Lincolnshire. They had: John, George, Richard, (10.) Thomas.

9. *Thomas*, [of Thomas, John, John, John, Wm., Geo., Wm.], citizen and apothecary of London, Eng., at the Three Fawns Old Bailey in 1628, b --------- d. 15 Apr., 1629; m. (1) 25 Feb., 1604-5, Anne Winthrop, dau. of Adam and Anne [Browne] Winthrop of Groton. She d. 16 May, 1618. He m. (2) 28 Aug., 1621, Priscilla, dau. of John Burgis, D. D., and widow of Bezaliell Shearman Will dated 14 Apr., 1629, proved at Doctors Commons, 29 Apr., named wife and John Winthrop executors. Son Samuel and daughters Elizabeth and Martha to be brought up by John Winthrop and ---- White, Esq., of the Temple, and dau. Mary by her mother Priscilla. All the children were minors.

Thomas and Anne [Winthrop] Fones had: (1.) Dorothy, b. 24 Oct., 1608, at Groton, Christened 2 Nov. (2.) Elizabeth, b. 21 Jan., 1609-10, d. ----; m. (1) 25 Apr., 1629, Henry Winthrop, s. of John and Mary (Forth) Winthrop. He d. 2 July, 1630. She m. (2) Lieut. Robert Feake. (See Feake, *Ante*.) She m. (3) William Hallett. (3.?) Martha, b. --------, she d. 14 May, 1634, at Agawam, (Ipswich,) Mass., s. p.; m. 8 Feb., 1630-31, John Winthrop, s. of John and Mary (Forth) Winthrop. (4.?) Samuel, b. 1616, his heir.

Thomas and Priscilla (Burgis) Fones had: (5.) Mary. (6.) Priscilla, called dead 1628.

(10.) *Thomas* *Fones*, [of Richard, John, John, John, Wm., Geo., Wm.], was of Plymouth, 1620; m. (1) Prudence, dau. of John Nicholes of Taverstock, county Devon; m. (2) Joane Heale, dau. of Walter Heale of Knaton, county Devon. By the first wife he had: (1.) Richard, b. 1602. (2.) Prudence. (3.) Mary. (4.) Joane. By the second wife he had: (5.) Sampson. (6.) John. (7.) Thomas. (8.) Elizabeth. (9.) Susan. (Copied, except as to (9.) Thomas, from N. E. Hist. and Gen. Register, XVIII., 182, Et Seq., as published from an old manuscript in the Winthrop family.)

WINTHROP.

1. ADAM WYNTROPE lived at Lavenham, Suffolk county, England. The parish register of this place began 1558, or more could probably be learned concerning him. He m. Joane Burton, but it is not certain whether the last name was that of her father or a former husband. They had a son (2) Adam, b. 9 Oct., 1498.

2. ADAM WYNTROPE, b. 9 Oct., 1498, d. 9 Nov., 1562. "He left his father's home at seventeen years of age and went to London, where he bound himself to Edward Altham as an apprentice for ten years. Altham was at this time a clothier or cloth-worker. He was afterward (1531) sheriff of London." In 1526, when he had completed his apprenticeship, Adam was admitted to citizenship in London, being sworn in on the 9th of Sept. "Under the mayorality of John Allen." He was master of the company of cloth workers 1551. In 1544 he received a grant of the Manor of Groton in Suffolk, whither he retired. Groton, Mass., was named after the English home of the Winthrops. He m. (1) 16 Nov., 1527, Alice Henry or Henny; he m. (2) 1534, Agnes Sharpe, b. 1516, d. 13 May, 1565, dau. of Robert Sharpe of Islington. After the death of Adam, his widow m. (2) William Mildmay of Springfield Barnes. Her stepson m. Alice Winthrop.

JOHN¹ WINTHROP,
Second Governor of Massachusetts,
Born 1587-8.

Arrived at Boston 1630; Governor there thenceforth with some interruptions until his death in 1649. Son of Adam¹ and Anne Browne Winthrop of Groton Manor, Eng. (descendant of Adam⁴, Adam¹', and brother to Anne¹ Winthrop Fones, 1585-6--161n; maternal grand-mother of the first wife of John¹ Bowne of Flushing, L. I., and of William² and Samuel² Hallett, also of Long Island.

Adam[2] and Alice (Henry) Wyntrope had:

1. *Thomas*, b. 8 Nov., 1528, d. ____ Apr., 1529.

2. *William*[3], b. 12 Nov., 1529, d. at London, Eng., 1 March, 1581, buried at St. Michael's church, Cornhill; m. Elizabeth ________, who d. in Kent, 2 June, 1578, and had: (1.) Jonathan. (2.) Adam. (3.) William. (4.) Joshua. (5.) Elizabeth. (6.) Sarah.

3. *Bridget*, b. 1 Jan., 1530–31, d. 1536.

4. *Christopher*, b. 4 Jan., 1531–2, d. __ Oct., 1532 in Parish of Stocke. Essex.

5. *Thomas*, b. __ June, 1533, at London; d. 1537.

Adam[2] and Agnes (Sharpe) Wyntrope had:

6. *Alice*[3], b. 15 Nov., 1539, d. 8 Nov., 1607; m. Sir Thomas Mildmay, and had: (1.) William. (2.) Francis. (3.) George. (4.) John. (5.) Henry. (6.) Thomas, who d. 1 Dec., 1602.

7. *Bridget*[3] (again), b. 3 May, 1543, d. in Tharfield, Herefordshire, 4 Nov., 1614; m. Roger Alabaster, of a distinguished Hadley family, and had: (1) William, was a doctor, and is described in Fuller's "Worthies" Vol. II., p. 343, as a "most rare poet as any our age or nation has produced: witness his 'Tragedy of Roxana,' etc. He was made prebendary of St. Paul's and rector of ye rich parsonage of Tharfield in Hartfordshire." R. C. Winthrop, says, "he had turned papist during a visit to Rome, and on that account, after coming back to England, had been imprisoned in the tower, but, of course, he had renounced the pope before obtaining the rich parsonage." He died 1640. (2.) George. (3.) John, (4.) Thomas. (5.) Sarah.

8. *Mary*, b. 1 March, 1544, m. Abraham Veysie.

9. *John*[3], b. 20 Jan., 1546, d. in Ireland 26 July, 1613; m. Elizabeth Risby, dau. of Robert Risby, and had descendants. (See life and letters of John Winthrop. Note on p. 16.)

10. *Adam*, b. 20 Jan., 1546, d. 1546, aged 6 mos.

11. *Adam*[3] (again), b. 10 Aug., 1548; d. at Groton Manor, 1623; buried 28 March; m. (1) 16 Dec., 1574, Alice Still, dau. of Wm., of Grautham, Lincolnshire, and sister to Dr. John Still, then master of Trinity college, Cambridge, and afterward bishop of Bath and Wells. She and first born child d. 24 Dec., 1577, and were buried together in Hadley church. He m. (2) 20 Feb., 1579–80, Anne Browne,* who d. 19 Apr., 1629, dau. of Henry and Agnes Browne of Edwardstone, and had: (2.) Anne, b. 5 Jan., 1580–81, d. 20 Jan., 1580–81. (3.) Anne[3] (again), b. 16 Jan., 1585–6, d. 16 May, 1618;

on 22 July, 1597, she returned to her father's from a visit to her uncle Mildmay's; on 10 May, 1602, she "had a new gown brought from London;" on 23 Feb., 1604–5, Thomas Fones came to her father's house; on 25th they were m; "27th departed toward London;" on 2 Sept., 1604, she was at Ipswich at marriage of the maid of her father's cousin Sparrow. On 8 May, 1605, she visited her father, and departed for home May 23, being there at the marriage feast of her brother John, May 9. On 1 Aug., 1605, he visited her father at Groton, probably with his wife. On 22 Oct., 1608, both were at Groton. On 24 Oct., their first child was born; and on 2 Nov. she was christened Dorothy. Sir Robert Crane and his lady were present, and she was witness with Mrs. Sampson and Mrs. Bronde and Adam Winthrop, the child's grandfather. On 19 Dec., the Fones family returned to London. She m. 25 Feb., 1604–5, Thomas[4] Fones, who d. 15 Apr., 1629, s. of Thomas[3], [of John[6], John[5], John[4], Wm[3]., Geo[2]., Wm[1].]. (See Fones, *Ante*.) (4.) John[4], b. 12 Jan., 1587–8, in Edwardstone. (Family later.) (5.) Jane, bapt. 17 June, 1592, m. 5 Jan., 1612, Thomas Gostling, a clothier of Suffolk Co. (6.) Lucy, b. 9 Jan., 1600–1, Christened 20 Jan. (Family later.)

12. *Catharine*, b. 17 May, 1550, d. probably before 20 Sept., 1562.

13. *Susanna*, b. 10 Dec., 1552, d. at Coventry, 9 Aug., 1604; m. D. Cottie and had children.

JOHN[1] WINTHROP, b. 12 Jan., 1587–8, in Edwardstone, Eng., d. Boston, Mass., 26 March, 1649, s. of Adam[2] and Anne (Browne) Winthrop, [of Adam[2], Adam[1]], m. (1) at Great Stambridge, Essex Co., Eng., 16 Apr., 1605, Mary Forth, b. 1 Jan., 1583–4, d. __ June, 1615, buried 26 June at Groton, dau. of John, and had:

1. *John*[2], b. at Groton, Eng., 12 Feb., 1605–6, d. in Boston, Mass., 5 Apr., 1676. Will recorded in Suffolk Co., Mass., and Hartford, Conn. He m. (1) 1631, his cousin Martha Fones, dau. of Thos. and Anne (Winthrop) Fones, and step-dau. of Rev. Henry Painter; she d. in Agawam (Ipswich), 1634, s. p. He m. (2) 1635, Elizabeth, dau. of Edward Reade of Wickford, Essex, Eng., step-dau. of Hugh Peters; she d. at Hartford, Con., 1672, leaving two sons and five daughters. "Much of correspondence of her husband and sons is printed in Pub. of Mass. Hist. Soc." For his portrait, see Barker's Hist. of N. E., p. 622. His eldest son, John[3], known as Fitz John, b. in Ipswich, Mass., 19 March, 1639, d. at Boston, 27 Nov., 1707; m. rather late in life, Elizabeth, dau. of Geo. Tongue of New London. He left an only child, Mary[4], who m. Col. John Livingston of Albany, but d., s. p.

Wait Still[5], a younger son of John[3], b. Boston, 27 Feb., 1643, d. there 7 Nov., 1717; was the jurist. He had an only son, John[4], b. 1681,

<hr>

* HENRY[1] BROWNE, of Edwardstone, Eng., was a clothier, b. 1520-21+, d. 8 Jan., 1596-7 (Saturday); m. Agnes, who d. 17 Dec., 1590, and had:
1. Anne, m. 20 Feb., 1579–80, Adam[2] Winthrop.
2. Johane, d. 8 Sept., 1597; m. Wm. Hilles, who d. 4 Aug., 1597; they probably had a dau. Joane, who m. 1600, Adam, son of Wm. Winthrop. Another sister probably m. Roger Weston; and still another probably m. John Snelling of Shimpling, and had Anna, who m. 1 Nov., 1596, John Duke.

d. 1747, who was graduated at Harvard, 1700. John[1] (of New London), had an only son, John Still[5], who had several sons; among them was Thos, Lindall[6], lieut. governor; his youngest son was Hon. Robert C[10]. Winthrop.

2. *Henry*[5], bapt. at Groton, 20 (or 19) Jan., 1607-8; d. 2 July, 1630; m. 25 Apr., 1629, his cousin, Elizabeth Fones, dau. of Thos. and Anne (Winthrop) Fones. "He designed to return to Virginia with his new wife." His views probably were changed by want of funds; and before the year ended, he undertook with his father the N. E. scheme of colonization. He was drowned 2 July, 1630, in a creek at Salem after his return from Barbadoes. Their dau., Martha Joanna, bapt. 9 May, 1630, at Groton, m. 1649, Thos. Lyon of Stamford, Conn., but d. ----------, s. p. The mother and child arrived in N. E. with Margaret Winthrop (wife of John[4]), -- Nov., 1631. She m. (2) in N. E. probably before 1632, Lieut. Robert Feake. (See Feake.)

3. *Forth*, b. 30 Dec., 1609, at Stambridge, in Essex; buried 23 Nov., 1630, unm; was engaged to Ursula, dau. of Bezaliell and Priscilla (Burgis) Shearman.

4. *Mary*, m. 1632, Rev. Samuel Dudley, s. of Gov. Thos. Dudley; he d. 12 Apr., 1643, leaving (two or four) children.

5. *Anne*, b. 26 Aug., 1614, d. in infancy.

6. *Anne*, (again), d. in infancy, buried 29 Jan., 1615.

JOHN[4] WINTHROP, 1587-8-1649, m. (2) 6 Dec., 1615, Thomasine Clopton, who d. 8 Dec., 1616, buried 11 Dec., dau. of Wm. Clopton, Esq., of Castleins, a seat near Groton. Their dau. ----------, b. 30 Nov., 1616, d. 2 Dec., 1616.

JOHN[4] WINTHROP, 1587-8-1649, m. (3) -- 1618, Margaret Tyndal, who d. 14 June, 1647, dau. of Sir John Tyndal, Knight of Great Maplestead, Essex Co., and had:

8. *Stephen*, b. 24 March, 1618-19.

9. *Adam*[5], b. 7 Apr., 1620; had a son Adam[6], who had a son Adam[7], who m. 1700, Ann Wainright, and had John[5], the distinguished professor of Harvard college.

10. *Dean*, b. 16 March, 1622-3, bapt. 23 March.

11. *Nathaniel*, bapt. 20 Feb., 1624-5, d. young.

12. *Samuel*, bapt. 26 Aug., 1627.

13. *Anne*, bapt. 29 Aug., or 20 Apr., 1630, d. 1631.

14. *William*, b. 14 Aug., 1632, d. young.

15. *Sarah*, bapt. 29, June, 1634, d. young.

JOHN[4] WINTHROP, 1587-8-1649, m. (4) -- Dec., 1647, Martha Nowell, wid. of Thos. Coytmore. John[4] Winthrop, d. 26 March, 1649. His widow m. 10 March, 1652, John Coggar. John[4] and Martha (Nowell) Winthrop, had:

16. *Joshua*, bapt. 17 Dec., 1648, d. young.

LUCY[4] WINTHROP, dau. of Adam[3] and Anne (Browne) Winthrop, [of Adam[2], Adam[1]], b. 9 Jan., 1600-1, christened 20 Jan., d. 9 Apr., 1629, m. 10 Apr., 1622, Emanuel Downing, a lawyer of the Inner Temple, London. His first wife was a dau. of Sir James Ware, and sister to the Sir James Ware who was called the Camden of Ireland. They had several children.

Emanuel Downing and wife Lucy came to America in 1638. He d. between 1653, and 9 Aug., 1656. Their children were:

1. *George*[5], b. 1624; he was of the first class of Harvard, graduated (1642). His diplomatic services under Cromwell and Charles II, are matters of history.

2. *Mary*, came to America -- May, 1633, with Gov. Coddington. She m. Thos. Barnardiston of the Old Knightly Family of Barnardistons at Kedington, Suffolk Co., Eng. The death of their son without issue secured the endowment of Downing college.

3. *James* came to America, 1630, in the Arbella with his Uncle John.

4. *Susan*, came to America with Mary.

5. *Ann Downing*, b. probably about 1633; m. -- Aug., 1656, Capt. Joseph Gardner, who was killed 19 Dec., 1675, by the Indians in the Narragansett fight, s. of Thomas and Margaret (Frier) Gardner, s. p. She m. (2) Gov. Simon Bradstreet. (See Register, Vol. XIII., p. 230, for her will. See also Register, April., 1894, for ancestry of Simon Bradstreet.

6. *Lucy.*

7. *John*, bapt. 1 March, 1640.

8. *Dorcas*, bapt. 7 Feb., 1641-2.

BIBLIOGRAHY.—Winthrop's Hist. of N. E., 2 Vols. Life and letters of John Winthrop by Robert C. Winthrop, 2 Vols. Encyclopedias. Harper's Monthly, Vol. LIII, contains exterior and interior views of the church at Groton, Eng., also illustration of the stone cup. For the most complete genealogy, see Suffolk Manorial Families, by Muskett, now being published at London.

SHOTWELL HOUSEHOLDS.

ALPHABETICALLY ARRANGED BY FATHERS' GIVEN NAMES.

[Continued.]

---

11. JOHN³ SHOTWELL, d. 1745±, of ......, N. J., supposed s. of Daniel² and Elizabeth Shotwell, of Staten Island, [of Abraham¹] whose wife *Lydia* was living in 1745, had:

1. *John*, b. 1729±.
2. *Benjamin*⁴, b. 17 July, 1731, m. 1754, Elizabeth Manning.
3. *Joseph*. These three sons were living at date of father's will in 1745.

18. JOHN⁴ SHOTWELL, 1712-1779±, of Plainfield, N. J., s. of John³ and Mary (Thorne) Shotwell, of Shotwell's Landing, N. J., [of John², Abraham¹], m. (1) 1734-5, *Elizabeth³ Smith*, b. 1718, dau. of Shobal² and Prudence (Fitz Randolph) Smith, of Woodbridge, N. J., [of Samuel¹], and had:

1. *Elizabeth*, b. 27 of 12 mo., 1736-7.
2. *John Smith*⁵, b. 8 of 12 mo., 1738-9, at Scotch Plains, near the present site of Plainfield, N. J., d. before 10 mo., 1801; m. (1) Plainfield, N. J., 22 of 9 mo., 1756, Mary' Webster, b. 9 of 4 mo., 1736, dau. of Wm²., Jr., and Susannah (Cowperthwaite) Webster, of borough of Elizabeth, N. J., [of Wm¹.]; he dw. in Somerset Co., N. J., when he m. (2) 23 of 5 mo., 1782, Phebe⁵ Shotwell, of Middlesex Co., N. J., sister to Perrytown Joseph and dau. of Joseph⁴ and Elizabeth (Jackson) Shotwell, of Woodbridge, N. J., [of Joseph³, Daniel², Abraham¹].

JOHN⁴ SHOTWELL, 1712-1779±, of Plainfield, N. J., [of John³, John², Abr¹.], m. (2) 1743, *Grace Webster*, b. 1725, dau. of Wm²., and Susannah (Cowperthwaite) Webster, of Essex Co., N. J., [of Wm¹.], and sister to the 1st wife of his son John Smith Shotwell, and had:

3. *Susannah*⁵, b. 2 of 1 mo., 1744, Plainfield, N. J.; m. in 1768, (between 16 of 3 and 20 of 4 mo.), John Townsend, b. 1734±, d. Essex Co., N. J., 8 of 4 mo., 1810, aged 76 yrs., buried at Plainfield. They became members of R. and P. M. M., 20 of 9 mo. 1769, by cert. from Flushing.
4. *Jacob*⁵, b. 29 of 8 mo., 1746, Plainfield, Essex Co., N. J., was disowned by R.

R. and P. M. M., 16 of 3 mo., 1780, on account of his reflections against John Webster; d. 15 Dec., 1815; he was of the borough of Elizabeth when he m. with unity of Friends in Plainfield, 22 of 3 mo., 1769, Bersheba⁴ Pound, b. 13 of 1 mo. 1747; d. ... Feb., 1823, dau. of Elijah³ and Elizabeth Pound of Piscataway, N. J., [of John², John¹].

Jacob⁵ Shotwell was a farmer and owned slaves, he bought land between Scotch Plains and Plainfield and settled each of his sons on a farm.

5. *William*⁵, b. 11 of 6 or 5 mo., 1748, Plainfield, was a valuable and consistent Friend, was appointed an Elder while yet a young man, and with many others, for his peace principles, suffered during the Revolutionary War, having property taken for fines, etc., for declining to perform military duty when called upon. The house in which he dwelt at Plainfield, is yet standing. One authority states that before his removal from New Jersey, he occupied a stone house that is still standing just outside the corporation limits of Dover and which is reported to have been finished on the day of the surrender of Cornwallis, 19 Oct., 1781.

In 1791, he accompanied Sarah Lundy and Elizabeth Martin on a religious visit to New England and Nova Scotia. He soon afterward removed from Scotch Plains with his family, except dau. Rachel, to the Tp. of Thorold, in Upper Canada, and settled on Chippewa Creek, near where the city of Welland now stands; d. at Pelham, C. W., 1841±, aged 93 yrs. He m. at Plainfield, 25 of 3 mo., 1772, Elizabeth⁴ Pound, b. 16 of 11 mo., 1754, dau. of Elijah³ and Elizabeth Pound of Piscataway, N. J., [of John², John¹], and sister to Jacob's wife.

6. *Isaiah*⁵, b. 20 of 11 mo., 1749-50, d. 13 of 3 mo., 1832; m. at Shrewsbury, (N. J.) Friends' Meeting House, 27 of 6 mo., 1772, Constant Lippencott, b. ... of 12 mo., 1753, d. at res. of her son Jediah in Plainfield, N. J., 8 of 11 mo., 1845, aged 92 yrs., 10 mo., 15 days, dau. of Remembrance⁴ Lippencott of Shrewsbury, who was b. at Rahway, 1723, [of Wm³., Remembrance², Richard¹]. Richard¹ Lippencott of Devonshire, Eng., and his wife Abigail, settled

at Shrewsbury, before 1674, and are believed to
have been the ancestors of all the Lippencotts
in America.

7. *James*, born 23 of 1 mo., (Jan.), 1752,
was a farmer, dw. Long Bridge, Independence
Tp., Sussex (now Warren) Co., N. J.; perhaps
the James who d. 4 of 6 mo., 1795; certainly d.
before the division of the county in 1824; was
spy and private agent under Washington in the
Revolution. His great-granddaughter Emma
(Shotwell) Wolverton, of Ashley, Mich., is
authority for the statement that he was mail
carrier under President Washington. He m.
Elsie (Smalley) Runyan, widow of Wm. Runyan
and dau. of Andrew Smalley, of Harris' Lane.
She was born 24 Jan., 1758.

8. *Sarah*, d. in 1850, aged about 94, several
yrs. earlier than her only dau. She m. (1)
Ralph Smith, who d. ...., s. p., s. of Ralph
Smith of Hanover, N. J.; she m. (2) Capt.
William Piatt, of the Revolution, who was
killed by the Indians, at General St. Clair's
defeat on the Miami in Ohio, 4 Nov., 1791, s. of
John Piatt from France; m. (3) .... Murray, a
native of Ireland, who deserted her, it is said,
because her pension as the captain's widow had
ceased; she was afterward restored to the pension roll.

9. *Mary*, m. John Stevens, and had one son
John; they removed from N. J. to Ky., in latter
part of the 18th century.

10. *Elizabeth*, m. .... Clayton.

11. *Martha*, m. Jonathan Hand Osborne,
son of Jonathan, of Scotch Plains, N. J.

12. *Hugh*, b. 19 Mch., 1764, at Plainfield,
Essex (now Union) Co., N. J., was a land surveyor, which calling he had learned from a wise
and generous old teacher in New Jersey, who,
it is said, had once upon a time, all unobserved,
watched the lad in company with other school
boys redressing some fancied grievance by
piling up their instructor's growing water-
melons. Among the family traditions are other
anecdotes of his youthful pranks, such as put-
ting a small quantity of gunpowder into the
tobacco pipe of his sister-in-law, Constant, in
whose family he lived for several years. His
brother-in-law, Capt. Wm. Piatt, is said to have
dissuaded him from joining the Continental
Army, giving him his military hat and powder-
horn as a reward for desisting from his purpose
so to do.

He emigrated from Sussex Co., N. J., with
his wife and two children to Pennsylvania, in the
autumn of 1794, at time of the Whisky Insurrec-
tion there, crossing the mountains with an ox
team and settling on Redstone Creek, Fayette
Co., near Brownsville, whence in the spring of
1813, he removed with the most of his large
family to Cadiz Tp., Harrison Co., O., in
which county he spent the remaining years
of his life, keeping for several years a
tavern about five miles east of Cadiz, which

was afterward kept by his son Joseph. He
d. at the home of his youngest son Arrison,
in Washington Tp., Harrison Co., O., 17 Mch.,
1854, at the age of 90 yrs. He was in early life
a member of the Society of Friends; but, on the
20 of 5 mo., 1784, he was disowned by R. and
P. M. M., for having been married by John
Miller, J. P., contrary to Friend's discipline, or,
as he expressed it, because he had "loved a
pretty girl" outside the Society. They afterward, in 1804, became members of the regular
Baptist church at Redstone, Pa., and in 1841,
Hugh was one of the constituent members of
the Corinth church, in which he remained a
consistent member till his death. "He saw his
children and his children's children prosperous
and happy around him and was even permitted
to behold the 4th generation of his offspring;
yet when his Master called, he was ready and
willing to go; death had no terrors for one who
had so nobly 'fought the good fight;' and we
cannot but rejoice that this aged veteran of the
Cross has gone to reap his reward."

He m. 23 Feb., 1783, Rosetta Arrison, of
Sussex Co., N. J., b. in N. J., 1764±, d. 1836, at
the home of her son Arrison, in whose possession the old bible and all the family records and
relics were left. She was dau. of John Arrison,
of Sussex Co., N. J., formerly of Wyoming, Pa.,
whence he was driven out by the Indians in the
time of the war of the Revolution.

Synopsis of the Children and Grand-children of John Shotwell, 1712–1779±,
of Plainfield, N. J.

JOHN SHOTWELL, b. 1712, s. of John and
Mary (Thorne) Shotwell, of Shotwell's Landing,
(Bricktown, now part of Rahway), N. J., [of
John, Abr.], m. (1) 1734-5, Elizabeth Smith,
b. 1718, dau. of Shobal and Prudence (F. Ran-
dolph) Smith, of Woodbridge, N. J., [of
Samuel], and had:

1. *Elizabeth*, b. 1736-7.

2. *John Smith Shotwell*, 173° -1801; m. (1)
1756, Mary Webster, b. 1736, [of Wm²., Wm¹.],
and had: (1.) John, d. unm. (2.) Wm. d.
1830±, unm. (3.) Samuel, m. Hetty (Cooper)
Davison, a wid., dau. of Nathan Cooper. (4.)
Susannah; m. David Martin, [of Alexander].
(5.) Elizabeth; m. Dennis Hughes. (6.) Sarah;
m. .... Hanison. John Smith Shotwell,
m. (2) 1782, Phebe Shotwell, [probably of
Joseph, Joseph, Daniel, Abraham], and had:
(7.) Joseph Smith Shotwell, an orthodox
Friend and merchant in New York city; m.
Deborah Fox, [of George]. (8.) Nathan, d.
unm. (9.) Mary; m. Daniel Shotwell, of Plainfield, N. J., [of Jacob, John, John, John,
Abraham].

JOHN SHOTWELL, b. 1712, [of Jno²., Jno².,
Abr.], m. (2) 1743, Grace Webster, b. 1725,
[of Wm²., Wm¹.], and had:

3. *Susannah*[3], b. 1744; m. 1768, John Townsend, 1734±-1810, and had: (1) Martha, b. 26 of 4 mo., 1769; m. (as 2d wife) James Powell, of Clinton, Dutchess Co., N. Y. (2.) Grace, b. 7 of 8 mo., 1770. (3.) Sarah, b. 23 of 10 mo., 1771; d. 1 of 4 mo., 1857, unm. (4.) Hugh, b. 11 of 8 mo., 1773; m. Mary Dell. (5.) Jotham, b. 19 of 12 mo., 1774. (6.) John, b. 18 of 8 mo., 1776.

4. *Jacob*[5] Shotwell, b. 1746; m. 1769, Bersheba[4] Pound, b. 1747, [of Elijah[3], John[2], John[1]], and had: (1.) Mary, an Orthodox minister. (2.) Sarah, b. 1772, d. unm. (3.) Ralph[6], 1773-1826, m. (1) Elizabeth Marsh, who d. 1812, dau. of Wm. of Ash Swamp; m. (2) Oay Tingley, [of Jacob], (4.) Daniel[6], 1775 1851, lived "on the hill," Plainfield, N. J.; m. (1) Mary[6] Shotwell, [of John Smith[5] Shotwell, John[4], John[3], John[2], Abraham[1]]; m. (2) Phebe Cole, [of Wm.]. (5.) John, b. 1779; m. Mercy Smith, [of Samuel]. (6.) Elijah[6] (twin of John),1779-1857; m. Jemima G. Piatt, dau. of Capt. Wm. and Sarah[5] (Shotwell) Piatt, (of John[4], John[3], John[2], Abraham[1]].

5. *William*[5] Shotwell, 1748-1841±, m. 1772, Elizabeth[4] Pound, b. 1754, [of Elijah[3], John[2], John[1]], and had: (1.) Rachel, b. 1773; m. Richard Dell, Jr., 1762-1845, of Dover, N. J., and Junius, N. Y., [of Richard]. (2.) Catharine, b. 1774; m. Benj. Burtsall. (3.) Anna, b. 1777, 2d wife of Jesse Willson, of Pelham, C. W. (4.) Phebe[6], b. 1779, wife of Isaac Willson, of Pelham, C. W. (5.) Elizabeth, b. 1781, wife of Joseph Adams, of Sussex Co., N. J. (6.) Elijah[6], b. 1783, m. Martha Burtsall, sister to Benj. (7.) John, b. 1785, m. (1) Grace Marsh, 1790-1827±, [of Joseph[2], John[1]], m. (2) 1833±, Matilda Heaton, [of Jonathan]. (8.) Smith[6], b. 1787, m. Mary Crawford, [of James]. (9.) Sarah, m. Levi Schooley. (10.) Mariam[6], b. 1791, m. Wm. Webster. (11.) Wm., b. 1795, d. unm.

6. *Isaiah*[5], 1749-1832, m. 1772, Constant[5] Lippencott, 1753-1845, [of Remembrance[4], Wm[3]., Remembrance[2], Richard[1]], and had: (1.) Mary, 1773-1842, m. 1793 (as 2d wife), Thos. Laing, 1759-1827, [of Isaac[3], John[2], John[1]]. (2.) Jediah, 1775-1847, m. 1796, Anna Pound, 1775 1851, [of Samuel[4], Elijah[3], John[2], John[1]]. (3.) Peter[6], 1777-1845, m. 1803, Phebe Vail, 1779-1866, dau. of Abraham and Margaret (F. Randolph) Vail, [of John[2], Samuel[1]]. (4.) Abel[6], 1779-1840, m. 1810, Elizabeth Vail, 1782-1866, sister to Phebe. (5.) Thos. L., 1781-1859, m. 1806, Elizabeth Satterthwait, 1786-1843, [of Joshua W.]. (6.) Wm., 1783-1846, d. unm. (7.) Grace, b. 1786, d. in infancy. (8.) Joseph L[6]., 1787-1871, m. 1809, Christiana Vail, 1788-1871, sister to Phebe and Elizabeth. (9.) Edmund[6], 1791-1866, m. Sarah R. Shepard, 1792-1860, [of Nathan]. (10). Samuel E., 1793-1823, m. 1817, Sarah

C. Rich, [of Joseph]. (11.) Hugh, b. 1795, m. Hannah Cole.

7. *James*[5], b. 1752, m. Elsie (Smalley) Runyan, b. 1758, dau. of Andrew Smalley, and had: (1.) Wm., b. 1783, m. Mary Ayres, [of Ezekiel]. (2.) Nancy, b. 1785; m. (1) John Green; m. (2) Wm. Vliet; m. (3) John Schmuck. (3.) Clarissa, b. 1787; m. David Vliet. (4.) Clarkson[6], b. 1789, m. Keziah Sutton. (5.) Charles, b. 1792, m. Ann Maines. (6.) Jonathan[6], 1795-1850, m. 1818, Phebe Willson, b. 1796, [of Mordecai].

8. *Sarah*, 1756±-1850, m. (1) Ralph Smith, [of Ralph]; m. (2) Capt. Wm. Piatt, d. 1791, [of John]; m. (3) --------- Murray; by the 2d husband, she had: (1.) Dr. Wm. Piatt, of New York. (2.) James Piatt of Cincinnati, O. (3.) Jemima G. Piatt, an orthodox minister who d. 1868±; m. her cousin Elijah Shotwell, who d. 1861±, s. of Jacob[5] and Bersheba (Pound) Shotwell, [of John[4], John[3], John[2], Abraham[1]].

9. *Mary*, m. John Stevens, and had one son, John.

10. *Elizabeth*, m. -------- Clayton.

11. *Martha*[5], m. Jonathan H. Osborn, of Scotch Plains, N. J., [of Jonathan], and had: (1) Dr. Cora Osborn of Westfield, N. J., who d. 1868. (2.) Letitia; m. Dennis Vail of Piscataway, N. J., [of Wm[4]., David[3], John[2], Samuel[1]].

12. *Hugh*[5], 1764-1854, of Harrison Co., O.; m. 1783, Rosetta Arrison, 1764±-1836, [of John], and had: (1.) John[6], 1784-1869; m. 1804, Sarah Shanklin, 1779-1851. (2.) Esther[6], 1785-1870; m. (1) 1803, Timothy Smith, Jr., [of Timothy]; m. (2) 1820 (as 2d wife), Maj. Geo. C. Seaton, 1783-1849, [of James]. (3.) Susanna[6], 1789-1874; m. 1809, Chas. Wintermute, 1784-1868, [of Geo.]. (4.) Charlotte[6], 1790-1827, m. 1816, Ephraim Sears. (5.) Nancy[6], 1795-1861; m. (1) 1815, Peter Van Dolah, 1787-1823; m. (2) 1826, Jacob Ebert, 1800-1854, [of John]. (6.) William[6], 1798-1855, m. 1819, Rhoda Beebe, 1792-1876, [of Stuart[2], Samuel[1]]. (7.) Joseph[6], 1801-1883, m. 1821, Mary Arrison, [of Jeptha]. (8.) Arrison[6], 1812-1893, m. 1835, Mary Dickerson, 1815-1894, [of Baruch[3], Thomas[2], Joshua[1]].

28. JOHN[4] SHOTWELL, 1727-1758, of Middlesex Co., N. J., s. of Abraham[3] and Elizabeth (Cowperthwaite) Shotwell, of Piscataway Tp., Middlesex Co., N. J., [of John[2], Abraham[1]], m. Anna -------- and had:

1. *John*[5], b. 6 Mar., 1753; removed with his family from Scotch Plains, N. J., about 1780, to the region known as "the bloody ground," as Kentucky was then called, stopping for a while at a place called Washington, now the seat of Mason county. He took up a large tract of land at Mayslick, eight

miles from Washington, and he and a hand proceeded to improve it, preparatory to moving his family thither. The Indians were then very hostile throughout the Ohio valley. His grandson Albert Shotwell, of Bowling Green, Mo., (b. 1811), is authority for the following two incidents:

One evening, after the day's work was done, the two—master and man—started to go back to Washington. Their course lay down a creek, running parallel with the road they traveled. Each had a gun, and, as game was then plentiful, they soon separated, following down the creek, one on each side, hoping to take fowl or vension on the way. After they had gone a short distance John Shotwell heard the report of a gun, which he supposed was his companion's; so he rode over to the spot, but, instead of the expected deer or turkey, he found his comrade dead and scalped; but, seeing no Indian and being a powerful man— about six feet in height—and of Herculean strength as well as courage, he lifted the dead man upon his own horse and, getting up behind, carried him a number of miles through the wilderness to Washington.

His wife was no less a heroine. During the Revolutionary period, the inhabitants had to build forts for protection from the Tories and hostile Indians. Mrs. Shotwell sat many a time at a port-hole, with gun in hand, watching for Indians. One night during the absence of her husband, three tories came to her house to take her brother, who lay sick in bed She had taken the precaution to barricade the door; and they undertook to force an entrance. She stood at the door, ax in hand, and as one had partly forced himself in, she killed him with the ax and drew him inside. She served the second in the same way. The third retreated.

Her husband used a good many barrels and did his own coopering. It is said that a friend, to have some fun at her expense one evening, put on a false face to frighten her. She happened to be where she got hold of a shaved hoop and commenced on the joker. He soon cried out "Stop!" and the fun turned the other way. She would pull teeth for her neighbors and friends, and often she would be sent for in case of sickness in preference to a doctor.

John and his wife continued to reside at Mayslick until the time of their death. Both belonged to the Baptist church, certainly from the earliest recollection of our informant. John was the leading member in a church of 700 members at Mayslick, and his house was called "the preacher's tavern." In early life, he worked at blacksmithing; and they used to tell it of him that he carried his anvil on his back all the way from New Jersey to Kentucky. He probably did his own blacksmithing for a time at Mayslick. Certainly his son William took up the trade and became an excellent workman.

John was an extensive farmer and owned quite a number of slaves, the men doing the labor on the farm, and the women the housework. He planted an orchard of many acres, and would distill his apples and peaches and make brandy and hundreds of barrels of cider. He would also distill his surplus corn and rye and make whisky out of it, and kept almost all kinds of drinks in his cellar. And yet, though it was common for almost every family to use different kinds of beverages, our informant states that "There were no drunken boys in those days."

The sale of personal property belonging to his estate after his death took three days. The widow gave up her interest in all the estate, and each of the eleven children was bound to pay her $35 annually, the amount, $385, being more than she had use for. All of the four sons and seven daughters were then married and had children. John⁵ died 9 Dec., 1826; m. 17 Sept., 1773, Abigail Shipman, b. 2 Mar., 1754; d. 9 Apr., 1835. They are said to have removed to Kentucky from Morris Co., N. J. His great-grandaughter, Mrs. E. T. Conway, of Henderson, Ky., is authority for the statement that he moved to Kentucky in 1788, having served the American cause throughout the Revolutionary War, and was postmaster at Mayslick, and a magistrate of Mason county for many years.

2. *Jasper*, mentioned in his father's will, 1758; removed from Scotch Plains during or soon after the Revolution to "the bloody ground," near the Ohio river during the Indian hostilities in that region. He is mentioned in an old history of Ohio (p. 97), as one of the settlers (1804) in and about Williamsburgh (formerly Lytlestown), Clermont Co., which was formed in the year 1800, the 18th county organized in the territory. He is said to have been from Kentucky; is believed to have had at least a son David, who visited his uncle and cousins at Mayslick, Ky., about 1820-24.

3. ------------, a daughter, m. --------Morris, and left descendants in Mason County, Ky.

55. JOHN SMITH⁵ SHOTWELL, 1738-9-1801-, of Somerset Co., N. J., s. of John⁴ and Elizabeth (Smith) Shotwell, of Plainfield, [of John³, John², Abraham¹], m. (1) 1756, *Mary*² *Webster*, b. 1736, dau. of Wm². Jr., and Suasannah (Cowperthwaite) Webster, of Essex Co., N. J., [of Wm¹.], and had:

1. *John*, d. unm.

2. *William*, known as "Turkey Billy," from the neighborhood in which he resided, Turkey, now New Providence, near Plainfield; was a farmer; had very odd ways, and of him various amusing anecdotes are related; d. 1830±, unm.

Littell states that William dwelt at Long Hill, near Franklin Place.

3. *Samuel*, went west; m. Hetty (Cooper) Davison, wid. of a Revolutionary officer, and dau. of Nathan Cooper of Chester, Morris Co., N. J.

4. *Susannah*, m. David Martin, s. of Alexander Martin of Long Hill, N. J.

5. *Elizabeth*, m. Dennis Hughes, a native of Ireland.

6. *Sarah*, m. ------ Hanison and had sons Henry and John, the latter of whom m. Sally Parker, dau. of Calvin of Long Hill, N. J.

JOHN SMITH[5] SHOTWELL, 1738-9-1801-, of Somerset Co., N. J., [of John[4], John[3], John[2], Abraham[1]], m. (2) 1782, *Phebe[5] Shotwell*, dau. of Joseph[4] and Elizabeth (Jackson) Shotwell, of Woodbridge, N. J., [of Joseph[3], Daniel[2], Abraham[1]], and had:

7. *Joseph Smith[6]*, was a prominent merchant, in N. Y. city, and a man of high standing; was apprenticed to Willet Hicks a wholesale dry goods merchant in New York, taking cert. of membership to the M. M. there from R. and P. M. M. dated 19 of 2 mo., 1806; was then a minor; after the separation in 1828, he was an Orthodox Friend. Reuben Haines of Orleans Co., N. Y., used to stop at his house while attending Yearly Meeting in New York, between 1814 and 1850; m. Deborah Fox, dau. of George Fox.

8. *Nathan*, was not smart; lived with his cousin Elijah Shotwell; d. unm.

9. *Mary*, died when only son was three years old; m. her cousin Daniel[6] Shotwell, of Plainfield, called "Daniel on the hill," b. 1775, s. of Jacob[5] and Bersheba (Pound) Shotwell, [of John[4], John[3], John[2], Abraham[1]]. Mary may have been dau. by first wife.

46. JOHN[5] SHOTWELL, 1743-4-1816, of Lower Rahway, N. J., s. of Joseph[4] and Sarah (Cock) Shotwell of Rahway, N. J., [of John[3], John[2], Abraham[1]], m. 1769, *Margaret Haydock*, 1752-1815, dau. of John Haydock of Rahway, and had:

1. *Jane[6]*, b. 3 of 5 mo., 1772; m. Wm. Smith.

2. *Sarah*, b. 20 of 3 mo., 1774.

3. *Margaret[6]*, b. 6 of 1 mo., 1776; m. Eden Haydock.

4. *Phebe*, b. 17 of 9 mo., 1780, received cert. of membership from R. and P. M. M. 20 of 2 mo., 1805, directed to the M. M. for northern district of Philadelphia; m. before 1806, Christopher Marshall.

5. *Joseph[6]*, b. 14 of 7 mo., 1783, called "Pigeon Joey," served an apprenticeship in N. Y., taking a cert. to the M. M. there, from R. and P. M. M. dated 20 of 1 mo., 1803; was a surveyor; dw. Rahway, N. J., and there d. 23 of 10 mo., 1863, aged 80 yrs., 3 mo., 9

days; m. 23 of 3 mo., 1820, Margaret Elston, b. 13 of 11 mo., 1797, d. Rahway, N. J., 1 of 3 mo., 1869, a teacher, dau. of Ambrose Elston, of Lower Rahway, N. J., a Middlesex county judge and a soldier in the Revolutionary War.

6. *Mary*, b. 14 of 8 mo., 1785, dw. Rahway, Middlesex Co., N. J., and there d. 26 of 7 mo., 1824, single.

7. *Elizabeth*, (twin of Mary), b. 14 of 8 mo., 1785, d. unm.

8. *Hannah*, b. 15 of 5 mo., 1787, d. Rahway, N. J., 26 of 9 mo., 1869, aged 82 yrs., 4 mo., 11 days; m. (1) ------ Knight; Hannah S. Knight took cert. of membership from R. and P. M. M. to Camden M. M. dated 26 of 5 mo., 1843. She m. (2) before 1852, John Corlies, who d. before 1869. Hannah S. Corlies took cert. from R. and P. M. M. 16 of 4 mo., 1851, to Shrewsbury, M. M.

9. *Rebecca*, b. 8 of 8 mo., 1789, d. Rahway, N. J., 6 of 3 mo., 1870, aged 80 yrs., 6 mo., 28 days, unm.

10. *Eleanor*, b. 28 of 10 mo., 1792, d. unm.

96. JOHN[5] SHOTWELL, 1753-1826, of Mayslick, Mason Co., Ky., s. of John[4] and Anna (----) Shotwell, [of Abraham[3], John[2], Abraham[1]], m. 1773, *Abigail Shipman*, 1754-1835, and had:

1. *Mary*, called Polly, b. 4 Aug., 1774; she and all her brothers and sisters were married and had children before the father's death in 1826; she d. 13 Nov., 1823; she m. 20 Jan., 1799, John Wise.

2. *Charlotte*, (twin of Mary), b. 4 Aug., 1774; m. (1) 30 Sept., 1790, ------ Wood; m. (2) Wm. Dye.

3. *Lydia*, b. 2 Aug., 1775; d. 20 July, 1857; m. 12 Feb., 1793, Sanford Mitchell.

4. *John[6]*, b. 29 Jan., 1777; was a farmer near Mayslick, Mason Co., Ky., and there d. 3 July, 1824; m. (1) 10 Mar., 1803, Rachel Dye, who d. about 1808, leaving two daughters; he m. (2) 26 Nov., 1809, Sally Burroughs, b. 15 Aug., 1780, in Maryland. In 1831, she removed with her family to Pike Co., Mo., and there d. 22 May, 1848. To her 2d son Albert[7] Shotwell (b. 1811), of Bowling Green, Mo., we are chiefly indebted for information concerning this branch.

5. *William[6]*, b. 12 Dec., 1779, in Morris Co., N. J.; was a farmer, blacksmith, wool carding-machine maker, manufacturer of cotton spinning machinery, etc., and ran a spinning factory in Mason county, Ky.; and there d. 12 May, 1834; m. 31 Jan., 1805, Fannie Triplett.

6. *Nathan[6]*, b. 2 Apr., 1782, was a farmer, removed with his 2d wife about 1827, from the vicinity of Mayslick, Ky., to St. Louis Co., Mo., and there d. soon afterward; m. (1) 10 Jan., 1806, ------ Grover, who d. in Mason

Co., Ky.; m. (2) Maria Bland, who d. .. Feb., 1885, aged 86 yrs.

7. *Anna*, b. 12 Jan., 1785, Mayslick, Mason Co., Ky.; d. 18 Sept., 1861; m. 11 Apr., 1802, -------- Webb, and had a dau., Elizabeth, wife of -------- Yancy, who dw. at Mayslick, Ky.

8. *Phcbe*, b. 17 Dec., 1789, m. Levi Van Camp.

9. *Jabez*[5], b. 23 Nov., 1791, Mayslick, Ky.; was a farmer near Mayslick for many years; removed about 1833, to Richmond, Ray county, Mo.; d. of typhoid fever, .. Nov., 1871, in Lexington, Mo., aged 80 years, less 18 days; m. about 1815, Eliza Warder.

10. *Abigail*, b. 20 Apr., 1795; m. Wm. Stewart.

11. *Priscilla*, b. 19 Jan., 1798; d. 20 Mar., 1866; m. Warner Wilson. Their s. John T. Wilson of Mayslick, Ky., m. a dau. of Dr. ---- Duke and granddaughter of his (J. T.'s) aunt Lydia[6] (Shotwell) Mitchell.

12. *Rachel*, b. 9 April, 1799.

13. *Jasper*, b. 18 July, 1800.

Nine of the foregoing children of John and Abigail (Shipman) Shotwell had sons named John.

JOHN[5] SHOTWELL, b. 1763, s. of Benj[4]. and Elizabeth (Manning) Shotwell, [of John[3], Daniel[2], Abr[1].], m. *Esther*[5] *Fitz Randolph*, dau. of Joseph[4] and Esther (Broderick) Fitz Randolph, [of Joseph[3], Joseph[2], Edward[1]], and had:

1. *Rachel*, b. 1797, d. 1881, unm.

2. *Randolph*, b. 4 Nov., 1801, d. 1828, unm.

3. *Elizabeth*, b. 1808; m. Rev. Buckley C. Morse, (no issue).

JOHN[5] SHOTWELL, of N. J., s. of Abraham[4] and Lydia (Hallet) Shotwell, of Essex county, N. J., [of John[3], John[2], Abraham[1]], m. -------- *Freeman*, and had:

1. *Abraham F*[6]., was from about 1857 to 1865 cashier of the Farmers and Merchants' Bank, organized 1828, and upon the organization of the National Bank of Rahway, afterward the Union County Bank, he became its President and so remained until 10 Nov., 1884; d. 28 Feb., 1885, in Linden Tp., Union county, N. J., on the homestead settled by his grandfather, near Shotwell's Landing, but separated from it by the boundary of Rahway city. He m. ----- who survived him, dw. Linden Tp., N. J.

2. --------------, a dau.; m. B. M. Price.

3. *Lydia*[6], m. Richard Townsend, of Baltimore, s. of -------- and Hester[5] (Shotwell) Townsend, [of Abraham[4], John[3], John[2], Abraham[1]].

JOHN[6] SHOTWELL, 1777-1824, of Mason Co., Ky., s. of John[5] and Abigail (Shipman) Shotwell of Mayslick, Ky., [of John[4], Abraham[3], John[2], Abraham[1]], m. (1) 1803, *Rachel Dye*, and had:

1. *Ann*, b. 28 Mar., 1805, in Mason Co., Ky., d. in spring of 1890; m. autumn of 1826, John Cash, b. 1804, in Kentucky; d. in autumn of 1840, s. of Thos. Sr., and Nancy (Burroughs) Cash of Pike Co., Mo.

2. *Lorana*, b. 22 July, 1806; d. 1 Oct., 1824, unm.

JOHN[6] SHOTWELL, 1777-1824, [of John[5], John[4], Abraham[3], John[2], Abraham[1]], m. (2) 1809, *Sally Burroughs*, 1780-1848, and had:

3. *Jasper*, b. 22 Aug., 1810, near Mayslick, Mason Co., Ky., was engaged in the manufacture of bagging and rope for baling cotton when he d. 12 Sept., 1849; he m. 15 Feb., 1843, Ann McMillen, b. --------, 1825, d. 1864±, having m. (2) about 1854, Wm. Smith; she was dau. of Kinzie and Isabel (Givens) McMillen.

4. *Albert*[7], b. 8 Dec., 1811, near Mayslick, Ky.; dw. Bowling Green, Pike Co., Mo. To him we are chiefly indebted for information concerning this branch, although since 1831, he has lived in Missouri, away from his Shotwell relatives. He was a farmer up to the commencement of the Civil War. Since that time he has not been engaged in any business, having lost all his servants.

In his boyhood, Kentucky had no free schools, and his parents being poor, he had to work on the farm when quite young. But, although his schooling was very limited, yet during the 65 yrs. of his residence in Missouri, he seems to have had on his "studying-cap" to good purpose, and, judging from the unusual excellence of his handwriting for one in his 85th year, and from the equally unimpaired clearness and accuracy of his statements concerning the history of the Mayslick, (Ky.), branch of the family, we are sure he must be an exceptionally well preserved old gentleman, although he has suffered much from poor health since early manhood. The war and the consequent abolition of negro slavery caused many to lose all they had and caused him to lose at least $15,000; and, had it not been for that unfortunate affair, he would undoubtedly have been rich, as he was in a good way to make a fortune and had considerable money loaned out. He is in religion a Christian (common called Campbellite), and in politics a Democrat. He m. (1) 14 Feb., 1836, Catharine Geery, b. 18 Jan., 1815, in Madison Co., Ky., d. in Pike Co., Mo., 1 Aug., 1892, dau. of James and Sally (Rice) Geery; m. (2) 10 May, 1893, Elizabeth (Biggs) Shotwell, b. 3 April, 1825, widow of his brother John, q. v.

5. *Nathan*[7], b. 4 July, 1813, near Mayslick, Ky.; dw. Frankford, Pike Co., Mo.; was a farmer until a few years ago; m. (1) 22 May, 1834, Catharine Geery, who d. --------, 1870; she was the mother of his nine children, all of

whom are now deceased, and was b. .. Apr., 1813, in Tenn., and d. 20 June, 1870, dau. of John and Elizabeth (Guthery) Geery. He m. (2) 9 Jan., 1871, his former wife's sister, Margaret Geery, b. 21 May, 1815, in Tenn., d. 28 May, 1880. He m. (3) 2 Mar., 1882, Mary (Fisher) Donovan, b. ---------, 1833±, in Pike Co., Mo., wid. of John Donovan, and dau. of Wm. and Eliza (Hostetter) Fisher.

6. *John*[7], b. 11 Dec., 1815, (where all were born), in Mason Co., Ky., was a farmer; d. --------; m. 12 Apr., 1840, Elizabeth Biggs, b. 3 Apr., 1825, in Pike Co., Mo., dau. of Wm. and Elizabeth (McCune) Biggs. Of their five sons and six daughters, three sons and four daughters are yet living. The widow m. (2) 1893, John's brother Albert, q. v.

7. *Permelia*, b. 2 Nov., 1817; m. 30 June, 1836, Thomas Cash, Jr., b. in spring of 1810, in Kentucky, d. -------- Mar., 1883, s. of Jno. and Elizabeth (Burroughs) Cash, of Pike Co., Mo. The two senior Cashes, John and Thomas, were brothers, and their wives were sisters.

179. JOHN[6] SHOTWELL, 1784-1869, of Franklin township, Fayette Co., Pa., s. of Hugh[5] and Rosetta (Arrison) Shotwell, of Harrison Co., O., [of John[4], John[3], John[2], Abr[1].], m. (1) 1804, *Sarah Shanklin*, of Fayette Co., Pa., 1779-1851, and had:

1. *Catharine*[7], b. 29 Dec., 1806; dw. 11th ward, Allegheny city, Pa.; d. in summer of 1890, two weeks after death of sister, Emily Shearer; m. Fayette Co., Pa., 20 Jan., 1825, Henry Bateman Goe, b. 1804±. The 50th anniversary of their marriage was pleasantly observed at their residence on Wednesday, Jan. 20, 1875. Their nine children were all present with about twenty grandchildren. The exercises of the evening were conducted by the Rev. Joseph King of the First Christian Church of Allegheny, of which the venerable couple were honored members. All their children are active members of the Christian Church. Similar festivities were held at the same place and season, ten years later, at which one son only was unexpectedly absent, not being then well enough for the trip. Four generations were in attendance. Flowers and evergreens decorated the spacious parlors. High up on the wall were the years "1825-1885." Many pleasant recollections were called up, questions about the past were asked and answered, congratulations were offered, mementoes and beautiful presents were given in friendship; and to all present a most memorable occasion was enjoyed.

2. *Rosetta*[7], b. 2 Feb., 1808, d. .. July, 1883; m. in Franklin Tp., Fayette Co., Pa., 4 Jan., 1827, Robert Smith, b. 1799, d. .. Nov., 1881, a farmer, dw. Franklin, Fayette Co., Pa.

3. *Emily*, b. 21 Feb., 1809, in Fayette Co., Pa.; dw. Cook's Mills, Fayette Co.; P. O., Tippecanoe, Pa., d. ---------, 1890; m. 27 Mar.,

19

1838, Jacob Shearer, b. 30 Jan., 1809, in Fayette Co., Pa., d. 27 June, 1884, s. of Frederick and Rebecca Shearer of Fayette Co., Pa.

4. *Susan C.*, b. 15 Mar., 1811, Fayette Co., Pa., d. at her home at South Uniontown Tp., Fayette Co., Pa., 31 Dec., 1894, two hours before the old year expired; was last surviving child of her parents; m. in Pennsylvania, 12 Apr., 1832, Eli Cope, b. 23 Apr., 1810, in Fayette Co., Pa., lived in Fayette city and Redstone Tp., until he was elected sheriff of Fayette Co., in 1860; after which time their home was in or near Uniontown.

5. *Caroline*[7], b. 2 Nov. 1813, in Uniontown, Pa., d. Connellsville, Fayette Co., Pa.; m. 30 Apr., 1835, Joel Strawn, who d.

244. JOHN[6] SHOTWELL, d. 1841, real estate, of N. Y., s. of Joseph[5] and Sarah (Wilson) Shotwell of Perrytown near Rahway, N. J., [of Joseph[4], Joseph[3], Daniel[2], Abraham[1]], m. 1809, *Phœbe Byron*, dau. of Wm. and Wilhelmina (Cannon) Byron, of London, and had:

1. *Joseph*, who d. -----.
2. *George*, d. 20 Jan. 1885.
3. *William*, d. .. Aug. 1847.
4. *Mary*, d. 4 July, 1847.
5. *Harriet*, d. 9 Sept. 1862; m. Dr. Norris of New York.
6. *Abraham*[7], d. 1891, aged 72 yrs., was manufacturer of cigars and tobacco in New York; m. Almyra Clark, of New York.
7. *John*[7], d. 1862, aged 45 yrs; founded the firm of Shotwell, Muller & Doscher, sugar refiners, of New York city, and was one of the founders of the Irving National Bank, and other similar institutions. He married Susan St. C. Stratton, dau. of Dr. James T. Stratton, of Brooklyn, N. Y. After John's death, the widow married Robert Currie, a dry goods merchant of New York.
8. *Sarah*, d. 10 Aug., 1852, m. Thomas Smith.
9. *Thomas*, d. ---------
10. *Byron*, d. ---------
11. *Phebe*, b. 7 March, 1834, at Rahway, N. J., dw. Yellow Springs, Green Co., Ohio; m. at Washington, D. C., 9 June, 1854, Isaiah Rynders, who d. 3 Jan., 1885, aged 81 yrs.

157. JOHN[6] SHOTWELL, b. 1785, of Goodland, Lapeer Co., Mich., formerly of Thorold, C. W., and Kans., s. of Wm[5]. and Elizabeth (Pound) Shotwell, of Upper Canada, formerly of Plainfield, N. J., [of John[4], John[3], John[2], Abraham[1]], m. (1) *Grace Marsh*, 1790-1827±, dau. of Joseph[2] and Anna (de Camp) Marsh, of Bertie, C. W., [of John[1]], and had:

1. *Joel*[7], b. 1810, Thorold, Upper Canada, dw. Garnett, Anderson Co., Kans., and there d. 9 of 11 mo., 1880, aged 70 yrs., 8 mos., 15 days; became member of Yarmouth M. M. of (Hic.) Friends, 16 of 8 mo., 1842, by cert. from Pelham M. M.; m. in Thorold, C. W., Sarah Jane

Blansfield, who after marriage, became member of Yarmouth M. M. 13 of 9 mo., 1848, by request; dw. (1887), Baldwin City, Leavenworth Co., Kans., a wd.

2. *Anna*, b. 1812, Thorold, C. W., d. Lobo, Ont., 9 of 9 mo.,1883, aged 71 yrs., 2 mo., 1 day, unm.

3. *Elizabeth'*, called Betsy, b. Thorold, C. W., d. Wainfleet, Ont.; m. in Pelham Friends Meeting House, Joseph Priestman, who dw. (1888) Wainfleet, Ont , P. O. 1893, Marshville; s. of Thomas and Ann Priestman.

4. *William'*, b. 18 of 12 mo., 1818, in Thorold, C. W., dw. Lobo, Ont., P. O., Coldstream; he or his cousin Wm., s. of Smith, became member of Yarmouth M. M. of (Hic.) Friends 9 of 6 mo., 1847, by cert.; he m. in Yarmouth, C. W., 3 May, 1846, Susannah Kester, b. 24 of 6 mo., 1825, dau. of Thomas R². and Beulah (Heaton) Kester, of Lobo, Ont., [of Harman']. She, with their children Anna M. and Thomas H., united with Yarmouth M. M. of (Hic.) Friends 14 of 3 mo., 1849.

5. *Joseph Marsh'*, b. Thorold, C. W., removed with his family in the winter of 1865–6, to Iowa, settling on the farm of 120 acres that he had bought several years previously; killed by a span of horses running away at Armour, Iowa, 24 of 3 Mo., 1874; m. in Lobo, Ont., 1860±, Martha Ferguson.

6. *John, Jr.*, b. Thorold, C. W., dw. Osceola Mills, Polk Co., Wis.; m. in Lobo, Ont., Catharine Blansfield, sister to the wife of Joel.

157. JOHN⁵ SHOTWELL, b. 1785, of Yarmouth, C. W., and Lapeer Co., Mich., [of Wm⁵.. Jno⁴., Jno³., Jno²., Abr'.], m. (2) 1833±, *Matilda Heaton*, dau. of Jonathan and Ann (....) Heaton, natives of Pennsylvania, and had:

7. *Isaac'*, b. 27 Sept., 1834, Thorold, C. W.; lived Yarmouth, C. W., 1840–1864; removed thence in 1864, to Oakland Co., Mich., thence in 1865, to Lapeer Co., Mich., thence in 1870, to Bancroft, Shiawassee Co., Mich., where he held the office of supervisor two terms, and finally in 1888 to Washington, settling at Puyallup; m. by a Methodist minister in Yarmouth, C. W., 1854, Mary Martha Nickerson, b. 24 Sept., 1834, Malahide, C. W., dau. of Nathaniel and Bethena (Miller) Nickerson, of Malahide, C. W.

JOHN SHOTWELL, of New York, and wife ...., had:
1. *Robert*, b. 1820, in New York, and there d. on Arundle St., 3 of 9 mo., 1821, aged 1 yr., 6 mos.; interred in N. Y. Friends' cemetery.

265. JOHN⁵ SHOTWELL, shoemaker, s. of Daniel⁴ and Keziah (Tarrill) Shotwell, of Woodbridge, [of Daniel⁴, Joseph³, Daniel², Abraham'], m. .... *Moore*, dau. of Joseph, of Turkey Hill, N. J., and had:
1. *Joseph*.

2. *Joel*, d. Rahway, N. J., unm.
3. *George*, dw. Rahway, N. J.
4. ...., a dau.; m. .... Winans, and had a son John who dw. Rahway, N. J.

JOHN T. SHOTWELL, b. 1813, of ...., Ohio, s. of Ralph⁶ and Osy (Tingley) Shotwell, of Plainfield, N. J., [of Jacob⁵, John⁴, John³, John², Abraham'], m. .... and had:
1. *William*.

JOHN⁷ SHOTWELL, b. 1815, s. of John⁶ and Sally (Burroughs) Shotwell, of Mayslick, Ky., [of John⁵, John⁴, Abr³. (?), John², Abr'.], m. (1) 1840, *Elizabeth Biggs*, b. 1825, dau. of Wm. and Elizabeth (McCune) Biggs, and had:
1. *William*, b. 24 Feb., 1841; dw. Spencersburg, Pike Co., Mo.; m. ... March, 1869, Jemima Liter.
2. *Montgomery'*, b. 16 Aug., 1842, dw. Frankford, Pike Co., Mo.; m. (1) 14 Feb., 1861, Elizabeth Robertson; m. (2) 1877±, Elizabeth Lewellen, who d. 1882±, s. p.; m. (3) 1882±, Cora Ellis, b. 1865±.
3. *Elizabeth* b. 14 Feb., 1844; d. 3 Oct., 1873; m. 2 Dec., 1860, Milton Hamilton.
4. *Ann Mary*, b. 18 Oct., 1848, dw. Mexico, Audrain Co., Mo.: m. (1) 22 Oct., 1865, George Layne; m. (2) 3 Feb., 1876, Frank Carter.
5. *Orwin*, b. 12 Sept., 1849, d. 1850.
6. *Ruth Ann*, b. 20 Aug., 1850, dw. Ashley, Pike Co., Mo.; m. 19 Nov., 1872, Claudius Cash.
7. *Emily*, b. 19 Dec., 1853; d. 7 July, 1857.
8. *Margaret L.*, b. 4 Dec., 1854; dw. Clarksville, Pike Co., Mo., m. 19 June, 1871, John Mantiply.
9. Unnamed, d. in infancy, 1 Dec., 1857.
10. *Fannie*, b. 10 Jan., 1861, dw. Bunceton, Cooper Co., Mo., m. (1) 25 Nov., 1885, Asa Strother; m. (2) 31 March, 1895, Wm. Strother.
11. *Dr. John Richard*, b. 17 June, 1869; dw. Spencersburg, Pike Co., Mo., unm. 1895.

JOHN⁷ SHOTWELL, 1817–1883, of Manchester, Mo., s. of Nathan⁶ and Maria (Bland) Shotwell, of St. Louis Co., Mo., [of Jno⁵., Jno⁴., Abr³. (?), John², Abr'.], m. (1) *Nancy Lollar*, 1823–1865, dau. of Reuben and Susannah Lollar, and had:
1. *Margaret*, b. 5 July, 1844, at Manchester, Mo., and there d. 28 Dec., 1864, unm.
2. *Nathan*, b. ... Dec., 1845, at Manchester, Mo., and d. St. Clair, Mo., 12 Oct., 1891, m. 17 Nov., 1878, Lizzie Stoy.
3. *Missouri*, b. 6 Oct., 1847, at Manchester, Mo., dw. Warrensburg, Mo., m. Chas. McQuerry.
4. *John*, b. 16 Aug., 1849, at Manchester, Mo., is a farmer, dw. St. Clair, Mo.; m. 1 Jan., 1888, Mollie Chesley.
5. *Kenneth*, b. 11 Oct., 1851, at Manchester, Mo., is a farmer, dw. Ellisville, Mo., about 20 miles from St. Louis; m. 19 Feb., 1878, Mary E. Stevens, [of Richard].

6. *William B.*, b. 22 Aug., 1853, at Manchester, Mo., is a farmer, dw. St. Clair, Mo.; m. 7 Oct., 1880, Margaret Signago.

7. *Susan*, b. 17 Mar., 1856, at Manchester, Mo.; dw. Oakland, Cal.; m. 6 Sept., 1876, Michael Hollocher.

8. *Martha Ann*, b. 23 Feb., 1858, at Manchester, Mo., dw., St. Paul, Mo.; m. 17 Oct., 1877, John Hollocher.

9. *Sarah*, b. 20 Mar., 1860, at Manchester, Mo.; dw. Warrensburg, Mo.; m. (1) James Graves; m. (2) Robert Graves.

10. *Stonewall Jackson*, b. -- Nov., 1861, at Manchester, Mo., and there d. -- Nov., 1864.

11. ---------, b. -- Apr., 1865, d. unnamed.

JOHN[7] SHOTWELL, 1817-1883, [of Nathan[6], Jno[5]., Jno[4]., Abr[3]., (?), Jno[2]. Abr[1].], m. (2) Martha (Brewer) Vaughn, b. 1843, wid. of James Vaughn, and had:

12. *Edwin*, b. 14 Dec., 1870, at Manchester, Mo., and there d. 10 Aug., 1892.

JOHN[7] SHOTWELL, 1817±-1862, sugar refiner, banker, etc., of New York City, s. of John[6] and Phœbe (Byron) Shotwell, [of Joseph[5], Joseph[4], Joseph[3], Daniel[2], Abraham[1]], m. *Susan St. C. Stratton*, dau. of Dr. James T. Stratton of Brooklyn, N. Y., and had:

1. *Emily*, m. Chas. Gœller, an attorney of New York City.

2. *Susan St. C.*, m. Wm. J. Pinckney, who is in the wholesale dry goods business, son of late Col. Stephen R. Pinckney.

3. *Marion*, m. John Quinlan, hardware merchant.

4. *John Byron*, is a practicing physician at No. 137 W. 49th St., New York City.

REV. JOHN M[7]. SHOTWELL, b. 1821, of Red Creek, Wayne Co., N. Y., formerly of Oramel, Allegany Co., N. Y., s. of Joseph[6] and Sarah (Randall) Shotwell, of Saratoga Co., N. Y., [of Caleb[5], Samuel[4], John[3], John[2], Abraham[1]], m. (1) 1842, *Salome Lucinda Stone*, 1823-1885, of Cayuga Co., N. Y., and had:

1. *Carlos Bacon*[8], b. 9 May, 1848, Meridian, town of Cato, Cayuga Co., N. Y., spent his boyhood with his parents at Westmoreland, Walesville, Little Falls, Belleville, Mannsville, Manchester, Wheatland and Angelica, N. Y., attending the common or district school until the age of 14 yrs., having at the age of 10 yrs. completed Adams' Arithmetic and begun the study of grammar and algebra; he was educated chiefly at the Angelica Academy, Genesee Valley Seminary, at Belfast, Allegany Co., and the Commercial College at Oswego, N. Y. At the age of 17 he commenced teaching at Ischua, about nine miles from his home; he afterward taught at Fillmore, at the Oswego Commercial College, and the Commercial College at Syracuse; went to Detroit in 1870, where he soon (Feb., 1871), took a position as bookkeeper with the Detroit White Lead Works, 101-109 Jones St., and where he has been nearly ever since. Is financial secretary, a stockholder and a director in that establishment; dw. 469 Third Ave., Cor. Bagg St.; in politics a republican; m. Oswego, N. Y., 13 Dec., 1871, Eliza Levinia Williams, who three years earlier had been one of his most amiable and unassuming pupils, b. Oswego, N. Y., 20 Aug., 1851, dau. of Nicholas and Sarah (Nichols) Williams, of Oswego, N. Y., natives of County Cornwall, England. Both are members of M. E. Church, Detroit.

2. *Theodore Frank*[8], b. 30 July, 1851, in Whitestown or Westmoreland, Oneida Co., N. Y.; educated at the Genesee Valley Seminary, and Oberlin College, graduated from the latter, classical course, 7 Aug., 1872, studied law in Norwalk, and Bucyrus, O.; admitted to the bar 1878, practiced his profession at Bucyrus for several years, but removed 1887, to Paulding, O., where he still resides, a lawyer and loan agent. He m. in Bucyrus, O., -- Nov., 1876, Amanda McKinstrey, of Bucyrus, Crawford, Co., O., dau. of James and Rebecca McKinstrey.

3. *William Edward*[8], b. 12 Oct., 1858, Meridian, Cayuga Co., N. Y.; educated at Genesee Valley Seminary, Geneseo Normal School, University Medical College, New York city, graduated from last named, 10 Mar., 1885. Settled in Dunellen, N. J.; went to Denver, Col., June, 1889, for his health, which greatly improved, and has since remained there in the practice of his profession as physician and surgeon. Residence 3103 Lafayette St.; in politics a republican, is an elder of Presbyterian Church, Hyde Park, Denver, Col.; m. by Rev. Newton W. Cadwell (Presbyterian), at Westfield, N. J., 1 Jan., 1885, Harriet Clark Pierson, (called Hattie), b. Crawford, N. J., 21 Oct., 1863, dau. of Everett M. and Elizabeth Wood (Williams) Pierson of Westfield, N. J.

JOHN W[7]. SHOTWELL, b. 1828, of Richmond, Ray Co., Mo., s. of Jabez[6] and Eliza (Warder) Shotwell of Richmond, Mo., [of John[5], John[4], Abraham[3] (?) John[2], Abr[1].], m. Julia E. Devlin, and had:

1. *Anna E.*, taught school and music at Orrick, Ray Co., Mo., about ten miles from her home; m. Geo. L. Mann, a lawyer of Osceola, Mo.

2. *John W., Jr.*, graduated from University of Michigan; dw. Richmond, Mo., cashier of Ray County Savings Bank there; m. Maud Bassett, and had two sons and one daughter.

3. *Joseph*, after spending one year in law department of U. of M. at Ann Arbor, he went to Albuquerque, N. M., in very feeble health, and there died, his brother Will going also to take care of him.

4. *William M.*, b. 1869, was at Albuquerque, N. M., 1891; dw. Richmond, Mo., 1896.

5. *Lizzie*, b. 1868.

6. *Benjamin E.*, b. 1871; was senior in college, 1891; is practicing law at Richmond, Mo., 1896.

7. *Horace*, b. 1880; freshman in Richmond graded school, 1896.

JOHN[7] SHOTWELL, JR., of Osceola Mills, Polk Co., Wis., s. of John[6] and Grace (Marsh) Shotwell; of Thorold, C. W., etc., [of Wm[5]., John[4], John[3], John[2], Abr[1].], m. *Catharine Blansfield*, and had:

1. *Sarah Elizabeth[8]*, b. Lobo, C. W., dw. Spooner, Washburn Co., Wis.; m. in Chatham, Ont., Jonathan Kent.

2. *Joseph Edward*, b. about 3 of 12 mo., 1852, Lobo, C. W., d. young in Chatham, C. W.

3. *John Parmely[8]*, b. in Ill., dw. Osceola Mills, Wis., m. ---------.

4. *Joel*, b. 1866±, Komoka, C. W.; dw. Osceola Mills, Wis., unm. (1888).

5. *Minnie Jane*, b. 1869±, Chatham, Ont.; dw. with father, Osceola Mills, Wis., unm. (1888).

JOHN[7] SHOTWELL, d. 1887±, of Oakland Co., Mich., s. of Clarkson[6] and Keziah (Freeman) Shotwell, of Oakland Co., Mich, [of James[5], John[4], John[3], John[2], Abraham[1]], m. *Sarah Johnson*, dau. of Ebenezer and Laura Johnson, and had:

1. *Emeline[8]*, b. 29 Apr., 1844, in Independence Tp., Oakland Co., Mich., dw. (1890), Ashley, Mich.; m. at Fentonville, Genesee Co., Mich., 13 June, 1864, John T. Wolverton, b. Tyrone Tp., Livingston Co., Mich., 29 Dec., 1838, was farmer, butcher, drayman, democratic alderman in city of Owosso several times; is proprietor of the Hotel Wolverton, Ashley, Mich., s. of Jonathan L. and Hannah (Tompkins) Wolverton.

2. *James*, dw. Owosso, Mich.

JOHN I[7]. SHOTWELL, of Colden, Erie Co., N. Y., formerly of Kans., s. of Smith[6] and Mary (Crawford) Shotwell, of Thorold, C. W., [of Wm[5]., John[4], John[3], John[2], Abr[1].], m. (1) ----------------, and had:

1. *Harvey II[8].*, dw. 312 Hampshire St., Buffalo, N. Y., formerly at Welland, Ont.; served on the Buffalo police force; m. ---------

JOHN BLANSFIELD[8] SHOTWELL, b. 1844±, of Strathroy, Ont., s. of Joel[7] and Sarah Jane (Blansfield) Shotwell, of Garnett, Kans., [of John[6], Wm[5]., John[4], John[3], John[2], Abr[1].], m. 1871, ----------------, and had:

1. *William*, b. 1872±, Caradoc, Ont.

2. *James*.

JOHN F[8]. SHOTWELL, b. 1858, of Canton, O., s. of Isaac[7] and Harriet (Hobbs) Shotwell, of Smyrna, O., [of Thos[6]., Titus[5], Daniel[4],

Joseph[3] ?, Daniel[2], Abr[1].], m. 1879, *Ella R. Starbuck*, b. 1860, dau. of Wm. Starbuck, of Belmont Co., O., and had:

1. *Earle Kibler*, b. 13 Feb., 1882, Barnesville, O.

2. *Edna Maud*, b. 28 May, 1883, in Barnesville, O.

3. *Erwa Hobbs*, b. 29 July, 1886, Canton, O.

JOHN PARMELY[8] SHOTWELL, of Osceola Mills, Wis., s. of John[7] and Catharine (Blansfield) Shotwell, of Polk Co., Wis., [of John[6], Wm[5]., John[4], John[3], John[2], Abraham[1]], m. ----------, and had children.

178. JONATHAN[6] SHOTWELL, 1795–1850, of Long Bridge, near Allamuchy, N. J., s. of James[5] and Elsie (Smalley) Shotwell, of Long Bridge, N. J., [John[4], John[3], John[2], Abraham[1]], m. 1818, *Phebe Willson*, b. 1796, dau. of Mordecai and Anna (Larison) Willson, and had:

1. *Mordecai W.*, b. 21 Apr., 1819, d. 4 Nov., 1864, s. p., m. Martha Richardson.

2. *James*, b. 13 Feb., 1821, d. 2 Feb., 1881; unm.

3. *Clarissa Ann*, called Elsie, b. 7 Jan., 1823, d. 30 Jan., 1881, m. Samuel Harden, d. at Johnsonburgh, Warren Co., N. J., early in 1888.

4. *Margaret[7]*, b. 31 Mar., 1825, d. 25 Sept., 1872; m. John A. Jones, of Buttzville, N. J.

5. *Emeline[7]*, b. 30 Mar., 1827, d. 10 Sept., 1866; m. William Hart, of Huntsville, Sussex Co., N. J., who d. 5 Sept., 1893.

6. *Charles*, b. 18 Sept., 1829, d. 17 June, 1852, at Long Bridge, N. J., unm.

7. *Caleb Lippencott*, b. 7 Nov., 1831, d. 14 Oct., 1873, in the "far west," unm.

8. *Josephine*, b. 11 Feb., 1834, d. 2 Oct., 1863, in Smoketown, N. J., s. p., m. Edwin Schmuck.

9. *Emelissa*, b. 23 Oct., 1835, owns the homestead of her father and grand-father at Long Bridge, N. J., dw. Johnsonsburg, N. J., unm. 1895.

10. *Austin*, b. 7 Apr., 1837, d. young.

11. *Anson[7]*, b. 1 June, 1839, dw. Genesee Co., Mich., P. O. Linden, formerly at Corunna, Mich., was some years since endeavoring to trace title to English property of a William Shotwell, who in early colonial days is said to have resided near Easton, Pa., a sea captain. Anson m. 30 May, 1863, Lucinda Jane Cummins, b. 18 Jan., 1841, dau. of William and Marie (Middlesworth) Cummins, [of Mathias]. Her great-grandfather, Machias Cummins, came from Holland in 1717, and settled at Vienna, N. J. Her mother, Marie, was dau. of John and Sarah (Reed) Middlesworth, of Johnsonsburg, N. J.

JONATHAN LUNDY[7] SHOTWELL, b. 1821, of Galen, N. Y., s. of Thomas[6] and Hannah

(Lundy) Shotwell, of Galen, N. Y., [of Benj⁵., Benj⁴., John³, John², Abr¹.], m. 1857, *Elizabeth Fitz Patrick*, b. 1838±, and had:

1. *Hannah Josephine*, b. 15 of 3 mo., 1858, Galen, N. Y., and there d. 19 Apr., 1861.

2. *Wm. Thomas*, b. 8 March, 1862, Galen, N. Y., and there d. 9 March, 1862.

3. *Frank Lundy*, b. 21 of 8 mo., 1864, dw. with parents, Galen, N. Y., unm. (1883).

9. JOSEPH¹ SHOTWELL, of Woodbridge, N. J., formerly of Staten Island, probably s. of Daniel² and Elizabeth Shotwell, of Staten Island, [of Abraham¹], m. 1716, *Mary Manning*, and had:

1. *Joseph¹ III*, called "Joseph ye 3d," to distinguish him from his 2d cousin, Joseph⁴, s. of John³, Jr., of the Landing; he was b. 26 of 4 mo., 1717, on Staten Island; was a tanner of Woodbridge, N. J., when he there m. 20 of 8 mo., 1743, Elizabeth Jackson, of Morris Co., N. J.; at the close of the Woodbridge M. M. which authorized their marriage in accordance with the discipline of Friends, they requested permission to proceed at once with the ceremony, and the minutes state that on account of "the distance of the way that sum of them came, Friends condesended to it;" and likewise to the marriage of Michael Liken and Sarah Schooly at the same time.

2. *Nicholas*, b. 29 of 10 mo., 1718, on Staten Island.

3. *Elizabeth*, b. 16 of 9 mo., 1720, on Staten Island, d. young.

4. *Mary⁴*, b. 30 of 11 mo., 1722–3, in Woodbridge; was probably the Mary Shotwell who m. with unity of Friends at Woodbridge, N. J., ----, 1745, (between 18 of 8 mo, and 21 of 9 mo., as 2d wife), Nathaniel Fitz Randolph, b. 21 of 3 mo., 1714, d. 23 July, 1780, s of Edward and Catharine (Hartshorne) Fitz Randolph.

5. *Daniel⁴*, b. 8 of 2 mo., 1725, in Woodbridge, N. J.; he dw. three miles from Rahway; he and Joseph Shotwell, Jr., were among the residents of Woodbridge Tp., who in 1757, contributed toward the building of a certain stone bridge there, subscribing seven shillings each; his bill for the care of Woodbridge Friends' Meeting House one year was allowed by the M. M. 21 of 4 mo , 1763, and a like bill 16 of 5 mo., 1764; m. at Plainfield with unity of Friends, 24 of 1 mo., 1753, Deborah⁴ Shotwell, of Piscataway, b. 12 of 3 mo., 1735, dau. of Abraham³ and Elizabeth (Cowperthwaite) Shotwell, [of John², Abraham¹].

6. *Abraham⁴*, b. 13 of 2 mo., 1726; dw. Woodbridge, when he there m. with unity of Friends, 28 of 12 mo., 1750–51, Mary Jackson, of Woodbridge.

7. *Isaac*, b. 8 of 5 mo., 1727, d. 7 of 5 mo., 1731.

8. *Jacob*, b. 25 of 2 mo., 1729; m. (1) before 6 mo., 1754, contrary to Friends' discipline, but making satisfactory acknowledgment to the M. M., 17 of 10 mo., 1754, retained his membership until he m. (2) again contrary to discipline before 19 of 4 mo., 1758, for which fault he was disowned by the Society, 20 of 7 mo., 1758.

9. *Elizabeth*, 2d of the name, b. 11 of 11 mo , 1731–2; m. with unity of Friends at Woodbridge, N. J., 27 of 5 mo., 1773 (as 2d wife) Samuel Smith, of the borough of Elizabeth, b. 21 of 11 mo., 1722–3, s. of Shobal² and Prudence (Fitz Randolph) Smith, of Woodbridge, N. J., [of Samuel¹].

17. JOSEPH⁴ SHOTWELL, 1710–1787, of Rahway, Middlesex (now Union) Co., N. J., s. of John³, Jr., and Mary (Thorne) Shotwell, of Shotwell's Landing, N. J., [of John², Abraham¹], m. (1) 1741–2, *Sarah³ Cock*, 1715–1759, dau. of Henry² and Mary (Feeks) Cock, of Matinicock, L. I., [of James¹], and had:

1. *John⁵*, b. 7 of 1 mo., 1743–4, Rahway, N. J., built the brick house opposite his father's res. and which was long occupied as a railway station house. He was a merchant, and in conjunction with his younger brother Henry, built the Milton Mill, and had the raceway dug, which at the time was considered a great undertaking; they also opened trade with Bristol Eng., their vessels sailing from Shotwell's Landing. He m. in Rahway Friends Meeting, 28 of 6 mo , 1769, Margaret Haydock, of Woodbridge Tp., b. 1752±, d. Middlesex Co., N. J., 2 of 1 mo., 1815, aged 63, buried at Rahway, dau. of John Haydock, of Rahway, N. J., formerly of Flushing, L. I. One John Shotwell of Middlesex Co., N. J , is recorded as having d. 23 of 8 mo., 1816, aged 74 yrs., buried at Rahway.

2. *Mary*, b. 28 of 3 mo., 1746, Rahway; m. at Rahway, 23 of 4 mo., 1766, John Haydock, of Rahway, who became member of that M. M. by cert. from Flushing M. M. dated 18 of 12 mo., 1765.

3. *Joseph*, b. 2 of 6 mo., 1747, Rahway, N. J., served apprenticeship in New York, becoming member of Friends Meeting there by cert. from R. and P. M. M. given 21 of 3 mo., 1764, but resumed membership at Rahway, 21 of 6 mo., 1769, by cert. from Flushing M. M. After retirement of his father, Joseph filled the position of clerk of the M. M. for many years. He dw. in the house afterward owned and occupied by his grand-nephew, Joseph S. Smith, grandson of his brother, John Shotwell, and there d. 13 of 4 mo., 1817, s. p., aged 70 years, buried at Rahway; was given cert. of clearness with respect to marriage engagements, 20 of 4 mo., 1774; m. in Philadelphia, Pa., ---------, 1774, Elizabeth Greenleaf, of Philadelphia.

4. *Sarah*, b. 6 of 5 mo., 1750; m. at Rahway, 8 of 5 mo., 1771, Thomas Burling, of New York, who brought cert. from Newtown, L. I., to R. and P. M. M. Sarah Burling took cert. of

membership to N. Y. M. M. from R. and P. M. M. dated 17 of 7 mo., 1771.

5. *Henry*[5], b. 28 or 25 of 4 mo., 1752, inherited the homestead on the site of the Rahway Bank Building at corner of Poplar and Main Sts. and bounded on the north by the Pa., R. R., the old buildings were entirely destroyed by fire in the spring of 1844; he took cert. of membership to N. Y. M. M. dated 18 of 8 mo., 1773, and accepted there 1st of 9 mo.; but afterward returned to Rahway, with cert. to Plainfield M. M. dated 3 of 6 mo., 1778. About 1821, he exchanged his half interest in the Milton mill for the farm of Joseph King at the head of "Duky's Lane,"—so called from Marmaduke Hunt—between the farms of Thomas Laing and James Hunt in the Tp. of Woodbridge, about one and one-half miles distant from the mill, and there d. 24 of 8 mo., 1824. He accompanied Isaac Martin of Rahway on several religious visits, (see Isaac Martin's Journal, pp. 18, 32, and 106); he m. 18 of 7 mo., 1781, Sarah Dobson, dau. of Thomas Dobson, of New York, and probably sister to the wife of Lindley Murray, the grammarian. They and their two children, Joseph and Sarah became members of R. and P. M. M. by cert. from New York, 16 of 9 mo., 1784.

6. *James*, b. 20 of 5 mo., 1754; was a school teacher at Rahway, 1796; probably d. unm.

7. *Thomas*, b. 9 of 5 mo., 1756, d. 30 of 6 mo., 1760.

8. *William*, b. 3 of 7 mo., 1759, probably d. young, if the record of Wm[5]. of Rahway and New York, as s. of Joseph and *Phebe*, and b. in 1762, be correct.

JOSEPH[4] SHOTWELL, 1710–1787, of Rahway, [of Jno[3]., Jno[2]., Abr[1].], m. (2) 1761, *Phebe Allen*, of Shrewsbury, N. J., and had:

9. William, b. _________, 1762, called "the governor," to distinguish him from his cousin Wm. at the Landing. In the first decade of the 19th century, he was the owner of some 30 acres of land adjoining the Shotwell homestead on the west and extending to the bank of Rahway river; on this he built what was then considered the largest and finest house in the neighborhood; rows of Lombardy poplars were planted on both sides of the avenue from the house to the river bank, where was a porter's lodge. It soon acquired the name of "Shotwell's Folly," which appellation it still retains, although the trees, avenue, and porter's lodge have long since disappeared; streets have been laid out through the land, and many less pretentious houses are now standing all around the "Folly House." The latter has had many owners since Wm.'s misfortunes compelled him to give up the place to his creditors about 1816. At the beginning of the war with Great Britain, he erected on Rahway river above tide water at the extreme upper part of the town a large brick building intended for the manufacture of coarse woolen goods; but peace with England soon afterward, ruined the business and its owner. After this it was occupied for various manufacturing purposes. Fires and the explosion of a steam boiler, about 1876, completely wrecked what was known as the "Taurino Factory." Some parts of the original wall yet stand and are regarded as another monument of the "Governor's Folly." He removed to New York, was a merchant there; visited Europe, not so common a thing to do early in the century as it is now.

He d. in Tiverton, R. I., about 1840; m. 1787, Sarah Hopkins, dau. of Samuel of Philadelphia. They and three minor children, Sarah, Hannah, and Wm. brought cert. from N. Y. M. M. to R. and P. M. M. dated 4 of 5 mo., 1796, and on 8 of 3 mo., 1802, they and six children, Sarah, Hannah, Wm., Mary, Elizabeth and Phebe, received a similar cert. from R. and P. M. M. to the meeting in New York.

33. JOSEPH[4] SHOTWELL, III., b. 1717, tanner, of Woodbridge, N. J., s. of Joseph[3] and Mary (Manning) Shotwell, of Woodbridge, N. J., [of Daniel[2], Abr[1].], m. 1743, *Elizabeth Jackson*, of Morris Co., N. J., and had:

1. *Margaret*, who m. John Freeman; she d. soon after marriage.

2. *Phebe*, sister to Perrytown Joseph, was of Middlesex Co., when she m. (1) 23 of 5 mo., 1782, (as 2d wife) John Smith Shotwell, of Somerset Co., N. J., b. 8 of 12 mo., 1738–9, s. of John[4] and Elizabeth (Smith) Shotwell, of Plainfield, Essex Co., N. J., [of John[3], John[2], Abraham[1]]; she m. (2) (as 2d wife) Henry Moore of Randolph and Rahway, N. J., b. 11 of 10 mo., 1755, s. of Enoch[2] and Grace (Brotherton) Moore, [of John[2], Samuel[1]].

3. *Joseph*[5], Deborah's son, Titus Shotwell I., called Joseph Shotwell, of Perrytown (near Uniontown), or his father, "Uncle;" but Titus' father's brother Joseph, b. 1717, was too old to be Perrytown Joseph, who d. 17 of 12 mo., 1831, age 77. He or his father, was appointed on a committee by a Woodbridge town meeting, 25 April, 1774, to investigate the right of suffrage among those who claimed the privilege of voting, and to make out a new list of the then present freeholders, etc. He was reappointed as one of the six trustees of the school land and money of the town of Woodbridge, 12 March, 1776. (Dally, p. 289.) One Joseph Shotwell, Jr., formerly of Perry Town, was disowned by New York M. M. 7 of 11 mo., 1781. It is said that he had a bad reputation for the part he took in the War of the Revolution, for which he was disowned by the Society of Friends. He was on one occasion challenged at the polls in Woodbridge for the part he took with Tories in time of the war. He was, however, restored to membership with Friends long before. his

decease. It is said that he closely resembled General Washington in appearance.

Joseph Shotwell of Perrytown, m. in New York, 15 Aug., 1781, Sarah Wilson, who d. Woodbridge Tp., N. J., 13 of 7 mo., 1828, aged 62 yrs. She was a native of England and an Episcopalian, but after marriage, united in membership with Friends, sending all her jewelry and gay clothing to members of her father's family, who after the Revolution, had settled near Little York, in Canada.

To Joseph's great-grandson, Dr. John Byron Shotwell of No. 137, W. 49th St., New York City (son of John), we are indebted for the following account of this branch:

The family of Joseph Shotwell of Philadelphia were Quakers; he was in business in New York City, an importer of teas, sugar and spices.

In the *New York World* newspaper of Nov. 10, 1890, appears an interesting article headed, "Taxes in 1820, when millionaires were few and personal taxes light." It goes on to say; "It is an interesting subject of study for New Yorkers to go back three-quarters of a century and compare the wealth of our grandsires with the latter day growth of metropolitan millionaires. Today they are as plenty as blackberries. The owner of half a million in personal estate was considered a veritable Crœsus seventy-five years ago. The receipts for taxes of this city for this year would amount to about one-half of the total assessed value of property of the city in 1820. In that year there were not more than one hundred and fifty individuals who were taxed on personal property above $20,000 in value." Among the names is that of Joseph Shotwell. The article ends by saying that "In those days rich men did not attempt to avoid payment of personal taxes."

The children of Joseph Shotwell were born in Rahway, N. J.

Mr. Biddle, of the firm of Bailey, Banks & Biddle, jewelers, of Philadelphia, and the families of Townsend, Dell, and many other prominent families of that city are closely related to the daughters of Joseph Shotwell.

John the eldest son was in business in New York City of the firm of Shotwell, Fox & Co., importers. He married Miss Phœbe Byron, daughter of William and Wilhelmina Byron, who were direct descendants* of Lord Byron. They were large owners of real estate in the lower and business portion of New York City and in Haverstraw on the Hudson. John and Phœbe Shotwell had nine children: John, Abraham, William, George, Byron, Mary, Sarah,—wife of Thomas Smith, has one son living, Dara, a builder—Harriet,—the wife of Dr. Norries,—and Phœbe, the youngest, who was married to Isaiah Rynders, at one time United States marshal for New York. Mrs. Rynders is now the only surviving child of John Shotwell.

Abraham Shotwell was engaged in the manufacture of cigars and tobaccos and made a fortune. He married Miss Almyra Clark, of New York, and died in 1891, aged 73 years. Their four children living are: Alonzo B.,

who continues his father's business; Belle; Ida, now Mrs. Chas. Pettengill, and Frank, who is in the railroad business. Alonzo B., has two daughters.

John Shotwell the second son of John Shotwell and Phœbe Byron, founded the firm of Shotwell, Muller & Doscher, sugar refiners of New York City. As an importer and refiner he made a large fortune. He married Susan St. C. Stratton, daughter of Dr. James T. Stratton, of Brooklyn, N. Y., for 40 years an eminent physician. Mr. Shotwell died in 1862, at 45 years of age. He was one of the founders of the Irving National Bank, the Irving Savings Bank, the North River Bank, and director of many other banks, insurance companies, and held offices of honor and trust. His widow is married to Robert Currie, a dry goods merchant in New York City.

The four children of John Shotwell, are: Emily, wife of Chas. Gœller, attorney, of New York City; Susan St. C., wife of Wm. J. Pinckney, who is in the wholesale drug business, son of the late Colonel Stephen R. Pinckney. In the Presbyterian church (Dr. Bradford), at Montclair, N. J., is a grand memorial window by Tiffany, representing St. George. It is dedicated to the memory of Wm. St. Clair Pinckney, son and only child of Wm. J. Pinckney and Susan St. C. (Shotwell) Pinckney, who died very suddenly on March 31, 1893, on the train at Wilmington, on their way home from Cape Charles. He was 16 years old, a young man of noble character and of great promise. He would have inherited a handsome fortune left by his grandfather John Shotwell. His parents have made an endowment to the hospital at Montclair in his memory.

Marion Shotwell married John Quinlan, hardware merchant. They have four children.

The only son of the late John Shotwell, is John Byron Shotwell, M. D., of New York City.

100. JOSEPH⁵ SHOTWELL, 1754±-1831, of Perrytown (now Iselin), near Uniontown, in Woodbridge Tp., Middlesex Co., N. J., s. of Joseph⁴ Shotwell, of Woodbridge, N. J., [of Joseph³, Daniel², Abraham¹], m. 1781, *Sarah Wilson*, 1766±-1828, and had:

1. *John⁶*, was a sugar refiner in N. Y., d. Rahway, N. J., 5 of 2 mo., 1841; m. Phœbe Byron, a relative of Lord Byron, the poet.

2. *Thomas*, lived in Jamaica, W. I., and there d. early in the century, unm.

3. *Wilson⁶*, dw. Moorestown, N. J., and there d.; m. (1) Sarah Marsh, who d.; m. (2) Fannie Marsh, sister to former wife.

4. *Joseph*, dw. Elizabeth City, N. C., and there d. _________, s. p.; m. in N. C., _________

5. *Elizabeth*, called "Betsy," b. 1794, near Rahway, N. J., d. at Springfield, O., __ Aug., 1882, s. p., interred in Hinkle cemetery; m. Springfield, O., 1848, (as second wife), her sister Margaret's widower, Alexander Dean, 1805-1870.

6. *Rebecca Wilson Shotwell*, b. near Rahway, N. J., d. Philadelphia, Pa., unm.

7. *Mary*, b. _________, 1800, d. Philadelphia, Pa., 1855; m. Richard Dell, b. 23 of 9 mo., 1798;

---

d. -- of 12 mo., 1884, s of Thomas (b. 23 of 11 mo., 1759, d. 25 of 2 mo., 1850), and grandson of Richard (b. 16 of 10 mo., 1726, d. 3 of 8 mo., 1804, m. 28 of 2 mo., 1754, Elizabeth Schooley).

8. *Isaac*, b. 1802, near Rahway, N. J., removed in Dec., 1816, from Philadelphia, Pa., to Cincinnati, O., and there kept a hat and fur store until 1851, when leaving his family in Cincinnati, he went to California, and there met with many reverses of fortune; he repeatedly lost all his property by fire, but still remained in California, hoping and striving for better things. He was a merchant at Columbia, Cal., and there died of conjetion, 9 Aug., 1864, aged 62, and was interred at Columbia, Cal.; m. "out of meeting," hence lost his membership in the Orthodox Society of Friends, and thereafter attended Hicksite Meeting, though he did not become a member of that branch; m. in Philadelphia, Pa., in -- Feb., 1828, Elizabeth A. West, b. ...., 1809, in Philadelphia, Pa., whither, after her husband's death, she returned from Cincinnati, and there d. ...., 1885, and was interred near Philadelphia, dau. of Samuel and Anna (Goncher) West.

9. *Catharine*, b. 5 of 9 mo., 1803, d. 28 of 12 mo., 1871; m. 28 of 9 mo., 1820, (as second wife) Jotham Townsend, b. 29 of 11 mo., 1797, d. 1 of 1 mo., 1876, s. of Hugh² and Mary (Dell) Townsend, [of John¹], a man who, like his wife, was of a "quiet, kind, and loving disposition." One of their thirteen children says of them, "Only sunshine and happiness filled their home always; and none ever left their door hungry or sorrowful or suffering. Would that all homes today over all our wide land were more as theirs was." They removed about 1853, from New Market, N. J., to Plainfield, N. J.

10. *Margaret*, b. 22 Oct., 1806, Middlesex Co., N. J.; d. of consumption, near Camden, N. J., 6 Sept., 1846, interred in Friend's cemetery near Camden; m. near Rahway, N. J., 1 June, 1825, (as first wife) Alexander Dean, b. 22 Jan., 1805, Orange, Essex Co., N. J., d. near Springfield, O., 13 Oct., 1870; was interred in Hinkle cemetery; was a shoemaker, s. of Alexander and Lydia (Fairchild) Dean.

11. *Sarah*, called "Sally," d. Rahway, N. J., 1832; m. at Rahway, N. J., Samuel Taylor, of New York City, who d. .... Their children John and Mary, died ....

12. *Alice*, d. Moorestown, N. J., unm.

118. JOSEPH⁶ SHOTWELL, 1783-1863, of Rahway, N. J., s. of John⁵ and Margaret (Haydock) Shotwell, of Lower Rahway, [of Joseph⁴, John³, John², Abr¹.], m. 1820, *Margaret Elston*, 1797-1869, dau. of Ambrose Elston, of Lower Rahway, and had:

1. *Margaret H*¹., b. 24 of 12 mo., 1821, took cert. of membership to Galen Meeting of Women Friends from R. and P. M. M. dated 15 of 12 mo., 1841; d. 25 of 6 mo., 1847; m. in Galen Friends Meeting 3 of 2 mo., 1842 (as 1st wife), Wm. S. Willson, of Waterloo, N. Y., b. 17 of 1 mo., 1821, s. of Asa² and Amy (Shotwell) Willson, of Junius, N. Y., etc., [of Gabriel⁴, Samuel¹]. They with their minor son Albert, took cert. to Adrian M. M. of (Hic.) Friends, from Junius M. M. dated 26 of 3 mo., 1845.

2. *Sarah*, b. 25 of 4 mo., 1823.

3. *Albert*, b. 25 of 10 mo., 1825, dw. Richmond, Va., formerly Asbury Park, N. J., was at St. Louis, mo., 1879, a Presbyterian minister.

4. *John Haydock*, b. 25 of 11 mo., 1827, dw. Asbury Park, N. J., whither he removed from Rahway after 1876, is a physician, and frequently speaks in Friends Meeting; m. Mary B. ....

5. *Frances Elizabeth*, b. 21 of 1 mo., 1831, dw. 1888, Los Angeles, Cal., formerly at Rahway, s. p., m. George Bayright, who dw. Los Angeles, Cal., s. of Augustus and Mary Bayright.

124. JOSEPH DOBSON⁶ SHOTWELL, of Rahway, N. J., s. of Henry⁵ and Sarah (Dobson) Shotwell, of Rahway, N. J., [of Joseph⁴, John³, John², Abr¹.], m. 1804, *Elizabeth Fitz Randolph*, dau. of Jacob and Anna (Webster) Fitz Randolph, and had:

1. *Henry Randolph*¹, b. 28 of 5 mo., 1806, was a prominent business man in Rahway, N. J., for more than 50 years, and there d. 18 of 7 mo., 1887, in 82d year of his age, and was buried in Hazlewood cemetery, Rahway, N. J., was paralyzed more than 12 years prior to his death, and was not afterward able to stand alone, but retained his faculties remarkably well; spent several weeks in the summer of 1886, near Reading, Pa. When the weather was fine frequently rode about the town in an easy chair on a push wagon; m. at Bristol, Pa., 11 of 11 mo., 1830, Margaret G. Laing, dau. of Wm⁵., and Martha (Freeman) Laing, [of Thomas⁴, Isaac³, John², John¹].

2. *Jacob Randolph*, b. 8 of 10 mo., 1813; an Orthodox Friend, and a prominent business man in Rahway, for more than half a century; d. 9 of 5 mo, 1894; m. (1) Elizabeth B. Hartshorne, who d. 1 of 5 mo., 1846; m. (2) Martha Stroud, of Stroudsburgh, Pa., who d. at Elmwood, Rahway, N. J., 22 of 1 mo., 1895, in the 79th year of her age. "A beloved member of Plainfield and Rahway Monthly Meeting. She was born in the town of Stroudsburg, Pa., (which was named for her father, Daniel Stroud), and married there in 1848. She came at once with her husband to Rahway; where her noble christian character, found active exercise, both in public and private, in devotion to the welfare of others; and her death leaves behind her in the community, the fragrance of a well-spent life; and in the hearts of all with whom she was closely associated, a lasting sorrow yet a precious memory." By first wife Jacob had two children who died young.

169. JOSEPH LIPPINCOTT[6] SHOTWELL, 1787–1871, of N. Plainfield, N. J., s. of Isaiah[5] and Constant (Lippincott) Shotwell, of Plainfield, N. J., [of John[4], John[3], John[2], Abraham[1]], m. 1809, *Christiana Vail*, 1788–1871, dau. of Abraham[3] and Margaret (Fitz Randolph) Vail, of Green Brook, N. J., [of John[2], Samuel[1]], and had:

1. *Abraham Vail*, b. 3 of 10 mo., 1810, in Plainfield, N. J., d. N. Plainfield, 30 of 3 mo., 1864, unm.; was a physician.

2. *George W.*, b. 28 of 9 mo., 1813, Plainfield, d. N. Plainfield, N. J., 23 of 10 mo., 1841, s. p.; m. Cor. Peace and Front Sts., Plainfield, N. J., -- Nov., 1839, Margaret Anderson, b. 18 Nov., 1817, dau. of Robert and Agnes Anderson, of Plainfield, N. J.

3. *Margaret V.*, b. 3 of 1 mo., 1817, Plainfield, d. Milton (now Rahway), N. J., 6 of 5 mo., 1819.

4. *Margaret V.*, (again), b. 12 of 3 mo., 1819 at Plainfield, N. J., d. N. Plainfield, N. J., 24 of 10 mo., 1863, unm.

5. *Alexander*, b. 22 of 4 mo., 1821, in Plainfield, N. J., dw. 42 Pearl St., N. Plainfield, N. J., s. p.; m. by John V. Morris, rector at Plainfield, N. J., 21, Apr., 1879, Elizabeth Thys, dau. of John Baptist and Mary A. Thys.

6. *Mary Perkins*[7], b. 4 of 5 mo., 1823, Plainfield, dw. St. Louis, Mo., m. in N. Y. City, Samuel M. Stelle, who is a merchant in St. Louis, Mo.

7. *Harriet Allen*[7], b. 31 of 10 mo., 1825, Plainfield, N. J., dw. Pontiac, Mich.; m. in 2d Presbyterian church, Plainfield, N. J., Dr. Washington G. Elliott.

8. *Elizabeth F.*, dw. with brother Alex., N. Plainfield, N. J., unm.

JOSEPH SHOTWELL, 1788–1863, of Eden, N. Y., s. of James and Ann (Moore) Shotwell, m. 1809, *Sarah[6] Thorn*, 1790–1837, dau. of Abraham[5] and Elizabeth (Smith) Thorn, of Junius, N. Y., [of Abraham[1], Abraham[3], Joseph[2], Wm[1].], and had:

1. *Eliza Ann*[7], b. 8 of 4 mo., 1810, in N. J.; removed with her parents in 1815 to Eden, Erie Co., N. Y., and there d. 9 Sept., 1861, suddenly, of apoplexy; m. 3 Apr. 1825, (as 1st wife) Joseph Willson Keater, b. 18 of 10 mo., 1803, Kingwood, N. J., d. Mt. Auburn, Blackhawk Co., Iowa, -- March, 1883, s. of Samuel[2] and Mary (Willson) Keater, of [Harman[1]].

214. JOSEPH[6] SHOTWELL, 1789–1869, of Saratoga Co., N. Y., s. of Caleb[5] and Phebe (Hinckston) Shotwell, of Saratoga Co., N. Y., [of Samuel[4] John[3], John[2], Abr.[1]], m. 1811, *Sarah Randall*, 1793–1877, and had:

1. *Samuel Randall*[7], b. 11 Oct., 1812, at or near Burnt Hills, in Saratoga Co., N. Y., graduated at Madison University, 1842; ordained, 1842, at Eaton, Madison Co., N. Y.;

served as pastor of Baptist church at Eaton, Jamesville, Saratoga, Co., Whitesboro and Taberg, Oneida Co.; d. at Taberg, N. Y., 12 or 6 Apr., 1853; m. 22 Aug., 1842, Patience Maria Bloss, who d. North Bay, Oneida Co., N. Y., 14 or 13 July, 1853, dau. of Samuel Bloss, of Oneida Co., N. Y.

2. *Caleb G.*, b. 12 July, 1815, Clifton Park, Saratoga, Co., N. Y., was a farmer and merchant; d. 24 June, 1873, at Barryville, Sullivan Co., N. Y., suddenly; m. in the town of Mentz, Cayuga Co., N. Y., 28 Sept., 1837, Sally Jane Corey, of Orange Co., N. Y.

3. *Sarah*[7], b. 25 July, 1817, in Clifton Park, N. Y., d. Port Byron, Cayuga Co., N. Y., 9 May, 1864; m. Greenfield, Saratoga Co., N. Y., 24 Oct., 1832, John Cornell.

4. *Phebe*, b. 28 Aug., 1819; d. 7 Sept., 1822.

5. *John Maxwell*[7], b. 22 Feb., 1821, in Half Moon, Saratoga Co., N. Y., about two miles east of Burnt Hills (now Clifton Park); received a common school and academiceducation; baptized in March, 1838, by Rev. Solomon Knapp into the Port Byron Baptist Church, Cayuga Co., N. Y., spent a few years after 1842 teaching in Boone Co., Ky., near Verona; was ordained in Walesville, Whitestown, Oneida Co., N. Y., 21 Jan., 1851; preached in Westmooreland, Whitestown, Little Falls, Belleville, Mannville, Manchester, Wheatland, and Angelica; removed 1 Apr., 1864, to Oramel, Allegany Co., N. Y., and has spent most of his time in lecturing, preaching, selling Bibles, and farming; he at one time (1858) had charge of a large school of several hundred students at Meridian, Cayuga Co., N. Y., which, however, was not a pecuniary success; he dwells (1895) Red Creek, Wayne Co., N. Y.; to him the compiler is indebted for valuable information respecting this branch of the family.

He m. (1) in Cato, N. Y., 14 Sept., 1842, Salome Lucinda Stone, a literary woman and a poetic writer, b. 25 or 28 Nov., 1823, in Ira, Cayuga Co., N. Y., d. 19 Apr., 1885, of pneumonia, very happy and without a struggle; was converted at age of 15, uniting with the M. E. Church; was baptised into the fellowship of the Baptist Church, Westmooreland, Oneida Co., N. Y., by Rev. Denison Alcott, in 1849. He m. (2) -------- Lydia Lucretia (Chamberlain) Jones, b. 9 June, 1836, in W. Sparta, Livingston Co., N. Y., fourth dau. of Harlam Chamberlain, J. P.; she was educated at Nunda Academy, engaged in teaching in Livingston Co., N. Y., and in Fondulac Co., Wis.; she m. (1) about 1858, -------- Jones; she was an earnest temperance worker, one of the leaders in the woman's crusade in her city, Ripon, Wis., was a student in Mr. Moody's Evangelistic School in Wis., 1889–90.

6. *Josiah*[7], b. 10 Dec., 1822, Clifton Park, N. Y., d. near Marshall, Mich., -- March,

1883; m. in Port Byron, N. Y., 4 Apr., 1850, Julia Cornell, who d.

7. *Dea Abel*[7], b. 12 June, 1825, in Saratoga Co., N. Y.; was a carpenter, grocer, and dealer in real estate; dw. on or near Alexander St., Detroit, Mich., and there d. 11 Sept., 1888; m. in Port Byron, N. Y., 9 Dec., 1847, Christi Ann Gordon.

8. *Phebe* (again), b. ...., 1827, Clifton Park, N. Y., dw. Toledo, O., s. p.; m. 9 May, 1848, Willis Coe, who is a merchant in Toledo, O.

9. *Mary*[7], b. 13 Aug., 1830, in Saratoga Co., N. Y., dw. Savannah, Wayne Co., N. Y.; m. 1 Jan., 1852, John Spoor, of Savannah, N. Y.

10. *Stephen C.*, b. 5 Sept., 1831; a farmer and peddler; dw. Sullivan Co., N. Y.; m. ....

11. *Charlotte*[7], b. .. Oct., 1834, in Saratoga Co., N. Y.; dw. Fosterville, Cayuga Co., N. Y., a wd. (1889); m. 8 Aug., 1852, Jehiel F. Pease, of Montezuma, Cayuga Co., N. Y.

142. JOSEPH SMITH[6] SHOTWELL, merchant of New York, s. of John Smith[5] and Phebe (Shotwell) Shotwell, of Somerset Co., N. J., [of John[4], John[3], John[2], Abr[1].], m. *Deborah Fox*, and had:
1. ...., a dau., dw. Plainfield, N. J., a wd.; m. .... Underhill.
2. ...., a dau.; m. .... Jenkens.
3. *Joseph F*[7]., b. 21 Jan., 1827, m. 22 Sept., 1847, Amy Titus.

JOSEPH H. SHOTWELL, of William St., New York, (parentage not ascertained), and wife ...., had:
1. *George*, b. 1815, d. William St., New York, 1815, interred in N. Y. Friends cemetery, 8 of 12 mo., 1815.

185. JOSEPH[6] SHOTWELL, 1801–1883, of Glenville, O., s. of Hugh[5] and Rosetta (Arrison) Shotwell, of Harrison Co., O., [of John[4], John[3], John[2], Abr[1].], m. (1) 1821, *Mary Arrison*, dau. of Jeptha Arrison of Delaware Co., O., and had:
1. *Jeptha*[7], b. 17 Nov., 1824, at Cadiz, O.; dw. Delphos, Allen Co., O.; P. O. (1882), Evandale, Hamilton Co., O.; occupation farmer; m. at Reading, Pa., 15 Feb., 1849, Nancy Cooper, b. 1825, dau. of Thomas and Hannah.
2. *George*, b. 1831; dw. ...., Ill., served in the Union Army during the War of the Rebellion; d. 1880; m. Catherine Martin.
3. *Louisa*; m. Thomas Gibson, of Carthage, O.; had one daughter now deceased.

266. JOSEPH[6] SHOTWELL, s. of Daniel[5] and Keziah (Terrill) Shotwell, of Middlesex Co., N. J., [of Daniel[4], Joseph[3], Daniel[2], Abr[1].], m. *Anne Ball*, and had among others:

1. *Gustavus*, removed with his father's family from N. J. to the west; dw. Woodlawn Park, Chicago, Ill.
2. *Henry Clay*, dw. Woodlawn Park, Chicago, Ill., an expert pen and ink artist.
3. *Harriet*, dw. Woodlawn Park, Chicago, Ill.; an artist; m. Chas. Peck, a portrait painter.
4. *John*, dw. Washington, D. C.

JOSEPH F[7]. SHOTWELL, b. 1827, s. of Joseph Smith[6] and Deborah (Fox) Shotwell, of New York, [of Jno. S[5]., Jno[4]., Jno[3]., Jno[2]., Abr[1].], m. 1847, *Amy Titus*, and had:
1. *William Titus*[8] *Shotwell*, b. 29 June, 1852; dw. 45 Waverly Ave., Brooklyn, N. Y.; m. 19 Oct., 1881, Ida Demarest Chapin.
2. *Walter Fox*[8], b. 21 March, 1856; m. .. Nov., 1892, Phebe Titus.
3. *Henry T*[8]., b. 31 Mar., 1862, dw. 72 Washington Ave., Brooklyn, N. Y., m. 15 Mar., 1886, Alice Gardner.

JOSEPH MARSH[7] SHOTWELL, d. 1874, of Iowa, s. of John[6] and Grace (Marsh) Shotwell, of Thorold, C. W., [of Wm[5]., John[4], John[3], John[2], Abr[1].], m. 1860±, *Martha Ferguson*, now of Martelle, Iowa, dau. of Peter and Martha Ferguson of Caradoc, Ont., formerly of Paisley, Scotland, and had:
1. *Emerson*,[8] b. Lobo, C. W., 19 March, 1864, dw. Martelle, Jones Co., Iowa; m. 14 Dec., 1893, Louisa Bishop, dau of Francis M. and Harriet Bishop, and had: Alma, b. 4 Sept., 1894.
2. *Louisa*, b. 26 June, 1870, in Jones Co., Iowa, d. 22 July, 1872.

JOSEPH MARSH[7] SHOTWELL, b. 1830, of San Francisco, Cal., s. of William M[6]. and Ann (Marsh) Shotwell, of Rahway, N. J., [of Aaron[5], Abraham[4], John[3], John[2], Abraham[1]], m. 1860, *Minnie Perrier*, b. 1845, and had:
1. *Ellsworth Earl*, b. 5 Feb., 1861.
2. *Mariane P.*, b. 6 Apr., 1862.
3. *Grace Darling*, b. 4 June, 1867.

JOSEPH D[7]. SHOTWELL, b. 1831, of Orange, N. J., s. of Henry R[6]. and Margaret G. (Laing) Shotwell, of Rahway, N. J., [of Joseph D[5]., Henry[4], Joseph[3], John[2], John[2], Abraham[1]], m. *Amelia Everit*, and had:
1. *Mary E.*, b. 3 of 10 mo., 1864.
2. *Margaret R.*, b. 10 of 9 mo., 1866.

JOSHUA[7] SHOTWELL, 1807–1866, of Crosswicks, N. J., s. of Thomas L[6]. and Elizabeth (Satterthwait) Shotwell, of Crosswicks, N. J., [of Isaiah[5], John[4], John[3], John[2], Abraham[1]], m. (1) 1834, *Sarah Ann Stillwell*, 1811–1837, dau. of Joseph M. and Hannah (Stillwell) Stillwell, and had:

1. *Hannah Ann*[1], b. 22 of 1 mo., 1836, at Crosswicks, N. J., dw., (1895), Freehold, Monmouth Co., N. J.; to her and her husband we are indebted for valuable data respecting this branch. She was married by Mayor Henry in Philadelphia, Pa., 14 May, 1862, to James T[1]. Burtis, born near New Egypt, N. J., 4 May, 1835; clerk in store in Freehold, 1851, merchant there since 1862; in politics a Democrat; compiler of the "Burtis Genealogical and Biographical Record;" son of Peter W[1]. and Margaret D. (Thompson) Burtis of Monmouth Co., N. J. The following is a concise lineage of their children: (1.) Elizabeth S., b. 13 Aug., 1864, d. ______, 1870. (2.) Emily S., b. 21 Aug., 1871. (3.) William Ryall[9] Burtis, born 21 Apr., 1876; James T[1]., b. 1835; Peter W[1]., b. 1812; James[6], b. 1777; William[5], b. 1740±; Richard[4] Alburtis [Burtis], b. 1700±; John[3] Alburtis, b. 1668±; Jan[2] Alberto [Alburtis], b. 1643; Pietro Cæsar[1] Alberto, a native of Venice, Italy, who came with the "Walloons" of Amsterdam in Holland, to Ft. Amsterdam, Nieuw Amsterdam (now New York), in 1636, and there married in 1642, Judith, daughter of Jan and Martha Chambœr Meynje of Amsterdam, Holland. His [W. R. B's] paternal grandmother, Margaret D. Thompson, b. 1815, was daughter of John F., b. 1773, [of Thomas Thomson, b. 1748, Thomas Tomson, b. 1720, Cornelius Tomson who lived near Freehold, Monmouth Co. N. J., as early as 1711), and descended from the Tomson family who settled at New Plymouth, Mass., about 1640.

JOSHUA[1] SHOTWELL, 1807-1866, of Crosswicks, N. J., [of Thomas L[5]., Isaiah[5], John[4], John[3], John[2], Abraham[1]], m. (2) 1842, *Rebecca A. Stillwell*, 1806-1861, sister to former wife, and had:

2. *Julia*[5], b. 27 of 6 mo., 1846, dw. Crosswicks, N. J.; m. 25 of 4 mo., 1866, Jervis S. Woolman, a descendant of John Woolman, the noted West Jersey Friend and anti-slavery philanthropist, and had: (1.) Henry M. (2.) Rebecca S. (3.) Margaret L. (4.) Helen R.

3. *Marietta*[5], b. 17 of 1 mo., 1849, dw. Crosswicks, Burlington Co., N. J.; m. 28 Nov., 1872, Isaac L. Woolman, brother to the husband of her sister Julia, and had: (1.) Jennie H. (2.) Edgar S.

JOSIAH[1] SHOTWELL, 1822-1883, of Calhoun Co., Mich., s. of Joseph[6] and Sarah (Randall) Shotwell, of Saratoga Co., N. Y., [of Caleb[5], Samuel[4], John[3], John[2], Abraham[1]], m. 1850, *Julia Cornell*, and had:
1. *Samuel*, d. suddenly.
2. *Sarah*.

KENNETH[6] SHOTWELL, b. 1851, of Ellisville, Mo., s. of John[7] and Nancy (Lollar) Shotwell of Manchester, Mo., [of Nathan[6], John[5], John[4], Abr[3]., John[2], Abr[1].], m. 1878, *Mary E. Stevens*, dau. of Richard and Lucinda [Triplet] Stevens, and had:
1. *Clarence L.*, b. 24 Dec., 1878.
2. *Kenneth D.*, b. 18 Jan., 1882.
3. *Willie S.*, b. 12 Dec., 1884.
4. *Floyd*, b. 10 Apr. 1887.
5. *Harry*, b. 4 July, 1889.

LEVI LUNDY[7] SHOTWELL, b. 1816, of Eaton Co., Mich., s. of Zachariah[6] and Elizabeth (Lundy) Shotwell, of Wayne Co., N. Y., [of Benjamin[5], Benjamin[4], John[3], John[2], Abr[1].], m. (1) *Nancy P. Pratt*, and had:
1. *Albert Edwin*, b. Elba, N. Y.; served three years in the 7th Michigan cavalry in the War of the Rebellion, carried the flag one summer, had two caps shot off his head, and several horses killed under him; dw. W. Windsor, Eaton Co., Mich.; m. (1) Anna Van Aukan, who d. about one week before death of Albert's mother; m. (2) Sophia Mills.
2. *Mary Elizabeth*[5], m. Madison Carman, of Eaton Co., Mich.

LEVI L[7]. SHOTWELL, b. 1816, of Eaton Co., Mich., [of Zachariah[6], Benj[5]., Benj[4]., John[3], John[2], Abr[1].], m. (2) *Aseneth Williams*, and had:
3. *Levi J.*, dw. W. Windsor, Mich.

LEVI S[7]. SHOTWELL, b. 1827, of Collins, Ionia Co., Mich., s. of Benjamin[6] and Sarah (Hoag) Shotwell, of Genesee and Monroe counties, N. Y., [of Richard[5], Benj[4]., John[3], John[2], Abr[1].], m. 1840, *Sarah Estes*, dau. of Allen Estes, of Wheatland, N. Y., and had:
1. *Elizabeth*, b. Wheatland, Monroe Co., N. Y.
2. *Freeman*, b. Wheatland, N. Y.

MAHLON[6] SHOTWELL, 1810-1859, of Barnesville, O., s. of Titus[5] and Deborah (Howell) Shotwell, [of Daniel[4], Joseph[3] ?, Daniel[2], Abr[1].], m. *Lucinda Lee*, and had nine children, among them:
1. *John C.*, b. in Warren Co., O., about four miles from Lebanon, the county seat; dw. at Cincinnati, O., address general delivery.

113 (c.) MANNING[6] SHOTWELL*, b 1758, s. of Benjamin[4] and Elizabeth (Manning) Shotwell, [of John[3], Daniel[2], Abr[1].], m. 1783±, *Mary Clarkson*, b. 1762±, dau. of Robert and Rebecca[4] (Fitz Randolph) Clarkson, and had:
1. *Robert*[6], b. 15 July, 1784; m. 22 Feb., 1812, Martha[7] Fitz Randolph, b. 20 Feb., 1796,

dau. of James[3] and Keziah (Kelly) F. Randolph, [of Jeremiah[5] and Rhoda (Ayers) F. Randolph, Jeremiah[4]- b. 1715—and Ruth (Dunn) F. Randolph, Joseph[3]—b. 1690—and Rebecca (Drake) F. Randolph, Joseph[2] and Hannah (Conger) F. Randolph, Edward[1] and Elizabeth (Blossom) Fitz Randolph].

2. *Daniel Clarkson[6] Shotwell*, called "Hatter Daniel," b. 19 July, 1791; dw. Plainfield, N. J., and there d. 3 Nov., 1875; m. .... Martha[6] Pound, dau. of Samuel[5] and Susannah (Webster) Pound, [of Zachariah[4], Elijah[3], John[2], John[1]].

3. *Elizabeth*, called Betsey, m. ....

4. *Lavinia*, m. Jas. Langstaff.

5. *Rachel*, never m.

6. *Clarkson*, m. Elizabeth Boice. (No issue).

MANNING[7] SHOTWELL, b. 1816, s. of Robert[6] and Martha (Fitz Randolph) Shotwell, [of Manning[5], Benj.[4], John[3], Daniel[2], Abr[1].], m. 1838, *Lucy Ann Cannon*, and had:

1. *George*, b. 15 of 1 mo., 1839.

2. *J. M. Shotwell*, b. 12 of 6 mo., 1842.

3. *Theodore*, b. 2 of 8 mo., 1846.

4. *J. Randolph Shotwell*, b. 18 of 11 mo., 1849.

McCLEERY J. SHOTWELL, b. 1855, of Knoxville, Tenn., s. of Rev. Dr. Nathan and Mary L. (McCleery) Shotwell, of Milroy, Pa., and elsewhere, [and grandson of Randolph and Mary H. (Gage) Shotwell, of Newark, N. J.], m. 1881, *Sarah M. Hardwick*, who d. 1894, and had:

1. *Margaret Susan*, b. 7 Sept., 1882.

2. *Mary McCleery*, b. 31 Aug., 1884.

3. *Nathan*, b. 14 Sept., 1886.

4. *Ralph*, b. 11 Aug., 1888.

5. *James*, b. ...., 1890; d. 1890, buried at Rogersville, Tenn.

6 and 7. (Twins), b. ...., 1892; buried at Rogersville, Tenn., unnamed.

MELANCTHON S. SHOTWELL, b. 1845, of Harrisburg, Pa., s. of Rev. Dr. Nathan and Martha Ann (Abbott) Shotwell, of W. Liberty, Va., [of Randolph and Mary H. (Gage) Shotwell of Newark, N. J.], m. 1887, *Caroline R[1]. Porter*, [of Dr. Geo. W[3]., Gov. David R[2]., Gen. Andrew[1]], and had:

1. *George Porter Shotwell*, b. 9 June, 1889.

2. *David Rittenhouse Shotwell*, b. 1 June, 1895.

MERRITT ELMER[6] SHOTWELL, 1859-1879, s. of Zachariah P[5]. and Margaret (Zavitz) Shotwell, of Galen, N. Y., and Lobo, Ont., [of Thomas[4], Benj[3]., Benj[4]., John[2], John[2], Abr[1].], m. 1877, *Sarah V. Bond*, b. 1859, dau. of John and Jane Bond, and had:

1. *Bertha May*, b. 31, of 12 mo., 1878, in Lobo, Ont.

MONTGOMERY[8] SHOTWELL, b. 1842, s. of John[7] and Elizabeth (Biggs) Shotwell, [of John[6], John[5], John[4], Abr[3]. ?, John[2], Abr[1].], m. (1) 1861, *Elizabeth Robertson*, and had:

1. *Dazarine*, b. .. Sept., 1862, d. 7 Oct., 1882.

2. *Elizabeth*, b. .. March, 1865, d 22 Feb., 1882.

3. *John Edward*, b. .. Oct., 1869, d. 15 Sept., 1883.

4. *Robert*, b. 31 Aug., 1875; m. 7 June, 1896, ...

MONTGOMERY[8] SHOTWELL, b. 1842, [of John[7], John[6], John[5], John[4], Abr[3]. ?, John[2], Abr[1].], m. (3) 1882±, *Cora Ellis*, b. 1865±, and had:

5. *Grover*, b. 28 Dec., 1884.

6. *Kenneth*, b. 1 Oct., 1887.

80. NATHAN[5] SHOTWELL, 1768-1848±, of Rahway and Blazing Star, N. J., and La Porte, Ind., s. of Jacob[4] and Katharine (Tilton) Shotwell, of Rahway, Middlesex Co., N. J., [of John[3], John[2], Abr[1].], m. 1798, *Sarah[4] Fitz Randolph*, 1782-1815, dau. of Jacob[3] and Anna (Webster) Fitz Randolph, of Blazing Star, N. J., [of Isaac[2], Jacob[1]], and had:

1. *Catharine Ann*, b. 18 of 3 mo., 1799, in Rahway, Middlesex Co., N. J.; when about 16 yrs. of age, her mother dying, she became her father's housekeeper; removed with him to La Porte Co., Ind., taking cert. of membership from R. and P. M. M. of (Hic.) Friends to Whitewater M. M. held at Richmond, Ind., dated 22 of 2 mo., 1843, was widely known in New York, New Jersey and Indiana, having spent much of her life in teaching the colored people and looking after their welfare; d. suddenly near Salem, Ala., 11 of 1 mo., 1877, unm., buried at Salem, Ala.; was followed to her grave by almost the entire black population of the neighborhood.

2. *Louisa[6]*, b. 8 of 12 mo., 1800, Rahway, N. J., became member of Friends Meeting in New York by cert. from R. and P. M. M. dated 21 of 12 mo., 1825, d. at the res. of her grandson Harvey S. Ogden, Orange, N. J., 4 of 3 mo., 1889, in 89th year of her age; buried at Rahway; was all her life a member of the Society of Friends. Though living for a long time far separated from Friends, and prevented in her later years by ill health from attending meetings, her attachment to the Society was deep and earnest, and her life that of a true and consistent member. She m. in Rahway, N. J., 25 of 12 mo., 1823, Harvey Shotwell, of New York, and afterward a druggist at Macon, Ga., b. 13 of 10 mo., 1800, Rahway, N. J., d. Macon, Ga., 6 of 1 mo., 1848, s. of Wm.[5] and Elizabeth (Moore) Shotwell, of Bricktown, Rahway, N. J., [of Benj[4]., John[3], John[2], Abr[1]].

3. *Alexander[6]*, b. 5 of 12 mo., 1802, Rahway, N. J., dw. for a time at Macon, Ga., and after-

ward for many years near Salem, Ala., and there d. 28 of 9 mo., 1884, in 82d year of his age, buried at Salem; m. Rahway, N. J., ________, 1825, or 1824, Eliza Smith, b. 1803, d. near Salem, Ala, 18 or 13 of 6 mo., 1879, aged 76 yrs., dau. of Wm. and Jane⁶ (Shotwell) Smith, [of John⁵, Joseph⁴, John³, John², Abr¹.]. In her memory among other affectionate expressions, her dau., Jennie S. Lamb, wrote as follows: "As we sat beside her in her dying moments, when she could no longer give utterance to words, oh! such thoughts as passed through our minds reflecting upon her past life, how kind and gentle she had been, how self sacrificing, how uncomplaining through long years of suffering! Her hand was ever ready to relieve those in distress and her heart beat in unison with those who were suffering. The loss of such a mother, oh! what a void it has left!"

4. *Jacob*, b. 7 of 9 mo., 1804, Rahway, N. J., d. in Miss., of exposure, aged 65 yrs.; m. Sarah Newhall.

5. *Susan R.*, b. __ of 8 mo., 1807, Rahway, N. J., dw. at La Porte, Ind., 1834–43, thence removed to Vincennes, Ind., where for many years she lived in the family of her sister, Mrs. Dr. Hitt; member of Whitewater M. M. by cert. from R. and P. M. M. dated 22 of 2 mo., 1843; never m.

"She was a member of the Society of Friends and exemplified in her life very many of the beautiful characteristics of that people; ignoring the usual adornments of person, she always wore that one which is the most beautiful of all, the ornament of a meek and quiet spirit. Her uniform gentleness and quiet dignity of character at once gained your truest respect. 'She lived 30 years in my family,' says Dr. H., 'and yet I never saw her manifest anger or speak harshly.' This is very rare testimony to human character. Her's was positive. She knew what she believed and was uncompromising in her principles. Having a weak and sickly body, her life was confined to the home, but its influence was felt by all who knew her, a silent, constant incentive to purity of life and integrity of purpose." About a year before her death, she, with her sister Catharine, went to visit their brother, Alexander, near Salem, Ala., vainly hoping that the change would permanently benefit her health. But while there, despite the best of care, on the 26 of 12 mo., 1874, she quietly fell asleep. Loving hearts followed her to the last resting place and how many of those who could not join in that sad procession look forward to the great reunion of the future, their hearts saying:

> "Amid the white robed multitude,
> We know that we shall find thee,
> For Jesus whispers, 'Where I am,
> There shall my servant be.'"

6. *Ellen Tilton*, b. ________, 1810, Rahway, N. J., dw. Vincennes, Knox Co., Ind.; m. Dr. Willis W. Hitt.

7. *Eden*, b. 5 of 8 mo., 1812, Rahway, Middlesex (now Union) Co., N. J., removed from La Porte, Ind., about 1856, to Loda, Iroquois Co., Ill., and subsequently to Lancaster Co., Neb., near Bennett, and there d. 3 of 3 mo., 1896, buried at Bennett; member of the Society of Friends in Ill. by cert. from R. and P. M. M. dated 21 of 9 mo., 1865; by occupation a farmer; to him the compiler is indebted for valuable items relating to this branch of the family. His exemplary life and earnest christian testimony were helpful to others during his lifetime, and should continue to exert a wholesome influence upon his kindred. He m. in Hanover, Jefferson Co., Ind., 26 of 6 mo., 1837, or 16 of 8 mo., 1837, Ann Mary Haas, b. 16 June, 1816, near Lynchburgh, Va., d. in Lancaster Co., Neb., 3 June, 1892, of la grippe, interred at Bennett, Neb., dau. of Jacob and Susanna (Goode) Haas.

8. *Sarah Elizabeth*, b. ________, 1814, Rahway, N. J.; member of Whitewater M. M. of (Hic.) Friends held at Richmond, Ind., by cert. from R. and P. M. M. dated 22 of 2 mo., 1843; had previously m. Wm. Allen, b. 1807, in Ind., d. 13 Dec., ____, in Mason City, Ill., where he had resided during the last 10 yrs. of his life, leaving an aged wife and four children; had removed from Indiana in 1854, to Havana, Mason Co., Ill.; was prominently identified with many of the public interests of that county and the State at large; had been for two terms a sheriff in Indiana, and once a member of the Indiana legislature; was a man whose marked characteristic was a firm and radical adherence to right; was a radical on every principle he espoused and always manifested his faith by his works; was uniformly looked up to with respect by his neighbors, and his counsel was sought on public matters. He was a member of the Presbyterian church prior to his removal to Illinois, from which time he was a member of the Methodist church. His funeral took place from the Presbyterian church on Wednesday morning, and was largely attended.

243 (f). NATHAN⁷ SHOTWELL, b. 1782, of Mason Co., Ky., afterwards of St. Louis Co., Mo., s. of John⁶ and Abigail (Shipman) Shotwell, of Mayslick, Ky., [of Jno⁴., Abr³. ?, Jno²., Abr¹.], m. (1) 1806, Grover, and had:

1. *Sanford*, believed to have d. young in Ky.

2. *Kenneth*, dw. Sapington, St. Louis Co., Mo., d. __ Oct., 1880, aged 71 yrs., 9 mos., unm.

3. *Zerelda*, d. __ July, 1883, s. p.; m. Jno. Baxter.

4. *Martha Ann*, d. 28 Feb., 1890, aged 76 yrs., s. p.; m. Joshua Harrison.

243 (f). NATHAN⁶ SHOTWELL, b. 1782, [of Jno⁵., Jno⁴., Abr³. ?, Jno², Abr¹.], m. (2) *Maria Bland*, 1799±–1885, and had:

5. *John¹*, b. 17 April, 1817, Mayslick, Mason Co., Ky.; emigrated to Manchester, Mo., there d. 25 June, 1883; was a farmer, a great hunter and rifle shot, while his brother Kenneth scarcely knew how to load a gun. Both were well-to-do men. John m. (1) in Glencoe, Mo., Nancy Lollar, b. 16 Sept., 1823, in Glencoe, St. Louis Co., Mo., d. Manchester, Mo., 9 April, 1865, the day that Lee surrendered, dau. of Reuben and ____ Lollar; he m. (2) Martha (Brewer) Vaughn, b. 3 May, 1843, living (1895), wid. of James Vaughn; she m. (3) ________ Quaile.

6. *Nathan*, b. ________, removed from Mason Co., Ky., to Manchester, Mo., d. ________, leaving a wife and 2 of their 4 children.

7. *Shipman*, was killed when about 21 yrs. of age.

8. *Margaret*, d. ________, m. ________Johnston, and had 1 dau.

9. *Sally*, d. ________, m. Wm. Darby, and has 2 sons living in Cal.

10. *Abagie*, d. ________, m. ________ Morgan, and has 5 daus. and 1 son.

11. *Mary*, d. ________, m. ________ Herrick, and had 1 dau. who is m. and lives in St. Louis.

REV. NATHAN SHOTWELL, D. D., 1806–1890, of Washington Co., Pa., afterward of W. Va., N. C., and Tenn., ____ s. of Randolph and Mary H. (Gage) Shotwell of Perth Amboy and Newark, N. J., m. (1) 1833 *Lydia Baldwin*, who d. 1840, and had:

1. *Samuel Randolph*, b. 20 Sept., 1835, in AlleghENY City, Pa., and there d. in childhood.

2. *Sarah Matilda*, b. 6 June, 1837, in Washington Co., Pa., and there d. in childhood.

3. *Alexander Hamilton*, b. 17 June, 1839, in Washington Co., Pa.; served as lieutenant and adjutant 34th regiment North Carolina cavalry in the Confederate army, being ordered off 3 Sept., 1861, and remained in the service until 11 July, 1862, when he was mortally wounded and d. in Richmond, Va.; was buried in Rutherfordton, N. C. "Alexander Hamilton Shotwell, M. D., was a highly educated, magnetic, sympathetic, brave gentleman, just starting on his practice when he was cut down. He had about a year before married a lovely and accomplished young lady of good family and independent fortune, who was soon to make him a father; and in all respects his life seemed bright and happy, and he looked forward with fond hopes to a useful career. That he died in full faith in the Redeemer was evinced by his dying words: After a tender mention of his beloved wife and his unseen boy [born a few weeks previously], he murmured softly as a child at prayer, 'Dear, dear Jesus,' and sank to sleep." He m. in Rutherfordton, N. C., 3 July, 1861, Jennie Eliza McEntire, who was born

and raised at Rutherfordton, N. C., and there remained with her son for more than 25 years, dau. of Dr. John McEntire, of Rutherfordton. To her we are indebted for valuable information concerning this branch. She now resides with her son at Smithwood, Knox Co., Tenn.

REV. DR. NATHAN SHOTWELL, 1806–1890, of Washington and Mifflin Cos., Pa., Ohio Co., W. Va., Rutherford Co., N. C., and Hawkins Co., Tenn., s. of Randolph and Mary H. (Gage) Shotwell, of Newark, N. J., m. (2) 1841 *Martha Ann¹ Abbott*, who d. 1849, dau. of Josiab³ Abbott, of Massachusetts, [of Samuel², Samuel¹], and had:

4. *Randolph Abbott Shotwell*, b. 13 Dec., 1843, W. Liberty, Ohio Co., Va. (now W. Va.); d. at Raleigh, N. C., 31 July, 1885, unm.; went at an early age to Media College, Pa., where he pursued a three years' course, it being his father's intention to prepare him for the senior class at Princeton, his father's *alma mater*; but, his state having seceded and the war coming on, he immediately left school to join in the defense of his southern home. On his way to Virginia he met with numerous adventures, traded a Yankee picket out of his skiff in order to cross the Potomac; was discovered, the boat shot to pieces, but he escaped to an island where he was subsequently rescued by a citizen; met the 8th Virginia volunteers just in time for the battle of Leesburg; he joined them and followed the confederate flag through 17 hard-fought battles; led the sharpshooters of a brigade—Pickett's division—in the fatal charge at Gettysburg, and for his valor and skill was tendered a special commission from Secretary Seddon by order of President Davis. Toward the last of the war he was captured as a spy; he made his escape from his captors, but was recaptured by another party, was taken to Fort Delaware and confined as a prisoner of war until three months after the southern flag was furled at Appomattox.

Going to North Carolina in 1866, his father's family having preceded him, they removed to Rutherfordton in Aug., 1869, he laid away the sword that he had honored with his courage and bravery, and chose as his future weapon of life's warfare, the pen, which he ever after wielded in the interest of those principles which he believed to be right. He went to Newbern, N. C., and with Col. Stephen D. Pool, established the Newbern "Journal of Commerce." After two years he removed to Rutherfordton and started the "Vindicator," through which he denounced in scathing terms the so called "carpet-baggers" of that region, and thus began the political warfare that ended only after he had suffered all the persecution that could be heaped upon him by his political enemies.

He went to Charlotte and engaged with Gen. D. H. Hill in the editorial management of the

"Southern Home." A few years later the people of Mecklenburg elected him a member of the legislature of 1876. In Jan., 1878, Capt. Shotwell went to Raleigh and associating himself with Jno. W. Dowd, bought the "Farmer and Mechanic," a paper previously published in the interest of the North Carolina patrons of husbandry; a few months later he became the sole owner, and soon won the confidence of the people. A few weeks prior to his death, the *State Chronicle* and the *Farmer and Mechanic* having been consolidated the name of *The State Chronicle* was retained, Capt. Shotwell becoming the editor-in-chief. Having been appointed State Librarian, he was, after years of struggle, just entering upon an era of success.

Randolph A. Shotwell d. in Raleigh, N. C., Friday, 31 July, 1885, of acute indigestion. From the memorial edition of the *State Chronicle*, Aug. 8, 1885, we have condensed most of the foregoing particulars. On the morning previous to his death he was the picture of robust health, alive to every interest that concerned his State and his people. His paper for the week had just been mailed to his readers, and the work for the coming issue undertaken, when suddenly he was stricken down and in a few hours passed away. For years he had lived by himself, doubtless from the sad disappointments he had endured. It is recorded of him that he was faithful to every trust and earnestly devoted to the defense of truth and honor. Early on the morning after his death, the remains of Capt. Shotwell were taken to the rotunda of the state capitol, where they "lay in state" for thirty-six hours, and were finally deposited in the soldier's burying ground, in Oakwood cemetery, Raleigh, N. C., twelve ex-confederate soldiers acting as pall bearers, and the funeral taking place from the First Presbyterian church of that city.

From a later notice, we take the following additional characterization: "Randolph Abbott Shotwell was a brave and noble man,—the soul of honor and the tongue of truth,—as soldier, editor, and statesman. He edited 'The Newberne Journal of Commerce,' 'The Vindicator,' 'The Citizen,' 'The Southern Home,' 'The Farmer and Mechanic,' and 'The State Chronicle. A brilliant young man, whose untimely end carried grief not only to his own family but to thousands of the best people of North Carolina. He would no doubt have been the next governor of North Carolina." He was a member of the legislature from Charlotte, Mecklenburg county. He was a brilliant, fearless writer,—never hinted, but said exactly what he thought, and stood by his convictions to the bitter end. No man of his years was ever beloved by North Carolinians more than he, and his memory is held most sacred by all the best people of the State, most of whom contributed to, and erected a handsome monument over his resting place in Raleigh, N. C. "His mother, Martha Ann Abbott, of Boston, Mass., was of a very large and widely connected family and most distinguished ancestry throughout that region and in London."

5. *Melancthon Schneider Shotwell*, b. 10 Apr., 1845, W. Liberty, Ohio Co., [W.] Va.; grad. from Princeton college, 1872; dw. Harrisburg, Pa.; occupation, car-builder and architect, manufacturer of "Shotwell's patent steel car-replacer;" address N. Front St., Harrisburg. To him we are indebted for much of the data here presented relating to this branch. He m. 28 Apr., 1887, Caroline Reily Porter, dau. of Dr. Geo. W. Porter, niece of Gen. Horace Porter of New York City, and Judge Wm. Porter of Philadelphia, and granddaughter of ex-Gov. David Rittenhouse Porter, who was a. of Gen Andrew Porter of the revolution.

6. *Dr. Frederick Addison Shotwell*, b. 14 Feb., 1847, W. Liberty, [W.] Va.; dw. Rogersville, Tenn.; m. 20 Sept., 1877, Lucy A. Kyle, dau. of Judge A. A. Kyle, of Rogersville, Hawkins, Co., Tenn.

7. *Ruth Eliza*, b. 3 Aug., 1849, W. Liberty, [W.] Va., and there d. in early childhood.

8. *Susan Janet*, (twin of Ruth Eliza), b. 3 Aug., 1849; d. young; buried at W. Liberty, [W.] Va.

Dr. Nathan Shotwell, 1806-1890, Presbyterian minister, of West Liberty, Va., (now W. Va.), afterwards for 15 years at Rutherfordton, N. C., and finally at Rogersville, Tenn., s. of Randolph and Mary H. (Gage) Shotwell of Newark, N. J., m. (3) at Milton, Pa., 23 Sept., 1852, *Mary L. McCleery*, who d. 28 Sept., 1853, and had:

9. *Mary McCleery Shotwell*, ·b. ———; 1853, Milroy, Mifflin Co., Pa.; d. young, buried at Milroy, Pa.

10. *McCleery Junkin Shotwell*, b. 8 Aug., 1855, Milroy, Pa.; dw. Knoxville, Tenn.; m. 1881, Sarah M. Hardwick, who d. 14 March, 1894.

Nathan[7] Shotwell, b. 1813, of Frankford, Mo., s. of John[6] and Sally (Burroughs) Shotwell of Mason Co., Ky., [of John[5], John[4], Abr[3]. ?, John[2], Abr[1].], m. 1834, *Catharine Geery*, 1813-1870, dau. of John and Elizabeth (Guthery) Geery, and had:

1. *Margaret Ann*, b. 27 June, 1835, d. 9 Aug., 1836.

2. *Emily*, b. 21 May, 1837; d. 2 July, 1889; m. 24 March, 1859, James Martin.

3. *John W.*, b. 28 June, 1839; d. 15 May, 1893; m. 24 May, 1876, Sarah Beckelheimer.

4. *Andrew M.*, b. 14 May, 1842; d. 16 Sept., 1845.

5. *Hiram*, b. 27 July, 1844; d. 7 May, 1849.

6. *David*, b. 12 Sept., 1846; d. 3 Jan., 1860.

7. *Mary*, b. 18 Aug., 1849, d. 16 Sept., 1885; m. 11 May, 1882, Warren S. Worsham.

8. *Sarah*, b. 9 Nov., 1850; d. 21 July, 1881; m. 8 Nov., 1868, Warren S. Worsham.

9. *Perry*, b. 6 March, 1853, d. 22 July, 1853.

NATHAN[7] SHOTWELL, b. 1826, of Concord, Jackson Co., Mich., formerly of Elba, Genesee Co., N. Y., s. of Isaac M[6]. and Edna C. (Pound) Shotwell, of Elba, formerly of Farmington, N. Y., [of Richard[5], Benjamin[4], John[3], John[2], Abraham[1]], m. 1850, *Bathsheba Phebe Gardner*, called Phebe B., b. 1831, dau. of George Washington[5] and Diana (Berry) Gardner, of Elba, N. Y., [of John[4], John[3], Wm[2]., George[1]], and had:

1. *Rozilla Phebe*, called Lilla P., b. 1 of 3 mo., 1851, in the log house in Elba, N. Y., to which on the day previous, her parents had removed from the G. Washington Gardner estate, and upon the place which was sold by her father one year later to Thomas Grayham, and which afterward came into the possession of the late Ambrose Douglass. She was a thoughtful, earnest child, fond of the beautiful in nature and in art. To the elementary education afforded in the primary schools of the neighborhood, she added several terms of academic training at her parents' *alma mater* in Careyville (now Oakfield), and at the union school in Concord, Mich. Having a taste for active and independent pursuits, she for a number of years owned and tilled several acres of land near the parental homestead, in Jackson Co., Mich. In 1875-6, she revisited her native neighborhood, whence seven years earlier the family had removed to their present residence in Concord, Mich. From 1876 to 1878 she kept house for and otherwise assisted her blind brother, Ambrose M., while prosecuting his studies at Ypsilanti. For several years thereafter, while aiding her mother in household cares at Concord, she kept bees and practiced portrait painting with a good degree of success. In the autumn and winter of 1885-6, she continued her art studies in Chicago under the instruction of Mr. C. F. Greiner. In Sept., 1886, she entered upon the duties of homekeeper in the family of her sister, in which capacity she was chiefly employed for several years. To her proficiency as her youngest brother's chief assistant bee-keeper and her skill as portrait painter, she added in 1896 the art of photography, under the tuition of D. J. Cook of Concord, Mich.

2. *Ambrose Milton*, b. 30 of 5 mo., 1853, in the house owned and occupied by his father from 1852 to 1857, and which is yet standing on the ridge in the northwestern part of the town of Elba, N. Y. The precise date of his birth is differently given in different records, varying from the 28th to the 31st of the month. At the early age when children begin to notice objects this child was seen to observe only the window,

the sunshine, the flame of a candle and other bright lights. For the optic nerve atrophe, hence inferred and which has proved only too persistent, no cause either immediate or prenatal was known, and no remedy has been found, but on the contrary the partial sight which he enjoyed during childhood has gradually declined to almost total blindness; nevertheless at the usual age, the boy was sent to the common district school in the neighborhood; and through the thoughtful aid and kind encouragement of teachers and classmates, as well as of his parents and elder sister, he made rapid progress in such branches as it was thought he could successfully pursue. He manifested great fondness for mathematical and scientific studies. He was a pupil in the N. Y. State Institution for the Blind at Batavia, from its first opening, 2 Sept., 1868, until June, 1873, when he delivered the valedictory. His revered preceptor, the late Dr. Asa D. Lord, certified that, "As a scholar, he ranked among the first in all his studies, and his deportment was invariably such as to command the esteem and confidence of all."

At Concord, Mich., where he had spent a portion of each summer vacation, he engaged for about two years in the manufacture of corn brooms, which trade he had learned at Batavia, and which he then taught for one year, 1875-6, to the young men in the Wisconsin Institution for the Blind at Janesville, where, during the same year, he acquired the art of cane chairseating. In the autumn of 1876, he entered the State Normal School at Ypsilanti, Mich., and two years later, having taught with success in the school of observation and practice, he was regularly graduated from the full English course.

In 1878-9, he successfully labored to secure the establishment of a separate school for the blind in Michigan, apart from the deaf and dumb, drafting, with his brother Manly's assistance, the bill (House Bill No. 13), introduced on 9 Jan., 1879, by Representative S. A. Strong, and which, in a modified form, subsequently became a law. In the summer of 1879, he acted as secretary of the first reunion of the officers, teachers and pupils of the N. Y. State Institution for the Blind, and prepared the report of its proceedings for publication in pamphlet form. He conducted for two years, 1879-81, a small bi-monthly paper in the interest of the blind; taught acceptably for three years, 1880-83, in the Arkansas School for the Blind; was for several years engaged in the book and news trade at Concord; for five years, 1887-92, acted as a voluntary observer for the Michigan weather service; and in the autumn of 1892, entered the Michigan School for the Blind, at Lansing, for the purpose of mastering the art of piano tuning and repairing, under the instruction of his friend and former associate,

Manly N. Shotwell

Son of Nathan and Phebe B. (Gardner Shotwell, of Concord, Mich., and
the compiler's chief assistant in the preparation of the "Annals
of our colonial ancestors and their descendants."

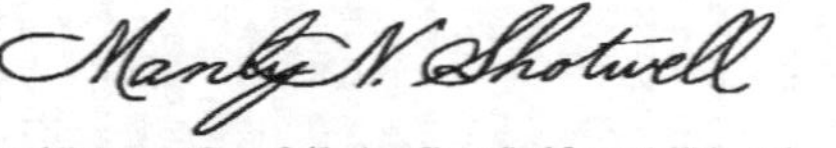

MISS LILLA P. SHOTWELL,

Daughter of Nathan[1] and Phebe B. Gardner Shotwell, of Concord.
Mich., and sister to the compiler of the Family Annals.

Mr. A. C. Blakeslee. And upon the introduction there of the American Braille (point) system of embossed writing and printing in the winter of 1893–4, he was appointed, and has since remained, as chief stereotype-maker for the school, an instrument, somewhat resembling a typewriter in essential structure, having been recently invented for the purpose of stamping upon metal plates, zinc or brass, the arbitrary groups of dots now extensively used by the blind to denote letters, figures, marks of punctuation, and certain short words and other combinations of letters of very frequent recurrence. From these embossed plates, lesson leaves, school text-books, and other literature for the use of sightless readers are printed in small editions and at comparatively little cost, as they may be needed for use in the school.

In the summer of 1886, he commenced the compilation of the present historico-genealogical account of his ancestors and their descendants, and two years later made a tour to New Jersey, New York, and Ontario, for the purpose of collecting materials for this record. He carried with him his New York point tablet, an apparatus by which he was enabled to write down in raised characters, and afterward read by the sense of touch, any information that might be communicated to him orally.

3. *Cassius Emmett*[2], b. 29 of 7 mo., 1855, Elba, N. Y., in the frame house on the ridge in the northern part of the town, built about 1835–6, by his father's cousin, Richard L. Aldrich, where also the older brother and younger sister were born. He early manifested a taste for barter and exchange and those firm and active traits that have often served to protect his interests and those of his friends in cases where people of less alertness and energy would have suffered loss. On 28 Nov., 1871, he left home and spent a little more than a year in Cook and DuPage counties, Ill., returning home in Jan., 1873; and for several years thereafter he continued to dig and repair wells, deal in pumps, notions, picture-frames, poultry and other property of various kinds, grafted and pruned apple orchards, and engaged in various minor enterprises. Since 1873, he has lived chiefly in Concord, but has made repeated journeys to Illinois and Wisconsin, and one in 1880, to Texas, whence he brought back a car load of horses. In the autumn of 1882, he engaged in the retail meat trade at Concord, and in the summer of the following year formed a partnership with Franklin A. Carpenter a hardware dealer. In the same year they erected the brick store on the east side of Main St., Concord. A few months later they disposed of their meat market and shortly afterward of their hardware stock, Cassius taking in exchange for the latter, his present residence on Hanover St. He has since manufactured picture frames in connection with various other minor pursuits. His

21

appreciation of the value of money has long been unmistakable, and in following out his business instincts, he has been active and enterprising.

He m. at the M. E. parsonage, Hanover, Mich., 19 Aug., 1885, Edith Myrtle Briggs, b. 5 Feb., 1866, in the northern part of the Tp. of Concord, Jackson Co., Mich., about two and one-half miles southwest of the village of Parma, dau. of Wm. C. and Elizabeth (Lewis) Briggs, of N. Concord, [of Richmond[3], Pardon[2], John[1]]. Her great-grandfather, Pardon[2] Briggs, s. of John and Zilpha (Madison) Briggs, of Connecticut, was b. there 9 June, 1783, removed with his family in 1830, to Livonia, Wayne Co., Mich., and there d. 28 Aug., 1861; m. Betsey Cook, b. 7 Jan., 1782, in Rhode Island, d. in Livonia, Mich., .. May, 1847, and had seven sons and four daughters, among them Richmond[3], who was b. 9 May, 1812, in the town of Sheldon, Wyoming Co., N. Y.; served for nine days about 1832, in the Michigan militia under Col. Holbrook, in the Blackhawk War; bought a farm of 160 acres in Sec. 2 in the Tp. of Spring Arbor (now Concord), Jackson Co., Mich., whither he removed in 1836, and there d. 28 Mar., 1891, having the respect and confidence of his neighbors. He was in 1872 elected justice of the peace, which office he continued to hold until 1881, when, on declining a renomination, his son William C., was chosen as his successor.

Richmond[3] Briggs m. (1) in Concord, Mich., 10 Apr., 1839, Caroline M. Chapman, b. 10 Apr., 1819, d. N. Concord, 13 Apr., 1843, dau. of Jesse and Belinda (Comstock) Chapman, by whom he had two sons, Wm. C[4]. and George W. He m. (2) 4 June, 1843, Mary Swift, b. 9 Feb., 1810, dau. of Theodosius and Polly (Winchester) Swift, by whom he had one dau., Louisa D., wife of Andrew LaFleur, of Parma, Mich.

William Cortland[4] Briggs, [of Richmond[3], Pardon[2], John[1]], was b. 19 Dec., 1840, at N. Concord, Mich., and there d. suddenly, 6 Nov., 1889; m. 25 Dec., 1860, Elizabeth Lewis, b. 4 Nov., 1839, Alden, Ingham Co., Mich., dau. of Jacob and Jane (Phillips) Lewis, by whom he had three daughters. (1.) Caroline Mary, b. 25 Nov., 1863; m. 15 Sept., 1880, Albert A. Peck, now of Wheatfield, Mich. (2.) Edith Myrtle, b. 5 Feb., 1866, in the old log house N. Concord, where her parents continued to reside until 1884; m. 19 Aug., 1885, Cassius E. Shotwell, as before stated. (3.) Nellie Elizabeth, b. 3 Oct., 1874.

4. *Ida Ann*[2], b. on 26th anniversary of her mother's birth, 23 of 2 mo., 1857, in Elba, N. Y., in the house sold the same year, by her father, to Robert Weeks; she was an active and energetic child, fond of reading and study and of social companionship as well. She commenced teaching school in Pulaski, Jackson Co.,

Mich., in 1873; entered the State Normal School at Ypsilanti, in 1875, worthily completed the academic and professional studies of the full English course, including all the elective mathematical and scientific branches therein, and was graduated therefrom in June, 1879; she has since taught almost continuously at Saugatuck, and Greenville, Mich., LaPorte, Ind., Bozeman, Mont., San Diego, Cal., Memphis, Tenn., Sioux Falls, S. D., Mobile, Ala., and Chicago, Ill.; m. by Prof. Joseph Estabrook, of Olivet college, a Congregational minister, formerly principal of the State Normal School at Ypsilanti, and at this time State Supt. of Public Instruction, at the res. of her parents in Concord, Mich., 8 July, 1886, Jehiel Kittridge Davis, an active and consistent member of the Baptist church, a congenial companion, and a capable and devoted teacher, who was b. 26 of 6 mo., 1848, in Troy, Oakland Co., Mich., s. of Jehiel³ and Phebe T. (Dean) Davis, of Troy, Mich., [of Kittridge², Thomas¹]. He lived with his parents, who were members of the Society of Friends, at Troy, Mich., until 19 years of age, with the exception of a few months in 1864–65, spent chiefly at Pontiac, Mich., Poughkeepsie, (where graduated at Eastman's business college), and New York City, N. Y., attended the Michigan State Normal School in Ypsilanti, at various times from 1868 to 1875, graduating there in 1874. He was principal of the Concord, (Mich.), union school for two years, 1869–71, and subsequently taught at Caro, Birmingham, and Chelsea, Mich., Rochester, Minn., Deadwood, Dak. T., Columbia, S. C., New Orleans, La., Butte City, and Bozeman, Mont., San Diego, Cal., Memphis, Tenn., Sioux Falls, S. D., and Mobile, Alabama. In his boyhood he spent a few months among the Shakers near Cleveland, O., and in July, 1896, in company with Ida, his 2d wife, he revisited that community, but found it in a less flourishing condition than when he left it in 1860. The two years, 1882–4, passed by him in the southern states, were occupied in laboring for and among the colored people in schools sustained by the American Baptist Home Mission Society, and in 1886, he was offered the presidency of Leland University in New Orleans, but having made other engagements for the year, he declined to change his plans, although the proffered compensation was considerably greater than that which he would receive in the position that he had accepted in the educational system of Montana. He was principal of, and his wife a teacher in, the Memphis Baptist Bible and Normal Institute, (for colored people) at Cor. Wellington and Frazer Sts., Memphis, Tenn., 1888–9, the year during which its noble founder and chief benefactor, Peter Howe, was murdered at his home in Winona, Ill. And in the autumn of 1892, they accepted like positions in the Emerson Normal Institute in Mobile, Ala., and remained there two years.

His father, Jehiel⁴ Davis, of Troy, Oakland, Co., Mich., formerly of Sweden, N. Y., s. of Kittridge³ Davis, of Wilbraham, Mass., [of Thomas¹], was b. in Wilbraham, Worcester Co., Mass., 12 July, 1787, was a farmer and after 2d marriage, a member of the Society of Friends, formerly a Methodist; removed about 1832, from Sweden, N. Y., to Troy, Mich., where he dw. for more than 40 yrs., and there d. 12 of 11 mo., 1872; m. (1) 16 Oct., 1810, Lydia T. Bentley, b. 30 Nov., 1792, in New Lebanon, N. Y., d. Troy, Mich., 12 Sept., 1842, by whom he had 12 children,—Alonzo, Levinus, Mary Ann, Ann, Jehiel B., Jane, Jehiel, Jr., Philo, Maryette S., Benjamin Franklin, Patrick Henry, and Francis Asbury.

Jehiel³ Davis, m. (2) in Waterford, Oakland Co., Mich., 17 Jan., 1843, Phebe Titus Dean, b. 11 of 5 mo. 1812, in Cornwall, N. Y., d. Troy, Mich., 12 of 3 mo., 1872, dau. of Daniel and Abigail (Carpenter) Dean, Quakers, of Scottsville, Monroe Co., N. Y., and had five children, —Charles Edward, Wm. Penn, (called Wm. B.), Jehiel Kittridge⁴, George Washington, and Mary Angeline (called Angie).

J. K⁴. Davis, b. 1848, m. (1) 10 March, 1874, Alma C. Donaldson, who d. in Saline, Mich., 2 Jan., 1881, aged about 34 yrs., dau. of Wm. and Almacy (Rouse) Donaldson, of Saline, Mich., and had one dau., Grace Bel, b. 17 Aug., 1875, in Saline, Mich. He m. (2) 8 July, 1886, Ida Ann⁸ Shotwell, dau. of Nathan⁷ and Phebe B. (Gardner) Shotwell, of Concord, Mich., [of Isaac M⁶., Richard⁵, Benjamin⁴, John³, John², Abraham¹], and had a son, Jehiel Shotwell Davis, called J. S., b. 5 March, 1892, at the res. of his maternal grandparents in Concord Tp., Jackson Co., Mich.

5. *Manly Nathan,* b. 1 of 11 Mo., 1858, in the house erected by his father in 1857, upon the farm (lot 2, sec. 7., tp. 13, range 2), previously purchased from the heirs of the G. Washington Gardner estate, in the town of Elba, Genesee Co., N. Y., removed with his parents from E. Oakfield, N. Y., in 1868, to Concord, Mich., where he has continued to reside, except during the autumn and winter of 1883–4, when he spent about six months in mastering the art of telegraphy in Ann Arbor. On account of congenitally defective elbow and knee joints and contracted muscles of the hands and shoulders he is unable to perform ordinary manual labor; but by holding a flattened penstock or pencil in his mouth, he has learned to write with considerable facility; he keeps his father's accounts and his own, reads for and otherwise assists his sightless brother, reducing to a perfectly legible form from dictation or from written or printed copy, the latter's correspondence or any matter intended for publication, etc. He was able, when in practice, to receive

by telegraph and write down 25 words per minute, "solid press," and to transmit fully 30 words per minute; but the difficulties in the way of obtaining a situation with few miscellaneous duties other than those at the key, have led him to turn his attention to other pursuits; he was for several years engaged in the rearing, buying, and shipping of poultry in Concord, and afterward in the sale of windmills, pumps, etc., is also proprietor of an excellent apiary and furnishes bee-keeper's supplies to others in the vicinity. For his kind, patient, and faithful cooperation with his senior brother in the arduous task of collecting, comparing, arranging, and transcribing the records of their kindred for publication, the appreciative reader, as well as the chief compiler of these pages, is under great and grateful obligation.

> "Let misfortune ne'er unman you,
> Deem not fate hath fixed your lot;
> Only think you can, then can you;
> Think you cannot, and you'll not.

> "Not the slothful, not the tiring,
> Shall obtain the golden prize;
> But the earnest, the aspiring,
> Shall alone to greatness rise.

> "Every age and every nation
> Teems with great men,—great of heart:—
> He is great who fills his station,
> Acting well his destined part."

NATHAN TILTON[1] SHOTWELL, b. 1842, of West Plains, Mo., s. of Eden[6] and Ann Mary (Haas) Shotwell, of Bennett, Neb., [of Nathan[5], Jacob[4], Jno[3]., Jno[2]., Abr[1].], m. (1) 1869, *Lizzie Smith*, dau. of Wm. and Jennie (Hinman) Smith, and had:

1. *Jennie May*, b. 28 Feb., 1870, in Bessville, Mo., d. 22 Dec., 1891; m. in West Plains, Mo., ———, 1888±, Glenroie McQueen.
2. *Wm. Eden*, b. 8 July, 1873, Bessville, Mo.
3. *Birdie Nellie*, b. 18 June, 1875, Ravenden Springs, Ark.
4. *Nathan John*, b. 7 Dec., 1880, Powhatan, Ark.
5. *Glenna Elsworth*, b. 18 Jan., 1888, West Plains, Mo.

164. PETER[6] SHOTWELL, 1777-1845, of Rahway, N. J., s. of Isaiah[5] and Constant (Lippincott) Shotwell, of Plainfield, N. J., [of John[4], John[3], John[2], Abraham[1]], m. 1803, *Phebe[6] Vail*, 1779-1866, dau. of Abraham[5] and Margaret (Fitz Randolph) Vail, of Greenbrook, N. J., [of John[2], Samuel[1]], and had:

1. *Harriet[7]*, b. 14 of 7 mo., 1804, in Rahway, Middlesex (now Union) Co., N. J., and there d. 18 June, 1872, buried in Hazlewood cemetery; member of New York M. M. by cert. from R. and P. M. M. dated 20 of 8 mo., 1823;

had previously m. at Rahway Friends meeting house, 26 of 12 mo., 1822, Joseph Williams Allen, b. 15 of 6 mo., 1796, Shrewsbury, N. J., d. Rahway, N. J., s. of Joseph and Elizabeth Allen.

2. *Margaret*, b. 3 of 10 mo., 1806, d. Rahway, N. J., 31 of 12 mo., 1814.

3. *Mary[7]*, b. 2 of 2 mo., 1809, found dead in her bed at Rahway, N. J., on the morning of 26 Dec., 1876, buried at Hazlewood cemetery, became member of Friends meeting at Flushing, L. I., by cert. from R. and P. M. M., dated 19 of 7 mo., 1827, had previously m. (1) at Rahway Friends meeting house, — of 3 mo., 1826, Benjamin Douglass Perkins, who d. at Flushing, L. I., 9 of 7 mo., or 7 of 9 mo., 1831, s. of Benjamin D., Sr., and Mary (Bowne) Perkins, of New York. One account states that his grandfather was John Murray, Jr., of New York, brother to Lindley Murray, the grammarian. She m. (2) by Cornelius Lawrence, mayor of New York, 29 Apr., 1835, Ellis Middleton, of Philadelphia, b. 16 of 4 mo., 1808, drowned in Delaware river, 1844, s. of Gabriel Middleton.

4. *Edward Randolph*, b. 19 of 8 mo., 1811, Rahway, Middlesex (now Union) Co., N. J.; engaged in mercantile business with B. M. Price, at Rahway, in 1840, removed with his family in Oct., 1845, to and settled in Bennington Tp., Delaware (now Morrow) Co., Ohio; removed from Marengo, O., in Nov., 1886, to Trenton, Grundy Co., Mo., and there d. 21 of 11 mo., 1887, in the 77th year of his age, the interment took place three days later in Marengo, O., where he had resided for more than 40 years. He and the late Abel V. Shotwell of Rahway, were double cousins, and a very close intimacy had always existed between them, and though residing far apart frequently corresponded. He m. (by John Swift, mayor of Philadelphia), 9 May, 1835, Margaret Hart Shotwell, b. 14 of 7 mo., 1816, Philadelphia, Pa., d. in Marengo, O., 12 Nov., 1882, dau. of Edmund[6] and Sarah R. (Shepard) Shotwell, of Rahway, N. J., [of Isaiah[5], John[4] John[3], John[2], Abr[1].].

5. *Julia Anna[7]*, b. 7 of 10 mo., 1813, d at Rahway, N. J., 20 of 2 mo., 1841, buried in Friends ground, Rahway, N. J.; m. by Jonathan Trotter, mayor of Brooklyn, N. Y., 4 Nov., 1836, Benjamin M. Price, b. 9 of 6 mo., 1809, at Elizabethtown, N. J.; dw. at Elizabeth, N. J.

6. *Jacob Vail*, b. 11 of 4 mo., 1817, Rahway, N. J., and there d. 14 of 11 mo., 1870, in 54th year, unm. Buried in Hazlewood cemetery.

147. RALPH[6] SHOTWELL, 1773-1826, of Plainfield, N. J., s. of Jacob[5] and Bathsheba (Pound) Shotwell, [of John[4], John[3], John[2], Abraham[1]],

m. *Elizabeth Marsh*, called Betsey, who d. 1812, and had:

1. *Sarah*, b. 16 of 10 mo., 1802, Plainfield, N. J., dw. Plainfield; m. Richard Manning.

2. *Jacob*[7], b. 2 or 7 of 11 mo., 1804; removed with large family to --------, Ill.; a farmer; m. Dorcas Drake, dau. of Noe Drake, of Washingtonville, near Plainfield, N. J.

3. *Bathsheba*[7], b. 14 of 7 mo., 1807, Plainfield, N. J., d. Stanhope, Morris Co., N. J., 2 of 7 mo., 1857, aged 49 yrs., buried at Plainfield; m. Isaac Line, s. of Amos and Phebe (Vail[4]) Line, [of David[3] Vail, John[2], Samuel[1]].

4. *Mary*, b. 18 of 8 mo., 1810, Plainfield, N. J., dw. French Creek, Pa.; m. Smith Line.

RALPH[6] SHOTWELL, 1773–1826, of Plainfield, N. J., [of Jacob[7], John[4], John[3], John[2], Abr[1]], m. (2) *Osy Tingley*, dau. of Jacob Tingley, and had:

5. *John T*[7]., b. 17 of 8 m., 1813, in Plainfield, dw. --------, Ohio; m. --------

6. *Betsy*, b. 19 of 9 mo., 1815, Plainfield; m. James Bullman.

7. *Ann*[7], b. 4 of 10 mo., 1818, Plainfield, N. J., dw. there, a wid, and m. there 4 of 10 mo., 1838, Alfred Berry, 1812–1885.

8. *David*[7], b. 20 of 11 or 10 mo., 1820; dw. --------, Cal., m. (1) in Westfield, N. J., Permelia Clark; m. (2) Ann Berry, dau. of John C. and Deborah (Cock) Berry. (The mother, Deborah Cock, was b. 1810.)

RANDOLPH SHOTWELL, b. 1 June, 1774, at Woodbridge, Middlesex Co., N. J., (said to have had a brother Jonathan and sister Charlotte), dw. at Perth Amboy and Newark, N. J.; m. -------- 1800, *Mary Harriott Gage*, b. 26 Oct., 1774, at Woodbridge, N. J., dau. of Philip Gage, thought to be a son of Lord John Gage, high constable of the tower of London, and whose wife -------- *nee* Pike, is said to have been an only dau., and to have carried important messages to the American forces when a girl, on horseback. Randolph's grandson, M. S. Shotwell of Harrisburg, Pa., is authority for the statement that his father, the late Rev. Dr. Nathan Shotwell, claimed to be the nearest heir to a block in London, and was second cousin to Col. Zebulon Montgomery Pike of New Jersey, (b. 1779), the trans-Mississippi explorer and valiant soldier who led the final assault and bravely fell upon the ramparts of York (now Toronto), U. C., 27 Apr., 1813, for whom Pike's Peak and counties in ten states have been named; a kinsman also of Gen. Albert Pike, the poet and confederate commander, and of Anderson Gage of Lawrenceburgh, Ind., Judge -------- Crowell of Cleveland, O., formerly of Rahway, N. J., and others. Rev. Nathan Shotwell's family Bible mentions also Urcilla Gage, Urcilla Bogar, and has this inscription: "Cornelius Jewell of Rahway, N. J., married our cousin Sarah."

Randolph and *Mary* (*Gage*) *Shotwell*, of Perth Amboy and Newark, N. J., natives of Woodbridge, N. J., b. 1774, m. 1800, had:

1. *Nathan*, b. 15 Oct., 1806, Perth Amboy, N. J.; was a Presbyterian minister; was a member of 1st Presb. church of Newark, N. J., and there preached one of his first sermons; dw. successively in Washington Co., Pa., Ohio Co., Va. (now W. Va.), Mifflin Co., Pa., Rutherford Co., N. C., Hawkins Co., Tenn., and elsewhere; d. Rogersville, Hawkins Co., Tenn., 10 Sept., 1890, aged nearly 84 years.

"Rev. Nathan Shotwell, D. D., was a man of rare talents and character. His paternal as well as maternal lineage traces to names once prominent in English and Scottish history. He was a descendant of the English dissenters who were banished on account of their religion. They were put into an unseaworthy vessel and sent out to perish on the ocean; but when left to themselves, 'they made for the first port, where the ship was put in condition to make the voyage across the ocean by being bound together with a large copper chain. They reached the coast of New Jersey, and they called their new home Perth Amboy.' This was his (Nathan's) own birthplace. On his mother's side, he was a descendant of Lord John Gage, high constable of the Tower of London in the reign of Queen Elizabeth. His mother was a pious Presbyterian.

"After graduating with high honors at Princeton College, he entered upon a prosperous career in Louisiana; but on being converted, immediately sacrificed all the bright prospects there to take up the humbler walk of the christian ministry. Studied theology at Allegheny Seminary, Pa., for three years, and pursued this high calling with unflinching faith and zeal for more than fifty years, despite many losses (being twice entirely burned out) and other afflictions. Venerable and careworn, loving and beloved, held in highest esteem by all whoever knew him, he went to a glorious reward from Rogersville, Tenn. He was once president of Oakland College, Natchez, Miss., and president of West Liberty [W.] Va. College (which was burned), and trustee of Davidson College, N. C.

"Dr. Nathan Shotwell was certainly a man of decided intellectual force, of earnest piety and deep convictions of truth and duty. He remained up to his death in the heartiest sympathy with our beloved Zion,—with all her institutions, and he loved her old-fashioned doctrines, her polity, and her worship. Not long before his death, he said to two of his younger brethren, 'Preach the gospel,—preach the gospel while you have the opportunity!' In later years, he spent much of his time on Saturdays praying for all pastors, that they might be prepared for the work, and come up to the house of God full of the Holy Ghost and faith, in order to accomplish much for the Master. He was a man of prayer, and spent his birthdays in fasting and prayer, from the time he was 25 years old to the end, and always seemed to get the answers. He was an affectionate man, yet always dignified. It was a real pleasure to take his hand and look into his face. All his faculties remained intact to the end. As he grew in years, he grew in grace. Who can calculate the value of such a life? As an old man, he was full and strong and tender and lovable, as charming an old gentleman, both to young and old, as you ever met."

He m. (1) (by Rev. Gideon N. Judd, D. D), in Bloomfield, Essex Co., N. J., 11 Sept., 1833, Lydia Baldwin, who d. at W. Liberty, Ohio Co., [W.] Va., 30 Jan., 1840. He m. (2) (by Rev. David Brigham), at Framingham, Mass., 19 July, 1841, Martha Ann Abbott, b. 28 Nov., 1815, at Framingham, Mass.; d. at W. Liberty, [W.] Va., 23 Sept., 1849, dau. of Josiah³ and Ruth (Easterbrook) Abbott of Framingham, Mass., [of Samuel², Samuel¹]. He m. (3) (by Rev. D. X. Junkin, D. D.), at Washington, D. C., 23 Sept., 1852, Mary Lytle McCleery, of Milton, Pa., who d. at Milroy, Mifflin Co., Pa. 28 Sept., 1855. He m. (4) (by Rev. O. M. Todd), at New Lisbon, Ohio., 16 Aug., 1859, Rebecca Prudence Thompson, b. 26 Nov., 1816, at New Lisbon, O.; d. 23 Sept., 1895, Rogersville, Hawkins Co., Tenn., dau. of Hon. W. Thompson, M. C.

2. *Edmund Kinsley Shotwell*, [s. of Randolph and Mary H. (Gage) Shotwell of Newark, N. J.], was b. 28 Aug., 1808, at Perth Amboy, N. J.; dw. Lawrenceburgh, Ind., d. --------; 1842.

3. *Olivia Harriet Watts*, b. 9 Sept., 1810, in New York City; d. at Elizabeth, N. J., 4 Dec., 1886.

4. *Jane Pike*, b. 4 Nov., 1812, Newark, N. J.,; d. 4 June, 1854, unm.

5. *Geo. Washington*, b. 8 Apr., 1815, Newark, N. J.; whereabouts unknown.

6. *Charlotte*, b. 30 Apr., 1817, Newark, N. J.; d. 30 Oct., 1817.

7. *Ann Pike*, b. 7 Jan., 1819, Newark, N. J.; d. .. Jan., 1819.

90. RICHARD⁵ SHOTWELL, 1756-1833, of Essex Co., N. J., Ontario and Genesee counties, N. Y., s. of Benjamin⁴ and Ame (Hallet) Shotwell, of Shotwell's Landing, N. J., [of John³, John², Abraham¹], m. 1782, *Mary Martin*, 1756-1844, dau. of Isaac and Elizabeth (Burling) Martin, of New York, and had:

1. *Elizabeth*, b. 12 of 1 mo., 1783, d. young.

2. *Amy⁶*, b. 4 of 10 mo., 1784, d. 20 of 10 mo., 1858, in Elba, Genesee Co., N. Y., having lived there about 40 yrs., dw. in Farmington, N. Y., when she there m. in a public meeting of Friends, 1 of 8 mo., 1805, Wanton Aldrich, b. 4 of 4 mo., 1780, in Northbridge, Worcester Co., Mass., d. Lenawee Co., Mich., at the home of his dau. Eliza Ann O'Dell, 5 of 8 mo., 1870, aged 90 yrs., buried in Friends' ground three

miles north of Adrian, s. of Asa and Susannah Aldrich, of Palmyra, N. Y.; he was in Ontario Co., N. Y., as early as 6 mo., 1802; removed from Junius, N. Y., in 1818, to the Holland Purchase, settling in the town of Batavia (now Elba), Genesee Co., N. Y., acquiring title to his homestead there, lot 2, sec. 3, about one-half mile west of Lancton's Corners, by deed from the Holland Co., dated 19 Nov., 1821; but he was certainly there as early as 30 July, 1819, being one of the trustees in the deed of the Friends' meeting house site and burial place of this date. He and wife Amy, and five minor children, Richard, Elizabeth, Asa, Jonathan and Mary S., became members of Farmington M. M. of Friends, by cert. from Junius M. M., dated 20 of 4 mo., 1818. After the death of his wife, he removed with his youngest dau., Eliza A., to Palmyra Tp., Lenawee Co., Mich., and there spent the remaining years of his life.

3. *Isaac Martin⁶*, b. 24 of 9 mo., 1786, in Springfield Tp., Essex (now Union) Co., N. J.; came with his parents in 1804, to Farmington, Ontario Co., N. Y., and thence with his family in 1818, to Batavia (now Elba), N. Y., locating on a farm one mile north of Pine Hill (now Elba village), purchasing the w. part of lot 7, sec. 11, town 13, range 1, by a conveyance deed dated 28 Sept., 1818, and recorded in the Genesee county clerk's office, liber 8, pp. 268-9; various additional pieces of land were subsequently purchased. The homestead was upon the west side of the Oak Orchard road a few rods south of what has long been known as Lancton's Corners,—so called from Aaron Lancton, a tanner, who about 1823, bought three small lots of Richard Shotwell, Isaac M. Shotwell and James Harris, situated upon three of the four corners, which have since borne his name, and whence in Dec., 1838, he removed to Wheatville, in the town of Alabama, N. Y., where in his 89th year he was visited by the writer in the autumn of 1888.

Isaac M. Shotwell was partially deaf and an invalid for many years; he d. at his res. in Elba, N. Y., 19 of 10 mo., 1860, aged 74 years, 25 days. Thousands in western New York are indebted to him for his skill and enterprise in the improvement of fruit by means of top grafting, as he was the first man who successfully introduced the practice into that part of the State. He and his family were birthright members of the Society of Friends and bore a prominent part in establishing and sustaining that branch of the christian church in Genesee Co. The first Batavia (now Elba) Friends meeting house was of log; but in 1834, the present stone structure was erected. A log schoolhouse also stood upon the meeting house lot, but this was destroyed by fire about 1823, and school was for a time kept in the meeting house: At the separation in 1828, the property remained in the possession of the orthodox society. The less numerous body held meetings for a time in an old house on the Sleeper place about one-half mile farther west, but soon built a meeting house on the estate of J. Hazard Gardner about one-half mile east of the present hamlet of East Oakfield, which after the suspension of the Hicksite Friends Meetings, was moved upon the adjoining farm recently purchased by Stephen Vail, and was long occupied as a dwelling.

Isaac M. was of Farmington, N. Y., when he there m. in a public meeting of Friends, 4 of 2 mo., 1813, Edna C. Pound, b. 2 of 1 mo., 1796, in Piscataway Tp., Middlesex Co., N. J., d. at the res. of her 2d son, Hugh P. Shotwell, in Elba, N. Y., 14 of 1 mo., 1872, of erysipelas, aged 76 years and 12 days, dau. of Hugh⁵ and Sarah (King) Pound, of Farmington, N. Y., [of Samuel⁴, Elijah³, John², John¹]. She distinctly remembered the incidents of the 14 days' journey taken by her parents, herself and brothers Nathan and Wm., when she was but seven years of age, in removing from the vicinity of Plainfield, N. J., to Ontario Co., N. Y.; it was made with two horse team, and covered wagon through deep mud and unbridged streams, the father forced at times to cut his road as he advanced. To make seven miles a day required in some instances the utmost diligence and hard labor. The writer has heard her relate that when in the vicinity of Cayuga lake, a band of warlike aborigines was encountered in full paint. With clubs uplifted they rushed out of the woods some distance ahead of the emigrants and arrayed themselves in a menacing attitude across the way as if contemplating mischief. The wife and children, as was natural, were greatly terrified, but the sturdy friend of the red man, in a calm and assured manner, continued to approach the savages, and when within easy speaking distance kindly greeted them speaking the familiar salutation, "shago shago! (how do-do) boys! you'll scare my horses." Whereupon, the Indians recognizing a friend, a man of peace, their fierce countenances relaxed, they threw down their clubs, came forward, shook hands in a very cordial manner, and after a pleasant conversation with these boasters of military prowess, the disciple of Penn, with his family and possessions, was permitted to pass on unharmed.

In 1818, Edna C., with her infant dau., Mary S., revisited her native place in New Jersey, after an absence of fifteen years, and later in the same year removed with her husband and daughters, Anna P. and Mary S., to the Holland Purchase as before stated. Both in Farmington and Elba, they were made unpleasantly familiar with the growl of the bear, the howl of the wolf, and the scream of the panther; but lived to witness a great transformation in the face of the country. After the death of her husband, in 1860, Edna lived mostly in the family of her son, Hugh P. Shotwell, in Elba. In the summer of 1871, she visited her sons. Nathan and David B., in Michigan, and while there had an attack of the ague.

4. *Benjamin*, b. 10 of 6 mo., 1788, d. shortly before the birth of 2d of the name, in 1793.

5. *Mary⁶*, b. 10 of 7 mo., 1790, Springfield Tp., Essex (now Union) Co., N. J., d. Farmington, near Victor, N. Y., 26 of 6 mo., 1868; m. (1) in Farmington, N. Y., 6 of 12 mo., 1812, Capt. David Smith, b. 10 of 4 mo., 1774, Gloucester, Providence Co., R. I., was elected Captain in the militia of Ontario county, under Lieut. Col. Asa Stanley, 23 May, 1811, was called out in the war of 1812, but resigned, as he said he could not draw his sword on any man. He d. W. Farmington, N. Y., 1 of 8 mo., 1842, s. of Joseph and Rhoda (Thornton) Smith, of Gloucester, R. I., and Farmington, N. Y., [of Samuel']. She m. (2) in Farmington (N. Y.), Friends meeting, 30 of 9 mo., 1852, (as 2d wife) James Peacock, b. 30 of 9 mo., 1784, in Scarborough, Yorkshire, Eng., d. Somerset, Niagara Co., N. Y., 8 of 3 mo., 1872, s. of Jonathan and Mabel Peacock.

6. *Elizabeth⁶*, b. 22 of 9 mo., 1791, in Springfield, N. J., dw., Farmington, N. Y., one-half mile north of the town house, and there d. 30 or 29 of 9 mo., 1874, aged 83 yrs.; m. in Farmington, N. Y., James Herendeen, b. 1 of 9 mo., 1788, Danby, Rutland Co., Vt., d. Farmington, N. Y., 19 of 5 mo., 1873, s. of Joshua and Pennsylvania (Herendeen) Herendeen, of Wm.]. United with Friends after marriage. The 60th anniversary of their marriage was pleasantly observed at their homestead in Farmington, N. Y.

7. *Benjamin⁶* (again), b. 10 of 4 mo., 1793, Springfield, N. J., removed about 1836-8, from Elba, N. Y., to Erie or Chautauqua Co., N. Y., and afterward to Wheatland, Monroe Co., N. Y., and there d. at the home of his dau., Desire Estes, 23 of 11 mo., 1865; was of Farmington, N. Y., when he m. in Palmyra (N. Y.), Friends Meeting, 29 of 11 mo., 1815, Sarah Hoag, b. 18 of 5 mo., 1799, d. in Wheatland, N. Y., 29 of 12 mo., 1869, dau. of Levi and Desire (Gardner) Hoag, of Palmyra, and Elba, N. Y.; after marriage they removed at once to Batavia (now Elba), N. Y., where all of their ten children were born, giving, including the parents, a birthday in every month of the year.

8. *Abbe⁶*, b. 25 of 1 mo., 1795, Mendham, Morris Co., N. J., d. at Adrian, Mich., 4 of 5 mo., 1878, she and her husband are buried in Friends ground three miles north of that city; her epitaph says she d. "May 4, 1878, aged 83 yrs., 3 mos., 19 days." She m. in Farmington (N. Y.), Friends meeting house, 23 of 2 mo., 1815, Smith Laing, of Junius N. Y., b. 18 of 11 mo., 1793, in borough of Elizabeth, Essex Co., or in Middlesex Co., N. J., d. Adrian, Mich., 1 of 5 mo., 1877, "aged 83 yrs., 5 mos., 13 days,"

buried in Friends ground, Adrian Valley, Mich., s. of Joseph' and Anna (Smith) Laing, of Seneca Co., N. Y., [of John', Samuel' ?, Wm'., John'].

The pearl wedding, or 60th anniversary of their marriage, was appropriately observed by their five surviving children, Sarah, Hannah, Joseph, Benjamin I., and Webster A., with ten of their thirteen grandchildren, and five of their eight great-grandchildren, together with thirty or forty other friends and neighbors. The Rev. A. F. Bourns, in behalf of the children, tendered the aged pair a number of well chosen presents, among them a photographic group of all their children then living, a scrap-bag, the handiwork of four grandchildren, etc. From an account of this event in the Adrian Daily Times of March 3, 1875, we gather the following particulars:

Smith Laing was b. at Plainfield, in Middlesex Co., N. J., 18 of 11 mo., 1793, removed with his parents in 1810, to Seneca Co., N. Y., settling near Waterloo, where the father secured a patent for 150 acres of forest land. After his m., Smith continued three years in Seneca Co., N. Y., whence in 1818, he removed with his family to the town of Batavia (now Elba), Genesee Co., N. Y., and there purchased 120 acres of wild land from the Holland Company, which had previously obtained from Robert Morris title to a large tract of land embracing several of the western counties of the State. In the spring of 1831 he went to Michigan prospecting, and took up from the government a quarter section of land in the Tp. of Raisin, Lenawee Co., Mich., (the farm now occupied by Stephen R. Harkness), to which one year later he moved his family, arriving at their new Michigan Home on the 8th of 7 mo., 1832, and here for the third time renewed pioneer life. Adrian was then a mere hamlet of perhaps half a dozen buildings, and the surrounding country was a great forest with here and there a log house in the midst of a little clearing.

Upon the marriage of their youngest son, Webster A., about 1856, the management of the farm was turned over to him; but when he in 1866, removed to Adrian, the parents remained for four years upon the homestead with their son, Benjamin I. When, however, the latter also moved, to the city, the parents again lived with their youngest son, Webster A., on Chestnut St., Adrian, Mich., and there spent their remaining years. According to the records of the Society of Friends, they and two minor children, Sarah Maria and Amy, having removed to the Holland Purchase, became members of Farmington M. M., by cert. from Junius M. M., dated 25 of 5 mo., 1818.

9. *Lydia*, b. 17 of 1 mo., 1797, who d.

10. *Sarah*, b. 5 of 3 mo., 1799, Mendham, Morris Co., N. J., d. in Lenawee Co., Mich., 8 of 12 mo., 1884, buried in Friends ground near Adrian; m. (1) 22 of 2 mo., 1821, Jacob Hoag, Jr., b. 8 of 8 mo., 1799, Cœymans, Albany Co., N. Y., dw. Elba, N. Y., a short distance east of Lancton's Corners, whence, with his family, he removed in 1831, to Raisin Tp., (formerly Logan), Lenawee Co., Mich., locating on the farm next east of that purchased the same year by Sarah's brother-in-law, Smith Laing, and there d. 30 or 10 of 5 mo., 1815, s. of Jacob and Elizabeth (Palmer) Hoag, of Dutchess and Wayne counties, N Y., [of Benjamin'], she m. (2) 20 of 2 mo., 1848, Nathan Chase. who d. Adrian, Mich., 30 of 5 mo., 1858, aged 67, member of Adrian M. M. by cert. from Farmington M. M., dated 27 of 11 mo., 1834, and at time of his death was an elder in the Adrian Friends Meeting, and his seat in meeting was seldom vacant except in illness.

SYNOPSIS OF THE CHILDREN AND GRANDCHILDREN OF RICHARD' SHOTWELL, OF ELBA, N. Y., [OF BENJAMIN', JOHN³, JOHN², ABRAHAM¹].

1. *Elizabeth*, b. 1783, d. young. (See No. 6).

2. *Amy*, 1784-1858, m. 1805, Wanton Aldrich, 1780-1870, [of Asa', Samuel', Seth', Jacob², George'], and had: (1.) Richard Levi, 1806-1876, m. 1827, Bathsheba S. Willson, 1809-1895, [of Asa]. (2.) Elizabeth, 1807±-1824. (3.) Asa, 1810-1892, m. (1) 1833, Abigail (Hoag) Robson, [of Levi Hoag]; m. (2) Susan Y. Fowler, 1825-1884. (4.) Isaac Martin, 1812-1812. (5.) Jonathan, b. 1813, m. (1) --------------; m. (2) 1840, Permela P. Mills, b. 1819. (6.) Mary S., 1815-1887, m. Thomas A. Slocum, b. 1810. (7.) Susannah, 1819-1887, m. (1) Michael Brininstool; m. (2) William Zaibel, or Seibel. (8.) Amy, 1822-1824. (9.) Isaac Martin, b. 1824, m. Betsey Sisson. (10.) Elizabeth Ann, called Eliza Ann, b. 1827, m. (1) 1850, Jacob Clayton; m. (2) 1858, Charles Odell, who d. 1894.

3. *Isaac Martin*, 1786-1860, of Elba, N. Y., m. 1813, Edna C. Pound, 1796-1872, [of Hugh', Samuel', Elijah³, John², John'], and had: (1.) Sarah P., 1814-1814. (2.) Anna P., 1815-1881, m. (1) 1830 Benjamin Hoag, d. 1831±, [of Levi], m. (2) 1833, Stephen Dillingham, 1809 1881, [of Silvanus]. (3.) Mary S, 1817-1893, m. 1839, John Reed, 1807-1888, [of Seley]. (4.) Isaac Martin, Jr., b. 1819, m. (1) 1843, Elvira L. Scofield, 1823-1852, [of Martin]; m. (2) 1854, Delia A. Mattice, b. 1825, [of Peter]. (5) Amy, 1821-1850. (6.) Hugh P., b. 1825, m. 1850, Hannah Haines, b. 1830, [of Reuben², Jesse']. (7.) Nathan', b. 1826, m. 1850, Phebe B. Gardner, b. 1831, [of George Washington', John', John', William², George']. (8.) Sarah Edna, 1830-1854.

(9.) David Benjamin, b. 1833, m. (1) 1860, Adaliza J. Wilder, 1839-1870; m. (2) 1880, Margery A. (McPherson) Mason, b. 1845. (10.) Catharine E., 1836-1857.

4. *Benjamin*, 1788-1793. (See No. 7).

5. *Mary⁶*, 1790-1862, m. (1) David Smith, b. 1774, and had: (1.) David Philander, 1814-1820±. (2.) Rebecca Thorn, 1819-1894; m. 1840, William Gray Lapham, [of John]. (3.) David Waterman, m. 1847, Lydia Cary, b. 1828. (4.) John Harvey, 1826-1852, m. 1850, Mary Jane Ferguson. (5.) Rhoda Mary, 1829-1859, m. 1850, Allen P. DeVol, b. 1825±. (6.) Isaac Benjamin, b. 1831, m. 1862, Rebecca S. Avery.

6. *Elizabeth⁶*, 1791-1874, m. James Herendeen, 1788-1873, [of Joshua², William¹], and had: (1.) Welcome, 1814-1816. (2.) Pennsylvania, called Vania, 1816-1888, m. 1839, Hartshorn Willson, 1818±-1888, [of David]. (3.) Mary, H., b. 1819, m. 1861, Benjamin Estes, Jr., 1811-1888, [of Benj.]. (4.) Richard Hallett, 1822-1875, m. 1855, Mary G. Bosworth, b. 1830, [of Seth and Catharine (Pound) Bosworth]. (5.) Elizabeth S., b. 1825. (6.) Amy Ann, b. 1829. (7.) James Wilkinson, b. 1831, m. Mary Alice Browning.

7. *Benjamin⁶*, 1793-1865, m. 1815, Sarah Hoag, 1799-1869, [of Levi and Desire (Gardner) Hoag], and had: (1.) David S., 1817-1872, m. 1838, Eliza S. Dillingham, b. 1820, [of Silvanus², John¹]. (2.) Desire, b. 1818, m. 1838, Robert Estes, 1814-1877, [of Benj.]. (3.) Bathsheba, 1820-1875, m. Edward Sherman. (4.) Mary Jane, b. 1822, m. Addison Smith, d. 1878. (5.) Richard, 1824-1832. (6.) Levi S., b. 1827, m. Sarah Estes, [of Allen]. (7.) Abigail, 1829-1858, m. Isaac Cox, b. 1825±, [of James⁶, Samuel⁵, Joseph⁴ Cock, Samuel³, Henry², James¹]. (8.) Benjamin H., b. 1832, m. ----------------. (9.) Sarah A., 1833-1853. (10.) Isaac M., b. 1835, m. Mary P. Estes, [of Allen].

8. *Abbe⁶*, 1795-1878, m. 1815, Smith Laing, 1793-1877, [of Joseph⁵, John⁴, Samuel³ ?, Wm²., John¹], and had: (1.) Sarah Maria, b. 1815, m. (1) 1834, David Harkness, who d. 1850; m. (2) 1856, Riley Harris, who d. 1864; m. (3) 1879, Abram Grant. (2.) Amy, 1817-1835, m. 1834, John Jay Doty. (3.) Phebe Ann, 1819-1845, m. 1841, Samuel Leeds. (4.) Hannah, b. 1823, m. 1845, Stephen Zeno. (5.) Joseph Smith, b. 1825, m. 1852, Jennette, or Jane⁴, Moultrop. (6.) Mary S., 1828-1838. (7.) Benjamin I., b. 1834, m. 1855, Mary Jane Cone. (8.) Webster Abram, 1836-1851, m. 1856, Almira A. Haviland, [of Charles].

9. *Lydia*, b. 1797.

10. *Sarah⁶*, 1799-1884, m. (1) Jacob Hoag, Jr., 1799-1845, and had: (1.) Elizabeth P., 1822-1845, m. 1843, Joseph Gibbons. (2.) Richard N., 1823-1830. (3.) Mary S., b. 1825, m. Seneca Haviland. (4.) Jacob Smith, 1828-

1817. (5.) Richard M., b. 1830. (6.) Sarah Jane, 1836-1880, m. 1858, Enoch D. Strang. (7.) Amy Ann, b. 1839, m. 1862, Joseph McRay.

280. ROBERT⁶ SHOTWELL, b. 1784, s. of Manning⁵ and Mary (Clarkson) Shotwell, [of Benj⁴., John³, Daniel², Abr¹.], m. 1812 *Martha⁷ Fitz Randolph*, b. 1796, dau of Jas⁶., and Keziah (Kelly) F. Randolph, [of Jeremiah⁵, Jeremiah⁴, Joseph³, Jos²., Edward¹], and had:

1. *Margaret⁷*, b. 29 March, 1812; m. 1833, Nicholas Mundy.

2. *Freeman⁷*, b. 26 Sept., 1814; d 13 April, 1893; m. 29 Sept., 1836, Nancy Nott, b. 5 Nov., 1817, d. 25 Oct., 1885.

3. *Manning⁷*, b. 17 Oct., 1816; m. 2 of 4 mo., 1838, Lucy Ann Cannon.

4. *Ann Maria*, b. 13 Sept., 1819; d. -----, 1823.

5. *Jas. F. R⁷.*, b. 13 Apr., 1822, married five times; m. (1) Julia Caroline Welch.

6. *Wm. B⁷.*, b. 13 March, 1824; m. 30 May, 1847, Phebe Compton, dau. of James of Perth Amboy, N. J.

7. *Mary E.*, b. 22 March, 1826; m (1) ------------; m. (2) -------------; m. (3) Andrew J. Clarkson.

8. *Robert C.*, b. 18 June, 1828; d. -------, 1831.

9. *Martha Ann*, b. 2 Aug., 1830; m. Geo. Goodwin.

23. SAMUEL¹ SHOTWELL, 1723-1777, of Rahway, Essex (now Union) Co., N. J., s. of John³, Jr., and Mary (Thorne) Shotwell of Shotwell's Landing, N. J., [of John², Abr¹.], m. 1748-9, *Ame* -------- of Mamaroneck, N. Y., who d. 29 Oct., 1762, and had:

1. *Caleb⁵*, b. 1 Dec. (?), 1749, at Rahway, in borough of Elizabeth, Essex (now Union) Co., N. J., was educated for an astronomer, was piously inclined and occasionally spoke in Friends meeting; but on the breaking out of the Revolutionary War, it is said that he enlisted in the American army and served as a soldier seven years and nine months. His parents were tories and nearly disinherited him, giving to his younger brother, David, the bulk of their confiscated real estate, which, in consideration of his mother's remonstrance, Caleb had restored to them. This partiality so wrought upon his mind and disheartened him, that he was not really himself afterward. Disposing of his 40 acres of marsh and his sloop, all he received from his father's estate, he bought a tract of nearly 500 acres, mostly wild land, in Sussex Co., N. J.; he afterward, about 1796, wandered to Balston, Saratoga Co., N. Y., and devoted his energies to the invention of a perpetual motion and supposed he had really succeeded, but after running 36 hours it stopped. It is said 500 people saw it in motion, though

the country was quite new and sparcely settled. He sent for his family in N. J., but little is known of his later history, as he wandered off and disappeared, his mind being doubtless deranged from intense application, disappointments, etc. When last heard from he was in Onondaga Co., N. Y. He m. Phebe (Hinckston) Gliddon, a wid. who d. in Centreville, Allegany Co., N. Y., about 1819-20.

He is said to have been greatly depressed by his parents' partiality, etc., and never fully regained his vivacity and mental equilibrium; and his children seemed impressed by their father's discouragement and there was a lack of animation so needful to make life useful and happy. But if the record that his mother died 29 Oct., 1762, be correct, the tradition reported by his grandson, Rev. John M². Shotwell, of Wayne Co., N. Y., (pp. 130 and 168), requires modification, at least in so far as relates to his having complied with her expressed wishes for the restoration of his parents' confiscated property. His name does not appear on the printed roll of the New Jersey soldiers who served in the Revolutionary War, nor in the roll of revolutionary pensioners; but the records of the Record and Pension Office of the War Department at Washington, D. C., shows that Caleb Shotwell served as a private in Capt. James Lawrie's Company, 1st Regiment of West Jersey Troops, commanded by Col. Wm. Maxwell, in the Revolutionary War; and, while the collection of Revolutionary War records on file in that bureau is far from complete, his name appears on the roll for the period from Oct. 28, 1777, to Jan. 15, 1778' which bears the remark, "Enlisted Nov. 13, 1775."

The dates of death of Samuel' and wife, Amy, have been obtained from an old bible in the possession of George T. Fish of Rochester, N. Y., which was used not only for their family record but also by their daughter, Elizabeth⁵ (Shotwell) Bills, for the record of her family; and as she was fifteen years old at the time of the Declaration of Independence she would probably have known if the dates of death of her parents were far out of the way. The date of her mother's death is a sufficient contradiction of the most romantic portion of the tradition referred to above. The remainder, like most traditions, may have little foundation. Quite likely the father was sorely distressed by his son's abandonment of the principles of peace, so dear to members of the Society of Friends. Samuel's granddaughter, Sarah D. (Bills) Fish, distinctly remembered that her mother told her of receiving little from her father's estate; also of the raids of both armies to which the people of New Jersey were subjected during the Revolutionary War, and of the fact that some of them buried their silverware and some other valuables and left them until the war was over.

22

2. *Thomas*, b. 22 of 2 mo. (April), 1752, Rahway, N. J., d. 9 of 11 mo., 1754.
3. *Sarah*⁵, b. 28 of 5 mo. (July), 1754, Rahway, Essex Co., N. J.; d. unm.
4. *Mary*, b. 26 of 7 mo., [record in family bible of later date, says Sept.], 1756, Rahway, N. J.
5. *David*⁵, b. 25 Feb., 1759, d. before 1798; was of Elizabeth, N. J., when he m. 24 of 6 mo., 1779, Elizabeth' Fitz Randolph, b. 23 of 2 mo., 1756, dau. of Hartshorne (b. 1723) and Ruth (Dennis) Fitz Randolph, [of Edward³ (b. 1670) and Catharine *nee* Hartshorne, Nathaniel² (b. 1642) and Mary *nee* Holley, Edward' and Elizabeth *nee* Blossom].
6. *Elizabeth*⁵, b. 28 of 7 mo., 1761; d. 10 of 8 mo., 1826; m. 1782±, (as 1st wife) Thomas Bills, b. 25 of 12 mo., 1760, Shrewsbury, Monmouth Co., N. J., d. 23 Oct., 1845, s. of Gershom and Margaret (Chamberlin) Bills; became members of Farmington M. M. of Friends.

72. SAMUEL⁵ SHOTWELL, b. 1759, of Rahway, N. J., s. of Abraham' and Mary (Potts) Shotwell, of Essex Co., N. J., [of John³, John², Abraham'], m. ------------ -----------; and had:
1. *Abigail*⁶, d. in Boston, Erie Co., N. Y., 17 of 4 mo., 1831; m. during war of 1812, (as 2d wife), Wm. Pound, b. 21 of 3 mo., 1784, in Piscataway, Middlesex Co., N. J., returned soon after this marriage to Boston, Erie Co., N. Y., where some years later he became member of Eden M. M. by cert. from R. and P. M. M., dated 23 of 2 mo., 1820. From Boston, he removed about 1845-50, to Aurora (now Elma), Erie Co., N. Y., settling on what is known as the Pound road and there d. 2 of 1 mo., 1857, s. of Samuel' and Catharine (Webster) Pound, [of of Elijah³, John², John'].

109. SAMUEL⁵ SHOTWELL, d. 1804, of Kingwood (now Quakertown), N. J., s. (?) of Abraham' and Mary (Jackson) Shotwell, of Woodbridge, N. J., [of Joseph³, Daniel², Abraham',], m. 1788, *Hannah Lundy*, of Piscataway, N. J., and had:
1. *Abraham* I'⁶, b. about 1789, went with parents that year to Hunterdon Co., N. J., becoming member of Kingwood M. M. by cert. from R. and P. M. M.
2. *Joseph*, said to have settled about seven miles from Wilkesbarre, Pa.
3. *James*, b. 30 of 5 mo., 1792, d. 1807; m. (1) Mary Van Gorder, m. (2) Sarah J. Roe.
4. *Mary*, dw. Sussex Co., N. J.; m. ------, Charles Van Gorder.
5. *Sarah*, called Sally, m. -------- Jacob Bales.

171. SAMUEL EMLIN⁶ SHOTWELL, 1793-1823, of Milton (now Rahway), N. J., s. of Isaiah⁵ and Constant (Lippincott) Shotwell, of Plainfield, [of John⁴, John³, John², Abraham'], m.

1817, *Sarah C. Rich*, dau. of Joseph and Elizabeth Rich, of Attleboro (now Langhorn), Pa., and had:

1. *Joseph Rich*, b. 3 of 12 mo., 1817, d. in Cherry St., New York, 5 of 12 mo., 1817, interred in N. Y. Friends' cemetery.

2. *Samuel Emlin*, b. 21 of 3 mo., 1819, Rahway, Middlesex Co., N. J., d. in Pa., 4 of 9 mo., 1841, unm.

3. *Elizabeth Rich*[7], b. 1 of 12 mo., 1822, Milton (now Rahway), N. J., she with her widowed mother and brother Samuel, became member of M. M. at Middletown, Pa., by cert. from R. and P. M. M., dated 20 of 5 mo., 1824; dw. 1409 N. 17th St., Philadelphia, Pa., m. in Middletown, Pa., Friends' meeting house, 17 of 2 mo., 1842, George Knorr Johnson, of Philadelphia, who d. 3 of 2 mo., 1891, s. of William and Catharine Johnson, of Philadelphia, Pa.

237. SAMUEL[6] SHOTWELL, b. 1802, of Elba and Galen, N. Y., and Ottawa, Ill., s. of Benjamin[5] and Bathsheba (Pound) Shotwell, of Wayne Co., N. Y., [of Benj[4]., John[3], John[2], Abr[1].], m. (1) 1821, *Phebe*[6] *Laing*, 1802–1824±, dau. of Joseph[3] and Anna (Smith) Laing, of Junius, N. Y., [of John[4], Samuel[3] (?), Wm[2]., John[1]], and had:

1. *Anna*, b. 14 of 6 mo., 1822, d. 30 of 9 mo., 1823.

2. *Joseph*, b. Galen, N. Y., and there d., aged about 15 years.

SAMUEL[6] SHOTWELL, b. 1802, of Elba, N. Y., and LaSalle Co., Ill., [of Benj[5]., Benj[4]., John[3], John[2], Abr[1].], m. (2) *Mercy*[3] *Pound*, dau. of Daniel[4] and Prudence (Jones) Pound, of Ridgeway, C. W., [of Elijah[3], John[2], John[1]], and had:

3. *Benjamin Franklin*, b. Elba (now Oakfield), N. Y., dw. Chicago, Ill., formerly Ottawa Ill., sp.; m. in Ill., _________ _________ Barnes.

4. *Hannah*[7], b. Elba, N. Y., dw. _________, Tex.; m. in Ill., Joseph Barnes.

5. *Sarah Elizabeth*[7], b. 20 of 1 mo., 1836, Galen, N. Y., dw. five miles from Ottawa, Ill., m. Aaron Barnes, brother to Joseph.

6. *Phebe Ann*, b. Galen, N. Y., was a hydropathic physician, studied under Dr. Troll, in N. Y. City, d. in Ill, unm.

7. *Emily*, b. Galen, N. Y.; died in Ill., s. p.

8. *Lydia*, d. in Ill.

211. SAMUEL[5] SHOTWELL, of Warren Co., N. J., s. of Caleb[3] and Phebe (Hinckston) Shotwell, of Saratoga Co., N. Y., [of Samuel[4], John[3], John[2], Abr[1].], m. _________________, and had quite a numerous family, of whom, however, we have not been able to obtain records.

REV. SAMUEL RANDALL[7] SHOTWELL, 1812–1853, of Saratoga and Oneida counties, N. Y., s. of Joseph[6] and Sarah (Randall) Shotwell, of Saratoga Co., N. Y., [of Caleb[5], Samuel[4], John[3], John[2], Abr[1].], m. 1842, *Patience Maria Bloss*, who d. 1853, dau. of Samuel Bloss, of Oneida Co., N. Y., and had:

1. *Samuel Bloss*[8], b. 25 July, 1845, Eaton, Madison Co., N. Y.; engineer for many years on Michigan Central railroad; afterward a farmer; dwelt Blissfield, Mich., and Napoleon, Jackson Co., Mich., whence he removed ______, m. at Fredonia, Calhoun Co. Mich., 21 Oct.; 1872, Sarah A. Lansing.

2. *Mary Jane*, b. 25 Nov., 1850, Oriskany, Oneida Co., N. Y., dw. Waco, Sedgwick Co., Kans.; m. __ April, 1874, or 1873, Wilbur A. Huff, of Caneadea, or Oramel, Allegany Co., N. Y.

SAMUEL P[7]. SHOTWELL, b. 1828, of Idana, Kans., s. of Benjamin[6] and Catharine (Pugsley) Shotwell, of Bedford, Mich., [of Benj[5]., Benj[4]., John[3], John[2]. Abr[1].], m. (1) 1851±, *Maria Watson*, of Junius, N. Y., who d. 1886, and had:

1. *Eliza B*[8]., dw. Clay Co., Kans., P. O. Clay Centre; m. Albert Wingrove, of W. Va.

2. *Mary Ellen*[8], dw. Idana, Clay Co., Kans. m. Samuel Isensee, from Pennsylvania.

3. *Celia M*[8]., dw. Idana, Kans.; m. George R. Rickert, from near Poughkeepsie, N. Y.

4. *Hattie*[8], m. Samuel Ober, of Pennsylvania.

5. *Clayton*, b. 3 Sept., 1874, Idana, Clay Co., Kans.

SAMUEL H[7]. SHOTWELL, b. 1836, of Gloversville N. Y., s. of Benjamin[6] and Mary (Hunt) Shotwell, [of Wm[4]., Benj[4]., John[3], John[2], Abraham[1]], m. 1874, *Jane Elizabeth Everit*, b. 1839, dau of Richard and Mary (Carle) Everit, and had:

1. *Marie Louise*, b. 2 Oct., 1875.

2. *Edward C.*, b. 14 May, 1877.

3. *Walter H.*, b. 24 May, 1884.

4. *Everit F.*, b. 20 April, 1886.

SAMUEL BLOSS[8] SHOTWELL, b. 1845, s. of Rev. Samuel R[7]. and Patience M. (Bloss) Shotwell, of Saratoga and Oneida counties, N. Y., [of Joseph[6], Caleb[5], Samuel[4], John[3], John[2], Abr[1].], m. 1872, *Sarah A. Lansing*, and had:

1. *Hattie May*, b. New Boston, Wayne Co., Mich.

158. SMITH[6] SHOTWELL, b. 1787, of Canada, s. of Wm[5]. and Elizabeth (Pound), Shotwell, of Upper Canada, [of John[4], John[3], John[2], Abr[1].], m. *Mary Crawford*, dau. of James and Amy (Heacock) Crawford, and had:

1. *Rachel*, b. Thorold, C. W.; d. unm.

2. *Amy*, d. unm.

3. *Phebe*, d. near Sparta, Kans., s. p.; m. in Yarmouth, C. W., James Andrew Town, who united with Yarmouth M. M. of (Hic.) Friends 9 of 4 mo., 1862; was drowned with his adopted son in Kansas, 27 of 3 mo., 1871.

4. *Martha*, d. Thorold, C. W., unm.

5. *Mary*, d. Welland, C. W., s. p.; m. in Thorold, C. W., James Bates.

6. *William*[7], b. Thorold, C. W., dw. (1879), at Sparta, McPherson Co., Kans., d. in that state; was a member of the Society of Friends; m. by Friends' ceremony in Malahide, C. W., Martha Elizabeth Taylor, who became member of Yarmouth M. M., 10 of 11 mo., 1841, by cert. and dw. (1888), Windham, McPherson Co., Kansas, formerly at Sparta, Ont., and Sparta, Kansas, dau. of John and Eliza (Shotwell[7]) Taylor, [of Elijah[4], Wm[5]., John[4], John[3], John[2], Abr[1].].

7. *Ruth*[7], dw. Toronto, Ont., d.; m. David White.

8. *James*[7], d. during the War of the Rebellion in a Union hospital or while returning therefrom; m. Matilda Seley.

9. *Elijah*, is a retired farmer; dw. Thorold, Ont., s. p., P. O. Welland; m. (1) Harriet --------; m. (2) --------------.

10. *John I*[7]., dw. Kansas, afterward (1896), Colden, Erie Co., N. Y.; thrice married.

STUART B[7]. SHOTWELL, 1819-1890, of Cadiz, O., s. of William[6] and Rhoda (Beebe) Shotwell, of Harrison Co., O., [of Hugh[5], John[4], John[3], John[2], Abraham[1]], m. 1851, *Nancy Gaston*, b. 1823, of Columbiana Co., O., dau. of James and Elizabeth (Kilgore) Gaston and granddaughter of Hugh and Grace (Gaston) Gaston and of Wm. and Nancy (Kelly) Kilgore, and had:

1. *Mary*, b. 8 May, 1853, at Cadiz, O., and there d. 2 March, 1854.

2. *Martha Beebe*, b. 2 Jan., 1855, Cadiz, O., dw. there, unm., graduated Franklin College, 1875, with highest honors of her class; is a member of Presbyterian church.

3. *Walter Gaston*[8], b. 27 Dec., 1856, Cadiz, O., graduated Franklin College, 1877, with first honors of his class, and at Yale University, June, 1878, studied law with his father, and was admitted to the bar in Oct., 1880, is a successful lawyer at Cadiz, O.; in politics a republican, was twice elected prosecuting attorney of Harrison Co., O., is a member of the Presbyterian church at Cadiz, O., m. at New Philadelphia, O., 24 Dec., 1883, Belle McIlvaine, b. New Philadelphia, O., 10 Dec., 1859, dau. of Judge Geo. W. and Caroline (Rinehart) McIlvaine of New Philadelphia, O., and granddaughter of Robert and Ann (Springer) McIlvaine, and of Joseph and Maria (Hudson) Rinehart.

4. *Stuart B*[8]., Jr., b. 9 Apr., 1861, Cadiz, O.; graduated Franklin College, 25 June, 1882, studied law with his father at Cadiz, O., was admitted to the bar by the supreme court of Ohio, 1 Nov., 1884; removed in Nov., 1884, to St. Paul, Minn., where he engaged in the practice of his profession; is vice president and treasurer of the Graves and Vinton Co., Investment Bankers, western managers of the Middlesex Banking Co.; also vice president of Crown Financial Co.; in politics a republican; m. in Philadelphia, Pa., 1892, Caroline R. McIlvaine, b. New Philadelphia, O., 30 Sept., 1864, dau. of Chief Justice Geo. W. McIlvaine, deceased, of New Philadelphia, O., and sister to the wife of his brother, Walter G.

5. *William James*, b. 15 May, 1863, Cadiz, O., and there d. 2 Sept., 1865.

STUART B[8]. SHOTWELL, JR., b. 1861, of St. Paul, Minn., investment banker, son of Stuart B[7]. and Nancy (Gaston) Shotwell, of Cadiz, O., [of William[6], Hugh[5], John[4], John[3], John[2], Abraham[1]], m. 1892, *Caroline R. McIlvaine*, b. 1864, dau. of Judge George W. McIlvaine of New Philadelphia, Ohio, and had:

1. *Stuart McIlvaine*, b. 16 Apr., 1893.

SYLVANUS D[8]. SHOTWELL, b. 1849, of Cortland Tp., Kent Co., Mich., s. of David S[7]. and Eliza (Dillingham) Shotwell, of Cortland, Mich., [of Benj[6]., Richard[5], Benj[4]., Jno[3]., Jno[2].. Abr[1].], m. 21 April, 1872, *Mary Whittall*, of Cortland, Mich., and had:

1. *Clarence A*., b. 14 Aug., 1873.

2. *Elmer C*., b. 26 Dec., 1877; lives with parents at the old homestead where his grandfather settled, in Cortland, Mich.

THEODORE[7] SHOTWELL, of Brooklyn, N. Y., s. of Daniel C[6]. and Martha (Pound) Shotwell, of Greenbrook, N. J., [of Manning[5], Benjamin[4], John[3], Daniel[2], Abr[1].], m. *Amelia Smith*, and had twin sons who died young, and afterward three daughters.

THEODORE[7] SHOTWELL, b. 1828, of Minneapolis, Minn., formerly of New York, and Cincinnati; s of Wm[6]., and Rhoda (Beebe) Shotwell, of Harrison Co., O., [of Hugh[5], John[4], John[3], John[2], Abr[1].] m. (1) 1852, *Sarah J. Lucas*, 1828-1891, dau. of Capt. Michael Ennis and Elizabeth (Nolan) Lucas, of Steubenville, O., and had:

1. *William Walter*, b. 12 Dec., 1855, Cincinnati, O.; a lawyer, in Minneapolis, Minn., manager of Northwestern Financial Agency—mercantile collections, mortgage loans—818 Guaranty Loan Building, Minneapolis, Minn., formerly practiced law in New York City, unm.

THEODORE F[7]. SHOTWELL, 1841-1870, of Alexandria, Minn., s. of Daniel[6], Jr., and Margaret (Force) Shotwell, [of Daniel[5], Daniel[4], Joseph[3] (?), Daniel[2], Abraham[1]], m. 1867, *Hattie A. Cambell*, b. 1849, dau. of Moses D. and Paulina (Whittemore) Cambell, [of David], and had:

1. *Horace Julian*, b. 13 Sept., 1868; began business with his cousin, Theodore Canfield, under the firm name of Canfield & Shotwell, sheet metal workers, and has a steadily increas-

ing business, at No. 525 Second Ave. S., Minneapolis, Minn., is unm. (1895).

2. *Theodora Azella*, b. 27 Aug., 1870, at Alexandria, Douglas Co., Minn., five weeks before the death of her father. She m. in Minneapolis, Minn., 22 June, 1892, William Wottage of Sauk Centre, Minn., a practical printer by trade; dw. 110 S. Robert St., St. Paul, Minn.

THEODORE FRANK[8] SHOTWELL, b. 1851, of Paulding, O., s. of Rev., John M[7]. and Saloma Lucinda (Stone) Shotwell, of Allegany Co., N. Y., etc., [of Joseph[6], Caleb[5], Samuel[4], John[3], John[2], Abr[1].], m. 1876, *Amanda McKinstrey*, daughter of James and Rebecca McKinstrey, of Crawford Co., O., and had:

1. *Carlos William*, b. ...., 1878.
2. *Becco*, b. ...., 1880.
3. *Herbert*, b. ...., 1883.

166. THOMAS LATHAM[6] SHOTWELL, 1785–1859, of Burlington Co., N. J., s. of Isaiah[5] and Constant (Lippincott) Shotwell, of Plainfield, N. J., [of John[4], John[3], John[2], Abraham[1]], m. 1806, *Elizabeth Satterthwait*, 1786–1843, dau. of Joshua W. and Ann (Middleton) Satterthwait, of Crosswicks, N. J., and had:

1. *Joshua[7]*, b. Crosswicks, Burlington Co., N. J., 6 of 9 mo., 1807, and there d. 18 of 2 mo., 1866, of fracture of skull, and interred in Presbyterian cemetery, Allentown, N. J., was by occupation a carpenter and farmer; m. (1) 13 of 11 mo., 1834, Sarah Ann Stillwell, b. Mercer Co., N. J., 6 of 4 mo., 1811, d. 30 of 8 mo., 1837, of brain fever, interred at Allentown, N. J., dau. of Joseph M. and Hannah (Stillwell) Stillwell (cousins); m. (2) 12 of 5 mo., 1842, her older sister, Rebecca A. Stillwell, b. 10 of 6 mo., 1806, d. 7 of 4 mo., 1861; m. (3) 5 of 11 mo., 1863, Hannah Lukens, b. 7 of 2 mo., 1821, d. 8 of 2 mo., 1880, dau. of David and Eliza W. Lukens. (No children by 3d wife.)

2. *Edmund[7]*, b. Crosswicks, N. J., 14 of 4 mo., 1811, was a contractor and builder in New York, whence, in 1842, he removed to Monmouth Co., N. J., engaging in farming; was justice of the peace at Key Port, Monmouth Co., 1855, and in 1863, removed to Crosswicks, Burlington Co., N. J., where he still resides at the old homestead, occupying every night the room in which he was born; m. in New York City, 23 of 12 mo., 1834, Adra Ann LaRue, who was b. 5 of 12 mo., 1815. d. 13 of 2 mo., 1887, and was buried in Old Tennent Churchyard near Monmouth battle ground, Monmouth Co., N. J.

3. *Ann M.*, b. 7 of 2 mo., 1816, d. 19 of 12 mo., 1823.

4. *Jediah[7]*, b. 15 of 11 mo., 1822, at Crosswicks, N. J., dw. 1896, with his only son, Thomas, near Hightstown, Mercer Co., N. J., m. 12 of 1 mo., 1845, Martha Ann Provost, who

lives mostly with only surviving daughter, Ella, wife of Emerson Pullen.

232. THOMAS[6] SHOTWELL, 1786–1857, of Galen, Wayne Co., N. Y., s. of Benjamin[5] and Bathsheba (Pound) Shotwell, of Essex Co., N. J., and Wayne Co., N. Y., [of Benj[4]., John[3], John[2], Abr[1].], m. (1) 1808 or 1807, *Tamer Lundy* 1786–1818, dau. of Jonathan and Rebecca (Heaton) Lundy, and had:

1. *Rebecca Lundy[7]*, b. 12 of 1 mo., 1809, in Hardwick, N. J.; member of Pelham M. M. by cert. from Junius M. M., dated 21 of 8 mo., 1827; d. Odell, Ill., 26 of 3 mo., 1875; m. in Galen (N. Y.) Friends' meeting, 26 of 5 mo., 1827, Benjamin Franklin[5] Pound, of Bertie Tp., Lincoln Co., U. C., b. 8 of 10 mo., 1805, Bertie, C. W., s. of Daniel[4] and Prudence (Jones) Pound, [of Elijah[3], John[2], John[1]], dw. Galen, N. Y., and Bertie, C. W.; they and their children, Tamer, Thos., Jacob, and Hannah E., returned to Wayne Co., N. Y., whence they removed to Odell, Ill., where the wife died; the family afterward removed to Ionia, Jewell Co., Kans.

2. *Zachariah Pound[7]*, b. 17 of 11 mo., 1811, near Hardwick Friends meeting house in Sussex (now Warren) Co., N. J.; dw. Galen and Oakfield, N. Y., acquiring title to a farm in Elba (now Oakfield), 25 July, 1839, removed in the spring of 1850, to Lobo, Middlesex Co., C. W., locating on a farm one mile southwest of Coldstream; was there visited by the compiler in the autumn of 1888, and was able to contribute valuable data for this work; P. O. Poplar Hall, Ont.; m. in Bertie (C. W.) Friends meeting house 10 of 10 mo., 1835, Margaret Zavitz, b. 6 of 8 mo., 1814, Bertie, U. C., d. Lobo, C. W., 20 of 10 mo., 1861, dau. of Jacob and Elizabeth (Pound[5]) Zavitz, of Canada, [of Daniel[4], Elijah[3], John[2], John[1]]. They and two minor children, Tamer Ann, and Thos. B., having removed to the Holland Purchase, became members of Rochester M. M. of (Hic.) Friends by cert. from Junius M. M., dated 26 of 6 mo., 1839; and they and their children became members of Yarmouth M. M., 8 of 1 mo., 1851, by cert.

3. *Benjamin Heaton[7]*, b. 9 of 1 mo., 1815, Hardwick, N. J.; dw. Hadley, Lapeer Co., Mich.; m. (1) in Junius, N. Y., Susan L. Thorn, b. 29 of 4 mo., 1819, in Junius, N. Y., and there d., dau. of Samuel and Rachel (Laing) Thorn, of Junius, Seneca Co., N. Y., [of Abraham[3], Abraham[2], Abraham[1]]; m. (2) in Michigan, Replina or Paulina (Richards) Davis, a wid.

4. *Rachel Heaton*, b. 7 of 4 mo., 1818 or 7 of 12 mo., 1817, Galen, N. Y., d. 20 of 2 mo., 1819.

THOMAS[6] SHOTWELL, 1786–1857, of Galen, N. Y., [of Benj[5]., Benj[4]., John[3], John[2], Abr[1].], m. (2) 1819, *Hannah Lundy*, 1789–1843, dau. of Daniel and Elizabeth (Laing) Lundy, of Independence, N. J., [of Samuel], and had:

5. *Jonathan Lundy*[1], b. 10 of 5 mo., 1821, in Galen, N. Y.; dw. on the farm on which his father lived many years, in the town of Galen, Wayne Co., N. Y., P. O., Marengo; m. Galen, N. Y., 25 of 2 mo., 1857, Elizabeth Fitz Patrick, b. in Down Patrick, County Down, Ireland, about 1838. To their kindness we are indebted for many items in this record. Thomas Shotwell's sons were all very short of stature, being each less than five feet in height.

259. Thomas[6] Shotwell, b. 1796, of Somerton, O., s. of Titus[5], Sr., and Deborah (Moore) Shotwell, of Pennsylvania and Ohio, [of Daniel[4], Joseph[3] (?) Daniel[2], Abraham[1]], m. *Ellen Brown*, and had:

1. *Mary Ann*[7], b. 21 April, 1818, Barnesville, O.; dw. there, a widow; m. 5 Oct., 1850, Edward S. Barnes, J. P., of Somerton, O., s. of Henry and Marion (Shotwell[6]) Barnes, [of Titus[5], Daniel[4], Joseph[3] (?), Daniel[2], Abraham[1]], he d. Barnesville, O.

2. *Jane*[7], b. 4 April, 1822, Barnesville, O.; m. 19 Jan., 1848, Joshua Barnes, who d. Barnesville, O.

3. *Eliza Ellen*[7], b. 1826, Barnesville, O.; dw. Barnesville, O.; m. 1851, James Fowler.

4. *Marion*[7] or Mariam *B.*, b. 21 Nov., 1829, Barnesville, O.; dw. there; m. -- Oct., 1855, John C. Bolon.

5. *Sarah*, b. Barnesville, O. d. ---------, O., unm.

6. *Isaac*, b. 1835±; dw. Smyrna, O., a farmer; m. (1) in Belmont Co., O., Harriet Hobbs, who d. 1866±; m. (2) Belmont Co., O., Sadie Fowler.

7. *William B.*, dw. Mt. Pleasant, Iowa; m. in Ohio.

8. *Joseph K.*, is a merchant at Somerton, Belmont Co., O.; m. (1) in Belmont Co. O., Minnie Lesley, who d. 1870±; m. (2) in Belmont Co., O., Jane Cloudy.

Thomas D[7]. Shotwell, s. of Isaac[6] and Catharine (Dell) Shotwell, of Philadelphia, Pa., [of Wilson[5], Joseph[5], Joseph[4], Joseph[3], Daniel[2], Abraham[1]], m. *Adele Picot*, and had:
1. *Helen.*

103. Titus[5] Shotwell, b. 1758, of Belmont Co, O., s. of Daniel[4] and Deborah (Shotwell) Shotwell, of Woodbridge, N. J., [of Joseph[3] (?), Daniel[2], Abraham[1]], m. (1) 1781, *Sarah Marsh*, and had:
1. *Hope*, b. 18 of 2 mo., 1782, in ---------, N. J.; m. in Pennsylvania, Joseph Woodard.
2. *Daniel*, b. 9 of 4 mo., 1784, ---------, N. J.

103. Titus[5] Shotwell, b. 1758, of Belmont Co., O., [of Daniel[4], Joseph[3] (?), Daniel[2], Abraham[1]], m. (2) 1787, *Deborah*[4] *Moore*, dau. of Edward[4] Moore of Lower Rahway, Middlesex (now Union) Co., N. J., [of Samuel[3], John[2], Samuel[1]], and had:

3. *Edward*[6], b. 12 of 11 mo., 1788, in N. J.; went with his parents to Pennsylvania in 1792, and afterward to Ohio; returned to Rahway, N. J.; while on a visit among his relatives in Athens Co., O., after his wife's death, he had a paralytic stroke which nearly deprived him of his speech, and he was nearly helpless the remaining years of his life; he d. Rahway, N. J., 17 of 1 mo., 1879, in the 92d year of his age; m. in New Jersey, his cousin, Miriam Moore, dau. of Edward[5], and --------- Moore, [of Edward[4], Samuel[3], John[2], Samuel[1]].

4. *Titus*[6], b. 19 of 5 mo., 1790, in New Jersey; was a soldier in the war of 1812, serving under Col. Lewis Cass, and for enlisting in the army was disowned by the Society of Friends; d. in Ohio, 22 March, 1852; m. 10 of 3 m., 1814, Susan Garret.

5. *Marion*[6], or Miriam, b. 16 of 7 mo., 1792, in New Jersey, m. Henry Barnes.

6. *Joseph*, b. 4 of 11 mo., 1794.

7. *Thomas*, b. 14 of 9 mo., 1796; removed from Fayette Co., Pa., to Somerton, Belmont, Co., O., and there d.; was a shoemaker; was disowned by the Society of Friends for joining the army in the war of 1812; m. Ellen Brown, who died.

8. *Isaac*[6], b. 14 of 12 mo., 1798, in Pennsylvania; was drowned 9 of 4 mo., 1845, by falling off a steamboat at the mouth of Hocking river about seven miles below Parkersburgh, on the Ohio River. At the division of the Society of Friends in 1828, he remained with those called Hicksite, and continued a faithful member until his death; was an active temperance man, and threw his whole soul into the anti-slavery enterprise, then in its infancy. He believed that the great curse of slavery would be wiped out by peaceable means. Negro slavery has been abolished, but not without the roaring of artillery, the crack of the musket, and the sacrifice of the lives of many thousands of America's bravest and noblest sons. How much better in all respects would have been the plan commended by our Quaker forefathers! Isaac m. after the manner of Friends, Hope Stanton, who d.

103. Titus[5] Shotwell, b. 1758, of Belmont Co., O., [of Daniel[4], Joseph[3] (?), Daniel[2], Abraham[1]], m. (3) 1807, *Deborah Howell*, and had:

9. *Rebecca*, b. 8 of 6 mo., 1808, d. 1830.

10. *Mahlon*[6], b. 2 of 4 mo., 1810, settled at Barnesville, about 30 miles from Cincinnati, O., d. -- of 6 mo., 1859; m. Lucinda Lee. Their son John C., states that they lived in Warren county, about four miles from Lebanon, O., and had nine children.

11. *Nathan*, last surviving son of Titus; b. 28 of 5 mo., 1812, dw. with a niece, Lucinda

McCarty, at Barnesville, Belmont Co., O., and there d. in the autumn of 1895, unm.; has latterly held with those called Wilber Friends.

12. *Sarah*, d. before 1826.

One account states that Mahlon and Nathan had sisters Amanda and Deborah.

256. TITUS[6] SHOTWELL, 1790-1852, of O., s. of Titus[5], Sr., and Deborah (Moore) Shotwell, of Belmont Co., O., [of Daniel[4], Joseph[3] (?), Daniel[2], Abraham[1]], m. 1814, *Susan Garrett*, and had:

1. *Priscilla*[7], b. 10 of 12 mo., 1814, d. 3 Dec., 1886; m. (1) 10 of 3 mo., 1842, Thomas McCarty, who left his family; she obtained a divorce and m. (2) 30 of 3 mo., 1850, Wm. G. Perry.

2. *Thomas M.*, b. 16 of 9 mo., 1817, d. 22 May, 1894; m. 25 of 11 mo., 1831, Nancy R. Thurston.

3. *John G.*, b. 30 of 1 mo., 1820, d. 25 Feb., 1837.

4. *Marion*[7], b. 2 of 1 mo., 1822, m. 10 of 3 mo., 1842, John Hollis.

5. *Allen*, b. 26 of 8 mo., or 2 Sept., 1824, d. 22 July, 1878.

6. *Rebecca*, b. 19 of 11 mo., 1826, d. 5 May, 1847.

7. *Isaac*, b. 19 of 8 mo., 1829, d. 4 Feb., 1830.

8. *Susan*, b. 27 of 12 mo., 1830, d. 26 Dec., 1894.

9. *Ellen*, b. 16 of 9 mo., 1833, d. 21 Sept., 1834.

TITUS[7] SHOTWELL, III., 1826-1896, of Latrobe, O., s. of Isaac[6] and Hope (Stanton) Shotwell, of O., [of Titus[5], Sr., Daniel[4], Joseph[3] (?), Daniel[2], Abr[1].], m. 1852, *Mary Doan*, and had:

1. _________, a dau., d. in infancy.

2. *Elias Whittier*, b. 16 of 10 mo., 1854.

3. *Enos Sumner*, b. 16 of 9 mo., 1856.

4. *William Ellery*[8], b. 19 of 10 mo., 1858; dw. Sioux Falls, S. D., m. _________.

5. *Emily Ann*, b. 17 of 9 mo., 1860; dw. with mother at Latrobe, Athens Co., Ohio, since 1888; m. John E. Moore, who d. 1888, leaving two small children, Ida and Frank.

6. *Sarah Asenath*, b. 11 of 3 mo., 1863.

7. *Isaac*, b. 10 of 9 mo , 1865.

8. *Effie Ellen*, b. 8 of 12 mo., 1867, m. _________ Dunfee, and dw. at the Titus Shotwell homestead at Latrobe, O., with mother and sister, Emily A. Moore.

9. *Edgar Thomas*, b. 6 of 6 mo., 1870.

WALTER L[7]. SHOTWELL, b. 1840, of Newark, N. J., s. of James[6] and Phebe (Ayres) Shotwell, of Hackettstown, N. J., [of Wm[5]., Jas[4]., John[4], John[3], John[2], Abr[1].], m. 1861±, *Harriet Decker*, and had:

1. *Nellie Vail*[8], b. 5 March, 1863, in Hackettstown, N. J.; dw. No. 66 Burnet St., Newark, N. J.; m. in the Halsey M. E. Church, Newark, N. J., 12 May, 1886, Wm. Edgar Langstroth, of Newark, N. J.

WALTER FOX[8] SHOTWELL, b. 1856, s. of Joseph F[7]. and Amy (Titus) Shotwell, of New York, [of Joseph S[6]., Jno. S[5]., Jno[4]., Jno[3]., Jno[2]., Abr[1].], m. 1892, Phebe Titus, and had:

1. *Samuel Titus Shotwell*, b. 14 Feb., 1895.

WALTER GASTON[8] SHOTWELL, b. 1856, of Cadiz, O., s. of Stuart B[7]. and Nancy (Gaston) Shotwell, of Cadiz, O., [of Wm[4]., Hugh[5], John[4], John[3], John[2], Abr[1].], m. 1883, *Belle McIlvaine*, b. 1859, and had:

1. *Margaretta McIlvaine*, b. 28 March, 1886, Cadiz, O.

WILLIAM[1] SHOTWELL, of Virginia—whose connection with the New Jersey and Staten Island branches of the family has not yet been definitely established—settled about the year 1750 (possibly as early as 1740), at what is now Criglersville, Madison Co., Va., on the farm now occupied by his great-grandson, Thomas N[4]. Shotwell, and there d. _________, having m. *Betsey Jurdine*, and had: two daughters—of whose names, marriages and descendants no records or traditions appear to have been preserved—and certainly one son,

3. JAMES[2], (son of the above), b. about 1759, entered the revolutionary army at 16 years of age, served seven years under General Washington, lived after the war for a few years in North Carolina, where according to tradition, he had uncles; he then returned to Virginia, settling on the Shotwell homestead in Culpepper (now Madison) Co., and there d. _ Dec., 1841, aged 82, his family were honorably reared, and his example as a good citizen still lives. He m. *Mary Crane*, who d. _ Sept., 1828, and had six sons and three daughters, born at the old homestead at Criglersville, Madison Co., Va., namely:

(1.) *Jerry*[3], b. 4 Jan., 1789, settled in Greene Co., Va., and there d. 28 Aug., 1864; m. Sarah Taylor of Madison Co., Va., b. 11 Jan., 1793, d. 13 March, 1878, and had:

(a) Miner, who d. _________; (b) Jerry, who d. _________; (c) Cazwell, dw. Burnleys, Albemarle Co., Va., was an officer in the Confederate Army for four years.

(2.) *Lewis*, settled in _________, Mo., m. _________, and raised a family, certainly one son served in the Confederate Army.

(3.) *Joshua*, settled in _________, Ohio, and there d.; was a successful hardware merchant; m. _________, but left no family.

(4.) *James*[3], *Jr.*, settled in Culpepper Co., Va., and there d. 1870±; m. (1) Mary Foushee or Martha Dunken, and had (a) James; (b) Elba or Emma.

Jas³., Jr., m. (2) Sarah Roberts, and had: (c) Wm., J., of Culpepper C. H., Va.; (d) Carter B.; (e) Jerry of Clarkston, Culpepper Co., Va.; (f) Mary; (g) Bettie; (h) Margarett. One of the daughters m. Ephraim Weaver, and had a son, James Weaver, said to reside in Washington, D. C.

(5.) *William³*, b. 4 May, 1810, remained at the old homestead at Criglersville, Madison Co., Va., and there d. 28 Aug., 1891, of a third stroke of paralysis; m. 30 Nov., 1831, Judith S. Garrett, b. 6 June, 1812, yet living at Criglersville, Va., dau., of Moses and Betsey (Leathers) Garrett of Criglersville, Va., and had 12 children of whom eight sons and three daughters lived to adult age, and eight are yet living. (Records later.)

(6.) *Margarette*, m. Abraham Carpenter, who settled in Missouri, and raised a family.

(7.) *Nancy³*, m. Allen McAllister, settled in Ohio and raised a family, among them a son Edwin.

(8.) *Betsy³*, m. Wm. Gaines, settled in Page Co., Va., and had three sons and four daughters; the former were: (a) Wm. E., who d. --------; (b) James, who d. --------, killed at first battle of Manassas; (c) John of Altoona, Pa.

(9.) *Jeckonias Yancy³ Shotwell*, "youngest and only living son," remained on a part of the old homestead at Criglersville, Va.; m. (1) Mary E. Utz, who d. .. Jan., 1862; m. (2) 10 March, 1870, Eliza Floyd, who d. 17 April, 1896, s. p. By the first wife he had four sons and six daughters, born and reared in Madison Co., Va., among them: (a) J. L. Shotwell, of Peola Mills, Madison Co., Va.; (b) J. F. Shotwell, of Lexington, Ill.; (c) Martha L., of Richmond, Mo., m. .. Feb., 1867, John Rush; (d) Mary F., m. .. Oct., 1860, James Gaines; (e) Julia A., of Oak Park, Madison Co., Va., m. .. Dec., 1866, Wm. Jenkins; (f) Adaline, of Criglersville, Va., m. Feb., 1870, E. A. Leathers; (g) Jane S., of Peola Mills, Va., m. Jan., 1875, Jas. H. Dulany.

The members of this branch, as of the other divisions of the Shotwell family, bore the reputation of having been honest and industrious citizens, honorable in the various relations of life.

WILLIAM² SHOTWELL, 1810–1891, of Criglersville, Madison Co., (formerly part of Culpepper Co.), Va., s. of James² and Mary (Crane) Shotwell of the same place, [of Wm¹. and Betsey (Jurdine) Shotwell]. m. 1831, *Judith S. Garrett*, b. 1812, dau of Moses and Betsey (Leathers) Garrett, of Criglersville; Va., and had:

1. *William Robert⁴*, b. 19 Jan., 1833, d. in El Paso, Texas, 15 Feb., 1888, of a wound received from a robber; was a successful miller; m. 3 Aug., 1858, Elizabeth F. Harrison of Kentucky, and had: (1) Wm. James, b. in Missouri, general agent of Denver & Rio Grande Railroad Co., San Francisco, Cal.; (2) Elizabeth Ratebel, dw. Salt Lake City, Utah, m. -------- --------.

2. *Ethelbert Lewis*, b. 5 April, 1835, dw. Front Royal,—the county seat of Warren Co., —Va.; occupation, tanner; m. 24 Dec., 1857, Judith F. Lillard, and had certainly four daughters and one son living, of whom two daughters are married.

3. *George Columbus*, b. 16 May, 1837, owns a farm near Denver, Colo.; by occupation a carpenter and cabinet builder; is unm.

4. *John Hamilton*, b. 6 Oct., 1839, d. 30 June, 1862, unm.; killed in battle at Seven Pines, Va.; was a cabinet builder when he entered the Confederate Army in 1861.

5. *Mary Elizabeth⁴*, b. 18 Oct., 1841, d. 4 Nov., 1862; m. 23 June, 1859, Augustus S. Utz, of Criglersville, Va., and had: (1.) John E., of Manchester, Va.; (2.) Joseph S. Utz, who dw. at Madison Court House, Va.

6. *Reuben Harrison*, b. 14 Oct., 1843, dw. Westport, Mo., a miller, unm.

7. *Albert Dallas*, b. 12 Jan., 1846, dw. Manchester, Va., is a manufacturer, formerly a tanner; m. 12 Jan., 1875, Mary S. Pulley, of Lunenburgh Co., Va. who d. .. June, 1891, and had five children.

8. *Lucetta E. L⁴*., b. 22 Oct., 1848; m. 22 Dec., 1866, Churchill B. Bates, dw. Criglersville, Va., and had: (1.) Seldon, of Manchester, Va.; (2.) Luther; (3.) Clarence; (4) Willie; (5) George; (6) Bessie; (7) Mary.

9. *Wilson Lanck⁴*, b. 27 June, 1850, dw. Westport, Mo.; occupation miller; to him and his younger brother, Thos. N., we are indebted for information concerning this branch; he m. (by an English Lutheran Minister) in Madison Co., Va., 24 Nov., 1882, Kate Lee Miller, of --------, Va., and had six children, four of whom are living; the two who d. were Wm. Luther and Grace Lillian.

10. *Thomas Newman⁴*, (twin), b. 10 Aug., 1852, lives on the old homestead at Criglersville, Va., where his great-grandparents, Wm. and Betsey (Jurdine) Shotwell, settled in the 18th century; is the only farmer among the eight sons; he m. 24 April, 1881, Annie Belle Murray of Criglersville, Va., dau. of Jno. W. and Jane (Thomas) Murray of Madison Co., Va., and had five children namely: (1.) Claude G., b. 17 March, 1885; (2.) Lizzie Lee, b. 15 Oct., 1886; (3.) Ethel May, b. 19 Sept., 1888; (4.) Robert Lucian, b. 16 Nov., 1890; (5.) Aubrey Murray, b. 20 Feb., 1893; (6.) Grace, b. 24 May, 1896.

11. *Sarah Frances⁴*, (twin), b. 10 Aug., 1852, dw. Criglersville, Va.; m. 31 Jan., 1889, Thos. W. Rosson, of Madison Co., Va., now a cabinet

builder at Criglersville, Va., and had: (1.) Rosa;
(2) Mamie.

12. *Luvenia Jane*, b. 28 Oct., 1854, d. 28
April, 1856.

58. WILLIAM[5] SHOTWELL, 1748-1841±, of
Plainfield, N. J., and Pelham, C. W., s. of John[4]
and Grace (Webster) Shotwell, of Plainfield, N.
J., [of John[3], John[2], Abr[1].], m. 1772, *Elizabeth[4]
Pound*, b. 1754, dau. of Elijah[3] and Elizabeth
Pound of Piscataway, N. J., [of John[2], John[1]],
and had:

1. *Rachel[6]*, b. 1 of 2 mo., 1773; remained
in New Jersey when her parents removed to
Canada; dw. Farmington and Junius, N. Y., d.
at res. of her son, Wm. S. Dell, Waterloo, N. Y.;
m. Richard Dell, Jr., b. 20 of 7 mo., 1762, Hanover, Morris Co., N. J., d. 3 of 1 mo., 1845,
having removed from Dover, N. J., about 1810,
to Junius, Seneca Co., N. Y., s. of Richard and
Elizabeth (Schooley) Dell, of Hanover, N. J.

2. *Catharine*, b. 21 of 9 mo., 1774, Plainfield, N. J.; dw. Thorold, U. C., east of Pelham,
and there d.; m. Benjamin Burtsall, who d.
Yarmouth, C. W.

3. *Anna[6]*, b. 31 of 8 mo., 1777; d. Pelham,
C. W.; m. (as 2d wife), Jesse Willson, of Pelham, who d. there, native of Sussex Co., N. J.

4. *Phebe[6]*, b. 13 of 8 mo., 1779, d. Pelham,
C. W.; m. Isaac Willson, of Pelham, U. C., b.
Sussex Co., N. J., and d. Pelham, C. W.,
and had brothers Lewis and Joseph.

5. *Elizabeth*, b. 27 of 9 mo., 1781, in N. J.;
m. Joseph Adams of Sussex Co., N. J.

6. *Elijah[6]*, b. 14 of 8 mo., 1783; dw. Thorold,
Tp., east of Pelham, C. W., d. Yarmouth, C.
W., when about 70 years of age; was minister
among Friends; m. at Pelham, U. C., Martha
Burtsall or Birdsall, sister to Benjamin. They
became members of Yarmouth M. M. of (Hic.)
Friends, 12 of 7 mo., 1843, by cert. from
Pelham.

7. *John[6]*, b. 29 of 5 mo., 1785, ..., N.
J., removed from Thorold, C. W., to ....,
Kansas, and thence with his youngest son,
Isaac, about 1869, to ...., Mich., d. God-
land Tp., Lapeer Co., Mich., 14 miles north of
Almont, when about 90 years of age; m. (1)
Grace Marsh, b. 3 of 11 mo., 1790; d. Thorold,
C. W., 1827±, dau. of Joseph and Anne
(de Camp) Marsh of Bertie, C. W., [of
John[1]]; m. (2) in Yarmouth Friends meeting
house, 1833±, Matilda Heaton, who d. at Oak
Openings, near Almont, Mich., dau. of Jona-
than and Ann Heaton. John and wife,
Matilda, and his three minor children, Joseph,
Wm., and Anna, became members of Yarmouth
M. M. of (Hic.) Friends, 10 of 9 mo., 1840, by
cert.

8. *Smith[6]*, b. 29 of 5 mo., 1787, in N. J., dw.
Thorold, C. W., and there d. aged about 70
years; was an active member of the Society of
Friends called Hicksite; attended New York
Yearly Meeting about 1850, and visited N. J.,
about 1856; m. Mary Crawford, who d., dau. of
James and Amy (Heacock) Crawford.

9. *Sarah*, b. 10 of 5 mo., 1788, or 13 of 3 mo.,
1789, in New Jersey; m. Levi Schooley.

10. *Miriam[6]*, or Marian, b. 19 of 9 mo., 1791,
in New Jersey; dw. Young St., C. W., and there
d.; m. William Webster.

11. *William*, b. 21 of 11 mo., 1795; was
killed when young by a tree falling upon him.

53. WILLIAM[5] SHOTWELL, 1762-1840±, of
Rahway, N. J., and New York City, (nicknamed
"Governor"), s. of Joseph[4] and Phebe (Allen)
Shotwell, [of John[3], John[2], Abr[1].], m. 1787, *Sarah
Hopkins*, dau. of Samuel, of Philadelphia, and
had:

1. *Sarah[6]*, b. before 1796; d. before 1850;
m. (as first wife) Morris Shipley, a native of
Utoxeter, Staffordshire, Eng., who m. (2) Ann
Eddy, of Rahway, N. J.; he afterward m. (3)
his first wife's sister, Mary Shotwell, Q. V.

2. Hannah, b. before 1796, m. Robert I.
Murray, of New York City.

3. *William*, b. before 1796.

4. *Mary*, b. 15 of 8 mo., 1796; dw. Fremont,
Westchester Co., N. Y., whence, in 1855, she
removed to West Farms, N. Y., and there d. ...
of 1 mo., 1876; m. at Westchester, N. Y., 14
Feb., 1856, (as third wife) her sister Sarah's
widower, Morris Shipley, who d. in 1859. She
had no children of her own, but adopted and
brought up from infancy a boy, called Charles
Akin Shotwell, b. in New York, 22 June,
1846, now of Philadelphia, giving him a home
until he showed an irrepressible inclination
toward a military career after the breaking
out of the War of the Rebellion. (See p. 100
ante.)

5. *Anna*, who d. unm.

6. *Elizabeth*, b. 17 of 8 mo., 1799; interred
in New York Friends cemetery, 10 of 8 mo.,
1804.

7. *Phebe*, b. 10 of 5 mo., 1801; interred in
New York Friends cemetery, 31 of 3 mo.,
1802, aged 8 years.

WILLIAM SHOTWELL, member of New York
M. M. (parentage not ascertained), m. *Mary
.........., and had:

1. *Sarah*, b. 15 of 9 mo., 1788.
2. *Hannah W.*, b. 5 of 3 mo., 1790.
3. *Samuel*, b. 20 of 7 mo., 1792.

94. WILLIAM[5] SHOTWELL, 1766-1855, of
Shotwell's Landing (Bricktown, now Rahway),
N. J., and Junius, N. Y., s. of Benjamin[4] and
Ame (Hallett) Shotwell, of the Landing, [of
John[3], John[2], Abr[1].], m. (1) 1792, *Elizabeth
Moore*, 1762±-1826, and had:

1. *Benjamin[6]*, b. 18 of 8 mo., 1793, at
Bricktown (now Rahway), N. J., dw. Blazing
Star in Woodbridge Tp., N. J., near mouth

of Rahway river, and there d. 20 of 1 mo., 1859, buried first in Rahway Friends' ground, afterward moved to Hazlewood cemetery in Middlesex Co., N. J.; m. Mary Hunt, b. 1800±, dw. Blazing Star, N. J., dau. of James' and Sarah Hunt of Rahway, N. J., [of Marmaduke', Solomon'].

2. *Elizabeth L'.*, b. 26 of 4 mo., 1795, d. -- of 6 mo., 1827; m. with unity of Friends at Rahway, N. J., 28 of 9 mo., 1815, (as 2d of three wives) Samuel Moore, Jr., of Falmouth, Mass., whence, about 1814, he removed to Piscataway, N. J., dw. for many years at the Six Roads about one mile south of Rahway; d. Milton (now Rahway), N. J., s. of Samuel' and Rachel (Stone) Moore of New Jersey, Nova Scotia, and Upper Canada, [of Samuel', John', Samuel'].

3. *William', Jr.*, b. 6 of 12 mo., 1798, dw. Bricktown (now Rahway), near the old homestead at the Landing, and there d. ...., 1876, was the last surviving son of his father, was always more or less engaged in brick making; was the last person engaged in that business in the vicinity of Rahway; he occupied for a time the Landing property, built there a lime kiln, kept a coal yard, and was interested in one or more vessels; was in some respects eccentric, but had the reputation of being a very honest and confiding man, and in this way was very often imposed upon. He m. (1) Catharine Pettit, a distant relative; m. (2) ....; m. (3) ...., who survived him.

4. *Harvey'*, b. 13 of 10 mo., 1800, in Bricktown, N. J., member of New York M. M., by cert. from R. and P. M. M., dated 21 of 2 mo., 1821; dw. on the homestead at the Landing; was a druggist in New York City, afterward at Macon, Ga., and there d. 6 of 1 mo., 1848; m. in Rahway, N. J., 25 of 12 mo., 1823, his father's cousin, Louisa Shotwell, b. 8 of 12 mo., 1800, d. 4 of 3 mo., 1880, dau. of Nathan' and Sarah (Fitz Randolph) Shotwell, of Rahway and Blazing Star, N. J., [of Jacob', John', John', Abraham'].

5. *David'*, dw. on the shore of Staten Island Sound, at the steamboat landing, called Red Bank, on Woodbridge Neck, about one mile from the town of Woodbridge, and there died about 1 of 2 mo., 1836; m. in Woodbridge, N. J., Margaret Prall, dau. of Isaac Prall, of Woodbridge; after David's death she m. (2) Azaliah Schooley, of Junius or Galen, N. Y.

173. WILLIAM' SHOTWELL, of Long Bridge, Independence Tp., Warren Co., N. J, s. of James' and Elsie (Smalley) Shotwell, of Long Bridge, N. J., [of John', John', John', Abr'.], m. *Mary Ayres*, dau. of Ezekiel Ayres, of Warren Co., N. J., and had:

1. *James'*, b. .. Dec., 1810, Long Bridge, Sussex (now Warren) Co., N. J., was a mer-

chant at Hackettstown, N. J., and there d. 14 June, 1845; m. at Allamuchy, Warren Co., N. J., 28 June, 1831, Phebe Ayres, b. 20 Apr., 1812, Allamuchy, N. J., dw. with son, Archibald, at Hackettstown, N. J., dau. of Archibald Ayres, of Allamuchy.

2. *Matilda'*, dw. Hackettstown, N. J., and there m. Isaac Sharp, a hotel clerk.

3. *Charlotte'*, dw. Stanhope, N. J.: and there d.; m. Geo. Wooley, a shoemaker, of Stanhope, N. J.

4. *Mary'*, dw. at or near Scranton, Pa., m. near Hackettstown, N. J., Simeon Saunders, a carpenter.

243 (e). WILLIAM' SHOTWELL, 1779–1834, of Mason Co., Ky., s. of John' and Abigail (Shipman) Shotwell of Mayslick, Ky., [of John', Abr'. (?), Jno'., Abr'.], m. 1805, *Frances Tripplet*, 1787–1863, and had:

1. *John Tripplet*, b. 10 Jan., 1806, near Mayslick, Ky., was an eminent physician and lecturer in a medical college in Cincinnati, and d. there of cholera, 23 July, 1850, s. p.; buried in Spring Grove cemetery, Cincinnati; m. Mary Foote, who survived him.

2. *Alfred Lawrence'*, b. 16 June, 1809, near Mayslick, Ky., was for many years a prominent commission merchant of Louisville, Ky.; afterward owned and operated an extensive coal mine near Louisville; was a man of large wealth and a leader in every public enterprise to build up the city of Louisville. He d. of paralysis of the brain, in Cincinnati, O., 16 May, 1893; interred in Louisville, Ky. He m. (by Rev. Thomas Henderson) at Georgetown, Ky., 30 July, 1829, Gabriella Jane Breckinridge, b. 13 June, 1812, in Georgetown, Ky., d. of dropsy, in Louisville, Ky., 20 Sept., 1872, interred in family lot, Louisville, Ky., dau. of Preston and Elizabeth (Trigg) Breckinridge, of Georgetown, Ky.

3. *Wm. Henry*, b. 26 Jan., 1816, in Mason Co., Ky., d. 1 Apr., 1843, unm.

Their grandfather, John' Shotwell and his brother Jasper, both of Morris Co., N. J., according to the roster of N. J., "Officers and Men in the Revolutionary War," p. 752, served as privates in the militia.

184. WILLIAM' SHOTWELL, 1798–1855, of Harrison Co., O., s. of Hugh' and Rosetta (Arrison) Shotwell, of Freeport, Harrison Co., O.. [of John', John', John', Abraham'], m. 1819, *Rhoda Beebe*, 1792–1876, and had:

1. *Stuart Beebe'*, b. 22 Nov., 1819, in Washington township, Harrison Co., O.; spent the early years of his life on a farm, removed to Cadiz, O., 1 Apr., 1837, received his education at the public school of his native township and at Franklin College, New Athens, Harrison Co., O.; studied law with the firm of Dewey & Stanton of Cadiz, O., and was there admitted to

the bar, 20 Oct., 1842. Shortly after this time, Edwin M. Stanton, who afterward became Secretary of War under President Lincoln, left Cadiz, moving to Steubenville, and S. B. Shotwell took his place as Chauncy Dewey's partner, and the business of the law firm of Dewey & Shotwell was continued until the retirement of Mr. Dewey from law practice, Mr. Shotwell continuing in the business of an attorney at Cadiz, O., until the time of his death, and attaining a high degree of success. His office in Cadiz was wrecked in 1887, by the Presbyterian church spire, thrown down by a cyclone, passing through it but a few feet from where he was standing at the time.

Stuart B. Shotwell, probably the largest land and property owner in Eastern Ohio, and one of the oldest and best known lawyers in the State, died at his home in Cadiz, O., on Wednesday morning, 3 Dec., 1890, at about 9 o'clock, of throat and lung trouble. His health had been failing for several months, but he had not been confined to the house except for a few days prior to his death.

He commenced the practice of law in Cadiz, long before the day of railroads and telegraphs, when the practitioner on horseback with his law books in the saddle-bags traveled from county to county. He was one of the last relics of the generation of the past, and a shadow of sorrow fell upon all as the announcement of his death was made. He was a patron of literature, an extensive reader, a good conversationalist, an ardent republican in politics, and a man who had the best welfare of society and his country always at heart. He took a great interest in education, and to him is Franklin College largely indebted for its present prosperity. In his home he was hospitable and generous, loving dearly the society of his friends; as husband and father, tender and indulgent; though strict in business affairs, no deserving appeal for charity was ever made to him in vain.

His funeral was held on Friday afternoon, Dec. 5, 1890, from his late residence. Among those in attendance were the members of the Cadiz Bar, who attended in a body; also his son, S. B. Shotwell, Jr., from St. Paul, his niece, Miss Minnie Sharon from Pittsburg, and Mr. W. B. Beebe, and his daughter, Mrs. Col. Norris, of Columbus. The pall-bearers were Hon. John A. Bingham, Judge J. S. Pearce, and Messrs. James B. Jamison, M. J. Brown, C. M. Hogg, and D. B. Welch. On Dec. 4, the day following his death, the Cadiz Bar Association held a meeting at the court house, at which the following resolutions were adopted:

The Cadiz Ohio Bar Association, of which the late Stuart B. Shotwell, LL D., was a most honorable member, now in memorial convention assembled, do unanimously resolve:

First, That we tender to the family and relatives of the deceased the sincere sympathy of his brethren, in this, their sad bereavement. While they mourn the loss of a faithful husband, a kind father, and a steadfast friend, this bar feels that by the decease of Stuart B. Shotwell, Esq., the eldest member of our circle, a distinguished name has been removed from our living roll. Another familiar form is missing from our court room. But we realize that in the life and memory of the deceased, there is left to us a high example of admirable courage, of remarkable diligence, and of unfailing devotion to his professional duties, which example commends itself to every lawyer who seeks distinction in his profession;

Second, That as a last mark of respect which we will have the privilege of paying to the mortal form of our deceased brother, this bar, as a body, will attend his funeral to the cemetery;

Third, That our secretary, J. M. Garvin, Esq., be requested to present a copy of these resolutions to the family of the deceased;

Fourth, That Hon. John A. Bingham be requested to present a copy of the same to the Common Pleas Court, and to the Circuit Court of Harrison county, Ohio, at the first following term of each of said courts, and to ask that in memory of Stuart B. Shotwell, Esq., the foregoing resolutions be entered upon the respective journals of said honorable court.

S. B. Shotwell, married 8 May, 1851, Nancy Gaston, b. 14 Nov., 1823, dwells Cadiz, Ohio, daughter of James and Elizabeth (Kilgore) Gaston, of Clarkson, Columbiana Co., Ohio [of Hugh], and a niece of Daniel Kilgore, at that time, 1851, a prominent business man of Cadiz. The Gastons were French Huguenots who fled their country in the time of the persecution of the Protestants in the sixteenth century, and settled in Ireland for a generation or two, whence Nancy's forefathers came to America. Her grandfather, Hugh Gaston, was born in New Jersey, 18 Jan., 1764, m. his cousin, Grace Gaston, who was born in New Jersey, 25 Nov., 1764. Their son, James, was born in eastern Pennsylvania, 20 Jan., 1793, removed to Columbiana Co., O., early in the nineteenth century; he married .... Kilgore, who was born in Washington Co., Pa., in 1794.

2. *John*, b. 3 June, 1821, Harrison Co., O., and there died 3 Aug., 1822.

3. *Samuel*, b. 7, Aug., 1823, Harrison Co., O., and there d. 30 Mch., 1824.

4. *William, Jr*, b. 2 Jan., 1825, Harrison Co., O.; graduated 1845, at Miami University, Oxford, Ind., where he was a classmate of Oliver P. Morton, the distinguished war governor of Ind.; he studied law with Dewey & Shotwell, at Cadiz, O.; admitted to the bar in Oct., 1847, and settled at Hamilton, Butler Co., O., where he practiced with good success for two years and there d. 1 Dec., 1849, unm. He was a fine scholar, and if he had lived would have made a high mark.

5. *Theodore*, b. 20 March, 1828, Harrison Co., O., dw. New York City, for many years, spending much of his time at Cincinnati, O., until about 1884, and afterward at Minneapolis, Minn., was senior partner in the mercantile house of Shotwell, Clerihew & Lothman; m. (1) 6 July, 1852, Sarah J. Lucas, of

Steubenville, O., b. 1 May, 1828, d. 16 Jan., 1891; dau. of Capt. Michael Ennis and Elizabeth (Nolan) Lucas, and sister to the wife of his cousin, Jonathan D. Seaton; m. (2) __ April, 1894, Anna G. (Seaton) Beckwith, granddaughter of Maj. George Seaton.

6. *Walter B.*, b. 3 June, 1831, Harrison Co., O., d. Cadiz, O., 21 May, 1847.

7. *Rhoda Lauretta*[7], b. 27 July, 1834, Harrison Co., O., dw. Cadiz, O.; m. 25 Dec., 1855, Smiley Sharon, who d. 15 Feb., 1870.

241. WILLIAM[6] SHOTWELL, 1798-1876, of Bricktown, (now Rahway), Essex (now Union) Co., N. J., s. of Wm[5]. and Elizabeth (Moore), Shotwell, of Shotwell's Landing, [of Benj[4]. John[3], John[2], Abr[1].], m. _________ _________, and had several daughters, living near Rahway, N. J.

193. WILLIAM M[6]. SHOTWELL, s. of Aaron[5] and _________ (Martin) Shotwell, of Rahway, N. J., [of Abr[4]., John[3], John[2], Abr[1].], m. *Ann Marsh*, and had:

1. *Joseph Marsh*[7], of the Merchants' Exchange Association, San Francisco, Cal., who was b. 15 Oct., 1830, at Rahway, N. J., and brought up in the Society of Friends; m. by Presbyterian clergyman, Oakland, Cal., 6 May, 1860, Minnie Perrier, b. 10 Feb., 1845, in Australia.

2. _________ a dau.; dw. on Staten Island, N. Y.

3. _________, other members of the family said to reside in New Orleans and Cincinnati.

WM. PIATT[7] SHOTWELL, b. 1802, of Scotch Plains, N. J., s. of Elijah[6] and Jemima Greene (Piatt) Shotwell, of Scotch Plains, N. J., [of Jacob[5], John[4], John[3], John[2], Abr[1].], m. *Harriet Parse*, and had:

1. *Greenleaf*[8], studied law under Chetwood, at Elizabeth, N. J.; d. _________; m. Elizabeth Cleveland, of Elizabethtown, N. J.

2. *Ellen P.*; d. _________ _________, s. p.; m. Henry T. Mc. Harg, of New York City.

3. *Caroline P.*, called Carrie P.; d. _________, 1894, s. p.; m. Charles N. Flanders, who has been since 1850 an oil manufacturer in Brooklyn, L. I., res. Scotch Plains, N. J.

4. *William P.* is captain on a steamer.

WILLIAM[7] SHOTWELL, b. 1818, of Lobo, Ont., s. of John[6] and Grace (Marsh) Shotwell, of Goodland, Mich., [of Wm[5]., John[4], John[3], John[2], Abr[1].], m. 1846, *Susannah Kester*, b. 1825, dau. of Thomas R. and Beulah (Heaton) Kester, of Lobo, C. W., [of Harman[1]], and had:

1. *Anna Marsh*, b. 1 of 11 mo., 1846, Lobo, C. W., and there d. 29 of 5 mo., 1880, unm.

2. *Thomas Hugh*, b. 27 of 1 mo., 1853, in Lobo, C. W., and there dw., s. p., P. O., Coldstream; m. in Strathroy, Ont., 29 of 11 mo., 1882, Phebe Ann Willson, b. 1 of 1 mo., 1864, Lobo, C. W., dau. of Thomas[3] and Caroline A. (Crealman) Willson, of Lobo, C. W., [of Richard[2], Jesse[1]].

3. *Mary Betsy*[4], b. 17 of 1 mo., 1862, in Lobo, C. W., dw. there, P. O., Coldstream, Ont.; m. in Strathroy, Ont., 25 of 4 mo., 1877, Fornando Thomas Willson, b. 25 Oct., 1855, dw. Lobo, s. of Thomas[3] and Caroline Amanda (Crealman) Willson, of Lobo, Ont., [of Richard[2], Jesse[1]].

WILLIAM[7] SHOTWELL, d. 1894, of Oxbow, Oakland Co., Mich., s. of Clarkson F.[6], and Keziah (Sutton) Shotwell, of Oakland Co., Mich., [of James[5], John[4], John[3], John[2], Abraham[1]], m. (1) *Theresa Linaberry*, who d. 8 March, 1858, and had three children, among them,—

1. *John L.*, dw. Whittlesey, Taylor Co., Wisconsin; has not seen any of the Shotwells since 1874.

WILLIAM[7] SHOTWELL, [of Clarkson F[6]., James[5], Jno[4]., Jno[3], Jno[2]., Abr[1].], m. (2) *Elizabeth Fitzgerald*, and had:

4. Lucy Louise, lived with aunt Orrilla.

5. Charles Winfield, lived with aunt Orrilla.

6. *Clarkson Fred*, adopted by his aunt, Orrilla Worden, and called Clarkson F. Worden, dw. White Lake Tp., Oakland Co., Mich.; P. O., Oxbow.

WILLIAM B[7]. SHOTWELL, b. 1824, s. of Robert[6] and Martha (Fitz Randolph) Shotwell, [of Manning[5], Benj[4]., John[3], Daniel[2], Abr[1].], m., 1847, *Phebe Compton*, dau. of Jas. Compton of Perth Amboy, N. J., and had:

1. *William Wright Shotwell*, b. 30 July, 1847; d. 17 Apr., 1850.

2. *Tyler Longstreet*, b. 1 July, 1850; m. Mary Taylor, and had: (1.) Ella. (2.) Anna. (3.) Flossie. (4.) Carrie. (5.) Agnes. (6.) Bremster. (7.) William.

3. *Manning*, b. 15 June, 1851; d. 13 Aug., 1865.

4. *Lewis, R.*, b. 13 June, 1853; m. Sarah Skinner. (No issue.)

5. *Robert Judson*, b. 13 March, 1854; d. 22 Sept., 1886.

6. *Carrie L.*, b. 19 Nov., 1856; d. 1 Feb., 1857.

7. *Agnes Anderson*, b. 26 June, 1858; m. Alex. Graham, and had: (1.) Lulu. (2.) William. (3.) Cora.

8. *Geo. Bradford*, b. 8 June, 1860; m. Carrie McKillie.

9. *Cornelia C.*, b. 16 Sept., 1861; d. 24 Feb., 1864.

10. *Chas. Compton*, b. 3 Aug., 1863; d. 4 Jan., 1870.

11. *Manning Hope*, b. 31 Aug., 1866; m. Lavina Jones, and had: (1.) Albert. (2.) Phebe.

12. *Hannah M.*, b. 16 Feb, 1873; d. 20 Feb., 1876.

WILLIAM MORRIS' SHOTWELL, b. 31 Jan., 1823, farmer Richmond, Mo., formerly school teacher, s. of Jabez⁶, and Eliza (Warder) Shotwell, of Richmond, Mo., [of John⁵, John⁴, Abraham³ (?), John², Abraham¹], m., near Camden, Mo., 31 Oct., 1855, *Amanda McGee*, and had:

1. *Chas. B.*, a practicing physician at Richmond, Mo., m. 1 Jan., 1885, Carrie Krieger of Chicago, Ill.

2. *Mamie*, m. 8 Nov., 1894, Dr. L. D. Greene, of Richmond Mo.

3. *Lucy*, teacher in academic course at Woodson Institute, Richmond, Mo.; dw. with parents on a farm one mile west of Richmond, unm. (1896).

4. *George*, is a farmer near Richmond, Mo., unm.

WILLIAM J'. SHOTWELL, of East Orange, N. J., s. of Benjamin⁴ and Mary (Hunt) Shotwell, [of William⁵, Benjamin⁴, John³, John², Abraham¹], m. 1862, *Mary N. Melick*, and had:

1. *William M.*, b. 27 July, 1865.

2. *Harriet Adelaide*, b. 28 Sept., 1870; m. 29 Jan., 1896, W. Harry Demarest, of Woodbridge, N. J.

3. *Frederic W.*, b. 5 Jan., 1875.

WILLIAM' SHOTWELL, d. at Sparta, Kans., s. of Smith⁶ and Mary (Crawford) Shotwell, of Thorold, C. W., [of Wm⁵., John⁴, John³, John², Abr¹.], m. *Martha Elizabeth⁴ Taylor*, who after her husband's death removed to Windom, Kans., and thence to Cushing, Oklahoma, dau. of John and Eliza (Shotwell⁷) Taylor, [of Elijah⁶, Wm⁵., John⁴, John³, John², Abr¹.], and had:

1. *Emily Ann⁴*, b. 24 of 2 mo., 1850, in Yarmouth, C. W.; dw. ...., Kans.; m. by Friends' Ceremony, in Yarmouth, Ont., Elijah Prior.

2. *Smith*, b. 30 of 3 mo., 1852, Yarmouth, C. W., dw. Odell formerly called Motor, Rooks Co., Kans.; m. at Sparta, Kans., Julia E. Reynolds.

3. *Elijah Bernard*, b. 28 of 1 mo., 1857, Yarmouth, C. W.; dw. Cushing, Oklahoma; m. at Sparta, Kans., Carrie Citgrim.

4. *Whitson Canby*, b. 22 of 12 mo., 1860, Yarmouth, C. W.; dw. Windham, Kans., afterward at Cushing, Oklahoma, m. in Windom, Kans.. Rachel Prior, sister to Elijah.

5. *Letitia A'.*, b. 17 of 12 mo., 1863, in Yarmouth, C. W.; dw. Sparta, Kans., afterward at Manchester, Oklahoma, there m. Zenas Scott.

WILLIAM HARVEY' SHOTWELL, of La Porte, Ind., s. of David⁶ and ...... (Prall) Shotwell, [of Wm⁵., Benj⁴., John³, John², Abr¹.], m. 1851, *Sarah Louisa' Shotwell*, b. 1827, dau. of Harvey⁶

and Louisa (Shotwell) Shotwell, [of Wm⁵., Benj⁴., John³, John², Abr¹.], and had:

1. *Clifford Alexander*, b. 19 of 7 mo., 1852, in La Porte, Ind., d. Verona, Mo., 10 of 7 mo., 1891.

2. *Birdie*, b. La Salle, Ill., d. in infancy.

3. *Lida Margaret*, b. 29 of 10 mo., 1858, La Salle, Ill.

4. *Marjory Josephine*, b. Chicago, Ill., d. in infancy.

5. *Ann F. R.* b. Rochester, N. Y.

6. *William Harvey*, b. Rochester, N. Y.

WILLIAM SEYMOUR' SHOTWELL, of Philadelphia, Pa., s. of Edmund⁶ and Sarah R. (Shepard) Shotwell, of Rahway, N. J., [of Isaiah⁵, John⁴, John³, John², Abr¹.], m.' ...., and had:

1. *William Seymour, Jr.*

WILLIAM' SHOTWELL, b. 1841, s. of John' and Elizabeth (Biggs) Shotwell, [of John⁴, John³, John⁴, Abr³. (?,) John², Abr¹.], m. 1869, *Jemima Liter*, and had:

1. *Bell.*

2. *Elizabeth.*

WILLIAM TITUS' SHOTWELL, b. 1852, of Brooklyn, N. Y., s of Joseph F'. and Amy (Titus) Shotwell of New York, [of Joseph S⁶., Jno. S³., Jno⁴., Jno³., Jno²., Abr¹.], m. 1881, *Ida D. Chapin*, and had:

1. *Amy Titus*, b. 15 Oct., 1882.

2. *Heman Chapin*, b. 24 Feb., 1887.

DR. WILLIAM EDWARD' SHOTWELL, b. 1858, of Denver, Colo., formerly of Dunellen, N. J., s. of Rev. John M'. and Salome L. (Stone) Shotwell, of Allegany Co., N. Y., etc., [of Joseph⁶, Caleb⁵, Samuel⁴, John³, John² Abr¹.], m. 1885, *Harriet C. Pierson*, b. 1863, dau. of Everett M. and Elizabeth W. (Williams) Pierson, of Westfield, N. J., and had:

1. *Harold Williams*, b. ...., 1885, Scottsburgh, Livingston Co., N. Y.

2. *Ethel May*, b. ...., 1887, Dunellen, N. J.

3. *Howard Ford*, b. ...., Denver, Colo.

4. *Robert Leslie*, b. ...., Denver, Colo.

WILLIAM ELLERY' SHOTWELL, b. 1858, of Sioux Falls, S. D., s. of Titus' and Mary (Doan) Shotwell, of Latrobe, Ohio, [of Isaac⁴, Titus³, Daniel⁴, Joseph³ ?, Daniel², Abr¹.] m. ...., and had:

1. *Titus*, b. early in 1895.

WM. P. G'. SHOTWELL, of 536 Swan St., Buffalo, N. Y., s. of Greenleaf⁶ and Elizabeth (Cleveland) Shotwell, [of Wm. P'., Elijah⁶, Jacob⁵, Jno⁴., Jno³., Jno²., Abr¹.], m.

Margaret R. Stevenson, of Milton, Pa., and had:

1. *James P.*, b. ----------, d. ----------
2. *Sadie P.*
3. *William P.*
4. *Mary P.*
5. *Laurence P.*
6. *Fannie P.*

WILLIAM[7] SHOTWELL, b. 1873, s. of Jas. L[6]. and Sallie (Magee) Shotwell, [of Albert[6], John[5], John[4], John[4], Abr[3]., John[2], Abr[1].], m. ------------, and had:

1. *Albert, b. -- Feb., 1892.*
2. *Willie B., b. -- Aug., 1894.*

246. WILSON[6] SHOTWELL, of Moorestown, N. J., s. of Joseph[5] and Sarah (Wilson) Shotwell, of Perrytown, N. J., [of Joseph[4], Joseph[3], Daniel[2], Abraham[1]], m. (1) *Sarah Marsh*, and had:

1. *Eden*, b. 16 of 1 mo., 1810, d. -- of 2 mo., 1843.
2. *Joseph*, b. 18 of 11 mo., 1816; d. 1844.
3. *Eliza*, b. 20 of 6 mo., 1820, d. 18 of 6 mo., 1871; m. John Elliott, who d. 8 of 5 mo., 1878.
4. *Isaac[7]*, b. -- of 5 mo., 1822 dw. 1508 N. 10th St., Philadelphia, Pa.; m. Catharine Dell, dau. of Richard and Mary[6] (Shotwell) Dell, [of Joseph[5] Shotwell, Joseph[4], Joseph[3], Daniel[2], Abr[1].].
5. *Margaret*, dw. Merchantville, N. J.; m. Ezra Haines, who d. 11 of 8 mo., 1890.
6. *Sarah Jane*, b. 10 of 1 mo., 1826, dw. Maple Shade, N. J.; m. George Darnell, who d. 17 of 11 mo., 1871, aged 41.
7. *Theodore*, b. 8 of 9 mo., 1827. d. 16 of 7 mo., 1868.
8. *Wilson*, b. 10 of 7 mo., 1829, d. 17 of 7 mo., 1844.

233. ZACHARIAH[6] SHOTWELL, 1788-1857, of Genesee and Wayne counties, N. Y., s. of Benjamin[5] and Bathsheba (Pound) Shotwell, of Wayne Co., N. Y., [of Benj[4]., John[3], John[2], Abr[1].], m. (1) *Elizabeth Lundy*, 1792-1816, dau. of Levi[3] and Sarah (Tomer) Lundy, of Hardwick, (now Independence), N. J., [of Samuel[1]], and had:

1. *Sarah Lundy[7]*, b. 16 of 9 mo., 1809, in Hardwick (now Independence), Sussex (now Warren) Co., N. J.; after the death of her mother in 1816, she and her two sisters went to live with her maternal grandfather who had removed with his daughter's family to the State of New York, but returned to New Jersey after Elizabeth's death, taking the three girls with him. Sarah L., d. 30 Dec., 1852; m. in a (Hic.) Friends meeting held in an old house on the Sleeper farm about one-half mile west of the stone meeting house, Elba, N. Y., ..., 1830, Jonathan L. Kester, b. 18 Aug., 1805,

Sussex (now Warren) Co., N. J.; became member of Farmington M. M., by cert. from Hardwick and Randolph M. M., dated 4 of 1 mo., 1827; on account of militia fines, he was imprisoned 4 of 2 mo., 1829, for seven days in the Ontario Co., (N. Y.), jail on a demand of $4,—Lyman Cowdry, marshal. Farmington M. M. of (Hic.) Friends gave him a cert. 26 of 3 mo., 1829, to enable him to proceed in m. with a member of Rochester M. M.; he became member of Elba M. M. of (Hic.) Friends by cert. from Farmington M. M. dated 22 of 4 mo., 1831; he afterward moved with his family to Wyandot Co., O., and there d. 30 Dec., 1852; both were buried in Friends' ground near Sycamore, O.

2. *Bathsheba Pound[7]*, b. 6 of 9 mo., 1811, Hardwick, N. J.; dw. with son Albert near Sycamore, O., P. O., Deunquat; went on a visit in autumn of 1874, to Erie, Neosho Co., Kans., m. in Hardwick Friends' meeting house, Warren Co., N. J., 7 of 12 mo., 1831, Jacob Lundy[4] Willson, b. 11 of 9 mo., 1810, d. 1 of 3 mo., 1863, s. of Abner[3] and Elizabeth (Lundy) Willson of Independence, (now Allamuchy), N. J., [of Gabriel[2], Samuel[1].]; removed two years after marriage from Warren Co., N. J., to Elba, N. Y., and thence in 1835, to Wyandot Co. Ohio.

3. *Huldah Dennis[7]*, b. 10 of 4 mo., 1814, Hardwick., N. J.; dw. Sycamore, O., m. by Friends' ceremony, Warren Co., N. J., -- of 5 mo., 1833, Elisha Willson, who removed in 1834 to Wyandot Co., O., and there died 18 of 5 mo., 1866, s. of Robert and Grace or Rhoda (Dell) Willson.

4. *Levi Lundy[7]*, b. 21 of 11 mo., 1816, Galen, N. Y.; spent several years of his early childhood in the family of John Laing in Wayne Co, N. Y., dw. Windsor Tp., Eaton Co., Mich., on the line of the Grand Trunk railroad, one mile from the P. O. of W. Windsor and three miles west of Dimondale; m. (1) Nancy P. Pratt, who d. in Windsor Tp., Mich., dau. of Elisha Pratt; he m. (2) in Charlotte, Eaton Co., Mich., Asenath Williams.

ZACHARIAH[6] SHOTWELL, 1788-1857, of Genesee and Wayne counties, N. Y., [of Benj[5]., Benj[4]., John[3], John[4], Abr[1].], m. (2) *Edna Lundy*, dau. of Daniel[2] and Elizabeth (Laing) Lundy, [of Samuel[1]], and had:

5. *Daniel L[7].*, b. 19 of 10 mo., 1819, Galen, Seneca (now Wayne) Co., N. Y., member of Rochester M. M. of (Hic.) Friends in 1840, by cert. from Farmington M. M.; dw. Richmond, Va., and afterward near Dowagiac, Cass Co., Mich., and there d. 31 Jan., 1890; m. in Johnstown, Barry Co., Mich., 12 June, 1844, Mary P. Iden, b. 26 June, 1820, in Richland, Bucks Co., Pa., dw. Dowagiac, Mich., dau. of Thomas and Rachel A. (Parry), Iden, the former one of the six sons and four daughters of George and Hannah (Foulk) Iden, and the latter, daughter of Philip and Mary (Armitage) Parry and all of

English Quaker ancestry. Rachel's ancestors came over with Wm. Penn, and trace back to the Peerage of old England, but pretty well Americanized by this time.

6. *Edwin Benjamin*[1], b. 28 of 11 mo., 1821, Galen, N. Y.; was a farmer; dw. successively in Barre, Elba, Buffalo, Elba (again), Rochester, N. Y., Bunker Hill, Ingham Co., Mich., Leslie, Mich., and Bunker Hill (again); m, by Judge Edgar C. Dibble, of the Genesee county court, in Batavia, N. Y., 20 Sept., 1846, Sarah Ann Harkness, b. 27 of 5 mo., 1825, in Wheatland, N. Y., dau. of Daniel and Beulah (Estes) Harkness, of Elba, N. Y.; postoffice, Fitchburg, Mich.

ZACHARIAH[6] SHOTWELL, 1788-1857, of Genesee and Wayne counties, N. Y., [of Benj[5]., Benj[4]., John[3], John[2], Abr[1].], m. (3) 1828, *Elizabeth H. Lundy*, 1800-1857, dau. of Samuel and Sarah (Lundy) Lundy, of Independence, N. J., and had:

7. *Samuel Lundy*, b. 21 of 11 mo., 1829, Elba, N. Y.; took a university course at Union College New York, afterwards was successfully engaged in teaching in Queens Co., N. Y., and received a gold medal for services rendered in establishing the graded Farr school system at Whitestone in said county. He taught in the Friends' school at Westbury, L. I., also in the Friends' Institute in New York City. He held a state teacher's certificate for New York granted by Henry S. Randall, and a principal's certificate for New York City granted by Samuel S. Randall. He was principal for several years of District School No. 8 in Kingston, N. Y. It is owing chiefly to his efforts the present educational system of Kingston was adopted. He removed to El Dorado, Butler Co., Kansas in 1869. Was county superintendent of schools for two years. Organized the Exchange Bank and was its cashier for several years.

In 1893 he was in the banking business in Minnesota, was taken with typhoid pneumonia and pleurisy, spent four months in the St. Mary's Hospital, and when able to travel removed to Escondide, Cal., where he has regained much of his former health though with lungs seriously engorged.

He there enjoys the respect and confidence of the community, being city clerk, city assessor, secretary of the board of trade, and secretary of the Escondide Mutual Building and Loan Association.

He has retained his firm faith in the tenets of Fox and Barclay, Penn and Woolman. A consistant republican, voting for Freemont and every republican candidate.

He was a good accountant, reliable, honest and trustworthy, he was always faithful to trusts reposed in him, and to the interest of those by whom he was employed. He m. Sarah (Smith) Underhill, of Amawalk, Westchester Co., N. Y.

8. *Edna Ann*, b. 30 of 5 mo., 1832, Elba, N. Y., member of Farmington M. M., 23 of 11 mo., 1854, d. a. p., soon after marriage; m. Jesse McKeel, a Friend, who lived at Amawalk, Westchester Co., N. Y.

ZACUARIAH POUND[7] SHOTWELL, b. 1811, d. at Poplar Hill, Ont., 17 of 12 mo., 1895, Lobo, C. W., s. of Thomas[6] and Tamer (Lundy) Shotwell, of Galen, Wayne Co., N. Y., [of Benj[5]., Benj[4]., John[3], John[2], Abr[1].], m. 1835, *Margaret Zavitz*, 1814-1861, dau. of Jacob and Elizabeth (Pound[5]) Zavitz, of Canada, [of Daniel[4], Elijah[3], John[2], John[1]], and had:

1. *Tamer Ann*, b. 25 of 7 mo., 1836, in Galen, N. Y.; dw. with her father at Lobo, Ont., and afterward with sister Emily near Garrison, Neb.

2. *Thomas Benjamin*, b. 22 of 4 mo., 1838; went twice from Michigan to California, dw. Seattle, Wash., d. at David City, Neb., 2 of 2 mo., 1895; was a farmer and carpenter, a great worker and accumulated a good property; he m. Galen, N. Y., 7 of 12 mo , 1864, Emily Rachel Thorn, b 25 of 2 mo., 1841, in Junius, N. Y., dw. Swartz Creek, Genesee Co., Mich., dau. of Isaac R[5]. and Rebecca (Palmer) Thorn, of Galen, N. Y., [of Joel[4], Abr[3]., Abr[2]., Abr[1].]. Their only child died when three days old.

3. *Jacob Zavitz*[4], b. 25 of 4 mo., 1840, Galen, N. Y., removed to Butler Co., Neb., taking cert. of membership from Yarmouth M. M. of (Hic.) Friends 9 of 4 mo., 1879; P. O., Garrison, Neb.; m. in Mendon, N. Y., 29 of 1 mo., 1870, Arabella J[5]. Cox, b. Scottsville, N. Y., 25 of 6 mo., 1840, dau. of Joseph[1], Jr., and Hannah (Briggs) Cox, of Wheatland, N. Y., (m. 1839) the former (1815-52), son of Joseph[6], and Dorothy (Farwell) Cox, of Wheatland, N. Y., [of Samuel[5], Joseph[4] Cock, Samuel[3], Henry[2], James[1]], and the latter (1814-50), dau. of James and Elizabeth (Quimby) Briggs of Westchester Co., N. Y.

4. *Daniel Pound*[4], b. 8 of 2 mo., 1842, Elba (now Oakfield) N. Y.; removed to Butler Co., Neb, from Lobo, Ont.; P. O., Garrison, Neb.; m. by Friends' order, Lobo, Ont., 10 of 2 mo., 1886, Sarah V. (Bond) Shotwell, wd. of his younger brother, Merritt E., q. v.

5. *Elizabeth Emily*, b. 31 of 5 mo., 1844, Oakfield, N. Y.; dw. Butler Co., Neb., unm.; P. O., Garrison.

6. *Eli Lundy*, b. 29 of 11 mo., 1847, in Oakfield, N. Y.; dw. Butler Co., Neb., s. p.; P. O., David City. To him and his father we are indebted for information kindly furnished. He m. near David City, Butler Co., Neb., 25 of 11 mo., 1875, Leah Bunting, b. 15 March, 1852, Millersburgh, Mercer Co., Ill., dau. of Ebenezer and Susan Bunting of Pennsylvania.

7. *Benjamin Heaton*[4], b. 23 of 8 mo., 1853, Lobo, C. W.; dw. Butler Co., Neb., P. O., Brainard; m. in Ontario, .. Feb., 1876, Melissa

Lowes, dau. of Caleb and Susannah Lowes, of Blenheim, Ont.

8. *Merritt Elmer*[5], b., 26 of 1 mo., 1859, in Lobo, C. W., and there d. 20 of 3 mo., 1879; was a school teacher; m. in Caradoc, Middlesex Co., Ont., 8 Dec., 1877, Sarah Vermiliar Bond, b. .. June, 1859, dw. Garrison, Neb., dau. of John and Jane Bond; united with Yarmouth M. M. of (Hic.) Friends 10 of 9 mo. 1879; she m (2) 10 of 2 mo., 1886, Merritt's older brother, Daniel P. Shotwell.

SHOTWELL ADDRESSES FROM AMERICAN CITY AND STATE DIRECTORIES, 1895.

1. *Shotwell &* Burt, mers., 19 White Hall St., New York City, N. Y.

2. *Shotwell,* A. D., & Co., tanners and sumac mfgrs., Perry St. & R. & P. R. R., Manchester, Va.; house 800 Cowardin Ave.

3. *Alexander,* retired; h. 30 Pearl St., N. Plainfield, N. J.

4. *Alonzo,* f'wd'g, 25 Liberty St., New York City, N. Y.

5. *Alonzo,* real estate, 14 S. Del. Ave., Philadelphia, Pa.; h. 1725 N. 31st St.

6. *Annie T.,* wid. Joseph F.; h. 241 Quincy St., Brooklyn, N. Y.

7. *Benjamin,* carpenter, bds. 197 Washington Boul., Chicago, Ill.

8. *Benj. F.,* real estate, h. s. s. Gridley, e of State St., Ottawa, Ill.

9. *Benj. W.,* dentist, Trenton, Mo.

10. *Byron A.,* clerk; h. 250 W. 84th St., New York City, N. Y.

11. *C. H.,* real estate, 2813 Dearborn St., Chicago, Ill.; h. Evanston, Ill.

12. *C. H.,* hod carrier; h. 452 Park Ave., Cincinnati, O.

13. *Carlos B.,* Sec. White Lead Wks.; h. 469 3rd Ave., Detroit, Mich.

14. *Caroline,* wid. Peter; h. 408 Gold St., Brooklyn, N. Y.

15. *Cassius,* bkpr., 98 Dearborn St., Chicago, Ill.; h. 642 W. 62nd St.

16. *Cassius, Jr.,* (Jno. Cheshire & Co.), 4304 Cottage Ave., Chicago, Ill.; h. 642 W. 62nd St.

17. *Catherine,* wid. Geo.; h. 3521 N. 11th St., St. Louis, Mo. (Removed. Mail so addressed returned 1896.)

18. *Charles,* coachman; h. 144 Linn St., Cincinnati, O.

19. *Chas A.,* grain, 18 Board of Trade Bld'g., Indianapolis, Ind.; h. s. w. cor. Cherry and Lawn Aves. (Irvington).

20. *Chas. H.,* phys., 200 n. Commerce St., Gainesville, Texas; h. 304 n. Commerce St.

21. *Charles M.,* clerk, 6 Van Pelt Ave., Erastina, Staten Island, N. Y.

22. *Chas. W.,* clerk, bds 349 Dearborn Ave., Chicago, Ill.

23. *Christina,* wid Abel, aged 67, died Aug. 8, 1894.

24. *Dee* (c.), servant, 106 Monroe St., Memphis, Tenn.

25. *Edmund D.,* stable boy, G. Kal.; bds. 432 E. 12th St., Sioux Falls, S. D.

26. *Edw'd D.,* clerk, Hackensack, N. J.; h. Passaic, n. N. 2d.

27. *Edw'd O.,* grain; h. 2740 Lucas Ave., St. Louis, Mo.

28. *Elizabeth,* h. 30 Pearl St., N. Plainfield, N. J.

29. *Elizabeth,* wid. Edmund; h. 148 E. 2nd St., Plainfield, N. J.

30. *Elizabeth,* wid. Wm.; h. 349 Dearborn Ave., Chicago, Ill.

31. *Elsworth, E.,* teller, Cal. Safe Deposit and Trust Co., San Francisco, Cal.; h. 622 Sutter St.

32. *Ezra M.,* dlr. in cattle; h. 432 E. 12th St., Sioux Falls, S. D.

33. *Ezra W.,* butter and eggs, Shotwell & Carver, (Jno. W. Carver), Lohrville, Iowa.

34. *Frank,* salesman, h. 1736 N. 29th St., Philadelphia, Pa.

35. *Frank C.,* engineer, 332 Genesee St., Trenton, N. J. (Mail so addressed returned from Columbia Station, 1896.)

36. *Frank W.,* draughtsman; h. 1129 9th St., New Orleans, La.

37. *Furman J.,* clerk; h. 26 Fairview Ave., N. Plainfield, N. J.

38. *Geo.,* inlayer, Hughes Ave., Bloomfield, Staten Island, N. Y. (No such P. O.)

39. *Geo.,* clerk, Cincinnati, O.; h. Bellevue, Ky.

40. *Geo. H.,* clerk, 25th St. and Liberty Ave., Pittsburgh, Pa.; h. Wilkinsburg, P. R. R.

41. *George M.,* policeman, 23 Erastina Pl., Erastina, Staten Island, N. Y.

42. *George M.,* liquors, 147 W. 23d St., New York City, N. Y.

43. *Geo. W.,* oysterman, 6 Van Pelt Ave., Erastina, Staten Island, N. Y.

44. *Geo. W.,* upholsterer; h. 132 Fillmore St., Nashville, Tenn.

45. *Green,* (c.) carp.; h. 41 Rice St., Lexington, Ky.

46. *Greene, Sr.;* h. s. w. c. Court and Baymiller Sts., Cincinnati, O.

47. *Greene, Jr.;* h. s. w. c. Court and Baymiller Sts., Cincinnati, O.

48. *Harvey H.,* patrolman 1st Precinct; h. 360 Plymouth Ave., Buffalo, N. Y.

49. *Mrs. Hattie A.;* h. 3109 Columbus Ave., Minneapolis, Minn.

50. *Henry,* hardwood, bds, 905 5th St., Louisville, Ky.

51. *H'y T.,* com. mer., 74 Washington Ave., Brooklyn, N. Y.; h. 159 Will'b'y Ave.

52. *Miss Hertha,* bds. 432 E. 12th St., Sioux Falls, S. D.

53. *Horace J.* (Canfield-Shotwell Co.), h. 3109 Columbus Ave., Minneapolis, Minn.

54. *Hugh W.*, mer., 19 Whitehall St., New York City, N. Y.; h. Hempstead, L. I.

55. *Isaac*, h. 1508 N. 10th St., Philadelphia, Pa.

56. *Isabella*, h. 102 W. 89th St., New York City, N. Y.

57. *J. B.*, trav., Whitman & Bm. Co., Kansas City, Mo. (Mail so addressed returned unclaimed, 1896.)

58. *J. H.*, physician, Asbury Park, N. J.; 3rd Ave. and B. St., Belmar.

59. *J. Loleo*, genl. store, Grapeland, Texas.

60. *J. Tudor*, clerk L. & N. R. R. frt. office, Cincinnati, O.; h. Bellevue, Ky.

61. *James*, asst. supt. Galv. Rope & Twine Factory, Galveston, Texas; h. 3807 Ave. L.

62. *Jas. A.*, clerk S. E. Olson Co., rms. 508 2nd Ave., Minneapolis, Minn.

63. *James B.*, com. trav.; h. 642 W. 62nd St., Chicago, Ill.

64. *Jay W.*, brakeman M. C. R. R.; h. 1324 E. Main St., Jackson, Mich. (Removed 1895 to Los Angeles, Cal.)

65. *John*, h. 851 S. Meridian St., Indianapolis., Ind.

66. *John B.*, reporter Cinn. Times-Star; h. c. 8th and Vine Sts., Cincinnati, O.

67. *John B*, physician, 137 W. 49th St.. New York City, N. Y.

68. *Jno. C.*, Shotwell & Pitts (H. B. Pitts), merchandise and cotton brokers, Marshall, Texas.

69. *John D.*, student; h. 2803 Thomas St., St. Louis, Mo.

70. *John F.* (Douglas & Shotwell); h. Starr Ave., e. of Cleveland Ave., Columbus, O.

71. *John H.*, h. 513 Asbury Ave., Asbury Park, N. J.

72. *John H.*, clerk (A. D. Shotwell & Co.); h. 300 Cowardin Ave., Manchester, Va.

73. *John L.*, moved from Memphis, Tenn. to Asbury Park, N. J.

74. *John W.*, 602 21st St., n. w. Washington, D. C.

75. *Joseph*, blacksmith; h. 37 Riddle St., Covington, Ky.

76. *Joseph D.*, teller Bowery Savings Bank, 130 Bowery, New York City; h. 82 Hillside Ave., Orange, N. J.

77. *Joseph H.*, iron worker, h. 1825 Taney St., Philadelphia, Pa.

78. *Joseph M.*, mgr. The Merchants Exchange Assn. of San Francisco, Merchants Exchange Bldg; h. Ross Valley, Marin Co., Cal.

79. *Julia*, h. 76 N. 11th St., Newark, N. J.

80. *Longstreet*, engineer, h. 116 N. Elliot Pl., Brooklyn, N. Y.

81. *Louis*, clerk; h. 197 Straight St., Paterson, N. J.

82. *Louis B.*, clk. Glass Blk.. Minneapolis, Minn.; h. 3109 Columbus Ave.

83. *Manning*, salesman, h. 118 Adelphi St., Brooklyn, N. Y.

84. *Mrs. Margt. H.*, Seattle, Wash.; bds. Margin St. n of Hawthorne Ave., Ross.

85. *Marie*, actress, h. 250 W. 84th St., New York City, N. Y.

86. *Mark*, lab.; h. 1510 Gay St., St. Louis, Mo.

87. *Mary*, wid. B. H., h. 424 Van Buren St., Milwaukee, Wis.

88. *Mrs. Mary A.*, prop. Shotwell Hotel, Lufkin, Texas.

89. *McClery J.*, works local frt. So. Ry., Knoxville, Tenn.; h. 433 Depot St., w.

90. *Mary E. A.*, wid. Geo. H., h. 40 Lawrence St., Cincinnati, O.

91. *Melancthon S.*, draftsman; h. Front St. c. Clinton Ave., Harrisburg, Pa.

92. *Miss Mollie*, printer; h. 349 Dearborn Ave., Chicago, Ill

93. *Nancy*, wid.; h. cor. Wayne and McDonald Sts., Lima, O.

94. *Norman E.*, piano tuner; h. 573 Springdale Ave., E. Orange, N. J.

95. *P. Northrup*, salesman, Hackensack, N. J.; h. Passaic n., N. 2nd.

96. *Randolph*, oysterman, Washington Ave., Summerville, Staten Island, N. Y.

97. *Reuben H.*, Sec. Board of Police Commissioners, Four Courts; h. 2740 Lucas Ave., St. Louis, Mo.

98. *Reuben H.*, flour mill, W'port Ave., c. Mill St., Kansas City, Mo.; h. W'port Ave., c. Jefferson.

99. *Robert*, stable foreman; h. 1917 McAllister St., San Francisco, Cal.

100. *Samuel H.*, imptr. French kid gloves, glovers material, dealer in domestic kid gloves, salted fleshers, etc., 55 S. Main St., Gloversville, N. Y.; h. 149 S. Main St.

101. *Sanford*, (c), lab.; h. 470 Market St., Lexington, Ky.

102. *Mrs. Sarah*, h. 76 11th St., Newark, N. J.

103. *Sarah*, wid. Geo. H., 1129 9th St., New Orleans, La.

104. *Sarah*, wid. Jobe; h. 824 N. Adams St., Peoria, Ill.

105. *Sarah R.*, wid. Robert; h. 75 Schenectady Ave., Brooklyn, N. Y.

106. *Seymour*, salesman; h. 742 Tehama St., San Francisco, Cal.

107. *Stuart B., Jr.*, Vice Pres. and Treas. Graves & Vinton Co.; h. 509 Holly Ave., St. Paul, Minn.

108. *Theo.*, b'keeper; h. 706 President St., Brooklyn, N. Y.

109. *Theo.*, Shotwell, Sprague & Dibble, (A. H. Sprague, F. D. Dibble,) gen. agts. Manhattan Life Ins. Co., 400 Kasota bldg., Minneapolis, Minn.; h. 902, s. e. 7th St.

110. *Theo. B*, carpenter, Richmond Ave., Graniteville, Staten Island, N. Y.

111. *Thomas*, laborer; h. 349 Linden St.. Brooklyn, N. Y.

SAMUEL L. SHOTWELL, BORN 1829.

At age of 30,

Latterly of Escondido, Cal., son of Zachariah[6] and Elizabeth H. Lundy Shotwell, of Genesee and Wayne Counties, N. Y., and grandson 1 of Benjamin[5] and Bathsheba (Pound Shotwell of Galen, N. Y., (of Benjamin[4], John[3], John[2], Abraham[1]), and 2) of Samuel and Sarah Lundy Lundy, of Independence. N. J.

112. *Thos. C.*, reporter Cinn. Times-Star; h. 308 Race St., Cincinnati, O.

113. *Thos. D.*, real estate, 905 Walnut St., Philadelphia, Pa.; h. Verbena Ave., Oak La Sta.

114. *Thos. J.*, fireman H. E. & W. T. Ry., Houston, Texas.

115. *Thos. M.*, 1150 N. Quincy St., Topeka, Kans.

116. *Townsend W.*, real estate, 2259 7th Ave., New York City, N. Y.; h. 21 E. 129th St.

117. *Trumbull S.*, horse dlv.; bds Transit House, Chicago, Ill.

118. *W. E.*, butter and eggs, Shotwell & Davis, (J. T. Davis) Perry, Iowa.

119. *Wallace*, porter, 11 Elsie Pl., Buffalo, N. Y.

120. *Walter E.*, tobacco, 41 Broad St., New York; h. 977 Laf. Ave., Brooklyn, N. Y.

121. *Walter L.*, salesman; h. 20 Eagles St., Newark, N. J.

122. *Wm.*, porter; h. 237 9th St., Cincinnati, O.

123. *Wm. B.*, h. 89 Bedford St., New York City, N. Y.

124. *Wm. B.*, salesman, 33 Bond Port, Richmond, Staten Island, N. Y.

125. *Wm. E.*, physician, 3403 Lafayette St., Denver, Col.

126. *Wm. E.*, yardman, Fullerton Lumber Co., Sioux Falls, S. D.; h. 9th St., w. of Western Ave.

127. *Wm. J.*, genl. agt. Denver & Rio Grande R. R. Co., 203 Front St., San Francisco, Cal.; h. Occidental Hotel.

128. *Wm. J.*, retired, 101 Grove St., East Orange, N. J.

129. *Wm. M.*, ins. agt.; h. 101 Grove St., E. Orange, N. J.

130. *Wm. P.*, asst. y'dmaster L. S. & M. S.; h. 847 Clinton St., Buffalo, N. Y.

131. *Wm. P., Jr.*, yard brakeman; h. 847 Clinton St., Buffalo, N. Y.

132. *Wm. W.*, supt. Crown Financial Co., St. Paul, Minn.; h. 905 s. e. 5th St., Minneapolis, Minn.

133. *Zack*, (c.), drayman; h. 40 Kinkead, Lexington, Ky.

NON-RESISTANT SHOTWELLS IN TIME OF THE REVOLUTION.

EXTRACTS FROM "AN ACCOUNT OF FRIENDS' SUFFERINGS WITHIN THE VERGE OF THIS (RAHWAY AND PLAINFIELD MONTHLY) MEETING, CHIEFLY FOR FINES AND TAXES FOR THE PURPOSES OF WAR," 1777–1780, COPIED FROM THE BOOK OF MINUTES.—*O. R. L.*

Benjamin Shotwell--
1 saddle, 1 cow	£8 10 0
2 cows, 1 mare, 1 hog, bed and bedding, plates and basins	30 5
2 calves, 2 cattle	8 10

Abraham Shotwell—
1 pair oxen	25
1 looking glass and cow	10
1 beast	3
1 beast	2 16 0

Isaiah Shotwell—
3 cows, 3 heifers, 1 steer, 2 calves	36 10
½ ton hay	2

William Shotwell—
1 wagon	17 0 0
2 cows, saddle, andirons, basins, plates	12 7
1 barrel cider spirits	11 0
5 sheep, 4 lambs	5
Hay	7

Isaac Shotwell—
Bed, bedding and clothing	£16 0 0
Looking glass, and andirons	5 10
Iron, axe, bible	8 12

Joseph Shotwell—
Feather bed, bolster, pillows, blankets, quilts, sheets	28 0 0
2 tables, plates, 8 chairs, 2 brass kettles, tea kettle	12 2 0

John Shotwell—
2 mahogany tables	7 15 0
Mahogany nest of drawers	12 0 0
2 looking glasses	8 0 0
Chairs	5 12 0
Household furniture	21 6 0
Kettles, pots, shovels, plates	10 9
3 feather beds, sheets	20 0

Joseph Shotwell—
1 mahogany table, 2 mahogany chairs	7 10 0
2 walnut tables, 13 chairs	13 11 0

Joseph Shotwell—*Continued.*				James Shotwell—			
1 desk and book case	£20	0	0	Feather bed, bedstead, trunk, andirons and kettle	£8	6	0
Looking glass	4	10	0				
Bed, bolster, sheets	12	0	0	Jacob Shotwell—			
Harness and saddle	10	0	0	One iron pot, pewter basin	0	17	9
Andirons, kettles, shovels, tongs, dishes, plates	21	17	6				

NOTE.—The valuation of the articles mentioned in the foregoing list was evidently expressed in a depreciated currency; but the hardship occasioned by the distraining and sale of such wares at a heavy sacrifice, was certainly sufficient to attest the sincerity of their profession of conscientious scruples against abetting military operations. Few reputable citizens would bid for the goods of their Quaker neighbors; and the latter did not feel free to redeem their own. Some of them had similarly suffered during the French War twenty years before for refusing to bear arms *for* Great Britain; they now suffered for refusing to fight or encourage others to fight *against* Great Britain. For belligerent Shotwells in that day, see pages 169 and 177.—A. M. S.

VITAL STATISTICS OF NEW JERSEY QUAKERS.

MARRIAGES MENTIONED IN THE BOOK OF MINUTES OF (AMBOY, WOODBRIDGE), RAH-
WAY AND PLAINFIELD MONTHLY MEETING OF MEN FRIENDS, PRIOR TO
THE YEAR 1785, AND KINDRED DATA FROM OTHER
RECORDS OF THE SOCIETY OF FRIENDS
IN UNION AND MIDDLESEX
COUNTIES, N. J.

NOTE.—The data here presented include marriages consummated in a manner contrary to the discipline of Friends, which required that the contracting parties should lay their intentions of marriage before two successive monthly meetings and secure the approbation of the Society, after which they were at liberty to marry themselves in a public meeting of Friends appointed for that purpose under the care of a special committee, who reported the "orderly" accomplishment of the same to the next monthly meeting. Copies of the certificates were usually preserved by the Society; and, so far as practicable, these transcripts have been consulted. In other cases, only approximate dates are given, the marriages having occurred between two successive monthly meetings of the dates specified. A few dates of births of Shotwells not elsewhere correctly entered in this volume, and a few Shotwell marriages of later date than 1785, are also given. For explanation of abbreviations, see page IV *ante*.

Allen, Joseph W., of New York, s. of Joseph and Elizabeth, of Monmouth Co., N. J., m. at Rahway, 12-26, 1822, to Harriet Shotwell, dau. of Peter and Phebe, of Middlesex Co., N. J.

Allen, Trustam, given certificate of membership and clearness 8-16, 1718, about to go to New England.

Alling [Allen], Samuel, m. between 2-20 and 3-18, 1732, Martha Shotwell, notwithstanding Sarah Bunn's opposition.

Ashton, Joseph, l. l. 7-20, 1711, to m. Mary Fitz Randolph.

Atkinson, Jno., with consent of his mother, Anna Gosney, m. between 12-15, 1727-8 and 1-21, 1727-8, to Susanna Haddon.

Bellangee, Aaron, of Woodbridge, s. of Thos. and Margaret, m. at Rahway, 3-3, 1825, to Margaret Shotwell, dau. of Henry and Sarah, of Woodbridge, N. J.

Bethell, Wm., given certificate of clearness from Amboy. (N. J.) m. m., 7-14, 1687, to m. a woman at Philadelphia.

Bloodgood, Abraham, m. before 4-16, 1761, to one not a Friend, contrary to discipline; disowned by W. R. & P. M. M., 7-16, 1761.

Bloodgood, Wm., m. between 1-16, 1726-7 and 2-20, 1727, to Mary Gach.

Bonnell, Jacob, m. between 11-24 and 12-18, 1760, to Mary Schooley.

Brooke, Chas., of Woodbridge, N. J., m. at Rahway, N. J., 8-28, 1788, to Ame Shotwell, of Elizabeth, N. J.

Brotherton, Henry, of Woodbridge, m. 6-25, 1713, at Woodbridge, Ann Shotwell, spinster of Richmond Co., N. Y. He was appointed Clerk of Woodbridge M. M. 12-17, 1714-15.

Brotherton, Henry, m. between 8-20 and 9-28, 1752, to Masse Schooley.

Brotherton, James, m. between 6-20 and 7-18. 1754, to Alice Schooley.

Burling, Thos., of New York City, with certificate of clearness from New Town (L. I.) M. M., m. at Rahway, N. J., 5-9, 1771, to Sarah Shotwell, of Woodbridge, N. J.

Carrill, James, member of Mendham Preparative Meeting, m. before 12-18, 1760, without unity of Friends; made acknowledgment to W. R. & P. M. M., 1-15, 1761.

Custer [Kester] Samuel, with certificate of clearness from Kingwood M. M., m. between 9-21 and 10-19, 1758, to Susannah Webster.

Chambers, Wm., l. l. 8-15, 1719. to m. Sarah Webster.

Clark, Jno., of Mendham Preparative Meeting, m. before 4-19, 1780, without unity of Friends; made acknowledgment to R. & P. M. M., 8-16, 1780.

Clark, Thos., of Mendham Preparative Meeting, m. before 4-19, 1780, without unity of Friends; made acknowledgment to R. & P. M. M., 8-16, 1780.

Clarkson, James, m. (1) before ...., 1740, without unity of Friends; he m. (2) before 1-21, 1744-5; again without the unity of Friends, and within two or three months after death of former wife; disowned 1-21, 1744-5. by Woodbridge M. M.

Cock, Jas., given certificate of clearness from W. R. & P. M. M., 6-19, 1761, to Westbury M. M.; m. Dorothy [Cock, of Hezekiah.]

Cohn, Peter, of Rahway, s. of Nicholas and Judith, m. at Rahway, 11-26, 1818, to Ann Shotwell, dau. of Henry and Sarah, of Woodbridge Tp., N. J.

Copeland, Cowperthwait, m. 2-26, 1750, to Susannah Atkinson.

Copland, Cowperthwaite, m. 4-1, 1772, to Margaret Flatt.

Cowperthwaite, John, of Mendham Preparative Meeting, m. before 10-19, 1774. without unity of Friends; disowned 11-16, 1774.

[*Craig*, John, m. in Pres. ch, New York City, 1-8, 1789, Hester Shotwell.]

Crane, Elizabeth, made acknowledgment to R. & P. M. M., 11-16, 1774, for having m. without unity of Friends.

Dell, Randolph, with parents' consent, m. between 2-17 and 3-17, 1763, to Anna (or Ann) Liken.

Dell, Richard, m. between 2-21 and 4-18, 1754, to Elizabeth Schooley.

Dell, Richard, Jr., of Hanover, N. J., m. at Plainfield, 11-21, 1792, to Rachel Shotwell, of Elizabeth, N. J.

Dorland, Philip, of Lenox Co., Upper Canada, s. of Samuel and Ann, m. at Rahway, 1-28, 1808, Lydia Shotwell, of Elizabeth, N. J., dau. of Benj. and Amy.

Fitz Randolph, Catherine, disowned by W. R. & P. M. M., 2-15, 1764, for having been m. to .... Shaver, by a priest.

Fitz Randolph, Edward, Jr., given cert. of cl. from Woodbridge M. M., 7-26, 1734, to Flushing M. M.; [m. 8-3. 1734, Phebe Jackson].

Fitz Randolph, Edward, m. between 11-12, and 12-18, 1782, to Mary Webster.

Fitz Randolph, Experience, m. before 4-.., 1717, to .... Moores, without the unity of Friends and without consent of parents.

Fitz Randolph, Hartshorn, m. before 11-15, 1746-7, [to Ruth ....,] without the unity of Friends; made acknowledgment to Woodbridge M. M., 1-17, 1746-7.

Fitz Randolph, Jas., disowned by W. R. & P. M. M., 1-15, 1761, for having m. without unity of Friends.

Fitz Randolph, Jno., of Woodbridge, N. J., m. at Rahway, 7-25, 1793, to Mary King, of Elizabethtown, [dau. of Nathan].

Fitz Randolph, Joseph, was at sea at time of Woodbridge M. M. 3-20, 1731, but m. between 3-27 and 4-17, 1731, to Elizabeth Kinsey.

Fitz Randolph, Mary, disowned by W. R. & P. M. M., 7-18, 1764, for having married her 1st cousin.

Fitz Randolph, Nathaniel, Jr., m. before 4-21, 1739, contrary to Friends' discipline; made acknowledgment 4-21, 1739.

Fitz Randolph, Nathaniel, [of Woodbridge], m. [8-22], 1745, to Mary Shotwell, [of Woodbridge, N. J.].

Fitz Randolph, Richard, given certificate of clearness from Woodbridge M. M. 6-28, 1735, to Shrewsbury M. M.; [m. Elizabeth ....].

Fitz Randolph, Robert, m. before 12-20, 1738-40, to his cousin Catherine Taylor, without the unity of Friends.

Fitz Randolph, Robert, Jr., disowned by W. R. & P. M. M., 1-15, 1761, for having m. his 1st cousin; reinstated 8-20, 1766.

Fitz Randolph, Robert, m. before 9-17, 1766, contrary to discipline; disowned 11-19, 1766.

Fitz Randolph, Robert. m. (2) before 4-20, 1768, without unity of Friends, 2nd time, for which disowned by W. R. & P. M. M., 5-18, 1768.

Fitz Randolph, Samuel, Jr., m. between 9-20 and 10-18, 1729, Johannah Kinsey.

Fitz Randolph, Samuel, Jr., given certificate of clearness from Woodbridge M. M., 5-17, 1753, to Nansemoud M. M., in Va.; another certificate of clearness given him 11-19, 1756.

Fitz Randolph, Taylor, of Plainfield Preparative Meeting, m. before 1-16, 1783, to Mary ...., without unity of Friends; both disowned by R. & P. M. M., 3-20, 1783.

Fitz Randolph, Thos., m. 11-23, 1763, to Abigail Vail.

Forrester, [Forster], Miles, l. l. at Amboy, N. J., 12-9, 1686-7, to m. Rebecca Laury [Lawrie]; had dau. Mary, b. 8-18, 1687.

Gach, Thos., l. l. 6-17, 1721, to m. Elizabeth Bloodgood.

Greuary, Thos., given certificate of clearness 4-18, 1719.

Griffith, Benj., l. l. 8-21, 1708, to m. Mary Hooper, who had one or more children by a former husband who had departed from her 14 years before and had not been heard from since.

Griffith, Jno., having certificate of clearness from Middletown M. M., in Bucks Co., Pa., l. l. 8-20, 1709, to m. Elizabeth Gach, (or Gauge,) a widow, who had children by former husband.

Haddon, Thos., m. between 1-16, 1726-7 and 2-20, 1727, to Margaret Fitz Randolph.

Hallet, Israel, of Queens Co., L. I., with certificate of clearness from Flushing M. M., m. at Rahway, N. J., 11-21, 1765, Naomy Shotwell, of Elizabeth, N. J., [dau. of Abraham'].

Hallet, Thomas, of Queens Co., L. I., with certificate of clearness from Flushing M. M., m. at Rahway, N. J., 9-22, 1763, Phebe Shotwell, of Elizabeth, N. J.

Hampton, Abner, m. between 1-15, 1743-4, and 2-19, 1744, Rachael Webster.

Hampton, Wm., of Elizabeth, N. J., member of W. R. & P. M. M., by certificate of clearness from Chesterfield M. M., m. at Rahway, N. J., 9-28, 1768, to Sarah Shotwell, of Elizabeth, N. J.

Hance, Isaac, with certificate of clearness from Shrewsbury M. M., m. between 10-21 and 11-18, 1772, to Catherine Miller, with their parents' consent.

Hance, Jno., m. between 12-17, 1777, and 1-21, 1778, Elizabeth Miller, with consent of their parents.

Harned, Jonathan, Jr., with fathers' approbation, m. 7-23, 1766, to Sarah Laing.

Harned, Jonathan, m. 3-24, 1768, Judah Bloodgood.

Harned, Nathaniel, m. between 4-17 and 5-15, 1742, to Annah Closson.

Harned, Nathaniel, l. l. 5-18, 1751, to m. Upham Alwood.

Haydock, James, with certificate of clearness from Flushing M. M., m. between 3-18 and 4-15, 1756, to Elizabeth Thorn.

Haydock, Jas., given certificate of clearness from W. R. & P. M. M., 1-16, 1765, to Shrewsbury M. M., to m. Phebe Tilton.

Haydock, James, Jr., given certificate of clearness from R. & P. M. M., 6-15, 1785, to N. Y. M. M.

Haydock, Jno., member of W. R. & P. M. M., 12-18, 1765, by certificate from Flushing M. M., m. at Rahway, N. J., 4-23, 1766, to Mary Shotwell, of Rahway, dau. of Joseph.

Heady, Ephraim, with his father's consent, l. l. 3-21, 1724, to m. Susannah Fitz Randolph.

Heborn, John, l. l. 1-21, 1733-4, to m. Sarah Laing, [of John and Elizabeth (Shotwell) Laing].

Heborn, John, m. before 3-18, 1756, without unity of Friends; disowned 3-18 1756.

Heddon, Thos., of Woodbridge, m. before 8-18, 1750, without the unity of Friends; disowned by Woodbridge M. M., 8-18, 1750.

Hedger, Eliakim, given certificate of clearness to Crosswick's M. M. 3-21, 1730.

Hedger, Jno., with certificate of clearness from Chesterfield M. M. and parents' consent, m. 2-27, 1765, Mary Fitz Randolph.

Hedger, Samuel, with father's consent, m. between 10-21 and 11-18, 1762, to Mary Vail.

Hicks, Samuel, of Westbury, N. Y., s. of Benj. and Phebe, m. at Rahway, 2-20, 1794, to Amy (Shotwell) Brook, of Rahway, wid. of Charles.

Hunt, Marmaduke, with certificate from Mamaroneck M. M. and his mother's consent, m. 7-17, 1761, Elizabeth Marsh.

Hunt, Solomon, with certificate of clearness, m. between 2-17 and 3-15, 1729, to Katherine Bishop.

Hunt, Solomon, given certificate of clearness from W. R. & P. M. M., 10-25, 1764, to the Falls M. M. in Pa., to m. wid. Mary Palmer.

Jelf, Catherine, made acknowledgment to R. & P. M. M., 1-16, 1783, for having been m. "before a hireling priest."

Kinsey, Benjamin, m. before 12-20, 1739-40, without the unity of Friends.

Kinsey, Edward, brought certificate from Newark, in Newcastle Co., Pa., l. l. 8-21, 1708, to m. Sarah Ogborn.

Kinsey, Jno., Jr., given certificate of clearness to Philadelphia M. M., in 5 mo., 1725.

Kinsey, Jonathan, m. before 6-17, 1739, without the unity of Friends; made acknowledgment to Woodbridge M. M., 6-17, 1739.

Kinsey, Mutry, m. 1-26, 1764 to Sarah Fitz Randolph.

Kirkbridge, Stacy, with certificate of clearness from Falls (Bucks Co., Pa.,) M. M., m. between 4-19 and 5-17, 1753, to Frances Smith.

Laing, David, m. between 9-19 and 10-17, 1741, to Mary Thorn.

Laing, David, of Piscataway, [s. of David], m. at Plainfield, 10-25, 1786, to Sarah Shotwell, of Piscataway, N. J.

Laing, David, m. at Plainfield, 7-23, 1794, Mary Thorn.

Laing, Elizabeth, made acknowledgment to W. R. & P. M. M., 3-20, 1760, for having m. contrary to discipline.

Laing, Isaac, m. before 2-16, 1747, without unity of Friends; disowned by Woodbridge M. M. 2-16, 1747.

Laing, Isaac, Jr., m. between 7-18 and 8-21, 1782, Rachel Moore.

Laing, Isaac, m. at Rahway, N. J., 2-28, 1788, to Grace Moore, both of Middlesex Co., N. J.

Laing, Isaac, Jr., m. at Rahway, N. J., 5-22, 1788, to Katherine Kinsey, both of Woodbridge.

Laing, Jacob, m. before 2-21, 1748, without unity of friends; restored to membership in Woodbridge M. M., 10-21, 1749.

Laing, Jacob, m. between 12-15, and 1-15, 1749-50, to Ann (or Anna) Copling [Copland?].

Laing, Jacob, given certificate of clearness from W. R. & P. M. M., 2-22, 1769, to ____ M. M.

Laing, Jacob, of Piscataway, m. at Plainfield, N. J., 5–24, 1780, to Rachel Shotwell, of Elizabeth, N. J.

Laing, John, Jr., of Piscataway, N. J., 1680 ± –1728, s. of John[1] and Margaret, of Middlesex Co., N. J., m. at Woodridge, N. J., ---- of 9 mo. (Nov.), 1705, Elizabeth[3] Shotwell, dau. of John[2] and Elizabeth (Burton) Shotwell, [of Abraham[1]], and had:—(1.) Sarah, b. 9–16, 1706. (2.) Elizabeth, b. 10–10, 1707; "present Elizabeth Shotwell his wife's mother." (3.) John, b. 2–28, 1709; "present Elizabeth Shotwell and her dau. Sarah." (4.) Margaret, b. 9–9, 1710 (5.) Ann, b. 1–7, 1712. [See also pp. 125, 127.]

Laing, John, m. between 3–21 and 4–18, 1741, to Sarah Smith.

Laing, Jno., m. between 5–17 and 6–21, 1759, to Elizabeth Webster.

Laing, Jno., m. before 1–16, 1765, his former wife's first cousin [Hannah ? ----------,] without unity of Friends; reinstated 11–15, 1769, in W. R. & P. M. M.

Laing, Jno., s. of David and Mary, m. 10–28, 1767, Susannah Webster.

Laing, John, of Middlesex Co., N. J., m. at Rahway, 4–28, 1803, Anne Shotwell, of Essex Co., N. J.

Laing, Joseph, with mother's consent, m. 8–26, 1784, to Sarah Marsh.

Laing, Joseph, of Piscataway, m. at Plainfield, 7–23, 1795, to Anna Webster, of Essex Co., N. J.

Laing, Samuel, m. between 1–16, 1737–8, and 2–20, 1738, Elizabeth Smith.

Laing, Thos., member of R. & P. M. M., 5–17, 1781, by request; m. between 5–17 and 6–20, 1781, Martha Webster.

Laing, Thos., of Woodbridge, m. at Plainfield, 1–23, 1793, to Mary Shotwell, of Essex Co., N. J.

Latham, Thos., m. 4–23, 1766, to Miriam Allen.

Liken, Michael, with his father's consent, m. at Woodbridge, N. J., 8–20, 1743, Sarah Schooley.

Liken, Michael, m. before 11–16, 1758, without unity of Friends; disowned by W. R. & P. M. M., 12–21, 1758.

Liken, Rebecca, disowned by R. & P. M. M., 3–21, 1782, for having m. ---------- Mills, without unity of Friends.

Liken, Wm., m. before 10–19, 1774, contrary to discipline.

Ludlam, Elizabeth, made acknowledgment to R. & P. M. M., 10–19, 1774, for having m. without unity of Friends.

Lues, [Lewis?], Thos., l. l. 8–20, 1748, to m. Elizabeth Hedger, with her father's consent.

Lufbarrow (or Loofbourrow), John, declared intention of marriage with Gartrand Holland at Amboy M. M. 9–9, 1687.

Lundy, Jacob, Jr., with certificate of clearness from Kingwood M. M. and parents consent, m. 9–25, 1783, to [wid.] Sarah [Shotwell] Hampton.

Lundy, Joseph, of Hardwick, N. J., m. at Rahway, 4–26, 1787, to Elizabeth Shotwell, of Elizabeth, N. J., [parents of Benjamin Lundy, the philanthropist].

Marsh, Benj., given certificate of clearness from R. & P. M. M., 10–16, 1782, to ---------- M. M.

Marsh, Elias, m. before 7–20, 1774, without unity of Friends; disowned by R. & P. M. M., 8–17, 1774.

Marsh, James, of Elizabethtown, m. at Rahway, 5–24, 1792, Margaret Elston, of Woodbridge, N. J.

Marsh, Jno., m. between 6–19 and 7–18, 1782, Sarah Fitz Randolph.

Marsh, Jno., m. at Rahway, N. J., 8–26, 1799, to Phebe Allen, both of Woodbridge, N. J.

Marsh, Joseph, of Woodbridge, m. at Woodbridge 6–22, 1750, Martha Webster, of Elizabethtown, N. J.

Marsh, Joseph, of Rahway, m. (2) before 6–21, 1759, without unity of Friends, soon after death of former wife; made acknowledgment to W. R. & P. M. M., 11–15, 1759.

Marsh, Joseph, m. between 11–21 and 12–19, 1770, to Mary Copeland, with their parents consent.

Marsh, Joseph, of Rahway Preparative Meeting, m. before 11–17, 1773, to Mary ----------; without unity of Friends; he was disowned by R. & P. M. M., 12–15, 1773; wife disowned 1–19, 1774.

Marsh, Mordecai, of Rahway, member of R. & P. M. M., 6–17, 1778, with two children, by request, m. (2) at Rahway, 10–29, 1778, to Mary Shotwell, of Elizabeth, N. J.

Marsh, Peter, disowned by Woodbridge M. M., 1–19, 1758, for having m. without unity of Friends.

Marsh, Samuel, of Woodbridge, m. in Borough of Elizabeth, N. J., 12–17, 1743–4, Mary Shotwell, of the Borough of Elizabeth.

Marsh, Samuel, m. between 6–21 and 7–20, 1780, Zipporah Fitz Randolph.

Marsh, Wm., Jr., m. before 8–16, 1775, by a justice of the peace; disowned 11–15, 1775.

Marsh, Wm., m. between 11–15 and 12–20, 1753, to Sarah Webster.

Marsh, Wm., m. between 2–16 and 3–16, 1780, Sarah Horton, who was received by R. & P. M. M., 2–16, 1780, by certificate from Harrison's Purchase.

Marshall, Christopher, Jr., of Philadelphia, s. of Benjamin and Sarah, m. at Rahway, N. J., 12–27, 1804, Phebe Shotwell, Jr., dau. of John and Margaret, of Rahway, N. J.

Miller, Adam, l. l. 8–16, 1746, to m. Mary Young.

Miller, Robert, m. 5–29, 1778, to Catherine Fitz Randolph.

Moore, Benj., m. between 1–21, 1727–8 and 2–18, 1728, to Elizabeth Shotwell, with consent of their parents.

Moore, Enoch, m. between 6-21 and 7 18, 1735, Grace Brothertou.

Moore, Enoch, m. before 7-20, 1763, without the unity of Friends; disowned by W. R. & P. M. M., 8-17. 1763.

Moore, Enoch, made acknowledgment to R. & P. M. M., 3-18, 1779, for having m. without unity of Friends.

Moore, Grace, dau. of Enoch, deceased, m. before 2 18, 1762, to .... Duany, by a priest, contrary to her mother's advice, for which disowned by W. R. & P. M. M., 2 18, 1762.

Moore, Henry, of Westfield, N. J., s. of Enoch and Grace, m. at Rahway, 9-22, 1803, to Phebe Shotwell, of Woodbridge, N. J.

Moore, James, of Rahway, m. before 1-19, 1774, [contrary to discipline].

Moore, James, of Rahway Preparative Meeting, m. before 12-21, 1774, contrary to discipline, disowned, 2-15, 1775.

Moore, James, of Poughkeepsie, N. Y., s. of John and Eleanor, m. at Rahway, 5-5, 1825, to Hannah Murray Shotwell, dau. of Henry and Sarah, of Woodbridge, N. J.

Moore, Jno., m. before 7-20, 1774, to his first cousin Hannah ...., without unity of Friends; disowned by R & P. M. M., 8-17, 1774.

Moore, Jno., with certificate of clearness from Kingwood, M. M. and parents consent, m. between 3 20 and 4-16, 1783, Hannah Copland.

Moore, Samuel, m. before 9-16, 1772, without unity of Friends; disowned by R. & P. M. M., 11 18, 1772.

Moore, Samuel, Jr., of Falmouth, Barnstable Co., Mass., s. of Samuel and Rachel, m. at Rahway, 9 28, 1815, to Elizabeth L Shotwell, dau. of William and Elizabeth, of Rahway, N. J.

Moore, Thos., of Rahway Preparative Meeting, m. before 12-20, 1775, without unity of Friends: disowned 1-17, 1776.

Morris, Joseph, m. before 4 15, 1772, contrary to discipline; disowned 5-20, 1772.

Morriss, Wm, m. between 10-18, 1746, and 12 19, 1746-7, Susannah Thorn.

Morrot, [Merriot?], Thomas, m. between 7-20 and 8-18, 1739, Sarah Smith.

Parker, George, of Shrewsbury, m. between 12-20 and 1 20, 1734-5, Elizabeth Laing, [of John and Elizabeth (Shotwell) Laing.]

Parker, Geo., Jr., m. 4-28, 1763, to Mathe Thorn.

Pound, Benj., m. 2-23, 1763, to Elizabeth Laing.

Pound, David, m. at Plainfield, N. J., 10-27, 1790, to Mary Shotwell, both of Piscataway, N. J.

Pound, Elijah, m. between 1-15 and 2-18, 1781, Isabel Sharp.

Pound, Samuel, m. 8 26, 1772, to Catherine Webster.

Pound, Zachariah, member of W. R. & P. M. M., by request, 11-24, 1760, m. between 1-15 and 2-19, 1761, to Elizabeth Smith.

Robinson, Elizabeth, given certificate of clearness from Woodbridge M. M. 1-17, 1708-9.

Robinson, Mary, m. before 9-19, 1716, from among Friends.

Robinson, Wm., m. before 10 18, 1712, "By ye Priest," contrary to discipline; disowned 6-19, 1714.

Schooley, Isaac, of Mendham P. Meeting, m. before 6-15, 1763, contrary to discipline; disowned 9-21, 1763, by W. R. & P. M. M.

Schooley, Richard, s. of Wm., given certificate of clearness from Woodbridge M. M., 8-18, 1750, to Chesterfield M. M.

Schooley, Robert, m. between 8-15 and 9-19, 1747, to Elizabeth Young.

Schooley, Wm., Jr., m. between 11-24 and 12-18, 1760, to Elizabeth Dell.

Shoemaker, Abraham, of New York City, m. at Rahway, 10-3, 1793, to Margaret Laing, of Woodbridge.

Shotwell, Abel, of Woodbridge, s. of Isaiah and Constant, of Essex Co., N. J., m. at Plainfield, 6-6, 1810, Elizabeth Vail, of Somerset Co., N. J., dau. of Abraham and Margaret.

Shotwell, Abraham, given certificate of clearness 9-23, 1712, to m. [Elizabeth Cowperthwaite].

Shotwell, Abraham, given certificate of clearness from Woodbridge M. M., 8-21, 1742, to Flushing M. M., [m. Mary Potts].

Shotwell, Abraham, [of Piscataway?] m. between 11-18 and 12-15, 1749-50, to Mary Hampton.

Shotwell, Abraham, of Woodbridge, m. at Woodbridge, N. J., 12-28, 1750-1, to Mary Jackson, of Woodbridge.

Shotwell, Abraham, of Woodbridge Preparative Meeting, given certificate of clearness from W. R. & P. M. M., 9-16, 1767, to Flushing M. M., to m. Lydia Hallet.

Shotwell, Alexander, s. of Nathan and Sarah, of Woodbridge, m. at Rahway, 5-5, 1825, to Eliza Smith, dau. of Wm. and Jane, of Woodbridge, N. J.

Shotwell, Ann, dau. of Henry and Sarah, b. 11 2, 1787.

Shotwell, Benjamin, given certificate of clearness from Woodbridge M. M., 7-18, 1746, to Flushing M. M.; [m. Ame Hallett, dau. of Richard of Newtown].

Shotwell, Benj., s. of Benj. and Amey, b. 4-21, 1759.

Shotwell, Benj., Jr., of Borough of Elizabeth, N. J., m. at Plainfield, 1-24, 1781, Bersheba Pound, of Elizabeth, N. J.

Shotwell, Daniel, requests certificate of clearness from Woodbridge M. M., 1 21, 1733-4, to Shrewsbury M. M.

Shotwell, Daniel, of Woodbridge, m. at Plainfield, N. J., 1 24, 1753, to Deborah Shotwell, of Piscataway.

Shotwell, Daniel, of Woodbridge, m. at Rahway, 10-25, 1787, to Margaret Alstone, of Woodbridge.

Shotwell, David, of Borough of Elizabeth, m. at Mendham, 6-24, 1779, Elizabeth Fitz Randolph, of Morris Co., N. J., with her father's consent.

Shotwell, Eden, s. of Jacob and Elliner, b. at Woodbridge, N. J., 4-7, 1751.

Shotwell, Elizabeth, made acknowledgment to R. & P. M. M., 10-20, 1784, for having m. ---------- Marsh, contrary to discipline.

Shotwell, Harvey, of New York, s. of Wm. and Elizabeth, of Essex Co., N. J., m. at Rahway, 12-25, 1823, to Louisa Shotwell, of Middlesex Co., N. J., dau. of Nathan and Sarah.

Shotwell, Hugh, m. before 2-18, 1784, [m. Feb. 23, 1783, to Rosetta Arrison,] without unity of Friends, for which disowned by R. & P. M. M., 5-20, 1784.

Shotwell, Isaac, of Woodbridge, N. J., m. at Rahway, N. J., 11-28, 1770, to Hannah Shotwell, of Woodbridge, N. J., with their parents' consent.

Shotwell, Isaac, m. at Rahway, 11-24, 1791, to Catherine Moore, both of Elizabeth, N. J.

Shotwell, Isaiah, s. of Jno. and Grace, b. 11-24, 1749.

Shotwell, Isaiah, given certificate of clearness from R. & P. M. M., 1-15, 1772, to Shrewsbury M. M., to m. Constant Lippincott; [m. 6-27, 1772].

Shotwell, Jacob, given certificate of clearness from Woodbridge M. M., 10-18, 1746, to Flushing (L. I.) M. M.; [m. 11-10, 1746, Eleanor Haydock].

Shotwell, Jacob, Jr., m. before 6-20, 1754, without unity of Friends; made acknowledgment 10-17, 1754.

Shotwell, Jacob, Jr., m. before 4-19, 1758, without unity of Friends, second time, for which disowned by Woodbridge M. M., 7-20, 1758.

Shotwell, Jacob, given certificate of clearness from W. R. & P. M. M., 8-20, 1766, to Shrewsbury M. M., to m. Catherine Tilton.

Shotwell, Jacob, Jr., of Elizabeth, N. J., m. at Plainfield, N. J., 3-22, 1769, to Barsheba Pound, of Piscataway, N. J.

Shotwell, James, of Borough of Elizabeth, m. at Rahway, N. J., 5-27, 1772, to Ann Moore, of Elizabeth, N. J.

Shotwell, Jediah, of Westfield, Tp., N. J., m. at Plainfield, 6-22, 1796, to Anna Pound, of Piscataway, [dau. of Samuel].

Shotwell, Jeremiah, disowned by N. Y. M. M., 8-1, 1781, for having m. [to Mary --------] without unity of Friends.

Shotwell, Jno., Jr., m. 10-9, 1709, Mary Thorne, Jr., in Long Island, certificate of clearness given by Woodbridge M. M., 8-20, 1709.

Shotwell, Jno., s. of Jno. Shotwell, Jr., and Mary, his wife, was b. at Rahway, 7-3, 1712.

Shotwell, John, m. between 11-16 and 12-20, 1734-5, Elizabeth Smith.

Shotwell, John, m. between 9-17 and 10-15, 1743, Grace Webster.

Shotwell, Jno., ye 3rd, of Woodbridge, N. J., m. at Rahway, N. J., 6-28, 1769, to Margaret Haydock, of Woodbridge, N. J.

Shotwell, John Laing, of Essex Co., N. J., m. at Plainfield, 9-25, 1799, to Mercy Smith, of Somerset Co., N. J.

Shotwell, Jno. Smith, of Elizabeth, N. J., m. at Plainfield, N. J., 9-22, 1756, to Mary Webster, of Borough of Elizabeth, N. J.

Shotwell, John Smith, of Somerset Co., N. J., m. at Rahway, N. J., 5-23, 1782, Phebe Shotwell, of Middlesex Co., N. J.

Shotwell, Joseph, l. l. 7-20, 1716, to m. Mary Manning, with consent of their parents.

Shotwell, Joseph, given certificate of clearness from Woodbridge M. M., 12-18, 1741-2, to Flushing M. M.; [m. Sarah Cock].

Shotwell, Joseph, of Woodbridge, a tanner, m. at Woodbridge, N. J., at close of Woodbridge M. M., 8-20, 1743, to Elizabeth Jackson, of Morris Co., N. J.

Shotwell, Joseph, given certificate of clearness from W. R. & P. M. M., 6-19, 1761, to Shrewsbury M. M., to m. Phebe Aline [Allen?].

Shotwell, Joseph, [Jr.], given certificate of clearness from R. & P. M. M., 4-20, 1774, to Philadelphia M. M., to m. Elizabeth Greenleaf.

Shotwell, Joseph, of Perry Town, N. J., m. before 12-17, 1783, [to Sarah ----------] without unity of Friends, for which disowned by R. & P. M. M., 1-15, 1784, [but afterward reinstated].

Shotwell, Joseph, of Westfield, N. J., s. of Isaiah, m. at Plainfield, 10-25, 1809, to Christian Vail, of Somerset Co., N. J.

Shotwell, Joseph, of Bridgetown, N. J., s. of Jno. and Margaret, m. at Rahway, 3-23, 1820, to Margaret Elston, dau. of Andrew and Sarah, of Rahway.

Shotwell, Joseph D., s. of Henry and Sarah, of Woodbridge Tp., N. J., m. at Rahway, 3-22, 1804, Elizabeth Fitz Randolph, dau. of Jacob and Anna, of Woodbridge.

Shotwell, Joseph Smith, of New York, s. of John S. and Phebe, m. at Rahway, 9-22, 1808, to Deborah Fox, dau. of Geo. and Esther.

Shotwell, Nathan, s. of Jacob and Katherine, b. 9-27, 1767.

Shotwell, Nathan, s. of Jacob and Catherine, m. at Rahway, 5-24, 1798, to Sarah Fitz Randolph, dau. of Jacob and Anna, all of Woodbridge, N. J.

Shotwell, Peter, of Essex Co., N. J., s. of Isaiah and Constant, m. at Plainfield, 8-31, 1803, Phebe Vail, dau. of Abraham and Margaret, of Somerset Co., N. J.

Shotwell, Samuel, given certificate of clearness from Woodbridge M. M., 1-2, 1748-9, to Mamaroneck M. M.; m. Ame ----------

Shotwell, Samuel, m. at Plainfield, N. J., 5-21, 1788, to Hannah Lundy, both of Piscataway, N. J.

Shotwell, Richard, given certificate of clearness from R. & P. M. M., 3-21, 1782, to N. Y. M. M., to m. Mary Martin; [m. 4-10, 1782].

Shotwell, Titus, of Woodbridge, m. at Rahway, N. J., 4-26, 1781. to Sarah Marsh, of Woodbridge Tp., N. J.

Shotwell, Titus. of Woodbridge, m. [2] at Rahway, 7-26, 1787, to Deborah Moore of Woodbridge, N. J.

Shotwell, Wm. of Borough of Elizabeth, N. J., m. at Plainfield, N. J., 3-25, 1772, to Elizabeth Pound, of Piscataway, N. J.

Shotwell, Wm., of Elizabeth, N. J., m. at Rahway, 10-25, 1792, to Elizabeth Moore, of Woodbridge, N. J.

Simcock, Jacob, m. before 3-15, 1781, without unity of Friends; had paid war fines contrary to discipline.

Smith, Abraham, l. l., 10-17, 1754, to m. Phebe Jackson. [Minutes of Woodbridge M. M. for 11th and 12th mos., 1754, and 1st mo. 1755, lost.]

Smith, Benj., l. l., 4-19, 1712, to m. Sarah Shotwell.

Smith, John, m. before 6-21, 1740, without the unity of Friends.

Smith, John, m. before 3-21, 1741, contrary to Friends' discipline; made acknowledgment to Woodbridge M. M., 3-21, 1741.

Smith, Ralph, with mother's consent, l. l., 8-23, 1746, to m. Elizabeth Williams.

Smith. Samuel, m. between 11-19 and 12-16, 1743-4, Masse Tailor.

Smith, Samuel, m. 3-27, 1769, to Sarah Pound.

Smith, Samuel, of Elizabeth, N. J., m. at Woodbridge, N. J., 5-27, 1773, to Elizabeth Shotwell, of Woodbridge, N. J.

Smith, Shobal, l. l., 3-17, 1716, to m. Prudence Fitz Randolph, having consent of parents.

Smith, Wm., m. between 1-18 and 2-15, 1753, to Elizabeth Heddon.

Smith, Wm., of Woodbridge, s. of Samuel and Sarah, m. at Rahway, 9-27, 1798, to Jane Shotwell, dau. of John and Margaret.

Stackhouse, Jno., lately from Falls M. M., m. before 6-19, 1776, without unity of Friends.

Thorne, Abraham, with certificate of clearness from Flushing M. M. and parents' consent, m. 7-19, 1717, Mary Shotwell.

Thorn, Abraham, m. 6-28, 1739. Ann Laing.

Thorn, Abraham, m. 6-22, 1750, Susannah Webster, dau. of Wm. and Susannah.

Thorn, Abraham, Jr., m. between 7-18 and 8-15, 1781. to Elizabeth Smith.

Thorn, Benj., of Woodbridge Tp., m. at Rahway, N. J., 11-23, 1786, to Mary Shotwell, of Woodbridge Tp.

Thorn, Hugh. of Plainfield Preparative Meeting. m. before 7-20, 1780, without unity of Friends; disowned 12-20, 1780.

Thorn, Isaac, m. 12-24, 1766, to Sarah Webster.

Thorn. Isaac, of Middlesex Co., N. J., m. at Rahway, 9-23, 1778, to Hannah Shotwell, of Middlesex Co., N. J.

Thorne, Jacob, with certificate of membership and clearness from Flushing M M., l. l. 4-20, 1723, to m. Susannah Shotwell.

Thorn, Jacob, m. before 1-17, 1770, contrary to discipline.

Thorn, Jno., of Woodbridge, N. J., m. at Woodbridge, 12-23, 1773, to Mary Shotwell, of Woodbridge, N. J.

Thorn, Webster, m. at Rahway, 6-27, 1793. to Elizabeth Martin, both of Woodbridge Tp., N. J.

Thorne, Wm., with certificate of clearness from Flushing M. M., m. between 1-20, 1728-9, and 2-17, 1729, to Mary Fitz Randolph.

Thorn, Wm., m. between 3-18 and 4-15, 1756, to Margaret Smith.

Thorn, Wm., of Plainfield Preparative Meeting, m. before 2-21, 1782, "by a priest."

Thorp, Geo., m. before 11-16, 1706-7, Margaret Robertson, [or Robinson,] (mother of Wm. Robinson), who removed to Philadelphia.

Townsend, John, of Queens Co., L. I., with certificate of clearness from Flushing M. M and father's consent, m. at Plainfield, N. J., 3-17, 1768, to Susannah Shotwell, of Elizabeth, N. J.

Townsend, Jotham, of Piscataway, N. J., s. of Hugh and Mary, m. at Bridgetown, N. J., 9-28, 1820, to Catherine Shotwell, dau. of Joseph and Sarah, of Woodbridge.

Vail, Abraham, m. 8-28, 1766, to Margaret Fitz Randolph.

Vail, Abraham, m. between 9-21 and 10-19, 1768, to Margaret Fitz Randolph.

Vail, Benj., m. before 2-21, 1760, contrary to Friends' discipline; made acknowledgment to W. R. & P. M. M., 4-17, 1760.

Vail, Daniel, of Plainfield Preparative Meeting, m. before 11-16, 1774, [to Mary ---------,] contrary to discip'ine; disowned 2-15, 1775.

Vail, David, m. 4-23, 1766, to Phebe Jackson.

Vail, Edward, of Bridgewater, N. J., m. at Rahway, 12-26, 1793, to Sarah Kinsey, of Woodbridge, N. J.

Vail, Isaac, m. some years before 1758, without unity of Friends.

Vail, Isaac, m. before 4-15, 1762, "by a priest," for which violation of Friends' discipline he made acknowledgment to W. R. & P. M. M., 10-21, 1762.

Vail, Isaac, of Somerset Co., N. J., m. at Rahway, 11-2, 1792, to Sarah Thorn, of Middlesex Co., N. J.

Vail, Isaac, of Woodbridge, s. of Jno. and Catherine, of Somerset Co., N. J., m. at Rahway, N. J., 11-29, 1810, to Sarah Shotwell, Jr., dau. of Henry and Sarah, of Woodbridge, N. J.

Vail, Jno., l. l., 3-15, 1712, to m. Martha Fitz Randolph.

GEORGE FOX,

FOUNDER OF THE SOCIETY OF FRIENDS,

Born at Brayton, Leicestershire, England, in 1624. Died in London, England, 13th of 11th Month January, 1690-91.

REPRODUCED BY PERMISSION OF THE OWNERS OF THE COPYRIGHT FROM A PHOTOGRAPH OF THE ORIGINAL PORTRAIT PAINTED BY SIR PETER LELY, NOW IN THE POSSESSION OF THE FRIENDS' HISTORICAL LIBRARY OF SWARTHMORE COLLEGE, SWARTHMORE, PA.

Vail, Jno., [Jr.], with certificate from Westchester, and his parents' consent, m. between 9-18 and 10-16, 1731, Margaret Laing.

Vail, Jno., Jr., m. (2) before 8-17, 1751, to his late wife's sister [Mary Laing], contrary to Friends' discipline, for which they were disowned by Woodbridge M. M., 10-15, 1751.

Vail, John, ye 3rd, m. before 12-20, 1739-40, without the unity of Friends; made acknowledgment to Woodbridge M. M., 12-20, 1739-40.

Vail, Jno., the 3rd, m. 4-23, 1760, to Catherine Fitz Randolph.

Vail, Joseph, m. before 9-20, 1740, without the unity of Friends; disowned by Woodbridge M. M., 11-21, 1741-2.

Vail, Mary, (*nee* Laing,) made acknowledgment to Woodbridge M. M., in 1757, for having m. her deceased sister's husband.

Vail, Nathaniel, m. before 5-21, 1748, without unity of Friends; made acknowledgment 4-15, 1749.

Vail, Rachel, given certificate of clearness 2-16, 1749.

Vail, Samuel, of Plainfield Preparative Meeting, m. before 12-20, 1775, by a priest; disowned 1-17, 1776.

Vail, Stephen, l. l., 11-17, 1733-4, to m. Esther Smith.

Vail, Stephen, Jr., m. between 11-19 and 12-16, 1761, to Rebeccah Jackson.

Vail, Stephen, Jr., m. 10-26, 1763, to Sarah Smith.

Vail, Stephen, Jr., m. (3) before 6-19, 1771, to his former wife's first cousin, for which they were disowned, 9-18, 1771, by R. & P. M. M.

Vail, Thos., l. l., 1-21, 1716-17, to m. Experience Fitz Randolph; but this marriage was never accomplished.

Vail, Thos., (continued) declared intention of m. 6-15, 1717, with Rachel Fitz Randolph, (probably sister to Experience).

Vail, Thomas, m. before 4-21, 1744, [Sarah Davis].

Vail, Thos., m. between 3-17 and 4-19, 1758, to Mary Drake.

Way, Jno., Jr., of L. I., with certificate of clearness from Newtown M. M., m. 10-20, 1768, to Mary (or Margaret) Marsh.

Webster, Hugh, m. between 11-15 and 12-20, 1753, to Sarah Marsh.

Webster, Isaac, of Elizabethtown, [s. of Hugh, Sr.,] m. at Plainfield, 10-24, 1757, to Mary Laing, of Piscataway, N. J.

Webster, John, m. 11-24, 1743-4, to Anna Tailor.

Webster, Jno., m. between 9-20 and 10-18, 1769, to Margaret Forde, with consent of her father, Thos. Forde.

Webster, Jno., the 3rd, m. before 12-20, 1775, [to Mary Morris?] by a priest; disowned 1-17, 1776.

Webster, Jno., Jr., m. 2-28, 1776, Christian Vail.

25

Webster, Joseph, m. between 9-15 and 10-20, 1733, Elizabeth Shotwell.

Webster, Taylor, m. between 2-15 and 3-15, 1769, to Hannah Jackson.

Webster, Wm., l.l, 3-16, 1717, to m. Susanna Copperthwait [Susannah Cowperthwaite].

Webster, Wm.'s dau. ——————, was m. before 12-15, 1726-7, by a priest, at her father's house, for permitting which he made satisfactory acknowledgment to Woodbridge M. M., 1-16, 1726-7.

Webster, Wm., given certificate of clearness from Woodbridge M. M, 8-18, 1745, to Flushing, L. I.

Webster, Wm., m. between 5-20 and 6-17, 1749, to Sarah Thorn.

Webster, Wm., Jr., m. between 5-17 and 6-21, 1775, to Sarah Smith.

Webster, Wm., disowned by N. Y. M. M, 9-5, 1781, for having m. without unity of Friends.

Webster, Wm., of New Town, L. I., m. 6-21, 1787, Susanna Laing, of Piscataway, N. J.

Willis, Jacob, given certificate of clearness from Woodbridge M. M., 2-16, 1747, to Hattenfield M. M.

Willis, Samuel, m. before 3-18, 1710, Sarah Pierce, before a priest, but made satisfactory acknowledgment to Woodbridge M. M., 3-17, 1711.

Willis, Wm., of Elizabethtown, m. before 4-20, 1706, Hannah ——————, who was not a member, but was received by request, 6-15, 1706.

Willis, Wm., given certificate of clearness from Woodbridge M M., 6-17, 1749, to Kingwood M. M.

Wills, Joseph, without his mother's consent, but with approval of R. & P. M. M., m. between 11-17, 1773, and 1-19, 1774, to Sarah Liken.

Wills, Thos., given certificate of clearness from W. R. & P. M. M., 8-16, 1759, to Kingwood M. M, to m. a young woman of the Meadows.

Wilson, Elia, of Independence, N. J., s. of Gabriel and Keziah, m. at Rahway, 10-16, 1800, to Mary Shotwell, of Elizabeth, N. J., dau. of James and Ann.

Wilson, James, with certificate from Chesterfield M. M., m. between 9-18, 1736, and 12-17, 1736-7, Martha Laing. (l. l., 9-18, 1736).

Wren, Peter, m. between 11-16, 1728-9, and 12-20, 1728-9, to Ann Brotherton, wid. of Henry Brotherton, by whom she had a ch.

Young, Jas., m. before 9-21, 1763, without unity of Friends; disowned by W. R. & P. M. M., 11-19, 1763.

Young, Morgan, made acknowledgment to Woodbridge M. M., 12-15, 1757, of his fault in marrying without unity of Friends, "some years since."

Young, Robert, m. before 6-17, 1732, from among Friends.

Young, Thos., m. before 1757, "some years since," without unity of Friends.

FRIENDS OR QUAKERS.

PLACE, DATE AND CIRCUMSTANCES OF THEIR ORIGIN, THE FACTS OF THEIR DEVELOP-
MENT, THE DISTINCTIVE POINTS OF THEIR BELIEF, THE CHIEF FEATURES
OF THEIR POLITY, THEIR PECULIAR USAGES, AND THE
STATISTICS OF THE VARIOUS BODIES.

FROM THE "REPORT ON STATISTICS OF CHURCHES IN THE UNITED STATES AT THE ELEVENTH CENSUS, 1890," BY
HENRY K. CARROLL, SPECIAL AGENT (pp. 381-391); AND FROM OTHER
PUBLICATIONS SEPARATELY CITED.

FRIENDS.

The Friends, or Quakers, as they are often called, own as their founder George Fox, an Englishman, born at Drayton, Leicestershire, in 1624. He began to preach experimental holiness of heart and life in 1647. He had large congregations, and in 1650 was assisted by 60 ministers. The first general meeting of Friends was held in London in 1668, the second in 1672. The yearly meeting was established in 1678. Encountering much opposition and severe persecution in England, many Friends emigrated to other lands, some of them arriving in this country at Boston in 1656, whence they were subsequently scattered by persecution.

The first yearly meeting in America is believed to have been held in Rhode Island in 1661. George Fox met with it in 1672, and in 1683 it was set off from the London yearly meeting. It was held regularly at Newport until 1878. Since that date it has alternated between Newport and Portland, Me.

Yearly meetings were organized in Maryland in 1672, in Pennsylvania and New Jersey in 1681, in North Carolina in 1708, and in Ohio in 1812.

The Friends have no creed, no liturgy, and no sacraments. They believe in a spiritual baptism and a spiritual communion, and hold that the outward rites are unnecessary. They accept the Old and the New Testament as the word of of God, and the doctrine of the atonement by Christ and sanctification by the Holy Spirit.

Belief in the "immediate influence of the Holy Spirit" is pronounced by President Chase, of Haverford college, the most distinctive feature of their faith. They believe in the guidance of the Holy Spirit in worship and all religious acts. Periods of silence occur in their meetings, when no one feels called upon to speak, and when each worshiper is engaged in communion with God and inward acts of devotion. The Friends believe that a direct call to the ministry comes to persons old or young or of either sex. Those who, after a sufficient probation, give evidence of a divine call, are acknowledged as ministers and allowed seats at the head of the meeting. Besides ministers, there are in the local meetings or congregations elders of both sexes, who are appointed by monthly meetings and who advise the ministers, and, if necessary, admonish them.

Their societies or congregations are usually called meetings, and their houses of worship meetinghouses. There are monthly meetings, embracing a number of local meetings. They deal with cases of discipline, accept or dissolve local meetings, and are subordinate to quarterly meetings, to which they send representatives. Quarterly meetings hear appeals from monthly meetings, record certificates of ministers, and institute or dissolve monthly meetings. The highest body is the yearly meeting. No quarterly meeting can be set up without its consent. It receives and determines appeals from quarterly meetings, and issues advice or extends care to subordinate meetings.

The Friends are divided into 4 bodies, popularly distinguished as the Orthodox, Hicksite, Wilburite, and Primitive.

FRIENDS (ORTHODOX).

These constitute by far the most numerous branch. In 1887, at a general conference of Orthodox Friends, held in Richmond, Ind., a "Declaration of Christian Doctrine" was adopted as an expression of "those fundamental doctrines of christian truth that have always been professed by our branch of the church of Christ." This declaration sets forth the evangelical view of the trinity, the scriptures, the fall of man, justification and regeneration, the resurrection and the final judgment, the issues of which are eternal. In the article on the Holy Spirit these sentences appear:

We own no principle of spiritual light, life, or holiness inherent by nature in the mind or heart of man. We believe in no principle of spiritual light, life, or holiness but the influence of the Holy Spirit of God bestowed on mankind in various measures and degrees through Jesus Christ our Lord.

The article on public worship recognizes "the value of silence not as an end but as a means toward the attainment of the end; a silence not of listlessness or of vacant musing, but of holy expectation before the Lord."

The discipline of the western yearly meeting makes as "disownable offenses," for which members are disowned, or excommunicated, denial of the divinity of Christ, the revelation of the Holy Spirit, the divine authority of the scriptures, engaging in the liquor traffic, drunkenness, profanity, joining the army, or encouraging war, betting, participating in lotteries, dishonesty, taking or administering oaths, etc.

Each yearly meeting has its own discipline, but fellowship is maintained between them by epistolary correspondence. There is also a general agreement between them on the fundamentals of doctrine and discipline. The Philadelphia yearly meeting, which is the oldest, has a discipline incorporating various decisions and advices adopted since its organization in 1681.

There are 10 yearly meetings, with 794 organizations, 725 church edifices, church property valued at $2,795,784, and 80,655 members.

FRIENDS (HICKSITE).

This body of Friends is so named from Elias Hicks, a minister who was foremost in preaching doctrines which became a cause of separation. They object to being called Hicksites. Elias Hicks was born in 1749 and died in 1830. He emphasized the principle of "obedience to the light within," and so stated the doctrines of the pre-existence, deity, incarnation, and vicarious atonement of Christ, of the personality of Satan, and of eternal punishment that he was charged with being more or less in sympathy with unitarianism.

Those identified with this body of Friends insist that Mr. Hicks' views were "exactly those of Robert Barclay," an English Friend of the seventeenth century, whose "Apology for the True Christian Divinity" is still regarded as a fair exposition of the doctrinal views of Friends. They decline to make orthodox theology a test of membership.

The separation took place in the Philadelphia yearly meeting in 1827, and in New York, Baltimore, Ohio, and Indiana in 1828. There was no separation in New England or North Carolina. The Genesee, in western New York, and the Illinois yearly meeting were formed many years later.

They have 7 yearly meetings, with 201 organizations, 213 church edifices, church property valued at $1,661,850, and 21,992 members.

FRIENDS (WILBURITE).

The Wilburite Friends are thus called because John Wilbur, of New England was their principal leader in opposing Joseph J. Gurney and his teaching. They separated from the orthodox body in the New England yearly meeting in 1845, in the Ohio in 1854, and in the Western, Iowa and Kansas in 1877. They are very conservative, and are unwilling to adopt the new methods devised, as the church became aggressive in evangelistic and missionary work. They make much of the doctrine of the light within, holding that every man, by reason of the atonement, has an inward seed or light given him, which, as it is heeded, will lead him to salvation. They deny instantaneous conversion and the resurrection of the body. The controlling portion of the Philadelphia yearly meeting hold to the views of Wilbur, but have never separated from the body of the church further than to decline epistolary correspondence with all branches. They are counted as orthodox, though not affiliating with that body.

They have 5 yearly meetings, with 52 organizations, 52 church edifices, church property valued at $67,000, and 4,329 members. They are represented in the states of Indiana, Iowa, Kansas, Massachusetts, Ohio, Pennsylvania, and Rhode Island.

The Primitive Friends are in faith and practice Wilburite. They separated from the Philadelphia yearly meeting because that body refused to correspond with the New England and Ohio (Wilbur) yearly meetings, and they do not affiliate with the latter, because they recognize the Philadelphia meeting by ministerial visitations and by exchanging certificates of membership.

They have 9 organizations, 5 church edifices, church property valued at $16,700, and 232 members. They are found only in Massachusets, New York, Pennsylvania, and Rhode Island.

NEW JERSEY IN 1675.

EXTRACTS FROM A LETTER WRITTEN BY RICHARD HARTSHORNE OF MIDDLETOWN, MONMOUTH COUNTY, N. J., TO A FRIEND IN ENGLAND.

DEAR FRIEND: My love is to thee and thy wife, desiring your welfare, both inward and outward: and that we may be found steadfast in that truth which is saving, for the welfare of our immortal souls.

*   *   *   *   *   *   *

Now, friend, I shall give thee some information concerning New Jersie, but time will not permit me to write at length.

Thou desirest to know how I live. Through the goodness of the Lord I live very well, keeping between 30 and 40 head of cows and 7 or 8 horses and mares to ride upon, etc.

There are 7 Towns settled in this Province, (Viz.) Shrewsbury and Midletown on the seaside, and along the riverside and up the creeks there is Piscattaway and Woodbridge, Elizabeth, Newark and Bergane. Most of these towns have about 100 families, and the least 40.

The country is very healthful. In Midletown, where I live, in 6 years and upwards there have died but one woman about 80, one man about 60, a boy about 5 years old, and one little infant or 2.

There are in this town, in twenty-five families, about 95 children, most of them under 12 years of age, and all of them lusty children.

The produce of the Province is chiefly wheat, barley, oates, beans, beef, pork, pease, tobacco, Indian corn, butter, cheese, hemp and flax, French beans, Strawberries, carrots, cabbidges, parsnips, turnips, radishes, onions, cucumbers, watermellons, mushmellons, squashes; also the soil is very fertile for apples, pears, plums, quinces, currans, red and white, gooseberries, cherries and peaches in abundance; having all sorts of green trash [truck] in Summer time; and the country is greatly supplied with creeks and rivers, which afford stores of fish, perch, roach, baste, sheepshead, oysters, clams, crabs, sturgeon, eels, and many other sorts of fish that I do not name.

You may buy as much fish of an Indian for half a pound of powder as will serve 6 or 8 men. Deer are also very plenty in this Province. We can buy a big buck of the Indians much bigger than the English deer for a pound and a half of powder, or lead, or any other trade equivolent; and a peck of strawberries the Indians will gether and bring home to us for the value of 6d; and our beef and pork is very fat and good.

The natural grass of the country is very much like that which grows in the woods in England, which is food enough for our cattle; but by the waterside we have fresh meadows and salt marshes.

We make English mead and beer; besides we have several sorts of drink; and travelling in the country and coming to any house, they will generally ask you to eat and drink and take tobacco; and their several sorts of drink they will offer you as confidently as if it were sack.

There are abundance of chestnuts, walnuts, mulberries and grapes, red and white.

Our horses and mares run in the woods, and we give them no meat winter or summer, unless we work them; but our cows must be looked after.

Our timber stands for fences about the land we manure. We plough our land with oxen for the most part. A husbandman here and in Old

England is all one, making most of our utensils of husbandry ourselves; and a man that has 3 or 4 sons or servants that can work along with him will down with timber amain, and get corn quickly.

The best coming to this country is at spring or fall. We make our soap and candles and all such things ourselves.

In the winter we make good fire and eat good meat, and our women and children are healthy. Sugar is cheap; Venison, geese, turkies, fowls, and fish plenty; and one great happiness we enjoy, which is we are very quiet.

I could give thee more information concerning this country, but time will not leave. In short, this is a rare place for any poor man, or others; and I am satisfied that people may live better here than they can in Old England, and eat more good meat.

The vessel is going away. I have no time to copy this over; therefore take the sense of it.

  My love salutes thee. Farewell,
    RICHARD HARTSHORNE.

New Jersie, Midletown, 12th of the 9th month, 1675.

Very many—probably a large majority—of the compiler's living relatives registered in this volume are descendants of the writer of the foregoing letter. Of his private life very little is known. Since the brief sketch at page 16

was put in type, we have obtained the following additional particulars from Mr. H. D. Vail of Santa Barbara, Cal.:

Richard Hartshorne was born, at a small town called Hathern—about 4 miles from Loughborough and 10 from Leicester—in Leicestershire, England, in 1641, came to East Jersey in 1669, and settled at Middletown. Sandy Hook was first held under a grant to him in 1677. Being a member of the Society of Friends, he was visited in 1672 by George Fox, who says in his journal: "Richard Hartshorne received us gladly at his house, where we refreshed ourselves; and thence he carried us and our horses in his own boat across a great water and set us on Long Island." He was appointed by William Penn and his associates one of the commissioners to lay out West Jersey, but whether he acted in that capacity or not is uncertain. In 1684 he was one of Gov. Laurie's council, in 1685 he was elected to represent Middletown in the Assembly; was chosen speaker of Assembly in 1686, when also he was again appointed a member of the Council. He retained his seat in the Assembly, and continued to hold both positions until the surrender of the Proprietary Government to the crown in 1702.[*]

<hr>

[*] Richard[1] and Margaret (Carr) Hartshorne's daughter Catharine married Edward[3] Fitz Randolph, [of Nathaniel[2], Edward[1]] and had Edward[4] whose son John[5] Fitz Randolph married Mary King, daughter of Nathan[4] and Sarah (Moore) King. [See p. 17, ante.]

HISTORICAL OUTLINE

OF THE ORIGIN OF

PLAINFIELD FRIENDS' MEETING,

PLAINFIELD, N. J.

BY O. B. L.

Among the earliest pioneers comprising the first English speaking settlement on New Jersey soil in 1665, were a few ardent followers of George Fox. But not till about twenty years after, when East Jersey was sold at public auction, did any considerable number of "Friends" make this part of the province their permanent home. The purchasers at this auction sale in London, on the 2d of February, 1682, were twelve Quakers headed by William Penn, who bought the land for the sum of 3,400 pounds sterling. The same year twelve others invested in equal shares with the original buyers, making 24 proprietors in all, who became the sole owners of East Jersey. There

was already a population of about 3,500 living in the few small towns along the salt water frontage from Shrewsbury to Hoboken. On scattered plantations just outside of these settlements, there were probably 1,000 more people, all of whom claimed title to their property (some 300,000 acres) by deeds from original patentees of the Lords Proprietors, Sir George Carteret and Lord John Berkley. To these two gentlemen the Duke of York had granted this and adjacent territory by virtue of a Royal Charter from his brother, King Charles II, dated March 12, 1663.

This Quaker syndicate, headed by William Penn, was not slow in soliciting settlers thither, especially those of their own religious sect. Their migration by thousands to the shores of the Jerseys, their occupation of the soil and management of the civil government became one of the most notable events in the closing years of the seventeenth century. Under their peaceful dispensation, the province greatly improved in commercial and agricultural advancement. They had always been foremost as advocates of free opinion, in the old world, and were no less inclined to independent thinking on religious subjects in the new world.

Their meetings in this province were early established at Shrewsbury in 1669, where the settlement was made up almost entirely of Quaker element, and at Amboy in 1686, where

hold meetings at the house of Nathaniel Fitz Randolph, in Woodbridge. Here they continued to meet till his death in 1713, during the fall of which year a meeting house was completed in the town.

For the convenience of many scattered members of the communion, meetings were permitted at the dwellings of several influential Friends in different localities. For those in the outskirts of Rahway they gathered at the house of William Robinson in 1707. Once in a while meetings were held in 1710, at John Shotwell's on Staten Island.

In the village of Rahway, as early as 1742, Friends began to hold meetings at the dwelling of Joseph Shotwell, and frequented his home

FRIENDS MEETING HOUSE AT PLAINFIELD, N. J., ERECTED IN 1788.

the disciples of the "Silent Communion" held influential power in local affairs. The official minutes of the Society state that in October, 1689: "It was agreed that the monthly meeting should be kept the third 5th day in every month, at Benjamin Griffith's in Woodbridge." Trouble occurred among the more worldly ambitious, who, not taking heed to the measure of grace in mercy, departed from the doctrines and discipline of the Society, as the following minutes confirm: "The aforesaid Monthly Meeting fell from ye year 1689 to ye year 1704, by reason of George Keith's separation." In this year, November 10, 1704, Friends began to

for religious services till 1757, when a meeting house was completed on the Main street. Then for the convenience of the more inland plantations beyond the hills in Morris county, there was a meeting occasionally at Mendham, where Richard Dell lived.

For the accommodation of several families living on farms along Greenbrook and Cedarbrook, there were meetings at the house of John Laing on Short Hills, near present city of Plainfield, in 1721, and till his death. At a meeting at Woodbridge, 1731, third month 27th day, the minutes record that "The Friends belonging to the meeting held at John Laing's, deceased, desire liberty to build a meeting house on the land given by the said John Laing for that purpose; this meeting grants their desire and orders that John Kinsey pay the money given by John Shotwell, deceased, to that use." The said house was built under the direction of Abraham Shotwell and Benjamin Smith, during the following months, and was known as the " Plainfield meeting house in the woods." The diminutive structure was " 24 foot square and 14 foot between joynts." It accommodated the worshipers for two generations, when it was torn down, and some of its timbers used in the erection of a new and enlarged meeting house on the plains. This memorable event occurred in 1787-8, when Plainfield was a small hamlet with less than two hundred souls living within a radius of three miles. The building is still standing, as originally built, in an excellent state of preservation, and near the center of the city now numbering almost 20,000 people.*

The Rahway and Plainfield meetings were permanently established and continued to increase, while the Society at Woodbridge, though the oldest and parent body, went into decline about the middle of the century, and by 1769 discontinued regular services altogether.

By the time the government of East Jersey passed into the hands of the Crown, 1702, and a decade or so thereafter, many farmers moved inland from the salt water frontage. Gradually one plantation after another was taken possession of, from these early colonial times, till the permanent settlements on the plains of the Society of Friends, at the opening of the 19th century, greatly outnumbered all other religious worshipers in the locality which is now embraced within the city of Plainfield. From the annals of their meetings and the public records of old Essex and Middlesex counties, the names of the following Quaker families are shown among those wh), over a hundred years ago, bought land in this vicinity, cleared the forest, built homes, and peopled the country with men and women who lived here and wrought and died and left worthy descendants to transmit their names to posterity. These are the family names of the founders of the Plainfield Society of Friends:

Shotwells, Moores, Laings, Thorns, Wilsons, Fitz Randolphs, Kinseys, Vails, Fields, Smiths, Marshes, Websters, Pounds, Robinsons, and others.

———

HISTORY OF

RAHWAY AND MENDHAM MEETINGS.

"At a Monthly Meeting at Nathaniel ffitz Randolph's in Woodbridge ye 18th Day of ye 7th Month 1707, * * * * * The Answer of the Meeting to the Motion of Benj'n Wade, Is that ffriends have not as yet Concluded To have a Meeting once a Month nearer [to Elizabethtown]. But agree to have a Meeting at the House of William Robertson [Robinson] at Rahway on the 12th Day of the 8th Month [October] be [being] the first day of the week."

"Att a Monthly Meeting held at Nathaniel fitz Randolph ye 16th of 12th Month 1709-10, * * * Our friend John Shotwell hath requested this Meeting to have a Meeting Settled at his house once every quarter to which this Meeting Consented and it is to begin ye first first day in ye next first Month and so to continue quarterly." On the 21st of 3rd Mo 1713, it is stated that "The Meeting y't was appointed att John Shotwell's att Statton Island is found Inconvenient to be on ye day it was appointed because it happened to come ye same day w'th ye quarterly Meeting att New York, therefore this meeting orders itt to be altered to ye Second first day in ye 4th 7th 10th and 1st Mo. till further orders."

It would appear that on the removal of his family to N. J., the meeting was continued at his house or that of his son John, as on 5th month 18th, 1728, we find a certain paper was directed to be read "at next meeting of friends held at John Shotwell's at Raway."

"At our Monthly Meeting held at our Meeting house in Woodbridge the 10th Day of the 10th Month, 1742, * * * * A motion was made by Divers friends from Rahway to have Liberty to hold a meeting for three Months at ye house of Joseph Shotwell and in Consideration its granted by this meeting that a meeting shall be held as aforesaid on ye first Days of the week." And under date of 12th Mo. 17th, 1742-3, "Friends at Rahway Requests that the Meeting at Rahway may continue one month Longer than appointment which this meeting grants."

Under date of 9th Mo. 17th, 1743, "Rahway friends Requests of this Meeting the Liberty of keeping a meeting at ye house of Joseph Shotwell from this Time to ye middle of the Second Month which Request was Taken under consideration and granted that the Meeting may be held Twice a weak on ye first and fourth Days of the weak for ye Time aforesaid." In 8th Mo., 1744, the same arrangement was made, "and whereas it is one mouth sooner in ye year than heretofore the reason whereof is that Divers friend are Infirm and Incapable of cumiug so far." On the 17th of 5th Mo., 1746, we find, "A Meeting is concluded to be held at the house of Joseph Shotwell at Rahway to begin half after three in the afternoon on first days from the middle of the 2nd month to the middle of the 8th month and at 12 o'clock from the middle of the 8th month to the middle of the 2nd month and a meeting on fourth days from the middle of the 8th mo. to the middle of the 2nd mo. which meetings are to continue till this meeting thinks proper to alter or drop them."

On the 16th of 5th Mo., 1747, it is stated that "Sum friends are desirous that a meeting house should be Erected at Rahway and some others are not easy therewith therefore this meeting Submits the consideration thereof to the quarterly Meeting And Sum friends at Woodbridge are not easy that the afternoon Meetings appointed at Rahway Should continue which is also Submitted." On the 15th of 8th Mo., '47, "Sum friends at Woodbridge Requests that the Meetings appointed to be held at the house of Joseph Shotwell at Rahway and the quarterly Meeting held at the house of John Shotwell (since 17—) Shall be all dropt except the quarterly Meeting Should be Removed to Woodbridge which Request is Referred to the consideration of next Monthly Meeting." On the 21st of 11th Mo., 1747-8, the subject was again considered. "Friends at Rahway & Plainfield Jenerally think proper To Continue the Meetings at Rahway according to the appointment made in the year 1746 at the house of Joseph Shotwell and that the quarterly meeting at John Shotwells Should be also continued. Friends in and about Woodbridge are oneasy and applies to the quarterly Meeting at Shrosbury." The Quarterly Meeting concluded, "that it will be moste to the advantage of Truth for to waite the building of the Meeting house until they are more unanimous amongst themselves & that the Meetings be continued as they are."

Under date of 2nd Mo. 21st, 1748, we find the following: "The Report of the overseers to this Meeting are that friends are mostly in loave and unity and Meetings at Rahway and plainfield are pretty well kep up but those at Woodbridge are not so well attended as could

be desired. This meeting have unanimously agreed to drop the afternoon Meeting at the house of Joseph Shotwell and that meetings shall be continued at S'd house on first and fourth days from ye 1st [of] 9th Mo. To ye 1st [of] 2nd Mo. yearly."

The Philadelphia yearly Meeting in 1755, "Ordered that a Meeting of Ministers and Elders Should be Established to be held once a month. Agreeable thereto it is agreed [by Woodbridge Monthly Meeting 11th-19th, 1755], to Establish such a Meeting to be held at Rahway and appoint John Shotwell, Joseph Shotwell, & John Webster, Mary Shotwell, Ame Shotwell, Elinor Shotwell, & Elizabeth Lewis for Elders to attend S'd Meeting and it is to be held at the house of John Vail on the third 2nd day of the week [Monthly] at Eleven O clock." And one month later, 12-18, '55, "The following Ministering Friends are appointed for Members of the Meeting of Ministers & Elders laitely Established to wit John Vail, Wm. Morriss, Sarah Shotwell, Robert Willis, and Abner Hamton."

On "the 20th [of] 1st Month 1757.—Friends at Rahway have Repeatedly made application to the Monthly Meeting for leave to build a Meeting house at that place which friends at Woodbridge are oneasy with and to put an end thereto it is Refered to the consideration of the Quarterly Meeting." That body accordingly "declared it to be the Solid Sense of that Meeting that a Meeting house ought to be built at Rahway."

The minutes of Woodbridge Monthly Meeting of 2nd Mo. 17th, 1757, proceed thus:— "This meeting desires Solomon Hunt, Samuel Marsh, Abraham Shotwell, & Benjamin Shotwell to purchase a lot of land at Rahway to build a Meeting house on and take a deed of Trust for it in the Meetings behalf .... Frances Bloodgood, Abner Hamton, & Robert Willis are desired to assist the friends in veying the ground and agreeing on the Quantity of land which they are to purchase. John Vail, Samuel Marsh, Joseph Shotwell, & Benjamin Moore are appointed to consider the Size of the house and compute the cost & promote Subscriptions & make Report thereof to next Monthly Meeting."

One mo. later 3-17, '57, "The friends appointed to take a deed for the land to build a Meeting house on at Rahway Report they have Taken a deed of Joseph Shotwell for one acre of land which he gave the Meeting for that Service and they have given a deed to this Meeting wherein they declare themselves Trustees therein. The Clerk is desired to take the care of the deed. The friends appointed to Size the Meeting house at Rahway * * * * agree that it Shall be 34 foot long & 30 foot wide which this Meeting concurs with * * * Samuel Marsh, Abraham Shotwell, Samuel

Shotwell, and Benjamin Shotwell are appointed to agree with tradesmen and provide materials for building ye Meeting house at Rahway and Joseph Shotwell is appointed to Receive the Subscriptions and pay for the Materials and the workmen Imployed therein as he shall be directed by the S'd friends."

On 4th mo. 21st, 1757, " A motion was made to this [the Woodbridge Monthly] Meeting for liberty to hold a meeting in the afternoon at Rahway on first days to begin at four O'clock which is agreed to."

On the 20th of 8th mo. 1761, we find—" The Establishing preparative Meetings has been weightily Considered and it is the Sense & Judgment of this Meeting that one should be held at Plainfield on the last week Day Meeting Preseding the Monthly Meeting and one at Woodbridge for Woodbridge & Rahway on the close of the week Day Meeting preseding the Monthly Meeting during the Time that Woodbridge & Rahway friends Meetes Together And one at Rahway for Woodbridge and Rahway friends During the Time that Rahway friends meets there separate from Woodbridge friends at the close of the week Day Meeting preseding the Monthly Meeting.

On the "27th 1st Mo. 1763, The Consideration of the Mo. Meeting being held Circular between Woodbridge, Plainfield and Rahway being Revived it is agreed on and Concluded to be Submitted to ye Quarterly Meeting for the approbation thereof. "The representatives to the Quarterly Meeting reported on the 19th of of 5th Mo. 1763 that they had 'Brot from thence the Judgment of that Meeting Respecting the holding our Monthly Meeting in future Viz to be held at Woodbridge the third fourth day of the fourth Month fifth Month Seventh Month and Eighth Month; at Plainfield the third fourth day in the third Month Sixth Month Ninth Month and Twelfth Month; at Rahway the third fourth Day in the first Month Second Month Tenth Month and Eleventh Month. And it is agreed there Shall be no weak Day Meeting held at Plainfield Woodbridge & Rahway on the weak that the Monthly Meeting is held Except that."

"Att our Monthly Meeting held att Rahway the 19th 10th Mo. 1763 * * * * It is agreed that the winter Meetings at Rahway This winter Shall begin at Ten and Two Oclock on first days."

In response to a request from the preparative Meeting at Rahway, the Monthly Meeting on 19th of 2nd Mo. 1766, did agree that two Meetings a day on the first days of the week be held at Rahway the one to begin at the Eleventh Hour and the other at three and that a Meeting be held on the fourth days of the week to begin at the Eleventh hour and it is Recommended to the preparative Meetings at Rahway and plainfield from time to time to appoint Some

of their Members to Visit the Meetings of Woodbridge."

At the Monthly Meeting held at Woodbridge 19th of 4th Mo. 1769, pursuant to a recommendation from the Woodbridge Preparative Meeting, it was "agreed by this Meeting that the preparative Meeting Should accordingly be Removed there [to Rahway] and the Removal of the Monthly Meeting from thence is Submitted to the Quarterly Meeting Eyther to be Settled at Rahway or Circular between Rahway and Plainfield." The Quarterly Meeting "ordered the Monthly Meeting Should be held next at Rahway and So held alternately at Rahway and Plainfield till next Quarterly Meeting."

On the 15th of 8th Mo. 1770, "The Friends appointed to Enlarge the Meeting House at Rahway Reporte it is Completed and that the Expense thereof is one Hundred & Sixty-One Pounds four Shillings & Sixpence which this Meeting desires the Quarterly Meeting to discharge." On the 21st of 11th Mo. '70, the Representatives Report that the Quarterly Meeting had agreed that Shrewsbury Monthly Meeting Should Pay the Sum of £46, 1. 4. & that Rahway & Plainfield Monthly Meeting the Sum of £115. 2. 8 for inlarging Rahway Meeting House in order to accommodate the Quarterly Meeting & have recommended to the Monthly Meetings to Discharge the same."

On the 21st of 10th Mo. 1778, the Monthly Meeting "Orders that the Week day Meeting at Rahway shall be held in future on the fifth day of the week And Likewise the Monthly Meetings there on the third fifth day of the Month and the Preparative Meetings at each place the week Preceding the Monthly Meeting."

MENDHAM MEETING.

At Woodbridge Monthly Meeting 3rd Mo. 15th 1740, "Sum friends in Morris County Request of this Meeting To grant them the Liberty of holding a Meeting once in three Months at the house of William Schooly in the county aforesaid, which Request is granted and concluded that S'd Meetings Shall be held on the Second first Dayes of the fourth Seventh Tenth & first Months."

At a Monthly Meeting at Woodbridge on the 18th of 7th Mo. 1746, "Sum friends from Hanover Township Requests To hold a Meeting on the first dayes of the weak at the house of William Schooley which this Meeting approves of." This was at Mendham; and on the 19th of 11th Mo. 1756, it was "agreed that a Week Day Meeting should be held there on the 5th Day of the Week and that a Preparative Meeting should be held once in three Months on the second day of the Week following the Circular Meeting there to begin at the Tenth Hour And on ye

26

[16th of] 6 Mo. 1758 it was agreed that a Meeting house should be built at Mendam which was Performed."

"At our Monthly Meeting held at Woodbridge the 19th 4th Mo. 1758   *   *   *   *
It is Requested that a Meeting house be built at Meudam and it is proposed to Set it on land belonging to Robert Schooley. John Vail Samuel Marsh Abraham Shotwell Robert Schooley Hartshorn Fitz Randolph & Jacob Laing are appointed to conclude on the Size of ye house & the manner of building it the quantity of land & when to be erected and com-

pute the cost & promote Subscriptions & leigh it before the succeeding Mo. Meeting." Two Mos. later, 6th 16th, '58, they "Report they think proper it should be 26 foot wide & 25 long & that it will Cost £73 or Sumthing over and that a Subscription is Raised that will be Sufficient to Compleat it which this meeting agrees to. James Brotherton & Jacob Laing are appointed to take a deed for the land where the Meeting house is to be built and to have the oversight of the building S'd house. And James Brotherton is desired to Collect the Subscription in."

FRIENDS ON LONG ISLAND.

In the [Hicksite] Friends' safe in 15th Street meeting house in New York, there are records of what is now New York Monthly Meeting from 1703 to the present time. Thirty years since an earlier book [1671-1703] was discovered in a garret in Flushing, which is now in the [Orthodox] Friends' safe at 20th St. meeting-house. George W. Cocks, of Glen Cove, L. I., and John Cox, Jr., of 308 W. 19th St., New York, are making an exact copy thereof for the 15th St. depository; and through their kindness, we here present a copy of the whole of page 2, as a picture of the times and life of our ancestors.* The first page [now remaining] has a deed of gift from Anthony Wright to the Quakers, of land for a meeting-house and burying-ground at Oyster Bay. This second page has the specification and contract for the house; also one of the earliest appearances of discipline and organization. This was in 1672, the year of George Fox's visit to Long Island. He spent the latter years of his life in getting the Society organized on the system he had thought out, largely, perhaps, during his last imprisonment. This paragraph on page 2 of the old record shows the effect of his presence here. The Quarterly Meeting, so organized, met about every two months for several years, before Monthly Meetings were established and the Quarterly Meeting was settled at fixed intervals of three months. Its present name is Westbury Quarter in the [Hicksite] body and New York Quarter in the [Orthodox] body. The minutes of the Yearly Meeting [now New York Y. M.] from 1696 to 1720 and of the Quarterly Meeting from 1671 to 1720 are recorded in this and the following books of the Monthly Meeting, which, with several mutations of name became in time New York Monthly Meeting. After 1720 the Yearly Meeting and Quarterly Meeting records were

kept separate from those of the Monthly Meeting. The "strong & Sufficient frame" which was erected at Oyster Bay in 1672 was taken down in 1693.—John Cox, Jr.†

[At a me]n & W[omens meeting at y' house of]
[Matthew Priar] in Kin[nin]g[worth[1]
[It w]as then & there Orde[red that y']
meeting house Jntended to be [built for y' use]
of ffriends in Oysterbaye shall be m[ade] 36[foote long]
& 24 foote wide & 12 foote y' stoode[2]
And Allsoe itt is by ffriends agreed that Samm[uel]
Andrewes & John ffeakes shall make & Sett
a strong & Sufficient frame every waye Sui[table]
and Answerable for the End & use affore sd [and]
they are to have the Summe of fifteene po[unds]
which Summ is to be p[d] in wheate att 4:6[d]
pease att 3':6[d] Jndian att 2':6[d] porke att [4[d] per lb]
to all w[ch] y' sd. John ffeakes & Sammuell [Andrews]
are Contented with and promise they s[hall endeavor]
to have itt upp for the further fi[nishing by]
y' 30th daye of the first[3] mon[th] : 73:
Jt is further agreed That for y' sd [sum Samuel]
and John shall make: 8: windowes [2 on]
one side the house, & 2 one the other side & 2 [in the]
ends belowe all made fitt for glasse, togeather [with]
window shutts & 2 windowes in the Gable ends [with]
Shutts likewise they are to make 2 Doors
One in one side of itt & the other in y' o[ther side]
Jtt is to bee understood both these doors a[re pro]
ber[t] duble doors with 2: dorment windowes
& for makeing all these they to have 5£ mor[e which]
makes y' Sum: 20£
To begin heare, Concluding that all
meetings Called men & womens
JenErall meetings ware Quarter
ly meetings wheather So named or
No Until Monthly meetins be named.

---

† For a more detailed account of " Early Long Island Records," the reader is referred to the five weekly issues of *Friends' Intelligencer and Journal* from 1st mo 20, to 2d mo. 27, 1897.—Editor.
1 Killingworth, afterward called Matinecock, the Indian name for " the land that overlooks " the adjacent country.
2 12 feet in the stud, i. e. height of frame.
3 March.
4 Proper i. e. complete.

JOHN BOWNE OF FLUSHING, 1627-1695.

WITH A SHORT ACCOUNT OF THE BI-CENTENNIAL ANNIVERSARY OF THE NEW YORK YEARLY MEETING OF FRIENDS, 1695-1895, AS OBSERVED AT FLUSHING, LONG ISLAND, IN FIFTH MONTH, 1895.

[Excerpts from pamphlet report of proceedings, published at expense of both yearly meetings, by Friends Book & Tract Committee, 45 East Tenth street, New York.]

In 1894 the Yearly Meetings of the two bodies of Friends in New York decided to observe with suitable exercises, in 1895, the two hundredth anniversary of the establishment of New York Yearly Meeting, and each referred the matter to its Representative Committee. Each of these appointed Special Committees with authority to arrange for a joint celebration. The meetings of these committees were characterized by much kindness and courtesy, and it was arranged to hold the celebration on the 29th of Fifth month, at Flushing, where the Yearly Meeting was held during its first eighty-two years. The Town Hall, having the largest audience room in the place, was secured for the purpose of the meeting. It was arranged that the exercises should consist of an historical address, a poem, and addresses upon "What Friends Have Done for the World" and "Woman's Position in the Society of Friends."

The meeting was held at the time designated. The attendance was very large, and the occasion proved of great interest. Robert S. Haviland, of Chappaqua, N. Y., presided, by the appointment of the Committee of Arrangements, and at the opening of the meeting made some appropriate remarks and read the 90th Psalm. After a time of silence, prayer was offered by Ruth S. Murray, of New England Yearly Meeting. The program was then carried out as arranged.

Opening Address.

ROBERT S. HAVILAND.

One of our wise men has said that if we are to hold a man to strict account for all his actions, he should have been allowed to choose his grandparents.

We have not been thus privileged, but it is our privilege to-day to ratify the choice that has been made for us and to rejoice in the memory of a godly ancestry, whose earnest efforts in the cause of truth have enriched our lives with so much that makes life of value.

Two hundred years of Minding the Light ought to have rewarded us with a strengthened and enlarged vision.

That the eye has been sufficiently single to effect these results we may well question of ourselves today.

We welcome you, Friends, all, to this joint celebration of the two hundredth anniversary of the establishment of New York Yearly Meeting of Friends.

We welcome you to this historic ground, where for nearly the first century of its existence the Yearly Meeting had its home, and from out whose peaceful shades the settlers early went forth to found new settlements of Friends in the wilds of Westchester and Dutchess and northerly to within the Canadian border. We welcome you as Friends in fact as well as in name.

Extracts from an Historical Sketch.

BY JAMES WOOD.

The progress of Christian doctrine in the Protestant Reformation in Great Britain was by slow and irregular stages. During the reign of Henry VIII, the departure from Rome was more in outward form and government than in real principles, and much that was gained under Edward VI. was lost during the reign of Mary. As freedom of thought and discussion asserted themselves during the following three-quarters of a century, there was great commotion in religious affairs, and a multitude of sects sprang into existence. The national church of England at first took but a short step in the new direction, and afterward increased the distance with great caution. The new sects took their stand with more or less disregard of the past, some upon one doctrine or practice, some upon another; but they were all, though in varying degrees, compromises with Rome, each retaining some doctrine or practice, some ordinances or ritual, that still identified it with the system of the old hierarchy.

If the crucial distinction between Catholicism and Protestantism is correctly expressed in the formula of Schleiermacher, that "Catholicism makes the believer's relation to Christ depend upon his relation to the church, while Protestantism makes the relation of the believer to the church depend upon his relation to Christ," then a remnant of Catholicism, more or less pronounced, was found wherever any churchly rite or ceremony was required, or wherever any trace of sacerdotalism was continued.

It was not until one hundred years had expired after the Reformation began, that it reached its culmination in the progress of doctrine by a severance from Catholicism that was complete and absolute. It was given to George Fox to see and to declare that the troubled soul can find access to and acceptance with God without the intervention of any human priest, or ordinance, or ceremony whatsoever. His presentation of the doctrine of the abiding of the Holy Spirit in the soul of the believer contained the most exalting truth ever announced to man as pertaining to his existence here. Thomas Carlyle has called this a revelation of "the divine idea of the universe," and it led him to declare that the preaching of Fox was "the most remarkable incident in modern history."

With the spread of the new doctrine in nearly all ranks of society in England, and the growth of the new organization until the kingdom swarmed with its adherents, it is not our present purpose to deal. It was not long before the advocates of the new doctrine crossed the Atlantic, and the history of Friends in America began. As is well known, its earliest chapters were darkened by persecution and blood, but they were made brilliant by steadfast faith and holy endurance. In considering these persecutions we must remember the times in which they occurred. Justice requires that we shall bear in mind how lightly human life was regarded, how little personal liberty was esteemed, and how hard was the public sense in regard to corporal punishment. In England there were almost numberless offenses punishable with death; and the stocks, the pillory and the whipping-post found victims with trivial excuse.

It is not necessary to speak in detail of the reception given them in Massachusetts. There were two sides to the dispute. From the Puritan standpoint the Quaker had no right to go there. The Puritans had come to Massachusetts to establish a religious, not a civil, commonwealth. Only members of their church were eligible to citizenship; all others were merely tolerated. The teachings of the Quaker were subversive of their order, and therefore he was excluded. The Quakers took broader ground. They claimed that as Englishmen they had the legal right to visit or to live wherever the English flag proclaimed English jurisdiction. This claim rested upon that clause in the Massachusetts charter which expressly guaranteed "all liberties and immunities of free and natural subjects of the realm; to all Englishmen which shall go to and inhabit Massachusetts," or "which shall happen to be born there, or on the seas in going thither or returning from thence." The Quaker stood upon the higher moral and legal ground—the Puritan had the physical power. The result was one of those sad episodes in history over which, in this age, it is better to throw the mantle of charity, with devout thankfulness that our lot is cast in better times.

The persecutions of the Quakers in Massachusetts turned the stream that continued to cross the Atlantic, and led to the settlement upon Long Island.

Very naturally the Friends looked to the Dutch for religious toleration. The Puritans themselves had gone to Holland to find religious liberty when they had been compelled to flee from England. Many others besides Friends came to Long Island from Massachusetts to escape the religious restraint there. The first who afterward became connected with Friends was Lady Deborah Moody. She settled in Lynn, Massachusetts, in 1640, and received a grant of four hundred acres of land. "She was a woman of consequence, and was treated with great respect till she fell under discipline and was excommunicated from the church for religious sentiments deemed heretical." Governor Winthrop thus speaks of her in his journal: "In 1643 Lady Moody was in the colony of Massachusetts, a wise and anciently religious woman; and being taken with the error of denying baptism to infants was dealt withal by many of the elders and others, and admonished by the church of Salem, whereof she was a member; but persisting still, and to avoid further trouble, etc., she removed to the Dutch against the advice of her friends." On Dec. 19, 1645, Gov. Kieft, of New Amsterdam, issued a general patent for the town of Gravesend, Long Island, to Lady Deborah Moody, Sir Henry Moody her son, George Baxter and James Hubbard, their heirs and successors, "to have and enjoy free liberty of conscience, according to the customs and manners of Holland, without molestation." Gravesend was planted entirely by English settlers from Massachusetts, and, unlike the "five Dutch towns," which constituted the rest of the county, the records were kept from the commencement of the settlement in the English language. The town was laid out on a very liberal scale, with streets radiating from a central square. For forty years it was the capital of Kings county, and there the courts were held. Friends came to Gravesend in considerable numbers in 1656 and '57, and their views met with favor. "Many of the inhabitants readily embraced their doctrines and discipline, and the first regular meeting on the island was organized and maintained here." Naturally, the views upon the rite of baptism which Lady Moody, and probably many of her associates, entertained, strengthened in their minds by the harsh treatment they had received both in Massachusetts and in Connecticut, when on their way to Long Island, prepared many of them to adopt the Quaker system when it was introduced among them. Croese says, "Meetings were held at the house of Lady Moody, who managed all things with such prudence and observance of time and place as to give no offense to any person of any other religion, so she and her people remained free from all molestation." Lady Moody received courteous consideration from the Dutch Governors, and for many years had the naming of the Gravesend magistrates. *Wm. Bowne*, a Friend, was a magistrate there in 1657.

Flushing was settled from the east, probably by dissenters who were impatient of religious restraint in Massachusetts, and who sought a larger liberty under the Dutch. They were careful to have inserted in their charter granted by Governor Kieft, October 10, 1645, a clause permitting them "to have and enjoy the liberty of conscience according to the manner and custom of Holland without molestation from any magistrate or any ecclesiastical minister that may pretend jurisdiction over them." For two years they had no minister. When Stuyvesant succeeded Kieft in the Dutch governorship in 1647, he urged upon their attention the propriety of calling a minister, and recommended the Rev. Francis Doughty. He soon settled there, but the people refused to pay his salary of 600 guilders, so that he was compelled to leave, and finally went to Virginia. It has been stated that he subsequently united with Friends, but I can find no evidence of his having done so. For many years there was no regular preaching at Flushing. The state of religion was thus described by the Dutch ministers, Megapolensis and Drisius, in 1657: "At Flushing they have heretofore had a Presbyterian preacher who conformed to our church, but many of the people became endowed with divers opinions, and it was with them *quot homines tot sententiæ*" (as many creeds as men).

It was in Eighth month, 1657, just ten years after George Fox began to preach in England, that ministering Friends came to Long Island and held meetings in Hempstead, Jamaica, Flushing and Gravesend. Robert Hodgson and Robert Fowler were among the number. Settlers of the sect had preceded them, among whom was Richard Smith. Now there began on the part of Governor Stuyvesant a persecution of the Quakers only second to that so much better known in Massachusetts. In the instructions given by the Directors of the Dutch West India Company the official oath required "the maintenance of the reform religion in con-

formity with the decrees of the Synod of Dortrecht, and not to tolerate in public any other sect." In this Stuyvesant had an excuse for a course of conduct which seemed suited to his character. In 1656 he imprisoned some Lutherans, and was sharply reproved therefor by the council of the West India Company. So far as appears, the ministration of the Friends provoked no immediate opposition from Governor Stuyvesant other than the posting of placards forbidding "the harboring of Quakers as disturbers of the public peace." The order was the subject of grave deliberation at a town meeting held in Flushing, Twelfth month 27th, 1657, at the house of Michael Milner; Tobias Feake, the sheriff, a New England man, drew up a remonstrance, which was signed by thirty of the townsmen. They declared that they could not in conscience lay violent hands upon the Quakers, but should give them free ingress and egress to their town and houses. The Governor was in a rage. He had most of the signers arrested. The sheriff was removed from his office, as also was the town clerk, who had signed the remonstrance. The immediate cause of the meeting was the arrest of Henry Townsend, who was fined and imprisoned for holding meetings at his house. Being a person of great worth and consideration, the people were deeply incensed. The signers of the remonstrance were imprisoned until the 26th of Third month, when they were released, and the Governor, in order to prevent as much as possible the consequences of Quaker influence among the people, resolved to change the municipal government of the town of Flushing. After formally pardoning the town for its mutinous resolutions, he abolished the town meetings and ordered that a council be chosen from certain respectable citizens. He stated that "in future I shall appoint a sheriff acquainted not only with the English and Dutch languages, but with Dutch practical law; that a tax of twelve stivers per morgen of land be laid upon the inhabitants for the support of the orthodox minister, and such as do not sign a written submission to the same in six weeks may dispose of their property and leave the soil of this government." Robert Hodgson, continuing his preaching, was seized and committed to prison on the accusation of holding conventicles. "A guard was sent from New Amsterdam to bring him before the Governor and council. Two women who had entertained him were also taken, one of whom had a young child. They were put into a cart, and Hodgson, having been fastened behind it, was dragged through the woods by night to the city and thrust into the dungeon of Fort Amsterdam. On being brought out the next day, he was examined, condemned and sentenced to two years' hard labor, or to pay a fine of 600 guilders. With the latter alternative he was either unable or unwilling to comply, and was again confined, without permission to see or converse with any one. Being afterwards chained to a wheelbarrow and commanded to work, he refused to do so, and was by order of the court beaten by a negro with a tarred rope till he fainted; the punishment was continued at intervals to one hundred lashes. After having been for some months confined and frequently scourged as before, he was liberated at the solicitation of Gov. Stuyvesant's sister, and banished from the province."

John Bowne was the leading member among Friends, and for many years was regarded as their representative member. The history of their establishment requires some special mention of his coming to America and his acceptance of the doctrines of Friends. He was born at Matlock, in Derbyshire, England, on the 9th of Third month, 1627, and was baptized in the parish church there on the 29th of the same month. His father was Thomas Bowne, who was baptized, as stated in the records, Fifth month 25th, 1595, and he came to America with his son and all his family, except one daughter, and died at Flushing. The family came to America early in 1649.

In Tenth month, 1650, John Bowne returned to England, and again arrived in America in 1651, landing at Boston, Fifth month 25th. On Sixth month 15th following, he visited Flushing in company with Edward Farrington, who is supposed to have married his sister Dorothy. The family soon after removed to Flushing and settled there. On Fifth month 7th, 1656, John Bowne and Hannah Field* were married at Flushing, and in 1661 he built the house which was used as a meeting-place for Friends for nearly forty years, which is still standing, an historic monument of Flushing, and which has been owned and occupied by his lineal descendants to the present time.

In the year of their marriage Hannah Bowne became acquainted with some of the Friends, who at that time were in the practice of holding meetings for worship in the woods. She soon after became a member. Her husband from curiosity attended a meeting, and was deeply impressed with the beauty and simplicity of their worship. He invited them to meet at his house, and soon after he joined in membership with them.

Meetings had not long been held at the house of John Bowne before complaints were made against him, as appears from the following translation from the Dutch records now preserved in Albany: "Complaints made 24th of August, 1662, by the magistrates of Flushing, that many of the inhabitants are followers of the Quakers who hold their meetings at the

* The Bowne records give the name Hannah Field, but it is believed by careful investigators that her name was Hannah Feake. See N. Y. Gen. and Biog. Record, vol. xi., p. 12.—[James Wood.]
It has been definitely settled that John Bowne's first wife was Hannah Feake, daughter of Robert and Elizabeth (Fones-Winthrop) Feake.—[George W. Cocks.]

house of John Bowne." An ordinance of the West India Company of 1662 provided that "besides the Reformed religion no conventicles should be holden in houses, barns, ships, woods or fields, under the penalty of fifty guilders for the first offense, double for the second, and arbitrary correction for every other."

Under the authority of this ordinance we find that great numbers, including many women, suffered severely, both by direct action of the Governor and by his courts held at Gravesend. John Bowne was arrested Ninth month 1st, 1662, charged with "harboring Quakers and permitting them to hold their meetings at his house." He was then taken a prisoner to Fort Amsterdam, and on the 14th of the same month the "court held by the Lords, Director General and Council at Fort Amsterdam in the Netherlands," entered the following judgment: "Because John Bowne, at present prisoner, dwelling at Flushing upon Long Island, has made no scruple in vilipendation of the orders and mandates of the Director General and Council of the New Netherlands, we do in justice to the high and mighty states of the United Provinces and the administrators of the West India Company of the Chamber of Amsterdam, having heard the demand of the substitutes, and the acknowledgment of the prisoner, have condemned and do condemn the said John Bowne by those present—boete—5 and 20 pounds Flemish with the charges of the Justician, and with express admonition and interdict to abstain from all such forementioned meetings and conventicles, or else for the second boete he be condemned in a double boete, and for the third boete to be banished out of this province of New Netherlands." John Bowne refused to pay the fine, and was then confined in a dungeon and restricted to bread and water, no person whatever being allowed to speak with him. As this did not change his steadfastness of purpose he was some time afterward taken to the Stadthaus and put in the prison-room there, and was allowed to see his wife and other friends. He was then notified that the Court had resolved that he must pay the fine that had been imposed or be sent out of the country, or he would be set free if he would promise to leave the country in three months. He still remained firm in his purpose not to compromise his principles in any way. On Tenth month 21st he was permitted to visit his friends under a promise to return in three days, and on the 31st of that month he was put on board ship and sent a prisoner to Holland. He arrived at Amsterdam on the 29th of Second month, 1663. The following statement was forwarded by the authorities of New Netherlands to the West India Company: "Honorable, Right Respectable Gentlemen. We omitted in our general letter the trouble and difficulties which we and many of our good inhabitants have since sometimes met with, and daily are renewed by the sect called Quakers, chiefly in the county and principally in the English villages, establishing forbidden conventicles and frequenting those against our published placards, and disturbing in a manner the public peace, in so far that several of our magistrates and well-affectioned subjects remonstrated and complained to us from time to time of their insufferable obstinacy, unwilling to obey our orders or judgment. Among others was one of their principal leaders named John Bowne, who for his transgressions was, in conformity to the placards, condemned to an amends of 150 Guilders in suevant, who has been now under arrest more than three months for his unwillingness to pay, obstinately persisting in his refusal, in which he still continues, so that we at last resolved, or were rather compelled, to transport him in this ship from this province in the hope that others by it be discouraged. If nevertheless by these means no more salutary impression is made upon others, we shall, though against our inclinations, be compelled to prosecute such persons in a more severe manner, and which we previously solicit to be favored with your Honours' wise and foreseeing judgment. With which after our cordial salutations we recommend your Honours to God's protection, and remain Honourable and Right Respectable Gentlemen, your Honour's faithful servants."

The officials of the West India Company considered the case and drew up a paper for John Bowne to sign. In reply he sent to the company the following dignified statement: "Friends, the paper drawn up for me to subscribe I have perused and weighed, and do find the same not according to that engagement to me through one of your members, viz.: that he or you would do therein by me as you would be done unto, and not otherwise. For which of you being taken from your wife and family, without just cause, would be bound from returning to them unless upon terms to act contrary to your conscience, and deny your faith and religion, yet this in effect do you require of me, and not less.

"But truly, I cannot think that you did in sober earnest ever think I would subscribe to any such thing, it being the very thing for which I rather chose freely to suffer want of the company of my dear wife and children, imprisonment of my person, the ruin of my estate in my absence there, and the loss of my goods here, than to yield or consent to such an unreasonable thing as you thereby would enjoin me unto.

"For which I am persuaded you will not only be judged in the sight of God, but by good and godly men, rather to have mocked at the oppressions of the oppressed and added afflictions to the afflicted than herein to have done to me as you in the like case would be done unto, which

the royal cause of our God requires. I have with patience and moderation waited several weeks expecting justice from you, but behold an addition to my oppression in the measure I receive.

"Wherefore I have this now to request for you, that the Lord will not lay this to your charge, but to give eyes to see and hearts to do justice, that you may find mercy with the Lord in the day of judgment.

"JOHN BOWNE."

In the Fourth month John Bowne was released. He returned to America by the way of England and the Island of Barbadoes, but did not reach Flushing until First month 30th, 1663.

The authorities in Amsterdam sent to the officials in New Netherlands the following decision, dated Amsterdam, April 16, 1663: "We, finally, did see from your last letter, that you had exiled and transported hither a certain Quaker named John Bowne, and although it is our cordial desire that similar and other sectarians might not be found there, yet as the contrary seems to be the case, we doubt very much if rigorous proceedings against them ought not to be discontinued except you intend to check and destroy your population, which, however, in the youth of your existence, ought rather to be encouraged by all possible means.

"Wherefore it is our opinion that some connivance would be useful that the consciences of men, at least, ought ever to remain free and unshackled. Let everyone be unmolested as long as he is modest, as long as his conduct in a political sense is unimpeachable, as long as he does not disturb others or oppose the government. This maxim of moderation has always been the guide of the magistrates of this city, and the consequence has been that from every land people have flocked to this asylum. Tread thus in their steps, and we doubt not you will be blessed.

"(Signed) The directors of the West India Company, Amsterdam Department.
"ABRAHAM WILMANDONK,
"DAVID VON BAERLE."

This document has peculiar historic interest because of the fact that it was the first official proclamation of religious liberty for any part of America, except Maryland. With this decree the persecution of Friends on Long Island ceased.

While in Holland John Bowne wrote letters to his wife and numbers of Friends, which are still preserved. They are remarkable for the illustrations they give of unflinching steadfastness of purpose, for the beautiful and lofty ideas expressed in them, and for their elegant and sometimes scholarly diction. In one of these he said: "Dear George Fox and many more Friends desire their dear love and tender salutations remembered to all Friends." From this we may infer that he was visited at Amsterdam by George Fox and others.

Hannah Bowne, wife of John Bowne, became a minister, and made two religious visits to England and Ireland, and one to Holland and Friesland. The letters of her husband sent to her there are admirable in their expressions of tender affection and of interest in her religious service. In one of these he quaintly remarks: "Dear heart, to particularize all that desire to be remembered to thee would be exceedingly large, but this I may say for all Friends in general, relations and neighbors, and people, the like largeness of love for one particular person I have seldom found amongst them, as it is for thee." John Bowne joined his wife in England in 1676, and accompanied her in her religious service until the Twelfth month, 1677, when she died in London. His testimony concerning her, given at her funeral at the Peel meeting, was remarkable for its tenderness and beauty.

The estimation in which John Bowne was held by Friends is shown by the following quaint certificate recorded upon the minutes of Flushing Monthly Meeting.

["In] the mens and womens me[eting] on long Island in America.

"These are to certif[y to all whom [it may c[oncerns that] our deare and well beloved friend John Bowne of fflus[hing on Long Island as afforesaid in the province of New Yorke i[nasmuch as] his occasions at this time Requireing his being in ould [England] by the first convaance, is for his Life ande [conversation] unblamable and of good Report and is likewise in treu [love and] unity with all friends in the truth heare, as by large & [long] expearince we have all found and wittnessed." Signed by many Friends.

The records of the same meeting nineteen years later contain the following minute. "John Bowne dyed 20 day of the 10 month, in the yeare 1695 and was bured ye 23 day of same being about sixty-eight yeares of age. he did Frely Expose himself his house and his estate to ye service of truth And had a constant meeting in his house near About forty yeares.

He was thrice married. His second wife was Hannah Bickerstaff, and his third was Mary Cock. Hee allso suffered very much for ye truth's sake."

The meeting-house* now standing in Flushing was erected in 1696. The circumstance of its erection is explained by a petition of Samuel Haight, of Flushing, bearing date June 17, 1697, preserved with the State archives at Albany, in which he says that his step-father-

in-law, Wm. Noble, lately deceased, and having no issue of his own body, left his estate to his widow during her life, and at her death to the people called Quakers, the land then being in the posession of the widow and the petitioner. In consideration of the request of the deceased, the petitioner had erected a meeting-house for the Quakers in that town at his own charge, and prays that certain tracts of land may be confirmed to him at the death of the widow. On the same date a patent was issued in accordance with the petition.

In O'Callahan's History of New Netherlands, it is stated that Wm. Noble was a magistrate in Flushing in 1658, and was one of the number arrested by Governor Stuyvesant for refusing to molest the Quakers.

From the journals of Friends' ministers who came to Long Island we find that the membership must have increased rapidly, as many meetings had become established. John Taylor says he passed through Long Island in the spring of 1659 and attended meetings at Setauket, Oyster Bay, Hempstead, Gravesend and other places. "Being joined in the winter by Mary Dyer, we had several brave meetings together, and the Lord's power was with us gloriously." George Wilson speaks of increasing numbers in 1661. William Edmundson says in the year 1672, "I went to Long Island, where there were many honest, tender Friends, and having several meetings with them there, we were well refreshed and comforted together in the Lord."

"In the year 1672 George Fox himself visited America, coming by way of the Barbadoes. He landed in Maryland in the early spring, and traveled northward through the wilderness to visit Friends on Long Island and in New England. He was accompanied by John Burnyeat Robert Widders and George Pattison, and also by John Jay, a planter and merchant of Barbadoes, and by others. He crossed the lower bay of New York, landed at Coney Island, visited Friends at Gravesend, Flushing and other points, and attended a Half-year meeting at Oyster Bay.* From the account in his journal it is evident there were a great number of Friends at these places. It is a remarkable fact, illustrating Friends' care not to glorify any man, that no mention is made of Fox's visit in any record of any meeting, although regular minutes were kept before the time of his visit. Afterward the attendance of all ministers from beyond the limits of the meeting was recorded, and the practice still continues. Fox went to Rhode Island, where he attended the Yearly Meeting for New England, and was entertained at the Governor's house. He returned to Long Island, and in his journal

---

* The meeting-house was erected in 1695 and the first meeting recorded as being held therein was a Quarterly Meeting, 25th of third month of that year. In 1702 Samuel Haight wrote in the record book an acknowledgment of having received the £10 he had laid out in building the house.—[John Cox, Jr.].

* It was the Fall Half-Year meeting, hold near the close of Ninth (now Eleventh) month, 1672, that George Fox attended, on his return from New England, as Bowden's and Thomas' Histories show.—[John Cox, Jr.].

FRIENDS' MEETING HOUSE AT FLUSHING, N. Y., ERECTED IN 1694.
Now occupied by Hicksite Friends.
Photo-Engraved for this work, through the kindness of John Cox, Jr., of New York, and George W. Cocks,
of Glen Cove, L. I.

INTERIOR OF FRIENDS' MEETING HOUSE AT FLUSHING, N. Y., ERECTED IN 1694
Reprinted by permission of Friends' Book and Tract Committee, New York.
From pamphlet report of proceedings (p. 38) at Bi-Centennial Celebration, 1895. Published at expense of
both Yearly Meetings by Friends' Book and Tract Committee, an Orthodox Organization.
NOTE. This high, story-and-a-half building, shingled on the sides, with the roof hipped from all sides,
has the doors on the side away from the present street and facing the grave-yard. Timber for this
house was cut in the winter of 1693-4, and a quarterly meeting was held in it on the 24th of ninth
month, 1694, as shown by the records. It was used during the Revolutionary War as a military

we read: "At Oyster Bay we had a very large meeting. The same day James Lancaster and Christopher Holden went over the bay to Rye, on the Continent, in Governor Winthrop's government, and had a meeting." These were the first Quakers, so far as known, who set foot in Westchester county. He states further, "from Oyster Bay we passed about thirty miles to Flushing, where we had a very large meeting, many hundreds of people being there, some of whom came about thirty miles to it. A glorious and heavenly meeting it was (praised be the Lord God), and the people were much satisfied."

Fox returned to Maryland, Philadelphia not having been then founded, without visiting the city of New York. Sewel and other historians have probably been in error as to his having visited the Governor there.

After leaving Long Island George Fox sent a letter to John Bowne from Maryland, 1st of Eleventh month, 1672, which concludes with, "Remember my dear love to Friends at Oyster Bay and Gravesend, and all the rest as though I named them, and for all of them to dwell in the word of God together as heirs of grace and life, and so the grace of our Lord Jesus Christ be in and with you all, Amen.

The meetings upon Long Island appear to have been established in the following order: those at Gravesend and Flushing in 1657, that at Oyster Bay in 1660, those at the Farms. the Kills and Newtown before 1676, Matinecock in 1684, Jamaica and Hempstead in 1692. In 1687 the Monthly Meeting ordered that meetings be held at Edmund Titus', Westbury, at Jericho, Bethpage and Jerusalem. Sequatogue was established in 1700, Cow Neck in 1703, Huntington in 1728, Rockaway in 1742, Setauket in 1743, and Stony Brook at some previous date.

The earlier meetings were soon organized into Monthly and Quarterly Meetings, and a half-year Meeting was held at Oyster Bay from 1665. The earliest records we can now find began in 1671.

The meetings of Long Island were organized into a Yearly Meeting, and became independent of New England, by the following minute of New England Yearly Meeting: "At a Yearly Meeting at the house of Walter Newberry, in Rhode Island, 14th of Fourth month, 1695, among the meetings called are Long Island. It is agreed that the meetings at Long Island be from this time a general Meeting, and that John Bowne and John Rodman shall take care to receive all such papers as shall come to the Yearly Meeting in Long Island, and correspond with Friends appointed in London." It was held at Flushing until 1777, when it was removed to Westbury, and in 1794 it was removed to New York city.   *   *   *

27

The records of the Yearly Meeting and Monthly Meetings contain many entries of great interest, some of them upon subjects of much importance. The earliest general concern of Friends upon Long Island seems to have been upon the use of tobacco, which the influence of their Dutch neighbors probably tended to increase. Under date of Eighth month 13th, 1685, we find the following: "This meeting hath drawn up a paper conserning the disorderly smooking of tobacco & have left ye care of it unto *John B rne*, Will Richardson & ffrancis Richardson, to see yt coppies be of ye sd paper be sents accordingly as ye desire of friends to be sent to ye meeting[s] of ye naboring provinces, & they to se ye Sd paper be recorded in a book." The neighboring province was New England, to whose Yearly Meeting the meetings on Long Island then belonged. On the second page of the records of the Yearly Meeting of Friends for New England we find the following under the date of Fourth mouth 14th, 1686. "At a general Yearly Meeting at the house of Wm. Coddington, R. I. The several meetings, to wit: Sandwich, Scituate, Salem, Piscataqua, Oyster Bay being called, the testimony of Friends at Oyster Bay against the immoderate use of tobacco being read in the meetings having unity with it, have agreed that copies of it be sent to the several meetings in New England, and all Friends are desired in the love of God everywhere to take heed of it." Friends steadily continued to oppose the use of tobacco. The Quarterly Meeting on Long Island recorded in 1774, "Friends are clear of chewing tobacco in meeting."   *
*   *   * Young Friends were educated to exercise great care in reference to marriage. This is interestingly illustrated in the following letter from *Hannah Bowne*, daughter of John Bowne, to her parents who were then in England: "And dear father and mother, I may also acquaint you, that one Benjamin Field, the youngest son of our friend Susanna Field, has tendered his love to me, the question he has indeed proposed is concerning marriage, the which as yet I have not at present rejected, nor given much way to, nor do I intend to proceed nor let out my affections too much toward him until I have well considered the thing, and have your and friends' advice and consent concerning it." Benjamin Field and *Hannah Bowne* were married in due time.   *   *   *   *

In 1771 the Yearly Meeting directed that £100 be raised and "paid to *Samuel Bowne*, merchant in New York, to be by him transmitted to the Meeting for Sufferings in London to defray the public expenses of the Society." Flushing Quarterly Meeting raised £90 of this sum, and Purchase Quarterly Meeting £40. Money was raised for the same purpose in other years.

POEM READ AT THE BI-CENTENNIAL OF THE
NEW YORK YEARLY MEETING, BY MARY
S. KIMBER OF NEW YORK.

THE BOWNE HOUSE.

1662—1895.

O quiet house, that now reposes
    So peacefully beneath the trees,
'Mid clustering vines and fragrant roses,
    And slumberous murmur of the bees.

No towering shaft,—no sculptured fane,
    Records the deeds that here were wrought,
The workers pass,—their works remain,
    The blessings of enfranchised thought.

There gathered round this ingle-side,
    In sixteen hundred sixty-two,
An earnest band, oft sorely tried,
    Reviled, proscribed, yet staunch and true.

They had left English hearth and home,
    And all the world would reckon dear,
With Him they loved, content to roam
    As strangers and as pilgrims here.

The woods had been their meeting-place,
    Their temple's arch the vaulted sky;
A living silence filled the space,
    Or prayer and praise ascended high.

But when upon this chosen site
    His homestead rose complete and fair,
John Bowne had claimed a brother's right
    With friends beloved, its cheer to share.

The fire glow fell on faces pale,
    Grave faces schooled in calm endurance,
Forms spent and worn in noisome gaol,
    But eyes alight with hope's assurance.

The patient faith that naught could daunt,
    Outlived at last the stern decree
Of Endicott and Stuyvesant,
    And Jesus set his people free.

Hither came in love and power
    The King's ambassadors of grace;
George Fox himself in happy hour
    Once tarried in this favored place.

Too long the tale, though sweet, to tell
    Of all who wrought the blest increase,
Who labored in the vineyard well,
    And passed to their eternal peace.

Fair lies the heritage they won,
    These loyal, fearless pioneers,
For them their Master's own "Well done"
    Comes echoing down two hundred years.

Let us, who enter on the fields
    So dearly bought for our possessing,
Garner the fruit our birthright yields,
    And seek in faith the promised blessing.

Sing softly, bird on leafy spray,—
    Spring green, O grass, around this door,
Breathe gently, winds from Rockaway,
    Spare this old house a century more.

NOTE—B. J. Lossing, in an illustrated article on
American Historical Trees in Harper's Monthly for
May, 1862, speaking of the "Fox Oak," says: "It is on
quiet Bowne Avenue." Referring to the religious service held by George Fox there in 1672 he quotes the
latter, "We had a meeting of many hundred people"
and adds, "There being no place of worship large enough
to hold the multitude, Fox preached in the shade of
two large white oak trees near the house of John
Bowne, a Quaker, who entertained him.
"Several years ago these venerable oaks showed signs
of decay; and one of them fell one pleasant breezy
afternoon in September, 1841. Its companion remains,
but life is extinct. I give a portrait of it as it appeared
in August, 1861. From the ascertained age of the other
one, it is supposed to be at least four hundred years old.
Its circumference two feet from the ground is sixteen
feet."
The "Fox Oaks" have long since disappeared. Their
site, on the other side of the street from, and nearly
opposite to, the Bowne house, is marked by a small
granite stone rising just above the sod, with the inscription "Fox Oaks" cut on the top.—[John Cox, Jr.].

APPENDIX

ADDENDA AND ERRATA

ABSTRACTS OF WILLS, DATA RECEIVED TOO LATE FOR INSERTION IN THE BODY OF
THIS WORK, LINEAGES OF SUBSCRIBING RELATIVES NOT ELSEWHERE
FULLY REGISTERED IN THIS VOLUME, ETC.

I.

ADDITIONAL DATA CONCERNING ANCESTORS AND OTHER RELATIVES OF THE AUTHOR'S PATERNAL GRAND-FATHER, ISAAC MARTIN⁶ SHOTWELL, 1786-1860.

SON OF RICHARD⁵ & MARY (MARTIN) SHOTWELL OF GENESEE CO., N. Y., AND GRANDSON
(1) OF BENJAMIN⁴ & AME (HALLETT) SHOTWELL OF BRICKTOWN, RAHWAY, N. J.,
[OF JOHN³ & MARY (THORNE) SHOTWELL, JOHN² & ELIZABETH (BURTON)
SHOTWELL, ABRAHAM¹ SHOTWELL], AND (2) OF ISAAC AND
ELIZABETH (BURLING) MARTIN OF
NEW YORK CITY.

ABSTRACTS OF SURROGATE RECORDS.

WILLS PROBATED, ADMINISTRATION OF INTESTATE ESTATES, APPOINTMENT OF GUARDIANSHIPS, ETC.,-
RELATING TO INHABITANTS OF NEW JERSEY NAMED SHOTWELL, 1705-1804,
PRESERVED IN THE OFFICE OF THE SECRETARY OF
STATE, TRENTON, N. J.

---

*1. Will of John Shotwell of Woobridg, dated 7th day of *first* [fifth] month called July 1719 (in the first part of will). In the latter part of the will the date is given as the fourteenth day of the fifth month called July. Proved Oct. 5, and Letters of Administration granted to John Kinsey one of ye Executors sometime in Oct. 1719. Mentions wife but does not give her name; sons, John and Abraham; daughters, Elezebeth Laing and Sarah Smith; witnesses, Isabel fich Randolph, Edward fitz raanlph, John Vail; executors, John Kinsey and son law John Laing; recorded in Liber A. of Wills, pages 134 &c.

*1. John¹ Shotwell, Sr., who d. in 1719, probably b. in England about 1650-58, s. of Abraham (pp. 85-7), and ancestor of the Essex (now Union) county (N. J.), Shotwells (pp. 124-7), and of a large majority of those now bearing this name in North America.

*2. Will of John Shotwell of the Borrough Elizabeth, Essex Co., dated the 10th day of the Second month 1759. Proved and Probate granted June 26th, 1762. Wife Mary; sons, John, Abraham, Samuel, Benjamin, Jacob, Joseph; daughter, Mary Marsh; executors, sons Joseph and Benjamin; witnesses, David Brant, Charles Howel, Benju Jenkins; recorded in Liber H. of Wills, pages 156 &c.

*2. John² Shotwell, Jr., 1686?-1762, of Shotwell's Landing, [of John², Abraham¹], (pp. 124-132).

*3. Will of Joseph Shotwell of Woodbridge, Rahway, Middlesex Co., dated 13th day of the ninth month, 1785. Proved and Probate granted September 20th, 1787. Wife Phebe; sons, John, Henry, Joseph, James, William; daughter, Mary Haydock; brother, Abraham; executors, sons John and Henry; witnesses, Isaac Martin, Joseph Latham, Anna Dobson; recorded in Liber 29 of Wills, pages 343 &c.

*3. Joseph[4] Shotwell, 1710-1787, s. of John[3], Jr., & Mary (Thorne) Shotwell of the Landing (pp. 127-9, 149-50).

*4. Will of John Shotwell of Elizabeth town, Essex Co., dated fifth day of the twelfth month 1776. Proved and Probate granted September 16, 1782. Sons, John Smith Shotwell, Hugh, Jacob, William, Isaiah, James; daughters, *Matthew*, Susannah Townsend, Mary Stevens, Sary Smith; grand-daughter, Mary Clayton, grand-daughter, Prudence Jones; executors, son John Smith Shotwell and Isaiah Shotwell and brother Samuel Shotwell; witnesses, Abraham Coles, Henry Line, William Shotwell; recorded in Liber M. of Wills, pages 113 &c.

*4. John[4] Shotwell, 1712-1779, "of Plainfield," (pp. 129, 139-141).

*5. Will of John Smith Shotwell of the township of Westfield, Essex Co., dated thirteenth day of the ninth month 1800. Proved and Probate granted April 30th, 1801. Wife Phebe; sons, Joseph Smith Shotwell, Nathan Shotwell, John Shotwell, William, Samuel; daughters, Mary Shotwell, Sarah Shotwell, Susanna Morton, Elizabeth Hughes; executrix, wife Phebe, brother Jacob Shotwell, and Isaac Vail, executors; witnesses, James Brown, John L. Shotwell, Joseph Cole, 3rd: recorded in Liber 39 of Wills, page 315.

*5. John Smith[5] Shotwell, 1759-1801, s. of John[4] & Elizabeth (Smith) Shotwell "of Plainfield," (pp. 140, 142-3).

*6. Letters of Guardianship were granted unto John Freeman, Junr., Guardian of Joseph S. Shotwell, child of John Smith Shotwell, late of Essex County, deceased; dated January 16th, 1804; recorded in Liber 40 of Wills, page 420.

*6. pp. 142-3, 154.

7. Letters of Guardianship were granted unto John Freeman, Junr., Guardian of Nathan Shotwell, child of John Smith Shotwell, late of Essex Co., deceased; dated January 16th, 1801; recorded in Liber 40 of Wills, page 420.

*8. Will of Abraham Shotwell of the borough of Elizabeth, Essex Co., dated the 23rd day of the seventh month 1800. There is an addition to the will dated the 28th day of the seventh month, 1800. Proved and Probate granted February 11th, 1801. Wife Lydia; sons, Jeremiah, Isaac, John, Aaron, Abraham; grand-children, William and Abigail, children of my son Samuel, deceased; executors, son Isaac and son in law Edward Moore; witnesses, Jeffrey Jones, Prudence Hand, Joseph DCamp; recorded in Liber 39 of Wills, pages 244 &c.

*8 Abraham[4] Shotwell, 1719 1801, [of John[3], John[2], Abraham[1]]. (See pp. 129-30, 88).

*9. Will of Abraham Shotwell, son of Abraham Shotwell, late of Elizabeth Town, Rahway, deceased, dated tenth day of the third month called March, 1801. Proved and Probate granted the 28th day of December, 1802. Mother, Lydia Shotwell; brothers, Isaac, Aaron and John; executors, brothers Isaac, Aaron and John; Witnesses, Thomas Bills, William Shotwell, Junier, Elizabeth Bills; recorded in Liber 40 of Wills, page 212.

*9. Abraham Shotwell, 1770-1801±, s. of Abraham[4] & Lydia (Hallett) Shotwell. (See p. 88.)

*10. Will of Jacob Shotwell of Bridgetown, Middlesex Co., dated the twenty seventh day of the fifth month, 1793. Proved and Probate granted July 8th, 1793. Wife Catherine; daughter, Hannah Shotwell, (wife of Isaac Shotwell); sons, Eden Shotwell, Nathan Shotwell; executrix, wife Catharine; executors, nephew John Shotwell of Bridgetown, Mercht., and son Nathan; witnesses, James Haydock, Joseph DCamp, Junr., Abel Gibbs; recorded in Liber 33 of Wills, page 228.

*10. Jacob[5] Shotwell, 1721-1793, s. of John[4], Jr., of the Landing. (See pp. 130, 121).

*11. Will of Samuel Shotwell of Elizabeth, Essex Co., dated 2nd of August, 1777. Proved and Probate granted April 7th, 1783. Sons, Caleb, David; daughters, Sarah Shotwell, Elizabeth Shotwell; John Shotwell, son of my Brother Joseph; Eden Shotwell, son of my Brother Jacob; Jeremiah Shotwell, son of my Brother Abraham; William Shotwell, son of my Brother Benjamin; executors, brothers Abraham Shotwell and Benjamin Shotwell; witnesses, Sarah Horton, Joseph Clarke, Joseph DCamp; recorded in Liber 24 of Wills, pages 320 &c.

*11. Samuel[4] Shotwell, 1723-1777, s. of John[3], Jr., of the Landing. (See pp. 130, 163-9).

*12. Letters of Administration were granted unto Elizabeth Shotwell, Administratrix, and Hartshorn Fitz Randolph and Richard Fitz Randolph, Administrators of David Shotwell, late of the county of Sussex, deceased; dated December 27th, 1788; recorded in Liber 31 of Wills, page 201.

*12. David[5] Shotwell, 1759-1788, s. of Samuel[4], [of John[3], John[2], Abraham[1]]. (See pp. 168-9, 105.)

*13. Will of Sarah Shotwell of the Borough of Elizabeth, County of Essex, dated the eighth day of the fifth month 1790. Proved and Probate granted the 7th day of June, 1790. Brother Caleb Shotwell and David Shotwell decd. and Elizabeth Bills my sister now the wife of Thomas Bills decd. amongst all their lawful children; executors, Uncle Marmaduke Hunt and Cousin Jeremiah Shotwell, son of Abraham; witnesses, Jacob Shotwell, Rhoda Morris, James

Shotwell; recorded in Liber 30 of Wills, page 338.

*13. Sarah, 1751-1790, dau. of Samuel⁴ Shotwell. (See p. 168.)

*14. Will of Benjamin Shotwell of Borough of Elizabeth, dated the eleventh day of the second month 1791. Proved and Probate granted May 17th, 1793. Wife, Amy Shotwell; sons, William, Richard, Benjamin; brother Abraham; daughters, Sarah Lundy, Mary, Elizabeth and Lydia, Amy, wife of Charles Brook; grandchildren, Amy, Benjamin, William and Sarah Hampton, Children of my daughter Sarah Lundy; father, John Shotwell, deceased; executors, son Benjamin, son William; witnesses, Samuel Marsh, Webster Wynn, Joseph DeCamp; recorded in Liber 33 of Wills, pages 196 &c.

*14. Benjamin⁴ Shotwell, 1738-1793, of the Landing. (See pp. 130-33, 91-95), the compiler's great-great-grandfather.

*15. Will of Abraham Shotwell of Piscatua, Middlesex Co., dated June 20th, 1757. Proved and Probate granted November 2nd, 1757. Sons, John, Abraham; daughters, Deborah Shotwell, Sarah Vail, Elizabeth Webster; grand-children, Hannah Shotwell, daughter of Daniel and Debory: Abraham Vail, son of John Vail and Sarah; Hannah Webster, daughter of Joseph Webster and Elizabeth; son-in-law, Daniel Shotwell; executors, son Abraham and son-in-law Daniel Shotwell and Nathaniel Fitz Randolph; witnesses, Agnes Bloomfield, Jacob Thorn, Joseph Shotwell, Jr.; Liber F. of Wills, pp. 465 &c.

*15. Abraham³ Shotwell, [of John², Abraham¹]. (See pp. 126, 88.)

*16. Will of John Shotwell of Woodbridge, Middlesex Co., dated November 17th, 1757. Proved and Probate granted January 3rd, 1758. Wife Anna; sons, John and Jasper; daughter, Mary; executors, Recompence Stanbery, James Clarkson, Wife, Anna Shotwell; witnesses, Jeremiah Wright, Benjamin Shotwell, Robert Clarkson; recorded in Liber F. of Wills, pages 481 &c.

*16. John⁴ Shotwell, [probably of Abraham³, John², Abraham¹]. (See pp. 88, 141-2.)

*17. Letters of Guardianship were granted to John Carle of Morris Town in the County of Morris, appointing him Guardian of Jasper Shotwell, son of John Shotwell, late of the County of Middlesex, deceased. Dated the twenty fifth of February, 1773; recorded in Liber K. of Wills, page 451.

*17. Jasper⁵ Shotwell, s. of John⁴ & Anna (———) Shotwell, [probably of Abraham³, John², Abraham¹]. (See pp. 142, 121.)

*18. Will of Daniel Shotwell of Woodbridge, Middlesex Co., dated Dec. 21st, 1732. Proved Jan. 30, 1735. Sons and Executors, Joseph, John and Abraham; daughters, Mary, Martha, Susannah, Elizabeth, Margaret; witnesses,

Martha Caujen, Sissell Sariant, Jno. Sarjant; recorded in Liber C. of Wills, pages 66 &c.

*18. Probably Daniel³ Shotwell, formerly of Staten Island. (See pp. 87-8., 101-2.) Daniel Shotwell took up 300 or more acres of land on Staten Island in 1694. In Shrewsbury Q. M. on 27 of 5 mo., 1713, he said: "Woodbridge friends proposed to this meeting to have our approbation to have a meeting once in three months at John Shotwell's on Staaten Island, and the meeting condescends unto it."
Dally, in his "History of Woodbridge," has the following:— "Sept. 20, (Nov. 20), 1729. This meeting recommends the oversight of the burying ground to Daniel Shotwell."

*19. Will of Daniel Shotwell of Woodbridge, Middlesex Co., dated April 18th, 1788. Proved and Probate granted April 13th, 1788. Wife Margit; sons, Titus, Daniel; daughters, Hannah Moore, Mary Thorn, Elizabeth Marsh, Sarah Shotwell; executors, Son Titus and son in law Daniel Moores; witnesses, Nathaniel Heard, William Heard, Joseph Shotwell, Junr., Joseph Shotwell; recorded in Liber 31 of Wills, page 220.

*19. Daniel⁴ Shotwell, 1725-1788, s. of Joseph³ & Mary (Manning) Shotwell. (See pp. 149, 103). He (not his son as intimated on p. 103), m. 1787, Margaret Alstone or Elston.

20. Will of Mary Shotwell of Elizabeth, Essex County, dated April 25th, 1770. Proved and Probate granted April 30th, 1772. Sons, Andrew Hamton, Abner Hamton, Jacob Hamton; daughters, Hannah Miller, Margaret Elston; Rachel Pangborn, Hannah Miller's daughter; Sarah, Mary and Anne, daughters of her son Jacob Hamton; her son Andrew Hamton's eldest son (name not given); his second son John Hamton; his two youngest daughters, Catharine and Margret; granddaughter, Hannah Elston; executors, son in law Samuel Elston; witnesses, John Thorn, Isaac Thorn, Benjamin Thorn; recorded in Liber K. of Wills, page 457.

*21. Will of Abraham Shotwell of Woodbridge, Middlesex Co., dated August 7th, 1775. Proved and Probate granted October 13th, 1775. Wife Mary; sons, James, Samuel; daughters, Susannah, Rachel, Sarah, Mary and Rebecker; executors, Brother Joseph Shotwell, and Brother Daniel Shotwell; witnesses, Benjamin Shotwell, Sarah Ross afd. Mary Compton; recorded in Liber L. of Wills, pages 300 &c.

*21. Abraham⁴ Shotwell, b. 1735, s. of Joseph³ & Mary (Manning) Shotwell. (See pp. 149, 88.) It thus appears that Abraham & Mary (Jackson) Shotwell, had several children not recorded at p. 88; among them was James, who may have been identical with the James Shotwell of Essex Co., N. J., who m., 1772, Anna Moore. (See p. 122.)

*22. Letters of Administration were granted unto John Moore, Administrator of James Shotwell, late of the County of Middlesex, Dec'd. Dated June 22nd, 1795; recorded in Liber 35 of Wills, page 201.

*22. James⁵ Shotwell, probably s. of Abraham⁴ & Mary (Jackson) Shotwell. (See pp. 88, 122.)

*23. Will of John Shotwell of Woodbridge, Middlesex Co., dated October 31, 1743. Proved February 14, 1745 6. Wife, Lydia; sons, John,

Benjamin, and Joseph; daughters, Elisabeth Shotwell, Johanah Stelle, Lydia Shotwell, Mary Shotwell and Prudence Shotwell; executors, son in law Benja. Stelle, Jr. and Edward Fitz Randolph, Jr; witnesses, John Clarkson, Jonathan Fitz Randolph, Benja: Stelle; recorded in Liber D. of Wills, pages 361 &c.

*21. John³ Shotwell, supposed s. of Daniel of Staten Island. (See pp. 101-3, 139.)

* 24. Will of Benjamin Shotwell of the township of Woodbridg, County of Middlesex, dated August 22nd, 1797. Proved and Probate granted the 26th of September, 1797. Wife, Elisabeth; sons, John, Manning; daughter, Elizabeth Drak; executors, son John and James Bonney; witnesses, Eli Miller, William Edgar, Shotwell Bishop; recorded in Liber 36 of Wills, page 514.

*24. Benjamin⁴ Shotwell, 1731-1797, s. of John³ & Lydia (——) Shotwell. (See pp. 139, 95.)

* 25. Will of Joseph Shotwell Junr. of Woodbridge, Middlesex Co., dated July 3rd, 1758. Proved and Probate granted July 29th, 1758. Wife, Rachel Shotwell; son, Benjamin; brother, Benjamin Shotwell; daughters, Rachel and Lyda; executors, Benjamin Shotwell (brother) and Peter Martain (brother); witnesses, James Fitz Randolph, Rebeckah Fitz Randolph, David Edgar; recorded in Liber F. of Wills, pages 541 &c.

*25. Joseph⁴ Shotwell, probably son of John³ & Lydia (——) Shotwell. (See p. 139.)

Note.—John³ Shotwell and wife Lydia had:—(1.) John, b. 1729±. (2.) Benjamin, b. 1731. (See abstract No. 24 ante and p. 139.) (3.) Joseph. (See abstract No. 25.) (4.) Johanna Shotwell, dw. Woodbridge, N, J., when she m. ——, 1739, (license dated Oct. 2, '39.) Benjamin Stelle, Jr., of Woodbridge, N. J., [See No. (6)], who was one of the executors named in his father-in-law's will of Oct. 31, 1743, proved Feb. 14, 1745-6, (5.) Elizabeth⁴ Shotwell, m. in June, 1748, (license dated June 11, '48). James Bishop, Jr., who had borrowed money of John Shotwell in 1744, giving a mortgage for three years (now in possession of James Bishop of New Brunswick, N. J.,) with a number of partial payments noted on the back, the latest in March, 1745-6. James Bishop, Jr., had, in 1778, executors, Benjamin and Daniel Shotwell,—probably Elizabeth's brother Benjamin and cousin Daniel⁴ [of Joseph³]. He was probably s. of James⁴ Bishop, Sr., [of John³, John², John¹]. James⁵, Jr., & Elizabeth (Shotwell) Bishop had an only daughter, Lydia, and a son, Shotwell⁶ Bishop, who served in the Revolutionary War. Shotwell⁶ Bishop's eldest daughter was named Lydia, and his son James was father of James Bishop, M. C., from New Jersey in 1851. (6.) Lydia Shotwell, dw. Woodbridge, N. J., when she m. ——, 1752, (license dated Aug. 14, '52), Benjamin Stelle of Piscataway, N. J., (probably widower of her sister Johanna.) (7.) Mary Shotwell, was of Woodbridge, N. J., when she

m. ——, 1753, (license dated May 26, '53), Gabriel Ogden of Morris Co., N. J. (8.) Prudence Shotwell, mentioned with foregoing children in father's will in 1743.

26. Peter Shotwell and Henry Baker, both of the County of Essex, Administrators of the estate of Abraham Shotwell late of the County of Essex deceased. Dated May 9th, A. D. 1750. Peter was the son of the deceased; recorded in Liber E. of Wills, page 397.

27. To James Marshall of Elizabeth Town, Principal Creditor of Peter Shotwell, late of said Elizabeth Town Labourer deceased. Dated Feb'y 12th, 1757; recorded in Liber F. of Wills, page 403.

28. Letters of Administration were granted unto Jacob Martin, Adm'r of Benjamin Shotwell, late of Middlesex, deceased. Dated October 29th, 1776; recorded in Liber 18 of Wills, page 54.

29. Letters of Administration were granted unto John Smith Shotwell and John Shotwell, Administrators of Joseph Shotwell late of Middlesex, deceased. Dated July 29th, 1793; recorded in Liber 33 of Wills, page 231.

30. Letters of Guardianship granted unto Jacob Martin, Guardian of Anna Shotwell. Dated December 24th, 1783; recorded in Liber 25 of Wills, page 225.

31. Letters of Guardianship were granted unto Jeremiah Clarkson, Guardian of Ann Shotwell. Dated February 23rd, 1791; recorded in Liber 32 of Wills, page 468.

NEW JERSEY MARRIAGE LICENSES.*

(a.) Benjamin Shotwell, Woodbridge, Elizabeth Shotwell, Woodbridge, 1753, Dec. 18.

(b.) Jacob Shotwell, Woodbridge, Esther Gach, Woodbridge, 1754, Apr. 3.

(c.) Jacob Shotwell, Woodbridge, Elizabeth Kinsey, Woodbridge, 1758, Feb. 22.

(d.) Manning Shotwell, Middlesex, Polly Clarkson, 1781, Feb. 27.

(e.) Nicholas Shotwell, Rachel Fitz Randolph, Woodbridge, 1744, June 2.

* These dates are supposed to be the dates of the licenses; and most of the marriages probably took place on the same day.

(*f.*) Elizabeth Shotwell, Middlesex, James Bishop, Middlesex, 1748, June 11.

(*g.*) Elizabeth Shotwell, Woodbridge, Benjamin Shotwell, Woodbridge, 1753, Dec. 18.

(*h.*) Elizabeth Shotwell, Essex, Henry Ludlam, Middlesex, 1772, Jan. 3.

(*i.*) Johanna Shotwell, Woodbridge, Benjamin Stelle, Woodbridge, 1739, Oct. 2.

(*j.*) Lydia Shotwell, Woodbridge, Benjamin Stelle, Piscataway, 1752, Aug. 14.

(*k.*) Mary Shotwell, Woodbridge, Gabriel Ogden, Morris, 1753, May 26.

(*l.*) Mary Shotwell, David Morris, Middlesex, 1769, Dec. 6.

NOTES TO FOREGOING.

(*a.*) Benjamin[4], s. of John & Lydia. Assumption (pp. 53, 95, 139), that wife's maiden name was *Manning* and that the marriage occurred in 1754, not confirmed.

(*b.*) Probably Jacob[4], b. 1720, s. of Joseph[3] & Mary (Manning) Shotwell, (p. 149).

(*c.*) Perhaps second marriage of above Jacob[4].

(*d.*) Son of Benjamin[4] & Elizabeth, (p. 95.) Date erroneously given (p. 54) as 1783.

(*e.*) Probably s., (b. 1718), of Joseph[3] & Mary (Manning) Shotwell. (See p. 149).

(*f.*) Daughter of John[3] & Lydia. (See " note" after abstract No. 25, p. 214).

(*g.*)=(a.) q. v.

(*i.*) Sister to Elizabeth— (f.) q. v.

(*j.*) Sister to (f.) and (i.) q. v.

(*k.*) Perhaps sister to the above. John Shotwell, of Woodbridge, (abstract No. 23, p. p. 213-14) ,in his will of 1743, mentions a daughter, Mary Shotwell, among other children.

LIST OF PERSONS WHO SERVED IN THE WAR OF THE REBELLION, COMPILED FROM RECORDS OF THE MICHIGAN NATIONAL GUARD, PRESERVED IN THE OFFICE OF THE ADJUTANT GENERAL AT LANSING.

Archibald Shotwell, enlisted at Detroit, Feb. 7, 1865, in Co. H, 24th regiment, Mich. Infantry; dismissed at Detroit, June 30, 1865.

Albert Shotwell, enlisted at Windsor, Sept. 13, 1862, in Co. D, 7th regiment, Mich. Cavalry; dismissed at Ft. Leavenworth, Kans., Dec. 15, 1865.

E. H. Shotwell, enlisted at Battle Creek, Mich., Jan. 29, 1861, in Co. H, regiment M. Horse. (No further record).

William Shotwell, enlisted Mt. Clemens, Mich., Mar. 26, 1863, in the eighth regiment, Mich. Cavalry. (No further record. Perhaps identical with the following).

William Shotwell, enlisted Arcadia, Mich., May 26, 1863, in Co. L, 8th regiment, Mich. Cavalry; dismissed at Detroit July 13, 1863.

ADDITIONAL SHOTWELL DATA

WITH BRIEF NOTICES OF CERTAIN ALLIED FAMILIES,

INCLUDING CONCISE LINEAGES OF VARIOUS SUBSCRIBING RELATIVES NOT BEARING
THE SHOTWELL NAME; TOGETHER WITH CORRECTED SHOTWELL RECORDS
RECEIVED TOO LATE FOR INSERTION IN PART II. OF THIS WORK.

AARON[5] SHOTWELL'S BRANCH.

[of Abraham[4], John[3], John[2], Abraham[1], (see pp.
88, 121-30, 124-5, 85-7, 84)].

George H[6]. Shotwell's widow, Mary E. A.,
has lived, since 1894, with her widowed daughter, Cordelia—Mrs. Dr. J. C. Campbell—of 234
Lawrence St., Cincinnati, Ohio. The son-in-
law, Dr. J. C. Campbell, formerly a practicing
physician and latterly engaged in real estate
business; d. in Cincinnati, Ohio, 1 Feb., 1894
(See p. 109.)

CASSIUS[7] SHOTWELL of Englewood, Ill., s. of
George H[6]. & Mary E. A. (Tudor) Shotwell of
Cincinnati, O., (see pp. 109, 81), [of Aaron[5],
Abraham[4], John[3], John[2], Abraham[1]], m. 1864,
Virginia D. Bone, of Cincinnati, O., and had:

1. *James Bone Shotwell.*
2. *George Harrison Shotwell,* (named for
his paternal grandfather), m. 1893, Viola
McLaughlin.
3. *Cassius Shotwell, Jr.,* m. 1895, Virginia
B. Huych.
4. *Alice Shotwell.*
5. *Stella Shotwell,* b. ...., d..........

BENJAMIN[5] SHOTWELL'S BRANCH

[of Benjamin[4], John[3], John[2], Abraham[1], (pp.
95-7)].

Ella May Shotwell, dau. of Benjamin H[7]. &
Paulina (Richards Davis) Shotwell (p. 98), [of
Thomas[6], Benjamin[5]], m. John Bush, Jr., of
Hadley, Mich.

John Seley & Mary Eliza (Shotwell) Reed,
of Perinton, N. Y., P. O., Egypt, (see synopsis,
pp. 117-18), the former, s. of John & Mary S[7].
(Shotwell) Reed, [of Isaac M[6]. Shotwell,
Richard[5], Benjamin[4], John[3], John[2], Abraham[1]],
and the latter, dau. of Edwin B[7]. & Sarah A.

(Harkness) Shotwell, of Ingham Co., Mich., (pp.
109, 181-2), [of Zachariah[6], Benj[5]., Benj[4]., John[3],
John[2], Abraham[1]], had among others (5.) Sarah
Edna Reed, who m. 25 Nov., 1896, Byron D.
Lapham of Macedon, N. Y., and (6.) Martha B.
Reed, who m. on the same date, 25 Nov., 1896,
O. H. Durfee Hoag of Macedon, N. Y., b. 12
Mar., 1875, Attica, N. Y., farmer, republican,
member of M. E. church, s. of Isaac R. & Mary
Ellen (Wright) Hoag of Macedon, N. Y., (m. 15
Mar., 1865),—the former, b. 8 Mar., 1838, s. of
Humphrey H. & (1st of 3 wives), Rachel
(Briggs) Hoag, (who were m. 13 Mar., 1834), and
the latter, dau. of Mark & Elizabeth (Simpson)
Wright of Bucks Co., Pa., Humphrey H. Hoag,
b. 22 Dec., 1810, m. (2) 11 Nov., 1852, Hannah
Mead; m. (3) 7 Nov., 1889, Esther Page. He
was son of Benj. & Anna (Smith) Hoag; (m.
11 Mar., 1810)—the former b. 10 Oct., 1788, s. of
Benj.

Asa & Amy[6] (Shotwell) Willson of Junius, N.
Y.,—the former, s. of Gabriel & Keziah (......)
Willson of Sussex (now Warren) Co., N. J., and
the latter, 1790-1876, dau. of Benj[5]. & Bathsheba (Pound) Shotwell of Wayne Co., N. Y.,
(pp. 95-7),—had: (1) Sarah, wife of Jacob
Bonnel. (2) Bathsheba Shotwell[7] Willson, b.
1 of 8 mo., 1809; d. 14 of 6 mo., 1895, at home
of dau., Amy S., wife of Stephen R. Harkness, in Raisin Tp., near Adrian, Mich., member of Hartland, (N. Y.), M. M, by certifi ate
from Junius M. M., dated 25 of 3 mo., 1828,
having m. in Junius Friends' Meeting, 31 of 10
mo., 1827, Richard L. Aldrich of Elba, N. Y.,
1806-1876, s. of Wanton & Amy[6] (Shotwell)
Aldrich of Elba, N. Y., [of Richard[5] Shotwell,
q. v., pp. 165, 167]. (3.) Amos Willson, dw.
Leslie, Mich., m. Anna Wares. (4.) Wm. S.,
removed to Michigan, 1845, m. (1) in Galen,
(N. Y.), Hicksite Friends' meeting, 3 of 2 mo.,
1842, Margaret H. Shotwell of Galen, N. Y.,
1821-1847, dau. of Joseph[6] & Margaret (Elston)

Shotwell of Rahway, N. J., [of John⁵, Joseph⁴, John³, John², Abr¹.]; m. (2) Elizabeth Mott. (5.) Elizabeth L., m. 1836, Joseph Cook of Macedon, afterwards of Williamson, N. Y. (6.) Benjamin, dw. Imlay City, Lapeer Co., Mich., m. (1) Martha Wares; m. (2) Charlotte Chase. (7.) Lydia, m. James Burton of Raisin, Mich. (8) Asa L., dw. Waterloo, N. Y., m. Angeline Scott. (9) Daniel S., m. Mary Robb.

Richard L⁷. Aldrich, b. 5-13, 1806, Palmyra, N. Y., d. Lenawee Co., Mich., 4-22, 1876, s. of Wanton & Amy⁶ (Shotwell) Aldrich of Elba, N. Y., [of Richard⁵ Shotwell, Benjamin⁴, John³, John², Abraham¹], m. 10-31, 1827, Bathsheba S⁷. Willson, 1809-1895, dau. of Asa & Amy⁶ (Shotwell) Willson of Junius, N. Y., and had: (1) Wanton, b. 2-8, 1829, in Elba, N. Y., and there d. 3-19, 1837. (2.) Asa Willson Aldrich, b. 12-18, 1831, in Elba, N. Y., in the log house built by his father in 1827, upon land adjoining the Aldrich homestead upon the west; dw. W. Maumee St., Adrian, Mich., member of firm of Wheeler & Aldrich, dealers in boots, shoes, and rubber goods, 10-12 Maumee St. E.; m. in Adrian, Mich., Oct. 24, 1860, Mary J. Smart, b. July 30, 1841, Adrian, Mich. (3.) Amy Shotwell⁷ Aldrich, b. 2-19, 1838, in the frame house on the Ridge in the northwestern part of the town of Elba, N. Y., built by her father about 1835-6; dw. Raisin, Mich. P. O. box 846, Adrian, Mich., m. in Raisin, Mich., Dec. 17, 1857, Stephen R. Harkness, s. of Daniel & Beulah (Estes) Harkness, of Elba, N. Y. (4.) George, b. 5-1, 1845, Raisin, Mich., and there d. 9-9, 1845. (5.) Sarah, b. 7-30, 1846, Raisin, Mich., m. after manner of Friends, in Raisin, Mich., 9-10, 1874, Asa Emury Jones, s. of Asa Augustus & Martha M. (Brooks) Jones.

Stephen R. & Amy S⁷. (Aldrich) Harkness, of Raisin Tp., Lenawee Co., Mich., [of Bathsheba S⁷. Willson, Amy⁶ Shotwell, Benjamin⁵, Benjamin⁴, John³, John², Abraham¹], had: (1.) Eva B⁸., b. 8-19, 1862, in Buffalo, N. Y., dw. Shaw, Mich., m. in Palmyra, Mich., Dec. 24, 1879, George N. Mudge, b. Dec. 1, 1859, and had: (a) Alfred E., b., Nov. 18, 1880, Palmyra, Mich. (b) Clara Ruth, b. Oct. 2, 1884, Raisin, Mich. (c) Emma A., b. Dec. 26, 1889, Allis, Tp., Presque Isle Co., Mich. (d) Floyd Raymond Mudge, b. May 26, 1894. (2.) Theodore D. R⁸. Harkness, b. Sept. 18, 1866, Madison, Lenawee Co., Mich., settled on a farm in Shaw, Presque Isle Co., Mich., m. at Adrian, Mich., Aug. 30, 1888, Flora E. Mudge, b. Feb. 26 (?), 1870, dau. of Henry & Martha (Kimball) Mudge of Adrian, Mich., and had: (a) Homer E., b. Jan. 8, 1890, Adrian, Mich. (b) Hazel M., b. June 19, 1892, in Raisin Tp., Mich. (c) Lester, b. July 7, 1894, Raisin, Mich. (d) Esther (twin), b. July 7, 1894. (3.) I. J. Stanley⁸ Harkness, b. May 20, 1868, Palmyra, Mich., d. Whittier, Cal., Sept. 26, 1894, m. Raisin Tp., Mich., Nov. 27, 1890, May V.

28

Benedict, dau. of James & Eliza (——) Benedict, and had: (a) Laura E., b. June 17, 1892, Adrian, Mich. (b) Lloyd Stanley Harkness, b. Sept. 13, 1893, Raisin Tp., Mich. (4.) Lydia, Emma, b. Jan. 18, 1872, Palmyra, Mich. (5.) Alfred Buckley Harkness, b. Sept. 5, 1874, Palmyra, Mich., and there d. Feb. 7, 1875.

CHARLES EDWIN⁴ SHOTWELL, b. 1849, of Dowagiac, Mich., s. of Daniel L⁷. & Mary P. (Iden) Shotwell, of Cass Co., Mich., (see p. 105), [of Zachariah⁶, Benj⁵., Benj⁴., Jno³., Jno²., Abr¹.], m. 1874, Caroline Hike, dau. of Henry & Docy (Robinson) Hike, and had:
1. Harry L., b. 26 Mar., 1876, in Bloomingdale, Van Buren Co., Mich.
2. Bertha H., b. 20 Apr., 1878.
3. Mabel C., b. 30 Nov., 1881.
4. Leo. R., b. 6 Sept., 1887.
5. Mattie Belle, b. 4 Apr., 1892, in Dowagiac, Cass Co., Mich.

ENOCH W. WATERHOUSE, of Clear Lake, Polk Co., Wis., m. 1881, Helen Edna⁴ Shotwell, b. 1846, dau. of Daniel L⁷. & Mary P. (Iden) Shotwell, of Cass Co., Mich., (see p. 105), [of Zachariah⁶, Benj⁵., Benj⁴., Jno³., Jno²., Abr¹.], and had:
1. Charles E., b. 19 Oct., 1888, d. young.

Albert & Eliza B⁴. (Shotwell) Wingrove, of Clay Centre, Kans., [of Samuel P⁷. & Maria (Watson) Shotwell of Idana, Kans., (p. 170), Benj⁶. & Catharine (Pugsley) Shotwell (pp. 95-7), Benj⁵., Benj⁴., John³, John², Abraham¹], had: (1.) Maude Maria, b. 1875, dw. Clay Centre, Kans., m. 3 Oct., 1895, George S. Peckham of Kans. (2.) Cora Clyde, b. 1877, m. 14 Feb., 1895, Roy Neil Rahn of Kans. (3.) Harry, b. 1878. (4.) Frances Ola, 1888-1889. (5.) Albert Linn, b. 1889. (6.) Jobe Lewis Loy, b. 1891.—All b. in Kansas.

Samuel P⁷. Shotwell, b. 1828, [of Benj⁶., Benj⁵., Benj⁴., John³, John², Abr¹.], m. (2) 1890, Florence Thompson of Piper City, Ill.

Edward H⁷. Shotwell of Monte Vista, Colo., s. of Benj⁶. & Catharine (Pugsley) Shotwell, [of Benj⁵., Benj⁴., John³, John², Abr¹. (pp. 98, 108-9)], & 2d wife, Eliza, nec Jones, had:
2. Emma Hortense⁸ (see p. 109), b. 1869, d. 6 Apr., 1892; m. 1887, Sigel Heilman, and had: (1.) Ziska, b. 7 Mar., 1888. (2.) Edward, b. 20 Nov., 1889. (3.) Manford, b. 3 Jan., 1892.
3. Edith Lydia⁸ Shotwell, b. 1871, m. 27 Sept., 1891, Samuel McOllough, and had: (1.) Laverne, b. 25 June, 1893. (2.) Clifford, b. 10 Dec., 1894.
4. Mary Blanch⁸, b. 30 Oct., 1872, m. 20 May, 1891, Frank Larick, and had: (1) Clarence, b. 27 Mar., 1892. (2.) Mabel, b. 18 Mar., 1894. (3.) ————, a dau., b. 31 Dec., 1895.
5. Albert Lee, d. in infancy.
6. Grace Edna⁸, b. 1876, (see p. 109), dw. Monte Vista, Colo.; m. 3 Feb., 1895, Joseph

Day, and had: (1.) Ralph Lee Roy Day, b. 13 July, 1896.

CALEB[5] SHOTWELL'S BRANCH

[of Samuel[4], John[3], John[2], Abraham[1]].

Caleb's grandson, Caleb G[7]. Shotwell—s. of Joseph[6] & Sarah (Randall) Shotwell of Saratoga Co., N. Y.—m. Sally Jane Corey (not *Carey* as printed at p. 99. See p. 153).

Clara Louise Shotwell, eldest daughter of Carlos B[8]. & Eliza L. (Williams) Shotwell, of No. 46 Lawrence Ave., Detroit, Mich. (p. 99), [of Rev. John M[7]. & S. Lucinda (Stone) Shotwell (p. 147), Joseph[6] & Sarah (Randall) Shotwell (p. 153), Caleb[5] & Phebe (Hinckston) Shotwell (p. 99), Samuel[4] & Ame (———) Shotwell (pp. 168-9), John[3] & Mary (Thorne) Shotwell (pp. 127-131), John[2] & Elizabeth (Burton) Shotwell (p. 124), Abraham[1] (85-8)], b. 17 Mar., 1873, m. 17 Mar., 1897, Rodman Hazard Cary of Detroit.

Thomas & Phebe[6] (Shotwell) Kerns (see p. 99), had certainly one son, Stephen Kerns, who dw. Port Byron, Cayuga Co., N. Y.

BILLS LINEAGE.

William[1] *Bills* was of Barnstable, Mass., 1640—one of the first settlers of Cape Cod. Quite likely he went there from Scituate with the congregation of Rev. John Lothrop. There is little or no doubt that Thomas was his son. Another son may have been Richard Bills, who was a soldier in the Great Swamp Fight, Dec. 19, 1675.

Thomas[2] *Bills*, d. 1721, April 2, in Shrewsbury township, N. J.; m. (1) 1672, Oct. 3, Anna Twining, who was b. about 1652, at Eastham, Mass.; d. 1675, Sept. 1; m. (2) 1676, May 2, Joanna Twining, b. 1657, May 30, at Eastham, Mass.; d. 1723, June 4, in Shrewsbury, N. J.; sister of his first wife and dau. of William, Jr. and Elizabeth (Deane) Twining.

Elizabeth Deane was dau. of Stephen Deane and Elizabeth—the dau. of Mary King, a widow of Plymouth, whom Goodwin in his *Pilgrim Republic* mentions as " a lady of prominence." Stephen Deane came to Plymouth in the second ship, *Fortune*, Nov. 1621, and built the first corn mill there.

Thomas Bills was one of the legal inhabitants of Eastham in 1695, but probably moved soon after to Shrewsbury, N. J. Some of his children quite likely settled in Bucks county, Penn. Children: (1) Anna, b. 1673, June 28; Elizabeth, b. 1675, Aug. 23; (2.) *Nathaniel*[3] b. 1677, June 25; Mercy, b. 1679, April 16; Mehitable, b. 1681, March 20; Thomas, b. 1685, March 22; Gershom, b. 1686, June 5; Joanna, b. 1688, Dec. 2.

Nathaniel[3] *Bills*, b. 1677, June 25, probably at Eastham, Mass.; d. 1729, in Shrewsbury township, Monmouth county, N. J. He bought lands in Manasquan, Shrewsbury township in 1722, and another parcel in 1726. See Book K 2 of Deeds, pp. 405 & 407, Trenton, N. J. As will recorded in Book B, p. 260, at Trenton, does not mention his wife, she probably d. before he did. Children: Thomas, *Gershom*[4], Daniel, b. 1716, Oct.; Mercy, Catharine, Joanna and Elizabeth.

Gershom[4] *Bills*, b. before 1715, probably in N. J., d. 1766, in Shrewsbury township, N. J., m. (1) ……… ………; m. (2) 1755, Margaret Chamberlin of Monmouth county, N. J., probably a descendant of John Chamberlin of Newport, R. I., two of whose sons according to Austin's Gen. Dict. of R. I., removed to Shrewsbury. He was a mariner and farmer and lived on the farm formerly owned by his father. Quite likely he was a member of the Society of Friends. His son Thomas was, and the deaths of Gershom's grandparents are recorded on the journal of the society. Will proved 1766, Sept. 27; recorded in Book I, p. 98, Trenton, N. J. Children: (1) Hannah, Daniel, Rebecca, Rachel, b. Jan., 1748, Sarah. (2.) Sylvanus, Sylvester, Thomas[5], b. 1760, Dec. 25, and Elizabeth.

Thomas[5] *Bills*, b. 1760, Dec. 25, in Shrewsbury township, Monmouth county, N. J.; d. 1845, Oct., 23, in Clarkson, Monroe county, N. Y.; m. (1) about 1782, Elizabeth Shotwell of Rahway, N. J., dau. of Samuel and Amy (——————) Shotwell. (See p. 169). She was b. 1761, July 28; d. 1826, Aug. 10, in Irondequoit, Monroe County, N. Y. He m. (2) Mary Webster, dau. of William and Susan (——) Webster. She had no children. His parents both died while he was a boy and he was brought up by his sisters, Hannah and Rachel.

Children all b. in east New Jersey, viz. :

I.   Samuel, b. 1783, Dec. 13; d. about 1784.

II.   Samuel Shotwell, b. 1785, Feb. 4.

III. Thomas, b. 1787, March 31; d. 1861, Aug. 17.

IV.   Mary Farrington, b. 1789, Sept. 13; d. 1845, June 16.

V.   David Shotwell, b. 1791, Oct. 15.

VI.   Eliza, b. 1794, Sept. 1; d. young.

VII. *Sarah Davids*[6], b. 1798, Sept. 11; m. Benjamin Fish. See Fish, p. 220.

VIII. Catharine Greenleaf, b. 1800, June 17; d. 1827, July 28.

IX.   Nathan Hunt, b. 1803, July 29.

X.   *Elizabeth*[6] *Shotwell*, b. 1806, Jan. 16; d. 1876, Jan. 28.

Elizabeth Shotwell[6] *Bills*, b. 1806, Jan. 16; d. 1876, Jan. 28, at Battle Creek, Mich.; m. ………, Platt Gilbert, b. 1802, at Salem, N. Y.; d. 1866, Nov. 18; son of Thomas Gilbert, who was b. at Salem, N. Y., and lived 84 years.

CHILDREN—GILBERT.

I. Mary Elizabeth, b. 1832; m. ______
Pitkin.
1. II. Charlotte Ann, b. 1835; m. D. Frank
Barber.
2. III. Charles Thomas, b. 1846, Aug. 31.
IV. George Howe, b. 1846, Aug. 31.

1. *Charlotte Ann Gilbert*, b. 1835; m. D.
Frank Barber.

CHILDREN—BARBER.

(3) I. Elizabeth Gilbert, b. 1866, Sept. 14.
II. Lottie Agnes, b. 1867.
III. Belle, b. 1868.

2. *Charles Thomas Gilbert*, b. 1846, Aug.
31; m. 1873, Nov. 27, Adelaide A. Cochrane.

CHILDREN—GILBERT.

I. George Curtis, b. 1875, Jan. 5; d.
1876, Nov. 10.
II. Ross Cochrane, b. 1879, Nov. 3.

3. *Elizabeth Gilbert Barber*, b. 1866, Sept.
14; m. 1892, Sept. 14, L. T. Dickason.

CHILDREN—DICKASON.

I. Dorothy Russell, b. 1894, Aug. 14.

FISH LINEAGE.

Thomas¹ Fish, and Mary, his wife, were
early settlers of Portsmouth, R. I. Land was
granted him in 1643. He was a freeman in
1655, and a member of Town Council in 1674.
He died 1687. She died 1699. Children:
Thomas², ________________; Mehitable, ______
________; Mary, ________________; Alice, ____
____________; John, ________________; Daniel,
and Robert.
Thomas² Fish, m. 1668, Dec. 10, Grizzel
Strange, dau. of John and Alice Strange, of
Portsmouth, R. I. He died 1684. Children:
Alice, b. 1671, Sept. 15; Grizzel, b. 1673, April
12; Hope, b. 1676, March 5; *Preserved²*, b.
1679, Aug. 12; Mehitable, b. 1684, July 22.
Preserved³, Fish, b. at Portsmouth, R. I.,
1679, Aug. 12. He was deeded land by his
grandfather Fish; d. 1745, July 15. Married,
1699, May 30, Ruth⁴ Cook, (John³, John²,
Thomas¹), of Tiverton, R. I., dau. of Ruth Shaw,
and granddaughter of Anthony and Alice
(Stonard) Shaw, of Portsmouth. Children:
Grizzel, b. 1700, March 16; Ruth, b. 1701, Nov.
30; Thomas, b. 1703, Dec. 1; Amy, b. 1706, Jan.
8; Sarah, b. 1708, Jan. 23; John, b. 1710, Feb.
23; Preserved, b. 1713, May 19; d. 1813, Feb.,
aged 99 years, 9 mo.; *Benjamin⁴*, b. 1716, April

14. He was doubtless a Friend as his death is
recorded on Friends' Journal.
Benjamin⁴ Fish, b. at Portsmouth, R. I.,
1716, April 14; died there 1793, Oct. 16.
Although a member of the Society of Friends,
he jammed and threw away a copper tea kettle
because his daughters made tea in it about the
time of throwing the tea overboard in Boston
harbor. He was a farmer. The diary of his
son Elisha says he died with a lingering disease
"which he bore with much patience and fortitude of mind." He married (1), 1739, Nov. 8,
Priscilla Arthur, dau. of John Arthur, Jr., and
Mary⁴ Folger, (Eleazer³, Peter², John¹), of Nantucket, Mass. Her mother, (Mary), was Benjamin Franklin's first cousin, and dau. of Sarah³
Gardner (Richard², Thomas¹). John Arthur,
Jr.'s, mother was Priscilla³ Gardner (John²,
Thomas¹). John² Gardner, m. Priscilla, dau. of
Joseph and Mary (More) Grafton, and granddaughter of Thomas and Anna Moore. Priscilla, wife of Benjamin Fish b. 1718, Nov. 2; d.
1774, April 1. He m. (2) 1776, April 3, Mrs.
Patience Sisson. Wife, Priscilla, was mother of
all his children, viz.; Sarah, b. 1740, Oct. 10;
Preserved, b. 1741, Dec. 13; Rhoda, b. 1743, Dec.
30; Stephen, b. 1745, Dec. 8; Peace, b. 1747,
Oct. 14; John, b. 1749, Aug. 17; Silas, b. 1751,
Sept. 24; Artemas, b. 1754, June 28; Elihu, b.
1756, Aug. 9; Elijah, b. 1759, Dec. 25; *Elisha⁵*,
b. 1762, Feb. 27; Gardner, b. 1765, Sept. 7.
Elisha⁵ Fish, b. at Portsmouth, R. I., 1762,
Feb. 27; d. 1833, June 25, at Jamestown, N. Y.,
his residence being Farmington, Ontario county,
N. Y. Married (1) 1788, Jan. 1, Hannah⁶
Sisson, (Joseph⁵, Richard⁴, Richard³, James²,
Richard¹), dau. of Ruth⁵ Sherman (Benjamin⁴,
Joseph³, Benjamin⁵, Philip⁵, Samuel⁴, Henry³,
Henry², Thomas¹). Her paternal grandmother
was Alice Soule, dau. of William and Hannah,
granddaughter of George and Deborah and
great granddaughter of George and Mary
(Becket) Soule, who were passengers of the
Mayflower and ship Ann respectively. Richard³
Sisson was grandson of Arthur Hathaway,
Jr., and Sarah Cooke, dau. of Pilgrims John
Cooke and Sarah Warren. The latter were
children of Francis Cooke and Richard Warren,
passengers of the Mayflower. Ruth Sherman
was dau. of Ruth Fish and granddaughter of
Preserved¹ Fish. The wife of Joseph³ Sherman
was Margaret Manchester, dau. of William and
Mary (Cook) Manchester, granddaughter of
Thomas and Margaret (Wood) Manchester, and
great-granddaughter of John Wood of Ports-
mouth. Mary (Cook) Manchester, was dau. of
John and Mary (Borden) Cook of Portsmouth.
Elisha Fish moved in 1778 from Portsmouth to
Foster, R. I., and in 1799, to Rensselaerville,
Albany county, N. Y., and in 1817, to Farmington, N. Y. He was a carpenter and also a
farmer during most of his life. He was an
excellent mathematician and understood sur-

veying. He was a member of the Society of Friends. On the division of that society in 1828, he adhered to the "Hicksite" branch. He was faithful in attendance at their meetings, as his diary, kept in a neat hand with more or less regularity from April, 1785, to June, 1804, attests. She was born 1763, March 30; died 1828, Sept. 6. He m. (2) Ruth⁴ Anthony, dau. of Jonathan³, (Jonathan², Jonathan¹), and Lydia⁵ Sisson (Joseph⁵). Children, (1) Hannah, b. 1788, Oct. 8; Elijah, b. 1790, Jan. 7; Elisha, b. 1791, Sept. 10; Susanna, b. 1793, July 30; Lydia, b. 1795, July 1; *Benjamin*⁶, b. 1797, June 25; Anna, b. 1799, July 31; Gardner, b. 1801, June 4. (2.) David, b. 1832, July 6; Avis, b. 1833, Oct. 18.

*Benjamin*⁶ *Fish*, b. 1797, June 25, at Foster, R. I.; d. 1882, Dec. 3, at Rochester, N. Y.; m. (1) 1822, Oct. 9, in Friends' meeting, Henrietta, N. Y., Sarah Davids Bills, dau. of Thomas and Elizabeth (Shotwell) Bills. She was b. 1798, Sept. 11; d. 1868, Nov. 7. She was second cousin to Benjamin Lundy, the philanthropist and pioneer abolition journalist. John Bowne, the eminent Quaker of Flushing, and successful champion of religious liberty in Long Island under Peter Stuyvesant, the Dutch governor, was her great-grandfather³. Anne (Winthrop) Fones, sister of John Winthrop, the first governor of Massachusetts, was her great-grandmother⁶, her great-grandfather⁵, being Thomas Fones, an apothecary of London, whose lineage is traced back for eight generations to Robert Hyelton, a Knight, who lived about 1400, A. D. See pp. 132-138 *ante.* Benjamin⁶ Fish, m. (2) 1871, Feb. 23, Louise M. Henck, who had no children. He with his father passed through the village of Rochester, in 1817, on their way to their new home, Farmington, N. Y.; moved to Rochester, 1828; lived at Sodus Bay, Wayne county, N. Y., from April, 1844, to April, 1847, (when he returned to Rochester), the first two years in an association which was first organized as the "Sodus Bay Phalanx," and which was similar in its scope to the "Brooke Farm Experiment." He was its president the first year. For the greater portion of his life he was a nurseryman and horticulturist. He and wife, Sarah were Hicksite Friends. He was several times fined and imprisoned for refusing to take part in military training. Later they affiliated with Progressive Friends. When it was thought that name sounded too much like an exclusive organization, he suggested "Friends of Human Progress," which name was adopted. It expressed in four words the character of the one who proposed the name, and that of his companion. They were abolitionists, prohibitionists, and "Land Reformers." They were opposed to capital punishment and in favor of equal suffrage, prison reform and of humane treatment of the Indians. They were optimists with not a belief, but an abiding confidence in the triumph of right. They believed that eternal life begins on earth and is destined to become more spiritual here, so that not only the few but the many on earth may commune with those who have crossed the river of time. Notwithstanding his Quaker ancestry, several of the following distinguished relatives were military men; Dr. Benjamin Franklin and he were first and fourth cousins; Hon. Roger Sherman (who was also a signer of the Declaration of Independence and of the United States Constitution) and he were fourth and eighth cousins; Gen. William T. Sherman and he were seventh and eighth cousins; Gen. Thomas W. Sherman and he were fifth and sixth cousins; Gen. James Warren, the Revolutionary patriot, and he were third and seventh cousins; Col. Benjamin Church, the hero of the Great Swamp Fight, and he were first and seventh cousins; Nathaniel Hawthorne and he were fifth cousins; Maria Mitchell, the astronomer, and he were fifth and fourth cousins; Lucretia Mott and he were fourth and third cousins.

CHILDREN.

(1) I.   Catharine Ann⁷, b. 1823, Aug. 17.
(2) II.   Mary Braithwaite, b. 1826, Feb. 26; d. 1873, Aug. 9.
III. Albert Carey, b. 1829, June 13; d. 1831, May 21.
(3) IV. Albert Carey, b. 1832, April 24; d. 1869, Oct. 26.
(4) V. Thomas Elisha, b. 1833, Nov. 26; d. 1870, Dec. 19.
(5) VI. *George Thompson*⁷, b. 1838, Aug. 1.

1. *Catharine Ann*⁷ *Fish*, b. 1823, Aug. 17, in Farmington, N. Y.; m. 1846, Aug. 17, at Sodus Bay, N. Y., Giles Badger Stebbins, son of Eldad and Lydia (Fitch) Stebbins, who was b. 1817, June 24, at Springfield, Mass. They reside in Detroit, Mich. He is a lecturer and author. She was the first school teacher in district No. 9, of Rochester, N. Y. From girlhood she has been a worker in reforms. Anti-slavery, temperance, anti-tobacco and equal suffrage movements have found her a faithful supporter. She was secretary of the first woman's rights meeting, the first session of which was held in Seneca Falls, and the second in Rochester, in the summer of 1848. She was secretary of the Rochester Anti Slavery Society, and had charge of the anti-slavery office. They are Unitarians. For brief sketch of her life with portrait, see "A Woman of the Century," by Frances E. Willard and Mary A. Livermore.

CHILDREN—STEBBINS.

I. Mary Wendelline, b. 1856, Dec. 10; d. 1859, Dec. 9.
II. Daughter (......), b. 1861, Oct. 4; d. 1861, Oct. 4.

2. *Mary Braithwaite' Fish*, b. 1826, Feb.
26, in Farmington, N. Y., died 1873, Aug. 9;
m. 1848, Oct. 5, as second wife, Joseph Curtis,
subsequently one of the founders and proprietors of the *Rochester Daily Union*. He
was b. 1817, May 27; d.1883, Sept. 14. They
were Unitarians. She was an active abolitionist
and friend of woman's suffrage, temperance,
and other reforms. For character sketch see
Rochester *Union and Advertiser*, 1873, Aug.
12. For sketch of his life see Rochester *Union
and Advertiser*, 1883, Sept. 15.

CHILDREN—CURTIS.

I. George Benjamin', b. 1851, Jan. 7;
d. 1852, March 4.
(6) II. Mary Elizabeth, b. 1853, Aug. 8.
(7) III. Catharine Fish, b. 1856, Sept. 30.
(8) IV. Wendell Joseph, b. 1863, April 22.

3. *Albert Carey' Fish*, b. 1832, April 24, at
Rochester, N. Y.; d. 1869, Oct. 26, at Denver,
Colorado, to which place he went hoping to prolong his life. He was a nurseryman and horticulturist. He was successful as a business man,
although disease, induced or aggravated by acci-
dents, left him but few years in which he
enjoyed good health. He was cheerful and
made life bright and pleasant for those about
him. He m. (1) 1855, Nov. 15. at Egypt,
Monroe county, N. Y., Lucy Ann Simpson, dau.
of Alexander and Melissa (Curtis) Simpson.
She was b. 1834; d. 1858, Aug. 25, aged 23
years, 9 months. He m. (2) 1867, Nov. 26, at
Rochester, N. Y., Julia Adeline Kershaw, dau.
of Seth and Julia Ann (________) Kershaw.
She was b. 1842, Feb. 18; d. 1879, at Thousand
Island Park, N. Y.

CHILDREN.

(1)

I. William Wendell', d. 1858, Aug. 21, aged
8 months.

(2)

II. Albert Carey, b. 1868, Aug. 23. Has a
family and lives at Syracuse, N. Y.

4. *Thomas Elisha' Fish*, b. 1833, Nov. 26,
Rochester, N. Y.; d. 1870, Dec. 19, at Minneapolis, Minn.; m. 1868, Dec. 24, in N. Y. City,
Isabella Douglas Marsh, dau. of Joseph Young
and Isabella Douglas (Vanderpool) Marsh. He
was a compositor by trade. Lived in Rochester
and Buffalo, N. Y., Chicago, Ill., Memphis,
Tenn., and during the latter part of his life in
New York City. He was for a time engaged in
the real estate business and published a real

estate journal. In 1861 he volunteered as
private in the Fifth N. Y. Regiment Duryee's
Souaves, Col. Abram Duryee, later under the
command of Col. Goveneur K. Warren. He
was enrolled May 9, and was in the following
engagements: Big Bethel, Siege of Yorktown,
Gaines Mills, Shepardstown Ford, Fredricks-
burgh and Chancellorsville, all in Virginia. He
was several times promoted and on retiring
from the service held the rank of first lieutenant.
He served in several capacities, and was acting
assistant inspector general of the brigade.
Left one child.
I. Charles Thomas' Fish, b. 1870, Jan. 16;
lives in New York City; m. 1895, Oct. 29, Sarah
Letitia Scott.
5. *George Thompson' Fish*, b. 1838, Aug. 1,
at Rochester, N. Y.; m. there 1867, Dec. 31,
Elizabeth Louise Vanderbeck, b. 1840, Dec. 22,
in Clarkson, Monroe county, N. Y., dau. of
Daniel and Susan (Bartholf) Vanderbeck. They
have been actively interested in the temperance
reform for thirty years, working within and
without the lines of the Independent Order of
Good Templars. As chairman of a committee
of Excelsior Lodge of that order, she led the
so-called "Temperance Crusade" of Rochester,
presenting a petition daily to the Board of
Excise. See Rochester daily papers from May
4, to July 8, 1874. He is author of the
American Manual of Parliamentary Law,
published by Harper and Brothers, 1880, and of
A Guide to the Conduct of Meetings, issued by
the same publishers in 1883. He is interested
in natural history studies and was the first
president of the Botanical Section (organized
April 13, 1881), of the Rochester Academy of
Science.

CHILDREN.

I. Clarence Vanderbeck', b. 1872, Sept. 11;
d. 1872, Sept. 11.
II. Clinton George, b. 1876, May 4.

6. *Mary Elizabeth Curtis*, b. 1853, Aug. 8,
Rochester, N. Y.; m. 1874, Sept. 1, Norman A.
Seymour, of Mt. Morris, N. Y.

CHILDREN.

I. Mary Francis, b. 1875, June 13, Mt.
Morris, N. Y.
II. Elizabeth Katharine, b. 1877, Nov. 10,
Mt. Morris, N. Y.
III. Charlotte, b. 1882, April 22, Mt. Morris,
N. Y.

7. *Catharine Fish Curtis*, b. 1856, Sept. 30,
Rochester, N. Y.; m. 1878, June 6, Horace
Crampton Brewster, of Rochester, N. Y., son of
H. Austin Brewster.

CHILDREN.

I.   Marrietta, b. 1880, Nov. 8.

8.   *Wendell Joseph Curtis*, b. 1863, April 22, Rochester, N. Y.; m. there 1885, Feb. 17, Margaret Breese Roby, dau. of Sidney B. and Sarah Eliza Roby.

CHILDREN.

I.   Wendell Joseph, b. 1886, Aug. 27.
III.   Catharine, b. 1891, Sept. 13.
III.   Ruth, b. 1895, Feb. 20.

DANIEL' SHOTWELL'S BRANCH

[of Daniel⁴, Joseph³, Daniel², Abr¹., (see pp. 103-5, 171-2)].

Horace Julian Shotwell of Minneapolis, Minn., s. of Theo. F⁷. & Hattie A. (Cambell) Shotwell, [of Daniel⁶], was b. Sept. 15, (not 13) as per p. 171), 1868; m. 24 June, 1896, Hetty Maud Lewis of Minneapolis. His sister, Theodora Azella, m. 22 June, 1892, William Nottage (not *Wottage*).

HENRY⁵ SHOTWELL'S BRANCH

[Joseph⁴, John³, John², Abr¹., (pp. 149-50, 110-11)].

Joseph D'. Shotwell, b. 1831, of 82 Hillside Ave., Orange, N. J., formerly of Rahway, N. J., paying teller of the Bowery Savings Bank, New York City, son of Henry R⁷. & Margaret G. (Laing) Shotwell, [of Joseph Dobson⁶ & Elizabeth (Fitz Randolph) Shotwell, Henry⁵ & Sarah (Dobson) Shotwell, Joseph⁴, Jno³., Jno²., Abr¹]. (See pp. 110, 111, 152, 154, *ante*.) He has two daughters, Mary Everit and Margaret Randolph.

Caroline Shotwell Wood, dau. of Henry R⁷. & Margaret G. (Laing) Shotwell of Rahway, (p. 111), [of Joseph D⁶, Henry⁵], was dean at Swarthmore college between 1878 and 1882. Her son, Henry Shotwell Wood, entered the Preparatory School there in Sept., 1873, graduated in the Engineering Dept., (degree—B. S.), in June, 1880; took second degree—C. E.—in 1883; address, 106 World Building, New York City, New York. His sister, Louise (Wood) Ferris, entered Preparatory School, Swarthmore, Pa., in Sept., 1878, took literary course in college there, but left before close of Junior year, about Mar., 1882; address, Claremont, Los Angeles, Cal.

Katharine S., dau. of Henry R⁷. & Margaret G⁶. (Laing) Shotwell, and wife of Edward J. Maginnis (p. 111), dw. 59 West 87th St., New York City, s. p.

HUGH⁵ SHOTWELL'S BRANCH

Descendants of Hugh⁵ & Rosetta (Arrison) Shotwell of Harrison Co., Ohio, [of John⁴ & Grace (Webster) Shotwell of Plainfield, N. J., John³ & Mary (Thorne) Shotwell, of Shotwell's Landing, Bricktown (now part of Rahway). N. J., John² & Elizabeth (Burton) Shotwell, of Staten Island, N. Y., and Woodbridge, N. J., Abraham¹ Shotwell, of Elizabeth Town, and New York, and of Wm². & Susannah (Cowperthwaite) Webster, of Woodbridge, N. J., Wm¹. & Mary (________) Webster, of Woodbridge, (see pp. 85-7, 124-141, 111-13, 11-15)].

Charles & Susanna⁶ (Shotwell) Wintermute's second child, Joseph R⁷. (b. 1811), & wife, Judith Ann (Shoemaker) Wintermute, (pp. 112-13), had: (*a*) Franklin C⁷., b. 3 Feb., 1841, dw. E. Mauch Chunk, Carbon Co., Penn.; m. 3 Apr., 1865, Kate Minor, b. 4 Dec., 1842, and had: (I.) Horace Minor Wintermute, b. 11 Aug., 1866. (II) Joseph E., b. 7 Dec., 1868. (III.) Maude E., b. 18 Apr., 1872. (IV.) Miriam, C., b. 17 Aug., 1875. (V.) Russel K., b. 12 May, 1881. (*b*) Cicero, b. 15 Oct., 1842, dw. Olathe, Kans.; m. 20 Mar., 1868, Missouri A. Hays, b. 23 Dec., 1847, and had: (I.) Frank, b. 21 Dec., 1868, dw. Albuquerque, New Mexico. (II.) Mary Etta (twin), b. 21 Dec., 1868, dw. Pierce, Ariz.; m. 15 Aug., 1892, John Towner, and had, Jesse W., b. 23 Dec., 1895. (III.) Myrtle, b. 1 June, 1880, dw. with parents, Olathe, Kans. (*c*) Cummins Harris Wintermute, b. 5 Oct., 1850, dw. Kansas City, Mo., m. 4 July, 1870, Susie Weller, who d. 8 May, 1887. (*d*.) Winfield Scott Wintermute, b. 7 Sept., 1854, dw. Arlington Springs, Col.; m. 24 Jan., 1878, Ellen Hoquet, b. 10 Aug., 1856.

Charles & Susanna⁶ (Shotwell) Wintermute's third child, Rosetta A. (Wintermute) Smith, dw. Hackettstown, N. J., (P. O. box 113), with step-daughter, Mary Smith, who m. 27 Nov., 1890, James B. Smith.

Charles & Susannah⁶ (Shotwell) Wintermute's fifth child, Esther S⁷., b. 1818; d. 12 July, 1888; m. 1843, Aaron B. Mitchell, who d. 15 July, 1888; s. of George & Anna (Bryant) Mitchell, and had nine children, among them (*b*) George I⁸. Mitchell, b. 23 Jan., 1849, Allamuchy, Warren Co., N. J., is a farmer and fruit-grower near Budd's Lake, N. J., address P. O. box 277, Hackettstown, N. J.; m. (by Rev. Peter Day), 23 Dec., 1874, Sarah Amelia Van Sickle, b. 14 Nov., 1845, Townsbury, Warren Co., N. J., dau. of Robert L. & Eliza (Morgan) Van Sickle of Townsbury, N. J., and had: (I.) Aaron B., b. 31 Dec. 1875, at Stone Mansion, Budd's Lake, N. J.; m. 16 Oct., 1895, Lizzie S. Frome. (II.) Alma, b. 18 Apr., 1880, Budd's Lake, N. J. (III.) Robert V., b. 28 Apr., 1881. (IV.) Charles M., b. 2 Nov., 1882. Also (*f*) Frank⁸ Mitchell, b. 27 July, 1859, dw. Washington, N. J.; m. 18 Oct.,

1882, Estella Davis, and had: Davis Mitchell, b. -- May, 1886.

Charles & Susanna' (Shotwell) Wintermute's tenth child, Abigail Roberts' Wintermute, b. 1826, d. at Johnsonsburgh, N. J., 28 Apr., 1892, m. 1847, Cummins O. Harris of Johnsonsburgh, b. 1811, and had: (a) Elwood C'., b. 30 Dec., 1847, grad. Princeton College, 1868, dw. Newark, N. J., counsellor at law, room 732, seventh floor, Prudential building, Newark; m. 22 Sept., 1874, Adelaide Duncklee and had: (I.) Mary L., b. -- July 1875. (II.) Albert W., b. -- Oct., 1876. (III.) Edith A., b -- June, 1881. (b) Dr. Philander A'., b. 29 Jan., 1852, at Johnsonsburgh, N. J.; graduated from Medical Dept., University of Michigan, 1872, and from College of Physicians and Surgeons, New York City, 1873; dw. 26 Church St., Paterson, N. J., practicing medicine and surgery; ex-Health Commissioner, city of Paterson, president of Passaic Co. District Medical Society, permanent member New Jersey Medical Society, member New York Medico-Surgical Society, fellow New York Academy of Medicine, fellow American Gynecological Society, member American Medical Association and corresponding fellow of Paris, (France), Obstetrical and Gynecological Society, etc.; m. 15 Nov., 1876, Margaret Rowson, b. 25 Oct., 1853, in Macclesfield, Eng., dau. of Thomas & Sarah (Ryle) Rowson, late of Paterson, N. J., natives of Macclesfield, England., and had: Grace Abby Harris, b. 9 Sept., 1877.

Fremont Shotwell, of Glenville, O., son of Arrison[6] & Mary (Dickerson) Shotwell, of Cuyahoga Co., O., (*q. v.*, pp. 90–91 *ante*), [of *Hugh*[5], Jno'., Jno³., Jno²., Abr']. Arrison's children were all born in Washington Tp., Harrison Co., O. His son, Adoniram J'. & wife, Martha H. (Graham) Shotwell, had also a dau. Susie, whose name was learned too late for insertion on p 91 *ante*.

Through the kindness of Mr. Wm. A. Eardeley Thomas formerly of Trinity College, Hartford, Conn., now of 5000 Woodland Ave., Philadelphia, Pa., who has in preparation (1895) a Chase and Fountain (Fontaine) Genealogy, also Perry and Maltby Genealogies, also editor of the Genealogical Department of the *Connecticut Quarterly* we are enabled to present the following concise synopsis (now printed, it is believed, for the first time) of the lineage of Lieut. Samuel' Beebe [of Jonathan[6], Jonathan[5], Samuel[4], John[3], John[2], Alexander[1]], paternal grandfather of Rhoda, wife of Wm[6]. Shotwell, (pp. 112–13, 177–9, 171, 174).

BEEBE.

1. Alexander' Beebe lived in Great Addington, Eng., and there d. in 1623. By his wife, Elizabeth, who d. in 1633, he had a son John² of Great Addington, who d. in 1634, in Eng.,

and who, by his wife, Alice, had a son John³, b. 1600, d. May 18, 1650, while on the way to America, leaving five sons and two daughters; a third dau., Mary, bapt. 1637, not mentioned in her father's will.

The third son was Samuel[4] Beebe, bap. in Broughton, Eng., 23 June, 1633, d. in New London, Conn., 1712. He was a wealthy and leading Rogerine Quaker, and got into much trouble with the Puritan authorities in New London. All his family and probably their connections were members of the Society of Friends. He m. (1) Agnes, d. prob. before 1662, and (2) before 1662, her sister, Mary, daughters of Wm. & Agnes Keeney. He had: (1.) Mary[5] b. abt. 1657, m. abt. 1678, Aaron Fountain (2.) Samuel, b. abt. 1659, m. Feb. 9, 1681-2, Elizabeth, dau. of James Rogers, the founder of the Rogerine Quakers. (3.) Susanna, b. abt. 1661, 2d wife of Aaron Fountain. (4.) William[5], b. abt. 1663, m. Ruth, dau. of Jonathan Rogers, [son of James]. (5.) Agnes[5], b. abt. 1665, m. Dec. 3, 1685, John Daniels. (6.) Nathaniel, b. 1667±, prob. m. July 2, 1697, Elizabeth Wheeler. (7.) Ann, b. 1670±, m. Apr. 23, 1700, Thomas Crocker. (8.) Jonathan[5], b. 1673±, was an early settler in East Haddam, Conn., m. abt. 1692, Bridget, dau. of Wolston & Hannah (Briggs) Brockway. (9.) Mercy, b. 1677±, m. Apr. 8, 1702, Richard Tozer. (10.) Thomas, b. 1680±; m. Dec. 17, 1707, Ann Hobson.

(For issue of Samuel[4] Beebe, see also *Connecticut Quarterly*, Vol. II, p. 397).

Jonathan[5] Beebe, of E. Haddam, Conn., b. 1673±, s. of Samuel[4], 1633–1712, of New London, Conn., [of John[3], John[2], Alexander[1]], m. twice; wife, Bridget, was mother of his 4 sons, viz: (1.) Jonathan[6], b. 1694, lived in E. Haddam, Conn., m. three times; m. 1720, Hannah, dau. of Peter & Hannah (Couch) Coley, who was mother of all his children. (2.) Wm[6]., b. in 1706, m. Eleanor _________ (3.) Joshua[6], b. 1713, m. Hannah Brockway, dau. of William & Prudence (Platt) Brockway. (4.) Caleb[6], b. 1717, m. Phebe Buckingham.

Jonathan[6] Beebe, of E. Haddam, Conn., b. 1694, [of Jonathan[5], Samuel[4], John[3], John[2], Alexander[1]], m. 1720, Hannah Coley, and had 6 sons and 3 daughters, viz.: (1.) Jonathan'. (2.) David. (3.) Lieut. Samuel' Beebe, d. 1786, aged 61; m. _________ _________, and had a son, Stuart' Beebe, whose dau., Rhoda³, m. Wm[6]. Shotwell, of Harrison Co., Ohio, [of Hugh[5], John[4], John[3], John[2], Abr'.], as elsewhere stated. (p. 112). (4.) Daniel. (5.) Ebenezer. (6.) Hannah. (7.) Rachel. (8.) Joshua. (9.) Elizabeth.

COPE.

The Cope family in America was planted in Pennsylvania by Oliver' Cope, who emigrated from Wiltshire, Eng., in 1687, coming with that large exodus of Quakers who followed William Penn. He settled in Chester Co., Pa.* Will proved 2 June, 1697; m. Rebecca, ———————; letters of administration granted 16 May, 1728. They had John[2] Cope of E. Bradford Tp., Chester Co., Pa., b. 1691; will proved 12 Mar., 1773; m. 13 of 9 mo. (Nov.), 1721, Charity Evans, who d. 1747; they had John[3] Cope of Jefferson Tp., Fayette Co., Pa., b. 1730, d. 31 July, 1812, m. 10 of 1 mo. (Jan.), 1760, Mary Dickinson, dau. of Joseph & Elizabeth Dickinson of Salisbury Tp., Lancaster Co., Pa., b. 10 Nov. (?), 1741, d. 5 June, 1805; they had James Dickinson[4] Cope of Jefferson Tp., Fayette Co., Pa., b. 21 Mar., 1780, Chester Co., Pa., settled in what is now Jefferson Tp., near Fayette City, then called Cookstown, in Fayette Co., Pa.; d. 10 May, 1832, m. 7 Apr., 1803, Rebecca[3] Cook, b. 18 Sept., 1783, d. 17 of 9 mo., 1864, [of Thomas[2], John[1],†], and had 11 children, 7 of whom are now deceased.

Eli[5] Cope, 4th of the 11 children of James D[4]. & Rebecca (Cook) Cope of Fayette Co., Pa., was b. 23 Apr., 1810, near Cookstown (now Fayette City), Pa., where, in early years, he was a butcher and tanner, later he moved to Redstone Tp., in the same Co., and engaged in farming and stock-dealing. He continued to buy and sell cattle at home and in the west during the remainder of his long and useful life. In Oct., 1859, he led the Republicans of his Co. to victory, being elected sheriff by a majority of about 400 over the Democratic candidate; removing then to Uniontown, and thereafter resided in that town or its vicinity. After his retirement from the sheriff's office, Provost Marshal Coulter of Greensburg, appointed him Deputy Provost Marshal for Fayette Co., and he served till the close of the War of the Rebellion, proving just the man for the emergency, and filling the position with great courage and efficiency. He was a terror to deserters and to those who, in any way, aided and abetted treason, and passed through many exciting experiences while making arrests in times when war passions ran high. On the expiration of his term as sheriff, he moved into what is now the Ruby property on Main St., near the court house, at present occupied as law offices. Later he moved into the large brick building at the corner of Fayette and Mill Sts., and there carried on the old tannery. In 1867 he bought the handsome North Union residence, where he resided for more than 20 years. Selling this he removed finally to South Union on the Pike, and there d. 15 June, 1896, of cancer of the stomach and was interred at Oak Grove Cemetery. He was an honest, good man and a member of the Christian Church. His deeds of kindness were many; he loved his neighbors and was beloved by them.

His ancestors were Quakers and he loved their quiet religious customs and habits. He was of quick temper, but quick also to regret and make amends for his heart was right, having no malice in it. He was a man of commanding presence and strong will. He was a vigorous, aggressive man, and his administration as sheriff and as Deputy Provost Marshal included an exciting period of local and national history. His official life, as his private life, was noted for devotion to duty and an honest purpose to discharge all obligations resting upon him.

Eli[5] Cope m. in Franklin Tp., Fayette Co., Pa., 12 Apr., 1832, Susan C[7]. Shotwell, b. 15 Feb., 1811, and they lived happily together for more than 62 yrs., until her death in S. Union, town, Fayette Co., Pa., 31 Dec., 1894. She was a consistent member of the Presbyterian Church, a faithful wife and mother, and dau. of John[5] & Sarah (Shanklin) Shotwell [of Hugh[5], John[4], John[3], John[2]. Abr[1]., (pp. 145, 111–113)]. Eli[5] & Susan C. (Shotwell) Cope had: (1.) Emelia Shotwell Cope, b. 14 Feb., 1833, d. 6 Apr., 1837. (2.) Rebecca, b. 15 March, 1836, d. 14 Oct., 1837. (3.) James Dickinson Cope, b. 18 Feb., 1838, d. 16 Oct., 1866. (4.) John Henry, b. 25 Apr., 1840, dw. Uniontown, Pa. (5.) Sarah Shotwell Cope, b. 11 March, 1842, dw. Uniontown, Pa. (6.) Wm. Lafferty Cope, b. 3 Oct., 1844, d. 19 Feb., 1876. (7.) Eli, Jr., b. 11 March; 1847, near Brownsville, Pa., dw. Streator, Ill.; a tanner; m. near New Salem, Pa., 13 Sept., 1871, Matilda R. Vankirk, b. 12 June, 1850, near New Salem, dau. of Theo. & Jane (Carothers) Vankirk of Fayette Co., Pa. (8.) Israel C., b. 4 March, 1849, dw. Streator, Ill., since 1869, formerly a druggist at Uniontown, Pa.; m. 31 May 1876, Fannie O. Ames, of Streator, Ill., b. 2 Nov., 1856, in Sunbury Tp., Livingston Co., Ill., dau. of Isaac & Aurelia (Moore) Ames of Streator, LaSalle Co., Ill., (9.) Susan Caroline, b. 14 Sept., 1851, dw. Streator, Ill.; m. 13 Dec., 1871, Dr. John Huston Finley, b. 7 Apr., 1847, near New Salem, Fayette Co., Pa., d. Streator, Ill., 16 Nov., 1883, son of Ebenezer & Phebe Finley, of New Salem, Pa. (10.) Ida C., b. 17 Feb., 1855; m. 22 Dec., 1881, Alexander J. H. Tait, now of Randall, W. Va., formerly of Uniontown, Pa.; b. 22 Dec., 1842, Aberdeen, Scotland, son of George & Jessie (Robertson) Tait, who d. in Bristol, Canada.

Eli[5] Cope, Jr., & wife, Matilda, nee Vankirk, had: (1.) Clara J., b. July 14, 1873, Uniontown, Fayette Co., Pa. (2.) Susan F., b. July 30, 1879, Streator, LaSalle Co., Ill. (3.) Ruth E., b. Feb. 17, 1887, Streator, Ill., d. Streator, Jan. 31, 1889.

Israel C[5]. & Fannie O. (Ames) Cope had: (1) Jessie O., b. Apr. 4, 1877, Streator, Ill. (2.) Elmer Ames Cope, b. Dec. 9, 1878, Streator, Ill.

Dr. J. H. & Susan C[5]. (Cope) Finley, had: (1.) Jessie Violet, b. 18 Aug., 1872, at Streator,

* Gilbert Cope's Cope Genealogy, 1861.

† John[1] Cook of Nottingham Tp., Chester Co., Pa., & wife, Rebecca, had Thomas[2], b. 28 of 7 mo., 1756, d. 14 of 2 mo., 1842, in Fayette Co., Pa.

Ill., d. 24 Oct., 1875. (2.) Susan Cope Finley, b. 23 Oct., 1876, at Streator, Ill.

Alex. H. & Ida C. (Cope) Tait, now of Randall, W. Va., formerly of Fayette Co., Pa., had: (1.) Eli Cope Tait, b. 9 Oct., 1882, Connellsville, Pa., d. 22 June, 1883. (2.) Sarah Cope Tait, b. 1 Sept., 1884, at Uniontown, Pa. (3.) John Finley Tait, b. 27 Feb., 1895, Homestead, Allegheny Co., Pa.

ISAIAH[5] SHOTWELL'S BRANCH

[of John[4], John[3], John[2], Abr[1]. (pp. 139-41, 119-20)].

Benjamin Warder[6] Shotwell, of Trenton, Mo., b. 1839, son of Edward R[5]. & Margaret H. (Shotwell) Shotwell, of Marengo, O., [of Peter[5] & Phebe (Vail) Shotwell, *Isaiah[5]* & Constant (Lippencott) Shotwell, Jno[4]. & Grace (Webster) Shotwell, Jno[3]. & Mary (Thorne) Shotwell, Jno[2]. & Elizabeth (Burton) Shotwell, Abraham[1] Shotwell, of Elizabeth Town, N. J., 1665], m. 1860, Mary Hoyle [of Edward]. (See pp. 98, 108, 163, *ante*.)

James T. & Hannah Ann[8] (Shotwell) Burtis, of Freehold, N. J., [of Joshua[7] Shotwell, Thomas L[6]., Isaiah[5] (p. 155)], had: (1.) Elizabeth S., who d. 23 July, 1870. (2.) Emily. (3.) Wm. Ryall, who was educated at Rutger's College, at New Brunswick, N. J.

Ella P., only living dau. of Jediah[7] & Martha Ann (Provost) Shotwell of Mercer Co., N. J., [of Thos. L[6]., Isaiah[5] (p. 123)], dw. near Perrineville, Monmouth Co., N. J., m. Emerson Pullen, and had: (1.) Isaac, b. 1890±.

Jediah[7] & Martha A. (Provost) Shotwell's only surviving son, Thomas[8] Shotwell, b. 1848, (p. 123), m. 1870, Elizabeth Stout, of Brooklyn, N. Y., and had 1 son, (1.) Jediah, and 4 daughters. (2.) Lillie. (3.) Anna. (4.) Nelly. (5.) Eva.

George Knorr Johnson, Jr., 4043 Walnut St., W. Philadelphia, Pa., of the firm of Belknap, Johnson & Powell, umbrella and parasol manufacturers, at 823 and 825 Filbert St., Philadelphia, and 532 & 534 Broadway, New York City, b. 11 of 12 mo., 1848, married at residence of bride's parents, Kaighns Point Ave., Camden, N. J., under care of Philadelphia M. M., 1 of 10 mo., 1873, Sallie Kaighn Cooper, dau. of John & Mary M. Cooper, of Camden, N. J. He was son of George K. & Elizabeth R[7]. (Shotwell) Johnson, of Philadelphia, [of Samuel E[6]. & Sarah C. (Rich) Shotwell, *Isaiah[5]* & Constant (Lippincott) Shotwell, John[4] & Grace (Webster) Shotwell, John[3] & Mary (Thorne) Shotwell, John[2] & Elizabeth (Burton) Shotwell, Abraham[1] Shotwell of Elizabeth Town, N. J., 1665, (see pp. 169-170, 119-120, *ante*).

George K. Johnson of Philadelphia, son of Wm. & Catharine of Philadelphia, m. 1842, Elizabeth R[7]. Shotwell, 1822-1897, and had: (1) Sarah Shotwell Johnson, b. 10 of 2 mo., 1843.

(2.) Wm[6]., b. 1 of 9 mo. 1844, dw. Bensalem, Bucks Co., Pa., m. 15 of 2 mo., 1866, Elizabeth Quinton Harper, by Friends' ceremony at the home of her parents, Jesse K. & Sarah K. Harper, Fallsington, Bucks Co., Pa., and had: (*a*) Albert H[7]., b. 12-18, 1868, m. 9-14, '93, Florence R. Seal, and had: (*a*) Arthur Seal Johnson, b. 28 of 5 mo., 1896, Philadelphia, Pa. (*b*) Rachel, b. 11-9, 1877. (3.) George Knorr, Jr., (see above.) (4.) Israel Howell Johnson, b. 10 of 12 mo., 1850, dw. 117 S. 42d St., Philadelphia, Pa.; m. 7 of 11 mo., 1878, Laura R. Woodruff, by the Rev. Richard C. Newton, at the home of her parents, Edward D. & Anna E. Woodruff, at 1708 Vine St., Philadelphia, Pa., and had Edward Woodruff Johnson, b. 11-1, 1879. (5.) Samuel Shotwell Johnson, who d. young. (6.) Joseph Barclay Johnson, b. 1 of 12 mo. 1852, dw. 1807 N. 18th St., Philadelphia, Pa.: m. 13 of 10 mo., 1881, Anna Carelake Furman, under the care of the Philadelphia M. M., at the house of her parents, Samuel T. & Abigail C. Furman, 1713 Girard Ave., Philadelphia, Pa., and had Elizabeth Edith, b. 12 6, 1885. (7.) Joshua Rowland Johnson, b. 6 of 12 mo., 1854, dw. 1222 N. 15th St., Philadelphia, Pa.; m. 27 of 10 mo., 1880, Alice James, by Friends' ceremony, at the home of her mother, 1526 Cherry St., Philadelphia, dau. of Wm. H. & Lydia A. James, and had: (*a*) George Clarence, b. 9-20, 1881. (*b*) Walter James, b. 11-25, 1883. (*c*) Edwin James, b. 3-11, 1888.

Geo. K., Jr. & Sallie K. (Cooper) Johnson of Phila., Pa., had: (1.) Howard Cooper Johnson, b. 18 of 1 mo., 1876. (2.) Mary C., b. 18 of 5 mo., 1880.

JACOB[5] SHOTWELL'S BRANCH

[of John[4], John[3], John[2], Abr[1]., (pp. 121-2, 139-41)].

Elijah[6] & Jemima G. (Piatt) Shotwell, of Scotch Plains, N. J., (pp. 109, 121-2, 140-41, 179), had: Wm. P[7]. Shotwell, (p. 179), who, by wife, Harriet, *nee* Parse, had: (1.) Greenleaf, b. 16 Dec., 1824, m. at Elizabeth, N. J., 11 May, 1846, Elizabeth Cleveland. (2.) Caroline, b. 24 Nov., 1828. (3.) Ellen J., b. 16 Nov., 1831. (4.) Wm. Piatt Shotwell, b. 6 Mar., 1841, was an officer in the U. S. Navy during the civil war; m. ...., who d. between 1860 and 1870.

Wm. P. G[8]., & Margaret R. (Stevensen) Shotwell, of Buffalo, N. Y., (pp. 180-1), [of Greenleaf[7], (p. 110), Wm. P[7]., Elijah[6], Jacob[5]], had: (1.) James Piatt Shotwell, b. 16 Jan., 1868, d. 6 Feb., 1869. (2.) Sadie P., b. 12 June, 1872, m. Rochester, Beaver Co., Pa., 4 Oct., 1893, Albert T. Bush. (3.) Wm. Piatt Shotwell, b. 18 Nov., 1873, dw. Buffalo, N. Y., unm. (1896). (4.) Mary P., b. 18 June, 1876, m. 11 Oct., 1893, George A. Robinson, of Conway, Beaver Co., Pa. (5.) Laurence Piatt, b. 15 Mar., 1878. (6.) Fannie P., b. 2 Jan., 1882.

JAMES⁶ SHOTWELL'S BRANCH

[of John⁴, John⁵, John², Abr¹., (pp. 148, 122)].

Clarkson F⁶. Shotwell's son, Wm³. Shotwell, (pp. 101, 179, "was an ordained minister and preached occasionally;" m. (1) Theresa Linabury, who d. 1858, leaving three children: (1.) John L., of Whittlesey, Wis. (2.) George⁴ who lives in Tillamook, Ore.; m. Mary Robinson, and had: (a) Maud Martha, who was raised by and lives with her great-aunt, Orrilla (Shotwell) Warden, in Oakland Co., Mich., P. O., Oxbow. George⁴ Shotwell, m. (2) Julia Serprise, and had six sons. (3.) Mary, (dau. of Wm³.), d. in Oakland Co., Mich. Wm³. Shotwell, m. (2) Libbie Fitchgark or Fitzgerald, who d. leaving three children, who were reared by their aunt Orrilla, in White Lake Tp., Oakland Co., Mich., viz.: (4.) Lucy Louise, who m. David Vanderhoof; they live in Cannon Co., Tenn., P. O., Martha. (5.) Charles Winfield, dw. Oakland Co., Mich., P. O., Oxbow. (6.) Clarkson Fred, called Fred Warden, dw. near Oxbow, Mich., m. __________ __________, and had: (a) Archie. (b) Clarence, b. __ Oct., 1890. Wm³. Shotwell, m. (3) __________ and had a son, (7) Austin W. Shotwell, who dw. at Almont, Lapeer Co., Mich. The third wife (now of Almont, Mich.), was found to have another living husband from whom she had not been legally divorced. They accordingly parted and the last marriage was set aside.

Clarkson F⁶. Shotwell's daughter, Clarissa A. (p. 101), m. Wm. Bailey, and had ten sons, among them, George Washington Bailey of __________, Oakland Co., Mich.

Clarkson F⁶. Shotwell's daughter, Caroline M. (Shotwell) Eastman, d. 16 June, 1896.

Josephine, 1834–1863, dau. of Jonathan⁶ & Phebe (Willson) Shotwell of Long Bridge, N. J., m. Edwin Schmuck, who dw. on his father's farm near "Big Meadows" in Warren Co., N. J., s. of Christopher & Elizabeth¹ (Laing) Schmuck and grandson of Samuel² & Edith (Lundy) Laing, [of John¹ & Hannah (Webster) Laing].

John T. & Emeline⁴ (Shotwell) Wolverton of Ashley, Mich., [of John¹ & Sarah (Johnson) Shotwell, (pp. 148, 101), Clarkson F⁶ & Keziah (Sutton, not Freeman as per p. 148) Shotwell, James⁶], had 4 children: (1.) Sarah H., dw. (1893), with parents, Ashley, Mich. (2.) James E. (3.) Wm. H. (4.) Mary Ann.

JEREMIAH⁵ SHOTWELL, s. of Abraham⁴ & Mary (Potts) Shotwell, [of John³, John², Abr¹., (pp. 88, 124)], m. in N. Y. City, 21 June, 1781, Mary Barron (as shown by New York marriage licenses).

JOHN SMITH⁵ SHOTWELL'S BRANCH

[of John⁴, John³, John², Abr¹. (pp. 139, 141–3, 154)].

HENRY T⁷. SHOTWELL, b. 1862, of Brooklyn, N. Y., (p. 111), [of Joseph F⁷., (p. 154), Joseph S⁶, Jno. S⁵., (pp. 142–143), Jno⁴., Jno³., Jno²., Abr¹.], m. 1886, Alice Gardner, and had:
1. Mary Titus Shotwell, b. __ Jan. 1887.
2. Willis Haviland, (see p. 111).
For other grandchildren of Joseph F⁶., see pp. 180, 174.

Joseph S⁶. Shotwell's son (Joseph F⁷. ?), settled at Skaneateles, N. Y., and had a son, __________, who was at one time a dealer in horses in Buffalo, N. Y.

Joseph S⁶. Shotwell's dau. __________ (p. 154), m. Abraham S. Underhill, of N. Y. City.

JOHN⁵ SHOTWELL'S BRANCH.

Descendants of John⁵ & Abigail (Shipman) Shotwell, of Mason Co., Kentucky, [of John⁴, Abr³.(?), John², Abr¹., (pp. 141–2, 143–4, 88)].

ALFRED LAWRENCE⁷ SHOTWELL, 1809–1893, commission merchant of Louisville, Ky., b. in Mason Co., Ky., 16 June, 1809, d. in Cincinnati, O., 16 May, 1893, interred in Louisville, Ky., s. of Wm. (1779–1834), & Frances (Tripplett) Shotwell of Mason Co., Ky., (see p. 177 ante), [of John⁵ (1753–1826) & Abigail (Shipman) Shotwell, of Mayslick, Ky., (p. 143) John⁴, Abraham³ (?), John², Abraham¹], went on his bridal tour to the east by buggy, having been married (by the Rev. Thos. Henderson) at Georgetown, Ky., on the morning of July 30, 1829, to Gabrella (Jones) Breckinridge of Georgetown, b. there 13 June, 1812, d. of dropsy 20 Sept., 1872, in Louisville, Ky., dau. of Preston & Elizabeth (Trigg) Breckinridge, of Georgetown, Ky., and had thirteen children, who with their respective families are recorded below. He owned a coal mine at Caseyville, Union Co., Ky., removed thither with his family from Louisville, Ky., in 1862, and lived there and at Louisville alternately for many years. Valuable family records were lost by the burning of his house at Louisville in 1863.

1. Stephen Breckinridge Shotwell, b. 29 Apr., 1830, at Georgetown, Ky., d. of heart failure at Louisville, Ky., 5 June, 1881, buried in Cave Hill cemetery, Louisville, Ky.; m. by Rev. W. L. Breckinridge, __________, Penelope Elston, and had a son, __________, who dw. at Henderson, Ky.
2. William Preston Shotwell, b. 15 Apr., 1835, at Georgetown, d. of typhoid fever at Louisville, Ky., 1 Mar., 1869, interred in Cave Hill cemetery, unm.
3. Betsey Trigg Shotwell, b. 15 Mar., 1838, Georgetown, Ky., d. in childbed, Chicago, Ill.,

25 Mar., 1873, both put in vault there and after moved to Louisville, Ky., and with her other two children placed in family lot at Cave Hill cemetery. She was m. by Rev. D. P. Henderson in Louisville, Ky., 10 Feb., 1859, to Robert McConnell Cannon, who after first wife's death, married a Chicago lady and moved to Minneapolis, Minn., where he is employed in the railroad service. The first wife left three living children (two of them now married), who dw. with or near their father. Robert M. and Bettie T. (Shotwell) Cannon, of Chicago, Ill., had: (1) ————————, who d. at birth, 23 Jan., 1860, unnamed. (2.) Gabriella Breckinridge Cannon, b. 22 Sept., 1861, d. Chicago, Ill., 2 Dec., 1863. (3.) Robert McConnell Cannon, Jr., b. 28 Sept., 1864. (4.) Alfred Lawrence Cannon, b. 30 Oct., 1866. (5.) Fannie Shotwell Cannon, b. 1 Dec., 1867, d. 5th Ave. Hotel, New York City, 25 Sept., 1868. (6.) Bettie Shotwell Cannon, b. 27 June, 1869.

4. *Mary Ann Shotwell*, b. ——————————, d. in early childhood before 1844, buried at Georgetown, afterwards moved to Louisville.

5. *William*, d. at birth.

6. *Alfred Ann' Shotwell*, b. 14 Nov., 1843, Georgetown, Ky., dw. 336 Alvasia St., Henderson., Ky.; m. (1) (by Rev. D. P. Henderson, of Christian church) in Louisville, Ky., 7 Feb., 1861, Gabriel Famsley Tate, b. 23 July, 1839, in Jefferson Co., Ky., d. of paralysis in Union Co., Ky., 14 Oct., 1886, interred in Henderson, Ky., was a capitalist of Henderson, s. of James & Sarah (Famsley) Erickson Tate, of Jefferson Co., Ky. She m. (2) Samuel Churchill; m. (3) Gabriel F. Tate, again; m. (4) Edwin Townshend Conway, of Henderson, Ky. By first husband she had: (1.) ————————, who d 25. Sept., 1862, Louisville, Ky., unnamed. (2.) Fanny Preston Tate, b. 2 May, 1863, in Union Co., Ky., and there d. May 28th, 1863, interred in Cave Hill cemetery, Louisville, Ky. (3.) Lilly Shotwell Tate, b. 1 April, 1864, at Shotwell Mines, Union Co., Ky., and there d. aged 1 day. (4.) Alfred L., b. 26 Oct., 1867, at Shotwell Mines, Union Co., Ky., m. 23 July, ——————, Virginia G. Edwards, and has two daughters, Virginia and Nannie H., and a son, Alfred L. S. Tate, Jr., b. 7 May, 1897. (5.) Gabriella Fannie Shotwell Tate, b. 28 May, 1869, Louisville, Ky., dw. Henderson, Ky., m. 1 April, 18.., James Harrison Hill, a farmer, and had one daughter, Elizabeth Virginia Hill, b. 1891±.

7. *Frances Triplett Shotwell*, b. 18 Feb., 1849, Louisville, Ky., and there d. 24 Dec., 1864, of heart failure, interred Louisville, unm.

8. ————————, (perhaps twin of 4, Mary Ann), d. in infancy, before 1844.

9. *John Triplett Shotwell*, b. 22 Feb., 1853, Louisville, Ky., m. by Rev. Louis Schifphaly (Episcopal), 1 June, 1875, Bell Manny.

The other five children died before 1844. The family record was lost by fire.

243 (*i*). JABEZ' SHOTWELL, 1791–1871, of Richmond, Ray Co., Mo., s. of John' & Abigail (Shipman) Shotwell, of Mayslick, Ky., [of John', Abr'., John², Abr'], (pp. 144, 120–1), served for a short time in the Indian War under Wm. H. Harrison; dw. near Mayslick, Ky., whence he removed with his family in 1833, to La Fayette Co., Mo., settling first near Lexington, but removing three years later to Richmond, Mo.; d. 10 Nov., 1871; was member of Baptist church for more than 60 years; m. near Mayslick, Ky., 27 May, 1814, Eliza Warder, who d. at Richmond, Mo., 8 Dec., 1852, of consumption.

Jabez⁶ & Eliza (Warder) Shotwell, had: (1.) Esther Ann, b. 28 Feb., 1817, in Mayslick, Ky.; d. 15 Nov., 1841, of consumption; member of Baptist church; m. 21 Feb., 1833, Luther F. Warder. (2.) John W. S., b. 10 Aug., 1820, d. 1 Oct., 1826. (3.) Wm. Morris' Shotwell, b. 31 Jan., 1823, taught school for several years before marriage but since 1853, has resided on a farm one mile west of Richmond, Mo., engaged in the pursuit of agriculture; member of Baptist church; m. near Camden, Mo., 31 Aug., 1855, Amanda McGee (for children, see page 182).* (4.) Benjamin E. Shotwell, b. 19 Nov., 1825, d. 2 May, 1849, of consumption; was preparing for the Baptist ministry. (5.) John Warder' Shotwell, b. 4 Apr., 1828, is a successful attorney and insurance agent at Richmond, Mo., m. Julia E. Devlin, and had 5 sons and 2 daughters, (pp. 121, 147–8). (6.) Jabez E'. Shotwell, b. 5 Dec., 1830, is a farmer at Odessa, La Fayette Co., Mo., member of Baptist church; m. 8 Jan., 1856, Bettie W. Hall. (7.) Charles H., b. 25 June, 1833, is a Methodist and a practicing physician at Gainesville, Texas; m. (1) Alice Mallock; m. (2) Mittie Miller, who d. ————————. (8.) Fannie E., b. 3 Apr., 1837, in Richmond, Mo.; dw. Lexington, Mo., m. Milton F. Royle, who is a merchant at Lexington, Mo.

Jabez E'. Shotwell, b. 1830, of Odessa, Mo., s. of Jabez⁶ & Eliza (Warder) Shotwell, (p. 121), m. 1856, Bettie W. Hall, and had: (1.) Anna A'., who m. Thomas Franklin Burchfield, of Odessa, Mo., a druggist there, and had: (*a*) Fannie. (*b*) Frank. (2.) Lizzie', who m. James Edward Ball, a lawyer at Richmond, Mo., and had; (*a*) Bessie Shotwell Ball. (*b*) Fannie Kertley Ball. (*c*) Ethel Bane Ball. (*d*) Ned. (*e*) Frank. (*f*) Harry Longeay. (3.) Alice' Shotwell, who m. Benjamin Elliott, a banker at

* To their daughter, Miss Lucy Shotwell, (p. 180), we are indebted for the corrected record of this family; and she reports the tradition that two brothers, named Shotwell, came to America from France, that the ancestor of this branch settled in New Jersey, and the other in New York. She also reports a modified version of the tradition given at page 142 concerning her great-grandmother, Abigail (Shipman) Shotwell, to the effect, that before the Revolutionary War, Abigail's young brother, —————— Shipman, went to England to learn a trade, that when the war with the colonies came on he was drafted and sent back to fight against home and native land, that, on arriving in America, he deserted and went to the home of his sister, Abigail Shotwell, that early one morning three British soldiers called him out, knocked him down and were dragging him off, when Mrs. Shotwell, seizing an ax, killed one soldier and wounded another, while the third was glad to make his escape.

Odessa, Mo., and had: (a) Lucy. (b) Lizzie. (4.) Susie Shotwell. (5.) Milton R'. Shotwell, is a druggist at Oak Grove, Mo., m. India Ella Willson of Woodstock, Ont., dau. of John H. & Caroline (Young) Willson, of Woodstock, Ont., —the mother a native of England—and had: Caroline Elizabeth, b. 8 Oct., 1895.

JOSEPH⁵ SHOTWELL'S BRANCH

[of Joseph⁴, Joseph³, Daniel², Abr¹. (pp. 149, 150-2, 101-3)].

Joseph⁵ Shotwell, 1754±-1831, of Perrytown, (now Iselin, near Uniontown and Rahway), in Woodbridge Tp., Middlesex Co. N. J.; m. 15 Aug., 1781, Sarah Wilson, 1766±-1828, and had:

I. John⁶, dw. Rahway, N. J., was a dealer in real estate, m. 1809, Phebe Byron, of N. Y., dau. of Wm. & Wilhelmina, (Cannon) Byron, of London, Eng.,—the former a cousin to Lord George Gordon Byron, and the latter a dau. of George Cannon, orator and statesman, and grand-daughter of Lady Norton, all of London, and had 13 children, (p. 145): (1.) Joseph, went to Cal., d. .... (2.) George, d. 20 Jan., 1885. (3.) Wm., d. .. Aug., 1847. (4.) Mary, d. 4 July, 1847. (5.) Harriet, d. 9 Sept., 1862, m. Dr. Thomas Norris, of N. Y. (6.) Abraham⁷, d. ...., 1891, aged 72, (p. 89). (7.) John⁷, d. 1862, aged 45, (p. 147). (8.) Sarah, d. 10 Aug., 1852, m. Thomas Smith. (9.) Thomas, went to Cal., d. .... (10.) Byron, d. .... (11.) Phebe. b. 7 Mar., 1834, at Rahway, N. J., dw. Yellow Springs, Greene Co., Ohio; m. at Washington, D. C., 9 June, 1854, Isaiah Rynders, who d. 3 Jan., 1885, aged 81.

II. Thomas Shotwell, d. in Jamaica, W. I., unm.

III. Wilson⁶ Shotwell, m. (1.) Sarah Marsh, (p. 181). Their daughter, Margaret⁷, m. Ezra Haines of Merchantville, N. J, and had: Ezra Shotwell Haines, now deceased. Sarah Jane⁷ Shotwell, [of Wilson⁶, Joseph⁵], m. George Darnell, of Maple Shade, N. J., and had: (a) Mary, who d. .... (b) Wilson, d. .... (c) Elizabeth. (d) Margaret. (e) Sarah. (f) Rebecca, d .... (See also p. 118).

IV. Joseph, dw. ...., North Carolina, and there d. ...., s. p.

V. Elizabeth⁶, 1791-1882, m. 1848, Alexander Dean, 1805-1870. (See X, Margaret F.).

VI. Rebecca W., d. 7-7, 1870, unm.

VII. Mary⁶, 1800-1855, m. Richard⁷ Dell, 1798-1884, [of Thomas², Richard¹]. and had: (1.) Catharine, m. Isaac⁷ Shotwell, s. of Wilson⁶ & Sarah (Marsh) Shotwell, (pp. 181, 118). (2.) Joseph S. Dell, b. 7-24, 1830, dw. Woodbury, N. J., d. 17 Feb., '84, m. 9-7, 1851, Catharine M. Cropper, and had 8 children. (3.) Thomas W., b. 6-11, 1836, is

executor and trustee, 12 Strawberry St., Philadelphia, dw. Woodbury, N. J., m. 10-26, 1859, Jeannette H. Vail, and has two children, Mary and Albert.

VIII. Isaac⁶ Shotwell, b. 1802, (see p. 152), m. 1828, Elizabeth Archer West, b. 9 of 1 mo., 1809, painted some fine pictures, d. 1885, dau. of Samuel* and Anna (Goucher) West, the latter of French extraction, and the former a nephew of the distinguished artist, Benjamin West, 1738-1820.

Isaac Shotwell was strictly temperate in his habits, avoided the use of tobacco in any form, and was thoroughly scrupulous in the words he uttered and in the life he led. He was an ardent admirer and supporter of Wm. Lloyd Garrison, Wendell Phillips and all the earnest workers in the anti-slavery cause, and though not himself a speaker, did his part in helping to work out the plans of the Anti-Slavery Society. After Fred Douglass escaped from slavery he was taken by friends to the home of Lucretia Mott in Philadelphia, a few doors from Isaac Shotwell's residence, and he was sent for to meet him and deliberate with other interested friends there assembled on plans of action for Fred's protection and education. Both Isaac and his wife were in the Anti-Slavery Hall (Pennsylvania Hall, Philadelphia), on the night when it was destroyed (fired) by a mob, because white and colored people were there assembled in the cause of human liberty. He was ever ready to do and dare for that cause. His eldest daughter was with him at meetings where stones, rotten eggs, and other offensive missiles were hurled through the windows at Cassius M. Clay, Abbie Kelley Foster and other speakers, and remembers having heard Lucretia Mott deliver an anti-slavery speech in (Hicksite) Friends' meeting and heard her rebuked by conservative members because it was First-day meeting. Others were likewise obliged to cease speaking on the subject in Friends' meetings. But the good seed already sown by Woolman, Hazzard, Hopper, Lundy, Whittier and other Friends brought forth at length a rich harvest.

Isaac was faithful in holding to the ancient Quaker ideas and customs, refused to recognize any titles, even *Mr.* and *Mrs.*, would not mention or observe birthdays or other holidays, even Christmas being passed unnoticed. In Philadelphia, half a century since, it was largely descent and family connection that secured position and recognition; and he thought that one should stand solely on one's own merits. Hence he did not care to talk of his ancestry nor to preserve genealogical records. So radical was he in his aversion to this species of "vanity" that on one occasion his daughter

---

* This branch of the West family is said to have been traced in an unbroken line to Lord Delaware who distinguished himself in the battle of Crecy under command of the Black Prince in the time of Richard II, and to ancestors located in Long Crandon, Buckinghamshire, as early as 1667, who embraced the tenets of the Society of Friends in 1800.

"saw him cut from a large family bible that he had purchased the pages intended for the insertion of records of births, marriages and deaths." Such instances of mistaken disregard for the proper sentiments, claims and records of heredity and kinship on the part of some of our relatives have rendered it difficult to obtain accurate vital statistics of certain branches for this work, but we may well be sincerely grateful for the systematic care of nearly all our Quaker forefathers in registering and safeguarding their family ties, and by precept and example, teaching a like wholesome concern on the part of their posterity.

Isaac[6] & Elizabeth A. (West) Shotwell, of Philadelphia, Pa., etc., had:

1. Sarah N. W.,* b., 1831, Philadelphia, Pa., dw. Vallejo, Solano Co., Cal.; possesses some ability as a writer and artist, attended school when a girl, at Plainfield and Rahway, living in the family of her uncle, John Shotwell; m. 1862±, Capt. William Austin Hutchinson, b. ---------- on Black Heath, County Kent, Eng.; graduated from the Naval School at Greenwich, Kent, Eng.; was for a time an officer in the British Navy, as had been his forefathers for several generations. He sailed for the Arctic regions from Woolwich, Eng., and was twice out on the ship *Enterprise*, in search of Sir John Franklin (with Capt. Collinson and with Sir James Ross). He was afterward captain of a ship sailing from Chili to California, but finally settled, about 1860, at Vallejo, Solano Co., Cal.; is conveyancer and notary public, real estate and insurance agent, auctioneer, fire and marine adjuster, member of the Society of California Pioneers, youngest son of John C. & Mary Rosina (McFarlane) Hutchinson,—the former b. about 1760, on the Hutchinson estate, Island of Shell Haven, in the River Thames, where the Capt's grandfather continued to reside until the estate was sold and converted into docks. Sarah N. W. (*nee* Shotwell) now of Vallejo, Cal., had: (*a*) Anna W., b. 1850±, who dw. No. 1066 S. 18th St., St. Louis, Mo.; m. Charles E. Graefen, of St. Louis. (*b*) Dora A., widow of Charles R. Heath. (*c*) May E. (Hutchinson) wife of Capt. Charles R. Reed, with whom she is at sea much of the time.

IX. *Catharine*[6] *Shotwell*, b. 9-5, 1803, d. 12-28, 1871, m. 9-28, 1820, (as second wife), Jotham Townsend, 1797-1876, s. of Hugh & Mary (Dell) Townsend of Middlesex Co., N. J., the former, s. of John & Susannah (Shotwell) Townsend, of Essex Co., N. J., formerly of Queens Co., L. I., (see pp. 139-141), and had:

1. Ruth Anna[7], b. 10-7,1821, dw. Rahway, N. J., m. 11-25, 1840, Jonathan Harned, b. 12-2, 1815, d. Rahway, N. J., 4-14, 1865, s of John & Phebe (Laing) Harned of Amboy, N. J., (m.

1811), the former, s. of Jonathan & Sarah[6] (Laing) Harned (m. 1766), of Jacob[3] Laing, John[2], John[1]], and the latter (b. 1790), dau. of Jacob[4] Laing, [of David[3], John[2], John[1]]. They and four minor children, Phebe, Julia, Jonathan S., and Franklin, became members of Kingwood M. M. (Hic.) by certificate from R. & P. M. M., dated 12-20, 1854. Jonathan & Ruth A. (Townsend) Harned had: (*a*) Phebe, b. 10-12, 1841. (*b*) Julia, b. 7-30, 1843, member of Shrewsbury M. M. (Hic.) by certificate from R. & P. M. M., dated 5-15, 1884, having m. 9-23, 1883, James Edward Borden. (*c*) Jeannette, b. 11-5, 1844, d. 5-14, 1847. (*d*) Catharine S., b. 12-17, 1848, dw. Rahway, N. J. (*e*) Franklin T., b. 9-15, 1850, d. 4-21, 1862.

2. Sarah S. Townsend[7], b. 9-21, 1823, dw. Philadelphia, Pa., m. 1-31, 1844, Jacob L. Harned, b. 5-24, 1818, d. --------, 1887, brother to Jonathan of Rahway. They and their 8 minor children, Catharine, Mary, Lizzie, William, Charles, Edward C., Laura, and Rachel, became members of Philadelphia M. M. (Hic.) by certificate from R. & P. M. M., dated 6-15, 1864.

3. Susannah[7], b. 11-22, 1825, d. 1-15, 1889, m. 4-20, 1853, Thomas Sexton, and had: (*a*) Elizabeth, who d. (*b*) Townsend. (*c*) Catharine.

4. Mary Jane[7], b. 2-3, 1828, d. 7-3, 1878, m. 3-9, 1852, Charles E. Gause, and had: (*a*) Ella T. (*b*) Townsend, who d. (*c*) Charles E., Jr.

5. Joseph S.[7], b. 7-28, 1830, was surveyor for the government; was sent to Gettysburg to survey the national cemetery, and had charge of burying the dead; was afterward sent into the oil lands of Pennsylvania as collector, and there d. of spotted fever, 3-26, 1865, m. 12-28, 1854, Mercy Wilson, an Orthodox Friend, who d. 7-12, 1861, aged 30, great-granddaughter of Capt. Wm. & Sarah[4] (Shotwell) Piatt, [of John[4] Shotwell, John[3], John[2], Abr[1].], and had: (*a*) Wilson, and (*b*) Alice S., both of whom live in West Virginia.

6. Wilhelmina B., b. 8-29, 1832, d. 12-30, 1832.

7. Wilhelmina[7] (again), b. 2-26, 1834, m. 11-24, 1864, Samuel Mason McCollin of Arch St., Philadelphia, Pa., a near re'ative of J. G. Whittier, and had: (*a*) Mary B., who m. Oliver P. Tatum. (*b*) James G., who d. (*c*) Catharine. (*d*) Samuel, who d.

8. Abigail Parker Townsend, b. 4-24, 1836, d. unm.

9. Rebecca S.[7], b. 9-28, 1838, m. 11-24, 1864, Edward E. Woolman, a descendant of John Woolman, the distinguished Quaker preacher and philanthropist, and had: (*a*) Josephine T. (*b*) Sarah N., who d. (*c*) Edward. (*d*) Henry N.

10. Jotham W., b. 1-29, 1842, d. 6-16, 1849.

11. Hugh S'., b. 11 22, 1844, d. 4-25, 1887, m. 5-18, 1868, Sarah J. Jones, and had: (*a*) Catharine, called Katie. (*b*) Henry. (*c*) Walter.

12. Mercie S', b. 7-18, 1847, dw. 44 N. 38th St., W. Philadelphia, Pa. To her and to her sister, Ruth A. Harned, of Rahway, we are indebted for valuable data concerning this branch. She m. 6-2, 1874, Jacob Parvin Masters, b. 8-2, 1847, s. of Joseph & Sarah (Edwards) Masters, who lived near Williamsport, Pa. Their only child, Ralph T. Masters, d. 10-20, 1879.

13. Jotham (again), b. 7-13, 1851, d. 5-15, 1852.

X. *Margaret Freeman⁶ Shotwell*, b. 22 Oct., 1806, in Middlesex Co., near Rahway, N. J.; d. of consumption in Camden Co., N. J., 6 Sept., 1846, interred in Friends' cemetery, near Camden, N. J., m. by Friends' ceremony, near Rahway, N. J., 6-1, 1825, Alexander Dean, b. 22 Jan., 1805, Orange, Essex Co., N. J., was a shoemaker, resided for twenty-three years at Springfield, Ohio, d. of consumption in Clark Co., near Springfield, Ohio, 13 Oct., 1870, interred in Hinkle cemetery, Springfield, Ohio, s. of Alexander & Lydia (Fairchild) Dean, of Orange, N. J., and had:

1. Jane Dean, b. 13 Oct., 1826, near Rahway, N. J., d. Patoka, Gibson Co., Ind., 23 June, 1875, m. .. Dec., 1849, Alexander Kitchell, a shoemaker.

2. Sarah S., b. 3 Jan., 1829, at Perth Amboy, N. J., dw. 195 (formerly at 211) Rice St., Springfield, Clark Co., Ohio, m. 12 Aug., 1856, Henry C. Rice, a farmer, who d. ...., and whose farm in Clark Co., has been surveyed into town lots and is now an addition to Springfield.

3. Alexander Dean, b. 28 Sept., 1832, Orange, Essex Co., N. J., is a teacher in Florida, m. 1860, Elma Willson or Millison.

4. Alice S. Dean, b. 29 Aug., 1836, Orange, N. J., m. 28 Apr., 1859, Michael Hinkle, a farmer.

5. Lydia, b. 30 Mar., 1839, Philadelphia, Pa., d. .. Aug., 1864, at Urbana, Champaign Co., Ohio, interred Springfield, Clark Co., Ohio; m. 1863, Moses Kitchell, a shoemaker.

6. Joseph S., b. 11 Mar., 1842, Haddonfield, near Camden, N. J., enlisted in 153d regiment of Ohio volunteers, infantry, was taken prisoner at South Branch, Md., 4 July, 1864, taken to military prison at Florence, S. C., and there kept until the following Dec., when he was exchanged and brought back to Annapolis, Md., and there d. the same month, .. Dec., 1864, of exposure and starvation endured while a prisoner, interred in Soldiers' Cemetery, Annapolis, Md., unm.

7. Walter, b. 20 Jan., 1845, near Camden, N. J., d. Springfield, Ohio, 10 July, 1870, of consumption, m. Sophronia Kimball.

XI. *Sarah*, called Sally, who d. ...., 1832, m. Samuel Taylor.

XII. *Alice*, who d. ...., unm.

MANNING⁵ SHOTWELL'S BRANCH

[of Benj⁴., John³, Daniel², Abr¹].

Nicholas & Margaret⁷ (Shotwell) Mundy, of Plainfield, N. J., (m. 1833), [of Robert⁶ Shotwell, Manning⁵], had 7 children, all of whom live in Plainfield, N. J., viz.: (1.) Clark. (2.) Robert. (3.) Wm. V. (4.) James L. (5.) Hannah M. (6.) George, d. (7.) Manning, d.

FREEMAN⁷ SHOTWELL, 1814-1893, s. of Robert⁶ and Martha (F. R.) Shotwell, [of *Manning⁵*], m. 1836, *Nancy Nott*, 1817-1885, and had:

1. *Harriet B.*, b. 17 Sept., 1839, d. ...., m. 19 Dec., 1860, J. Smith Garretson.

2. *William H⁸*., b. 30 May, 1841, dw. Plainfield, N. J., a grocer; m. 8 Sept., 1864, Miriam Staats, and had Freeman J. See pp. 155-166, 168, 169.

Mary E⁷. Shotwell, b. 1826, dau. of Robert⁶ & Martha (Fitz Randolph) Shotwell, (p. 168), m. (1) Nathan Terrell, and had: (1.) Charles. (2.) Clara. Mary E⁷., m. (2) .... Seaman; m. (3) Andrew J. Clarkson, dw. Plainfield, N. J.

Martha Ann⁷ Shotwell, b. 1830, [of Robert⁶, Manning⁵], m. George Goodwin, and had: (1.) Hattie M., who d. .... (2) Robert S., d. .... (3.) George W., d. .... (4.) G. Wesley, d. .... (5.) Norma. (6.) Ida Louisa. (7.) Anna A., d. .... (8.) John Insley. (9.) Hattie M.

Lavinia⁶ Shotwell, dau. of Manning⁵ & Mary (Clarkson) Shotwell, (pp. 155-6), m. James Langstaff, and had: (1.) Henry. (2.) Caroline. (3.) Matilda. (4.) Mary.

NATHAN⁵ SHOTWELL'S BRANCH

[of John⁴, John³, John², Abraham¹].

Eden⁶ Shotwell's daughter, Sarah F. R., m. 1864, Charles W. Long, a wagon-maker of Loda, Ill.

His second daughter, Susan Haas, m. 1859, James Welch, who is a real estate agent and speculator at Webster City, Iowa.

His fifth child, Catharine Ann, m. (2) 1885, James H. Mussetter, who keeps a feed store and stable at University Place, Lancaster Co., Nebraska, 18 miles from the late residence of Eden⁶ Shotwell near Bennett, Neb.

His sixth child, Jacob Alexander, was a blacksmith while in Kansas, but has been farming for sixteen years in Wanatchee, Wash.

Glenroie & Jennie May⁶ (Shotwell) McQueen, [of Nathan T⁵. Shotwell, (see page 163 *ante*), Eden⁶, Nathan⁵, Jacob⁴, John³, John², Abraham¹], had: (1.) Glenna Udell, b. 17 July, 1889, at Spencerport, N. Y. (2.) Lyman Shotwell McQueen, b. 21 Mar., 1893, at Princeton, Ill. (3.) Donald Gene, b. 18 Dec., 1894, Princeton, Ill, whence the family have since removed.

RICHARD[1] SHOTWELL'S BRANCH

[of Benj[4]., John[3], John[2], Abr[1]. pp. 92-3, 95, 165-8)].

Elizabeth[4] Shotwell, 1791-1874, m. 2 Apr., 1812, James Herendeen,* 1788-1873, (said by dau. Mary H. Estes, to have been b. in Berkshire Co., Mass.), was brought to Farmington, N. Y., in 1790,—his younger brother, Welcome Herendeen, b. 17 Sept., 1790, being the first white child b. in the town of Farmington, (see pp. 166, 168). They had: (1.) ...., a son, who d. aged 5 days. (2.) Welcome, b. 1814, d. Farmington, N. Y., 1816, aged 18 mos. (3.) Pennsylvania, called Vania, b. 30 Nov., 1817, Farmington, N. Y., and there d. 5 June, 1883, s. p., m. in Farmington (Orth.) Friends' Meeting House, 11-28, 1839, Hartshorn Willson, b. 1818±, d. 23 Aug., 1888, Farmington, N. Y., s. of David of Farmington. (4.) Mary H., b. 20 Sept., 1819, dw. Farmington, N. Y., s. p., m. Farmington, N. Y., 10 Jan., 1861, (as 2d wife) Benjamin Estes, Jr., b. 11-5, 1811, in Maine, d. Farmington, N. Y., 2-10, 1883, s. of Benj. & Sarah of Wheatland, N. Y. (5.) Richard Hallett, b. 28 Apr., 1822, Farmington, N. Y., and there d. 29 Dec., 1875, s. p.; m. in Perinton, N. Y., 1 Jan., 1855, Mary G. Bosworth, b. 2-3, 1830, d. Rochester, N. Y., .. Jan., 1893, dau. of Seth & Catharine E. (Pound) Bosworth of Rochester, N. Y., (p. 11). (6.) Elizabeth Shotwell Herendeen, b. 1 mo., (Jan.), 11, 1825, d. Farmington, N. Y., 17 June, 1893. unm. (7.) Amy Ann, b. 11 of 3 mo. (Mar.), 1829, dw. on the homestead, Farmington, N. Y., unm. (8.) James Wilkinson[7] Herendeen, b. 18 Apr., 1831, dw. Farmington, N. Y., d. 26 March, 1875; m. in Zion Episcopal church, Palmyra, N. Y., 11 Sept., 1860, Mary Alice Browning, who dw. Farmington, N. Y., P. O., Manchester, box 99, dau. of Joseph, and had: (a) James, b. 12 June, 1861, Farmington, N. Y., and there d. 10 Apr., 1862. (b) James Hallett, called Hallett, b. 23 Mar., 1863, dw. Farmington, Ontario Co., N. Y., P. O Box 99, Manchester, N. Y., is a school teacher, graduated at Brockport Normal School, June 23, 1892, and at Gen. Theological Sem., N. Y. City, June 2, 1897; ordained deacon of the P. E. church, June 5, 1897, at Zion P. E. church, Palmyra, N. Y. To him and his aunts we are indebted for data concerning this branch. (c) Mary Sophia, b. 2 Sept., 1864, grad. Brockport Normal School, 1888, taught school, dw. Victor, N. Y.; m. in Episcopal church of the Good Shepherd, Victor, N. Y., 14 Feb., 1888, Horace Jonathan Calkins, and had: Robert Marsh Calkins, b. 5 Sept., 1890; Jay Horace, b. 26 Dec., 1891, d. aged 4 mos., and Alice Browning, b. Mar., 29, 1897. (d) Elizabeth Vania Herendeen, b. 16 Mar., 1866, dw. Farmington, N. Y., a teacher, graduated at Brockport Normal School, 1891. (e) Josephine Morey Herendeen, b. 21 Aug., 1867, dw. Farmington, N. Y., a teacher. (f) Sarah Alice, b. 25 May, 1869, d. 11 Oct., 1873. (g) Fannie Browning Herendeen, b. 16 Aug., 1870, d. 11 Oct., 1870. (h) Jane Effie, b. 25 Sept., 1871, dw. Farmington, N. Y., a teacher at Jamica, L. I., graduated at Brockport Normal School, 1894. (i) Joseph Morey Browning Herendeen, b. 11 Sept., 1873, dw. Farmington, N. Y., a farmer. (j) Richard Wilkinson, b. 30 Apr., 1875, a farmer, dw. Farmington, N. Y., P. O., Victor, m. in Zion P. E. church, 31 Jan., 1894, Minnie M. Gaylord, dau. of Charles & Mary R. (Bortle) Gaylord, and had: Mary Alice, b. 9 May, 1896.

Mary Jane Dillingham, b. 1835, (p. 117), dau. of Stephen & Anna P[1]. (Shotwell-Hoag) Dillingham, of Elba, N. Y., [of Isaac M[2]. Shotwell, Richard[1]], m. 1859, Lewis Genung, b. 1828, and had: (1) Lizzie A. Genung, b. 4 Sept., 1860, d. 5 Dec., 1893; m. 12 Sept., 1889, S. W. Randall, s. of Jackson A. & Juliette (King) Randall, and had: (a) Lewis Willard, b. 26 Aug., 1890. (b) Mary Edna, b. 29 Jan., 1893. (2.) Carl D. Genung, b. 1 Jan., 1866, m. 25 Oct., 1894, Mary A. Hill, dau. of Horacio & Hettie (Bodine) Hill, of W. Barre, N. Y., and had: (a) Margaret Lucile, b. 28 Dec., 1895. (3.) Clara C. Genung, (twin), b. 1 Jan., 1866, dw. Barre Centre, Orleans Co., N. Y., m. 10 Mar., 1892, Wm. H. Stoney, b. 2 Nov., 1865, s. of Wm. H. & Susan (Webster) Stoney, and had: (a). Warren Genung Stoney, b. 9 Jan., 1896. (4.) Mary Edith Genung, b. 17 Feb., 1870, m. 2 Feb., 1893, Webster Defendorf.

Oscar Dillingham, 1841-1895, s. of Stephen & Anna P. (Shotwell Hoag) Dillingham, (p. 117), d. 8 of 2 mo., 1895. At Elba Monthly Meeting held at Batavia, N. Y., 20 of 2 mo., 1895, "Much tender sympathy was expressed for the bereaved family of our late dear friend, Oscar Dillingham, and there were loving testimonies as to his steadfast christian walk, his earnest zeal, and the great loss the church has sustained." "Write, blessed are the dead who die in the Lord from henceforth; yea, saith the Spirit, that they may rest from their labors; and their works do follow them."

Stephen N. Dillingham of Oakfield, Genesee Co., N. Y., b. 2-27, 1843, son of Stephen[3] & Anna P. (Shotwell Hoag) Dillingham,—the former a native of Saratoga Co., N. Y., son of Silvanus[2] & Judith (Marshel) Dillingham, [of John[1]], and the latter, a native of Ontario Co.,

* James Herendeen was s. of Joshua & Pennsylvania (Herendeen) Herendeen of Farmington, N. Y.,—the former b. 1-30, 1761, in Cumberland, Providence Co., R. I., d. 2-14, 1851, s. of Wm. & Bethia (......... ...) Herendeen, and the latter, b. 1-13, 1765, in Smithfield, Providence Co., R. I., dau. of Nathan & Huldah (..........) Herendeen. His sister, Huldah (Herendeen) Whipple, was b. 5-19, 1784, in Danby, Rutland Co., Vt.

N. Y., dau. of Isaac M[6]. & Edna C. (Pound) Shotwell, of Elba, N. Y., of New Jersey Quaker ancestry,—m. July 26, 1863, Emeline E[7]. Porter, b. March 18, 1844, dau. of John K[2]. & Deliverance (Hicks) Porter, of Genesee Co., N. Y., [of John[1]].

John[1] Porter, b. about 1780, removed in 1815, from New Hampshire to Oneida Co., N. Y.; d. in Camden, Oswego Co., N. Y., ----------, 1854; m. Eleanor Doten, who d. in Camden, N. Y., April 27, 1869, aged 85 years, and had: John K[2]. Porter, b. May 31, 1803, in Camden, Grafton Co., N. H., d. in Elba, N. Y., Aug., 31, 1876; m. Oct. --, 1829, Deliverance Hicks, b. Sept. 28, 1812, in Herkimer Co., N. Y., d. June 11, 1891, dau. of Stephen & Elizabeth (Nichols) Hicks,—the former b. about 1770, in Vermont, d. 1812, and the latter, b. April 11, 1771, in Vermont, d. Aug., 31, 1845,—and had: Emeline E[7]. Porter, wife of S. N. Dillingham, of the town of Oakfield, N. Y.

Stephen N. & Emeline E. (Porter) Dillingham's son, Wm., 1865-1891, (p. 117), took a business course, taught school for two winters, d. 1-1, 1891, of inflammation of the brain caused mainly by an injury; was of a retiring disposition, appreciated most by those who knew him best; member of Friends' church, Elba, N. Y. For children of his sister, Anna D., & her husband, Henry A. Vail, see outlines of Vail family later.

John H. & Rosetta M. (Dillingham) Field, (p. 117), had: Helen, b. April 13, 1893.

David B[7]. & Adaliza J. (Wilder) Shotwell's eldest daughter, Edna A[8]., 1861-1883, (pp. 106, 118), m. 1832, (as 1st wife) William Fred[6] Smith, b. 1855, now of St. Paul, Minn., s. of Charles[5] (1812-1882) & Clarissa H. (DeWolf, d. 1869) Smith, of Barry Tp., Barry Co., Mich. His paternal grandmother, Sophia[4] (Gardner) Smith, is said to have been a descendant of Lord Gardner of England, in the following line:

Stephen[1] Gardner, from England, settled at Greenwich, Conn., about 1701; by wife, Amy, he had twelve children, the fifth of whom, Daniel[2], b. 14 Dec., 1709, by wife, Bathsheba, had eight children, the third being James[3], who, at the age of 26, m. in Vermont, Kesiah Washburn and settled at Skaneateles, N. Y., where Sophia[4] (Gardner) Smith, second of their seven children, latterly resided. Charles[5] Smith, eldest of her six children, m. Clarissa H. DeWolf, of French ancestry, and said to have been related to President Jackson, and had three children; the second of these, William Fred[6] Smith, (p. 106), m. (2) Morenci, Mich., 28 July, 1887, Agnes L[7]., (b. 1863), dau. of Orin E[5]. & -------- Green, of Morenci, Lenawee Co., Mich., [of Hon. Noah K.[3] (b. 1808), & Esther E. (Baldwin) Green, of Medina Tp., Lenawee Co., Mich., Hon. Noah[2] (b. 1761, J. P., etc.), & (2d of 3 wives), Sarah (Davis) Green, of Berk-

shire Co., Mass., Hezekiah[3]* (1733-1826) & Alice (Leavens) Greene, Henry[2] & Juda (Giles) Greene, of Windham Co., Conn., Henry[1] from Greenwich, Eng., said to have settled at Salem, Mass., about 1629].

Sarah Jane[5] Shotwell, called Jane, b. 1839, dau. of David S[4]. & Eliza (Dillingham(Shotwell, of Kent Co., Mich., (of Benj[6], Richard[5]], m. (1) 1858, Isaac M. Hunting, and had: (1.) Luella Hunting, b. 1-22, 1862, d. 3 1, 1883. (2) H. Seymour Hunting, b. 4 29, 1863. (3.) Elmer, b. June --, 1864. (4.) Julia B., b. May 5, 1867. (5.) David S., (twin), b. July 31, 1868. (6.) Eliza S., (twin), b. July 31, 1868. (7.) Elbert Isaac, called Isaac, b. ----------, 1869. (8.) Barton D., b. Mar., 19, 1873. (9.) Lura A., b. June 29, 1874; P. O., Rockford, Mich.

Judith Ann[x] Shotwell, b. 1840, P. O., Cedar Springs, Mich., dau. of David S[7]. & Eliza (Dillingham) Shotwell, (p. 106), m. 1860, A. J. Provin, of Kent Co., Mich., and had: (1) Irving C., b. Oct., 19, 1861. (2.) William A., b. ----------, 1866. (3.) Eliza S. (4.) Martha J. (5.) Warren L.

Elmer C. Shotwell, youngest child of Sylvanus D[7]. & Mary (Whittall) Shotwell of Cortland Tp., Kent Co., Mich., (p. 171), was b. 27 Dec., 1877, dw. Cortland, Mich.

TITUS[5] SHOTWELL'S BRANCH.

[of Daniel[4], Joseph[3], Daniel[2], Abr[1]. (pp. 118, 173-4, 180)].

TITUS[7] SHOTWELL III, of Latrobe, Athens Co., Ohio, s. of Isaac[6] & Hope (Stanton) Shotwell, [of *Titus[5]* & Deborah (Moore) Shotwell, Daniel[4], & Deborah (Shotwell) Shotwell, Joseph[3] & Mary (Manning) Shotwell, Daniel[2], Abr[1].], d. at Latrobe, O., 18 Jan., 1896, had been a life-long sufferer from asthma, and for several years from heart trouble; was in religion a liberal, and in politics a republican, having been a strong anti-slavery man prior to the War of the Rebellion. By his will, Titus left all his property to his widow during her life time, then to the children equally, appointing her his sole executrix without security. The sleeve-buttons mentioned on page 118 *ante*, go to his grandson, Titus, (b. 1895, ---- son of William --------), who is the only known descendant of the first Titus now bearing this name.

(See pp. 118, 173-4 *ante*).

Titus[6] & Mary (Doan) Shotwell, of Athens Co., Ohio., had: (1.) Elias Whittier Shotwell, b. 1854; P. O., Twin Creek, Osborne Co., Kans., m. -- of 11 mo., 1890, Annie Moore of Osborne Co., Kans. (2.) Enos Sumner[7], b 1856, P. O., Museville, Muskingum Co., Ohio; m. 12 of 1 mo., 1881, Rose E. Mitchell, of Muskingum Co.,

----

* The tradition that Hezekiah was cousin to Gen. Nathaniel[5] Greene of Revolutionary fame, [of Nathaniel[4], Jabez[3], James[2], John[1]], has not been confirmed.

Ohio, and had: (*a*) Gertie, b. 10 of 5 mo, 1881. (*b*) Georgie (a dau.), b. 15 of 8 mo., 1883. (3) Wm. E⁵., b. 1858, P. O., Sioux Falls, S. D., m. 1888, Minnie Bernard, of Sioux Falls, S. D., and had: (*a*) Etta Mary. (*b*) Emma Sadie. (*c*) Titus, b. 1895. (4.) Emily Ann⁵, b. 1860, P. O., Torch, Athens Co., Ohio; m. 4 of 11 mo., 1880, John E. Moore, of Athens Co., Ohio, who d., 25 of 1 mo., 1888, s. of Ezekiel & (2d wife) Margaret (Elliot) Moore of Athens Co., Ohio, and had: (*a*) Ida May, b. 24 of 3 mo., 1883. (b) Frank E., b. 7 of 12 mo., 1885. (5.) Sarah Asenath, b. 1863, dw. Sioux Falls, S. D., a teacher, unm. (1896). (6.) Isaac⁵, b. 1865, m. Vivia Sherman of Seneca, Nemaha Co., Kans., and had: (*a*) Emma May. (*b*) Sadie. (7.) Effie Ellen⁵, b. 1867, P. O., Torch, Ohio; m. -- of 9 mo., 1888, Walter Dunfee, of Athens Co., Ohio, and had: (*a*) Hazel Belle, b. 20 of 1 mo., 1890. (b) Zola Marine, b. 17 of 12 mo, 1891. (c) Nellie Ruth, b. 21 of 5 mo., 1894. (8.) Edgar Thomas⁵ Shotwell, b. 1870, P. O., Marietta, Ohio; m. 7 of 1 mo., 1893, Lillian Johnson, of Washington, Ohio, and had: (*a*) Oscar E., b. 5 of 8 mo., 1894, d. 5 of 6 mo., 1895.

WILLIAM⁵ SHOTWELL'S BRANCH

[of John⁴, John³, John², Abr¹., (pp. 139-41, 176)].

Elijah⁶ & Martha (Burtsall) Shotwell, (p. 109), had: Elizabeth B⁷., who m. (2) Amos Canby, and had: Mary Letitia⁸ Canby, who m. Elijah D. Scott, and had: Emma Louisa⁹ Scott, b. 1861, who m. 1881, H. Jacob Vogt, and had: Carl Edwin and Ada Letitia.

Emerson⁸ Shotwell, of Martelle, Iowa, s. of Joseph⁷ & Martha (Ferguson) Shotwell, [of John⁶], (p. 154), by wife Louisa *nee* Bishop, had also (2.) Francis Joseph, b. 15 Nov., 1896.

Emily Ann⁸ *nee* Shotwell, wife of Elijah Prior, and dau. of Wm⁷. & Martha Elizabeth (Taylor) Shotwell, of Sparta, Kans., (p. 180), [of Smith⁶, Wm⁵, of Canada, John⁴, John³, John², Abr¹.], dw. Windom, McPherson Co., Kans.

WILLIAM⁵ SHOTWELL'S BRANCH.

[of Benj⁴., John³, John², Abr¹., (pp. 93-4, 176-7)].

William⁶ Shotwell, Jr., 1798-1876, of Bricktown, Rahway, N. J., manufacturer of brick and lime, dealer in coal, etc., s of Wm⁵. & (1st wife), Elizabeth (Moore) Shotwell, m. (1) 28 June, 1826, Catherine Pettit, who d. 28 Aug., 1830, and had: (1) Ann Elizabeth, b 22 Aug., 1828, dw. Union Co., N. J. (2.) Joseph, b. 22 July, 1830, d. 3 Sept., 1830. Wm⁶. Shotwell, 1798-1876, m. (2) Mary Prall, b. 2 Mar., 1793, d. 20 Jan., 1867, and had (only) (3.) Harriet, b. 7 Apr., 1836, dw. Rahway, N. J., unm.

William J⁷. Shotwell, of 101 N. Grove St., E. Orange, N. J., s. of Benj⁶. & Mary (Hunt) Shotwell, m. 16 Sept., 1862, Mary N. Melick, (pp. 97-8, 180).

COCK, COCKS, COX.

REVISED OUTLINE OF FOUR GENERATIONS, WITH LINEAGES OF CERTAIN DESCENDANTS.

James¹ Cock first appears on public record Aug. 6, 1659, at Cromwell's Bay alias Setauke (Setauket, Suffolk Co.), on Long Island, province of New Netherland, (afterward New York), as one of those who applied to the colonial authorities of Hartford, Conn., for the extension of their governmental jurisdiction over the settlement at Setauket, this being the initial settlement of the township of Brookhaven. In 1661, he had an allotment of more land there. Whence he came or when he arrived in America, has not been ascertained. There is the usual " three brothers " tradition, all of which may be true, but we have no record evidence. His great-great-grandson, Samuel⁵ Cock (1765-1855), [of Clark⁴, Samuel³, James², James¹], " used to recount a tradition that the vessel in which James came over encountered a severe storm and was obliged to put into Bermuda for repairs; that during the storm when everything seemed disastrous, a severe shock was felt as of striking a rock, and the vessel leaked badly; but the united and persistent prayers of the passengers so prevailed that the ship was brought to land, and on being ' hove out,' it was discovered that its side had been penetrated by the weapon of a great swordfish, which was broken by the shock and remained therein imbedded."

In 1662 he removed to Oyster Bay, Queens Co., L. I., where he remained about seven years. In 1669 he bought of the Indian proprietors a tract of land at " Killingworth upon Matinecock " in the township of Oyster Bay, some of which remains in the possession of descendants of his youngest son, Henry. His nearest neighbor at Killingworth was Matthew Priar (as he wrote it), who had also been at Setauket. Matthew's settlement at Matinecock, L. I., was determined by some claims he had upon the notorious adventurer, Capt. John Scott.* James Cock's next nearest neighbor was Henry Birdsall, next Capt. John Underhill and John Feke, all of whom seem to have settled there about the same date.

James Cock appears to have been a substantial citizen, having a good showing on the tax list and being employed in such matters of trust as heading various arbitrations and a commission to purchase the remainder of Matinecock lands. He died about 1698. His wife, Sarah, d. 16 of 10 mo., 1715.

For the following summary of three generations of descendants of James¹ and Sarah Cock of Matinecock, L. I., we are chiefly indebted to George Wm. Cocks of Glen Cove, L. I., as also for the use of a chart from which we have compiled the alphabetical synopsis of his (G. W. C.'s) ancestors and those of his wife, presented at the close of this exhibit. James¹ and Sarah Cock had:

I. *Mary²* b. 1 of 1 mo. (Mar.), 1655-6, d. --------; m. 26 of 4 mo., 1693, (as 3d wife) John² Bowne of Flushing, L. I., (see pp. 133-4 and 208), and had two children:

1. Amy³, b. 1 Apr., 1694; m. 1717, (as 1st wife) Richard³ Hallett, (of Newtown, L. I.), b. 17 Nov., 1691, d. --------; s. of William² & Sarah (Woolsey) Hallett, [of Wm¹.], and had: (a) Mary, b. 1719. (b) Richard, b. 1721. (c) Sarah, b. 1723. (d) William, b. 10 of 12 mo., 1725. (e) Ame⁴, b. 5 of 3 mo., 1727, d. 1796; m. 1746, Benjamin⁴ Shotwell, 1726-1793, [of John³, John², Abraham¹].
2. Ruth Bowne, b. 30 Jan., 1695-6, d. young.

II. *Thomas² Cock,* b. 15 of 10 mo., 1658, d. 1685; m. Esther Williams, dau. of Robert & Sarah (Washbourne) Williams, and had:

1. John.
2. Charity.

III. *Martha Cock,* b. .. of 7 mo., 1661, d. 1670.

IV. *John² Cock,* b. 22 of 1 mo., 1666, d. 1716-17; m. (1) -------- --------, and had by her two children:

1. Thomas³, b. 1689; m. Hannah --------, and had: (a) Sarah, who m. Joseph Ludlam. (b) Joanna, who m. Michael Weekes.
2. Hannah³ Cock, b. 1692; m. Matthew Prier, and had: (a) Hannah, b. 1720. (b) Mary, b. 1723-4; m. 1748, George Townsend. (c) Matthew, b. 1729; m. 1754, Ann Pearsall.

John² Cock, 1666-1716-17, m. (2) Dorothy Harcourt, dau. of Richard & Isabel (Potter) Harcourt, and had:

* See Thompson's History of Long Island, also G. D. Scull's "Dorothea Scott."

3. John, b. 1698, d. --------, unm.
4. Daniel³ Cock, b. 1699; m. (1) Levinah Rushmore, and had: (a) Sarah, b. 1748; m. 1765, Jacob Coles. Daniel³ Cock, b. 1699; m. (2) Susannah (Prince) Youngs, wid. of Thomas Youngs.
5. Meribah³ Cock, b. 1701-2; m. Joshua Townsend, and had: (a) Noah, who married Margaret Wright.
6. Hezekiah³ Cock, b. 1703; m. Roseannah Townsend, and had: (a) Penn, b. 1733. (b) John, b. 1735. (c) Violetta. (d) Dorothy, b. 1742. (e) Sarah, b. 1750. (f) Gabriel, b. 1755.
7. James³ Cock, b. 1708; m. Deborah Feke, and had: (a) Lorette. (b) Phiany. (c) Daniel, who m. 1768, Roseannah Townsend, dau. of Wm. & Elizabeth (Cock) Townsend, [of Henry², James¹].

V. *Hannah² Cock,* b. 22 of 1 mo., 1669; m. 28 of 6 mo., 1692, James de la Plaine, and had:

1. Joshua³ de la Plaine, who m. Hester Zane, and had: (a) Elizabeth, b. 1718. (b) Joshua, b. 1721. (c) Joseph.

VI. *Sarah² Cock,* b. 20 of 9 mo., 1672, d. 1750; m. Henry Franklin, [of Matthew], and had:

1. Matthew, b. 1698-9; m. 1722-3, Deborah Cornwell.
2. Sarah³ Franklin, b. 1700; m. 1716, Samuel Bowne, Jr. and had: (a) William, b. 1719. (b) Samuel, b. 1721. (c) Mary, b. 1724. (d) Sarah. (e) Abigail. (f) James.
3. Henry³ Franklin, b. 1702; m. 1723, Sarah Cornwell, and had: (a) Elizabeth. (b) Thomas.
4. Thomas³ Franklin, b. 1703-4; m. 1726, Mary Pearsall, and had: (a) Walter. (b) Sarah. (c) John. (d) Thomas. (e) Mary. (f) Samuel. (g) James.
5. Elizabeth, b. 1706-7, d. --------, unm.

VII. *James² Cock,* b. 4 of 4 mo., 1674, d. 1728; m. 1 of 10 mo, 1698, Hannah Feke, b. 1675, d. 1750, dau. of John & Elizabeth (Prier) Feke, and had;

1. Sarah, b. 1700, d. 1786±.
2. Samuel³ Cock, b. 1702; m. Martha Alling, and had: (a) Hannah, b. 1731. (b) Samuel, b. 1734. (c) Anne, b. 1736. (d) Clark, b. 1738. (e) Penelope, b. 1741.
3. Joshua, b. 1704, d. 1778, unm.
4. Elizabeth, b. 1706.
5. Josiah³ Cock, b. 1709; m. Rebecca Frost, and had: (a) James, b. 1731. (b) Deborah, b. 1734. (c) Jacob, b. 1736. (d) George, b. 1739. (e) Isaac, b. 1741. (f) Rhoda. (g) Martha, b. 1747. (h) Hannah. (i) Elizabeth.
6. Jacob, d. 1726.
7. Robert³ Cock, m. -------- --------, and had: (a) Joshua, b. 1755. (b) Jordan. (c) Mary. (d) Hannah.
8. Martha³ Cock, m. Joseph Frost, and had: (a) Ame. (b) Caleb. (c) Jacob. (d) Michael.

(e) Elizabeth. (f) Wright. (g) Hannah. (h) Sarah.

9. Mary[1] Cock, m. 1737-8, Isaac[3] Frost, b. 1716, s. of Wm[2]. & Hannah (Prier) Frost, [of Wm[1]. & Rebecca (Wright) Frost, and of John[2] & Elizabeth (Bowne) Prier], and had: (a) James. (b) Rhoda. (c) Elizabeth. (d) Isaac. (e) Obadiah. (f) Jordan (g) Solomon. (h) George. (i) Mordecai. (j) Mary. (k) Anna. (l) Ethelanah. (m) Sarah. (n) Hannah.

10. Hannah, d. 1759, unm.

VIII. *Henry[2] Cock*, b. 1 of 4 mo., 1678. As was frequently the case in those times, the elder sons were otherwise provided for and the homestead at Matinecock, L. I., passed to the youngest son. He there died 1733; m (1) at Matinecock in the bounds of Oyster Bay, L. I., 28 of 6 mo. (Aug.), 1699, "Mary[3] ffeakes, daughter of John and Elizabeth (Prier) ffeakes, all of Matinecock;" she d. 30 of 10 mo., 1715, and the Friends' Records further state that "She sometimes had a few words in testimony and prayer in meeting." Henry[2] & Mary (Feke) Cock, had:

1. Joseph, b. 1701, d. in Pennsylvania, s. p.

2. Benjamin[3] Cock, b. 1703; m. 1730, Ann Brinton, and had: (a) James, b. 1733. (b) John, b. 1735. (c) Benjamin, b. 1737. (d) Mary, b. 1739. (e) Moses, b. 1742. (f) Ann, b. 1745. (g) Joseph Brinton Cock, b. 1755.

3. John[3] Cock, b. 1705; m. Sarah Carpenter, and had: (a) Mary, b. 1730. (b) William, b. 1732. (c) Henry, b. 1735. (d) Rees, b. 1738. (e) Elizabeth, b. 1740. (f) Ann, b. 1743. (g) Elijah, b. 1745. (h) Sarah, b. 1748. (i) Benjamin, b. 1754. (j) Amy, b. 1756.

4. James, 1707-1733.

5. Amy[3] Cock, b. 1708-9; m. Rees Jones of Pennsylvania, and had: (a) Henry Jones. (b) John Richard Jones. (c) Joseph. (d) Benjamin. (e) Jane. (f) Mary. (g) Sarah. (h) Evan.

6. Mary[3] Cock, b. 1711; m. 1735, Nathan Bane, and had: (a) Ame. (b) Sarah. (c) Elizabeth. (d) James. (e) Abigail. (f) Hannah. (g) Deborah.

7. Henry[3] Cock, b. 1713; m. 1736, Mary Bowne, and had: (a) Thomas. (b) Sarah. (c) Daniel. (d) Hannah. (e) Mary. (f) Henry. (g) Anne. (h) Abraham.

8. Sarah[3] Cock, b. 1715, m. 1742, Joseph[1] Shotwell, 1710-1787, s. of John[3], Jr., & Mary (Thorne) Shotwell, [of John[2], Abraham[1]], and had: (a) John, (see page 149). (b) Mary. (c) Joseph. (d) Sarah. (e) Henry. (f) James. (g) Thomas. (h) William. (See pp. 149-50).

9. Elizabeth[3] Cock (twin), b. 1715, m. William Townsend, and had: (a) James, b. 1742; m. 1762, Freelove Wilmot. (b) Roseannah, b. 1751; m. 1768, Daniel[1] Cock, s. of James[3] & Deborah (Feke) Cock, [of John[2], James[1]].

Henry[2] Cock, 1678-1733; m. (2) Martha Pearsall, b. 10 of 10 mo., 1681, dau. of Nathaniel[2] & Martha (Seaman) Pearsall, the former (who d. 1703), s. of Henry[1] & Anne (----------) Pearsall, and the latter (who d. 1712), dau. of Capt. John[1] & Martha (Moore) Seaman and grand-daughter of Thomas[2] & Martha (Younga) Moore, [of Thomas[1] & Anna (----------) Moore, of Salem, Mass.], and had:

10. Thomas Cock, b. 1718, d. 1724.

11. Samuel[3] Cock, b. 1720±, d. 1755±; m. ---------- ----------, and had: (a) Joseph[4] Cock, who m. Rhoda[4] Frost, dau. of Isaac[3] & Mary (Cock[3]) Frost, the *former* b. 1716, s. of Wm[2]. Frost, 1675-1728, b. at Maitnecock, & wife, Hannah[3], *nee* Prier, 1681-1771, (m. 1700), and grandson (1) of Wm[1]. Frost, a native of England, who d. 1720±, wife, Rebecca[2], *nee* Wright, (m. 1672), [of Nicholas[1] & Ann (----------) Wright], and (2) of John[2] & Elizabeth (Bowne[3]) Prier, [of Matthew[1] & Mary (----------) Priar, and great-grandson of John[2] & Hannah (Feke) Bowne, of Flushing, L. I., and the *latter*, dau. of James[2] Cock, b. 4 of 2 mo., 1674, d. 26 of 3 mo., 1728, & wife, Hannah[1], *nee* Feke, and grand-daughter (1) of James[1] & Sarah (----------) Cock, and (2) of John[2] & Elizabeth (Prier) Feke, [of Lieut. Robert[1] & Elizabeth (Fones) Feake]. (b) Levi Cock. (c) Zoar. (d) Martha. (e) Samuel.

IX *Martha[2] Cock*, b. 13 of 2 mo., 1680, m. (?) Isaac Davis, [s. of John, whose wife, Mercy, was Widow Banbury], and had:

1. Thomas Davis, who m. Hannah Cock.

2. Joseph Davis, who m. ---------- ----------.

3 Abraham, b. 1721.

4. Mary, b. 1723.

SYNOPSIS OF THE ANCESTRY

OF

GEORGE W. & MATILDA K. (TOWNSEND) COCKS,

OF GLEN COVE, QUEENS CO., N. Y.

ALLING.

Abraham[1], of Oyster Bay, L. I., m. Mary

Abraham[2]† 1697, m. Mary (Hawxhurst) Townsend.
Martha[3], d. 1742, m. Samuel[3] Cock, 1702–1741.

ALMY.

William[1], 1601–1676, of Rhode Island, m. Audrey ...., 1603–1676.
Col. Job[2], d. 1684, m. Mary[2] Unthank, d. 1725±.
Audrey[3], b. 1669, m. James[3] Townsend, ..., d. 1729+.

BILLOPP.

Capt. Christopher[1], of Staten Island, N. Y.
Joseph[2], m. (?) Ann[2] Stillwell.
Anna[3], m. Thomas[1] Farmer.
Thomas Farmer[4] Billopp, m. Sarah............
Col. Christopher[5] Billopp, m. 1762, Frances[3] Willett, b. 1765, d. 1811.   Sarah[6], m. 1784, Henry Seaman, 1761–1799.

BUTLER.

Richard[1], Stratford, Conn., m. ....
Mary[2], m. (1) John Washbourne, m. (2) Thomas[3] Hicks, 1659, Setauket, 1663, Oyster Bay.

COCK.

of Killingworth now Matinecock, L. I., 1669.
James[1], d. 1698, m. Sarah ...., d. 16 of 10 mo., 1715.
James[2], 1674–1728, m. 1698, Hannah[3] Feke, 1675–1750.
Samuel[3], 1702–1741, m. Martha[3] Alling, d. 1742.
Clark[4], 1738–1822, m. 1760, Elizabeth[4] Pearce, 1743–1835.

Samuel[5],* 1765–1855, m. 1785, Elizabeth[5] Cock, 1769–1859.
Clark[6], 1790–1866, m. 1816, Catharine[7] Feeks, 1793–1875.
George William[7] Cocks, 1829, of Glen Cove, L. I., m. 1858, Matilda Katharine[8] Townsend, b. 1826.
Frances Seaman[8] Cocks, b. 1859, & Robert Feeks[8] Cox, b. 1863.
James[1] Cock, d. 1698, m. Sarah ...., d. 1715.
John[2], b, 22 of 11 mo., 1666, d. 1717, m. Dorothy[2] Harcutt, d. 1739.
James[3], 1708–1746, m. Deborah[4] Feke, d. 1794.
Daniel[4], m. 1768, Roseannah[3] Townsend, 1751–1831.
Elizabeth[5], 1769–1859, m. 1785, Samuel[5] Cock, 1765–1855.
James[1] Cock, d. 1698, m. Sarah ...., d. 1715.
Henry[2] 1678–1733, m. 1699, Mary[3] Feke, 1678–1715.
Elizabeth[3], b. 14 Dec., 1715, d. 13 Nov., 1794, m. William[4] Townsend, b. 13 Feb., 1716, d. 5 May, 1777.

---

*Clark[6] Cock's brother, William Townsend[6] Cock. [of Samuel[5], Clark[4], Samuel[3], James[2], James[1]], b. 11-26, 1803, at Buckram, L. I., m. at Westbury, L. I., Elizabeth Hicks,—dau. of Isaac & Sarah (Doughty) Hicks and a descendant of Sir Ellis Hicks who was Knighted by Edward the Black Prince,—and had: Isaac Hicks[7] Cocks, b. 8-31, 1836, m. at Westbury, L. I., 6-15, 1859, Mary Titus[9] Willets, b. 3-22, 1837,—dau. of William (1808-1839 ±) & Elizabeth Powell[8] (Titus) Willets of Westbury, L. I., the latter b. 10-14, 1815, d. 12-29, 1884, [of Samuel[7] & Mary (Powell) Titus, Stephen[6] & Phebe (Willets) Titus, Stephen[5] & Sarah (Mott) Titus, Samuel & Mary[4] (Jackson) Titus, John & Elizabeth[3] (Hallett) Jackson, Samuel[2] Hallett (whose wife's name is unknown, though it has sometimes been called Bridget Blackwell), William[1] & Elizabeth (Fones-Winthrop-Feake) Hallett], and said to be a descendant of Wm. Coddington, First Gov. of R. I., and of Thos. Willet, first mayor of New York, and had: (1.) Wm. Willets Cocks, b. 7-24, 1861. (2.) Elizabeth Hicks[8] Cocks, b. 7-5, 1865, dw. at "Beech Hill," Great Neck, L. I., m. at Westbury, L. I., under care of Friends' meeting there, 6-14, 1892, Geo. Alex. Thayer, Jr., of an early New England family, and had a son, Geo. Alex. Thayer, 3d, b. 12-22, 1893. (3.) Frederick Hicks Cocks, (name changed to Frederick Cocks Hicks), b. 3-6, 1872.

COLES.

Robert[1], Mass. Bay, Warwick, R. I., d. 1654, m. Mary[1] Hawxhurst.

Elizabeth[2], m. John[1] Townsend, d. 1669.

Robert[1], d. 1654, m. Mary[1] Hawxhurst.

Nathaniel[2], d. 1712±, m. Martha[2] Jackson, d. 1668.

Nathaniel[3], 1668-1705, m. Rose[1] Wright.

Martha[4], d. 1723, m. Jotham[3] Townsend, d. 1752±.

Nathaniel[3], 1668-1705, m. Rose[1] Wright.

Roseannah[4], 1691-1757, m. 1711 George[3] Townsend, 1687-1762.

Robert[1] d. 1654, m. Mary Hawxhurst.

Anna[2], m. Henry[1] Townsend, d. 1695.

Robert[1], d. 1654, m. Mary Hawxhurst.

Daniel[2], d. 1692, m. Maha-Shalal-Hasbaz[2] Gorton.

Joseph[3], 1675-1767, m. Elizabeth[3] Wright.

Joseph[4], d. 1781, m. 1736, Freelove Weekes.

Elizabeth[5], 1742-1824, m. 1764, Daniel[*] Feke, 1739-1824.

COVERT.

Jacob, Peeks Kill, N. Y., m. Mary Bancker, descended from Teunis Janse Coevert from Hemstede, Holland, settled at Bedford now Brooklyn, L. I.

Mary[2], 1765-1848, m. Robert[6] Feeks, 1766-1830.

DARVALL.

William[1], N. Y. City, m. 1670, Rebecca[2] Delaval.

Frances[2], bap. 1651, m. 30 Mar. 1703, Richard[1] Willett.

DELAVAL.

Capt. Thomas, N. Y. City.

Rebecca[2]. m. 1670, William[1] Darvall.

DICKINSON.

Capt. John[1], Oyster Bay, m. Elizabeth Howland

Elizabeth[2], m. Caleb[2] Wright, 1645-1695+.

DOUGHTY.

Rev. Francis[1], Flushing, m. Bridget ? Stone.

Elias[2], b. 1635±, d. 1690±, m. 1658±, Sarah d. 1726.

Charles[3], b. 1667, m. 1688±, Elizabeth[3] Jackson, 1668±-1758.

Martha[4], m. Samuel[5] Hicks.

FEAKE. *

Robert[1] *Feake*, d. 1662, Saugus, Mass., Greenwich, Conn., m. 1631, Elizabeth[2] Fones.

* Feake, Feke, Feeks, according to period.

John[2] Feke, d. 1724, m. 1670, Elizabeth[2] Prier, 1656-1701.

Hannah[3], 1675-1750, m. 1698, James[2] Cock, 1674-1728.

John[2], d. 1724, m. 1670, Elizabeth[2] Prier, 1656-1701.

Rev. Robert[3], 1683-1773, m. Clemence[3] Ludlam, 1684-1760.

Deborah[4], d. 1794, m. James[3] Cock, 1708-1746.

John[2], d. 1724, m. 1670, Elizabeth[2] Prier, 1656-1701.

Mary[3], 1678-1715, m. 1699, Henry[2] Cock, 1678-1733.

Rev. Robert[3], 1683-1773, m. Clemence[3] Ludlam, 1684-1760.

Charles[4], b. 1718, d. 1799, m. Catharine[4] Tiller, 1719-1805.

Daniel[5], 1739-1824, m. Elizabeth[5] Coles, 1742-1824.

Robert[6] Feeks, 1766-1830, m. Mary[2] Covert, 1765-1848.

Catharine[7], 1793-1875, m. 1816, Clark[4] Cock, 1790-1866.

FONES.

Thomas[1], London, Eng., m. Anna[1] Winthrop, dau. of Adam[1].

Elizabeth[2], m. 1631, Robert[1] Feake, d. 1662.

GORTON.

Samuel[1], R. I., m. Mary Mayplett.

Maha-Shalal-Hasbaz[2], m. Daniel[2] Coles, d. 1692.

HARCUTT.

Richard[1], R. I., m. ________ ________

Susannah[2] Harcourt, m. John Townsend.

Richard[1], m. Elizabeth[2] Potter.

Dorothy[2], will dated 31 of 1 mo., 1739, m. John[2] Cock, b. 22 of 11 m., 1666, d. 1717.

HAWXHURST.

Christopher[1], Oyster Bay, m. Mary[2] Reddough.

Mary[3], m. (1) George[2] Townsend, (2) Abr[2]. Alling.

HICKS.

Robert[1], m. Elizabeth[1] Morgan.

John[2], m. Horod[1] or Hored Long.

Thomas[3], m. Mary (Butler[2]) Washbourne, wid. of John.

Jacob[4], m. Hannah[1] Carpenter.

Samuel[5], m. Martha[1] Doughty.

Mary[6], m. Dr. James[5] Townsend, 1729-1790.

JACKSON.

Robert[1], Hempstead, m. Agnes[1] Washbourne.

Martha[2], m. Nathaniel[2] Coles.

Robert[1], m. Agnes[1] Washbourne.

Col. John[2], m. Elizabeth[3] Seaman.
Elizabeth[3], 1669±-1758, m. 1680±, Charles[2] Doughty, b. 1667.

LUDLAM.

William[1], Southampton, Oyster Bay, m. Clemence ----------.
Joseph[2], d. 1698, m. Elizabeth[3] Townsend.
Clemence[3], 1684-1760, m. Rev. Robert[3] Feke, 1683-1773.

MOTT.

Adam[1], Hempstead, m. Sarah ----------.
Adam[2], 1619-1686, m. 1647, Jane[1] Hulet.
Joseph[3], 1661±-1735, m. Mary (Smith ?).
Jane[4], m. Benjamin[3] Seaman, 1685-1729.
Adam[2], 1619-1686, m. 1647, Jane[1] Hulet.
Adam[3], b. 1649, m. 1678, Mary[2] Stillwell.
Adam[4], m. Elizabeth[4] Mott.
Elizabeth[5], 1720-1781, m. Benjamin[4] Seaman, 1719 1781.
Adam[1], m. Sarah ----------.
Adam[2],1619-1686, m. 1667, Elizabeth Richbill.
Richbell[3], 1668-1734, m. 1696, Elizabeth[3] Thorne, d. 1739.
Elizabeth[4], m. Adam[4] Mott.

PEARCE.

Richard[1], 1615-1678, R. I., m. Susannah Wright, d. 1678+.
William[2], 1664, m. ---------- ----------.
James[3], b. 1700, m. 1723, Elizabeth (Lawrence ?), b. 1705.
Elizabeth[4], 1743-1835, m. 1760, Clark[4] Cock, 1738 1822.

POTTER.

Robert[1], R. I., m. Isabel ----------.
Elizabeth[2], m. Richard[1] Harcutt.

PRIAR. *

Matthew[1], Setauket, Killingworth, m. Mary ----------, d. 1700.
Elizabeth[2], 1656-1701, m. 1670, John[2] Feke, d. 1724.

REDDOUGH.

Henry[1], R. I. and Matinecock, d. 1674 —, m. Mabel[1] Burroughs.
Mary[2], m. 1674 —, m. Christopher[1] Hawxhurst.
Henry[1], m. Mabel[1] Burroughs.
Elizabeth[2], m. 1674 —, Samuel[2] Weekes.

RICHBELL.

John[1], Oyster Bay, m. Ann Parsons.
Elizabeth[2] m. 1667, Adam[2] Mott, 1619-1686.

* Priar or Prier, as per period.

SEAMAN.

Capt. John[1], Hempstead, m. Elizabeth[2] Strickland.
Benjamin[2], b. 1650, m. Martha[3] Titus, 1663.
Phebe[3], d. 1733, m. Jacob[4] Townsend, 1692-1742.
Capt. John[1], m. ? Elizabeth Strickland.
Elizabeth[2], m. Col. John[2] Jackson.
Benjamin[2], b. 1650, m. Martha[3] Titus, d. 1663.
Benjamin[3], b. 1685, d. 1733, m. Jane[4] Mott, 1682-1729.
Benjamin[4], b. 1719, d. 1781, m. Elizabeth[5] Mott, 1720-1781.
Henry[5], 1761-1799, m. 1784, Sarah[4] Billopp, 1765-1811.
Frances Jane[6], 1797-1854, m. 1 Feb., 1817, William W. Townsend, b. 1795, d. 1828.

SIMKINS.

Nicholas[1], Oyster Bay, m. Elizabeth Weekes.
Mary[2], m. 26 Sept. 1678, Samuel[2] Tillear.

SMITH.

Abraham[1], Hempstead, m. ---------- ----------.
Hester[2], d. 1749+, m. 1680+, John[3] Townsend, d. 1705.

STILLWELL.

Nicholas[1], Brooklyn, m. Anne[1] Van Dyke.
Mary[2], m. Adam[3] Mott.
Thomas[1], m. Martha[1] Batieu.
Ann[2], m. Joseph[2] Billopp.

STRICKLAND.

John[1], Hempstead, m. ---------- ----------.
Elizabeth[2], m. Capt. John[1] Seaman.

THORNE.

William[1], Flushing, m. Sarah ----------.
William[2], m. Winifred ----------.
Elizabeth[3], m. 1696, Richbell[3] Mott, 1668 1734.

TILLEY*.

Jan Letelier, of Normandy ?, Bushwick, L. I., m. 1665, Christina Pieters, of Flanders.
Samuel[2] Tillear, m. 26 Sept., 1678, Mary[2] Simkins.
David[3] Tillear, m. ---------- ----------.
Catharine[4] Tilley, 1719-1805, m. Chas[4]. Feke, 1718-1799.

TITUS.

Robert[1] Hempstead, m. Hannah ----------.
Edmond[2], m. Martha[3] Washbourne.
Martha[3], d. 1663, m. Benjamin[3] Seaman, 1650-1773.

* Tiller or Tilley, as per period.

TOWNSEND.

John¹, d. 1669, Oyster Bay, m. Elizabeth² Coles.

George², d. 1697, m. Mary² Hawxhurst.

George³, 1687–1762, m. 18 March, 1711, Roseannah⁴ Coles, 1691–1757.

William⁴, b. 13 Feb., 1716, d. 5 May, 1777, m. Elizabeth³ Cock. b. 14 Dec., 1715, d. 30 Nov., 1794.

Roseannah⁵, 1751–1831, m. 1768, Daniel⁴ Cock, b. 1747, d. 1804.

William⁴, 1716–1777, m. Elizabeth¹ Cock, 1715–1794.

James⁵, b. 16 Apr., 1742, d. 12 Sept., 1798, m. 4 Feb., 1762, Freelove³ Wilmot, b. 25 Feb., 1744, d. 21 of 7 mo., 1809.

William⁶, b. 12 Sept, 1769, d. 23 Aug., 1834, m. 8 Feb., 1792, Margaret⁶ Townsend. b. 6 Feb., 1772, d. 11 Oct., 1818.

William W⁷., 1795–1828, m. 12 Feb., 1817, Frances Jane⁶ Seaman, 1797–1854.

Matilda Katharine⁸, b. 1826, m. 1858, George William⁷ Cocks, b. 1829.

John¹, d. 1669, m. Elizabeth² Coles.

John², m. Susannah² Harcourt, d. 1698.

James³, d. 1729+, m. Audrey³ Almy, b. 1669.

Jacob⁴, 1692–1742, m. Phebe Seaman, 1696–1774.

Dr. James⁵, 1729–1790, m. 1757, Mary Hicks, d. 1796.

Margaret⁶, b. 6 Feb., 1772, d. 11 Oct., 1818, m. 8 Feb., 1792, William⁶ Townsend, 1769–1834.

Henry¹, d. 1695, m. Anne² Coles.

John², d. 1705, m. 1680+, Hester² Smith, d. 1749+.

Jotham³, m. Martha⁴, Coles. d. 1723 —

Freelove⁴, 1721–1744, m. Rev. Walter² Wilmot, 1709–1744.

Henry¹, d. 1695, m. Anne² Coles.

Henry², m. Deborah² Underhill, 1659.

Elizabeth³ ?, m. Joseph² Ludlam, d. 1698.

Henry¹, d. 1695, m. Anne² Coles.

Mary², m. John² Wright.

UNDERHILL.

Capt. John¹, Killingworth, m. Elizabeth Feke.

Deborah², 1659–1698, m. Henry² Townsend.

UNTHANK.

Christopher, R. I., m. Susannah ________,

Mary², d. 1725+, m. Col. Job² Almy.

WASHBOURNE.

William¹, Hempstead, m. Jane ________,

Martha², m. Edmond² Titus.

WEEKES.

Francis¹, Oyster Bay, m. Elizabeth Luther.

Elizabeth², m. Nicholas¹ Simkins.

Francis¹, m. Elizabeth Luther.

Samuel², m. Elizabeth Reddough.

Samuel³, m. Anna ________,

Freelove⁴, m. 1736, Joseph⁴ Coles, d. 1781.

WILLETT.

Richard¹, N. Y. City, m. 30 Mar., 1703, Frances² Darvall, bap. 1681.

Thomas², m. 1737, Elizabeth¹ Lawrence.

Frances³, m. 1762, Col. Christopher⁶ Billopp.

WILMOT.

Alexander¹, d. 1720–21, Southampton, L. I., m. Mary ________

Rev. Walter², 1709–1744, m. Freelove⁴ Townsend, 1721–1744.

Freelove³, b. 25 Feb., 1744, d. 21 of 7 mo., 1809, m. 4 Feb., 1762, James⁵ Townsend, b. 16 Apr., 1742, d. 12 Sept., 1798.

WINTHROP.

Adam³, 1548–1623, m. Anna Browne.

Anna⁴, 1585–6–1618, m. Thomas Fones.

WRIGHT.

Nicholas¹, b. 1619, Oyster Bay, m. Anne ________,

John², m. Mary² Townsend.

Rose³, m. Nathaniel³ Coles, d. 1712+.

Nicholas¹, b. 1619, m. Anne ________,

Caleb², 1645–1695+, m. Elizabeth² ? Dickinson.

Elizabeth³, m. Joseph² Coles, 1675–1767.

LINEAGE OF JOHN COX, JR.,

of 308 W. 19th St., New York City, [of John⁶ Cox, Isaac⁵ Cocks, Joseph⁴ Cock, Samuel³, Henry², James¹].

Isaac⁵ Cocks, s. of Joseph⁴ & Rhoda (Frost) Cock of Crum Elbow, Dutchess Co., N. Y., [of Samuel³, Henry², James¹, and of Isaac & Mary³ (Cock) Frost, James² Cock, James¹], was b. 4 of 5 mo., 1764, at Crum Elbow, N. Y., was a farmer and a Friend; dw. at Clinton, Dutchess Co., N. Y., afterward owned a farm in Yorktown, Westchester Co., near the Croton river, and later, another near Amawalk, Westchester Co., N. Y.; d. in Yorktown, N. Y., 7–26, 1834, buried in Friends' cemetery, Amawalk, N. Y.; chosen elder of Amawalk M. M. 1832, and used to sit at the head of the meeting and was frequently appointed on committees of that meeting. He never voted. His brothers spelled the name *Cocks* and *Cox* and his descendants spell it *Cox.* He m. (1) 11-17, 1790, Phebe Underhill, b. 11-6, 1764, d. in Yorktown, N. Y., 4-24, 1817, dau. of Thomas & Sarah (Weeks) Underhill of Salem, Westchester Co., N. Y., by whom he had 8 children,—Zilpha, Martha C., Thomas, Henry, Jesse, Sarah, Abel and Mary C. He m. (2) at Chappaqua Meeting House, 11-19, 1818, Hannah (Fowler) Thorn, widow of John Thorn and dau. of Stephen & Elizabeth (Dickinson) Fowler, of North Castle, Westchester Co., N. Y., and Manhattan Island. She was b. 10-18, 1778, on Manhattan Island, d. Rush, Monroe Co., N. Y., 4-4, 1862. Isaac[5] & Hannah (Fowler-Thorne) Cocks had 2 children, —John[6] & Stephen.

John[6] Cox, now of Scottsville, N. Y., [of Isaac[5] Cocks, Joseph[4] Cock, Samuel[3], Henry[2], James[1]], b. 8-31, 1819, Yorktown, Westchester Co., N. Y., whence he removed May, 1844, to Chili, Monroe Co., N. Y., and thence in March, 1854, to their present residence, Wheatland, Monroe Co., N. Y., P. O., Scottsville; m. at Peekskill, Westchester Co., N. Y., 10-5, 1842, Mary C. Cunningham, b. 11-15, 1822, North Castle, N. Y., dau. of Oliver & Ann (Mosher) Cunningham, of North Castle, N. Y., and had: (1) Stephen Wm[1]. Cox, b. 2-5, 1844, Yorktown, N. Y., is a farmer; dw. Wheatland, N. Y., P. O., Caledonia; m. at E. Hamburg, Erie Co., N. Y., 3-13, 1867, Catharine R. Hampton, dau. of Asa[4] & Catharine S. (Pound) Hampton, and granddaughter (1) of Wm[3]. & Mary (Pound) Hampton, and (2) of Wm[3]. & Mary (Vail) Pound, of Erie Co., N. Y., (see pp. 9, 13 and 241). She became member of Rochester M. M. of (Hic.) Friends, 6-28, 1872, by certificate from Hamburg M. M; (Children later). (2.) Isaac, b. 3-12, 1846; m. (1) 2-9, 1870, Lydia Lucelia Martin; m. (2) 11-29, 1883, Lucy Ward. (3.) Henry E., b. 10-28, 1850; m. 10-6, 1875, Alice L. Bowerman. (4.) Wm. James, b. 4-2, 1855; m. 3-21, 1876, Amelia Hyde. (5.) John, Jr., b. 11-1, 1860, Wheatland, N. Y.; present address. 308 W. 19th St., New York City, unm.; is recording secretary of the Young Friends' Aid Association of New York, now (1897) in its 21th year of work in assisting the worthy poor of the city. To him we are indebted for valuable data.

HAMPTON.

Wm[3]. Hampton, b. 25 of 12 mo., 1776, dw. Eden and E. Hamburg, N. Y., was a blacksmith, farmer, and sawyer; d. E. Hamburg, N. Y., 23 of 5 mo., 1859, son of Wm[2]. & Sarah (Shotwell) Hampton, and grandson (1) of Abner & Rachel[3] (Webster) Hampton, and (2) of Benj.[4] & Ame (Hallett) Shotwell of Shotwell's Landing (now Rahway), N. J., [of Jno[3]., Jno[2]., Abr[1].], married in Hardwick, N. J., 10 of 10 mo., 1798, Mary Pound, b. 9 of 6 mo., 1777, d. 10 of 8 mo., 1846, dau. of Benj[4]. & Elizabeth (Laing) Pound, [of Elijah[3], John[2], John[1]], and had: (1.) Jacob Hampton, b. 10 of 4 mo., 1799, d. aged about 4 months. (2.) Joseph, b. 21 of 12 mo., 1800, d. E. Hamburg, N. Y., 7 of 10 mo., 1877; m. by Friends' order in Erie Co., N. Y., Rebecca Hampton, b. 21 of 4 mo., 1804, d. E. Hamburg, N. Y., .. of 8 mo., 188 , dau. of Aaron & Jane (Slater) Hampton, of Boston, N. Y. (3.) Benjamin, b. 5 of 1 mo., 1804, Farmington, N. Y., d. aged 4 yrs. 6 mos. (4.) Andrew, (twin), b. 5 of 1 mo., 1804, d. E. Hamburg, N. Y., 5 of 2 mo., 1886, s. p.; m. at Bertie, C. W., 3 of 1 mo., 1856, Elizabeth Pound of Pelham, Ont., dau. of Wm[5]. & Susannah (Crawford) Pound, [of Daniel[4], Elijah[3]. Jno[2]., Jno[1].]. (5.) Asa, b. 20 of 4 mo., 1806, in Farmington, N. Y., removed about 1845 from Eden, N. Y., to E. Hamburg, N. Y., and there d. 23 of 7 mo.. 1886; was an elder among (Hicksite) Friends; m. in Plainfield, (N. J.), Friends' Meeting House, 30 of 11 mo., 1831, Catharine S[6]. Pound, 1810-1889, dau. of Wm[5]. & Mary (Vail) Pound, [of Samuel[4] & Catharine (Webster) Pound, Elijah[3], Jno[2]., Jno[1].]. (6.) John, b. 14 of 4 mo., 1809, d. Junius, N. Y., 28 of 9 mo.. 1884; m. Tamar Lundy, b. 1 of 3 mo., 1814, dau. of Jacob[2] and Anna (Bunting) Lundy, [of Jonathan[1]]. (7.) Hugh, b. 30 of 6 mo.. 1811, d. Wabash, Ind.; m. Julia Ann Kester, b. 25 of 2 mo., 1818, dau. of Stephen & Sarah Kester. (8.) Sarah Ann, b. 3 of 3 mo., 1814, in Eden, N. Y., d. 9 of 2 mo., 1879, s. p.; m. (1) 25 of 7 mo., 1840, Willets Lundy, [of Jesse of N. J.]; m. (2) at Orchard Park, N. Y., 10 of 9 mo., 1874, (as 2d wife) Joseph Willson Kester, son of Samuel & Mary (Willson) Kester. His former wife was Eliza Ann, dau. of Joseph & Sarah (Thorn) Shotwell, of Eden, N. Y. (9.) Wm., b. 27 of 9 mo., 1816, d. Buffalo, N. Y., s. p.; m. 2 of 9 mo., 1855, Betsey Wilcox, a widow. (10.) Mary L., b. 5 of 1 mo., 1819; P. O., Covert, Van Buren Co., Mich.; m. 7 of 4 mo., 1843, Ezra C. Manchester.

Asa[4] Hampton, 1806-1886, of E. Hamburg, Erie Co., N. Y., m. 1831, Catharine S[6]. Pound, 1810-1889, and had: (1.) Mary Ann, b. 2 of 12 mo., 1832, Eden, Erie Co., N. Y., d. E. Hamburg, N. Y., 18 of 7 mo., 1864, unm. (2.) Anna S., b. 2 of 11 mo., 1836, Eden, N. Y., dw. Lobo, Ont., P. O., Coldstream; m. by Friends' order, E. Hamburg, N. Y., 2 of 6 mo., 1855, George O. Zavitz, who became member of Norwich, (C. W.) M. M. of (Hicksite) Friends by certificate, 8 of 9 mo., 1858, son of Henry & Catharine, and had: Mary Eliza, b. in Lobo, C. W., 4 of 9 mo., 1859. (3.) Elizabeth B., b. 2 of 12 mo., 1839, Plainfield, N. J., dw. E. Hamburg, N. Y., P. O., Orchard Park. (4.) Jediah Shotwell Hampton. (twin), b. 10 of 10 mo., 1842, Eden, N. Y., dw. E. Hamburg, N. Y.; m. by David Avery, J. P., Eden, N. Y., 19 of 10 mo., 1868, Mary Elizabeth Willson, b. 30 of 11 mo., 1841, dau. of Gabriel & Sarah K. (Kester)

Willson, [of Eber & Mary (Shotwell) Willson], and had: (a) Merton L., b. 18 of 10 mo., 1871, E. Hamburg, N. Y. (b) Anna May, b. 2 of 2 mo., 1878, E. Hamburg, N. Y., and there d. 25 of 4 mo., 1884. (c) Enos Willson Hampton, b. 29 of 10 mo., 1881, E. Hamburg, N. Y. (5.) Catharine R., (twin). b. 10 of 10 mo., 1842, dw. Monroe Co., N. Y., P. O., Caledonia, Livingston Co.; m. by Wm. Hamilton in E. Hamburg, N. Y., 13 of 3 mo., 1867, Stephen W. Cox, and had: (a) Mary, b. 12-9, 1869. (b) Elizabeth Catharine, b. 3-15, 1872. (c) Wm. H., b. 3-9, 1874. All b. in Wheatland, Monroe Co., N. Y.

William² & Sarah (Shotwell) Hampton (see pp. 91, 95), had: Benjamin³ Hampton [of Wm²., Abner¹], b. 20 of 2 mo., 1775, in Elizabeth, Essex (now Union) Co., N. J., became member of Rochester (N. Y.), M. M. of (Hic.) Friends by certificate from Junius M. M., dated 25 of 12 mo., 1833, m. in a public meeting of Friends at Junius, N. Y., 9 of 12 mo., 1807, Mary (Cox) Jackson, b. 19 of 7 mo., 1768, in Stafford, Monmouth Co., N. J., dau. of Jonathan and Hannah Cox, of Junius, Seneca Co., N. Y., and had: Sarah Lundy Hampton, b. 26 of 3 mo., 1810, in Junius, N. Y., dw. Waterloo, N. Y., when she m., with unity of Junius M. M. of (Hic.) Friends, 26 of 1 mo., 1832, Wm. Jackson, of Rochester, in town of Gates, N. Y., s. of Micajah W. and Catharine (........) Jackson.

Wm. & Sarah (Shotwell) Hampton's dau. Amy⁶ m. Wm. Clifton, and had: Amy⁷ Clifton, who m. Morris Hampton, and had: S. Elizabeth Hampton, who dw. Quakertown, N. J., d. -- March, 1897; m. George D. Leaver, who d. -- Jan., 1897. To her kindness we are indebted for valuable information concerning the life of Benjamin Lundy.

Jacob & Sarah (Shotwell-Hampton) Lundy had Elizabeth Lundy, who m. Abner Willson and had Abijah Willson, the addresses of whose 14 children are as follows: (1.) Ezra Willson, Johnsonsburgh, Warren Co., N. J. (2.) Mary L. Staley, Huntsville, Sussex Co., N. J. (3.) Sarah Lovett, Amity, Orange Co., N. Y. (4.) Elizabeth Lewis, Fredon, Sussex Co., N. J. (5.) Mercy A. Gibbs, Hope, Warren Co., N. J. (6.) Abner Willson, Amity, N. Y. (7.) Amy L. Labar, Sugarloaf, Orange Co., N. Y. (8.) James Willson, ----, Mich. (9.) Amos Willson, Erie, Neosho Co., Kans. (10.) Asa Willson, Erie, Kans. (11.) Belinda B. Willson, Spring Brook, Erie Co., N. Y. (12.) Frank W. Willson, Vancouver, Clark Co., Wash. (13.) Lucy D. Bail, La Fayette, Sussex Co., N. J. (14.) Grace May Willson, La Fayette, N. J.

FROST.

Wm¹. Frost, Shipwright and farmer at Matinecock, L. I., b. England; d. about 1718-19; m., about 1673, Rebecca Wright,

dau. of Nicholas & Ann (........) Wright and divorced from Eleazer Leverich, and had: William² Frost, b. about 1675, d. Nov. 29, 1728, farmer at Matinecock, L. I.; m., about 1700, Hannah Prier, b. 8-22, 1681, d. 12-18, 1771, dau. of John² & Elizabeth (Bowne) Prier, [of Matthew¹ & Mary (......) Priar], and had: Samuel¹ Frost, b. 2-25, 1706, farmer at S. Oysterbay, Peekskill or Crom Pond; m. Keziah ...., and had: Samuel⁴ Frost, b. 10-28, 1736, d. 5-28, 1775, probably farmer in Westchester Co., N. Y.; m. 8-29, 1760, Mary⁴ Cock, b. 7-24, 1741, dau. of Robert³ & .... (........) Cock [of James² & Hannah (Feke) Cock, James¹ & Sarah (........) Cock], and had Samuel R⁵. Frost, b. 8-18, 1775, d. 7-14, 1862, farmer, Yorktown, Westchester Co., N. Y., and Henrietta, Monroe Co., N. Y.; m. 10-18, 1815, Zilpha⁶ Cocks, b. 8-23, 1791, Clinton, N. Y., d. in Henrietta, Monroe Co., N. Y., 5-26, 1873, dau. and eldest child of Isaac³ & (1st wife) Phebe (Underhill) Cock, of Clinton, Dutchess Co., and Yorktown, Westchester Co., N. Y.—members of Amawalk M. M. of Friends—[of Joseph⁴ & Rhoda (Frost) Cock, of Crum Elbow, N. Y., Samuel³, Henry², James¹], and had: Prier⁶ Frost, b. 12-14, 1817, d. 11-8, 1874, farmer, owned his father's farm in Henrietta, N. Y.; m. 12-13, 1843, Millicent Elvira Martin, b. 11-29, 1822, d. 8-29, 1895, dau. of James K. & Fanny H. (Bristol) Martin, of Rush, Monroe Co., N. Y., and had: James Samuel⁷ Frost, b. 10-1, 1854, in Henrietta, Monroe Co., N. Y., is a farmer, owns and occupies his grandfather's farm in Henrietta, N. Y.; P. O., N. Rush, N. Y.; m. (by Rev. Thomas Delamater) in Marshall, Mich., Sept. 27, 1881, Ida May Diver, of Marshall, Mich., b. 3-26, 1855, in Henrietta, N. Y., dau. of Robert & Frances E. (Griswold) Diver, of Henrietta, N. Y., and Marshall, Mich., and had two children: (1.) Edith May, b. 7-17, 1883, in Henrietta, N. Y. (2.) Vincent James, b. 12-14, 1886, in Henrietta, N. Y.

WILLSON.

Robert¹ Willson came from Yorkshire, Eng., with William Penn, in 1682, and settled in Philadelphia, whence he is said to have removed to Burlington Co., N. J., within the limits of Chesterfield M. M. of Friends, where he probably engaged in farming, d. 1709. He m., about 1672, Anne Hogg ?, who came with him to America. Several articles brought with them from their English home, are still cherished as heirlooms in the families of some of their descendants, among them a well-worn Bible which bears on one of its blank leaves the autograph of Robert Willson, in Old English characters. They had 4 children: (1.) Sarah, b. 14 of 12 mo., 1673, d. 1700, buried 30 of 9 mo., 1700, at Chesterfield, Burlington Co., N. J.; m. Cornelius Empson. (2.) Deborah, b. 21 of 9 mo., 1674, d. 1687,

31

buried 18 of 6 mo., 1687, probably at Chester-field, N. J. (3.) Rebecca, b. 14 of 2 mo., 1677, d. about 1760, and probably buried in Friends' Ground at Kingwood (now Quaker-town), N. J.; m. Samuel Large, a minister among Friends. They removed from Burlington Co., in 1729, to Hunterdon Co., N. J., where their 5 children left numerous descendants. (4.) *Samuel² Willson*, b. 1 of 5 mo., 1681, in Scarborough, Eng., removed in 1730 from Burl-ington Co., N. J., to Hunterdon Co., in com-pany with the Emley, Large and perhaps other families, where he purchased of Jacob Doughty a tract of 600 acres of land in Bethlehem Tp. for the sum of £300, the deed bearing date, Jan.

wood. He m., ____ of 11 mo., 1705, Hester or Esther, Overton, b. 10-26, 1682, dau. of Samuel & Hannah (________) Overton. They had 8 children, all born in Chesterfield, Burlington Co., N. J.

James' Willson, b. 21 of 11 mo., 1713, [of Samuel², Robert¹], m. 18 of 9 mo , 1736, Martha³ Laing, b. 1715, dau. of John² & Elizabeth² (Shotwell) Laing, of Piscataway, [of John¹ (p. 127)], and had: *James⁴ Willson*, b. 1-20, 1760, m., 1781, Lucretia Freeman, and had *Samuel⁵ Willson*, b. 11-27, 1782, dw. Franklin Tp., near Kingwood (now Quakertown), N. J., m. Hannah Mason, dau. of John Mason, and had *James⁶ Willson*, b. 11-2, 1811, in Kingwood (now

22, 1730. In 1735 he built thereon a stone dwelling, which is still standing in a fair state of preservation and is still owned and occupied by his descendants, never having passed out of the possession of the family and not until recently out of the name. The Large home-stead was near, and it is related of Samuel Will-son and his sister Rebecca that in their old age they frequently visited each other and played together like children, the one visited always accompanying the visitor on the homeward way as far as "the stile," where they would separate with tears. He was a minister among Friends for many years; d. 19 or 13 of 12 mo., 1761, and was buried in Friends' Burial Ground at King-

Franklin) Tp., Hunterdon Co., N. J., engaged in farming there, and there d., 3-21. 1881, of angina pectoris, m. by Joseph Cougle, J. P., 2-3, 1836, Mary Allen⁵ Laing, b. 8-24, 1810, near Metuchen in Piscataway Tp., Middlesex Co., N. J., d. in Franklin Tp., Hunterdon Co., N. J., 4-14, 1870, of Heart Failure, interred at Quakertown, dau. of David⁵ & Elizabeth (Allen) Laing, of Hunterdon Co., N. J., formerly of Middlesex Co., N. J.,—the former, s. of Jacob⁴ & Rachel (Shotwell) Laing (m. 1780), [of David³ & Mary (Thorne) Laing, John² & Elizabeth (Shotwell) Laing, John¹ & Margaret (________) Laing (p. 127)], and the latter, dau. of John⁷ Allen [of Joseph¹], and had: (1.) Annie E.

Willson, b. 8–26, 1837, near Quakertown, N. J., dw. Vancouver, Wash.; m. 12–13, 1867, W. D. Wolverton, M. D. (2.) Samuel T., b. 1–30, 1840, Hunterdon Co., N. J., m. 1–29, 1870, Victoria Lundy, dau. of George William Augustus Courtney Lundy, called Courtney, and wife Sarah Ann *nee* King, and granddaughter of Amos[3] & Abigail (Stockton) Lundy, [of Isaac[4] & Anna (Large) Lundy, Samuel[3] & Anne (Schooley) Lundy, Richard[2] & Elizabeth (........) Lundy, Richard[1] & Jane (Lyon) Lundy]. (3.) Mary Caroline, b. 11–20, 1842, near Quakertown, N. J., dw. Quakertown, N. J. To her we are indebted for much valuable information presented in these pages. She was m. by Friends' ceremony at her father's residence near Quakertown, 9–19, 1866, to John H[6]. Vail, of Forest Hill, Md., afterward for many years a merchant and postmaster at Quakertown, N. J., s. of Lindley M[5]. & Rachel (Harned) Vail, of Forest Hill, Md., [of James[4], David[3], John[2], Samuel[1]].

Gabriel[3] Willson, b. 23 Nov., 1725, s. of Samuel[2] (1681–1761) & Esther (Overton) Willson, of Hunterdon Co., N. J., [of Robert[1] & Annie (Hogg) Willson, of Burlington Co., N. J.], m. Elizabeth[3] Lundy, b. 10 Mar. (?), 1730, dau. of Richard[2] & Elizabeth (........) Lundy, [of Richard[1]], and had: Gabriel[4] Willson, 1752–1815.

Abner & Elizabeth (Lundy) Willson, the former b. 1785, s. of Gabriel & Keziah (Decker) Willson, [of Samuel], and the latter dau. of Jacob & Sarah (Shotwell-Hampton) Lundy (pp. 91–2, 95), had: (1.) Jacob Lundy Willson, b. 9–11, 1810, in Independence (now Allamuchy), Sussex (now Warren) Co., N. J., d. in Sycamore Tp., Wyandot Co., Ohio, 3–1, 1863, having removed, 1835, from western New York to Wyandot Co., Ohio, was a farmer, a Republican, a member of the Society of Friends; m. in Independence, Warren Co., N. J., 12–7, 1831, Bathsheba P[7]. Shotwell, b. 1811, dau. of Zachariah[6] & Elizabeth (Lundy) Shotwell [of Benj[5]., Benj[4]., John[3], John[2], Abr[1]. (p. 181)]. (2.) Abijah, 1812–1878, m. Margaret Emeline Willson, dau. of Amos & Sarah (Groff) Willson, of Independence, N. J., [of David, Ebenezer]. (3.) Joel Stevenson Willson, 1814–1882, dw. Stark Co., Ill., m. Dulcena Young. (4.) Mercy Stevenson Willson, 1817–1889, wife of Alfred Buckley, of Allamuchy, N. J. (5.) Ezra, b. 1819, dw. Elma, Erie Co., N. Y., P. O. Spring Brook; m., 1842, Anna Ashton Kester, dau. of Arnold & Mary (Kester) Kester. (6.) Lydia Derling Willson, 1821–1866, wife of Jacob Riker, of Tymocty Tp., Wyandot Co., Ohio. (7.) Belinda, b. 1823, wife of Joel Turner Buckley, of Streator, Ill.

Jacob L. Willson, 1810–1863, of Wyandot Co., Ohio, s. of Abner & Elizabeth (Lundy) Willson, m., 1831, Bathsheba P[7]. Shotwell, b. 1811, dau. of Zachariah[6] & Elizabeth (Lundy) Shotwell (p. 181), and had: (1.) Elizabeth Edna, b. 7–9,

1833, in Warren Co., N. J., d. Wyandot Co., Ohio, 4–1, 1863; m. 10–13, 1857, Charles Rouse, of Wyandot Co., Ohio. (2.) Abner, b. 10–12, 1835, d. in the Union Army, 11–17, 1861. (3.) Albert Zachariah, b. 8–20, 1837, Wyandot Co., Ohio, dw. Sycamore Tp., P. O., Deunquat, Ohio, served in the War of the Rebellion; m. 6–16, 1859, Frances Brown, who d. 11–6, 1873. (4.) Levi Lundy Willson, b. 4–16, 1839, served in the Union Army, d. 8–22, 1866, m. 5–3, 1860, Elizabeth Lupton, who d. 4–1, 1873. (5.) George, b. 6–9, 1844, dw. Neosho Co., Kans., with son Levi, P. O., Erie, was a soldier in the war for the Union; m. 8–20, 1865, Margaret Brown; they removed in 1884 to Neosho Co., Kans. (6.) Edwin Samuel, b. 2–16, 1846, dw. Wyandot Co., Kans., served as a Union soldier in the War of the Rebellion, owns the 100 acres first bought by his parents near Sycamore*; m. 3–1, 1866, Eliza C. Price, b. 7–7, 1848. (7.) Walter, b. 5–30, 1854, removed with family in 3 mo., 1884, to Sycamore, Butler Co., Kans., and there d. 3–6, 1885, buried near Sycamore Springs, Kans.; m. 9–10, 1874, Monirah M. Danby, b. 1–25, 1854, near Farmersville, Canada. The widow m. (2) 11 Aug., 1887, Rev. Edward Cameron, Sec'y and Prin. of Preparatory Dept. of Lincoln College, Lincoln, Kans., where her children attended school.

VAIL.

FOUR GENERATIONS IN NEW JERSEY.

The name of the immigrant forefather of the Quaker Vails of the vicinity of Plainfield, N. J., has not been ascertained; but the family was planted in Westchester Co., N. Y., at a very early date, certainly before 1678.—Vail (the name was often anciently written Veal) married Elizabeth ...., who (b. 1657±), d. in Woodbridge, N. J., 3 Nov., 1747, having m. (2) .... Gach, and m. (3) John Griffith. .... and Elizabeth (........) Vail, of Westchester Co., N. Y., had: (1.) Samuel[1] Vail, a synopsis of whose children, grand-children and great-grand-children is here presented. (2.) Martha. (3.) John, Sr., the Quaker preacher. (4.) Daniel. (5.) Arthur. (6.) Thomas.

Samuel[1] Vail, b. 21 of 10 mo. (Dec.), 1678, in West Chester, N. Y., d. Woodbridge, N. J., 26 of 4 mo. (June), 1733; m. (1) Abigail ...., b. 1685±, d. West Chester, N. Y., 14 of 8 mo. (Oct.), 1724, and had:

I. John[2] Vail Jr., (so-called to distinguish him from his uncle, John Vail, the Quaker preacher), b. 21 of 2 mo. (April), 1708, West Chester, N. Y., d. at Plainfield, N. J., 17 of 5 mo. (May), 1754; m. (1) ...., 1731, (between 18 of 9 mo. and 16 of 10 mo.), Margaret[3] Laing, b. 9 of 9 mo., 1710, at old

* The 100 acres bought later is now owned by a granddaughter, Edith V. (Willson) Ranck.

Plainfield, Piscataway Tp., Middlesex Co., N. J., d. before 1751, dau. of John² & Elizabeth (Shotwell) Laing, and granddaughter (1.) of John¹ & Margaret (________) Laing, and (2.) of John² & Elizabeth (Burton) Shotwell, [of Abraham¹ Shotwell], and had:

1. Samuel Vail, b. 1732, d. 12 of 8 mo., 1753.

2. John³ Vail, b. 29 of 6 mo. (Aug.), 1734, near Plainfield, N. J., inherited the homestead—the southern-most part of his father's estate—in Greenbrook, Somerset Co., N. J., and there d. 13 of 1 mo., 1814, buried at Plainfield. On one occasion, during the Revolutionary War, General Washington, with an escort, rode up to his house and engaged his brother-in-law, Edward Fitz Randolph, as a guide to take them to an eminence on the face of the mountain whence a good view of Greenbrook and vicinity could be obtained. The horse of this volunteer guide being in a distant field, an aide or orderly vacated his saddle, which Edward took and led the general and his party to the top of a high rock, since known as Washington's Rock, whence the desired view of the plain below was had. In the meantime a boy had been sent to the pasture for the horse, which the waiting attendant at once mounted and hastened off in pursuit of General Washington and staff. John³ Vail m. (1) 23 of 4 mo., 1760, Catharine Fitz Randolph, b. 20 of 9 mo. (Nov.), 1739, Woodbridge, N. J., d. Greenbrook, N. J., 20 of 3 mo., 1809, dau. of Edward⁴, Jr., & Phebe (________) Fitz Randolph of Greenbrook, [of Edward³, Nathaniel², Edward¹], and had:

(*a*) Margaret Vail, b. 5 of 1 mo., 1762, d. 27 of 2 mo., 1831; m. Benjamin Nichols, of Middlesex Co., N. J., an old Revolutionary soldier, who afterward united with Friends and became very zealous in the work of the Society; after the separation in 1828, he remained with Hicksite Friends.

(*b*) Edward Vail, b. 27 of 3 mo., 1764, dw. Greenbrook, N. J., was " of Bridgewater " when he married at Rahway, N. J., 26 of 12 mo., 1793, Sarah Kinsey of Woodbridge, N. J., who d. at Plainfield. N. J., 2 of 5 mo., 1863, aged 92 yrs., 8 mos., 25 days, dau. of Mootry & Sarah (Fitz Randolph) Kinsey, and granddaughter of Capt. Robert Fitz Randolph.

(*c*) Amos¹ Vail, b. 31 of 7 mo., 1766, m. in Plainfield, N. J., ________, 1795, Phebe Smith, b 13 of 3 mo., 1771, dau. of Abraham³ & ________ Smith, [of Benjamin² & Sarah (Shotwell) Smith, of Samuel¹ & Esther (________) Smith].

(*d*) Isaac Vail, b. 1 of 8 mo., 1770, assisted in building the Plainfield Friends' Meeting House, the centennial of the occupancy of which in 1788 was appropriately celebrated on the 20th of 8 mo., 1888, and built the Rahway Friends' Meeting House in 1803. (See p. ...) Soon after Black Hawk War he settled on a farm near La Port, Ind., and there d. 1 of 10 mo., 1839; was of Somerset Co., N. J. when he m. (1) at Rahway, N. J., 2 of 11 mo., 1792, Sarah Thorn of Middlesex Co., N. J., dau. of John⁴ & Mary (Shotwell) Thorn, [of Abraham³ & Ann (Laing) Thorne, Joseph² & Mary (Bowne) Thorne, Wm¹. & Sarah (________) Thorne.] (See pp. 132–3.) He was of Woodbridge when he m. (2) at Rahway, N. J., 29 of 11 mo., 1810, Sarah Shotwell of Woodbridge, N. J., b. 2 of 1 mo., 1784, dau. of Henry⁵ & Sarah (Dobson) Shotwell, [of Joseph⁴, John³, John², Abraham¹].

(*e*) Nathan⁴ Vail, b. 3 of 5 mo., 1777, Greenbrook, N. J., dw. Plainfield, N. J., and there d. 14 of 5 mo., 1857, was an elder among Orthodox Friends; m. in Plainfield, N. J., 24 of 6 mo., 1801, Annah⁵ Webster, b. 5 of 6 mo., 1783, d. at Philadelphia, Pa., 18 of 3 mo., 1875, dau. of Hugh⁴, Jr., & Sarah (Moore) Webster, [of John³ & Anna (Taylor) Webster, Wm². & Susannah (Cowperthwaite) Webster, Wm¹. & Mary (________) Webster, (see pp. 12–15)], and had nine children. Hugh D⁵. Vail, one of their sons, b. 12 April, 1818, a student at Westown, (Pa.), School, 1833 & '34, a teacher of mathematics there 1838 to 1847; and at Haverford, (Pa.), College, 1848 to 1854; and afterwards from 1860 to 1882, one of the directors of it, residing then in Philadelphia; removed in 1882 to Santa Barbara, Cal.; m. at Rahway, 4 May, 1871, Miriam L. Vail, dau. of Benjamin F.¹ & Martha (Parker) Vail of Rahway, N. J., the former of Benj². & Margaret (Clarkson) Vail, [of John², Samuel¹], and the latter, dau. of Jacob Parker of Rahway, and had 2 sons, born in Philadelphia, Hugh F. R., and Edward R. To his kindness we are indebted for valuable data concerning several early N. J. settlers and their families.

(*f*) Joel¹ Vail b. 7 of 1 mo., 1780, dw. near Greenbrook, N. J., was a farmer, hatter and merchant, d. in Delaware Co., Ohio, ________, 1829, while traveling; m. Catharine K. Miller, whose maternal grandfather was Capt. Robert Fitz Randolph.

3. Daniel² Vail, [of John², Jr., Samuel¹], b. 7 of 1 mo., 1735–6, d. ________, 1823, was member of Plainfield Preparative Meeting of Friends, when he m. (before 16 of 11 mo.), 1774, Mary Tu, and for having m. contrary to Friends' discipline he was disowned by the M. M., 15 of 2 mo., 1775. They had:

(*a*) Prudence Vail.

4. Isaac³ Vail, [of John², Jr., Samuel¹], b. 27 of 11 mo., 1737–8, dw. Basking Ridge, N. J.; m. ________, 1762, (before 15 of 4 mo., '62), " by a priest," for which violation of the discipline of Friends he made satisfactory acknowledgment to the (W., R., & P.,) M. M., 21 of 10 mo., 1762; they had:

(*a*) James Vail, who m. ________ ________.

5. David³ Vail, [of John², Jr., Samuel¹], b. 6 of 4 mo., 1740, dw Greenbrook, Somerset Co.,

N. J., and there d. 7 of 8 mo., 1823, buried at Plainfield, N. J., was a slave-holder, but freed his negroes when other N. J. Friends did the same. He m. at Plainfield, N. J., 23 of 4 mo., 1766, Phebe Jackson, of Woodbridge, N. J., probably the Phebe Vail of Middlesex Co., N. J., who d. 5 of 3 mo., 1820, aged 73 and was buried at Plainfield. David's wife, Phebe, was dau. of Wm. & Prudence (Smith) Jackson, and granddaughter of James & Rebecca (Hallett) Jackson. David³ & Phebe (Jackson) Vail, had:

(*a*) William Vail, b. 4 of 2 mo., 1767, Greenbrook, N. J., dw. New Market, N. J., d. .. of 2 mo., 1837, m. Jemima Cole, of Scotch Plains, N. J.

(*b*) John Vail, b. 4 of 10 mo., 1768, Greenbrook, N. J., and there d. unm.

(*c*) Prudence Vail, b. 6 of 3 mo., 1770, Greenbrook, N. J., and there d. 25 of 9 mo., 1849; m. Samuel Vail, (distinguished as "Ohio Samuel,") 1765–1830, s. of Stephen³ & Sarah (Smith) Vail, [of Stephen², Samuel¹]. Both were elders in Plainfield Friends' meeting.

(*d*) James' Vail, b. 29 of 8 mo., 1772, Greenbrook, N. J., dw. near Plainfield, killed by being thrown from a horse in Rahway, Middlesex (now Union) Co., N. J. ------------; m. 6 of 1 mo., 1811, Rachel Line, b. 26 of 11 mo., 1779, Plainfield, N. J., d. Quakertown, Hunterdon Co., N. J., 29 of 11 mo., 1863, having became member of the (Hic.) Friends' Meeting at Kingwood, N. J., by certificate from R. & P. M. M., dated 25 of 5 mo., 1848, dau. of Henry & Mary (Cole) Line, of Plainfield.

(*e*) Daniel Vail, b. 7 of 4 mo., 1774, dw. Philadelphia, Pa., was a hatter there, and there d. -----------; m. at Greenbrook, N. J., --------, Hannah Marcelius, of --------, N. J.

(*f*) David Vail, b. 7 of 12 mo., 1775, Greenbrook, N. J., dw. Plainfield, Essex (now Union) Co., N. J., d. 2 of 7 mo., 1815, interred at Philadelphia, Pa.; m. 23 of 7 mo., 1794, Elizabeth Webster, called Lizzie, dau. of Wm⁴, & Sarah (Smith) Webster, [of Hugh³, Sr., & Sarah (Marsh) Webster, Wm²., Wm¹., (see p. 13)].

(*g*) Rebecca⁴ Vail, b. 7 of 5 mo., 1778, Greenbrook, N. J., dw. Plainfield, N. J., d. in N. Y. City, --------; m. at Plainfield, 26 of 11 mo., 1794, Marsh⁴ Webster, b. 27 of 8 mo., 1771, Plainfield, N. J., d. 28 of 10 mo., 1819, s. of Hugh³, Sr., & Sarah (Marsh) Webster, [of Wm¹., Wm¹., (see pp. 12–14)], and had: Phebe⁵ Webster, who m. Joel Vail, resided in Ontario Co., N. Y., and had: the late Joseph W. Vail, who m. Elizabeth D'. Shotwell, b. 1823, dau. of Daniel C⁵. & Martha (Pound) Shotwell, [of Manning⁴, Benjamin⁴, John⁴, Daniel², Abraham¹ (see pp. 104, 155 (6)], and had: J. Thompson Vail, real estate agent, Plainfield, N. J.

(*h*) Margaret Vail, b. 18 of 8 mo., 1780, Greenbrook, N. J., d. young. [See (*m*)].

(*i*) Smith Vail, b. 5 of 2 mo., 1782, Greenbrook, N. J., dw. Plainfield, N. J., and there d. 23 of 7 mo., 1855; m. Deborah Marsh, who d. Plainfield, N. J.

(*j*) Phebe Vail, b. 20 of 4 mo., 1783, Greenbrook, N. J., dw. in Crawford Co., Pa., near Meadville; m. at Plainfield, N. J., -----------, Amos Line, b. 21 of 8 mo., 1776, Plainfield, N. J., d. near Meadville, Pa., --------, s. of Henry & Mary (Cole) Line, of Plainfield, N. J.

(*k*) Mary Vail, b. 17 of 1 mo., 1787, Greenbrook, N. J., dw. Boston, Erie Co., N. Y., and there d. 20 of 12 mo., 1811; m. (as 1st wife) Wm⁵. Pound, s. of Samuel⁴ & Catharine (Webster) Pound, of Piscataway, N. J., [of Elijah³, John². John¹]. (See pp. 9–10).

(*l*) Joseph Vail, b. 2 of 3 mo. 1788, m. Mary Fitz Randolph, b. 23 of 5 mo., 1789, dau. of Edward & Mary (Webster) Fitz Randolph and granddaughter of Hugh¹ & Sarah (Marsh) Webster.

(*m*) Margaret (again), b. 18 of 1 mo., 1791, removed with her husband and family from N. J. in 1817 and settled within the limits of Norwich (U. C.) M. M., which meeting she served in the capacity of an overseer for several years; d. at Norwich, C. W., 15 of 5 mo., 1861, an elder among Orthodox Friends (see "Anual Monitor" for 1862, p. 222); m. at Plainfield Friends' Meeting House, --------, Crowel Webster, s. of Hugh⁴, Jr., & Sarah (Moore) Webster, of Norwich, U. C., [of John³, Wm²., Wm¹.].

6. Jacob Vail, [of John⁴, Jr., Samuel¹], b. 3 of 7 mo., 1742, dw. Basking Ridge, Somerset Co., N. J., and afterward, with his nephew, Israel Vail, near the Wind Mill in Westfield, Essex (now Union) Co., N. J., and there d. 8 of 7 mo., 1823, buried at Plainfield, never m.

7. Abraham³ Vail, [seventh son of John₁₁ Jr.], b. 22 of 7 mo. (Sept.), 1744, dw at Green Brook, in Warren Tp., Somerset Co., N. J., built there in 1775—"the year the war broke out in Boston"—what was, for many years, the only two-story house between Green Brook and Brunswick Landing; d. in Barnard Tp. (now North Plainfield), Somerset Co., N. J., 11 of 9 mo., 1824; m. in Friends' Meeting at Woodbridge, N. J., 28 of 8 mo., 1766, or 28 of 9 mo., 1768, Margaret Fitz Randolph, dau. of Edward & Phebe (Jackson) Fitz Randolph and sister to the wife of his brother, John Vail, and had:

(*a*) James Vail, b. 1 of 7 mo., 1769, d. at Greenbrook, N. J., 9 of 5 mo., 1773.

(*b*) Daniel, b. 1 of 5 mo., 1771, d. -------- of 8 mo., 1774.

(*c*) James (again), b. 25 of 1 mo., 1773, dw. Plainfield, N. J., d. 28 of 6 mo., 1850; m. on Long Island, --------, Maria Jackson, dau. of Samuel & Phebe (--------) Jackson.

(*d*) Mercy Vail, b. 19 of 2 mo., 1775, d. Greenbrook, N. J., 13 of 11 mo., 1872, aged 97 yrs., 8 mo., 24 da., never m.

(e) John A'. Vail, b. 9 of 2 mo., 1777, in the neighborhood called Green Brook, was a hatter, dw. Green Brook. near Dunellen, Middlesex Co., N. J., and there d. 28 of 6 mo., 1832, of consumption; m. (1), in Plainfield Friends' Meeting House. 23 of 6 mo.. 1803, Rachel Webster, dau. of Hugh', Jr., & Sarah (Moore) Webster. [of John³, Wm²., Wm'.]; m. (2), in Rahway Friends' Meeting House, 27 of 3 mo., 1817, Deborah Harned. b. 6-16, 1788, at Amboy, Middlesex Co., N. J., aunt to former wife, and dau. of Jonathan & Sarah (Laing) Harned and granddaughter of Jacob Laing [of John³, John'], she d. 12-6, 1861, Plainfield, N. J., of paralysis.

(f) Phebe' Vail, b. 16 of 5 mo., 1779, Green Brook, N. J., d. at Rahway, N. J., 19 of 9 mo., 1866; m. at Plainfield Friends' Meeting House, 31 of 8 mo., 1803, Peter⁶ Shotwell, 1777-1845, of Rahway. N. J., s. of Isaiah³ & Constant (Lippincott) Shotwell [of John', John³, John², Abraham']. (See pp. 119 & 163).

(g) Elizabeth, b. 17 of 2 mo., 1782, Green Brook, N. J., d. Rahway, N. J., 15 of 8 mo., 1866; m. 6 of 6 mo.. 1810, Abel⁶ Shotwell, 1779-1840, of Woodbridge Tp. (now part of Rahway), N. J., brother to Peter Shotwell. (See pp. 84-5 & 119).

(h) Ephraim Martin Vail, b. 4 of 4 mo., 1784, Greenbrook, Warren Tp., Somerset Co., N. J., and there d. 26 of 4 mo., 1878. He was so named for Colonel Ephraim Martin. whose timely interference saved the father from being hung at Morristown for having harbored supposed spies—Tories from Staten Island, who had merely come over for a friendly visit with John Marcelus and lodged in Abraham Vail's barn without permission or knowledge of the owner. He m. at Plainfield. N. J., 21 of 3 mo., 1810, Rebecca Vail, dau. of Samuel' & Prudence (Vail) Vail [of Stephen', Jr., Stephen², Samuel'].

(i) Margaret Vail, b. 23 of 5 mo., 1786. Greenbrook, N. J. d. Rahway, N. J., 22 of 4 mo., 1805, was of Bridgewater, N. J., when she m. 30 of 5 mo., 1804. (as 1st wife). David' Laing. of Woodbridge Tp., N. J.. b. 3 of 1 mo., 1782, s. of Thomas' & Martha (Webster) Laing, [of Isaac², John', John'].

(j) Christiana' Vail, b. 11 of 12 mo., 1788, Greenbrook, N. J., d. 29 of 11 mo., 1871, m. 25 of 10 mo, 1809, Joseph L'. Shotwell, 1787-1871, brother to Peter and Abel. (See pp. 119-120).

The united ages of five members of this family, at time of death, exceeded 144 years, - Christiana, 82; Elizabeth, 84; Phebe. 87; Ephraim, 94, and Mercy. 97. (Average 89). Three younger children died with an aggregate age of 151 years. The relatives of this family spoke of them as "the cousins from under the mountain."

8. Benjamin³ Vail, [of John', Jr., Samuel'], b. 3 of 8 mo., 1745. dw. on a farm in Essex (now Union) Co., near Rahway, N. J., and there

d. 5 of 10 mo., 1820, buried at Plainfield; m. Margaret Clarkson, and had:

(a) Bethiah Vail, b. 8 of 6 mo., 1790, d. --------, unm.

(b) Clarkson, b. 8 of 10 mo., 1792, d. July 31, 1877, was of Woodbridge, Tp., N. J., when he m. (1) at Rahway, N. J., 22 of 9 mo., 1814, Sarah Laing, dau. of Isaac⁴ & Catharine (Kinsey) Laing, of Woodbridge Tp., N. J., [of Isaac³, John², John']; he m. (2) Violetta Morgan.

(c) Christianna Vail, b. 10 of 10 mo., 1794; m. 26 Nov., 1817, Abel Marsh.

(d) Robert Vail. b. 23 of 8 mo., 1799, d. 1881; m. (1) Sarah Marsh; m. (2) --------

(e) Benjamin F'. Vail, b. 17 of 11 mo., 1803, d. Rahway, N. J., 10 Dec., 1866; m. 23 Dec., 1830, Martha Parker.

(f) Abel C. Vail, b. 21 of 5 mo , 1806, d. --------, unm.

(g) Margaret C. Vail, b. 8 of 11 mo., 1808; m. Robert Henderson.

John² Vail Jr., 1708–1754, of Plainfield, N. J., s. of Samuel' & Abigail (--------) Vail of West Chester, N. Y.; m. (2) -------- --------, 1751±. (before 17 of 8 mo., '51), his former wife's sister, Mary³ Laing, b. 1717, contrary to the discipline of Friends, for which fault they were disowned, 15 of 10 mo. (Dec.), 1751; but on 19 of 5 mo., 1757, Mary made satisfactory acknowledge of her fault to the M. M. and was restored to membership. A committee composed of Solomon Hunt, Francis Bloodgood, Samuel Marsh, Joseph Shotwell, Abner Hamton, and Shobel Smith, reported to the Woodbridge M. M., on 17 of 7 mo., 1755, recommending a continuance of the prohibition to marry a deceased wife's cousin. On 20 of 10 mo., 1773, James Shotwell of Plainfield Preparative Meeting, (son of John), was dealt with by the M. M., for having been present at a marriage consummated contrary to the rules of the discipline of Friends. John², Jr., & Mary (Laing) Vail, had:

9. Joseph Vail, b. 12 of 6 mo., 1752, d. unm. His stepfather, Samuel Hedger, & wife, on the 15th of 2 mo., 1764, requested that the latter's son, "Joseph Vail, be taken under notice of Friends," i. e., into membership, in W., R., & P. M. M. Joseph Vail and 3 of his 7 older half-brothers, John, David and Abraham, occupied adjoining farms in Somerset Co., N. J., on the westerly side of the Greenbrook road. His other 4 half-brothers, Isaac, Daniel, Jacob and Benjamin Vail, owned farms at Basking Ridge, near the residence and valuable estate of Lord Wm. Alex. Sterling.

10. Christianna Vail, b. 10 of 12 mo., 1753, d. 1776, s. p.; m. 28 of 2 mo., 1776, John Webster, Jr., s. of John³ & Anna (Taylor) Webster, [of Wm.³, Wm.'].

11. Stephen³ Vail, s. of Samuel' & Abigail (--------) Vail, dw. near Greenbrook, N. J.,

whence he removed to the west and left descendants principally in Ohio. He m. --------, 1733-4, [passed meeting 17 of 11 mo. (Jan.), 1733-4], Esther Smith, b. 1713, dau. of Benjamin & Sarah (Shotwell) Smith, and granddaughter (1) of Samuel & Esther (--------) Smith and (2) of John[2] & Elizabeth (Burton) Shotwell, [of Abraham' Shotwell], (see pp. 125-7), and had:

1. Thomas Vail, b. 9 of 1 mo. (Mar.), 1734-5. On the 19th of 2 mo., 1756, "complaint was made [to the Woodbridge M. M. of Friends], that Stephen Vail [had] employed a person in the place of his son who was prest to go to ye frontears in order to build block houses."

2. Stephen Vail, b. 23 of 6 mo., 1738, d. 14 of 7 mo., 1738.

3. Stephen[3] Vail, Jr., (again), b. 19 of 10 mo., 1739; m. (1) --------, 1761, (between 11-19 & 12-16), Rebecca Jackson; m. (2) 26 of 10 mo., 1763, Sarah Smith, who d. 31 of 8 mo., 1769, dau. of Shobel Smith,—probably the Sarah Smith, b. 2 of 9 mo., 1720; and had:

(a) Samuel' Vail, b. 20 of 10 mo., 1765, called "Ohio Samuel;" dw. Green Brook, Somerset Co., N. J., and there d. 12 of 4 mo., 1830; resided near his grist-mill and saw-mill, and owned a saw-mill at Coon Town; was also a clothier. His fulling-mill was the first cloth-dressing establishment in that part of the country, and the carding-machine in connection with it was a great convenience to the inhabitants, as the farmers' families then made their own cloth. He m. 21 of 11 mo., 1787, Prudence' Vail, 1770-1849, dau. of David[3] & Phebe (Jackson) Vail, [of John[2], Jr., Samuel'].

(b) Moses Vail, b. 24 of 8 mo., 1767, member of Chesterfield M. M., by certificate from R. & P. M. M., dated 18 of 11 mo., 1784.

(c) Shobel or Shubal Vail, b. 13 of 6 mo., 1769.

Stephen[3] Vail, b. 1739, [of Stephen[2], Samuel'], m. (3) 1771, (before 6-19, '71), his former wife's cousin, for which violation of Friends' discipline they were disowned by the W., R., & P. M. M., 18 of 9 mo , 1771; they had:

(d) Rebecca Vail.   (g) Mary.
(e) Aaron.   (h) Hugh.
(f) Randall.   (i) Catharine.

4. Abigail Vail, b. 14 of 2 mo., 1742, was of Somerset Co., N. J., when she m. at Plainfield, N. J., 23 of 11 mo., 1763, Thomas Fitz Randolph, of Middlesex Co., N. J., b. 21 of 10 mo., 1740, s. of Richard & Elizabeth (Corlies..) Fitz Randolph, and grandson of Catharine nee Hartshorne.

5. Abraham Vail, (called Black Abraham, to distinguish him from his cousin, Abraham', s. of John[2], Jr.), b. 25 of 5 mo., 1746, removed about 1793, to western Pennsylvania, settling at Redstone and becoming member of Friends' Meeting at Westland, Pa., by certificate from R. & P. M. M., dated 4 of 7 mo., 1793, for himself; wife, Margaret; children, Benjamin and Mary—then of age and clear with respect to marriage engagements—and younger children, Margaret, Samuel, Stephen, Catharine and Taylor. Abraham m. --------, 1768. (between 9-21 and 10 19, '68), or probably in 1766, (see I. 7, p. 245 ante), Margaret Fitz Randolph, dau. of Capt. Robert & Catharine (Taylor) Fitz Randolph, and granddaughter of Catharine nee Hartshorne.

6. Sarah Vail, (twin of Abraham), b. 25 of 5 mo., 1746.

III. Samuel Vail, (s. of Samuel' & Abigail).

IV. Phebe Vail, was murdered by a British soldier during the Revolutionary War; m. Daniel Turner, who d. before the Revolution; both left wills but no issue.

V. Thomas[2] Vail, settled in Westchester Co., N. Y., m. Mary Griffin, and had 10 children whose records, however, we have not obtained.

VI. Isaac Vail.

VII. Joseph.

VIII. Abigail.

Samuel' Vail, 1678-1733, m. (2) Apr. 8, 1725, Sarah, dau. of Matthew Farrington, and had:

IX. Matthew Vail, who d. 18 of 4 mo., 1766.

X. Sarah.

XI. Elizabeth.

Samuel' Vail's brother, John' Vail, Sr., the Quaker preacher, also left descendants in N. J.; among them was Alfred Vail, the distinguished electrician, to whose researches we are indebted for valuable data.

Lindley M'. Vail, of Forest Hill, Md., s. of James' & Rachel (Line) Vail, [of David[3], John[2], Samuel'], m. 12-24, 1835, Rachel Harned, b. 9-3, 1813, who became member of Friends' Meeting at Upper Springfield, by certificate from R. & P. M. M. (Hic.), dated 4-20, 1836, dau. of John & Phebe (Laing) Harned, (m. 1811), of Amboy, N. J., the former, s. of Jonathan & Sarah (Laing) Harned, and the latter (b. 1790), dau. of Jacob' Laing, [of David', John[2], John'], and had: John H[6]. Vail, b. 12-28, 1844, near Quakertown, N. J., lived 1865-7, at Forest Hill, Md., but returned to Quakertown the year after his marriage; was a merchant there; in politics a republican, and for 15 years, postmaster at Quakertown, N. J., member of the Society of Friends; m. by Friends' ceremony at the residence of the bride's father near Quakertown, N. J., 9-19, 1866, Mary Caroline' Willson, b. 1842, dau., of James[2] and Mary A. (Laing) Willson, of Franklin Tp., Hunterdon Co., N. J., [of Samuel[5], James', James[3], Samuel[2], Robert'], and had: (a) Willis W. Vail. (b) Evangeline. (c) James L.

Amos' (b. 1766) & Phebe (Smith) Vail, [of John' & Catharine (Fitz Randolph) Vail, John[2] & Margaret (Laing) Vail, Samuel' & Abigail (--------) Vail], had: Jonah' Vail, b. 8-6, 1799, at Green Brook. Somerset Co., near Plainfield, N. J., and there d. 6-7, 1880, interred at

Plainfield, was a hatter and farmer at Green Brook; m. by Friends' ceremony, at Plainfield, N. J., 5-3, 1819, Rachel Pound, b. 2-21, 1799, in Middlesex Co., N. J., d. Green Brook, N. J., 12-16, 1881, of pneumonia, interred at Plainfield, dau. of Samuel[5] & Susannah (Webster) Pound, [of Zachariah[4], Elijah[3], John[2], John[1]], and had: (*a*) Theodore Vail, who d. in infancy. (*b*) Sidna P., b. 6-30, 1821, Green Brook, N. J., m. 5-27, 1841, Edward R. Vail, a hatter. (*c*) Theodore (again), b. 7-8, 1823, d. Plainfield, N. J., 12-13, 1887, was teacher and store-keeper; m. 5-15, 1845, Phebe Harned. (*d*) Jane Dell Vail, b. 8-5, 1825, Green Brook, N. J., m. 5-16, 1845, Abram R. Vail, a farmer and nurseryman, who dw. Quakertown, N. J., s. of John A[4]. & (2d wife) Deborah (Harned) Vail, [of Abraham[3] & Margaret (Fitz Randolph) Vail, John[2], Samuel[1]]. (*e*) Adelbert, b. 5-31, 1834, clerk in bank and in store, m. (1) 6-17, 1874, Cornelia; m. (2) Gertrude Adams. (*f*) Amos, b. 5-28, 1836, is a truck-farmer, m. 6-28, 1880, Lina Sutton. (*g*) Isabella R., b. 9-19, 1839, is unm. All 7 b. at Green Brook.

John A[4]. Vail, 1777-1832, of Middlesex Co., N. J., [of Abraham[3] & Margaret (Fitz Randolph) Vail, John[2] & Margaret (Laing) Vail, Samuel[1] & Abigail (........) Vail], by 1st wife, Rachel, *nec* Webster, had: (1.) Hugh W. Vail, b. 8-7, 1804, near New Market, N. J., d. Plainfield, N. J., 10-13, 1879.

John A[4]. Vail, 1777-1832, [of Abraham[3], John[2], Samuel[1]], by 2d wife, Deborah, *nec* Harned, 1788-1861, had: (2.) Jonathan H. Vail, b. 2-23, 1818, near New Market, Middlesex, Co., N. J., was a tailor and clothier, afterward a daguerreotype operator, d. at Three Mile Run near New Brunswick, N. J., 6-15, 1852, buried at Plainfield, m. (1) Margaret Laing; m. (2) Catharine Outkelt. (3.) Gilbert, b. 10-23, 1819, d. Keokuk, Iowa, 6-5, 1855, was a stave maker, formerly in a woolen mill; m. May Mount. (4.) Rachel W., b. 3-23, 1821, d. Plainfield, N. J., 9-5, 1860, m. (as 1st wife) George R[4]. Pound, of Plainfield, [of Samuel L[5]., Samuel[4], Elijah[3], John[2], John[1]]. (5.) Abram Randolph[5], b. 2-16, 1823, near New Market, N. J., is a farmer and nurseryman at Quakertown, N. J., m. 5-16, 1845, Jane Dell Vail, b. 1825, dau. of Jonah[5] & Rachel (Pound) Vail, [of Amos[4], John[3], John[2], Samuel[1]]. (6.) John Elwood Vail, b. 5-12, 1824, d. Dover, N. J., 2-22, 1896, was a truck-farmer, and at one time weigh-master at iron mines, Dover, Morris Co., N. J., m. 6-18, 1848, Rachel Brotherton. (7.) Jacob L., b. 3-10, 1831, a machinist, m. Susan Brown.

Samuel[4] Vail, 1765-1830, of Green Brook, N. J., s. of Stephen[3] & Sarah (Smith) Vail, [of Stephen[2] & Esther (Smith) Vail, Samuel[1] & Abigail (........) Vail], m. 1787, Prudence[4] Vail, 1770-1849, dau. of David[3] & Phebe (Jackson) Vail, [of John[2], Jr., Samuel[1]], and

had, among other children, *Moses[5] Vail*, b. 4-5, 1796, at Green Brook, in Warren Tp., Somerset Co., N. J., removed in spring of 1834, from Green Brook, N. J., to Elba (now Oakfield), Genesee Co., N. Y., and thence in 1865, to Lobo, Middlesex Co., Ont., and there d. 3-12, 1871; m. (1) in Plainfield, N. J., 9-25, 1816, Mercy[6] Pound, who d. 1850±, dau. of Samuel[5] & Susannah (Webster) Pound, of Sandy Hill, Green Brook, N. J., [of Zachariah[4], Elijah[3], John[2], John[1]]. They and their 8 minor children, Prudence, Samuel, Emeline, Eli, Susan, Phebe, Sarah Elizabeth, and Jonah, became members of Rochester M. M. of (Hic.) Friends, by certificate from R. & P. M. M., dated 20 of 11 mo., 1734. He m. (2) (by Friends' ceremony) in Pittsford, N. Y., 3-26, 1853, Harriet (Toby) Wood, b. 12-17, 1795, d. Lobo, Ont., 7-13, 1880, wid. of Rufus Wood. They became members of Norwich, (Ont.), M. M. of (Hic.) Friends by certificate, 9 of 8 mo., 1865. Of this family (of Moses[5] Vail, b. 1796). (5.) Susan Webster[6] Vail, b. 5-16, 1827, in Essex (now Union) Co., near Green Brook, N. J., dw. Lobo, Ont., P. O., Coldstream; m. by Friends' ceremony in E. Oakfield, N. Y., 2-2, 1847, Daniel Zavitz, s. of Jacob & Elizabeth[5] (Pound) Zavitz, [of Daniel[4] Pound, (see p. 8), Elijah[3], John[2], John[1]]. (7.) Sarah Elizabeth[6] Vail, b. 1-6, 1830, Green Brook, N. J., dw. Lobo, Ont., P. O., Coldstream; m. by Friends' order at the residence of John Cornell in Mendon, N. Y., 1-23, 1853, Isaac Zavitz of Lobo, C. W., s. of Jacob & Elizabeth (Pound) Zavitz. (9.) Ephraim Martain[6] Vail, b. 10-21, 1838, in Elba (now Oakfield), N. Y., dw. E. Oakfield, a farmer and fruit-dryer, elected town-assessor of Oakfield, 1885, and at expiration of term, re-elected for three years; appointed postmaster at E. Oakfield, in Jan., 1892; m. (1) Nov. 10, 1858, Mary Elizabeth Nash, b. Oct. 18, 1837, at Pine Hill in the town of Barre, Orleans Co., N. Y., d. in Oakfield, N. Y., Dec. 19, 1864, dau. of Whitman & Elizabeth (Begerall) Nash, of E. Oakfield, N. Y., formerly of Wheatfield, Niagara Co., N. Y. He m. (2) in Medina, N. Y., Dec. 21, 1865, Christabelle Stewart.

Ephraim M[6]. & Mary E. (Nash) Vail, of E. Oakfield, N. Y., had: (*a*) Carrie Belle, b. Apr. 21, 1860, Oakfield, N. Y., dw. Alabama, Genesee Co., N. Y., m. in Medina, N. Y., Nov. ..., 1882, Joseph Ellis, b. in Barre, N. Y. (*b*) Clara Estella, b. July 2, 1861, Oakfield, N. Y., dw. Elba, N. Y., m. (by Rev. Charles E. Sweet, of Elba, N. Y., a minister of the Society of Friends), in Oakfield, N. Y., 9-24, 1886, Andrew Balfour, b. in Scotland. (*c*) Henry Amerisa[7] Vail, b. July 18, 1864, Oakfield, N. Y., dw. E. Oakfield, N. Y., m. (by Rev. Charles E. Sweet), in Oakfield, N. Y., 9-24, 1886, Anna D. Dillingham, eldest dau. of Stephen N. & Emeline E. (Porter) Dillingham, of N. Oakfield, N. Y., (see p. 117), had: Ephraim S. Vail, b. May 21, 1889.

1789-1839,

ANTI-SLAVERY EDITOR, LECTURER AND TRAVELER,

Son of Joseph and Elizabeth (Shotwell) Lundy, of Hardwick, N. J.

FROM MINIATURE PAINTED IN 1829, BY A. DICKINSON.

BENJAMIN LUNDY, THE PHILANTHROPIST.

HIS ANCESTORS, DESCENDANTS, OTHER NEAR RELATIVES, AND A SKETCH OF HIS LIFE AND PUBLIC SERVICES.

Richard[1] Lundy,* a member of the Society of Friends, came from Devonshire, Eng., and settled in Bucks Co., Pa. He was in New England from 1676 to 1682. In 1485 he took a patent for 200 acres of land in Bucks Co., Pa. He m. (1), in 1684, Elizabeth Bennet, who d. 6-14, 1687. He m. (2) at the Falls M. M., 4-21, 1691, Jane Lyon, who had come to America with Wm. Penn's steward, who lived at "Penn's Manor," in Bucks Co., Pa., near the Falls Meeting.

From "Arrivals in Bucks Co., Pa., prior to 1687," in the *Pennsylvania Magazine of History and Biography*, Vol. 14, page 232, we quote the following: "Richard Lundy of Axminister, in the Co. of Devon, son of Sylvester Lundy, of the said town in old England, came in a Catch from Bristol (the master, Wm. Browne) for Boston in New England, in the 6th mo., 1676, and from thence came for this river [Delaware] the 19th of the 3rd mo., 1682. Elizabeth Bennet, daughter of Wm. Bennet, late of the Co. of Bucks, and now wife to the aforesaid Richard Lundy, came from Longford, in the Co. of Middlesex, in the ship Concord, of London, the master, Wm. Jefferay, arrived in this river in the 8th mo., 1683. Richard and Elizabeth were married in 1684 and she died 6-14, 1687. Richard married 2nd, Jane Lyon, of Bucks Co., Pa., 4-21, 1691, at Falls Mo. Meeting, and their son, Richard[3], was born 3-20, 1692."

Jane Lyon is said to have come to America with James Harrison, who was Wm. Penn's steward and lived at Pennsbury near the Falls Meeting, and, as Jane Lyon may be supposed to have shared in the vicissitudes of the Harrison family, we quote the following from "Watson's Annals of Philadelphia and Pennsylvania in the Olden Time," Vol. 1, page 47: "The Harrison and Pemberton families [intermarried] came over together among 50 passengers in the ship Submission, Capt. James Settle, from Liverpool. The terms of passage were £4 5s. for all persons over twelve years of age, for all children £2 2s. 6d., and for all goods, £30 per

ton. Their contract was 'to proceed to Delaware river or elsewhere in Pennsylvania to the best conveniency of freighters.' It may serve to know the execution of such voyages to learn that by distress of weather, they were landed in the 'Potuxen River in Maryland,' whence they came to Philadelphia and proceeded thence to Pennsbury neighborhood, where they settled and occupied places of distinguished trust. When James Harrison and his son-in-law, Phineas Pemberton, first entered Philadelphia on horseback, from Choptank in Md., the latter records that at that time (Nov., 1682,) they could not procure entertainment there for their horses; 'they therefore spancelled them' and turned them out in the woods! They sought them next morning in vain, and after two days search they were obliged to take a boat to proceed up the river to Bucks Co. One of those horses was not found till the succeeding January!"

Richard[2] Lundy, called Richard Lundy, Sr., of Hardwick, N. J., b. 20 of 3 mo., O. S., 1692, s. of Richard[1] & Jane (Lyon) Lundy of Bucks Co., Pa. On the 8 of 4 mo., 1749, Richard Lundy, Sr., was appointed an elder of the meeting at Great Meadows (Hardwick), by Kingwood (now Quakertown, N. J.,) M. M; settled at Buckingham, Pa.; removed thence to Berks Co., (near Reading), Pa., becoming member of Exeter M. M. at Maiden Creek, 9-24, 1737, by cert. from Buckingham M. M. Ten years later, 8-8, 1747, he and his wife, Elizabeth, with some minor children, became members of Bethlehem (afterward called Kingwood, now Quakertown, N. J.), M. M., by certificate from Exeter M. M. They settled at Hardwick (then in Morris Co., afterward Sussex now Warren Co.), the meeting there being a branch of Bethlehem (Kingwood) M. M. He d. there 28 of 2 mo., 1772.*

---

* The fact that the name, Richard Lundy, appears in several successive generations makes it often difficult to discriminate between their respective records and traditions. One account states that Richard[1] Lundy was mainly "instrumental in establishing three churches in the wilderness," the first at Buckingham, Bucks Co., Pa., the second at Plumstead, Pa., the third at Hardwick, Sussex (now Warren) Co., N. J., but this was undoubtedly Richard[2], Sr., son of Richard[1].

* Mr. J. Wilmer Lundy of Mt. Holly, Burlington Co., N. J., (to whom we are indebted for valuable data, especially relating to descendants of Joseph[4] Lundy, [of Thomas[3], Richard[2], Richard[1]]), states that Richard Lundy, from Falls Meeting in Bucks Co., Pa., first settler at what was long known as Great Meadows in Sussex Co., N. J., built on a bluff which comes boldly up to the Meadows. The house was back (north and east) from the Meadows, a quarter of a mile from what is now known as the "Egypt School-house." In 1886 the site of the graveyard on the old place was still plainly visible. The meeting-house was rebuilt of stone about three miles up the valley, near the head waters of the stream that drained the Meadows, and the name of the meeting was changed from Great Meadows to Hardwick.

From the records of Kingwood M. M., the following memorial has been copied:

CONCERNING OUR ANCIENT FRIEND AND ELDER, RICHARD LUNDY.

He was son of Richard and Jane Lundy of Bucks county in Pennsylvania, professors of the truth with us, born 20th of 3 mo., 1692, a man much esteemed among Friends and others, being of a meek and quiet spirit, exemplary in life and conversation, and a pattern of plainness and simplicity, diligent in attending meetings for worship and dicipline, duly observing the hour appointed; and in contribution for the service thereof gave freely according to his ability. He often gave up to attend monthly, quarterly and yearly meetings with great willingness, even in his declining years, until the indisposition of his wife rendered that service impracticable. He was an affectionate husband, a tender father, and kind friend, punctual and just in his dealings among men, evidencing to the world that he was concerned to do to others as he would have others do to him. His house was freely opened for those who traveled in the work of the ministry, whose company he greatly valued, and often cheerfully traveled with such as a guide to other meetings. He lived in the fear of the Lord, and was much concerned that love and unity might be obtained among Friends, and deeply affected when anything of a contrary nature arose to obstruct it. In his last illness, which was but short, he entirely refused the help of any physician, signifying his resignation to the Divine will, whether in life or death, and continued in a patient frame of mind, when sensible, till his departure, which was on the 28th of 2d mo., 1772, aged near 80 years; and although our loss is great, we are comforted in the hope that he has gone to inherit the crown immortal which is laid up for all those who love and fear the Lord. He was decently buried in Friends' burying-ground at Hardwick the 29th of the same [month], attended by a large number of Friends and others.

Signed by order of s'd meeting at Hardwick, 13th day of the 8th mo., 1772, by

JACOB SMITH, Clerk.

Richard², Sr., 1692-1772, and wife, Elizabeth (-----------) Lundy, of Hardwick, N. J., had certainly sons, Jacob and Samuel, and were probably the parents also of Richard, Jr., Joseph, Thomas, John, Mary & Martha, Elizabeth & Margaret. Upon this assumption the third generation is recorded as follows:

I. Mary³ Lundy was of Buckingham when she m. with approval of Chesterfield M. M. in 6 mo., 1734, Robert² Willson [of Samuel², Robert¹]; they became members of Bethlehem (N. J.) M. M. by certificate from Exeter (Pa.) M. M., granted 28 of 11 mo., O. S., 1747-8.

II. Richard³ Lundy, Jr., m. at Exeter, Pa., in 7 mo., 1739 (l. l. 6-30, 1739), Ann³ Willson [of Samuel², Robert¹]. They produced a certificate of membership in Bethlehem (afterward called Kingwood) M. M., 12 of 4 mo., 1746, from Exeter M. M. It is said that one Richard

Lundy d. 7 of 11 mo., 1757, and was buried at Hardwick, N. J.

III. Joseph, m. at Exeter, Pa., in 1743 (l. l. 1-31, 1743), Susanna Hutton, became members of Bethlehem M. M., 6-12, 1745, by certificate from Exeter M. M.

IV. Jacob³, became member of Bethlehem M. M., 12 of 6 mo., 1745, by certificate from Exeter M. M.; m. in 1748, Mary Willson; passed Kingwood Meeting 8-13, 1748.

V. Thomas³, b. 14 of 6 mo., 1725, became member of Bethlehem M. M., 3-13, 1745, by certificate from Exeter M. M.;* m. at Hardwick, N. J., in 1750, Joanna Doan; passed Meeting 3-10, 1750.

VI. Samuel³, of Hardwick, N. J., m. (1) 1751, (declared intention 7-19, 1751), Anne Schooley.

VII. John, member of Bethlehem (Kingwood) M. M., 1-14, 1751, by certificate from Gwynedd M. M. (Montgomery Co., Pa.).

VIII. Martha Lundy, member of Bethlehem (Kingwood) M. M. by certificate from Exeter M. M., granted 12-28, O. S., 1744-5, the date when Thomas Lundy obtained a like certificate.

IX. Elizabeth Lundy, m. at Hardwick, N. J., 1749, Gabriel Willson.

X. Margaret, m. at Hardwick, N. J., 1750, John Willson, s. of Samuel.

IV. JACOB³ LUNDY'S BRANCH

[of Richard², Richard¹, (pp. 91-2, 240 (?))].

Jacob⁴ Lundy, Jr., of Hardwick, N. J., b. 7-30, 1751, d. 3-22, 1806, s. of Jacob³ & Mary (Willson) Lundy of Great Meadows (Hardwick), N. J., [of Richard², Richard¹],† was member of Kingwood M. M., when he m. 9-25, 1783, Sarah (Shotwell) Hampton, b. 1748, wid. of Wm. Hampton, and dau. of Benj⁴, & Ame (Hallett) Shotwell, of Essex Co., N. J. From Friends' Miscellany," Vol. VI., 1835, pp. 141-3, we take the following:

JACOB LUNDY, 1751-1806.

"Jacob Lundy was descended of sober, honest, and respectable parents, Jacob and Mary Lundy, of the Society of Friends, members of Hardwick monthly meeting, New Jersey. He was a dutiful and affectionate son, and lived with his parents in much harmony, and in the decline of life, he was a comfort and staff for them to lean upon. May others be engaged to go and do likewise, that they may reap the reward of an approving conscience, which appeared to be his happy experience. Being for some time in poor health, he told his physician

---

*This is the earliest Lundy name found on Kingwood M. M. records, which date from 1744. Thomas & Joanna were probably parents of the Thomas Lundy, Jr., who m., in 1779, Elizabeth Stockton. One Dr. Thomas Lundy, a minister among Friends, had brothers, Jacob and Eli.

†His is the first Lundy name mentioned in the minutes of Rahway & Plainfield M. M., and is 1st given in connection with his application respecting marriage with Sarah (Shotwell) Hampton, 5-20, 1783. In A. V. Shotwell's copy of the book of minutes, under date of 9-18, 1783, this name is erroneously given as Jacob Laing.

to speak his mind plainly, for he did not fear. After he was confined to his room, he remarked to those present, that he did not expect to go out until he was carried out. About two weeks before his decease, he desired to have his children sent for, his step-daughter being one of them, to whom he had extended a parental care, and to whom he expressed himself tenderly, saying, 'Dear child, I am glad to see thee again;' and repeated it twice. He appeared to bear his bodily suffering, which was great, without a murmur,—was very patient and quiet, as though his day's work was done, except bearing the pain of the mortal body; yet sometimes, when in great distress through oppression, he would say, 'what can be done? I fear I am not patient enough.'

"He was favored throughout with his rational faculties without much change; and, near half an hour before he departed, he fell into a quiet sleep, and drew his breath shorter and shorter, until he expired without a sigh or groan, or the least motion, so calm and easy that death seemed disarmed of his terrors. At this solemn period, his aged mother standing by, bore this testimony, 'Why should we wish his stay, seeing his way is made so easy.'

"He was an example of piety and virtue; and in early life, was called upon to fill very important stations in the Society. He was for many years, clerk of the monthly meeting. In 1772, he was chosen to the station of an Elder; the duties of which he was careful to fulfill with dignity and uprightness, to the end of his days. In the year 1783 he was married to Sarah, the widow of William Hampton, of Rahway; she being a minister to whom he was a helpmate in her christian exercises; and when she was concerned to travel on Truth's account, he endeavored to open the way for her to fulfill the work she believed herself called unto, by assisting her freely.

"Jacob Lundy also traveled in the service of Truth, on his own concern, to visit Friends in their meetings for discipline. In the second month of the year 1801, he was furnished with a minute of the unity of his friends, to attend a few meetings for discipline, in the remote parts of Pennsylvania.—Again, in 1805, the monthly meeting set him at liberty to attend Redstone Quarter, and the monthly meetings composing it, stating in his certificate, that he was 'an elder in good esteem.'

"He was very diligent in the attendance of all our religious meetings, those near home as well as monthly, Quarterly, and Yearly Meetings; encouraging his family also in this important duty. He was a careful neighbor, and careful over his own house to make them comfortable. He was of a tender spirit, so that, at times, when reading, or hearing others read the Bible, he has appeared to be affected, even to tears. He was ever ready to entertain strangers, particularly those who were traveling on Truth's account, who found him kind and hospitable, to the comforting, as well as refreshing of the weary, so that oft times, the visitors and the visited have had to rejoice together, feeding, as it were, at the banqueting table of heavenly love."

Jacob[4] & Sarah (Shotwell Hampton) Lundy, had: (a) Mary, b. 6-26, 1784, m. (1) John Stevenson; m. (2) David[4] Willson, Jr., who dw. in Ontario Co., N. Y., s. of David[3] & Mary (Ware) Willson, [of Ebenezer[1]]. (b) Elizabeth, b. 11-10, 1787, d. in Independence, N. J., 3-16, 1838; m. in Hardwick Friends' Meeting, 6-8, 1808, Abner Willson, s. of Gabriel & Keziah (Decker) Willson, of Independence, N. J., [of Samuel]. (c) Lydia, d. about 1815, m. Thomas Brotherton, b. 2-16, 1786, s. of Wm. & Sarah (Dell) Brotherton.

Jonathan[4] Lundy,[*] brother to Jacob, Jr., m. Rebecca Heaton, and had: (a) Jacob, b. 7-11, 1784, dw. Eden and Junius, N. Y., d. about 1818; m. Anna Bunting, sister to Levi, of Eden, N. Y., [of Israel]. (b) Tamer, b. 3-27, 1786, d. Galen, Seneca (now Wayne) Co., N. Y., 7-3, 1818, m. 3-1, 1808, (as 1st wife) Thomas[5] Shotwell, 1786-1857, of Galen, N. Y., s of Benjamin[5] & Bathsheba (Pound) Shotwell, (p. 96). (c) Eli, dw. Independence (now Allamuchy), N. J., d. 1887±, aged about 90, m. --------- Dickinson.

<h3>V. THOMAS[3] LUNDY'S BRANCH,</h3>

<h4>[of Richard[2], Richard[1]].</h4>

Joseph[4] Lundy, b. in Hardwick, N. J., 3-29, 1762, probably s. of Thomas[3] and Joanna (Doan) Lundy [of Richard[2], Richard[1]], dw. for a time in Hardwick, Sussex Co., N. J., whence, in 1805, he, with his 2d wife and family, went down into Burlington Co., N. J., and settled on the north bank of Rancocas River, where his grandson, Joseph[6] Lundy (s. of Richard[5]) now lives, obtaining deed to the "plantation" there in 1810, and there d. 1-13, 1846. The homestead at Rancocas was one of the stations on "the underground railway." He m. (1), at Rahway, N. J., 4-26, 1787, Elizabeth[4] Shotwell, b. 1762, dau. of Benj[3]. & Ame (Hallett) Shotwell, of Shotwell's Landing (Bricktown, now part of Rahway), N. J., [of John[1], John[2], Abr[3]. (p. 93)], and had: (a) Benj[5]. Lundy, the eminent anti-slavery leader, b. 1-4, 1789, in Hardwick Tp., Sussex Co., N. J., d. of bilious fever in Lowell, La Salle Co., Ill., 8-22, 1839, and was buried in the graveyard adjacent to the old Clear Creek (Hicksite) Friends' Meeting House, 1½ mi. from the new. The graves of some of his grandchildren are near by. (Fuller sketch and descendants later.) His eldest and only living child, Susan M. (Lundy) Wierman, who, with her son Isaac P. Wierman and family, lives near the old Clear Creek Meeting House, has an excellent miniature of her father, painted by A. Dickinson in Baltimore, in 1820, showing his fine features, blue eyes and light curly hair, with a countenance indicating the philanthropist. Through the kindness of the family we are pleased to be able to present to our readers a half-tone reproduction of this portrait. His grandnephew, J. Wilmer Lundy, of Mt. Holly, N. J., has a

---

[*] Called by one correspondent "Uncle to Anti-Slavery Benjamin."

smaller picture of him which shows a slight deformity in the left hand between the thumb and forefinger.

Joseph⁴ Lundy, 1762–1846, [of Thomas³(?), Richard², Richard¹], m. (2) 1–15, 1795, Mary Titus, and had one more son, Richard, and six daughters, all now deceased, viz.:

(b) Abigail. b. 9–30, 1795, d. ----, m. (as 2d wife) Daniel Woolston, and lived till her death in a house built on the old place at Rancocas.

(c) Richard⁵ Lundy, b. 7–30, 1797, in Sussex Co., N. J., d. ----, m. ----, Mary Ward,* and had:

(I) George W⁶., m. Maria Haines, and had, among other children: (1.) Mary, who m. Joseph Burrough, (2.) G. Howard, (3.) Ellen.

(II) Edith⁶, m. (1.) John H. Bryant (no issue); m. (2.) Isaac S. Wright, and had: (1.) Walter Scott Lundy Wright; (2.) Mary Ellen, m. George Betts; (3.) Ruth Anna.

(III) Joseph⁶ Lundy, m. Mary Evans, and had: (1.) Maurice E., m. Laura Thomson; (2.) J. Wilmer, to whom we are indebted for valuable data concerning this branch, dw. Mt. Holly, Burlington Co., N. J., m. Bessie Roberts.

(IV) Charles, m. (1.) --------, m. (2.) --------, (no issue).

(d) Elizabeth, b. 6-2, 1799, d. 9–21, 1840, unm.

(e) Phebe, b. 2–6, 1802, d. --------, m. 12 8, 1825, Wm. Hilton, and had 7 children:

(I) Joseph⁶ Hilton, m. (1.) --------; m. (2.) --------; he had: (1.) Mary; (2.) Emma, who m. Clifford Budd; (3.) Annie, d. unm.; (4.) Joseph, m. Etta Moore; (5.) Hannah.

(II) Lydia, d. young.

(III) Ellen M.

(IV) Deborah L.

(V) Caroline Hilton, m. Isaac Lippincott.

(VI) Titus, d. young.

(VII) Abigail W⁶., m. Edward Sutton, and had a son, Edward.

(f) Lydia⁵ Lundy, b. 7–25, 1804, d. --------, m. Joel Wireman, and had 3 daughters who live in Pennsylvania, viz.:

(I) Hannah.

(II) Lucretia.

(III) Phœbe.

(g) Deborah, b. 4-29, 1806, at Rancocas, Burlington Co., N. J., dw. at Moorestown and there d. 5–7, 1896, m. Ezra Walton (no issue).

(h) Asseneth, b. 2–27, 1808, d. 8–6, 1809.

(i) Mary⁵ Lundy, b. 3–26, 1811, d. --------, m. Wm. Barnard, and had:

(I) Joseph, d. young.

(II) Mary Ella, dw. in Pennsylvania.

(III) Philena, dw. Pennsylvania.

VI. SAMUEL³ LUNDY'S BRANCH,

[of Richard², Sr., & Elizabeth (--------) Lundy of Great Meadows (Hardwick), N. J., Richard¹ & Jane (Lyon) Lundy of Buckingham, Pa.].

* Their descendants, with one exception, live in Burlington Co., N. J.

Concerning Samuel³ Lundy we quote from the Armstrong Record: "Samuel Lundy was collector of Sussex County for 13 years, 1759–64, 1767–76. In 1765 there was a great scarcity of bread-stuff throughout Sussex County, and the Legislature decided to loan money to the sufferers to buy food and seed, and appointed Samuel Lundy on a committee to supervise the loaning of the provincial funds. He was collector of Independence Township and was a judge of the court of common pleas of Sussex County, having been appointed on October 27, 1772, by Gov. William Franklin. He had eleven children."

Judge Samuel³ Lundy of Independence, Sussex Co., N. J., [of Richard², Richard¹], m. (1), in the autumn of 1751, Anne Schooley, and had:

1. Isaac⁴, dw. Hunterdon Co., N. J., m. Anna Large, of Hunterdon Co., N. J., and had: Amos⁵, b. 3–26, 1778, near Great Meadows in Sussex (now Warren) Co., N. J., d. near Quakertown, Hunterdon Co., N. J., m. Abbey (or Abigail) Stockton. Elizabeth⁵ Lundy. b. 10–11, 1779, d. in Independence (now Allamuchy), N. J., about 23 Nov., 1856, aged 77; m. Eli Willson, s. of Samuel & Deborah (Collins) Willson of Independence, N. J., Amos & Abbey (Stockton) Lundy had Amy, a teacher who dw. near Clinton, Hunterdon Co., N. J., m. Hugh Exton.

2. George⁴, m. with the concurrence of Kingwood (Hunterdon Co.) & Hardwick (Sussex) M. Ms., 1780, Esther Willson, [of Samuel³, Samuel², Robert¹], and had 9 children, 7 of whom m. and left families living in different states, among them David⁵ Lundy, b. Oct. 8, 1791, d. Sept. 19, 1853, m. in the winter of 1824–5, Sarah Wildrick, and had 5 children, 17 grandchildren and 23 great-grandchildren, the 4th of the 5 children being Esther Ann, b. Jan. 10, 1836, Independence (now Frelinghuysen), N. J., dw. there; P. O., Johnsonburgh, Warren Co., N. J., m. Richard Turner⁴ Armstrong, s. of John³ & Lydia (Kirkpatrick) Armstrong, [of George² & Sarah (Hunt) Armstrong, Nathan¹ & Euphemia (Wright) Armstrong], and had 3 sons, among them Wm. Clinton Armstrong, of New Brunswick, N. J., author of "A Genealogical Record of Descendants of Nathan Armstrong, an Early Settler of Warren Co., N. J.," (200 pp.,) with brief notices of associated families.

3. Daniel⁴, d. in Sussex Co., N. J., about 1818, m. Elizabeth Laing, dau. of John⁴ & Hannah (Webster) Laing, [of Samuel³ (?), Wm²., John¹], and had: (a) Edna⁵ Lundy, second wife of Zachariah⁶ Shotwell, [of Benj⁵., Benj.⁴, John³, John², Abr¹., (pp. 96, 181–2)]. (b) Daniel, Jr., who m. his cousin, Anna Laing, dau. of John⁵ & Achsah (Lundy) Laing, and granddaughter (1) of John⁴ & Hannah (Webster) Laing, and (2) of Samuel & Sarah (Willets) Lundy; she m. (2) Joseph Gardner of Elba (now Oakfield), N. Y., (p. 31). (c) Hannah

Lundy, b. 2-27, 1789, d. Galen, N. Y., 3-26, 1843, m. 12-13, 1819, Thomas⁶ Shotwell, 1786-1857, [of Benj⁵., Benj⁴., John³, John², Abr¹. (pp. 96, 172-3)]. (d) Anna, m. in Hardwick Friends' meeting, Jesse Dell, of Randolph, N. J., s. of Thomas Dell, the surveyor, and had 2 sons.

Judge Samuel³ Lundy, of Independence Tp., Sussex (now Warren) Co., N. J., [of Richard², Richard¹], m. (2) Sarah Willets, and had:

4. Ann, b. 8-10, 1766, m. (1) John Patterson, (2) John Hance.

5. Levi⁴ Lundy, b. 3-24, 1770, in Sussex (now Warren) Co., N. J., learned the blacksmith trade in early life, but poor health, a few years later, forced him to change his occupation for that of a farmer; he removed from Sussex Co., N. J., to Galen, Seneca (now Wayne) Co., N. Y., but a few years later returned to N. J., becoming member of Hardwick & Randolph M. M., by certificate from Junius, (N. Y.), M. M., dated 5-22, 1820, which mentions also his wife Sarah, son Willits, and minor granddaughters, Sarah L., Bathsheba P., and Huldah D., children of Zachariah⁶ Shotwell. He removed in 1834 from Warren Co., N. J., to Belle Vernon, Wyandot Co., Ohio, and there d. 3-26, 1850. He m. Sarah Tomer, b. ---------, in Sussex, (now Warren) Co., N. J., united with Friends after her marriage, d. Wyandot Co., Ohio, 6-9, 1856, aged 92 (?), buried beside her husband in Friends' grounds, near Sycamore, Ohio, dau. of C------ & Elizabeth (Webster) Tomer, the former of German descent. Levi⁴ and Sarah (Tomer) Lundy, had: (a) John who m. (1) ------- -------, m. (2) Elizabeth Willson, dau. of Gabriel & Grace (Brotherton) Willson, and had many children, among them, Sarah, b. 5-24, 1815, Independence, N. J., d. there 9-17, 1852; m. there 3-12, 1835, (as 1st wife) Jesse Adams, of Independence (now Allamuchy), N. J., s. of Joseph and Amy (Lundy) Adams, of the same township. (b) Elizabeth⁵ Lundy, b. 6-27, 1792, Sussex, now Warren Co., N. J., d. Galen, Wayne Co., N. Y., 12-13, 1816, m. in Hardwick Friends' Meeting house, (as 1st wife) Zachariah⁶ Shotwell, 1788-1857, s. of Benjamin⁵ & Bathsheba (Pound) Shotwell, (pp. 96, 181). (c) Christiana. (d) Willits.

6. Edith, b. 6-9, 1773, dw. near Log Jail, (now Johnsonburgh), N. J., m. Samuel Laing, s. of John & Hannah (Webster) Laing.

7. Samuel, b. 5-18, 1775, removed from Hardwick, N. J., to Junius (now Waterloo), N. Y., locating near the Junius town line, and there d. of a cancer; m. in N. J., Elizabeth⁵ Shotwell, 1781-1857, dau. of Benj⁵. & Bathsheba (Pound) Shotwell, (pp. 95-6).

8. Achsah⁴, b. 3-21, 1777, dw. Junius, N. Y., d. 9-26, 1854, m. (1) John Laing, s. of John & Hannah (Webster) Laing; m. (2) in Junius, N. Y., 9-27, 1827, Wm⁵. Shotwell, s. of Benj⁴.

& Ame (Hallett) Shotwell, of the Landing, (p. 94).

9. Jesse, b. 8 10, 1779, dw. Independence, N. J.; m. (1), -------- Bunn, and had many children; m. (2), in Independence (now Allamuchy), N. J., Mariam Adams, dau. of Joseph, and had 6 more children; removed with 2d wife to Upper Canada, where her grandfather resided, near Pelham, they becoming members of Pelham M. M. (Hic.) by certificate from R. & P. M. M., dated 1-17, 1839, also 3 minor children, Elizabeth, Ozias, & Joseph.

10. Sarah, b. 6-26, 1781, dw. Independence, now Allamuchy, N. J., m. Samuel Lundy, of Muncy, Pa., called "Muncy Sammy."

11. Amy, b. 9-20, 1785, Independence (now Allamuchy) Tp., Sussex (now Warren) Co., N. J., d. there; m. in Hardwick Friends' Meeting there, Joseph Adams, who d. there in 8 mo., 1827±.

THOMAS¹ LUNDY'S BRANCH (CONTINUED).

Line of Benjamin², Joseph¹ (pp. 251-2, ante).

It has been truly remarked that "There are periods in the history of our country which we would almost be glad to forget. There are periods, the history of which has not been properly written; and the life and times of Benjamin Lundy will come under this head." Horace Greeley in his "History of the American Conflict," (Vol. I, p. 111), opens an excellent account of the life of this devoted leader of the cause of emancipation (condensed from a biography by Thomas Earle) with these words: "Benjamin Lundy deserves the high honor of ranking as the pioneer of direct and distinctive anti-slavery in America." In the *Northern Monthly* (New York and Newark, Vol. II, No. 5, March, 1868, p. 501), appeared an account of his life and relations with his disciple and associate, William Loyd Garrison, from the pen of Dr. A. E. Snodgrass. Briefer articles of interest have appeared in other periodicals, and in a sketch of William Loyd Garrison, by Sarah K. Bolton, in her book "Poor Boys Who Became Famous," (p. 159), there is a short account of Lundy to which we are indebted for a few particulars. He was slightly built but his indomitable will raised him above many difficulties. He had no advantages of education save those afforded by the common schools, but was imbued with a keen thirst for knowledge and read eagerly such books as were within his reach.

From an article in *The Cosmopolitan*, New York, for May, 1889, by Frank B. Sanborn, of Concord, Mass., (author of a Life of John Brown), re-printed in *Friends' Intelligencer and Journal*, of Fifth Month, 18 and 25, 1889, (pp. 308-10, 325-7), we copy the following account of the

LIFE AND CHARACTER OF BENJAMIN LUNDY.

There is something in Quakerism exceedingly favorable to philanthropy, and the New Jersey Quakers appear to have been the most persistent anti-slavery men in America. John Woolman, setting forth from his humble home at Mount Holly, before 1750, traveled south and north, showing kindness to the negroes, and bearing testimony against slavery. Even earlier than he, an eccentric English Quaker, Benjamin Lay, tormented the meetings in New Jersey and Pennsylvania by violent and theatrical declamations against negro slavery. It was the Quakers of Philadelphia who stood with Franklin as members of an abolition society there in 1775, or earlier; but neither this society nor others of the same sort accomplished much for emancipation until another New Jersey Quaker, Benjamin Lundy, took the field about 1818, as a missionary of emancipation, and planted the seeds of that great movement which, under Garrison, Phillips, John Brown, Gerrit Smith, and other courageous leaders, finally achieved, in war, the downfall of American slavery. The name of Lundy is remembered, but that is almost all that the public generally know of him. He deserves a better biographer than he has found, for his life was romantic, adventurous, and full of danger and hardship. The road taken by Garrison before 1830 was, in fact, "Lundy's Lane," for into that straight and narrow path did it turn aside from the time that Benjamin Lundy, in 1827-8 9, visited Boston and addressed himself to the heart and conscience of his young disciple. In *The Liberator* of September 20, 1839, Garrison noticed the death of Lundy, and said:

"To Benjamin Lundy, more than to any other human being, am I indebted for having my attention called to the wretched condition of the slaves in this liberty-worshiping, slavery-idolizing country. He it was who first informed, quickened, inflamed my mind on the subject of American slavery, and by whom I was induced to consecrate my life to the overthrow of that dreadful system of iniquity. If, therefore, anything has been achieved in the cause of liberty through my instrumentality, let him have all due credit. But I am not the only person who has to acknowledge the personal impulse that was given by his benevolent example and earnest entreaty. Thousands stand ready to testify how much they are indebted to him, under God, for their conversion to the side of emancipation, from a state of total apathy to its success."

That this was no mere obituary compliment, but literally and exactly true, will appear when we see who Lundy was, and what he had accomplished before he ever saw Garrison, as well as what they did together, and what share Lundy had in directing the attention of the world to the true character of the Texan revolt from Mexico, and the annexation of Texas to the United States. Benjamin Lundy was born January 4, 1789, at Hardwick, Sussex County, in New Jersey—now a township of six hundred people in Warren county, which, about 1820, was set off from the old county of Sussex. At the time of his birth there were but twenty thousand people in the whole two counties—mostly farmers, mechanics, and small traders, and with many Quakers among them. Sussex is the extreme northwestern county of New Jersey, extending along the Delaware river from Orange county in New York to Northampton county in Pennsylvania; and Hardwick is not far from the romantic scenery of the Delaware Water Gap. Lundy's English and Welch ancestors came early to America, and branches of the family have been found in North Carolina, Pennsylvania, and wherever the Quakers settled. Richard Lundy was living at Burlington, N. J., in 1822, Thomas Lundy at Rockford, N. C., the same year, and at Huntsville, N. C., in 1833—no doubt brothers or cousins of Benjamin Lundy.* His own family were not rich, and he received but little education, though he afterward taught himself a good English style, with some smattering of Latin, French and Spanish. At the age of nineteen he emigrated to Wheeling on the upper Ohio River, then a town of but a thousand or two inhabitants, where he learned the trade of a saddler, and about 1810 set up in business for himself, accumulating a small property by industry and thrift. Wheeling was then one of the great thoroughfares of the domestic slave trade; the breeders of Maryland and Virginia, and the kidnappers of Delaware, New Jersey, and Pennsylvania, sending their chained coffles of negroes and mulattoes down the river from that point. During Lundy's four years' residence in Wheeling he was a constant witness of the horrors of the traffic. Twenty years later, in November, 1832, he said of Wheeling:

"That was the place where his youthful eye first caught a view of the 'cursed whip' and the 'hellish manacle,' where he first saw the slaves in chains forced along like brutes to the Southern markets for human flesh and blood! Then did his young heart bound within his bosom, and his heated blood boil in his veins, on seeing droves of a dozen or twenty ragged men, chained together and driven through the streets, *bareheaded and bare-footed, in mud and snow*, by the remorseless 'SOUL SELLERS,' with horsewhips and bludgeons in their hands!! It was the frequent repetition of such scenes as these, *in the town of* WHEELING, *Virginia*, that made those durable impressions on his mind relative to the horors of the slave system which have induced him to devote himself to the cause of of *Universal Emancipation*. During an apprenticeship with a respectable mechanic of that

* Richard was a younger half brother to Benjamin[5]; Thomas of N. C., was brother to Joseph[4].—A. M. S.

place, he was, by these and other means, made acquainted with the cruelties and the despotism of slavery, as tolerated in this land; and he *made a solemn vow to Almighty God*, that, if favored with health and strength, he would break at least one link of that ponderous chain of oppression when he should become a man."*

Lundy was eleven years older than John Brown (who was born May 9, 1800), and therefore his vow against American slavery was naturally registered earlier than Brown's, say in 1809. But it was not long after this same period (during the war with England, 1812–15) that Brown, then a mere boy, was led, as he says in his autobiography,† to "declare or swear eternal war with slavery." A friend of John's, a slave boy, "very active, intelligent, and good feeling," was beaten before the lad's eyes "with iron shovels, or anything that first came to hand." This brought John to reflect, he says, "on the wretched, hopeless condition of fatherless and motherless slave children. He sometimes would raise the question, *Is God their father?*" A like question rose in the heart of Lundy, and the principles of his humane and devout religion soon taught him how it should be answered. He left slave holding Virginia, moved, and settled at St. Clairsville, Belmont county, Ohio, still pursuing his saddler trade, and there, in 1815, he organized an emancipation society, which, beginning with himself and a few other members, soon grew to five hundred. This was the first anti-slavery association organized in the United States during the present century. It was called the "Union Humane Society," and became the parent of many others. The older abolition societies founded by Franklin and other Philadelphia Quakers (1775), by Jay and the colonists of New York (in 1785), and by the Quakers, of New Jersey, Delaware, Maryland, Virginia, Rhode Island, etc., from 1788 to 1795, had gone to sleep with their fathers. Lundy's relatives in New Jersey had, no doubt, belonged to some of these organizations; and he notices with satisfaction, in 1833, that "the patriarch, Benjamin Lay, lived to witness the abolition of slavery by that very society (the Quakers) which almost unanimously condemned him for advocating abolition."‡ But with the spread of slavery and of cotton-planting, the early enthusiasm of the eighteenth century abolitionists died out. Franklin was in his grave; Jefferson had just written to Edward Coles (Aug. 25, 1814), —"I have overlived the generation with which mutual labors and perils begot mutual confidence and influence. The hour of emancipation is advancing. This enterprise is for the young; for those who can follow it up and bear it through to its consummation; it shall have all my prayers, and these are the only weapons of an old man." Jefferson was then seventy-one. His young friend did check the spread of slavery over Illinois, and those other young men and boys, Benjamin Lundy, John Brown, Garrison, and Gerrit Smith, Wendell Phillips, Charles Sumner, Abraham Lincoln, Whittier, and Theodore Parker—all living when Jefferson wrote—did in their turn "follow up and bear through to its consummation" the cause of liberty. It was less than a year after Jefferson's letter was written when Lundy organized his emancipation society on the Ohio river, and began to dispel the apathy which had caused even the sanguine temper of the great Virginia democrat to despair.§

A few years of domestic quiet on the banks of the Beautiful river alone remained to Benjamin Lundy. In 1818 he came to the resolution to sell all he had and follow his Master. He joined with Charles Osborn at Mount Pleasant, near St. Clairsville, in the management of a journal called *The Philanthropist*, and to qualify him for this he went to St. Louis in 1819 to dispose of his stock in the saddler's trade, and put himself in funds. It took him a year or two to do this, and to struggle as he could against the admission of Missouri as a slave state, which was carried by Henry Clay in 1820. His property was sold at a ruinous sacrifice, and he returned to Ohio to find that *The Philanthropist* had also been sold. Meanwhile Elihu Embree, a Tennessee Quaker, who in 1820 had begun a monthly publication against slavery (*The Emancipator*), at Jonesborough, Tenn., had died, just as Lundy was planning to aid him. He, therefore, established a paper of his own, with an absurd but memorable title (*The Genius of Universal Emancipation*), at Mount Pleasant, and issued his first number July 4, 1821. It was begun without a dollar of capital, with only six subscribers, and with a hired printer, for in 1821 Lundy had not learned the "art preservative of arts." For a time he walked each month twenty miles to Steubenville (where young Edwin Stanton, then seven years old, was growing up to torment the slave oligarchy) and brought back to Mount Pleasant the whole edition of his monthly on his back, from the printing office where it was

---

* This passage from *The Genius of Universal Emancipation*, then printed in Washington, is given with the Italics, capitals, and exclamation points of the writer, and is a good example of his style, both of writing and printing, at the age of forty-three.

† "Life and Letters of John Brown" (Roberts Brothers, Boston), page 14. The incident narrated must have happened not very far from Wheeling.

‡ *Genius of Universal Emancipation*. Vol. XII., p. 201. The passage occurs in a notice by Lundy of Rev. George Bourne, a Presbyterian, who was living in 1833. A Presbyterian clergyman in Ohio had lately informed Lundy "that he once stood alone in Bourne's favor, when he was called before a council under a charge of heresy, in combating the sin of slave-holding. He was condemned—as was *the apostle of emancipation, Benjamin Lay, at an early period by the Quakers*." Then follows the passage above.

§ "Your solitary but welcome voice, is the first which has brought this sound to my ear," wrote Jefferson to Coles in the same letter; "and I have considered the general silence which prevails on the subject as indicating an apathy unfavorable to every hope. I had always hoped that the generous temperament of youth, analogous to the motion of their blood, and above the suggestion of avarice, would have sympathized with the oppressed wherever found, and proved their love of liberty beyond their own share of it."

put in type. Stanton told Henry Wilson* that Lundy was a frequent visitor at his father's house, and that "he had often sat on his knee when a child and listened to his words."† Before July, 1822, Lundy removed his journal to Greenville, Tennessee, where it was printed for some years on the press of Elihu Embree's deceased *Emancipator*, and where he learned to set type himself and became a reasonably good printer. He traveled the five hundred miles from Mount Pleasant to the East Tennessee mountains on foot, leaving his wife and children to follow him later in the year 1822. He remained in Greenville for two or three years, and then removed his journal to Baltimore, where he was living in 1827, when he made his first visit to New England and found young Garrison ready to receive his instruction at Boston.

The twelve monthly numbers of *The Genius of Universal Emancipation* for the year July, 1822–June, 1823, lie before me as I write. It is a magazine of sixteen double column octavo pages, each page containing some eight hundred words, and the whole second volume (which this is) making one hundred and ninety-two pages. There are a few rude engravings on wood or copper—one twice used, representing a slave coffle, with the slave-trader on horseback, brandishing a whip, following a little cart full of black pickaninnies, while half a dozen full-grown blacks follow the horseman, one of them carrying the Stars and Stripes. Over this cut is the motto: "HAIL COLUMBIA! HAPPY LAND," and beneath it, "SHALL THY FAIR BANNERS O'ER OPPRESSION WAVE?"

Reference is made to a preceding page, on which, from a Kentucky newspaper, (*The Western Citizen*), appears this statement, signed "Philanthropist": "Having business in Paris, (Ky.), on Tuesday, 17th inst., I there witnessed a scene more shocking to humanity than any that has ever come within my notice. I there beheld between seventy-five and a hundred miserable wretches galling under the yoke of despots, doomed to leave their homes, their country, and their friends. Chained and guarded, they were driven, like other stock, from their native land. They were paraded on the public square, in front of the court house, the seat of justice. Over their unhappy heads *that banner waved* under which our forefathers fought and bled for the liberty and independence which they attained," etc. It is quite possible that this scene was witnessed by Lundy himself; for Paris, the chief town of Bourbon county, is on the road from Greeneville to Cincinnati, which the Quaker missionary printer had frequent occasion to travel, as he founded

anti-slavery societies and collected subscriptions for his magazine. It was also one of the routes by which the Virginia slave-breeders sent their human cattle to the southwest. This traffic, beginning early in the century had increased by 1822 to several thousand slaves in a year. In 1832 it was estimated to be six thousand a year from Virginia alone, and in 1836 rose to forty or fifty thousand.

While such "incendiary" matter was coming out in East Tennessee, Lundy's newspaper and cause had agents, whose names he published, in twelve of the slave-holding states and territories,—at Baltimore, Richmond, Winchester, Wheeling, Louisville, Nashville, St. Louis, Little Rock; at Huntsville, Ala., Pensacola, four towns in North Carolina, and even one agent in South Carolina. In 1832 he had twenty-nine agents in ten of the slave states. And in the interval from 1820 to 1830 he had perambulated a large portion of the south, besides twice visiting Hayti; and from 1830 to 1835 he twice visited Texas, where he hoped to establish colonies of free colored persons under the anti-slavery laws of Mexico. In 1830 he said in his *Genius*, then publishing at Baltimore, where Garrison was his associate:

"I have, within ten years, sacrificed several thousand dollars of my own hard earnings; have traveled upward of five thousand miles on foot, and more than twenty thousand in other ways; have visited nineteen of the states of the Union" (there were then but twenty-four), "and held more than two hundred public meetings, with the view of making known our object; and in addition to this have performed two voyages to the West Indies, by which means the liberation of a considerable number of slaves has been effected, and I hope the way paved for the enlargement of many more." And he added, with pardonable pride: "There is not another periodical work published by a citizen of the United States, whose conductors *dare* treat upon the subject of slavery as its nature requires and its importance demands." This was a year before Garrison began to print his *Liberator* in Boston, and after the early emancipation organs —*The Abolition Intelligencer*, in Missouri, a newspaper in North Carolina, etc.,—had been silenced.

What, then, was the bodily presence of this hero, who almost alone had, for a dozen years, sustained the contest against negro slavery in the United States? Garrison, writing in 1828, a year after he had seen Lundy, said: "Instead of being able to withstand the tide of public opinion, it would at first seem doubtful whether he could sustain a temporary conflict with the winds of heaven." After his death, Garrison said in *The Liberator* (September 20, 1839): "In his personal appearance friend Lundy, like the Apostle Paul, was 'weak and contemptible.' In my imagination I had given to him in shape

---

* *Atlantic Monthly*, Vol. XXV., p. 243. This article has been ascribed erroneously to J. G. Wilson, and not to the Massachusetts senator.

† The families were intimate, Lundy's wife's brother having married a sister to Stanton's father.—A. M. S.

and size the figure of a Hercules; and my disappointment was great in finding him far below the average of mankind in bulk and stature. I was almost tempted to say to him, as a beloved Irish correspondent of Dr. Watts, on seeing that mighty dwarf for the first time, remarked to him: ' Why, sir, you don't look as if you could say *Boo* to a goose!' ' Boo!' was the clever retort of the doctor; and I should have received as good a one in return had I resorted to that pleasant banter, for Lundy was a ready wit and could make capital repartees. He was not a good public speaker. His voice was too feeble, his utterance too rapid to interest or inform an audience; yet he never spoke wholly in vain. In private life his habits were social and communicative; but his infirmity of deafness rendered it difficult to engage with him in protracted conversation. How, with that infirmity upon him, he could think of traveling all over the country, exploring Canada and Texas, and making voyages to Hayti, is, indeed, a matter of astonishment. But it shows, in bold relief, what the spirit of philanthropy can dare and conquer."

Sir Humphrey Davy, the famous discoverer in chemistry, said: "My greatest discovery was Michael Faraday"; and so Lundy might have said, and perhaps did say (for he was generous), that his chief work as an emancipator, was to unchain the pent-up force of Garrison, and open to him his true career. This Lundy did, and the story has been often told. He drew Garrison to Baltimore, where the master and disciple united in issuing the two hundred and twenty-seventh number of the *Genius*, September 2, 1829. It had become a weekly journal in September, 1825, and so continued during the stormy time that Garrison edited it—just six months, for the last weekly issue was dated March 5, 1830, when the partship between Lundy and Garrison was dissolved, and the senior partner went on with his paper as a monthly, or rather a "semi-occasional" publication. They parted good friends, and on the 17th of April Garrison was committed to the Baltimore jail, for a libel on two Massachusetts men, Francis Todd, owner, and Nicholas Brown, master of the ship *France*, engaged in the domestic slave-trade. Lundy visited him often in the jail, from which he was released June 5, 1830, his fine being paid through Lundy, by Arthur Tappan, of New York. Seven months afterward (January 1, 1831), Garrison began to publish his *Liberator* in Boston, while Lundy had removed his *Genius* to Washington (October, 1830), where it was printed until 1834, when it made its last remove but one to Philadelphia, expiring there in 1838, amid the flames of Pennsylvania Hall, which was burnt by the mob in May, 1838. He removed next to Illinois, where Lovejoy, the anti-slavery martyr, had been killed by a mob in November, 1837,

and, while laboring there against slavery, died at Lowell, an obscure village in La Salle county, August 22, 1839. His *Genius* had been printed there for some months, and its final number announced his death.

During the period between Garrison's imprisonment and Lundy's death, the latter had three times visited Texas, and explored its possibilities as a home for free colored people, nearly losing his life there by cholera in 1832. He became better acquainted than any northern man with that state, both while it was subject to Mexico and while revolting; and he exposed fully and freely the plot formed before 1830, to increase the area of slave territory by annexing Texas. His pamphlet on " The War in Texas," (Philadelphia, 1836), is not only the best account, up to that time, of the Texas Conspiracy, but closes with the remarkable prediction of the Southern Confederacy, which established itself twenty-five years later. "Our countrymen, in fighting for the union of Texas with the United States, will be fighting for that which at no distant period will inevitably *dissolve the Union*. The slave states, having the eligible addition to their land of bondage, will ere long cut asunder the federal tie, and confederate a new and distinct slaveholding republic in opposition to the whole free republic of the north. Thus early will be fulfilled the prediction of the old politicians of Europe, that our Union could not remain one century entire; and then also will the maxim be exemplified in our history, that liberty and slavery can not long inhabit the same soil."

Lundy died, as he had lived, in the firm belief that American slavery would be abolished before 1900, and he contributed more to that result than many—perhaps than any—of his contemporaries. He did not always agree with Garrison in opinion—being more sensible though far less forcible; but his best eulogy is that written by Garrison, who in his first year as editor of *The Liberator* had printed there this sonnet to his teacher and friend:

TO BENJAMIN LUNDY

The Veteran Advocate of Negro Emancipation.

Self-taught, unaided, poor, reviled, contemned,
  Beset with enemies, by friends betrayed.
As madman and fanatic oft condemned,
  Yet in thy noble cause still undismayed!

Leonidas thy courage could not boast;
  Less numerous were his foes, his hand more strong;
Alone, unto a more than Persian host,
  Thou hast undauntedly given battle long.

Nor shalt thou singly wage the unequal strife;
  And to thy aid with spear and shield I rush,
And freely do I offer up my life.
  And bid my heart's blood find a wound to gush!

New volunteers are trooping to the field—
  To die we are prepared, but not an inch to yield.
—FRANK B. SANBORN.

Prof. Veytrus R. Williams, Supt. of Schools at Streator, Ill., who had read Thomas Earle's Life of Lundy, in Chicago Library, attended Ill., Yearly Meeting of Friends (Hicksite) held at Clear Creek, 9th mo. 16, 1895, and "expressed a concern in reference to a suitable *monument* to the memory of that great and good man, Benjamin Lundy," whose grave is in the yard adjacent to the old meeting house there, though he thought a desirable place for the monument was outside the Friends' Ground. "He was listened to with interest and a committee was appointed to consider the subject and confer with Clear Creek Monthly Meeting."

Lundy's eldest and only surviving child, in a recent letter, remarks: "His descendants are not blessed with a superabundance of this world's goods or the monument would be erected, as we all feel that he richly deserves to be gratefully remembered by posterity." We believe the Lundy Monument Association has not yet

Yet, shame upon them!—there they sit,
  Men of the North, subdued and still,
Meek, pliant poltroons, only fit
  To work a master's will.

Sold,—bargained off for Southern votes,—
  A passive herd of Northern mules,
Just braying through their purchased throats
  Whate'er their owner rules.

*   *   *   *   *   *   *

Look we at home!—our noble hall,
  To Freedom's holy purpose given,
Now rears its black and ruined wall,
  Beneath the wintry heaven,—

Telling the story of its doom,—
  The fiendish mob,—the prostrate law,—
The fiery jet through midnight's gloom,
  Our gazing thousands saw.

Yet well did Whittier sing in 1839 in the poem, "The New Year," from which we have quoted above, a prophecy whose fulfillment was deferred for a quarter of a century:—

·DWELLING BUILT BY BENJAMIN LUNDY AT LOWELL, LA SALLE CO., ILL., 1839.

been incorporated though opinions on the subject are all highly favorable.

Mrs. Wierman, in the letter cited above, said also: "There was a small volume published shortly after father's death, compiled by Thomas Earle of Philadelphia; but the materials for such a work were very meagre, as his papers and everything else he possessed were destroyed by the mob that burned Pennsylvania Hall in 1838 [May 17], he having stored them there in preparation for removal to Illinois, where we, his children, were already settled. One small valise containing his journal, kept on his trip through Texas and Mexico was all that was saved."

Still round our country's proudest hall
  The trade in human flesh is driven,
And at each careless hammer-fall
  A human heart is riven.

And this, too, sanctioned by the men,
  Vested with power to shield the right,
And throw each vile and robber den
  Wide open to the light.

And all who now are bound beneath
  Our banner's shade, our eagle's wing,
From Slavery's night of moral death
  To light and life shall spring.

Broken the bondman's chain, and gone
  The master's guilt, and hate, and fear,
And unto both alike shall dawn,
  A New and Happy Year.

IN LUNDY'S LAND.

BY WENDELL PHILLIPS GARRISON.

Reprinted from the Pennsylvania Magazine of History and Biography, October, 1895.

PRINTER! do not make it *Lane.* A genius for blundering might do worse, but could not possibly do better, for there is a close connection between Lundy's Lane and the Jersey uplands we are going to view. Between the Hero of Lundy's Lane, also, and *our* hero there is a relation which will bear the telling. Still, for all that, Printer, in your jargon (which was Lundy's likewise), *stet*—let it stand as written: *Land*.

And yet we will, if you please, begin with the Lane. An easy walk will bring you to it from the Canadian side of Niagara Falls; or you may take a horse-car which runs beside the Canada Southern tracks at the head of the street between Dufferin Park and the Clifton House. You are now on high but level ground, and when the car presently turns southward at a right angle, you alight at the foot of a short rise to a flat-topped sand-bank. The by no means narrow road still bears the name of Lundy's Lane, and the Lundys are amongst the oldest families residing about the Falls. The contest for the sand-bank was the battle of Lundy's Lane, fought on July 25, 1814. A semblance of earthworks, with two mounted guns, marks the spot, which is crowned by an observatory commanding a wide prospect.* The ridge falls away abruptly in the rear, owing, as it would seem, to extensive quarrying for sand in this historic mound. The view northward is over a broad plain showing few houses, but pleasingly diversified with a stream, groves, vineyards, orchards, and market-gardens. Southward, directly across the Lane, Death has reasserted his claim to this field, for a post-bellum graveyard adjoins a Presbyterian church.

There were no "Quaker guns" in the bloody battle, but the Lane divided the farms of two Quaker brothers Lundy, who removed to what is called the Peninsula of Upper Canada from the State of New Jersey. It was their fence-rails which were piled upon the heaps of slain for a rude cremation that long whitened the ground. Some ten miles west, at Pelham, certain of their posterity may still attend the century-old Friends' Meeting, but such as bear their name about the Falls have become mingled with the "world's people." The emigrant Lundys came from Johnsonburg, now in the township of Frelinghuysen, Warren County, New Jersey. The records of Pelham Meeting might reveal their identity among the numerous progeny of Richard Lundy, of the township of Buckingham, Bucks County, Province of Pennsylvania, who helped form the "Quaker Settlement" in Hardwick, Sussex County, New Jersey. We read in the minutes of Hardwick and Mendham Meeting, Eighth month 3, 1797:

"This Meeting appears to be at a loss concerning Friends who have removed from Hardwick to Niagary, whether they are to be considered as members of this Meeting or of Kingwood. Therefore the Meeting requests the judgment of the Quarterly Meeting concerning them."

The Quarterly Meeting hopefully decided that they belonged to "this Meeting." Accordingly, Seventh month 4, 1799, we come upon the case of one Thomas D—— in Upper Canada, "visited but could not be seen; to remonstrate against his priestly marriage and drinking to excess and other disorderly ways." Nothing could be done but to record a "Testification" against him, drawn up by the practised hand of Joseph Lundy, whom we take to have been the grandson of Richard aforesaid; if so, in his eightieth year. In 1800, Seventh month 3, Sarah Lundy, "she being a minister in good esteem with us," lays before Hardwick and Mendham Meeting a "concern that had rested on her mind for some time past to pay a religious visit to Friends in Upper Canada;" and Elizabeth Shotwell would fain accompany her. In the same year Friend Willson removes to Upper Canada, and dismissals to Pelham Monthly Meeting steadily follow, —Mercy Brotherton and others in 1801, William Shotwell in 1803, Mary Shotwell (wife of Richard) and Amy Shotwell in 1804, Schooley Dennis in 1807, Richard D. Willson in 1823.

Lundy's Land was getting depopulated, and the extinction of Hardwick Meeting was clearly foreshadowed. Lundy himself, greatest of his name, had gone out from the Quaker Settlement, though not from the Society of Friends, to which he was an honor as few others have been since George Fox laid the foundations of it. At the Monthly Meeting Seventh month 6, 1809, Joseph[4] Lundy, son of Thomas[3] (born Sixth month 14, 1725), the son of Richard[2] (died Eleventh month 7, 1757,* and buried at Hardwick) and grandson of Richard[1], requests a certificate of removal for his son BENJAMIN (born First month 4, 1789) to the Monthly Meeting of Westland, Pennsylvania. Such a certificate was reported (Ninth month 7) "not quite satisfactory as first drawn," and was finally (Tenth month 5) addressed to the Monthly-Meeting of Concord, Ohio, having been "requested for Benjamin Lundy, a minor, who has gone to reside within the limits of your meeting." Attest, Levi Lundy, Clerk.

The Lundys had been dispersing since 1794 at least. mostly to Pennsylvania; and a Thomas Lundy† (1796) to Westfield, North Carolina. Joseph himself made an exit immediately upon that of his and our Benjamin, to Burlington (New Jersey) Monthly Meeting, with a certificate bearing date of Eleventh month 1, 1810. He was born Third month 19, 1762, and married Elizabeth Shotwell (perhaps in 1788, but a Joseph and Elizabeth Lundy are witnesses to a marriage in 1787).‡ The records are silent as to this ceremony, as they are concerning his second marriage about 1794 to Mary (surname unknown).§ With her and his minor children, Abigail, Richard, Elizabeth, Phœbe, Lydia S. (afterwards Mrs. Wierman) and Deborah, Joseph withdrew to Rancocas, New Jersey, and

---

* Since this paper was written and put in type, a monument has been erected (in July, 1895) to commemorate the battle from the Canadian point of view.

* Joseph[4] Lundy's grandfather, Richard[2], d. 2-28, 1772.—A. M. S.
† Thomas was brother to Joseph[4].—A. M. S.
‡ They were m. at Rahway, 26 of 4 mo., 1787, (see pp. 90, 189)—A. M. S.
§ She was Mary Titus, of Jericho, L. I.—A. M. S.

there survived the sole offspring of his first marriage. Henceforth, for us, Lundy's Land is but a realm of ghosts.

It was like ghost-hunting, or flea-hunting, to find our way thither. We had, to begin with, the doubly and trebly misleading statement by Benjamin Lundy in the Life of him compiled, with little skill and many errors, by Thomas Earle (Philadelphia, 1847): "My native place was the county of Sussex, New Jersey. . . . It was at Handwich that my father and myself were born." The printer's *Handwich* we had already corrected to Hardwick, and our first step was to locate this in the admirable State Atlas. Hardwick we found, but in Warren, not in Sussex County; there was a Hardwick Township, with a Hardwick cross-roads and a Hardwick Centre, lying among the foot-hills of the Kittatinny Mountain, say from three to five miles from the Delaware River. Clinging fast to the local name, we rightly conjectured a change of boundary by which Sussex County had been the loser, one or other of the Hardwick hamlets we regarded as the certain Mecca of our pilgrimage.

How else should such a pilgrimage be made, except on foot? Was not Lundy the most unwearied of pedestrians in his holy crusade against American slavery? This little man, so slight you might think he would be blown away, traversed a large part of the Union without a conveyance. "Rivers and mountains," said an admiring disciple, "vanish in his path; midnight finds him wending his solitary way over an unfrequented road; the sun is anticipated in his rising." When he founded his *Genius of Universal Emancipation* in Ohio,—it was in 1824, upon the heels of the Missouri Compromise,—he had the paper printed at a distance of twenty miles from the place of publication, and trudged to and fro, carrying the printed sheets home upon his back. Later, as he sought to extend his subscription-list while preaching the gospel of freedom, his practice was "to pack up in his carpet-bag his direction-book, his title-letter, head-lines and column-rules, leads and standing-matter;" and, knapsack on back and carpet-bag in hand, stopping to lecture, to get subscribers, and to form anti-slavery societies, he would pursue his journey "till, publication day coming round, and getting at a country printing-office, he would hire a number of his paper printed, mail it, and pass on," and then repeat the performance,—the *Genius* being all the time dated at Baltimore. In Texas in 1833 we see him pouring the water from his shoes and wringing out his stockings three times before breakfast, on account of the dewey grass; at night reposing on the same grass by the roadside, "my knapsack serving for a pillow, and my small thin coat for sheets and counterpane, while my hat, staff, and my pistol smartly charged [against panthers, alligators, and rattlesnakes] lay at arm's length from my person."

Afoot, then, let us go to the birthplace of Benjamin Lundy. We start, no matter where, and we arrive at Washington's head-quarters in Morristown. No landmark this for non-resistant Quakerdom; have we lost our way? "Wayfarer," responds the Genius of the place, "have you forgotten Washington, who detested the domestic slave-trade and who died an abolitionist?" The omen grows as we next encounter Mount Freedom, from whose western slope we have spread before us the ravishing panorama of the Succasunna Plains. On the second day we reach Waterloo at the foot of Allamuchy Mountain. If one of these names seems remote from our Quaker abolitionist, it was Toussaint who ruined Napoleon's dream of a Central American empire, and it was Toussaint's free Hayti that Lundy twice visited in order to settle there emancipated slaves. On the other hand, the Spanish-sounding Allamuchy recalls Lundy's subsequent vain efforts in the then Mexican province of Texas to erect a cordon of free-negro colonies against the southwestern extension of the slave-power, and in refutation of the libel that the black man would not work, except under the lash. It was this Texas which General Scott, still mindful of his wound at Lundy's Lane whenever he tugged at his overcoat, would presently help to annex to "the land of the free," and so prolong for another generation the life of the "peculiar institution."

The road over the Allamuchy Mountain is sandy and unshaded. As we reach the summit, for a mile or more we are obtrusively attended on the left by a high board fence entirely cutting off the forest view, and sheltering a preserve of wild animals owned by the wealthy New York proprietor of the adjoining manor. The irritation caused by this unsightly enclosure and by the destruction (for prudential reasons) of the trees between it and the road is a good preparation for the view of Lundy's Land which bursts upon us as we emerge upon the valley of the Pequest,—grander and more extensive, but less lovely, than the landscape in which Succasunna lies. The great wall of the Kittatinny Mountain, stretching indefinitely northward from the Delaware Water Gap, forms the background. A southward-flowing stream drains the hither valley between it and Allamuchy Mountain. Why did not some hand detain us at the bridge over the Pequest, and an inner voice admonish us to take off our shoes as if on holy ground? Why did we pass without heeding on the left the dilapidated burying-ground; why the grove just beyond, with the school-house, on a little knoll? Hardwick cross-roads, Hardwick Centre, proved but a delusion and a snare to our feet, and the third day found us, better advised, retracing our steps through Johnsonburg, whence the Lundy brothers—whether in search of a more generous soil and larger possessions, or whether (though Sabine makes no note of them among his Loyalists) in some disaffection to the government that succeeded George the Third's—migrated to the shores of the great river of the mist and the rainbow, to "Lundy's Lane."

The "Quaker Settlement," as it is still called, centred at the meeting-house in the grove near the west branch of the Pequest. This house, of blue limestone, exists no longer, but its foundation (on which a truthful hand has scratched the date 1764) now supports a frame building with its gable and entrance towards the west; a school-house below, a non-Quaker meeting-house above. The ground about it is shaded mostly by white oaks, one of which, newly felled, we perceived must have been standing when the boy Lundy frequented these sacred precincts, and looked off upon the Allamuchy Mountain for the last time, perhaps, when the certificate of removal to Ohio was granted him. From this grove we entered the old Friends' burying-ground from the rear,—clambering the brick wall, we must confess, since we had failed to observe the main entrance. The spot is sadly neglected, with stones prostrate or out of plumb, with gruesome holes, but also with some sign of comparatively recent interment, and with fine un-Quakerlike monuments erected by a child in memory of David Lundy and Sarah his wife, contemporaries and kinsfolk of Benjamin's. Other Lundy stones there are, with graves of Shotwell and Adams of the extinct Society.

The records of this Society have found their way to Plainfield. Besides the family names already adduced, one meets with Hampton, Hance, Laing, Parker, Patterson, Pound, Stockton, Willits, and many more now hardly to be met with in the Quaker Settlement.

* * * * *

It is three miles from the meeting-house to Lundy's birthplace, which must be sought in Sussex County, at Greensville, in Green Township. The road marches with the river Pequest for two-thirds of the way, when it bends at a right angle northwesterly. We have crossed a low divide between the alluvial lands, covered with thriving farms, and a rugged glacial tract, more picturesque if less fertile. To the right rises a fine, rather sheer ridge, clothed not too thickly with evergreens. To the left and in front of us lies the hamlet of Greensville. It has, for our purpose, a far too modern look. The eye rests on no building that might have been Lundy's birthplace,—that Lundy might have seen, perhaps. In truth, the house in which he saw the light is no longer standing. It was on the left of the road by which we have entered the village. A drawing from the description of it given by Eli Lundy, a cousin of Benjamin's, is all that preserves the memory of it. A plain, unpainted frame structure, two-storied in the gable, with an extension at the east end and a chimney at the west end, it pre-

sented its long side to the road, and offered a door to the cold blasts from northeast and northwest; to the south the outbuildings formed two sides of a quadrangle. The farm had passed, some sixty years ago, to Colonel John Drake, who had doubtless been "active at military trainings," and was bought on his death by his son Samuel, who sold it to his brother-in-law, Timothy H. Cook. This owner in turn died, when Jacob Vass purchased the estate, and at this writing it is the property of his widow and his daughter (Mrs. Joseph Durling).

Our pilgrimage, therefore, was but to the Land, not the home. "Argos was there for Lundy," was all that we could say. We turned our back on the quiet neighborhood in which the oldest inhabitant knew not Benjamin, nor held in his crumbling memory any tradition of the birthplace. We passed on our left, at the foot of the ridge which greeted us on entering, the little post-office of Lincoln,—a name substituted of late years for Greensville, and not inapt for the cradle of the forgotten apostle of emancipation. We turned not at the bend in the road, but traversed the lovely intervale of the Pequest in which the village of Tranquillity leads a smiling existence, under the shelter of Allamuchy Mountain; peaceful in its designation, if not strictly a part of the Quaker Settlement.

> "Tranquillity! thou better name
> Than all the family of fame,"

sings Coleridge. Fame was earned, and the inward tranquillity, by Lundy; but his body never knew rest from the time he asked himself, "What can I do?" to redress the wrongs of the slave. This was in the year 1816, at St. Clairsville, Ohio, when the saddler's trade which he had learned at Wheeling, Virginia, was making him a man of property, if not of independent means. Wheeling, as Lundy says, was "a great thoroughfare for the traffickers in human flesh. Their *coffles* passed through the place frequently. My heart was deeply grieved at the gross abomination; I heard the wail of the captive; I felt his pang of distress; and the iron entered my soul." Hence the giving up of every worldly prospect, a stable home, the good repute of his fellow-countrymen, for the honor of being the first American to lay aside all other business to plead the cause of the oppressed.

We spoke of Lundy's fame; but how many of our readers will hear for the first time the name of him whose statue ought to be one of New Jersey's two in the old Senate Chamber of the Capitol at Washington, although his very existence is ignored by most of our history writers for young and old, by most of our biographical dictionary-makers!

"He was not a good public speaker. His voice was too feeble, his utterance too rapid, to interest or inform an audience; yet he never spoke wholly in vain. In private life his habits were social and communicative, but his infirmity of deafness rendered it difficult to engage with him in protracted conversation."

So testified at Lundy's death the then editor of the *Liberator*, who heard him for the first time in Boston, on March 17, 1828, when his appeal to the clergymen present to organize an anti-slavery society was "wholly in vain," but to the layman was like a mandate from the Almighty. Garrison was drawn irresistibly to Baltimore to assist in editing the *Genius of Universal Emancipation*, and there gave his pledge to Lundy to write his biography in case the younger philanthropist outlived the elder. When the time came, in 1839, to redeem this promise, opposition was manifested by the father, Joseph Lundy, speaking on behalf of the family, but really as the mouth-piece of his daughter Lydia, who controlled the Life as finally compiled by Thomas Earle. There lies before us a letter, hitherto unpublished, from B. C. Lundy, a son of Benjamin, addressed to William Lloyd Garrison. The date is five years later than that of the Life:

"Mt. Palatine, Putnam Co., Ill., June 25, 1852.

"Respected Sir—You will remember that some time ago a work was published in Philadelphia by William D. Parish, entitled 'The Life and Opinions of Benjamin Lundy,' and purporting to have been issued under the supervision and by request of his children. This was all a false statement. His children had no control whatever of the work, nor were they even consulted on any important point relative to the compilation or publication. A half-sister of my father's, Lydia Wierman, assumed all the responsibility. . . .

"The reason for these relatives acting as they did was this, they feared the children would put the MS. into your hands, which they were opposed to—I know not why. It was the choice of the children that you should write the biography. One reason, because you were more intimately acquainted with his life than any other man, another because we had learned that an understanding existed between yourself and our father that the survivor should be the other's biographer. Yet all father's journals and important papers were in the hands of this half-sister, and . . . [she] was enabled to act immediately on her resolves. I was then young and just commencing my studies, and could not resist the movement to any advantage. I however resolved to some day right the wrong so far as the unfavorable circumstances would allow. I have now to propose to you to commence the work which you should have had an opportunity to commence years ago. If you think there is the least prospect that you would be justified in so doing, we would be glad to have you 'write a book.'

"Please let me know soon your opinions relative to my proposal. I am the youngest son of Benjamin Lundy, have a family, and been engaged in the practice of medicine about two years. I have a brother and two sisters yet living, they reside near me.

"Yours truly,
"B. C. Lundy."

It was no longer possible for Mr. Garrison to comply with this request, but he never, to the end of his days, ceased to render to Lundy the grateful homage of a disciple, and to claim for him an imperishable renown in the annals of American and of universal philanthropy.

BENJAMIN⁵ LUNDY'S FAMILY AND DESCENDANTS.

Benjamin⁵ Lundy, 1789-1839, of Saint Clairsville, Ohio, Baltimore, Md., Lowell, Ill., [of Joseph⁴, Thomas³ (?), Richard², Richard¹], m. by Friends' ceremony, 2-13, 1815, Esther Lewis, b. 3-26, 1793, in Washington Co., Pa., d. in Baltimore, Md., 4-5, 1826, a few hours after birth of twins, buried at Baltimore, Md., dau. of Henry & Susanna (Hoge) Lewis, and had 5 children. His living descendants reside in Illinois, Iowa, Kansas, and Texas, and include 1 daughter, 6 grandchildren, 18 great-grand-children, and 10 great-great-grand-children, but only 1 male descendant bearing the name of Lundy,—a grandson living in Iowa. Benjamin⁵ & Esther (Lewis) Lundy, had:

I. Susan Maria⁶, b. 11-18, 1815, Saint Clairsville, Ohio, dw. with son, Isaac P⁷. Wierman, in Clear Creek Tp., Putnam Co., Ill., P. O., Mt. Palatine; m. 1-31, 1833, Wm. C. Wierman, of Mangola, Ill., b. 1-21, 1799, York Springs, Adams Co., Pa., d. 2-12, 1863, buried at Clear Creek, Ill., s. of Wm. & Sarah (Cleaver) Wierman, of Adams Co., Pa., and had:

1. Esther M. b. 12-13, 1833, d. 9-20, 1850, buried at Clear Creek, Ill., unm.

2. Sarah Katharine⁷ Wierman, b. 5-19, 1836, in Adams Co., Pa., d. of consumption, 4-5, 1864, buried at Clear Creek, Ill., m. 11-13, 1856, Levi Gunn, b. 7-2, 1833, in Franklin Co., Mass., P. O., Great Bend, Barton Co., Kans., and had: (a) *Wm. W⁸. Gunn*, b. 11-14, 1857, at La Salle, Ill., dw. Webber, Kans., is farmer and township assessor (1897); had his right hand caught in the cogs of a feed mill, a few years since, and thereby lost all the fingers of that hand except the little finger, which was broken and remains stiff, and half the thumb, yet he can hold a pen, or write with either hand. To him and his grandmother, Susan M. (Lundy) Wierman, of Clear Creek, Ill., we are chiefly indebted for the data relating to Benj⁵. Lundy's descendants. He m. 10-16, 1879, Mary E. Vale, b. 2-25, 1858, at Mangola, Ill., dau. of Isaac Vale, of Webber, Kans., and had: (I.) Charles Chester Gunn, b. 4-1, 1882, Great

Bend, Kans. (II.) Lucian Lundy Gunn, b. 3-24, 1884, Webber, Kans. (III.) Sarah K., b. 8-11, 1888, Webber, Kans. (IV.) Wm. W., Jr., b. 1-25, 1892, Great Bend. Kans. (V.) Ralph Raymond Gunn, b. 4-29, 1894, Webber, Kans. (b) *Charles Lundy* Gunn, b. 8-24, 1859, at Mt. Palatine, Putnam Co., Ill.; P. O., Heisler, Kans.; m. 3-5, 1882, Frances A. Lee, b. 12-27, 1862, Winterset, Iowa, and had: (I.) Walter L., b. 4-10, 1883, Great Bend, Kans. (II.) Leonard, b. 9-17, 1884, Great Bend, Kans. (III.) Grace Katharine, b. 9-4, 1888, Great Bend, Kans. (IV.) Edwin Ray, b. 5-18, 1895, Heizer, Kans. (c) *Francis Levi* Gunn, b. 12-14, 1863, La Salle, Ill., dw. Great Bend, Kans., m. there 6-1, 1892, Edna McDowell, of Iowa, b. 7-21, 1871, and had: (I.) Susan Kathryn, b. 8-7, 1894, Great Bend, Kans.

3. Mary Sabina Wierman, b. 8-15, 1838, d. 3-28, 1857, of consumption, buried Clear Creek, Ill., unm.

4. Joseph Wm. Wierman, b. 5-19, 1841, d. 2-20, 1864, of consumption, buried Clear Creek, Ill., unm.

5. Benjamin Lewis Wierman, b. 12-15, 1843, d. 3-31, 1876, of consumption, buried Clear Creek, Ill., unm.

6. Isaac P'. Wierman, b. 8-18, 1846, Magnolia, Ill., dw. Clear Creek, Putnam Co., Ill., P. O., Mt. Palatine, is a healthy man and a member of the Society of Friends; m. 4-4, 1872, Isabelle W. Merritt, b. 6-8, 1847, at Saint Clairsville, Ohio, and had: (a) Mary Emma Wierman, b. 5-22, 1874, Magnolia, Ill., is a school teacher. (b) Susan Edna, b. 8-30, 1876, Magnolia, Ill., is a teacher. (c) Charles L., b. 5-30, 1879, Great Bend, Kans. (d) Wm. Henry, b. 11-18, 1881, Ottawa, Kans. (e) Harry Wilson Wierman, b. 9-21, 1884, Ottawa, Kans. (f) Herbert L., b. 7-9, 1890, Ottawa, Kans.

7. Charles Francis Wierman, b. 5-9, 1850, d. 8-14, 1850, buried at Clear Creek, Ill.

II. Elizabeth Shotwell[6] Lundy, called Eliza, b. 10-3, 1818, Saint Clairsville, Belmont Co., Ohio, d. 1-22, 1879, buried Greenwood, Mo., m. in 2 mo., 1838, Isaac Griffith, of Magnolia, Ill., b. 2-29, 1816, at Newbury, York Co., Pa., d. 12-1, 1895, buried at Des Moines, Iowa. s. of George & Sarah (Kirke) Griffith, who emigrated in 1836, from Harrison Co., Ohio, to La Salle Co., Ill., and had:

1. Benjamin Lundy[7] Griffith, b. 11-9, 1839, at Clear Creek, Putnam Co., Ill., dw., 536 Pine St., Des Moines, Iowa, m. 6-17, 1868, Rebecca J. Fisher, b. 3-30, 1842. and had: (a) Allen Melville Griffith, b. 1-3, 1870, d. .... (b) Charles Talmage Griffith. b. 12-24, 1871. (c) Nettie May, b. 6-27, 1876 (d) Adelle Louise, b. 9-25, 1878. (e) Edna Peryl, b. 8-3, 1882.

2. George Edward[7] Griffith, b. 2-5, 1843, at Clear Creek, Ill., where all this family were born; dw. Des Moines, Iowa; m. (1) 2-22, 1872, Sarah J. Hartley, b. 4-15, 1848, in Bucks Co., Pa., d. 3-27, 1890, and had: (a) Leland Clyde, b 9-4, 1874. (b) Harry Orville, b. 11-4, 1876. (c) George Hartley. b. 6-6, 1879. (d) Ethel, b. 1-17, 1888. George Edward[7] Griffith, (b. 1843), of Des Moines, Iowa; m. (2) 5-10, 1891, Eva A. Billinger, b. 1848, and had: (e) Harold Crosby Griffith, b. 5-27, 1892.

3. Robert A Griffith, b. at Clear Creek, Ill., m. Jessie Filo, (since divorced), and had 3 children, 2 of whom are deceased. (c) Mable Filo, b. 9-25, 1878.

III. Charles Talmage Lundy, b. 12-28, 1821, Mt. Pleasant, Jefferson Co., Ohio, dw. in the vicinity of Magnolia, Ill., d. in Putnam Co., Ill., in 10 mo., 1858, buried at Clear Creek, Ill., s. p.; m. Eleanor Mears, dw. Greenville, Bond Co., Ill.

IV. Esther Lewis Lundy (twin), b. 4-4, 1826, Baltimore Md.; d. Putnam Co., Ill., 12-26, 1846, buried at Clear Creek, Ill., unm.

V. Benjamin Clarkson[6] Lundy, (twin), b. 4-4, 1826, Baltimore, Md., was a practicing physician in Putnam Co., in the vicinity of Magnolia, Ill., d. 9-16, 1861, buried at Magnolia, Ill., m. 3-27, 1850, Catharine Haines, of Springboro, Ohio, and had:

1. Annie L., b. 1-26, 1851, d. 1-23, 1859, buried at Magnolia, Ill.

2. Charles L., b. 4-24, 1852, d. 9-27, 1854, buried at Magnolia, Ill.

3. Mary Alice, b. 7-18, 1854, d. 10-24, 1872, buried at Lacon, Marshall Co., Ill., unm.

4. Wm. L'. Lundy, b. 3-3, 1856, is the only living male representative of the .name, dw. Clarinda, Page Co., Iowa, m. 10-21, 1885, Alice Clement, b. 3-21, 1861, and had: (a) Lorene, b. 9-26, 1891.

5. Benjamin C., Jr., b. 7-6, 1858, d. 6-5, 1859, buried at Magnolia, Ill.

6. Catharine H., b. 3-14, 1860, dw. Clarinda, Page Co., Iowa.

NOTE.—The following data arrived too late for insertion in page 262:—Joseph[4] Lundy & family removed from Sussex (now Warren) Co., to Rancocas, Burlington Co., N. J., about 1810, acquiring title to his "plantation" there in that year. His eldest dau., Abigail, died 14 of 5 mo., 1874. His grandson, Joseph[6] Lundy, [of Richard[5]], m. Mary Evans, dau. of Darling & Rachel (Matlack) Evans, and had Maurice E'. Lundy, who m. Laura Thomson, dau. of Alex. & Rebecca (Scattergood) Thomson, and had Florence T. Lundy. J. Wilmer[7] Lundy, of Mt. Holly, N. J., [of Jos[6]., Richard[5]], m. Bessie Roberts, dau. of Stacy & Harriet (Roberts) Roberts, of Haddonfield, N. J. Charles[6] Lundy, [of Richard[5]], m. (1) Sue Cooper; m. (2) Lizzie Dunk. Phebe[5] (Lundy) Hilton, b. 1802, [of Jos'. Lundy], d. in 5th mo., 1849. The eldest of her *eight* children was Mary L. The second child, Jos[6]. Hilton, m. (1) Hannah Lippincott; m. (2) Rachel Dudley. His second child, Emma[7] Hilton, m. Clifford Budd, and had one child. The 4th ch., Jos'. Hilton, m. Etta Moore, and had two children. The 5th ch., Hannah Hilton, is unm. Lydia[5] Lundy, b. 1804, [of Jos'.], d. 5-27, 1884. Mary Ella[6], dau. of Wm. & Mary[5] (Lundy) Barnard, b. Sept. 18, 1850, m. Aug. 3, 1876, Rev. G. F. Wiswell, D. D. Her sister, Philena Ruth, d. Oct. 10, 1887, s. p.

HALLETT.

William[1] Hallett, b. about 1616, in Dorset-shire, Eng., emigrated to Greenwich, Conn., where, in 1647, he, with Elizabeth Feake, had charge of the property of her insane husband, Lieut. Robert Feake, (pp. 134–6), and thence in 1649, with Elizabeth, removed to Newtown, L. I.; the next year William Hallett & Elizabeth Hallett conveyed to Jeffise Ferris all of his and his wife's interest in land purchased by Daniel Patrick and Robert Feake at Greenwich, Conn. William Hallett was in Hellgate in 1652. On 14 May, 1652, William Hallett bought of Thomas Baxter the house and plantation which Baxter had bought of his father. A few years later (1654±), he settled on what is known as Hallett's Cove, where he is said to have lived to the age of ninety years, and died leaving sons, William and Samuel.*

I.   *William[2] Hallett*, b. 1648±, eldest son of William[1], was justice of the peace and Capt. of Foot Company; d. 18 Aug., 1729; m. Sarah Woolsey, dau. of George & Rebecca (Cornell ?) Woolsey, of Jamaica, L. I., and had: (1.) Wm., b. 10, Dec., 1670, m. Ruth .... (2.) Sarah, b. 19 Mar., 1673, m. Rev. George Phillips, of Brookhaven, Suffolk Co., N. Y. (3.) Rebecca[3], b. 31 Aug., 1675, m. James Jackson, of Rocky Hill, L. I., name mentioned in New York M. M. records, lived much nearer to Flushing than to Jericho, L. I., son of Col. John[2] & Elizabeth (Seaman) Jackson, [of Robert[1]]. (4.) Joseph, b. 4 Mar., 1678. (5.) Moses, b. 19 Jan., 1681, m. .... Fitch. (6.) George, b. 5 Apr., 1683. (7.) Charity, b. 16 Mar., 1685, m. Samuel Moore. (8.) Mary, b. 22 Oct., 1687, m. Jacob Blackwell. (9.) Elizabeth, b. 12 Apr., 1689, m. John Fish. (10.) *Richard[3]*, b. 17 Nov., 1691, dw. Newtown, L. I., and there d. 19 of 5 mo. (May), 1769, bought in 1717, the farm of John Denman (deceased), at English Kills; embraced the principles of Friends, which many of his descendants yet profess. (See Riker's quotation "Annals of Newtown, L. I."); m. (1) at Flushing, L. I., 14 of 9 mo. (Nov.), 1717, Amey[3] Bowne, b. 1694, at Flushing, L. I., "deceased ye 7th of ye 9th mo., 1733, and was buried in ffriends' burying ground in New-towne," dau. of John[2] & (3rd wife) Mary (Cock) Bowne, of Flushing, L. I., [of Thomas[1]]; m. (2) at Birmingham, Conn., ..., 1739, Anne (Gilpin) Miller, who d. 15 of 9 mo., 1759, widow of Joseph Miller, and dau. of Joseph & Hannah (......) Gilpin. "y't was of Pennsylvan'a." (Children later).

From Benjamin C. Dwight's paper on the Woolsey Family, published in the *N. Y. Genealogical and Biographical Record*, (IV p. 143 et. seq.), we learn that *George[1] Woolsey*, the settler, b. at Yarmouth, Eng., Oct. 27, 1610,

went first to Holland with his father, Benjamin[1], s. of Thomas[1]; came to America, 1623, with Dutch emigrants; Aug. 19, 1647, he bought land at Flushing; subsequently removed to Jamaica, where he died Aug. 17, 1693, at 87. Will[2] mentions wife, Rebecca* (Cornell ?); daus., Sarah[4] (Hallett), Mary Woolsey and Rebecca (Wiggins); and he probably had sons, George, Thomas, and John.

II.   Samuel[2] Hallett, b. 1649±, brother to William[2], [of Wm[1].], d. 27 Dec., 1724; m. .. .., and had: (1.) Hannah, who who m. John Washborne. (2.) Elizabeth, m. John Jackson.† (3.) Grace, m. Lewis Hewlett. (4.) Mercy, m. .... Cornell. (5.) Martha, m. James Hazard. (6.) Samuel, d. 7 March, 1756, m. Bridget Blackwell, dau. of Robert and Mary Blackwell.

Richard[3] Hallet, 1691–1769, of Newtown, L. I., son of William[2] & Sarah (Woolsey) Hallett, of Newtown, L. I., [of Wm[1].], m. (1) 1717, Amey[3] Bowne, 1694–1733, dau. of John[2] & Mary (Cock) Bowne of Flushing, L. I., [of Thomas[1]], and had: (1.) Mary, b. 12 of 11 mo. (Jan.), 1719, d. .. of 10 mo., 1724, in Newtown, L. I. (2.) Richard, Jr[4]., b. 31st of 10 mo. (Dec.), 1721, was killed by falling of a tree limb, ye 13 of 5 mo., 1757, and buried ye 15th in Friends' burying ground; m. Mary[4] Way, [of Samuel[3], John[2], James[1]], and had: (a) June, b. 8-21, 1752, m. Anthony Betts. (b) Jonah, b. 10-31, 1754, settled at Whitestown, Oneida Co., N. Y.; was member of assembly; d. Oct. 2, 1811. (3.) Sarah, b. ye 5 of ye 6 mo. (Aug.), 1723, m. at Newtown, L. I., 13 of 9 mo., 1745, William Webster, of Elizabethtown, N. J. In the marriage certificate, her name was written "Sarah Hallock of Newtown." (4.) William, b. 10 of 12 mo., 1725; probably d. young. (5.) Ame[4], b. ye 5th of 3rd mo. (May), 1727, d. 15 of 9 mo., 1796, m. in 8 mo., 1746, Benjamin[4] Shotwell, 1726–1793, of John[3], John[2], Abr[1]. (pp. 130, 91–95)].

Richard[3] Hallett, 1691–1769, of Newtown, L. I., [of Wm[2]., Wm[1].], m. (2) 1739, Anne (Gilpin) Miller, who d. 1759, [of Joseph Gilpin], and had: (6.) Thomas[4], b. 24 of 1 mo. (March), 1740; d. Aug. 22, 1780; m. at Rahway, N. J., 9-22, 1763, Phebe Shotwell, of Elizabeth, N. J., b. 1744, [of Abr[4]., John[3], John[2], Abr[1]. (p. 88)], and had: Gideon, b. Dec. 8, 1773. (7.) Lydia[4], b. 12 of 7 mo., 1744, d. 19, of 9 mo., 1815, m.

* The name is smoet mo- written Hallock.

* George Woolsey's wife, Rebecca, was doubtless dau. of Thomas Cornell, of Cornell's Neck, Westchester Co., N. Y., who, b. about 1593, in Essex, Eng., came to Boston about 1636. (See Austin's R. I. Gen. Dic.)

† Col. John Jackson & wife, Elizabeth[3] *nee* Hallett, [of Sam'l[2], Wm[1].], had John[4] Jackson, who m. Keziah[4] Mott, dau. of Richbell & Elizabeth[3] (Thorne) Mott, [of Wm[2]. & Winifred (Livingston) Thorne, Wm[1]. & Sarah (......) Thorne of ......, L. I., (p. 133)], and had Elizabeth[5] Jackson, who m. Capt. John Sands, and had Sarah[6] Sands, who m. Geo. Downing, and had Augustus Cornwall[7] Downing, b. July 28, 1817, dw. New York City, d. Apr. 2, 1895, m. Eliza Bloodgood Rogers, a native of Albany, N. Y., and had Lizzie[8] Downing, who m. H. O. Spear, and now (1897) resides at No. 34 Gramercy Park, N. Y. City; all of her ancestors mentioned above dwelt in the Province or State of New York.

1767, (as 2nd wife) Abraham⁴ Shotwell, 1719–1801, [of John³, John², Abr¹. (pp. 88, 129–130)].
(8.) Isarel⁴, b. 5 of 3 mo. 1742, d. Oct. 1, 1776, m. at Rahway, N. J., 11–21, 1765, Naomy Shotwell, b. 1749, [of Abr¹., John³, John², Abr¹. (pp. 68, 188)], and had four sons, Richard, Abraham, Jeremiah, and James.

Rebecca² Hallett, b. 1675, dau. of Captain William² & Sarah (Woolsey) Hallett, of Newtown, L. I., [of Wm¹.]; m. James³ Jackson, of Rocky Hill, L. I.. [son of Col. John² & Elizabeth (Seaman) Jackson, grandson (1) of Robert¹ & Agnes (Washbourne) Jackson, early settlers of Hempstead, L. I., and (2) of Capt. John & Elizabeth (Strickland) Seaman, early of Hempstead, and great-grandson of William & Jane (---------) Washbourne, early settlers of Oysterbay and Hempstead, L. I., and of John Strickland, early of Hempstead], and had 21 children, nineteen of whom lived to rear families of their own. They were the following:

1. Thomas⁴ Jackson, b. 4 of (Dec. ·?), 1694; m. Mary Townsend, dau. of James & Audrey (Almy) Townsend.

2. Mary⁴ b. 20 Nov. ?, 1696; m. (1) Jacob Willets, of Richard & Abigail (Powell) Willits; m. (2) Nathaniel Townsend, s. of James as above. (Children by both husbands.)

3. Sarah⁴, b. 11 of 11 mo., 1697; m. Samuel Clements, (probably son of Joseph at Flushing, 1698).

4. Rebecca⁴, b. 20 Feb. ?, 1699; m. Sylvanius Seaman, s. of Thomas & Mary.

5. John⁴, b. 9 March, 1701; m. Sarah Doty, of Joseph & Sarah.

6. Charity⁴, b. 26 Feb., 1702; m. John Dingee, probably son of Robert.

34

7. Elizabeth⁴, b. 20 March, 1703; m. Nathaniel Field, son of Robert² of Newtown.

8. James⁴, b. 4 June, 1704; m. (1) Sarah Thorne, dau. of Joseph & Mary (Bowne) Thorne; m. (2) Mary Thorne, dau. (probably) of John & Katharine of Flushing, Chesterfield and Crosswicks.

9. William, b. 6 July, 1705; probably d. young.

10. Hannah⁴, b. 5 Aug., 1706; m. John Hicks.

11. William⁴ (again), b. 4 Oct., 1707; m. Prudence Smith.

12. Nathan, b. 26 Jan., 1709.

13. Joseph⁴, b. 9 Feb., 1710; m. Mary Rogers.

14. Richard⁴, b. 20 March, 1711; m. Mary Wright.

15. Martha⁴, b. ---------; m. Wm. Green.

16. Phebe⁴, b. 3 May, 1712; m. at Flushing, L. I., 3 of 8 mo. (Oct.), 1734, Edward Fitz Randolph, of Woodbridge, N. J., s. of Edward & Catharine (Hartshorne) Fitz Randolph.

17. Robert⁴, b. 15 of 5 mo., 1713; m. Sarah Hallett, dau. (probably) of Joseph & Lydia (Blackwell) Hallett, although no daus. are named by Riker.

18. Jemima⁴, b. 25 of 7 mo., 1714; m. Henry Hicks.

19. Samuel⁴, b. 21 of 9 mo., 1715; m. Sarah Carpenter, dau. (probably) of Increase Carpenter, of Jamaica—she having son Increase.

20. Stephen⁴, b. 17 of 7 mo., 1717; m. Mary Lewis.

21. Benjamin⁴, b. 26 of 2 mo., 1719; m. widow, Amy Paul, (perhaps Powell).

II.

ADDITIONAL DATA CONCERNING ANCESTORS AND OTHER RELATIVES OF THE AUTHOR'S PATERNAL GRANDMOTHER, EDNA C². POUND SHOTWELL, 1796-1872.

DAUGHTER OF HUGH⁵ & SARAH (KING⁵) POUND, OF FARMINGTON, N. Y., AND GRANDDAUGHTER (1.) OF SAMUEL⁴ & CATHARINE (WEBSTER⁴) POUND, OF PISCATAWAY, MIDDLESEX CO., N. J., [OF ELIJAH³ POUND, JOHN², JOHN¹, AND OF JOHN³ & ANNA (TAYLOR), WEBSTER, WILLIAM² & SUSANNAH (COWPERTHWAITE) WEBSTER, WILLIAM¹, WITH ADAMS, HARTSHORNE, AND CARR FOREFATHERS, AND (2.) OF NATHAN⁴ & SARAH (MOORE³) KING OF AMWELL, AND RAILWAY, N. J., [OF JOSEPH³ KING, JOSEPH², HARMANUS¹, AND OF JOSEPH⁴ & CHRISTIANA (BISHOP) MOORE, SAMUEL³, JOHN², SAMUEL¹], (PP. 6-24, 50, 53, 56, 186-193, 196-7).

DANIEL⁴ POUND'S BRANCH,

[of Elijah³, John², John¹, (p. 8)].

William⁵ & (second wife) Susannah (Crawford) Pound of Humberston and Bertie, C. W., had: (2.) Elizabeth (again), wife of Andrew Hampton, son of William & Mary⁵ (Pound) Hampton, [of Benjamin⁴ Pound, Elijah³, John², John¹, (p. 8)]. (3.) Prudence, Widow of John Fritz, of Bertie, Ont. (4.) James⁶ (see below). (5.) Amy, wife of George Bidner. (6.) Rachel, widow of Simon Zavitz (7.) Samuel.

James⁶ Pound [of William⁵, Daniel⁴], b. 4-25, 1818, in Bertie, County of Lincoln (now Welland), U. C., m., in Bertie Friends' Meeting-house, 5-13, 1841, Rebecca S. Zavitz, b. 5-19, 1822, in Bertie, U. C., dau. of Henry & Catharine Zavitz, and had: (1.) Asa, b. 11-13, 1843, dw. Yarmouth, Elgin County, Ont., P. O. Sparta; m. at residence of bride's father in Macedon, N. Y., by Friends' ceremony, 12-23, 1870, Anna Seaman, of Macedon, N. Y., b. 8-3, 1851, Macedon, N. Y., dau. of John & Elizabeth Seaman, of Macedon. (2.) Catharine, b. 3-1, 1846, Yarmouth, C. W., dw. Bennett, Neb., whither she removed with her family about 1851; m. in Yarmouth Friends' Meeting House, 10-26, 1868, Michael Aaron Depeel. (3.) Rachel Ann, b. 2-10, 1849, dw. Yarmouth, Ont., P. O. Sparta; m. by Friends' order in Yarmouth, Ont., 1869, Stephen Baily, b. 1839. (4.) William Samuel, b. 3-20, 1852, Yarmouth, C. W., dw. Sparta, Elgin County, Ontario, formerly at Lexington, Ky., m. in St. Thomas, -- Jan., 1875, Jennie Edwards, a native of England, who d. ------ -------, and had: (a) George Alfred, b. 5-8, 1878; (b) Elsie May, b. 5-7, 1881. (5.)

Tryphena Jane, b. 2-18, 1857, dw. St. Thomas, Ont.; m. by Friends' order at Kennett Square, Pa., 5-9, 1878, Henry H. Way, b. 7-26, 1848, is a dentist at 533½ Talbot St., St. Thomas, Ont., whither he removed in the autumn of 1882 from Lincoln, Neb., formerly of Kennett Square, Pa. (6.) Irena Malissa, b. 2-4, 1860, dw. Ames, Story Co., Iowa; attended Swarthmore College, 1879-80; m. by Friends' ceremony in Aylmer, in Malahide Tp., Ont., 4-14, 1885, George Lewis McKay, now instructor in Dairy Dep't, Iowa State Agr'l Col., Ames, Iowa. (7.) Serena Eliza, b. 9-22, 1865, dw. Yarmouth, Ont., P. O. Sparta.

HUGH⁵ POUND'S BRANCH,

[of Samuel⁴, Elijah³, John², John¹, (pp. 8-11)].

Nathan K⁶. Pound, b. 18 of 1 mo., 1798, in Middlesex Co., N. J., came with his parents in 1803, to Farmington, Ontario Co., N. Y., where he passed his youth and early manhood, assisting his father in clearing up the woodland from what is known as the Pound homestead. In 1835 he settled in Ontario, Wayne Co., N. Y., and there resided until his death, which occurred 3 of 1 mo., 1882. He m., 24 Nov., 1824, Hannah G. Lane, b. 25 June, 1799, in the Mohawk Valley, N. Y., whence, when quite young, she removed with her parents to the vicinity of Lundy's Lane in Upper Canada; she d. 15 Sept., 1880. During the War of 1812, her father was drafted into the British service, but, as his sons were serving in the American army, he deserted to the United States; and at the close of the war, all his Canadian property, including 300 acres of land, was confiscated and his family were sent out of the dominion.

Addison T'. Pound, b. 6-13, 1826, son of Nathan K'. Hannah G. (Lane) Pound (p. 10), m. 12-11, 1845, Chloe Gurnee, who d. 11-29, 1888; they had: (1.) Marion Gurnee Pound, b. 1-13, 1847, d. 1849. (2.) Hannah L., b. 9-27, 1848, m. 1866, Christopher Meyers and had one child, Chloe, b. 5-4, 1869, m., 1886, S. E. Haughey. (3.) Mary A. Pound, b. 1-24, 1855, m. 12-24, 1875, Alanson Penoyer and had: (a) Addison Penoyer, b. 6-23, 1878; (b) Eliza, b. 5-2, 1880; (c) Roscoe, b. 2-15, 1883; (d) Louisa, b. 7-30, 1888.

Edward Hugh' Pound, b. 2-9, 1828, dw. Ontario, N. Y., and there d. June 23, 1893; m. May 20, 1868, Lucy Pease, who dw. Ontario, N. Y., and had a son, Charles Edward Pound, b. July 15, 1868, m. Nov. 12, 1891, Lizzie Norman Woodam, and had Norma May Pound, b. Nov. 30, 1893.

Jacob M., son of Nathan K. & Hannah G. (Lane) Pound, enlisted in Sept., 1861, in the 11th Mich. regiment volunteer infantry, company K., Col. Stoughton, 2d brigade, 2d division, Gen. Negley, 14th army corps, Gen. Thomas. He was wounded and taken prisoner, Dec. 31, 1862, at the battle of Stone River or Murfeesborough, Tenn., and d. Jan. 3, 1863, at Atlanta, Georgia, while undergoing a surgical operation. He had m. in 1861, Maud Braman.

Stephen Bosworth' Pound, son of Nathan K'. & Hannah G (Lane) Pound (p. 10), was b. Jan. 14, 1833, in Ontario Co., N. Y., went with his parents in 1836 to Ontario, Wayne Co., N. Y., studied at Walworth and Macedon Academies, graduated at Union College in 1859; was admitted to the bar in 1863; entered into a partuership in 1864 with Judge Lyman H. Sherwood, of Lyons, N. Y., continuing in this firm until the death of Judge Sherwood in 1866. In 1867 he located at Lancaster (now Lincoln) the capital of Nebraska, where he yet resides at 1632 L St. In 1869 he was elected probate judge, was a member of the State Senate in 1872-3, and of the Constitutional Convention of 1875. In the fall of the latter year, he was elected district judge of the second judicial district of Nebraska, and served for three successive terms. In the fall of 1887, becoming tired of the routine, he resigned and resumed the practice of law at Lincoln, Nebraska. He m., Jan. 21, 1869, Laura' Biddlecome, b. May 15, 1841, in Phelps, Ontario Co., N. Y., educated at Macedon Academy and Lombard University, dau. of Joab Stafford' Biddlecome & wife Olivia (Mathewson) Biddlecome, (m. Jan. 8, 1843),—*the former* b. Nov. 29, 1803, son of Thomas' (b. April 7, 1769, d. Oct. 16, 1861), & wife Sarah, *nee* Read [dau. of Daniel & Elinor* (Southwick) Read, of Uxbridge, Mass.], and grandson of *Thomas²* *Biddlecome*, 1726-1813—of. Warwick Neck, R.

I., Adams, Berkshire Co., Mass., and Oneida Co., N. Y., a Revolutionary soldier from Rhode Island and prisoner on English prison-ship at Halifax, N. S., *and* (2d of his two wives, who were sisters, Mary and) *Sarah Burlingame*, and great-grandson of Thomas' Biddlecome, who came from Devonshire, Eng., and settled at Warwick Neck, R. I., and *the latter* (b. Aug. 15, 1808, d. Feb. 25, 1885, m. Jan. 8, 1833), dau. of Philip⁵ Mathewson (b. 4-26, 1765), & wife, Deirdama, *nee* Phillips, and granddaughter of Philip⁴ Mathewson (b. 9-4, 1737), & wife, Lydia, *nee* Angell (b. 3-15, 1739), and great-granddaughter (1) of Thomas³ & Sarah (.........) Mathewson, [of Thomas² (b. 4-1, 1673, d. 10-23, 1735) & Martha (Sheldon) Mathewson, James' (d. 1682) & Ruth (Field—who died 1703) Mathewson, of Providence, R. I.], and (2) of Jeremiah⁴ Angell (b. 1-29, 1707,) & wife Mary ....., [of Thomas³ Angell (b. 3-25, 1672) & wife Sarah, *nee* Brown (m. 4-4, 1700), John² Angell (b. 1646, d. 7-27, 1720) & wife Ruth, *nee* Field (m. 1-7, 1669), Thomas' Angell (1618-1694) who came in ship *Lyon*, which left Bristol, Eng., in Dec. 1630, arriving at Boston, Feb. 5, 1631, and soon went to Salem, whence, after spending the winter of 1635-6, at Seekonk, he, with Roger Williams and four others, removed to Providence, R. I., being a signer of the first written compact of the Providence Plantations, and his wife, Alice ...., who d. in 1695].

Judge Stephen B'. & Laura B. (Biddlecome) Pound, of Lincoln, Nebraska, had: (1.) Roscoe, b. Oct. 27, 1870, graduated at University of Nebraska, 1888, was assistant in the Botanical Laboratory, 1888-9; received degree of A. M., 1889, and Ph. D. 1897; studied · at Harvard Law School, 1889-90; admitted to the bar in Lincoln, Neb., in autumn of 1890; director of Botanical Survey of Nebraska; member of the law firm of S. B. Pound & Roscoe Pound, Lincoln, Neb. (2.) Louise, b. June 30, 1872, graduated at University of Nebraska, 1892; received degree of A. M., 1895; is assistant in Department of English Literature in University of Nebraska. (3.) Olivia, b. April 30, 1874, graduated at University of Nebraska, 1895, received degree of A. M. 1897.

Dr. Jacob & Anna S'. (Pound) Rickabaugh, of Chester Valley, Pa., P. O., Warren Tavern, Chester Co., Pa., [the latter a descendant of *Jediah Shotwell⁶ Pound* (p. 10), Hugh⁵, Samuel⁴, Elijah³, John². John'], had: (1) Walter, b. Sept. 22, 1862. (2) Mary E., born Sept. 25, 1864, m. in Chester Valley, Pa., 1886, Dr. O. J. Roberts, of New Centerville, Chester Co., Pa., and had a son, J. Alan Roberts, b. June 17, 1887. (3.) .... (4.) Sarah E., Rickabaugh, called Sally, born March 19, 1868.

William H. Bosworth, b. 8-9, 1832, in Perrin-

<hr>

* Daniel Read's wife, Elinor⁵, *nee* Southwick, was a lineal descendant (through Daniel⁴, Daniel³, & Daniel²), of Lawrence & Cassandra (......) Southwick, who came to New England in 1630, settled at Salem, Mass., and were fined, whipped, and imprisoned at Boston because of their fidelity to the profession of Quakerism during the Puritan persecution of the Friends there in the 17th century. See Whittier's poem, "Cassandra Southwick"; also Sewel's History, Vol. 1., pp. 225, 226, 419.

ton, Monroe Co., N. Y., son of Seth W. & Catharine E. (Pound) Bosworth, of Rochester, N. Y., and grandson (2.) of Hugh[5] & Sarah (King) Pound of Farmington, N. Y., [of Samuel[4] & Catharine (Webster) Pound, of Piscataway, Middlesex Co., N. J., Elijah[3], John[2], John[1] (p. 11)], graduated 1858, at Hamilton College, Clinton, N. Y., was principal of public school No. 9, Rochester, N. Y., from 1864, until his death, which occurred in Rochester, N. Y., Jan. 14, 1885; buried in Mt. Hope cemetery, Rochester, N. Y., under the Masonic order; m. by a justice of the peace in Farmington, N. Y., Dec. 27, 1860, Susan Jennings, and had: (1.) Edward Jennings Bosworth, b. Nov. 10, 1862, is job printer—firm of E. J. Bosworth & Co.,—125 & 127 N. Water St., Rochester, N. Y., m. in Adrian, Mich., Oct. 12, 1887, Allie Louise Evans, dau. of Prof. U. R. Evans, of Adrian, Mich. (2.) Frank Williston Bosworth, b. May 25, 1867, is a druggist at Astoria, Oregon, m. ....

JOHN[2] POUND'S BRANCH,

[of Samuel[4], Elijah[3], John[2], John[1] (p. 11)].

Waterman S[7]. & Addie (McNiel) Pound, of 45 Niagara St., Lockport, N. Y., [of Samuel[6], (b. 1810), John[5], of Lockport, N. Y., (p. 11)], had: George W. Pound, of 49 Niagara Ave., Lockport, N. Y., attorney, office in Farmers and Mechanic's Savings Bank Building, Lockport; president of Grant Club, Lockport, attended dedication of the Grant monument in New York, April 22, 1897.

Hon. John E[7]. Pound, counsellor at law, Lockport, Niagara Co., N. Y., son of Alexander[6] (b. 1812) & Almina (Whipple) Pound, of Lockport, N. Y., [of John[5] & Alice (Smith) Pound, of Lockport, (p. 11)], was b. in the city of Lockport, N. Y. Aug., 23, 1843, graduated from Lockport union school, and took a course of training at Brown University. During the War of the Rebellion, he was connected with the quartermaster's department, and rose to the position of chief clerk of the property department under Gen. Crane, quartermaster of the military railroads at Nashville, Tenn. He soon afterward began the study of the law with L. F. & G. W. Bowen, and was admitted to the bar in 1867; and in the practice of his profession as an attorney, he has made an excellent record. He is a staunch Republican and has the distinguished honor of having been one of the renowned 306 delegates, who stood by Gen. Grant in the National Republican Convention of 1880, until "the sun of hope had set behind the level waters of disappointment."

When Lockport Council, No. 307, of the Royal Arcanum, was instituted, April 10, 1879, with 19 charter members, he was elected regent; and in the course of the next 16 years, he rose to the highest office in the gift of the order, that of Supreme Regent,—when the order was said to have over 195,000 members; and at the 19th annual session of the Supreme Council, May 20–25, 1896, he was unanimously re-elected to the same position. He has also served his fellow citizens as supervisor, as a state assemblyman, as mayor of Lockport, as assistant U. S. attorney, and for about 20 years as U. S. commissioner. He is president of the Home for the Friendless, one of the commissioners of the Buffalo State Hospital, and a member of the board of education, Lockport.

He married Catharine W. Hurd, and had an only daughter, Almina Catharine Pound, in whose memory there was erected in Grace Episcopal Church, Lockport, N. Y.,—Rev. Wm. F. Faber, rector—a very beautiful stained glass window—a double light lancet from the studio of Messrs. J. & R. Lamb, of New York, designed by their head artist, Frederick Stymetz Lamb,—being unveiled on Easter Day, April 18, 1897. The figures selected for the window —two of a series which will be ultimately completed along the sides of the church—are those of St. Andrew and St. Stephen. Under the former is the personal inscription,—"To the glory of God and in loving memory of Almina Catharine Pound, born August 8, 1872, died November 8, 1893"; while under St. Stephen are the words, "In Memoriam Almina Catharine Pound, 1872–1893," and the well-known quotation of Tennyson's latest poem,—

> " I hope to see my Pilot face to face,
> When I have crossed the Bar."

John W[6]. (b. 1818) & Catharine Lucretia (Wilson) Pound, of Lockport, N. Y., (p. 11), had William R. W. Pound, a druggist at 224 W. Water St., Elmira, N. Y. (formerly at 244 Pine St., Lockport, N. Y.).

SAMUEL L[5]. POUND'S BRANCH,

[of Samuel[4], Elijah[3], John[2], John[1], (p. 10)].

George R[6]. & Rachel W. (Vail) Pound, of Plainfield, N. J., had: (1.) Samuel, b. Plainfield, N. J., and there died, aged about two years. (2.) Robinson[7] Pound, b. 11–3, 1857, Plainfield, N. J., entered preparatory school at Swarthmore, Pa., in Sept., 1872, took an irregular course in Swarthmore College, remaining there until June, 1880; dw. at 255, E. 2d St., (formerly at 37 E. 31 St), Plainfield, N. J.; was given an interest, in 1884, in his father's business—as dealer in hides, etc.—in Plainfield, N. J., m. under care of R. & P. M. M. of (Hic.) Friends, at the residence of the bride's father on 2d St., Plainfield, N. J., 3–23, 1867, Mary Jane Griffen, called Jennie M., b. at Plainfield, N. J., dau. of Dr. John F. Griffen, of Plainfield, and had: (a) George Henry Pound, b. 5–30, 1888, Plainfield, N. J. (b) Mary Elizabeth, b. 8–4, 1889.

COWPERTHWAITE.

Hugh[1] Cowperthwaite * and wife Elizabeth, ministers of the Society of Friends, settled about 1674 at Flushing, L. I., and there died.

John[2] Cowperthwaite, of West Jersey, son of Hugh and Elizabeth (--------) Cowperthwaite, of Flushing, L. I., m. in January, 1690–91, Sarah Adams, of Flushing, L. I., and had: (1.) Thomas. (2.) John. (3.) Hugh. (4.) Elizabeth, who m., in 1712, Abraham[3] Shotwell, of Middlesex Co., N. J., (called Shadwell in the Cowperthwaite genealogy), [of John[2], Abr[1]. (pp 126, 88 ante)]. (5.) Susanna, who m., in 1717, Wm[2]. Webster, Jr., of Woodbridge, N. J. (pp. 3, 11-15, 56, 193). (6.) Hannah. (7.) Deborah, who m. Ambrose Copeland.

WEBSTER.

Lineage of certain descendants of William & Mary (--------) Webster,† of Woodbridge, N. J. (pp. 11-15, 56, 193).

William T[5]. Webster, 12th child of Hugh[4], Jr., & Sarah (Moore) Webster, of Norwich, Upper Canada (Canada West, now Ontario), [of John[3], Wm[2]., Wm[1]., (see pp. 11-15, 18-24)], b. 10-18, 1801, at Plainfield, N. J, went with his parents to Canada when about 17 years of age, removed in 1836 to Somerset, Hillsdale Co, Mich., where he bought several hundred acres of wild land, built a sawmill, and cleared a large farm. Selling this in 1863, he removed to Ypsilanti, Mich., and there d., 3-31, 1867; was an esteemed member and Elder of the Society of Friends (Orthodox); m. at Norwich, C. W., Sept. 10, 1827, Mary Stover, b. Feb. 15, 1807, Westerlo, Albany Co., N. Y., d. in Hillsdale Co., Mich., -------- May, 1876, dau. of Michael & Polly (Siple) Stover, of Norwich, C. W., [of Adam] (p. 15), and had 10 ch., 5 born at Norwich, C. W., & 5 in Somerset, Mich., namely: (1.) Susan S., b. 9-12, 1828, d. Lansing, Mich., Feb., 1890, unm. (2.) Elizabeth, b. 3-20, 1830, d. Norwich, C. W., 7-26, 1833. (3.) Charles, b. 1-6, 1832, d. Norwich, C. W., 7-22, 1833. (4.) Mary S[5]., b. 10-23, 1833, Norwich, C. W. (now Ont.), dw. Somerset, Hillsdale Co., Mich., P. O. Addison, Lenawee Co., Mich., m. at Wheatland, Mich., 1 Jan., 1859, Garret T. Fisk, b. 6 Oct., 1826, in Chemung Co., N. Y., and had: (a) Thaddeus K. Fisk, b. 20 Nov., 1859; (b) Charles H, b. 30 July, 1861, dw. in Hillsdale Co., Mich., (c) William W., b. 11 Aug., 1869, dw. Somerset, Mich.,—where all 3 were born—P. O. Addison, Mich. (5.) Sarah Webster, b. 7-1, 1836, Norwich, C. W., and there d. 6-10, 1837,

* It is from this Hugh Cowperthwaite that the name of Hugh became so common among the descendants of William[2] Webster, Jr., who married his (Hugh's) granddaughter, Susanna[3] Cowperthwaite, in 1717.

† The relationship, if any, between this family and that of John[1] and Mary (Shotwell) Webster, of Ipswich, Mass., has not been traced, nor has any connection been found between the Shotwells of New Jersey and the family of John Shotwell, or Shotwell, who, with wife Joanna, arrived at Ipswich, Mass., in 1638, was deacon of the First Congregational Church there, and there died in 1647.

(6.) Phebe, b. 10-13, 1838, Somerset, Mich., and there d. 6-26, 1840. (7.) Catharine, b. 11-3, 1840, dw. near Lansing, Mich., whither she removed in 1870, from Ypsilanti, Mich., attended Raisin Valley Seminary 4 years, gaining honors as composer of prose and verse; m. (by Elder -------- Gunn), at Leslie, Mich., 1 Jan., 1871, Henry Clay Everett, b. in Perinton, Monroe Co., N. Y., -------- son of Capt. Roswell & Rosamond (Packard) Everett, from Connecticut. (8.) John, b. 8-31, 1842, dw. near Lansing, Mich., m. Fannie Holmes, niece of Henry C. Everett. (9.) William T., Jr., b. 11-21, 1846, dw. near Lansing, Mich., a gardener; m. (1) Sarah Williams, who d. about 3 years later, s. p.; m. (2) Myra Hardy. (10) Thomas, b. 3-12, 1849, d. Somerset, Mich., 3-30, 1850.

Oliver B. Leonard, of 915 Madison Ave., Plainfield, N. J, with the Lawrence Cement Co., No. 1, Broadway, New York City, b. 1839, (m, 1865, Elizabeth Blossom Marsh), son of James & Mary[5] (Webster) Leonard, [of Morris[5], Webster, John[4], Hugh[3], Wm[2]., Wm[1].]. (See pp. 12-13, ante).

John[4] Webster, III., b. 1756±, d. 1817, [of Hugh[3], Sr.,] m. (1), about 1775, Mary Morris, and had: (1.) Morris[5], b. 19 July, 1777, dwelt in southern part of Essex Co., N. J., on the narrow strip which, by recent survey, falls in Middlesex Co., N. J., d. before 4th mo., 1854; m. (1), 1804, Sarah Line; m. (2), 28 of 9 mo., 1815, Hannah Marsh, dau. of Samuel[5] & Ann (Middleton) Marsh, [of Samuel & Mary[4] (Shotwell) Marsh, John[3] Shotwell, John[2], Abraham[1]]. (2.) Hannah, b. 22 June, 1783, m. at Rahway, 26 of 9 mo., 1805, Job Burdsall, of Woodbridge. (3.) James, b. 1785, m. Ann Marsh. (4.) Rachel, b. 16 May, 1788, d. in Lower Rahway, N. J., 2 of 1 mo., 1857, aged 69±, unm. (5.) Mary, b. 2 Feb. 1792, d. Rahway, N. J., 23 of 4 mo., 1868, aged 76 yrs. 2 mos. 10 days. (6.) Ann, b. May 1, 1794, m. James C. Ayers. (7.) John, b. 3 July, 1796. (8.) Lydia, b. 13 Aug., 1799, m. (1) George Brown; m. (2) William Briggs. John[4] Webster, III., m. (2) 1809, Isabel Smith, b. 1783, dau. of Chas. & Lydia Smith, and had: (9.) Hugh, b. 4 of 9 mo., 1809, Farmington, N. Y. (10.) Joseph, b. 21 of 1 mo., 1814. (11.) Betsy, b. 26 of 9 mo, 1815.

Morris[5] Webster, b. 1777, (p. 13), and 1st wife Sarah, nee Line, had: (1.) Mary, b. 1805, m. 1824± (certainly before 20 of 1 mo., 1825, contrary to the discipline of Friends), James Leonard. Morris[5] Webster, b. 1777, and 2nd wife, Hannah, nee Marsh, had: (2.) Sarah, b. 7 of 8 mo., 1816; m. Thomas H. Force. (3.) Samuel, b. 18 of 5 mo., 1819; m. Phebe F. Randolph. (4.) Ann, b. 22 of 6 mo., 1820; m. David Lenox. (5.) Reuben, b. 10 of 12 mo., 1821. (6.) Elizabeth, b. 13 of 11 mo., 1824. (7.) Susan, b. 23 of 5 mo., 1827, d. ---- of 2 mo., 1829.

Samuel[4] Webster, 1762-1843, son of Hugh[3] (b. 1730) & Sarah (Marsh) Webster, [the former of Wm[2]. & Susanna (Cowperthwaite) Webster, Wm[1]. and Mary (________) Webster, and the latter of Samuel[2] and Mary (________) Marsh, Joseph[2] & Sarah (Clark ?) Marsh, Samuel[1] & Comfort (__________) Marsh, of New Haven, Conn.], m. (2), Martha Thorn, and had: Mary[5] Webster, who m. Wm. Estil, and had: Hugh Mulford Estil, a bookseller, of Plainfield, N. J., et al.

BENJAMIN[2] WEBSTER'S BRANCH,

[of Wm[1]. & Mary (______) Webster, of Wood-bridge, N. J., (pp. 12, 56, 193)].

Benj[2]. Webster, 8th ch. of Wm[1]. & Mary (________) Webster, of Woodbridge, N. J., was b. 4 of 2 mo. (Apr.), 1709, became member of Kingwood (N. J.), Monthly Meeting of Friends by certificate from Woodbridge M. M., dated 8-17, 1751, but brought back a similar certificate 5 years later (10-21, '56); m. Rachel ____*, and had at least five children,—Susanna, Skinner, Joseph, Hannah & Anna,—and perhaps also Samuel, Sr.

I. Susanna[3] Webster [of Benj[2]. Wm[1].], b. 10-11, 1736, d. 2-24, 1832, was member of Woodbridge (N. J.) M. M. of Friends when she m., at Plainfield, in 1753 (between 9-21 & 10-19, '58), Samuel Kester, who had brought a certificate of membership and clearness with respect to marriage engagements from Kingwood M. M. He was b. 9-26, 1737, and d. 3-8, 1801, son of Harmanus & Ann (________) Kester. Five of their children,— Benjamin, Ann, Rachel[1], Hannah, and Mary Webster,—married 5 children of Stephen & Hannah (Paxson) Hambleton, of Bucks Co., Pa. Rachel's grandson, Chalkley J. Hambleton, Esq., of Chicago, has compiled a genealogy of the Hambleton family.

NOTE.—It has been supposed that this Susanna, wife of Samuel Kester, was sister also to the Samuel Webster, Sr., who married under care of Kingwood (N. J.) M. M. of Friends in 1755 (having declared intention 7-10, '55, with) Susanna Kester, who was b. 9-10, 1733, and d. ________, 1796, and had, among other children, Samuel Webster, b. 8-3, 1759, who m. in 1786, Rachel Willson, of Hardwick, N. J., and became member of Eden M. M. (in Erie Co., N. Y.), by certificate granted by Kingwood M. M., 4-11, 1816, for himself, wife and two minor children, Peter and Rachel,—as did also Samuel Webster, Jr., (probably an older son). Samuel & Rachel (Willson) Webster's children were: (a) John, b. 12-11, 1787; (b) Mary, b. 4-15, 1790; (c) Samuel [Jr.], b. 7-8, 1792; (d) Asa, b. 12-21, 1794; (e) Peter, b. 8-31, 1797; and (f) Rachel, b. 1-28, 1802. Samuel & Susanna (Kester) Webster's son Joseph[4], b. 11-22, 1769, m. Phebe Mac Crary, b. 11-2, 1765, dau. of Andrew & Phebe (________) Mac-Crary, and with 5 minor children acquired membership in Eden (N. Y.) M. M. by cert. from Kingwood (N. J.) M. M., granted 4-11, 1816. The children were: (a) William, b. 5-20, 1793; (b) Charles, b. 4-30, 1795; (c) Mary Ann, b. 5-23, 1797; (d) Thomas, b. 6-15, 1799; (e) Andrew, b. 5-29, 1801; (f) Susanna, b. 6-24, 1804; and (g) Phebe, b. 4-23, 1808, d. 1-18, 1812. One William Webster, Jr., had transferred his membership to Eden M. M. by certificate granted by Kingwood M. M., 6-9, 1814,—about two years

* It is supposed that this marriage was registered on the lost records of Abington (Pa.) M. M. whose books from 1697 to about 1730 are missing.

prior to the migration thither of these two families of his relatives. Samuel & Susanna (Kester) Webster's dau. Rebecca m. (1), in 1794, Thomas Stevenson, who d. in 1798, son of John & Mercy (King) Stevenson. Their membership, with that of their young dau. Susanna, had been transferred to Hardwick & Randolph M. M. by cert. dated 4-12, 1793; but Rebecca & dau. brought back a cert. to Kingwood M. M the same year; she m. (2), in 1810, John Freeman, of Woodbridge, Middlesex Co., N. J. One Joseph Webster was made a member of a committee of Kingwood M. M. in 1749, but his relationship to Samuel & Susanna has not been ascertained.

Samuel & Susanna (Webster) Kester, of Kingwood, N. J., had: (1.) Elizabeth, m. (1) Benj[3]. Hamilton [of Wm[2]., Jas[1].], b. 12-7, 1757, a farmer, of Solebury, Bucks Co., Pa., who d. about 1811; she m. (2), Reuben Paxson. (2.) Benj. removed, 1812, from Kingwood, N. J., to Boston, Erie Co., N. Y., and there d. in 1819; m., 6-19, 1782, Rachel[3] Hambleton, b. 3-7, 1765, d. 3-6, 1858, dau. of Stephen[2] & Hannah (Paxson) Hambleton, of Bucks Co., Pa., and granddaughter of James[1] Hambleton, of Solebury, Pa., member of Buckingham M. M. of Friends at its establishment in 1720, who d. in 1751, & wife Mary nee Greenleaf. (3.) Rachel, b. 8-2, 1762, d. 12-15, 1856, m. 11-23, 1780, John[3] Hambleton [of Stephen[2], Jas[1].], b. 6-14, 1755, in Solebury, Pa., removed, 1793, to a farm of 294 acres in Upper Oxford Tp., Chester Co., Pa., and there d. 10-8, 1834, an Orthodox Friend, though all his sons were Hicksite Friends. (4.) Mary, b. 5-21, 1764, d. 8-8, 1803, m. 11-24, 1785, Wm[3]. Hambelton [of Stephen[2] Jas[1].], b. 10-23, 1758, in Solebury, Pa, employed for a time at Ellicott's Mills, Baltimore, Md., settled 1802 on a farm in Little Britain, Lancaster Co., Pa, whence, after first wife's death, he removed in 1806 to a farm near Flushing, Belmont Co, O., and there d. 7-16, 1837. (5.) Anna, m. Jonas[3] Hambleton, b. 10-17, 1760, [of Stephen[2], Jas[1].]. (6.) Sarah, m. Joseph Palmer, of Chester Co., Pa. (7.) Susannah, dw. Rahway, N. J., and there d. in her 99th year, m. Jos. Stevenson. (8.) Hannah, m. Aaron Hambleton, b. 1-21, 1770, [of Stephen[2], Jas[1].].

II. Skinner[3] Webster, [of Benj[2]., Wm[1].], was of West Bradford Tp., Chester Co., in the "Province" of Pennsylvania, when he m. at Buckingham Friends' Meeting, in Bucks Co., Pa., 5-23, 1781, Jane Hambleton, of Solebury, Bucks Co., Pa., dau. of Stephen & Hannah (________) Hambleton, and had: (1.) Stephen, who m. Mary Thorpe. (2.) Hannah, who m. Jabez Thorpe. (3) Benjamin, who d. young. (4.) Aaron. (5) John, who d. young. (6.) Rachel. (7.) Wm[4]., 1794-1879, m. Elizabeth Thorpe. (8.) John[4] (again) m. Hannah Horner. (9.) Mary, m. (1) Jesse Holt; m. (2) Thos. Baines.

William[4] Webster [of Skinner[3], Benj[2]., Wm[1].], b. 11-21, 1794, d. 3-10, 1879, m. at Frankford, (Pa), Friends' Meeting, 9-25, 1821, Elizabeth Thorpe, dau. of Thos. & Elizabeth (________) Thorpe, and had: Edmund[5] Webster, b. 1-31,

1829, dw. 1156 S. Broad St., Phila., Pa., member of the Society of Friends (Hicksite). Member of executive committee of the board of managers of Swarthmore College, and of its committees on building and finance and on trusts, endowments and scholarships; m. 3-28, 1861, Rebecca N. Sheppard, dau. of Josiah Foster & Mary M. (--------) Sheppard.

John[4] Webster [of Skinner[3], Benj[2]., Wm[1].], b. 7-11, 1797, d. ------, buried in the grounds of Merion (Montgomery Co., Pa.,) Friends' Meeting; m. Dec. 1, 1819, Hannah Horner, and had 12 children: Julia Ann (1820-1852), Annabella C., Stephen G., Mary J., Sarah G., Edmund G., Isaac Spencer[3] (1830-1893), Rebecca G., William, Hannah H., John, and Keziah B.

Isaac Spencer[3] Webster [of John[4], Skinner[3], Benj[2]., Wm[1].], b. Dec. 7, 1830, d. Dec. 8, 1893, m., July 4, 1853, Sarah Catharine Ritch, "of the Rittenhouse family," and had 5 children,— Sarah B., Ida Theresa, Wm. Henry, Chas. Franklin, and A. Lincoln, the last of whom, b. July 7, 1869, dw. at No. 26 S. 15th St, Phila., Pa., unm. (1897).

III. Joseph[3] Webster [of Benj[2]., Wm[1].], b. 4-3, 1743, member of Friends' Meeting at Haverford, Pa., by cert. from Kingwood (now Quakertown, N. J.), M. M., m. Rebecca Kester, b. 12-12, 1738; membership transferred to meeting at Concord, Pa. by cert. from Haverford M. M., dated 6-4, 1788, for Jos. & wife, Rebecca, and children, Mary, Wm., Ruth, & Jos., one of same date and corresponding tenor being granted to their older dau. Rachel. Thence on 3-9, 1791. Joseph & wife and children, Wm., Ruth, & Jos. took a cert. directed to Chester Meeting, followed one month later by one for Rachel & Mary. The children were born as follows: (1) Rachel, b. 1-20, 1770. (2) Samuel, b. 5-10, 1771. (3.) Mary, b. 3-6, 1773. (4.) Wm., b. 11-24, 1774. (5.) Benj., b. 12-29, 1776. (6.) Jos., b. 8-4, 1781, d. 1-11, 1867.

William[4] Webster, [of Jos[3]., Benj[2]., Wm[1].], b. 11-24, 1774, m. (1) 12-4, 1800, Lydia Sharpless, and had 5 children: Mary, Rebecca, Sarah, Jos., & Lydia. He m. (2) 10-31, 1811, Agnes Yarnall, and had 4 children more, namely: Phebe, Wm., Jr., Caleb, & Ruth.

Wm[5]. Webster, Jr., [of Wm[4]., Jos[3]., Benj[2]., Wm[1].], b. 9-23, 1815, m. at Chichester (Pa.) Friends' Meeting House, 11-15, 1838, Elizabeth Larkin, dau. of Salkeld & Sarah Pennell Larkin, and had 11 children: Hannah, Sarah L., Nathan, Rebecca, Edward, Ruth Anna, William[6], Pennell L., Owen Y., Elizabeth & Richard.

Wm[6]. Webster, [of Wm[5]., Jr., Wm[4]., Jos[3]., Benj[2]., Wm[1].], b. 3-6, 1851, dw. 3226 Woodland Ave., W. Phila., Pa., m. by Friends' ceremony at the res. of the bride's father, No. 3224 Woodland Ave., W. Phila., Pa., on Fifth-day afternoon, 5th of Fifth-month, 1881, Cynthia Dora[6] Kester, dau. of John[5] & Ann T. (John) Kester, [of Jos. K[4]., & Mary (Wood) Kester, John & Hannah[3] (Webster) Kester, Benj[2]., Wm[1].], and had: (1) William, b. 10-16, 1882; and (2.) Dora Edna, b. 12-20, 1883.

IV. Hannah[3] Webster, [of Benj[2]., Wm[1].], b. 3-19, 1747, m. John Kester, b. 7-31, 1744, d. 7---, 1825, son of Paul[3] & Ruth (----) Kester, [of Johannes[2], Paulus[1], Kuester.*] In 1787 they and their children transferred their membership from Bradford (Pa.) M. M. of Friends to Concord Meeting in Chester Co., Pa., and thence to Exeter M. M. in Berks Co., Pa., by a certificate dated 12-5, 1792, which mentions beside, John Kester & wife Hannah, their children, Samuel, Mary, William, John, Benjamin, Ruth, Joseph, & Aaron. They removed to Mt. Pleasant Tp., Northumberland (now Columbia) Co, Pa.,— nearer to which place, on 4-23, 1796, Exeter M. M. established Catawissa M. M., which, in turn, in 1799, organized Muncy M. M. (name changed in 1856 to Fishing Creek M. M., held at Millville, Pa., and more recently to Millville M. M.)

Joseph K[4]. Kester†[of John & Hannah[3] (Webster) Kester, Benj[2]. Webster, Wm[1].], b. 6-14, 1785, d. 2-17, 1852, interred in Friends' Burial Ground at Fishing Creek, Pa.; m. (1) in Frankford (Pa.) Friends' Meeting House, 3-6, 1810, Mary Wood, b. 4-21, 1791, d. 11-15, 1820, buried in Millville (Pa.) Friends' Ground, dau. of Jas. & Sarah (Dicks) Wood, of Providence Tp, Delaware Co., Pa., and had 5 children, Mary, Ann, James W., John[5], and Elijah. He m. (2) 11-14, 1821, Rachel Musgrave, and had 12 children more,— Sarah M., Joseph W., Aaron, Wm. B., Septimus, Hannah M., Ruth, Rachel, Elizabeth, Mercy Ellis, Thos. Chalkley, & Benj. Franklin.

John[5] Kester [of Jos. K[4]., Hannah[3] (nee Webster), Benj[2]., Wm[1].], b. 8-21, 1817, in Mt. Pleasant Tp., Columbia Co., Pa., d. 4-3, 1893, suddenly, of paralysis, buried on the 7th in Darby Friends' Burial Ground in Delaware Co., Pa.; m. at Shamokin (Pa.) Friends' Meeting-House, 12-18, 1845, Ann Thomas John, b. 4-27, 1823, d. 3-8, 1864, of lockjaw, dau. of Asa Townsend John & wife, Mary, nee Thomas, and had 7 children: Joseph J., Townsend Wood, Mary Anna, Cynthia Dora[6], b. 8-20, 1853, in Locust Tp., Columbia Co., Pa., dw. 3226 Woodland Ave., W. Phila., Pa.; m. by Friends' Ceremony at the res. of her father in W. Phila., Pa., 5-5, 1881, Wm[6]. Webster, son of Wm[5]., Jr., & Elizabeth (Larkin) Webster, [of Wm[4]., Jos[3]., Benj[2]., Wm[1].], and had two children, Wm. & Dora E.

V. Anna[3] Webster, [of Benj[2]., Wm[1].], m. Paul Kester, of Fishing Creek, Pa., brother to Sam'l & Harmanus, of Hunterdon Co., N. J.,

---

* It is said that Paulus Köster (or Köster) with wife Gertrude, and three sons, Harmanus, Johannes, and Arnold, from Crefeld, Germany, came over in the time of William Penn with a shipload of German Quakers, and settled first at Germantown (now part of the city of Philadelphia). The son, Johannes[2] Knester (Kester) married, in 1692, Elizabeth Castle (Cassel), and their descendants and the Webster and Hambleton families intermarried and were closely allied for several generations.

† The K. was inserted to distinguish his name from that of his double cousin, Joseph, son of Paul & Anna[3] (Webster) Kester.

and had: Rachel, who m. Chandlee Eves; Joseph, who d. in Canada; & Arnold, who m. at Kingwood, N. J., Mary Kester, dau. of Benj. & Rachel (Hambleton) Kester, of Kingwood, N. J., afterward of Boston, Erie Co., N. Y., and granddau. of Sam'l & Susanna[2] (Webster) Kester, [of Benj[2]. Webster, Wm[1].], and of Stephen[2] & Hannah (Paxson) Hambleton, [of Jas[1].].

A certain William[2] Webster, of Abington, (Philadelphia Co.), Pa., son of John[1], of Abington, Pa., [and possibly grandson of the first William & Mary (_________) Webster, of Woodbridge, N. J., see p. 12], married with approbation of Abington (Pa.) M. M. between the dates of the meetings of 7-29 & 8-27, 1740, Ann Phips, and had: (1.) Tamer, b. 9-18, 1741. (2.) John, b. 2-23, 1744. (3.) Elizabeth, b. 11-7, 1746-7. (4.) Naylor[3] Webster, b. 6-26, 1749, dwelt at Horsham, Montgomery Co., Pa., and there d. in 1830, m. Martha Fisher. (5.) Martha, b. 7-9, 1752, (6.) William, b. 7-3, 1755. One William Webster produced in Abington M. M., 6-26, 1780, a written acknowledgment of the error of his conduct in paying fines in lieu of taking the test of allegiance and abjuration, which, after being "read and solidly considered," was accepted. One George Webster (perhaps of this family) m. before 10-31, 1774, (wife's name not stated), as on that date Friends report to Abington (Pa) M. M. that "George Webster has accomplished his marriage contrary to the rules of our Society, with one not in membership with us, by the assistance of a priest," and a testimony of denial against him and his said conduct was ordered to be drawn for approbation at the next monthly meeting. One George Webster, removed from Montgomery Co., Pa., to Lancaster Co., Pa., had sons: (1.) Naylor, who settled in Ohio, and there died; (2.) Jesse, who m. Elizabeth Lukens, and had: (a) Elizabeth, whose present address is, Melos House, Atlantic City, N. J.; (b) Jesse, of Parkesburg, Chester Co., Pa.; & (c) Lukens, who dw. in Philadelphia, Pa. (3.) William, who m. Sarah Lukens. (4.) George, who m. Ann Walton; and daughters, Patience, Martha, & Hannah.

For some infraction of Friends' discipline,—probably the voluntary payment of fine imposed for his refusal to take the oath of allegiance,—he was suspended from membership, but was restored to membership in Abington M. M., 1-26, 1778, having at that time presented a satisfactory written acknowledgment and condemnation of his misconduct, whatever it may have been.

Naylor[3] (1749-1830) & wife Martha (Fisher) Webster, of Horsham, Pa., had Sarah[4] Webster, 1789-1861, who m. Joseph Parry and had Mordecai[5] Parry, 1818-1892, who m. Gulielma Henley, and had Webster[6] Parry, of 2 0 N. Ninth St., Richmond, Ind., b. 1818, Notary Public, Real Estate & Loans, stockholder of the Richmond Nut Lock Co., 210 N. 9th St., Richmond, Ind., member of the Society of Friends (Orthodox), is collecting data relating to Naylor Webster's ancestry and kindred.

KING.

Harmanus[1] King & wife Marcia, with a colony of Friends from Holland, whither he had gone from England to escape religious persecution, came to America about the year 1676 and settled in Burlington Co., West Jersey. They had sons, Joseph[2], Sr.,* and John.

Joseph[2] King, Sr., was a farmer in Burlington Co., N. J., afterward in Piscataway, Middlesex Co., whence he finally removed, in 1729, to what is now Franklin Township, in the central part of Hunterdon Co., N. J., where he purchased of Mary Tomkins 954 acres of land situated along the south branch of Raritan River, and settled on it, building there, in 1733, a grist-mill about four miles from Kingwood Friends' Meeting-House. He was one of the first trustees of the Meeting property there, associated with Edward Rockhill, John Stevenson, Samuel Willson, & Samuel Large; he was appointed an Elder in Kingwood M. M., 14 of 11 mo., 1744, and an overseer 12 of 7 mo., 1745. A Meeting for worship was begun in this part of Hunterdon Co., about the year 1729, and Bethlehem (afterward called Kingwood) Monthly Meeting was established as early as 1744. The oldest records of the meeting, dating from this time, are kept at Newtown, Pa. Hardwick meeting for worship was established in 1745, but it continued to be a branch of Kingwood Monthly Meeting until 1797. Among the Elders for that M. M. in 1756, beside Joseph King, Sr., for the Hunterdon Co. Friends, Richard Lundy and Thomas Lundy were named for the Hardwick Branch.

A memorial of the time of Death & Burial of Joseph King, Senior, [1683±-1761].

Our antient Friend Joseph King departed this Life the 10th day of the 12th month 1761, In the Seventy-eighth year of his age, and was Inter'd in Friends Burying Ground at Kingwood the Eleventh day of the same Month. He was not, as could be perceived, attended with any Violent illness, and he departed quietly as one going to Sleep. He was esteem'd amongst us to be an Honest, Sober, Innocent, well-minded man, a good & Inoffensive Neighbor, well beloved of Friends & others, for which reasons he was appointed an Elder amongst us before the Select meeting was settled here, and for the same reasons hath been continued an Elder amongst us ever since until his Death, and we doubt not but that he is gone to Eternal rest.

Copied from records of Kingwood Monthly Meeting.

*The Joseph[2] King, Sr., of this article is identical with the Joseph[1] King mentioned in earlier pages of this work; and Nathan[4] King of this Appendix is identical with Nathan[3] King, of Part I, pp. 16-18.

HIRAM EDMUND⁴ DEATS, OF FLEMINGTON, N. J., BORN 1870.

SON OF HIRAM AND ELMIRA³ (STEVENSON) DEATS,

Of Flemington, Hunterdon Co., N. J., and grandson 2 of John⁵ and Hannah⁶ (Willson Stevenson, the former a descendant of Joseph⁴ and Susannah (Kester Stevenson, Joseph and Mercy³ King Stevenson, of Hardwick, N. J., Joseph⁵ and Mary (·) King, Joseph² and Mercy Nicholson King, Harmanus¹, and the latter of Gabriel and Grace⁴ Brotherton, Willson, James³ and Alice Schooley Brotherton, Henry and Ann² Shotwell Brotherton, of Woodbridge, N. J., Daniel² Shotwell, of Staten Island, Abraham Shotwell, of Elizabethtown, N. J., 1665.

Joseph[2] King, Sr., m., 1707, (declared intention of marriage 4-5, 1707, at Chesterfield M. M., Burlington Co., N. J.), Marcy [Mercy] Nicholson, b. 13 of 12 mo., 1687, dau. of George & Hannah.

Joseph[2] King, Sr., & wife Marcy [Mercy] (Nicholson) King had certainly 3 children, namely: 1, Joseph[3], Jr., b. 1712; 2, William[3], b. 4-1, 1714, dw. Kingston, N. J., m. 1737±, Abigail Doughty; 3, Hannah, b. 1717. And perhaps another daughter,—the Elizabeth King who declared intention of marriage, in Kingwood M. M., 8 of 2 mo., 1753, with Thomas Coat.

Joseph[3] King, Jr., b. 1712, & wife, Mary (________) King, members of Kingwood M. M., had 8 children, all b. in that part of Amwell Tp., Hunterdon Co., N. J., which was set off in or about the year 1748 to form the township of Kingwood, namely:

1. Mary King, Jr., b. 3 of 3 mo., 1738, declared intention of marriage, in Kingwood M. M., 12 of 2 mo., 1756, with David Marsh.

2. Mercy, b. 26 of 10 mo., 1739, (not always easily distinguishable, with certainty, from records of her cousin, Mercy, dau. of Wm., King, q. v.); m. in winter of 1760-61, (declared intention of marriage in Kingwood M. M., 12-7, 1760, with) John Stevenson, b. 22 Jan., 1732, who removed with wife "Mary" [Mercy] about 1778, to Hardwick, N. J., and there d. 12 Apr., 1812, son of Thomas (b. 1707) & Sarah (Whitehead) Stevenson (who were m. 29 Apr., 1730), and had, among other children, a son Joseph[3] Stevenson, b. 1767. (One line of descendants later.)

3. Jane, b. 29 of 10 mo., 1741.

4. George, b. 21 of 10 mo., 1743, was under dealing, in Kingwood M. M., 14 of 2 mo., 1771, for having m. out of the Society of Friends.

5. Anne, b. 28 of 2 mo., 1746, d. 24 of 8 mo., N. S., 1759.

6. Hannah, b. 10 of 5 mo., 1748.

7. Nathan[4] King, b. 3 of 5 mo., O. S., 1750, Kingwood, Hunterdon Co., N. J.; was appointed an overseer in Kingwood M. M. in 1781; released from that office at his own request in 1785. He m. 2-19, 1771, Sarah Moore, [of Jos'., Sam'l', Jno[2]., Sam'l', (see pp. 16-24)]. They and daughters, Mary and Ann,—then of mature age,—and minor children, Sarah, John, Joseph, Amy, Asher and Christiana, became members of R. & P. M. M., by cert. from Kingwood M. M., dated 7-12, 1792.

8. Alice Maria, b. 28 of 9 mo., N. S, 1752.

John & Mercy (King) Stevenson had Joseph[3] Stevenson, b. 19 Mar., 1767, d. 4 Aug., 1841, m. (1) in 1793, Ann Willson of Hardwick, N. J.; m. (2) 22 Sept., 1796, Susanna Kester, and had John[4] Stevenson, b. 16 May, 1801, d. 12 Mar., 1854, m. 12 May, 1824, Hannah Willsou, b. 29 Oct., 1802, d. 20 Mar., 1869, dau. of Gabriel & Grace (Brotherton) Willson,—the former b. 29 Oct., 1752, d. 10 Mar., 1835, s. of Gabriel[3] & Elizabeth (Lundy) Willson [of Samuel[2], Robert'], and the latter, dau. of James[2] (b. 28 Aug.(?), 1726), & Alice (Schooley) Brotherton, [of Henry' (see pp. 101-3)], and had Elmira[3] Stevenson, b. 12 Dec., 1830, m. 28 Nov., 1865, Hiram Deats, b. 12 April, 1810, d. 22 Nov., 1887, s. of John' & Ursila (Barton) Deats,—the former b. 1 Feb., 1769, d 1 May, 1841, and the latter b. 20 Jan., 1767, d. 8 Oct., 1853, dau. of Elisha & Jemima (________) Barton. Elisha, b. Oct. 5, 1729, d. May 31, 1823, was a Captain in the Morris Militia, of N. J., in the Revolutionary War.

Hiram & Elmira (Stevenson) Deats, of Flemington, N. J., had an only son, Hiram Edmund Deats, whose portrait is herewith presented, b. 20 May, 1870, at Brookville, Hunterdon Co., N. J.; was a close student at Peddie Institute, Hightstown, N. J., and graduated with honors in June, 1891. His father gave largely of his means to Peddie, and the son has likewise taken a deep interest in the welfare of the school and is one of its earnest supporters and liberal benefactors, being secretary of its board of corporators. He established, in 1891, *The Jerseyman*, a magazine of local history, which he still publishes at Flemington, N. J. He is a born collector, and while interested in all branches of collecting, pays particular attention to the Postage and Revenue Stamps of the United States, of which he has one of the finest collections in this country. He has also a large library of the literature of the subject, which ranks second among similar collections. He lives on a farm, formerly the Reading homestead, near Flemington. The locality was a favorite Indian resort, and Mr. Deats has gathered a large collection of stone implements along the Mineakoning Creek, which flows through his property. He is a member of the Sons of the American Revolution, the Order of the Founders and Patriots of America, and of numerous Historical, Scientific, and Philatelic Societies.

H. E. Deats, of Flemington, N. J., m. 27 Sept., 1893, Eva Augusta Taylor, b. 25 Aug., 1870, dau. of James Grover & Elizabeth Ely (Perrine) Taylor, who were m. 1869, the former b. 31 May, 1830, and the latter, b. 15 Mar., 1842, descendants of early Monmouth Co. (N. J.) families,—and had Elsie May Deats, b. 31 July, 1894.

James Grover Taylor, b. 31 May, 1830, d. 22 Feb., 1897,—son of James Grover Taylor and wife Sarah, *nee* Morford, the former b. 2 Jan., 1805, d. 7 Dec., 1854, and the latter b. 18 Dec., 1802, d. 25 Sept., 1884,—m. 9 Dec., 1869, Elizabeth Ely Perrine, b. 15 March, 1842,—dau. of James Wm. Perrine & wife Deborah Ann, *nee* Dey (who were m. 8 March, 1838), the former b. 24 July, 1813, d. 2 June, 1893, and the latter b. 16 Nov., 1816, dau. of David Baird Dey & wife Elizabeth, *nee* Ely (who were m. in 1811), [the former b. 10 March, 1789, d. 7 June, 1860, and the latter b. 30 Jan., 1794, d. 27 Apr., 1828], and granddaughter of John Dey & wife Mary, nee Baird,—the former b. 28 Dec., 1741, d. 26 Apr., 1829, was a Captain in the Second Regiment from Middlesex Co., N. J., in the Revolutionary War, and the latter b. 30 Sept., 1747, d. 17 Apr., 1836.

Christiana King, b. 1789, dau. of Nathan[4] & Sarah (Moore) King, of Woodbridge Tp., N. J., [of Joseph[3], Joseph[2], Harmanus[1]], m. at Rahway, N. J., 23 of 6 mo., 1830, (as 2d wife) Jonathan Harned (see p. 18).

Joseph[5] King, 1782-1859, of Granville, O., [of Nathan[4] & Sarah (Moore) King, of Amwell, Plainfield, and Rahway, N. J., [of Joseph[3], Jos[2]., Harmanus[1]], (see pp. 16, 17, 13, 127)], m., 1805, Catharine[5] Laing, 1787-1841, [of Thomas[4] & Martha (Webster) Laing, Isaac[3], John[2], John[1]]. Their son, Thomas L[6]. King, 1808-1894, late of Topeka, Kans. (pp. 17-18), m. (2) 3 June, 1863, Alice Gray, b. 18 Aug., 1847, dau. of John & Rebecca (Livingston) Gray, who d. at Lawrencebury, Ind., the former b. 14 Feb. 1784, in Scotland, and the latter b. 18 Jan., 1813, dau. of Associate Justice John Livingston, of Wilmington, Ind., who was b. 30 Nov., 1774, in New York, and d. 3 Jan., 1846, of distinguished Scotch ancestry, & wife Rebecca, nee Allen, b 7 Nov., 1782, niece of Ethan & Ira Allen, of revolutionary fame.

Martha L[6]. King, b. 1813, dau. of Jos[5]. & Catharine (Laing[5]) King, of Granville, Ohio, (p. 17), d. at Newark, O, 13 Jan., 1895, aged 81; m., 1837, James Knight, b. 31 March, 1805, at New Athens, Harrison Co, O., son of John & Nancy (........) Knight, and had Joseph King Knight, D. D. S., of 145 W. River St., Hyde Park, Mass.

William[3] King, of Kingston, N. J, b. 4-1, 1714, [of Jos[2]., Harmanus[1]], m. 1737±, Abigail[3] Doughty, b. 10-3, 1716,—said to have been one of the 12 daughters of Jacob[2] & Amy (Whitehead) Doughty, to each of whom a silver spoon was given, marked with the parental initials, J. A. D.,—sister to Amy Doughty who m. in 1719, Samuel Stockton, and to Deborah & Daniel who are mentioned in the will of Jacob Doughty, 1737, and granddaughter (1) of Elias & Sarah (........) Doughty, of Long Island, and (2) of Maj. Daniel Whitehead, patentee of Jamaica, L. I., and wife Abigail, nee Stevenson, whose dau. Amy[2] (Whitehead) Doughty, b. 6-17, 1676, d. in 1742. William[3] & Abigail (Doughty) King became members of Chesterfield (N. J) M. M. by cert. from Kingwood M. M., dated 14 of 12 mo., N. S., 1752. They had issue:

1. Marcia [Mercy], b. 6-4, 1738, m. John Potts.

2. Amy[4] King, b. 10-12, 1739, d. 3-16, 1819, m. John[3] Stockton, of Princeton, N. J, 1732-1800, son of Richard[3] (1692-3—1760) & Esther (Smith) Stockton, [of Richard[2] & Susannah (Witham Robinson) Stockton, Richard[1] & Abigail (........) Stockton, who arrived at Flush-

ing, L I., prior to 8 Nov., 1656, and supposed to have been a descendant of John Stockton, Esq, of Keddington, in the parish of Malpas, and county of Chester, Eng., who m., about 1550, Eleanor Clayton], and had: Abigail[7] Stockton, b. 2-25, 1776, d. 2-6, 1864, m. Amos[5] Lundy, b. 3-26, 1778, d. 6-26, 1851, son of Isaac[4] (b. 12-26, 1752, d. 12-6, 1779), & Anne (Large) Lundy, of Hardwick, N. J.,—the former of Samuel[3] & Anna (Schooley) Lundy, Richard[2], Richard[1], (see pp. 249-52), and the latter, dau. of Jacob[3] (1714-1799) & Mary (Bunting) Large, [of Samuel[2] (1688-1761) & Rebecca (Willson) Large, of Hunterdon Co, N. J.], and had Amy Stockton[6] Lundy, b. 6-9, 1807, d 9-5, 1894, m. Hugh[6] Exton, son of Hugh[5] & Mary (........) Exton, natives of England, [of Hugh[4], John[3], John[2], John[1]], and had Henrietta Louisa Exton, M. D., of Clinton, Hunterdon Co., N. J.

3. Anne King.

4. Joseph[4] King, b. 4-12, O. S., 1745, m. (1) Sarah Willson; m. (2) Anne (Large) Lundy; m. (3) Sarah (Scott) Stockton. By the 2d wife he had a son, William Large[5] King, b. 2-12, 1789, d. ...... 1869, m. Elizabeth Large, dau. of Samuel & Mary. His only surviving child, Mrs. James P. Huffman, dwells at Clinton, Hunterdon Co., N. J.

ROBINS.

Daniel[1] Robins, of Woodbridge, N. J., & wife Hope, According to Woodbridge Town Records, has issue: (1.) Lydia, b. 25 July, 1668. (2.) Joseph, b. 12 March, 1670. (3.) Richard, b. 14 Feb., 1673. (4.) Hope, b. 15 July, 1674 [probably d. young]. (5.) Nathaniel, b. 22 March, 1676. (6.) Moses, b. 27 March, 1679. (7.) Hope[2] (again), b. 10 Dec., 1681, m. at Woodbridge, N. J, 18 March 1699, John[2] Moore, son of Samuel (see pp. 18-21). (8.) Farrington, b. 24 May, 1683. (9.) Benj., b. 5 June, 1686. There was probably an older son, Daniel, namely the Daniel Robins who married in Woodbridge, N. J., 27 Nov., 1691, Mary Parker.

MOORE *

The following are abstracts of three *wills* from surrogate records preserved at Trenton, N. J., namely, those of (1) John[2] Moore, son of Samuel & Mary (Ilsley) Moore, of Woodbridge, N. J., formerly of Newbury, Mass.; (2) Samuel[3] Moore, son of John[2] & Hope (Robins) Moore, [of Samuel[1]]; and (3) Joseph[4] Moore, of Hunterdon Co, N. J., formerly of Middlesex Co., son of Samuel[3] & Mary (........) Moore [of John[2], Samuel[1]], and brother to Edward[4] Moore, of Lower Rahway, N. J., and to Samuel[4] Moore, of Upper Canada:

Will of John Moore, of Woodbridge, Middlesex Co., dated March 13th, 1735. Proved April

_____
* See also pp. 18-24, ante.

20th, 1736. Wife, Mary. Sons, Benjamin, Enoch, Samuel, Daniel. William, John. Daughters, Rachel, Mary, Hannah, Deborah, Sarah, Elizabeth. Hope, Frances. Executor: Son Benjamin; wife Mary, Executrix. Witnesses: Joseph Conger, Joseph Oliver, Benj. Sharp, J. Stevens. Recorded in Liber C. of Wills, page 85.

Will of Samuel Moore, of Woodbridge, Middlesex Co., dated May 3rd, 1750. Proved, &c, June 1st, 1751. Wife, Mary. Sons, Joseph, Edward, Isaac, John, Samuel. Executors: Wife Mary Moore and brother Enoch Moore, of Essex Co. Witnesses: Robart Moores, Michael Moore, Isaac Prall, Nugient Kelly. He was in his fortieth year when he made his will. Recorded in Liber E. of Wills, page 529.

Will of Joseph Moore, of the Township of Amwell, Hunterdon Co, dated 22nd day of the Second mouth, 1793. Proved &c., Nov. 8th, 1793. Wife not mentioned. Sons: Samuel Moore, John Moore, Benjamin Moore. Daughters: Huldah Moore, Anna Moore, Miranda Moore, Sarah King. Rachel Head, Hannah Cary. Executors: Henry Clifton, Samuel Kester, Robert Emley. Witnesses: Isaac Still, John Hogland, Abraham Hogland. Sister, Mary Decamp. Recorded in Liber 33 of Wills, page 287.

The following, from a History of Hunterdon County, N. J., was copied from the Records of Kingwood (now Quakertown) M. M.:

"A brief account of Friends' sufferings belonging to Kingwood Preparative Meeting, in the years 1776-78, for not complying with the u just requisitions of men to become instruments in the shedding of human blood. Our worthy Friend Joseph Moore, for refusing to take the test of allegiance to the State of New Jersey—so called—& abjuring the king of Great Brittain, was confined in Trenton Jail near 6 weeks, & had the test tendered to him again by the court, but he, refusing to comply, was fined in the sum of £60, & discharged from confinement, for which sum the following chattels were distrained: 1 yoke of oxen & 1 mare, worth £10. For militia fines & tax, 1 yoke oxen, 2 cows, 1 mare & 1 colt, worth £61."

Joseph¹ Moore, an approved minister of the Society of Friends, son of Samuel" & Mary (..........) Moore, of Lower Rahway, in the part of Woodbridge Tp., Middlesex Co, now within the city of Rahway, Union Co., N. J, grandson of John² & (first wife) Hope (Robins) Moore, and great grandson (1) of Samuel¹ & (2d of 3 wives) Mary (Ilsley) Moore & (2) of Daniel & Hope (........) Robins, all of Woodbridge, N. J.,—dwelt for many years in Amwell Tp., Hunterdon Co., N. J., probably within the present Township of Raritan, which was erected in 1838, from part of the territory of the original Township of Amwell. The precise location of his dwelling has not been ascertained, no one in

the neighborhood seeming to have any recollection of having heard of the family. The house in which his intimate friend, Thomas Atkinson, resided, is yet standing, and in a very good state of preservation. It is about two and a half miles east of Flemington, in the Township of Raritan, and is built of stone in the side of a steep hill and presents to view two stories in front and one at the back. The public road runs near and in front of it, between it and the south branch of the Raritan River, on which, almost opposite his dwelling, Thomas Atkinson built, in 1742, a mill, which was rebuilt in 1853 by Jacob Rockafellow, and is now the property of Mr. Alex. S. Rockafellow, who resides near the old Atkinson homestead.

Joseph¹ Moore and family having settled in this vicinity, became members of Kingwood (now Quakertown, N. J.,) Monthly Meeting of Friends on the 10th of 7th mo., 1766, by certificate from Rahway & Plainfield M. M. On 6th mo. 12th, 1783, Kingwood M. M. granted certificates to his daughter Ann and to Joseph for himself, wife, & 3 minor children, Benj., Hannah, & Miranda, directed to the M. M. at Chesterfield, Burlington Co., N. J., but these were returned to Kingwood M. M. 6 mo. 10, 1784; and Joseph and his household continued to worship at Kingwood until his death, which occurred in the autumn of 1793, at the close of his arduous service of several months on the expedition to Detroit, undertaken under care of Philadelphia Yearly Meeting of Friends in conjunc'ion with a government commission appointed in the hope of being able to negotiate a general treaty of peace with the various Indian tribes northwest of the Ohio River. (See pp. 21-24.)

One Samuel Moore was reported to Kingwood M. M. 9-8, 1808, for having neglected the attendance of meetings and for intemperance, which latter he denied; he was treated with for his delinquencies, and was finally disowned by the Society, 11-9, 1809. Joseph¹ Moore's son Samuel, had m. in 1781, Amelia Prall, dau. of the Benj. Prall who d. 17 Nov., 1791. John Moore and family transferred their membership to Rahway & Plainfield M. M. by cert. from Kingwood M. M., granted 9-8, 1787. Benj. Moore, in 7th mo., 1790, brought to Kingwood M. M. a cert. of membership from Buckingham (Pa.) M. M.; but, having m. contrary to Friends' Discipline, etc., he was disowned. He was, however, restored to membership in 1st mo., 1807, after making satisfactory acknowledgment of his transgressions, and thereupon transferred his membership to Buckingham M. M. by cert. granted by Kingwood M. M., 2-9, 1807. Miranda Moore became member of Buckingham (Pa) M. M. by cert. from Kingwood M. M., granted 5-9, 1793. And after the father's death, Huldah & Ann Moore, having also moved thither, acquired membership in the same meeting by cert. from Kingwood M. M., granted 6-12, 1794.

Edward[4] Moore, [of Samuel[3], John[2], Samuel[1]], b. 6 Nov., 1733, probably in the part of Woodbridge Tp., Middlesex Co., now within the city of Rahway, Union Co., N. J., was a carpenter in Lower Rahway, became member of the Society of Friends there by request, 15 of 8 mo., 1764, and there d., 8 of 3 mo., 1822; m. (1) _ _ _ _ _ _ _ _ and had:

1. Thomas, b. 6 Jan., 1755, at Lower Rahway, N. J., was a Loyalist or Tory in time of the Revolutionary War, and settled about 1782 in Nova Scotia, d. _ _ _ _ _ _ _ _ _ _ _ _; m. about 1775 _ _ _ _ _ _ _ _ _ _ _ _ _, and had 5 children: (a) John, who m. _ _ _ _ _ _ _ _ _, and had 1 son & 3 daughters; (b) Esther; (c) Edward[6], who m. twice and had 16 children; he m. (1) Rebecca Dakin, and had 9 children,—Abraham, Deborah, Rachel, Thomas, William, John[7], (b. 1816±, living, 1896, with dau., Miss L. Moore, at Bear River, N. S.), James, Daniel & Sarah. Edward[6] Moore m. (2) _ _ _ _ _ _ _ _ _ _ _, and had 7 children more,—Esther, Samuel, Isaac, Charles, Robinson, Joseph & Edward. (d) Rachel; (e) Joseph, who m. _ _ _ _ _ _ _ _ _ _ _ and had one daughter.

2. Mary, b. 26 Apr., 1757, (probably d. young).

3. Rachel, b. 8 Oct., 1758.

4. Deborah[5], b. 19 May, 1761, d. _ _ _ _ _ _ _ _ _ _ _; m. 26 of 7 mo., 1787, (as 2d wife) Titus[5] Shotwell, 1, 1759-1835, son of Daniel[4] & Deborah (Shotwell) Shotwell, [of Joseph[3], Daniel[2], Abraham[1]] (see pp. 103, 173. *ante*).

5. Mary (again), b. 7 May, 1764.

6. Sarah, b. 1 June, 1765.

7. Samuel, b. 9 March, 1768.

8. Isaac[5], b. 2 Oct., 1772, was a surveyor & examiner, dw. at the homestead in Lower Rahway, N. J., and there d. 25 Oct., 1850; m. (1), about 1831, Elizabeth G. _ _ _ _ _ _ _ _ _, who d. 21 of 10 mo., 1831, aged 55; he m. (2), 15 May, 1833, Hannah[3] Price, b. 4 May, 1806, d. 9 March, 1870, dau. of Ichabod & Susan[5] (Moore) Price, (m. in New York, 12 May, 1804),—the former, b. 4 Oct., 1781, in Elizabethtown, N. J, d. 22 Feb., 1802, and the latter b. 10 Feb., 1784, at Rahway, N. J., d. 4 May, 1871, dau. of John[3] & Hannah (Copeland) Moore, (m. 1781), [of Jos[4]., Sam'l[3], John[2], Sam'l[1]], and had: (a) Edward, b. 9 June, 1834. (b) Benton P[5]., b. 11 Aug, 1835, m. 18 Oct., 1860. Jane E. Christina, (and had: Henry, b. 29 Oct., 1861; Charles, b. 2 June, 1864; Hannah, b. 24 Sept., 1865; & Margaret, b. 8 Oct., 1867). (c) Charles, b. 7 July, 1838. (d) Walter, b. 5 Aug., 1841.

9. Edward, b. 14 Apr., 1774.

10. Marion, b. 21 Feb., 1776.

Samuel[4] (b. 4 Apr., 1742,) and Rachel (Stone) Moore (m. 8 Nov., 1763,) of Norwich, C. W., [of Samuel[3], John[2], Samuel[1] (pp. 18-21)], had among others, Samuel[5] Moore, b. 23 of 3 mo., 1784, m. (2) 28 Sept., 1815, Elizabeth L[6]. Shot-well, 1795-1827, dau. of Wm[5]. & Elizabeth (Moore) Shotwell, of Bricktown, now Rahway, [of Benj[4]., Jno[3]., Jno[2]., Abr[1].], and had Harvey Shotwell[6] Moore, b. 19 July, 1820, m. (2) 23 Aug., 1853, Susan Van Winkle, and had Wm. Harvey Moore, b. 19 Aug., 1854; dw. 28 Sanford Ave., Plainfield, Union Co., N. J., an electrician; is collecting data relating to the genealogy of the Moore family, and invites correspondence with any members of the same. He m. 17 Nov., 1886, Mary C. Rocap.

KESTER ADDENDA.

The following additional items were received too late for insertion (between the last two paragraphs) on page 271:

The younger three children of John[5] and Ann T. [John] Kester of West Philadelphia, Pa., are: (5.) Roselda, who dwells at Kennett Square, Chester Co, Pa., having m. Edward P. Cloud, who is editor and proprietor of the "Kennett (Weekly) Republican," and of "Cloud's Poultry News," and had one child, John Kester Cloud. (6.) Annie who dwells at the homestead, unm. (7.) William W. Kester, who is engaged in the milk business, and resides near Darby, Pa.

The father, John[5] Kester, 1817-1895, of No. 3224 (now 3226) Woodland ave., W. Phila., Pa., owned at time of his death the oldest milk route in the city, retaining to the last, customers who had patronized him when he first embarked in the business nearly fifty years before. He was one of the four originators of the Philadelphia Milk Exchange. He was also identified with other successful business operations; and, though his early struggles were somewhat handicapped by disasters, he was able by hard work, frugality, and carefulness to accumulate a goodly competence. He was a devout and consistent member of the Society of Friends (Hicksite), and elder of Darby Monthly Meeting, a representative to Philadelphia Yearly Meeting from Fishing Creek Half Year's Meeting. Was accustomed to welcome to his house Friends attending the Y. M. from a distance. He was a kind and faithful husband and father, nobly endeavoring to discharge to his seven children after the death of their mother in 1864, the tender offices of both parents. A careful adviser to the many who sought his counsel, an honest, upright christian, and a friend to the oppressed of all races and conditions. He was a firm advocate of peaceful arbitration as the wisest way to settle difficulties which rise between governments and in neighborhooods. But he is probably most widely remembered as "an earnest and staunch advocate of prohibition and total abstinence." In politics, originally a whig, afterward a republican, and steadfastly favorable to the recognition of the equal political and other rights of women.

III.

ADDITIONAL DATA CONCERNING RELATIVES OF THE COMPILER'S MATERNAL GRANDFATHER, GEORGE WASHINGTON[3] GARDNER, 1785-1849, OF ELBA, GENESEE CO., N. Y.,

SON OF JOHN[4] & BATHSHEBA (WATSON) GARDNER, OF WASHINGTON CO., R. I., AND LIVINGSTON CO., N. Y. [OF JOHN[3], WILLIAM[2], GEORGE[1]]: ADDENDA TO RECORDS PRESENTED IN PART I., PP. 24-37

GARDNER.

Sunderland Pattison[4] Gardner, of Farmington, N. Y., son of Elisha W[3]. & Sarah (Pattison) Gardner, of Farmington, N. Y., [of William[4] & Sarah (Watson) Gardner, John[3], William[2], George[1], (p. 30)], b. 4 of 7 mo., 1802, at Rensselaerville, Albany Co., N. Y., was first recorder of Farmington (N. Y.) Monthly Meeting of (Hicksite) Friends, 1828. On account of a demand (by L. Cowdry, Marshall) for $4 for military fines on the 5 of 2 mo., 1829, he was imprisoned for 11 days in Ontario Co., (N. Y.) jail, and again in 1830. He was a farmer, and for about 50 years an esteemed Minister of the Society of Friends, and traveled much in the ministry, attending in that time no less than 2300 funerals. He d. at Farmington, N. Y., ..., 1893. He m., at his residence in Farmington, N. Y., 23 of 5 mo., 1863, Annette H. Bell, of Farmington, N. Y., dau. of Wm. & Sarah H. (........) Bell, and had: (1) Sunderland P., Jr., b. 12-23, 1869. (2) Oscar Bell Gardner, b. 6-18, 1871. (3) Anson L., b. 2-7, 1873.

[For Elisha Watson[4] Gardner, bro. to S. P., see page 10].

John C[7]. Gardner, 2d, of Alexander, N. Y., son of Joel[6] & Bathsheba[6] (Gardner) Gardner, of Elba, N. Y.,—the former, son of Abiel[5] & Polly (Jewell) Gardner, of Hector, N. Y., [of Thomas[4], Wm[3]., Wm[2]., Geo[1].], and the latter, dau. of Jeffrey Watson[5] & Freelove (Gardner) Gardner, of Elba, N. Y., and granddau. (1) of John[4] & Bathsheba (Watson) Gardner, [of John[3], Wm[2]., Geo[1].], and (2) of Clark[4] & Amy (Lillibridge) Gardner, [of Wm[3]., Wm[2]., Geo[1].], (see p. 31), was b. in Elba, N. Y., ... 1826, d. at his residence in the eastern part of the town of Alexander, Genesee Co., N. Y., 28 July, 1893, aged 67 years, having resided upon his farm there since his removal in 1875 from that of his uncle, Jeffrey W. Gardner, in the western part of the town of Elba; interred at Batavia cemetery. He was an exemplary member, and for many years a deacon, of the Free Baptist Church at West Bethany. He left a widow, S. Maria (Judd) Gardner, 5 sons, Jeffrey W.,

Herbert J. (since deceased), & Fred G., of Batavia, Luther W. & Otis J., at home in Alexander, and 4 daughters, Mrs. Herbert Harding, of Bethany, Miss Cora Gardner, of Batavia, & Misses Myrtle & Grace, of Alexander.

Jeffrey W[6]. & Martha M. (Turner Atwater) Gardner, of Elba, N Y., (p. 31) had two children: (1) Jeffrey Turner Gardner, b. 22 Oct., 1876, Elba, N. Y, and there d. 21 March, 1877. (2) Grace Freelove, b. 28 Nov., 1878, Elba, N. Y., inherited the homestead of her father and grandfather in Elba, N. Y.

George Milton[6] Gardner, Sr., of 211 Clinton St., Jackson, Mich., b. 1835, son of George Washington[5] & Diana (Berry) Gardner, of Elba, N. Y., (pp. 34-5), [of John[4], John[3], Wm[2]., Geo[1].], (for his ancestors and their immediate households, see pp. 24-49), m., 1857, Jane E[1]. Gardner, b. 1840, a descendant of Geo[6]., Abiel[5], Capt. Thomas[4], Wm[3]. (p. 29), Wm[2]., Geo[1]. Gardner, of Newport, R. I.

Capt. Thomas[4] Gardner, of S. Kingstown, R I., and Rensselaerville, N. Y., b. in March, 1738-9, son of William[3], Jr., & Freelove (Joslin) Gardner, of S. Kingstown, R. I., (perhaps identical with the Thos. Gardner who there m., in 1765, Abigail Parker), had (some of them probably by a former wife): (1.) Abiel[5], b. about 1758-9, said to have served at age of 17 under his father in the R. I. Militia during the Revolutionary War in defense of a certain bridge on Boston Neck, R. I.; settled about 1797 at Rensselaerville, Albany Co., N Y.; removed about the beginning of the century to the town of Durham, Greene Co., N. Y, and thence, about 1817, to Hector, Tompkins (now Schuyler) Co., N. Y., and there d. 22 Jan., 1836,—before the organization of the county of Schuyler from parts of Tompkins, Steuben, Chemung, and Tioga Counties. He m., 23 Feb., 1797, Polly Jewell, b. 5 May, 1779, d. at Hector, N. Y., 28 May, 1818, dau. of Jos. Jewell, 1744-1822, & descendant of Thomas[1] Jewell, of Braintree, Mass., in the 5th generation, line of Nathaniel (see Jewell Register, 1860, No. 1406, p. 70), and had 12 children (recorded in following paragraphs). (2.) ...., a son, d. young. (3) Sally, m.

either Silas or Gratton H. Wheeler, of Wheeler, Steuben Co., N. Y., and had a large family. (4.) Dorcas, m. ...., and had numerous children. (5.) Ruth, m. Nathan Rose. and had a numerous family. (6.) Sarah, m. Wm. Holmes. (7.) Polly, m. .... Sweet. These daughters and their families dwelt mostly in Steuben Co., N. Y.

Abiel[5] & Polly (Jewell) Gardner, of Rensselaerville, Durham, and Hector, N. Y., [of Capt. Thomas[4], Wm[3]., Wm[2]., Geo[1].], had issue:

1. Joel[6], b. 12 Feb., 1798, at Rensselaerville, N. Y., purchased on 29 July, 1834, the farm lying just northeast of that of his father-in-law in Elba, N. Y.; d. in Alexander, N. Y., 5 May, 1878; m. (1) in Elba, N. Y., 19 Dec., 1820, Bathsheba[6] Gardner, who d. in Elba, N. Y., 22 Jan. 1836, dau. of Jeffrey Watson[5] & Freelove (Gardner) Gardner, of Elba, N. Y.,—the former a son of John[4] & Bathsheba (Watson) Gardner, [of John[3], Wm[2]. Geo[1]. (p. 31)], and the latter a dau. of Clark[4] & Amie (Lillibridge) Gardner, [of Wm[3]., Wm[2]., Geo[1].]. He m. (2) ....:.... 1836, Lydia Smith, who d. about 1885, dau. of John & Lucy (Mallison) Smith, of Middlebury, N. Y.,—the former b. 23 Nov., 1789±, at Coeymans, Albany Co., N. Y., d. at the residence of his son-in-law, Abiel Gardner, in Stafford, Genesee Co., N. Y., 28 Nov., 1861, and the latter, b. 14 July, 1785, also in Coeymans, N. Y., d. in Stafford. N. Y., 11 Nov., 1872.

2. James, b. 22 May, 1800, d. at Alabama Centre, N. Y., 27 July, 1853, m. 1 Jan., 1832, Betsey Wood.

3. Jehiel, b. 3 July, 1801, was a carpenter, dw. in ...., Genesee Co., N. Y., and latterly at Saginaw, Mich., and there d. ....; m. (1) 30 Oct., 1838, Sally Toby; m. (2) ....

4. Harriet, b. 11 Dec., 1802, d. at res. of brother John in Oakfield, N. Y., 9 March, 1851, unm.

5. Nancy, b. 8 March, 1804, dw. N. Pembroke, N. Y., d. ....; m. (1), 2 May, 1826, (as 2d wife) Scott E. Fuller, who d. ....; m. (2), 12 Oct., 1833, John Gustavus Vader, of Elba (now Oakfield), N. Y., who d. in Sherwood, Mich., ..., son of Peter & Catharine (Howard) Vader, natives of N. Y. State,—the former, of Dutch, and the latter of Hessian ancestry.

6. Abiel, Jr., b. 29 Aug., 1805, d. of smallpox in Durham, N. Y., 8 May, 1811.

7 William, b. 9 Dec., 1806, dw. Reynoldsville. N. Y., m. at Newfield, Tompkins Co., N. Y., 17 Feb., 1831, Dorcas C. West, dau. of Jonathan West, of Newfield, N. Y.

8. George[6], b. 22 Sept., 1808, in Durham. Greene Co., N. Y. On 12 Nov., 1838, he and his brothers Joel & Abiel jointly purchased lots 1, 2 & 4, in Sec. 4, & lots 1 & 2 in Sec. 3, Town 13, Range 2, Elba, N. Y. He owned and operated for several years the sawmill at what is now the hamlet of East Oakfield, N. Y. He

bought of Wm. Craft, about 1866, the house erected in 1827 by G. Washington Gardner, in Elba, N. Y., with 60 acres of the central portion of the Gardner homestead. Selling this in 1868 to the present owner, Stephen Vail, he removed to the Township of Scipio, Hillsdale Co., Mich., and there d. 6 March, 1880, on the farm where his only surviving son, Leroy T. Gardner, still abides. George Gardner m. (by Eden McIntyre, Esq., J. P.), in Batavia, N. Y., 23 Dec., 1835, Mary V. Pugsley, b. 29 Jan., 1815, in the Town of De Ruyter, Madison Co., N. Y., d. in Scipio Tp., Hillsdale Co., Mich., 21 Jan., 1892, dau. of Samuel V. (who d. 1850) & Delila (Williams — who d. 1868) Pugsley, of Milo and Rose, N. Y., granddau. of Samuel and Mary (Vail) Pugsley, and had 5 children: (a) Jane Elizabeth, b. 19 Feb., 1840, on what is known as the Peedy Place on the ridge north of the Friends' Meeting House, Elba, N. Y.; m. 28 Feb. 1857, Geo. Milton[6] Gardner, now of Jackson, Mich., (see pp. 34-5). (b) ...., a son, d. 1 Apr., 1843, unnamed. (c) Lafayette, b. 3 Oct., 1845, d. at E. Oakfield, N. Y., 12 Nov., 1847. (d) Leroy Taylor[7] Gardner, b. 11 Jan., 1850, E. Oakfield, N. Y., dw. Scipio, Mich., P. O., Litchfield; m. at Homer, Mich., 18 Jan., 1871, Emma Van Wert. (e) Samuel Addison, b. 28 Feb., 1856, d. E. Oakfield, N. Y., 20 Feb., 1857.

9. John[6] b. 25 Dec., 1810, Durham, N. Y., settled about 1850 in Oakfield, N. Y., purchasing about 300 acres of land on Drake St.; removed thence in the autumn of 1869, to a farm on Sec. 12 in Litchfield (Tp. 5 S., of Range 4 W.), Hillsdale Co., Mich., and there d. 23 Jan., 1892; m. in Middlebury, Genesee (now Wyoming) Co., N. Y., 4 July, 1842, Maranda Smith, b. 21 May, 1819, at Ashtabula, Ohio, dau. of John & Lucy (Mallison) Smith, of Middlebury, N. Y.

10. Abiel (again), b. 1 Apr., 1812, was a carpenter & farmer, dw. Elba, Batavia, & Stafford, N. Y., d. ...., 1879; m., in Elba, N. Y., 4 Dec., 1836, Amanda Smith, 1811-1884, sister to wives of Joel & John.

11. Sarah Ann, b. 15 Aug., 1814, dw. Rutland, Pa.; m. 22 Oct., 1837, Alanson Palmer, of Austinville, Bradford Co., Pa., b. 8 June, 1814.

12. Thomas, b. 19 Aug., 1817, at Hector, N. Y., dw. Rutland, Pa., a millwright; m. in Roseville, Pa., ..., and went to Oregon.

George W[6]. & Miriam F. (Grimes) Gardner, of E. Oakfield, N. Y., [of J. Hazzard[5] & Harriet (Pattison) Gardner, of Genesee Co., N. Y., John[4], John[3], Wm[2]. Geo[1]. (p. 32)], had: (1.) Clarissa Maria, b. 29 Nov., 1839, in Elba (now Oakfield), N. Y., and there d. 29 Jan., 1854, aged 14 yrs. (2) Harriet, b. 1 Feb., 1842, Oakfield, N. Y., at the homestead of her father and grandfather, which she inherited and there dwells, P. O., E. Oakfield; m. (by Rev. R. Martin) 16 June, 1867, Amerisa Everett Nash, called Mett, b. at Pine Hill, in the town of Barre, Orleans Co., N. Y., 10 Oct., 1828, son of Whitman & Elizabeth (Baggerly) Nash of E. Oakfie d, N Y., and had: Miriam Forbush Nash, b. 25 March, 1868, at E. Oakfield, N. Y. Mrs. Nash is authority for the statement that her grandfather came to Batavia (now Oakfield) in 1808, went back to Ontario Co. in 1809, and returned with his family in 1812, his widow having often been heard to tell of meeting the moving troops in the war of 1812, but possibly this may have been in the latter part of the war, after the burning of Buffalo and the subsidence of the universal alarm among the settlers, over the expected incursion of hostile Indians from Canada.

John W⁶. Gardner, b. 1824, son of J. Hazzard⁵ & Harr:et (Pattison) Gardner, of Genesee Co., N. Y. (p. 32), d. of a cancer, 22 Dec., 1895, leaving wife Ellen, and one dau. ....

Sunderland Pattison⁶ Gardner, 1821-1884 (p. 32), married (1), 1842, Sarah Ann Churchill, who d. 1860 (see p. 32), and had: (1.) Wm. Earl', called Earl, b. 1 Feb., 1844, in the town of Batavia, N. Y., dwelt Oakfield, N. Y., whence, in May, 1879, he removed with his family to Penfield, Monroe Co., N. Y., and thence in Apr., 1887, to Fairport, N. Y.; m., in Penfield, N. Y., Isabell Lovett, dau. of James, and had: (a) Fred Earl, b. .. Sept., 1877, Oakfield, N Y ; (b) Flora Elizabeth, b. 28 Nov., 1880, Penfield, N. Y.; (c) Lotta May, b. 2 Apr., 1885, Penfield, N. Y. (2) Ara Dan, b. 8 of 9 mo., 1846, Oakfield, N. Y.; d. Parma, Mich., 11 Feb., 1867. (3) Sarah Adelia, b. .. May, 1853, dw. Fairport, N. Y.; m Dr. John Franklin Tubbs, a practicing physician at Fairport, N. Y.

PATTISON.

It is said that three brothers, Thomas, John & William Pattison, from the north of Ireland, came to America about the middle of the 18th century and settled in Connecticut, that John & William were the first in America who made up tin, but that one of these subsequently went south and left descendants in Baltimore and elsewhere.

Thomas' Pattison, b 2 Feb., 1725-6, d. ....; m. (1) Elizabeth Sunderland, b. 1722±, who d. on Tuesday, 27 Sept., 1763, aged 41 yrs.; m. (2) 2 Apr., 1766, Irena ...., b. 1724±, who d. 19 Aug., 1792, aged 68 yrs.

Thomas' Pattison, b. 1725 6, by 1st wife, Elizabeth, nee Sunderland, had:

1. Anna, b. Sunday, 19 Feb., 1744.*
2. Elizabeth, b. Monday, 5 Jan., 1746-7.
3. Hannah, b. Wednesday (?), 20 Dec., 1748.
4. Sunderland, b. Wednesday, 16 Jan., 1750-51, d. young.

* The interrogation point (?) is inserted where there is an apparent discrepancy between the given day of the week and the assigned date of birth. Feb. 19, O. S., 1743-4, fell on Sunday.

5. Sarah, b. Friday, 2 Oct., O. S., 1752.
6. James, b. Wednesday (?), 26 Dec., 1754.
7. Sunderland² (again), b. Thursday (?), 25 Jan., 1757, d. in Elba (now Oakfield), N. Y., 7 Feb., 1842, aged 85 years 13 days; m. (1), 14 May, 1778, Sarah Utter, b. 1753, who d. at Rensaelaerville, N Y., on Thursday, 3 Dec., 1801; m. (2), .. July, 1802, Rhoda Worden, b. 7 July, 1754, d. 1 Sept., 1811, aged 57; m. (3), .. Feb., 1812, Amy Gardner, who d. .... and was buried in the Gardner family burying ground, Elba, N. Y., dau. of C ark & Amie (Lillibridge) Gardner.
8. William, b. Saturday, 24 March, 1759. There is a tradition that either this William or his brother James was killed near Lake George during the French and Indian war.
9. Hannah, b Sunday, 9 Aug., 1761.
10. Chloe, b. Monday, 12 Sept., 1763.

Thomas' Pattison, b. 1725-6, by 2d wife, Irena. 1724±-1792 (m. 1766), had:

11. ...., b. Sunday, 29 March, 1767, (unnamed).
12. Irena, b. Sunday, 11 Nov., 1770.

Sunderland² Pattison, 1757-1842, by 1st wife, Sarah, nee Utter (1753-1801, m. 1778), of Dutchess Co., N. Y., [of Thomas' & Elizabeth (Sunderland) Pattison], had:

1. Sunderland', Jr., b. Friday, 19 of 2 mo., 1779, at Amenia, Dutchess Co., N. Y., was a miller in Farmington, Ontario Co., N. Y.; removed about 1837 to Marengo, Calhoun Co., Mich., and there d. ....; m. ...., Dorcas' Gardner, dau. of John' & Bathsheba (Watson) Gardner (p. 33).
2. Elizabeth, b. Thursday, .. Nov., 1780, d. 2 Jan., 1781.
3. Thomas, b. Wednesday, 13 of 2 mo., 1782, Amenia, N. Y., d. in Michigan; m. 20 Apr., 1809, Hannah Flint, b. 13 of 1 mo., 1780, at Stanford, Dutchess Co., N. Y., dau. of Moses & Tabathy (.........) Fisher.
4. ...., a son, who d. (unnamed).
5. Sarah, b. Friday (?), 8 July, 1785, d. ....; m. 19 of 4 mo., 1801, Elisha W⁵. Gardner, son of William' & Sarah (Watson) Gardner (p. 30), [of John³, Wm²., Geo'.].
6. Margaret, b. Wednesday (?), 28 Nov., 1788, d. ...., buried in the village of Oakfield, N. Y.; m. Smith Hopkins, who was buried at Oakfield, N. Y.
7. Harriet, b. 12 of 12, 1792, d. 22 of 2 mo., 1878, at E. Oakfield, N. Y.; m. Jeremiah Hazzard' Gardner, bro. to Sunderland's wife, Dorcas (see p. 32).

Sunderland² Pattison, 1757 1842, [of Thomas'] by 3d wife, Amy, nee Gardner, [of Clark', Wm²., Geo'.], had:

8. Amy, b. 25 of 9 mo., 1812, in Farmington, N. Y., d. .. Sept., 1813.

HICKS.

Horod Long* married (1), in London, Eng., about 1638, John² Hicks, who, about 1642, removed from New England to Long Island, son of Robert¹ & Elizabeth (Morgan) Hicks, of Bermondesey St., Southwark, London, Eng.,† and grandson of James Hicks, who was lineally descended from Sir Ellis Hicks, who was knighted by Edward, the Black Prince, on the battlefield of Poictiers, Sept. 9, 1356, for bravery in capturing a set of colors from the French. John² & Horod (Long) Hicks had 3 children, Thomas³, Hannah & Elizabeth. By his 2d wife, Rachel, née Starr, he had no children. Thomas³ Hicks m. (1), Mary Washburn and had Thomas & Jacob⁴; he m. (2), Mary Doughty and had Isaac, William, Stephen, John, Charles, Benjamin, Phebe, Charity, Mary & Elizabeth. Jacob⁴ Hicks m. Hannah Carpenter and had Samuel, Stephen, Thomas, Joseph, Jacob, Benjamin⁵, Elizabeth & John. Benjamin⁵ Hicks m. Phebe Titus and had Silas, Benjamin, Samuel⁶, Sarah and Phebe. Samuel⁶ Hicks m. Phebe Seaman and had Isaac⁷, Elizabeth, Samuel, Valentine & Phebe. Isaac⁷ Hicks m. Sarah Doughty and had John D., Robert, Benjamin D⁸., Isaac, Elizabeth⁸,‡ & Mary. Benjamin D⁸. Hicks m. Elizabeth T. Hicks and had Marianna & Benjamin D⁹., of Old Westbury, Queens Co., L. I, who for the past thirty years has been engaged in preparing, and expects soon to publish, a genealogy of the Hicks family; he m. (1), Maria Louise Herrick (a descendant also of the Hicks family); m. (2), Alice Albertson (likewise a descendant of the Hicks family); had no children.

---

* For her persecution for Quakerism in New England, her descendants by second husband—George Gardner—etc., see pp. 24-37, ante.

† Robert¹ Hicks, a leather-dresser, from London, ancestor of the Hicks family in America, arrived at Plymouth, Mass., 11 Nov., 1621, in the ship Fortune, which brought over the parts of families left behind the year before by the passengers of the Mayflower. He had m. (2) Margaret Winslow, who, with her children, Samuel, Ephraim, Lydia & Phebe, came over in the ship Ann, which arrived at Plymouth in June, 1623; and the family, with two of the former wife's four children, Elizabeth & Thomas, settled at Duxbury, Mass., the other two sons, John² & Stephen, going subsequently (642 ±) to Long Island.

‡ Paternal grandmother of Mrs. Elizabeth H. C¹⁰. Thayer, of Great Neck. Queens Co, L. I., dau. of Isaac II⁹. Cock (see foot note, p. 236, ante).

IV.

ADDITIONAL DATA CONCERNING RELATIVES OF THE COMPILER'S MATERNAL GRANDMOTHER, DIANA (BERRY) GARDNER, B. 1810, SECOND WIFE OF GEORGE WASHINGTON GARDNER, OF ELBA, N. Y.,

DAUGHTER OF JONATHAN & BATHSHEBA (GREENE) BERRY OF RENSSELAER CO., N. Y., & LENAWEE CO, MICH., AND GRANDDAU. (2), OF LANGFORD & ABIGAIL (THOMAS) GREENE, OF STEVENTOWN, N. Y., [OF JOSEPH⁴ & PHOEBE (LANGFORD) GREENE, JOHN⁵ & MARY (ALLEN) GREENE, JAMES² & ELIZABETH (ANTHONY) GREENE, JOHN¹ GREENE, SURGEON, OF WARWICK, R. I.], WITH HOLDEN, LATHAM, AND OTHER ANCESTORS SKETCHED IN PART I., PP. 37-50.

BERRY & PARK.

Langford Greene Berry, 1812-1878, son of Jonathan & Bathsheba⁸ (Greene) Berry, of Lenawee Co., Mich., (p. 39), was active in the formation of the Congregational Church, of Adrian, and a liberal supporter and member of the board of control of Adrian College. His dau. Gertrude M. (Berry) Seager (p. 39), m. (2), ... McCabe, and dwells at Brookline, Mass.

Ambrose Spencer Berry, 1814 1878, (p. 39), d. of typhoid fever at Corning, Ark.

Mrs. A. Emily (Berry) Park, b. 1818, sister to above, d. at her home in Adrian, Mich., 18 July, 1896.

Ambrose B. Park, son of Jonathan S. & A. Emily (Berry) Park, of Adrian, Mich., b. 12 Nov., 1852, in Adrian, Mich (p. 39), dwells at No. 33 Church St., Adrian, Mich., is a dry goods merchant at No. 17 S. Main St., Adrian; m. in Adrian, Mich., 19 Nov., 1879, Emma M. Young, b. 26 Apr., 1858, Adrian, Mich., dau. of Charles & Rhoda (Aldrich) Young, of Adrian, Mich., and had: (1) Robert Charles, b. 22 Aug., 1881. (2) Frederick Edwin, b. 2 July, 1883. (3) Florence Helen, b. 25 March, 1893.

GREENE.

Lineage of George H. Greene.

John¹ Greene, b. Feb. 9, 1596-7, Eng., d. 1658, R. I.; m. Joanna Tattersall, and had: James², bap. June 21, 1626, Eng., d. April 27, 1698, R. I.; m. Deliverance Potter [of Robert] and had James³, b. June 1, 1659, d. Mar. 12, 1712; m. Mary Fones [of John], and had: Fones⁴, b. Mar. 23, 1689-90, d. July 29, 1758; m. Rebecca Tibbitts [of Henry], and had: Job⁵., b. Aug. 8, 1717, d. Mar. 29, 1798; m. Marcy⁵ Greene,

36

[of William¹, Peter³, John², John¹], and had: Stephen⁶, b. Jan. 9, 1757, d. Sept. 5, 1829; m. Sarah Chace [of Abraham], and had: Seneca⁷, b. Nov. 14, 1782, d. Aug. 6, 1815; m. Nancy Peake [of William]. and had: Augustus Weeden⁸, b. Mar. 13, 1813, d. June 6, 1879; m. Amy Jenkins Davis [of David], and had: George Henry⁹, b. Oct. 12, 1836, dw. 114 Shiawassee St., W., Lansing, Michigan; m. Julia Lucretia Baldwin. He is secretary of the Michigan Pioneer and Historical Society, etc. has given much attention to the genealogy of the Greene family, and has kindly contributed much valuable material for use in this work.

Lineage of Marcy Greene, who married Job, of Coventry, above.

John¹, b. Feb. 9, 1596-7, d. 1658; m. Joanna Tattersall and had: John², bap. Aug. 15, 1620, d. Nov. 27, 1708; m. Ann Almy [of Wm.], and had: Peter³, b. Feb. 7, 1654 5, d. Aug. 12, 1723, m. Elizabeth Arnold [of Stephen], and had: William⁴, b. July 29, 1690, d. Mar. 17, 1766; m. Sarah Medbury, and had: Marcy⁵, b. Oct. 31, 1725, d. April 8, 1800; m. Job⁵ Greene [of Fones⁴, James³, James², John¹].

Lineage of Sarah Ann, nee Budlong,

Wife of Abel Whitney, of Adrian, Mich.

John¹ Greene, surgeon, 1597-1658, of Warwick, R. I., m. 1619, Joanna Tattersall, and had: (Dep. Gov.) John² Greene, b. 1620, who d. 27 Nov., 1708, m. Ann Almy, [of Wm. & Audry]. and had (as 4th of their 11 children): Peter³ Greene, b. 7 Feb., 1655, who m. Elizabeth Arnold, dau. of Stephen & Sarah (Smith) Arnold, and granddau. of Wm.* & Christiana

---

*The ancestry of this William¹ Arnold has been traced through 16 generations before his own to the early kings of Wales.

(Peak) Arnold, of Hingham, Mass., and Providence, R. I. The 5th of their 7 children was William⁴ Greene, b. 29 July, 1690, m. Sarah Medbury [of Wm. & Sarah], and had: Sarah⁵ Greene, b. 17 Sept., 1718, d. 14 Nov., 1776; m. Capt. John Rhodes, b. 5 May, 1716, son of Maj. John & Catharine⁴ (Holden) Rhodes, [of Catharine³, nee Greene, John², John¹], and grandson (1) of (Elder) John & Wait (Waterman) Rhodes and (2) of Charles & Catharine (Greene) Holden, and had: Sarah⁶ Rhodes, b. 15 March, 1750, who d. 21 Sept., 1841, m. Daniel Budlong, son of Daniel & Rebecca (Davis) Budlong, grandson of John & Isabel (Potter) Budlong, and great-grandson of Francis Budlong of Warwick, R. I., (whose wife was Rebecca Lippitt, widow of Joseph Howard), and had: Daniel⁷, b. 14 Jan., 1771, at Warwick, R. I., who d. at Adrian, Mich., 24 Jan., 1853; m. 17 March, 1797, Martha Campbell, b. 25 Apr., 1772, at Voluntown, Conn., d. at Adrian, Mich., 11 Oct., 1849, dau. of Moses & Sarah (Dixon) Campbell, and had: (a)Sarah Ann, nee Budlong, wife of Abel Whitney, of Adrian, Mich.; & (b) Almira M. Budlong.

HOLDEN.

Randall¹ Holden, 1612-1692, of Warwick, R. I. (pp. 47-8), m., 1648, Frances Dungan, b. 1630, in London, Eng., d. 1697, dau. of William & Frances (Latham) Dungan, and granddau. of Hon. Lewis Latham, of Elstow, County Bedford, Eng., who d. May 16, 1655, aged 100 years, Falconer to King Charles I. (pp. 47-8), and had: Randall² Holden, b. Apr. 4, 1660, at Warwick, R. I., d. 1726 (p. 47), m., 1687, Bethiah Waterman, 1664±-1742 [of Nathaniel], and had: Randall³, b. Jan. 2, 1694, Warwick, R. I., m. Jan. 3, 1724, Rose Wickes, and had: Randall⁴, b. Nov. 25, 1726, Warwick, R. I, m. Jan. 14, 1749, Naomi Potter, and had: Randall⁵, b. July 18, 1754, Warwick, R. I., m. Oct. 19, 1777, Elizabeth Warner, and had: Randall⁶, b. Sept. 3, 1792, Providence, R. I., m. Sept. 10, 1829, Catharine Morgan Deming, and had: (Maj.) Frederic Augustus⁷ Holden, b. July 4, 1830, Providence, R. I., dw. "Rose Lawn" Hyattsville, Md., Sec. of the Co-operative Town Co. of Tennessee, Washington, D. C., and Elizabethton, Tenn., has published genealogies of "the Capron Family" and "the Lockwood Family" and sketches, more or less lengthy, of several other Rhode Island pedigrees. The work of his life has been the genealogy of persons of every name descending from Holdens; he has compiled material sufficient for a large volume, mentioning about 50,000 persons, and hopes ere long to have it printed.

ADDRESSES OF PATRONS OF THIS WORK,

WITH PAGE REFERENCES TO THEIR RESPECTIVE RECORDS AND THOSE OF THEIR DIRECT ANCESTORS AND IMMEDIATE FAMILIES.

See also Condensed Lineage Table (pp. 50–57), and the General Index to Personal Names at close of the volume. The numbers preceding certain families in Part II. are identical with those prefixed to the corresponding names in the "Synopsis of Six Generations," given at pages 81–83.

William C. Armstrong, New Brunswick, N. J., p. 252.

William Harris Arnold, 120 Franklin St., New York City, N. Y.

Mrs. John R. Bellis, No. 6 W. 66th St., New York City,—Mary Louise⁵, *nee* Shotwell, [of James', William⁶, Jas³., John⁴, John³, John², Abr'.], pp. 123, 177.

NOTE.—James⁷ Shotwell, of Allamuchy, N. J., son of Wm⁶. & Mary (Ayers) Shotwell, of Independence, Warren Co., N. J. (p. 177), m. Phebe Ayres, b. 1811±, who dw. (1897) at Hackettstown, N. J., and had: (1.) Archibald Ayres Shotwell, of Hackettstown, N. J. (2.) Emma Elizabeth³, who d. in 1884, m. Theo. Crane, M. D., of Hackettstown, N. J, and had 7 children, the eldest being Mrs. Ethel Louise (Crane) Havens, of Point Pleasant, N. J. (3.) Mary Louise⁵, b. 1837, dw. No. 6 W. 66th St., New York City; m. Nov. 24, 1859, John Rockafelow Bellis, b. 1826, then (1859) a druggist at Hackettstown, N. J., having started the first drug store established in that town, is now (1897) a druggist in New York; they had three sons and one dau., two of whom are m. and two single. (4.) Walter L. Shotwell, of No. 77 Roseville Ave., Newark, N. J., & (5) Fannie, who dw. in New York City, m. C. F. Roddy.

Mrs. Eliza (Sh.) Biggs, Kirkwood, Mo., p. 123.

Edward J. Bosworth, 127 N. Water St., Rochester, N. Y., pp. 11, 267–8.

Miss Elizabeth Bowne, 134 E. 36th St., New York City, pp. 133–4.

Mrs. Harriett H. (Shotwell) Brown, St. Clair, Mich., p. 97.

Mrs. Hannah A. (Shotwell) Burtis, Freehold, N. J., pp. 155, 172, 225.

Mrs. Sarah Isabel (Shotwell) Caldwell, Kansas City, Mo., p. 123.

Daniel H. Carpenter, Maplewood, Essex Co., N. J.

Mrs. Ruth A. (Sh.) Cash, Ashley, Mo., p. 146.

George William Cocks, Glen Cove, Queens Co., N. Y., pp. 233–41.

Mrs. E. T. Conway, Henderson, Ky., p. 226–7.

Eli Cope, Jr., Streator, Ill., pp. 112, 145, 224.

John H. Cope and sister, Sarah S. Cope, Uniontown, Pa., pp. 112, 145, 223–5.

John Cox, Jr., 308 W. 19th St., N. Y. City, pp. 5–6, 233–41.

Wendell J. Curtis, Rochester, N. Y., pp. 221–2.

Mrs. Ida A. S. Davis, 805 Lunt Ave., Chicago, Ill., pp. 161–2, 115–18, 165–8, 5, 7, 25, 38, 50–57, 85, 124–5, 127, 130–38, 91–93, 95.

H. Edmund Deats, Flemington, N. J., p. 273-4.

Thomas W. Dell, 12 Strawberry St., Philadelphia, Pa., pp. 151–2, 229.

Stephen N. Dillingham, Oakfield, N. Y., pp. 1–37, 85, 114–15, 117–18, 231–2.

Mrs. Mary H. Estes, Farmington, N. Y., pp. 165–8, 230.

Hugh Mulford Estil, Plainfield, N. J., p. 270.

George T. Fish, 9 Beckley St., Rochester, N. Y., pp. 168–9, 218–222.

Mrs. Mary S. (Webster) Fisk, Addison, Hillsdale Co., Mich., pp. 15, 21, 269.

H. C. Fitz Randolph, 174 W. 58th St., New York City.

Friends' Historical Library, Swarthmore College, Swarthmore, Pa.

James S. Frost, North Rush, N. Y., p. 241.

Supt. Gardner Fuller, N. Y. S. School for Blind, Batavia, N. Y.

George Milton Gardner, Sr., 211 Clinton St., Jackson, Mich., pp. 34, 24–49, 277–8.

J. H. Gardner, Centreville, St. Joseph Co., Mich., pp. 33-4, 24–37.

Mrs. Martha M. Gardner, Elba, Genesee Co., N. Y., pp. 31, 277.

Mrs. Anna W. Graefen, *nee* Bonney, b. 1850, 1016 S. 18th St., St. Louis, Mo., pp. 151–2, 114, 229.

George H. Greene, 114 Shiawassee St., W., Lansing, Mich., pp. 40, 281-2.

W. W. Gunn, Webber, Kans., pp. 262–3.

Miss Elizabeth B. Hampton, Orchard Park, Erie Co., N. Y., pp. 9–10, 240.

Mrs. Amy S. Harkness, Box 846, Adrian, Mich., pp. 165–8, 216–17.

Elwood C. Harris, 732 Prudential Bldg., Newark, N. J., pp. 111-13, 223.

Dr. Philander A. Harris, 26 Church St., Paterson, N. J., visiting physician to the Paterson General Hospital, surgeon-in-chief to department for diseases of women in Passaic Hospital, etc., pp. 111-13, 223.

Benjamin D. Hicks, Old Westbury, Queens Co., N. Y., (New York address, 1046 Broadway), p. 280.

Mrs. G. Fannie (Tate) Hill, 700 2d St., Henderson, Ky., and mother, Mrs. E. T. Conway, Henderson, Ky., pp. 143, 226-7.

Maj. Fred'c A. Holden, "Rose Lawn," Hyattsville, Md., pp. 47, 282.

Gardner L. Hunn, Parma, Jackson Co., Mich., pp. 24-49.

Mrs. Capt. W. A. Hutchinson, Vallejo, Solano Co., Cal., pp. 151-2, 228-9.

George K. Johnson, Jr., 4043 Walnut St., Philadelphia, Pa., pp. 170, 119-20, 225.

Mrs. Annie F. (Sh.) Keeler, 23 Church St., Paterson, N. J., pp. 104, 222.

Mrs. Alice G. King, 223 8th Ave., Topeka, Kans., pp. 18, 274.

Dr. Joseph King Knight, 145 W. River St., Hyde Park, Mass., pp. 16, 17, 13, 127, 274.

Mrs. Jemima P. Lenox, Box 106, New Brunswick, N. J., pp. 104, 121-2.

Oliver B. Leonard, 915 Madison Ave., Plainfield, N. J., pp. 12-15, 269.

Charles R. Loomis, Sherburne, Chenango Co., N. Y., pp. 107, 117-18.

Mrs. Sarah Lovett, Amity, Orange Co., N. Y., p. 241.

J. Wilmer Lundy, Mt. Holly, N. J., pp. 252, 263.

Emory McClintock, 32 Nassau St., N. Y., pp. 213-15.

Dr. S. Mason McCollin, Arch St., Philadelphia, Pa., p. 229.

Mrs. Maggie Mantiply, Clarksville, Pike Co., Mo., p. 146.

Mrs. Mercie S. Masters, 44 N. 38th St., W. Philadelphia, Pa., pp. 152, 229-30.

George I. Mitchell, Box 277, Hackettstown, N. J., pp. 112-13, 222-3.

Mrs. Emily A. (Sh.) Moore, Torch, Athens Co., Ohio, pp. 174, 232-3.

Prof. J. W. Moore, Dept. of Physics, Lafayette College, Easton, Pa.

Wm. H. Moore, 28 Sanford Ave., Plainfield, N. J., pp. 18-24, 276.

Mrs. C. A. (Sh.) Mussetter, Box 35, University Place, Lancaster Co., Neb., pp. 107, 156-7, 230.

Mrs. Hattie (Gardner) Nash, E. Oakfield, Genesee Co., N. Y., pp. 32, 278-9.

Ambrose B. Park, Adrian, Mich., pp. 36-8, 231.

Webster Parry, 1004 Main St., Richmond, Ind., p. 272.

George W. Pattison, "Orchard Hill," Birmingham, Mich., pp. 33, 280.

Mrs. Harriet W. (Sh.) Polhemus, 79 W. Mulberry St., Springfield, Ohio, pp. 114, 152, 228-9.

George W. Pound, 49 Niagara Ave., Lockport, N. Y., p. 11.

H. H. Pound & Co., Williamson, N. Y., p. 10.

Hon. John E. Pound, 345 High St., Lockport, N. Y., pp. 11, 268.

Robinson Pound*, 255 E. 2d St., Plainfield, N. J., pp. 10, 268.

Roscoe Pound, 1632 L St., Lincoln, Neb., p. 267.

S. B. Pound, 1632 L St., Lincoln, Neb., pp. 10, 267.

Wm. R. W. Pound, 224 W. Water St., Elmira, N. Y., son of John W°. & Catharine Lucretia (*Wilson*) Pound, of Lockport, N. Y., pp. 11, 52.

Wm. S. Pound, Sparta, Elgin Co., Ontario, Canada, pp. 8, 266.

John S. Reed, Egypt, Monroe Co., N. Y., pp. 117, 167, 216.

Mrs. Sarah S. Rice, Marysville, Union Co., Ohio, care of Harry Rice, pp. 152, 230.

Mrs. Anna P. Rickabaugh, Warren Tavern, Chester Co., Pa., pp. 10, 267.

Mrs. Abel V. Shotwell–Rosetta S. (Ebert) Shotwell, Rahway, N. J., pp. 84-5, 112-13.

Albert Shotwell, Bowling Green, Pike Co., Mo., pp. 144, 89.

Dr. A. N. Shotwell, 98 Cass Bvd., Mt. Clemens, Mich., pp. 119, 146.

A. T. Shotwell, Box 1662, Fargo, N. D., pp. 90, 108, 155-6.

Benjamin F. Shotwell, Cortland Centre, Kent Co., Mich., pp. 106, 99, 97, 165-8, 232.

B. W. Shotwell, Box 987, Trenton, Grundy Co., Mo., pp. 108, 98, 163, 119, 225.

Benjamin [H.] Shotwell, Brainard, Butler Co., Nebr., pp. 98-9, 172-3, 216.

Carlos B. Shotwell, 469 3rd Ave., Detroit, Mich., pp. 147, 99, 153, 218.

C. A. Shotwell, 3501 Mather St., Phila., Pa., pp. 99-100, 176.

Eden Shotwell's family, Bennett, Nebr., pp. 107, 156-7, 121, 230.

Edward R. Shotwell, Elba, N. Y., 113-14, 4-24, 85.

Miss Emelissa Shotwell, Johnsonburgh, N. J., pp. 148, 122.

Emerson Shotwell, Martelle, Jones Co., Iowa, pp. 154, 145-6, 233.

Frank L. Shotwell, Marengo, Wayne Co., N. Y., pp. 148-9, 172-3.

Fremont Shotwell, Glenville, Ohio, pp. 90-91, 112, 223.

George M. Shotwell, 29-31, W. 42d St., N. Y. City, pp. 118-19, 115.

Harvey E. Shotwell, Mission, Wash., pp. 107, 156-7.

Mrs. Hattie A. Shotwell, 303 E. Lake St., S. Minneapolis, Minn., pp. 104-5, 171-2, 123, 222.

Henry T. Shotwell, 72 Washington Ave., Brooklyn, N. Y., pp. 154, 111, 226.

H. P. Shotwell, Elba, Genesee Co., N. Y., pp. 113-15, 165-8.

I. M. Shotwell, Batavia, N. Y., (d. Nov. 1, 1897) pp. 115, 117, 118-19, 5-24, 85-7, 165-7.

* His father Geo. R. Pound, d. 28 of 6 mo., 1803, buried at Plainfield, N. J.

Jacob Z Shotwell, Garrison, Nebr., pp. 122, 172-3.

J. L. Shotwell, Farber, Mo., pp. 89, 144-5.

James H. Shotwell, Box 509, Seattle, Wash.

Jas. Harrison Shotwell, E. Stroudsburg, Pa.

Dr. J. R. Shotwell, Spencersburg, Mo., pp 144-6.

Dr. J. B. Shotwell, 137 W. 49th St., N. Y. City, pp. 147, 145, 151-2, 228.

John B. Shotwell, Carthage, Hamilton Co., Ohio, pp. 123-4, 154.

John L. Shotwell, Whittlesey, Taylor Co., Wis., pp. 101, 226.

Rev. John M. Shotwell, Westbury, Wayne Co., N. Y., pp. 153-4, 147, 218.

John T. Shotwell, Deadwood, S. D., pp. 90-1, 111-13.

John W. Shotwell, Richmond, Ray Co., Mo., pp. 120-21, 143-4, 227-8.

J. D. Shotwell, paying teller of the Bowery Savings Bank, N. Y. City for 27 years; d. at his residence, Hillside Ave., Orange, N. J., 7 mo. 4, 1897, of apoplexy; pp. 110-11, 154, 152, 222.

J. M. Shotwell, Merchants' Exchange Assoc'n, San Francisco, Cal., (d. Nov. 11, 1897) pp. 154, 84.

Kenneth Shotwell, Ellisville, St. Louis Co., Mo., pp. 146-7, 155.

Miss L. P. Shotwell, 805 Lunt Ave., Station Y, Rogers Park, Chicago, Ill., pp. 160, 115-16.

Miss Lucy Shotwell, Richmond, Mo., pp. 120-1, 180, 227-8.

M. N. Shotwell, Concord, Jackson Co., Mich., pp. 160-3, 115-18, 165-8, 1-5, 7, 25, 38, 50-7, 85, 124-5, 127, 130 8. 91-3, 95.

Miss Martha B. Shotwell, Cadiz, Ohio, pp. 171, 223.

Melancthon S. Shotwell, N. Front St, Harrisburg, Pa., 158-9, 156, 164-5.

M. R. Shotwell, Oak Grove, Mo, pp. 121, 227-8.

Murray A. Shotwell, Elba, Genesee Co., N. Y., pp. 113-14, 4-24, 115, 165-6.

Mrs. Nancy G Shotwell, Cadiz, O., pp. 171, 223.

Nathan Shotwell, Box 195, Concord, Mich., pp. 115-16, 160-3, 165-8, 92-3, 130-1, 124-5, 132-8, 85-7, 1-24.

Mrs. P. B. Shotwell, Concord, Mich., pp. 115-16, 24-49.

Miss Phebe M. Shotwell, Linden, Mich., pp. 90, 148.

Romolia A. Shotwell, Walsdorf Hotel, N. Y. City.

Samuel H. Shotwell, 105 S. Main St., Gloversville, N. Y., pp. 97-8, 170, 176-7.

Sam'l L Shotwell, Escondido, Cal., pp. 182, 95-7.

Stuart B. Shotwell, Jr., (Graves & Vinton Co.) 819 Pioneer Press Building, St. Paul, Minn., pp. 171, 177, 111-13, 139-41, 124-138, 85-7, 11-13, 223.

Theo. F. Shotwell, Paulding, Ohio, pp. 147, 153-4, 99, 168-9.

Titus Shotwell III., (d. 1896) (family of), Latrobe, Athens Co., Ohio, pp. 173-4, 118, 232.

Townsend W. Shotwell, 2259 7th Ave., N. Y. City.

W. G. Shotwell, Cadiz, Ohio, pp. 171, 177, 174, 111-13, 139-41, 124-38, 85-7, 11-13, 223.

Wm. H. Shotwell, Plainfield, N. J., pp. 109, 230.

Wm. J. Shotwell, 101 N. Grove St., E. Orange, N. J., pp. 97-8, 233.

Wm. J. Shotwell, 314 California St., San Francisco, Cal., pp. 174-6.

Wm. P. G. Shotwell, 536 Swan St., Buffalo, N. Y., pp. 110, 225 6, 179-81, 109, 121-2, 139-41, 124.

Wm. T. Shotwell, 45 Waverly Ave., Brooklyn, N. Y., pp. 154, 180.

Wm. W. Shotwell, 905 5th St., S. E., Minneapolis, Minn., pp. 171, 223.

Wm. Fred Smith, 93 E. 4th St., St. Paul, Minn., pp. 106, 118, 232.

Mrs. Laura (Blair) Snyder, wife of W. V. Snyder of 697-705 Broad Street., Newark, N. J.

H. D. Spears, 34 Gramercy Park, New York, City, p. 264.

Mrs. Annie Strothers, Bunceton, Cooper Co., Mo., pp. 144-5.

Elizabeth H. C. Thayer, "Beach Hill," Great Neck, L. I., pp. 236, 280.

Abram R. Vail, Quakertown, Hunterdon Co., N. J., p. 243.

H. D. Vail, Santa Barbara, Cal., pp. 243-8.

Mrs. Mary C. Vail, Quakertown, N. J., pp. 241-8.

Mrs. Ruth (Sh.) Vickers, Seneca, Nemaha Co., Kans., p. 118.

Mrs. Cynthia D. K. Webster, nee Kester, 3226 Woodland Ave., Philadelphia, Pa., pp. 11-15, 270-1.

Edmund Webster, 1156 S. Broad St., Philadelphia, Pa., pp. 270-1.

Abel Whitney, 40 E. Maumee St., Adrian, Mich., p. 282.

Mrs. William W. Willett, Allamuchy, Warren Co., N. J., granddaughter of Peter & Esther (Rhodes) Wintermute, pp. 112-13.

Mrs. Bathsheba P. (Sh.) Willson, Deunquat, Wyandot Co., Ohio, pp. 253, 241-3.

Mrs. Eliza B. Wingrove, Clay Centre, Kan-as, pp. 170, 98, 96-7, 93, 130-31, 124-5, 85-7, 132-8, 217.

Cicero Wintermute, Olathe, Kans., pp. 112-13, 222-3.

Frank C. Wintermute, E. Mauch Chunk, Carbon Co., Pa., pp. 112-13, 222-3.

Mrs. Annie E. Wolverton, Vancouver Barracks, Vancouver, Wash., p. 243.

Mrs. Emeline (Sh.) Wolverton, Ashley, Gratiot Co., Mich., pp. 148, 101, 122, 226.

Mrs. Caroline S. Wood, Claremont, Los Angeles Co., Cal., pp. 111, 222.

H. S. Wood, 106 World Bld'g, N. Y. City, p. 222.

Mrs. Minnie Worsham, Frankford, Mo., p. 160.

ALPHABETICAL TABLE OF CONTENTS.*

*For more detailed references, see indexes to surnames and Shotwell given names at the close of the volume and the list of Patrons' addresses with references to their respective lineages, etc., at pages 283-5. See also the condensed lineage table of heads of families at pp. 50-57. Synopsis of six generations of Shotwells at pp. 81-3. Shotwell addresses from directories [1895], pp. 182 4. Eighteenth-century marriages of Friends at Woodbridge, Rahway, and Plainfield, N. J., pp. 186 193. Eighteenth-century wills, etc., of Shotwells in New Jersey, pp. 211 215, and the charts and synopses at pages 4, 5, 7, 25, 38, 40-1, 44-46, 95, 102-3, 112-3, 117-8, 127, 131-8, 140-1, 187-8, 236 9, 243 8, 280-2.

INDEX TO GIVEN NAMES

OF BORN SHOTWELLS.

NOTE.—In this index, no attempt is made to distinguish between different persons bearing the same name, nor between the pages whereon they are severally sketched and those where they are merely mentioned in lineages or otherwise. To find the records of a particular Benjamin, Daniel, John, Joseph, or William Shotwell or other person for whose name the index gives several references, the reader may seek the family name of such person's wife, husband, or mother in the foregoing index to surnames, or some less familiar given name of a brother or sister in this list.

* Single figures following larger numbers take the same tens' and hundreds' figures as the preceding number thus. pp. "113, 9" denotes pages 113 and 119.

† Abraham (sometimes, though rarely, written Abram), occurs in the outline lineages in nearly all of the synoptic clauses with which the several households sketched in Part II. are introduced. For personal sketches see pp. 84-7, 126, 7, 9, 132, 144, 5, 9, 169.

‡B The compiler's lineage is elsewhere frequently alluded to for convenience of reference merely. Brief notices of his various direct ancestors and their brothers and sisters chiefly occupy Part I., pp. 1-50; also pages 85-8, 91-5, 114-7, 124-136, 165-7, 196-7, 208-215, 233-5, 244-5, 289-290.

¶ See foot note to John, p. 297.   ' See foot note to Mary, p. 298.

*See foot note to John, p. 297.   † See foot note to Mary, p. 298.

38

* For data concerning a particular Mary Shotwell, consult references to her husband's surname or mother's maiden name in preceding index, or account of her father's family in its alphabetical order in Part II.
† See foot note to John, p. 297.   ‡ See foot note to Mary.

LIST OF ILLUSTRATIONS.

NOTE.—In this old colonial residence, yet standing in Bowne avenue, lived six successive John Bownes, the last one dying in 1804; and here were the headquarters of the Hessian officers stationed in Flushing during the Revolutionary war. The original proprietor, John[2] Bowne, 1627-1695, was grandfather alike [1] of Mary[3], nee Thorne, wife of John[3] Shotwell, Jr., of Shotwell's Landing [Bricktown, now part of Rahway City] in Essex [now Union] county, N. J., and [2] of their daughter-in-law Amei, nee Hallett, wife of Benjamin[4] Shotwell [likewise of the Landing], and was thus an ancestor of a majority of the Shotwells now living in America.*

Under the two white oak trees shown at the left, George Fox [1624-1691, founder of the Society of Friends] preached during his visit to America in 1672. These trees have disappeared since 1841. A stone with the inscription "Fox Oaks" now marks the site of these historic trees, one of which is estimated to have been standing half a century before Columbus discovered America

*Benjamin[4] Shotwell's children were likewise doubly descended from Elizabeth, nee Fones, niece of Gov. John[4] Winthrop, of Boston, [see plates 13 and 14, pp. 129A and 136B.]

† Lacking the use of his hands (see page 162), he writes by taking his penholder in his mouth.

9 783337 154455